Y0-BLZ-690

MICROECONOMICS

Microeconomics

E. WARREN SHOWS and ROBERT H. BURTON
University of South Florida

D. C. HEATH AND COMPANY
Lexington, Massachusetts   Toronto   London

Copyright © 1972 by D. C. Heath and Company.

All rights reserved. No part of this publication may be reproduced or transmitted in any form or by any means, electronic or mechanical, including photocopy, recording, or any information storage or retrieval system, without permission in writing from the publisher.

Published simultaneously in Canada.

Printed in the United States of America.

International Standard Book Number: 0-669-61564-1

Library of Congress Catalog Card Number: 70-171951

PREFACE

This book is written for the undergraduate course in intermediate microeconomics. Our basic objective is to present the theory of microeconomics as concisely yet understandably as possible so the book can be covered from beginning to end in one term. In our experience with the intermediate theory course, it is possible to devote so much time to the theories of consumer and firm behavior that only cursory treatment is accorded the theory of distribution, general equilibrium theory, and welfare. Microeconomics is not complete, however, unless the theories of output and resource price are integrated with general equilibrium theory and the notions of economic efficiency and welfare. We hope this text will enable its users to cover the essentials of these topics within the time constraints of the typical intermediate course.

To help convince students of the relevance and usefulness of microeconomics, we have included in appendices at the ends of chapters selected readings and case materials that are applications of the theories presented in the text. Of course the text stands alone, and most or all of the appendices can be skipped without loss of continuity in the presentation of micro theory. But we hope most students will read some, if not all, of the appended material, for it serves to complement the theory. The selected readings are written at a level that should pose little difficulty for the undergraduate.

In addition, we have written the text in recognition of several new trends in economics: (1) There is a growing awareness that the division of economic theory into watertight micro and macro compartments is arbitrary and sometimes misleading. In fact, microeconomics and macroeconomics overlap in several important respects. For example, microeconomics is not just concerned with the theory of individual producers and consumers, but more vitally with how the economy operates as a whole to allocate scarce resources; also, micro and macroeconomics are directly complementary in the area of aggregate expenditure theory. (2) Economists have become increasingly aware in recent years that their analytical tools are an aid to the businessman in decision-making. Linear programming is one of the most useful decision tools, so we have integrated it into the theory of production. (3) Economists have questioned recently the appropriateness of profit maximization models with their focus on allocative efficiency. Firms often seek growth, or simply survival, first before pursuing profit maximization objectives. If economic models of the firm are to have predictive efficiency, the goals assumed to apply to firm behavior ought to be representative of those of firms in the real world.

To cover the essentials of microeconomics in a space of moderate dimensions, without being encyclopedic, we have chosen to simplify the theoretical models as much as possible. We avoid complex theoretical and mathematical constructions, since these usually are very time-consuming and best left for graduate courses. An advantage gained is that the student needs only a background in basic algebra to handle the material in the text.

E. W. S.
R. H. B.

CONTENTS

PART I INTRODUCTION

1 Introduction 3
What Is Economics? • Economic Methodology • Plan of the Book
Appendix
The Economic Organization of a Prisoner of War Camp
  by R. A. Radford 14

2 Supply and Demand 27
Classification of Markets • Supply and Demand—Competition • The Functions of Price Briefly Introduced • The Role of Information • An Application of Supply and Demand Analysis: Taxes • Conclusion
Problems 37
Appendix
Abundance—Scarcity by Frederic Bastiat 40

PART II THE THEORY OF CONSUMER BEHAVIOR AND DEMAND

3 Two Theories of Consumer Behavior 49
Marginal Utility Theory • Indifference Curve Theory • Summary
Problems 88

Appendix
The Experimental Determination of Indifference Curves
 by K. R. MacCrimmon and M. Toda 91

4 The Theory of Market Demand 114
Partial Equilibrium and *ceteris paribus* • The Nature of an
 Industry or Market • The Geographic Market Area • Market
 Demand and Its Measurement • The Market Demand Curve
 and the Demand Function • Summary
Problems 139
Appendix
The Pope and the Price of Fish *by Frederick W. Bell* 142
Change and Innovation in the Technology of Consumption
 by Kelvin Lancaster 148

PART III A THEORY OF PRODUCER BEHAVIOR

5 The Theory of Production: Marginal Productivity Analysis 159
The Theory of Production • Cost Curves • Short-Run Unit
 Costs • Long-Run Costs
Problems 190
Appendix
A Long-Run Cost Function for the Local Service Airline
 Industry: An Experiment in Non-Linear Estimation
 by George Eads, Marc Nerlove, and William Raduchel 192

6 Isoquant–Isocost Analysis and Linear Programming 212
Isoquant–Isocost Functions • The Determination of Firm
 Costs • Linear Programming • Summary and Conclusion
Problems 239
Appendix
An Introduction to the Simplex Solution to Linear Programming
 Problems *by E. Warren Shows and Robert H. Burton* 242
Economies of Scale in High School Operation
 by John Riew 249
Economies of Scale, Expansion Path, and Growth of Plants
 by T. Y. Shen 262

7 The Theory of Competition: The Firm and the Industry 278
The Rationale for a Competitive Model • The Characteristics
 of the Competitive Model • Conclusion: Long-Run
 Equilibrium Output Under Perfect Competition • Summary

Problems   303
Appendix
A Competitive Theory of the Housing Market
   by Edgar O. Olsen   306

8 **Monopoly**   320
A Definition of Monopoly • Importance of Monopoly Theory • The Theory of Pure Monopoly • Nonprofit-Maximizing Behavior • Summary
Problems   349
Appendix
A Case Study in Monopoly Price Setting: The Chesapeake Bay Bridge and Tunnel Commission *by E. Warren Shows and Robert H. Burton*   352
Allocative Efficiency vs. "X-Efficiency"
   by Harvey Leibenstein   355

9 **Imperfect Competition: Monopolistic Competition and Oligopoly**   377
Monopolistic Competition • Oligopoly • Summary
Problems   395
Appendix
Oligopoly: An Example and a Contrast *by E. Warren Shows and Robert H. Burton*   399
Duopoly, Oligopoly, and Emerging Competition
   by G. Warren Nutter   401

PART IV   THE THEORY OF DISTRIBUTION

10 **The Theory of Resource Price**   419
The Supply and Demand for Resources in Competitive Markets • Imperfect Competition—Resource and Output Markets • Summary and Conclusion
Problems   438
Appendix
A Universe of Commodities *by Kenneth E. Boulding*   440

11 **Rents and Wages**   458
The Classical and Modern Theories of Rent • Wages • Wages and Rent in the Long Run in Classical Theory • Conclusion
Problems   482
Appendix
The Negative Income Tax and the Supply of Work Effort
   by Michael Jay Boskin   484

The Negative Income Tax and the Supply of Work Effort:
  Comment *by Jonathan Kesselman*   505

12 **Interest and Profits**   512
Interest • Profits
Problems   528
Appendix
The Optimum Lifetime Distribution of Consumption
  Expenditures *by Lester C. Thurow*   531
Student Finance in Higher Education *by Stephen Merrett*   539

PART V   GENERAL EQUILIBRIUM

13 **General Equilibrium and Social Welfare Theory**   557
General Equilibrium Analysis: A Two-Commodity–Two-Resource Model • The Existence of a Unique General Equilibrium • General Equilibrium and Economic Efficiency • Welfare Economics
Problems   583
Appendix
Production, Consumption, and Externalities *by Robert U. Ayres and Allen V. Kneese*   586

Answers to Problems   608

Index   613

MICROECONOMICS

PART I. INTRODUCTION

1
INTRODUCTION

WHAT IS ECONOMICS?

A well-known economist, Jacob Viner, reportedly answered the question "What is economics?" with the response, "Economics is what economists do." For one important reason that statement provides a useful approach to an understanding of economics. As evidenced by economists' activities and interests at various times, economics seems to be continuously changing. In one period, depression and unemployment are the chief problems and receive the most attention. In another, economists' interest focuses on inflation or antitrust policy, and in still another, on full capacity growth or foreign trade. A list of economists' activities at any one time might, therefore, serve as the best guide to what economics is all about. However, a complete list of the activities of those people identified as economists might fill this book without helping very much to limit its scope.

A more useful definition proposes that *economics is the study of how best to satisfy relatively unlimited human wants with relatively scarce resources.* This definition identifies the ultimate objectives of economics, whatever current problems are receiving economists' attention. It is also a general definition applicable to all economies at all times. It is well to investigate why.

Human Needs and Wants

A fundamental proposition in economics is that human wants are unlimited relative to the economy's capacity at any one time to satisfy these wants. Some writers have questioned this proposition. One argument reasons that since there is a limit to how much one person can consume of any one commodity (a maximum amount of food one can eat, a maximum number of clothes one can wear, and so forth) an individual's total wants are also limited. The argument is true as far as it goes. Human wants at any given point in time are limited. If everyone were polled today and a list were compiled of all their wants, it would be finite. However, the list would certainly contain aggregate quantities of different goods and services well beyond the capacity of the economic system to supply. The economy can only produce a small fraction of the goods and services that would be required to satisfy completely every person's wants. Human wants are unlimited, therefore, when related to our capacity to produce.

Human wants are unlimited in another sense involving the time dimension and human development. All of us require not only the life-sustaining necessities, air, water, food, and the like, but also those amenities peculiar to humans only. These include chilled or heated air depending on the season, *haute cuisine*, sports, plays, literature, and sculpture. The most "human" consumption activities are physiologically the least necessary for survival, yet they require a large proportion of an economy's resources to satisfy. But most important, these latter wants tend to increase over time with the evolution of culture. As new products and services become socially acceptable, more and more individuals develop tastes and desires for them. Society is always experimenting with new ideas for products and services, some existing for only a brief span, others lasting much longer.

Modern man has been referred to, often with scorn, as "homo economicus," a title which contains a large element of truth, since most of us devote much of our time and most of our energy to economic pursuits. And when men are deprived of their economic pursuits, they do not revert to savagery or to philosophy. Rather, when deprived of economic relationships, modern men create new ones, as the paradigm in the appendix of this chapter illustrates. Perhaps the central importance of economics in our society is due to the overwhelming pervasiveness of economic intercourse.

The average American family of today lives in luxury undreamed of by the wealthiest nobles of the Middle Ages. Central heating and air conditioning, diversified diets and health services, and higher education are all generally available because our appetites for these goods and services increased commensurately with our ability to produce them. Sometimes our appetites for increased consumption stimulate increased production, while in other instances our expanding productive ability, aided by advertising and promotion efforts of entrepreneurs who introduce new products, stimulates our demand for consumption. The process will undoubtedly continue. The demand for personal services, travel, education, and a host of commodities, now unknown, seems capable of expansion without bound.

Summarizing, we may say that aggregate demand is unlimited because (1) at any time, people would like to consume more than the economy can produce and (2) throughout history, our capacity and desire to consume has continuously expanded as new products and services have been assimilated into society.

Limited Resources and the Fundamental Economic Problem

What are the "scarce resources" referred to in our definition of economics? A resource may be defined as anything used to produce goods or services. Resources may be tangible, such as pig iron, machine tools, and computers, or intangible, such as the services of labor. Resources include all the inputs which may be combined to produce outputs, where the outputs may be either consumer goods or inputs to other producers, while production may be defined as the process itself. The original and fundamental resource in every economy is the human mind, which develops the technology or the knowledge for combining resources most efficiently to produce useful commodities, and through time, technology has expanded as man has experimented with completely new ways to produce, or has improved existing techniques. However, at any point in time, the existing stock of knowledge or the state of industrial technology is *given*, and the quantity of tangible and intangible resources is *fixed* in amount. Even if all resources are used at maximum efficiency, the economy can produce only so much. In general, the volume of output possible with an economy's existing resources and available technology is circumscribed at every point in time.

When the fact of unlimited consumer demand is coupled with that of limited resources and technology, we are faced with the fundamental problem of economics: *allocating scarce resources among alternative uses for these resources*. It is conceivable that human ingenuity will ultimately prove greater in production than in consumption, that there will someday be enough resources, and the technology to use them, to satiate completely all consumers in society. If so, scarcity will be at an end, and economics will be obsolete. Until this occurs, however, societies will have to face the age-old problem of allocating their scarce resources among the alternative uses for these resources, in a way that is socially optimal. This fundamental economic problem in turn gives rise to five basic questions which all societies must answer:

1. What commodities to produce?
2. How much of each to produce?
3. What productive techniques to use and how to provide incentives?
4. How to distribute the output among the various members of society?
5. What provision to make for the future?

Though our interest is principally in a *market* economy, these five questions will be answered by every society, whether it consciously seeks to answer them or not. In addition, these questions are applicable to all societies, regardless of whether they are directed by tradition, as are primitive societies, by central planning, as are socialistic societies, by market decisions, as are capitalistic societies, or by a combination of all of the above, as are most real-world societies. A purely market economy automatically provides answers to all of these questions, although the market's solution to question 4 is not always considered ethically correct, and the market system may not always provide answers to 1, 2, and 5 that are socially acceptable. In our economy, a major proportion of the decisions on the basic questions are made in output and resource markets. For example, the number of automobiles to produce each year is essentially market determined. However, for many decisions bearing on the basic questions, the market is provided with special inducements to encourage the use of more resources in a given activity, or with restrictions to reduce the use of resources in another. At other points decisions are made centrally, for example, the quantity of legal heroin to be produced and consumed in our economy is determined by central authorities, presumably on the basis of medical needs.

ECONOMIC METHODOLOGY

The Role of Theory

Microeconomics developed, after long effort, as a theoretical system for analyzing how a market economy functions to answer the five fundamental questions. The models or theories (the terms are interchangeable) that developed to explain consumer, producer, and market behavior are artificial, abstract constructions apparently divorced from reality. It is a strange quirk of history that the father of modern economics, Adam Smith, an ivory-tower political philosopher and professor, stressed the practical side of the new science (his *Wealth of Nations* contains many practical examples), while David Ricardo, a very practical man of affairs and an economist as well, used in his work a theoretical approach nearly devoid of examples or illustrations. Ricardo, born some six years before the publication in 1776 of *Wealth of Nations*, was not only a most eminent English economist but also a successful businessman and politician. But despite having both feet planted firmly in the world of business and politics, Ricardo's approach to economics was extremely abstract and theoretical. For instance, he was the first to make the simplifying assumption of a homogeneous labor force; today such assumptions are commonplace. Ricardo's major work, *The Principles of Political Economy and Taxation*, contains little of a descriptive nature; it is almost completely theoretical.

Ricardo recognized that description of economic behavior is an inadequate basis for a science of economics. Description alone does not produce generalizations about economic behavior, without which prediction is not possible. But the ability to predict is the main test of any science from astronomy to zoology. In economics, prediction serves as the basis for control or economic policy. Therefore, political economy must be supported by sound generalized theories of how the economy operates. Only then can it be effective. For example, it makes little sense to propose that tariffs should be generally lowered unless we are prepared to say with some assurance what the effects of lower tariffs will be on the economy. Perhaps only the most practical men, such as Ricardo, can completely appreciate the value of pure theory.

Some people become impatient with theory and question its usefulness, sometimes with the remark, "I don't want theories—only facts." However, most economic events contain more facts than any observer could possibly detail if he spent his entire life on the job. Consider a simple transaction. Say you ordered bacon, eggs, toast, and coffee for breakfast. A nutrition expert might try to detail the calories, protein, vitamins, minerals, and the like, in the bacon, eggs, and toast, and in the cream and sugar in the coffee, and describe their utilization by the human body. A chemist would be interested in a whole different set of facts, as would a physicist, a psychologist, an accountant, or a specialist in any number of areas who might have a legitimate interest in the "facts" of your breakfast. The economist might be interested only in the prices at which these goods were sold, disregarding all the other facts involved.

Those who ask for facts, not theories, must really be asking for relevant facts—so they are necessarily proceeding according to some unconscious, implicit theory. Moreover, even if the facts are collected, they are useless unless they lead to meaningful statements or hypotheses about economic behavior. In economic analysis, hypotheses that prove sound graduate to the position of theories, tentatively accepted as a basis for predicting economic behavior. Only by means of theories can economics offer suggestions for changes in public policy designed to improve the economy's performance. Thus, theories are the basic tools of analysis in economics, while facts are necessary both to stimulate the discovery of theories and to test their validity.

Partial and General Equilibrium Analysis

Our objective in this book is to describe the way that a market-directed economy functions to answer the five basic economic questions. We have been using the term "economy" up to now without giving it a definition. We may start by defining an economy as all of the systems in a society which are involved in the process whereby scarce resources and commodities are allocated among their alternative uses. In a market economy these "systems" are principally the markets for goods and services and resources. The principal objects of economic analysis are the participants in these markets, including the individuals who demand products and supply resources and the firms which produce and supply these products. Other individuals and institutions that may be significant in economic analysis are government agencies and nonprofit institutions.

General Equilibrium Analysis. One approach to economics is to study the economy in its entirety, to see how all consumers and firms relate to each other. This is the methodology of *general equilibrium analysis*. General equilibrium analysis seeks answers to such questions as, "What pattern of output and input prices, including the prices of all consumer goods and all resources, would produce stability or equilibrium?" "Is stability possible at all?" "What would happen to the whole myriad of interrelationships in the economy if a disturbance occurred in one sector?" For example, if consumer demand for entertainment services increases, what effect will this have not only on the entertainment sector but also on all other portions of the economy, including resource markets? In short, general equilibrium analysis works within the framework of a comprehensive model of the entire economy.

Partial Equilibrium Analysis. The most extensively used methodology in economics has been partial rather than general equilibrium analysis. Developed by Alfred Marshall, the famous British economist of the late nineteenth century, partial equilibrium analysis has proved a highly successful technique and is extensively used in economic theory. The first objective of partial equilibrium analysis is an understanding of the behavior of individual segments or sectors of the economy rather than the whole economy. Partial equilibrium analysis focuses therefore on the behavior of consumers, firms, and markets separately, rather than the behavior of the whole economy. Although partial equilibrium analysis admits the interrelatedness of all sectors in an economy, in developing models of economic behavior, it makes a sweeping assumption, called the *ceteris paribus* assumption, which holds constant those forces which do not have a direct bearing on the sector under investigation. One of the sectors investigated most in partial equilibrium analysis is the industry or market for some single consumer good and the relationship of the industry to the individual firm, in which case, all other markets and industries in the economy are effectively ignored by making the *ceteris paribus* assumption. As another example, if we are concerned with a consumer's allocation of his available income among the possible consumer goods that he might purchase, we hold constant all factors such as output prices, allowing to vary only the quantities of the goods that the consumer purchases.

The second objective of partial equilibrium analysis, like general equilibrium analysis, is an understanding of how an economy functions as a whole. The principal difference between the two methods is that partial equilibrium analysis studies first the components of the system, then tackles the broader question of how the parts fit together within the over-all economy. The use of one approach does not preclude the use of the other, however, and we will use both.

The method employed throughout most of this book is partial equilibrium analysis. Given an understanding of the way consumers and firms operate in isolation, we then make use of general equilibrium analysis to see how the whole economy functions. As the book progresses, we will see that partial equilibrium analysis provides a useful theoretical framework for analyzing a wide range of economic questions, and when combined with general equilibrium analysis at the end of the book, provides the necessary analytical tools for studying the economy in its entirety.

The Concept of Equilibrium. Equilibrium in economics is synonymous with stability, and equilibrium analysis is the study of the forces that determine stability, e.g., those values of relevant economic variables which tend to produce stability, either in a single sector of the economy, as in partial equilibrium analysis, or in the whole economy, as in general equilibrium analysis. For example, regarding the former, equilibrium analysis focuses on those values of price and quantity in a given market which, given the conditions of supply and demand, will have a tendency to be stable through time. If something is disturbed in the sector (say, demand increases), equilibrium analysis investigates the whole process whereby new conditions of stability are reached. General equilibrium analysis, on the other hand, is concerned with the entire set of output prices and resource prices in the economy and their respective quantities, which will result in over-all economic stability, e.g., no tendency for any price or quantity in the economy to vary.

Equilibrium values of relevant variables are singled out as having special importance in economic theory, because if these values are disturbed, the system, if generally stable, will generate forces which restore them. Most economists believe that the economy, and most industries within the economy, are inherently stable, so that the equilibrium values of economic variables are the norm, or at least the system tends toward the equilibrium values. Of course, at any one time the system is probably out of equilibrium in at least some of its sectors. Even so, the *tendency* is for equilibrium to be restored whether it is ever completely restored or not. It is the tendency of economic systems to reach an equilibrium which provides the basis for predicting what changes will occur. In short, disequilibrium is a basis for predicting change in a given direction, whereas equilibrium is a basis for predicting no further changes. Thus, not only does equilibrium analysis predict what the pattern or prices in an economy will be but it also provides the tools for understanding the forces which determine price.

Statics and Dynamics

If a stable equilibrium condition exists in a market for a time, followed by a disturbance which upsets the equilibrium, it will take time before a new equilibrium condition is restored. For example, the height of the Tarpon Springs, Florida, sponge-diving industry was in the 1920's just before the discovery of a process for producing cheap synthetic sponges. The new process caused a decline in the demand for natural sponges that has virtually destroyed the natural sponge industry. If we took an "economic" picture of the sponge-diving industry just before the new process was introduced, waited and took another picture a year or so later, we would be able to make a number of revealing comparisons regarding price, quantity, the number of divers and boats, and other related factors. On the other hand, if we took continuous pictures of the industry (a movie), we could observe not only the values of such variables as price and quantity at the beginning and ending points of periods of elapsed time, but also the values of the important variables as they changed from day to day, or even hour to hour. The approach which we use almost exclusively in this book is illustrated by the before–after pictures and is called *comparative statics*. The latter approach, that of taking a moving picture of the economic phenomena through time, is called economic *dynamics*. Comparative statics, in many ways the weaker of the two approaches, has nevertheless been proved the most efficient approach for a wide variety of purposes. Economic dynamics reveals much more about the interworkings of the adjustment process than comparative statics, yet it is more cumbersome to apply. For many problems our main aim is to predict the direction and magnitude of changes expected to occur after an elapsed period of time, and for this purpose, comparative statics is adequate.

Normative Versus Positive Economics

The study of an economic system *as it is* is called *positive economics*, whereas *normative economics* is that area or subdivision of economics concerned with the socially desirable or socially optimum forms of economic organization. To put it more simply, positive economics is concerned with *what is*; normative economics is concerned with what *ought to be*.

The first task of economic analysis is to understand how an economic system functions, that is, to understand the institutions in existence and the mechanisms which determine how they interact to establish relative prices, output levels, and the distribution of output. Only by first understanding the nature of an economic system *as it exists* can there be a foundation for proposing changes in the system. Positive economics therefore logically precedes public policy.

Public policy has the over-all objective of achieving the best or optimal allocation of scarce resources among alternative uses for these resources, where the optimal allocation is one which maximizes social well-being. This involves not only the specific allocation of resources to determine what is to be produced and in what numbers, but also how output is to be distributed. But criteria are needed for determining when social well-being has been improved. Normative economics provides such criteria. Normative economics supplies the missing link, for it provides a conceptual model of the economy or parts of the economy, which is ideal or best from the standpoint of society. Normative models may not always describe economic structures as they in fact exist. In fact, it is the existence of a difference between the normative model and the positive model that indicates the need for change. The normative model can be compared with the situation which in fact exists, to provide a basis for enlightened public policy, e.g., to encourage or force the real world to conform to the normative conception.

For most of this book our concern will be with positive economics. We will develop theories or generalizations about economic behavior which give us a picture of how the system actually works. These positive models will then be compared with normative ones to establish a basis for economic policy. We will find that the normative models are more difficult to develop and are subject to question largely because of the difficulties involved in establishing criteria for social well-being. Nevertheless, we will be able to make some positive–normative comparisons which will in turn lead to guarded suggestions for economic policy.

Comments on the Use of Mathematics

Microeconomics draws heavily upon a few basic mathematical concepts, especially functional relationships which can be graphed in two dimensions, and simple algebraic equations. For example, economists are interested in the relationship between the number of units of a good consumed by a consumer and the total satisfaction or utility which he enjoys as a result.

In addition, economic analysis has tended to focus on the effects of small adjustments to the relevant variables, more than on the total magnitudes. For example, as will be developed more fully in Chapter 3, the most important consideration for analysis of consumer behavior is the additional satisfaction derived from the last unit of a commodity consumed, rather than the total satisfaction from consuming all units of the commodity. One can argue that the total satisfaction gained from the consumption of air is very considerable, since without it we would die, yet the last breath in any given time period is a matter of indifference. Whether you take twelve, thirteen, or fourteen breaths a minute, the total satisfaction you derive from air will be about the same. The extra satisfaction or what economists call "the marginal utility" of the thirteenth or fourteenth breath of air per minute is, therefore, close to zero, and it is no coincidence that so is its price. However, suppose for some reason you were restricted to two breaths a minute (for example, if air pollution became so severe you had to buy bottled air to breathe, and you could afford only a small amount). Then the extra utility of the second breath each minute would be very high indeed, and so too would be the price you would be willing to pay for it (or for a third or fourth breath in any given minute). The technique of analyzing what happens when we make small adjustments to the important variables in a model is called *marginal analysis*.

Marginal analysis is employed to study firm behavior as well as consumer behavior. Since firms react to opportunities for profit and growth, marginal analysis focuses upon the effects of the firm's decisions to raise or lower output on its total costs, total revenues, and growth rate. For example, marginal cost, developed in Chapter 5, measures the increase in total costs which results when an additional unit of output is produced.

Mathematically inclined readers will recognize the idea of marginal analysis as an economic application of the derivative, the fundamental concept of the calculus. However, a knowledge of calculus is not required to understand microeconomics and is not required to handle the material in this text.

PLAN OF THE BOOK

This book shows how a market economy answers the five basic questions facing every society. Although our economy employs a mixture of private and public decision-making, we focus largely on the functions of a pure market system to provide a theoretical basis for economic policies. As a preview of the use of the basic tools of economic theory, the concepts of supply and demand are introduced in Chapter 2.

Part II is concerned with demand, and since we assume that the purpose of all production is ultimately consumption, we begin our analysis with the theory of individual consumer behavior in Chapter 3. In Chapter 4, we develop the concept of market demand as an aggregation of individual consumer demand.

Part III develops the theory of supply and, by combining the theory of supply with that of demand, completes the theory of price. First, Chapters 5 and 6 are devoted to the principles of production and costs, which provide the foundation for the theory of the firm. Firm behavior is then analyzed in the four types of markets, including competition (Chapter 7) and monopoly (Chapter 8) at the extremes. The two types of imperfect competition, oligopoly and monopolistic competition, the typical market structures, are investigated in Chapter 9.

Part IV is concerned with price determination in markets for productive resources. Chapter 10 develops the basic theoretical tools necessary for analyzing resource pricing, and these tools are employed in Chapters 11 and 12 to analyze price determination for rents and wages. Chapter 12 concludes this section with a discussion of the role of interest and profits in a market system.

Part V summarizes the theory of microeconomics by pulling together the general conclusions of the four previous parts of the book, focusing on those conditions which bring about efficient resource use.

Our objective is to cover the entire field of price theory concisely enough to allow it to be completed in one course. It seemed important, nevertheless, to include recent developments, for example, to relate microeconomics more closely to macroeconomics, especially in the matter of aggregate demand and investment theory, and to recognize that decision models such as linear programming are not only extremely practical adjuncts to business planning but can also be integrated into the heart of economic theory. In addition, we have included a discussion of the goals of management in large enterprises, because, where ownership and control are divorced, profit maximization models of firm behavior can be misleading.

REFERENCES

BLACK, DUNCAN, "The Unity of Economic and Political Science," *Economic Journal*, 60 (September 1950), 506–514.

FRIEDMAN, MILTON, "The Methodology of Positive Economics," *Essays in Positive Economics*. Chicago: University of Chicago Press, 1953, 1–43.

KEYNES, J. M., *The Scope and Method of Political Economy*, 4th ed. London: Macmillan, 1930.

KOOPMANS, TJALLING C., *Three Essays on the State of Economic Science*. New York: McGraw-Hill, Inc., 1957, 129–149.

LANGE, O., "The Scope and Methods of Economics," *Review of Economic Studies*, 13 (1945–1946), 19–32.

LIEBHAFSKY, H. H., *The Nature of Price Theory*. Homewood, Ill.: The Dorsey Press, Inc., 1963. Chap. 10.

MILL, J. S., *Principles of Political Economy* (1848). London: Longmans, Green & Co., 1929.

ROBBINS, LIONEL, *An Essay on the Nature and Significance of Economic Science*, 2nd ed. New York: Macmillan, 1935.

APPENDIX TO CHAPTER 1

The Economic Organization of a Prisoner of War Camp

R. A. RADFORD

Every student is encouraged to read Radford's "The Economic Organization of a Prisoner of War Camp." Radford shows how a system of markets quickly emerged in a war camp society as a means of efficiently allocating the limited commodities available to prisoners. The latter included rations, canned goods, cigarettes, and the like supplied by Red Cross packages. Cigarettes became the universally acceptable medium of exchange, quickly replacing barter exchange. Prices were determined by supply and demand forces except for one period when prices were fixed. Radford describes how the markets functioned smoothly and efficiently in periods of ample supplies of commodities and cigarettes, but became disorganized and inefficient when supplies of commodities increased or decreased relative to cigarettes.

INTRODUCTION

After allowance has been made for abnormal circumstances, the social institutions, ideas and habits of groups in the outside world are to be found reflected in a Prisoner of War Camp. It is an unusual but a vital society. . . .

One aspect of social organization is to be found in economic activity, and this, along with other manifestations of a group existence, is to be found in any P.O.W. camp. True, a prisoner is not dependent on his exertions for the provision of the necessaries, or even the luxuries of life, but through his economic activity, the exchange of goods and services, his standard of material comfort is considerably enhanced. . . .

Nevertheless, it cannot be too strongly emphasized that economic activities do not bulk so large in prison society as they do in the larger world. There can be little production; as has been said, the prisoner is independent of his exertions for the provision of the necessities and luxuries of life; the emphasis lies in exchange and the media of exchange. . . . Everyone receives a roughly

From *Economica*, XII (November 1945), 189–201. Reprinted by permission.

equal share of essentials; it is by trade that individual preferences are given expression and comfort increased. All at some time, and most people regularly, make exchanges of one sort or another.

Although a P.O.W. camp provides a living example of a simple economy which might be used as an alternative to the Robinson Crusoe economy beloved by the textbooks, and its simplicity renders the demonstration of certain economic hypotheses both amusing and instructive, it is suggested that the principal significance is sociological. True, there is interest in observing the growth of economic institutions and customs in a brand-new society, small and simple enough to prevent detail from obscuring the basic pattern and disequilibrium from obscuring the working of the system. But the essential interest lies in the universality and the spontaneity of this economic life; it came into existence not by conscious imitation but as a response to the immediate needs and circumstances. Any similarity between prison organization and outside organization arises from similar stimuli evoking similar responses.

The following is as brief an account of the essential data as may render the narrative intelligible. The camps of which the writer had experience were Oflags and consequently the economy was not complicated by payments for work by the detaining power. They consisted normally of between 1,200 and 2,500 people, housed in a number of separate but intercommunicating bungalows, one company of 200 or so to a building. Each company formed a group within the main organization and inside the company, the room and the messing syndicate, a voluntary and spontaneous group who fed together, formed the constituent units.

Between individuals there was active trading in all consumer goods and in some services. Most trading was for food against cigarettes or other foodstuffs; cigarettes rose from the status of a normal commodity to that of currency. RMK.s existed but had no circulation save for gambling debts, as few articles could be purchased with them from the canteen.

Our supplies consisted of rations provided by the detaining power and (principally) the contents of Red Cross food parcels—tinned milk, jam, butter, biscuits, bully, chocolate, sugar, etc., and cigarettes. So far the supplies to each person were equal and regular. Private parcels of clothing, toilet requisites and cigarettes were also received, and here equality ceased owing to the different numbers despatched and the vagaries of the post. All these articles were the subject of trade and exchange.

THE DEVELOPMENT AND ORGANIZATION OF THE MARKET

Very soon after capture people realized that it was both undesirable and unnecessary, in view of the limited size and the equality of supplies, to give away or to accept gifts of cigarettes or food. "Goodwill" developed into trading as a more equitable means of maximizing individual satisfaction.

We reached a transit camp in Italy about a fortnight after capture and received one fourth of a Red Cross food parcel each a week later. At once exchanges, already established, multiplied in volume. Starting with simple direct barter, such as a nonsmoker giving a smoker friend his cigarette issue in exchange for a chocolate ration, more complex exchanges soon became an accepted custom. Stories circulated of a padre who started off round the camp with a tin of cheese and five cigarettes and returned to his bed with a complete parcel in addition to his original cheese and cigarettes; the market was not yet perfect. Within a week or two, as the volume of trade grew, rough scales of exchange values came into existence. Sikhs, who had at first exchanged tinned beef for practically any other foodstuff, began to insist on jam and margarine. It was realized that a tin of jam was worth one half lb. of margarine plus something else, that a cigarette issue was worth several chocolate issues, and a tin of diced carrots was worth practically nothing.

In this camp we did not visit other bungalows very much and prices varied from place to place; hence the germ of truth in the story of the itinerant priest. By the end of a month, when we reached our permanent camp, there was a lively trade in all commodities and their relative values were well known, and expressed not in terms of one another—one didn't quote bully in terms of sugar—but in terms of cigarettes. The cigarette became the standard of value. In the permanent camp people started by wandering through the bungalows calling their offers—"cheese for seven" (cigarettes)—and the hours after parcel issue were Bedlam. The inconveniences of this system soon led to its replacement by an Exchange and Mart notice board in every bungalow, where under the headings "name," "room number," "wanted," and "offered" sales and wants were advertised. When a deal went through, it was crossed off the board. The public and semipermanent records of transactions led to cigarette prices being well known and thus tending to equality throughout the camp, although there were always opportunities for an astute trader to make a profit from arbitrage. With this development everyone, including nonsmokers, was willing to sell for cigarettes, using them to buy at another time and place. Cigarettes became the normal currency, though, of course, barter was never extinguished.

The unity of the market and the prevalence of a single price varied directly with the general level of organization and comfort in the camp. A transit camp was always chaotic and uncomfortable: People were overcrowded, no one knew where anyone else was living, and few took the trouble to find out. Organization was too slender to include an Exchange and Mart board, and private advertisements were the most that appeared. Consequently a transit camp was not one market but many. The price of a tin of salmon is known to have varied by two cigarettes in 20 between one end of a hut and the other. Despite a high level of organization in Italy, the market was morcellated in this manner at the first transit camp we reached after our removal to Germany in the autumn of 1943. In this camp—Stalag VIIA at Moosburg in Bavaria—there were up to 50,000 prisoners of all nationalities. French, Russians, Italians, and Jugo-Slavs were free to move about within the camp: British and Americans were confined to their compounds, although a few cigarettes given to a sentry would always procure permission for one or two men to visit other compounds. The people who first visited the highly organized French trading center, with its stalls and known prices, found coffee extract—relatively cheap among the tea-drinking English—commanding a fancy price in biscuits or cigarettes, and some enterprising people made small fortunes that way. (Incidentally we found out later that much of the coffee went "over the wire" and sold for phenomenal prices at black market cafés in Munich: Some of the French prisoners were said to have made substantial sums in RMk.s. This was one of the few occasions on which our normally closed economy came into contact with other economic worlds.)

Eventually public opinion grew hostile to these monopoly profits—not everyone could make contact with the French—and trading with them was put on a regulated basis. Each group of beds was given a quota of articles to offer and the transaction was carried out by accredited representatives from the British compound, with monopoly rights. The same method was used for trading with sentries elsewhere, as in this trade, secrecy and reasonable prices had a peculiar importance, but as is ever the case with regulated companies, the interloper proved too strong.

The permanent camps in Germany saw the highest level of commercial organization. In addition to the Exchange and Mart notice boards, a shop was organized as a public utility, controlled by representatives of the Senior British Officer, on a no profit basis. People left their surplus clothing, toilet requisites and food there until they were sold at a fixed price in cigarettes. Only sales in cigarettes were accepted—there was no barter—and there was no higgling. For food at least there were standard prices: Clothing is less homogeneous and the price was decided around a norm by the seller and the shop manager in agreement; shirts would average say 80, ranging from 60 to 120 according to quality and age. Of food, the shop carried small stocks for convenience; the capital was provided by a loan from the bulk store of Red Cross cigarettes and repaid by a small commission taken on the first transactions. Thus the cigarette attained its fullest currency status, and the market was almost completely unified.

It is thus to be seen that a market came into existence without labor or production. The B.R.C.S. [British Red Cross Society] may be considered as "Nature" of the textbook, and the articles of trade—food, clothing and cigarettes—as free gifts—land or manna. Despite this, and despite a roughly equal distribution of resources, a market came into spontaneous operation, and prices were fixed by the operation of supply and demand. It is difficult to reconcile this fact with the labor theory of value.

Actually there was an embryo labor market. Even when cigarettes were not scarce, there was usually some unlucky person willing to perform services for them. Laundrymen advertised at two cigarettes a garment. Battle dress was scrubbed and pressed and a pair of trousers lent for the interim period for twelve. A good pastel portrait cost thirty or a tin of "Kam." Odd tailoring and other jobs similarly had their prices.

There were also entrepreneurial services. There was a coffee stall owner who sold tea, coffee or cocoa at two cigarettes a cup, buying his raw materials at market prices and hiring labor to gather fuel and to stoke; he actually enjoyed the services of a chartered accountant at one stage. After a period of great prosperity he overreached himself and failed disastrously for several hundred cigarettes. Such large-scale private enterprise was rare but several middlemen or professional traders existed. The padre in Italy, or the men at Moosburg who opened trading relations with the French, are examples: The more subdivided the market, the less perfect the advertisement of prices, and the less stable the prices, the greater was the scope for these operators. One man capitalized his knowledge of Urdu by buying meat from the Sikhs and selling butter and jam in return: As his operations became better known, more and more people entered this trade, prices in the Indian Wing approximated more nearly to those elsewhere, though to the end a "contact" among the Indians was valuable, as linguistic difficulties prevented the trade from being quite free. Some were specialists in the Indian trade, the food, clothing, or even the watch trade. Middlemen traded on their own account or on commission. Price rings and agreements were suspected and the traders certainly cooperated. Nor did they welcome newcomers. Unfortunately the writer knows little of the workings of these people: Public opinion was hostile and the professionals were usually of a retiring disposition.

One trader in food and cigarettes, operating in a period of dearth, enjoyed a high reputation. His capital, carefully saved, was originally about 50 cigarettes, with which he bought rations on issue days and held them until the price rose just before the next issue. He also picked up a little by arbitrage; several times a day he visited every Exchange or Mart notice board and took advantage of every discrepancy between prices of goods offered and wanted. His knowledge of prices, markets and names of those who had received cigarette parcels was phenomenal. By these means he kept himself smoking steadily—his profits—while his capital remained intact.

Sugar was issued on Saturday. About Tuesday two of us used to visit Sam and make a deal; as old customers he would advance as much of the price as he could spare then, and entered the transaction in a book. On Saturday morning he left cocoa tins on our beds for the ration, and picked them up on Saturday afternoon. We were hoping for a calendar at Christmas, but Sam failed too. He was left holding a big black treacle issue when the price fell, and in this weakened state was unable to withstand an unexpected arrival of parcels and the consequent price fluctuations. He paid in full, but from his capital. The next Tuesday, when I paid my usual visit he was out of business.

Credit entered into many, perhaps into most, transactions, in one form or another. Sam paid in advance as a rule for his purchases of future deliveries of sugar, but many buyers asked for credit, whether the commodity was sold spot or future. Naturally prices varied according to the terms of sale. A treacle ration might be advertized for four cigarettes now or five next week. And in the future market "bread now" was a vastly different thing from "bread Thursday." Bread was issued on Thursday and Monday, four and three days' rations respectively, and by Wednesday and Sunday night it had risen at least one cigarette per ration, from seven to eight, by supper time. One man always saved a ration to sell then at the peak price: His offer of "bread now" stood out on the board among a number of "bread Monday's" fetching one or two less, or not selling at all—and he always smoked on Sunday night.

THE CIGARETTE CURRENCY

Although cigarettes as currency exhibited certain peculiarities, they performed all the functions of a metallic currency as a unit of account, as a measure of value, and as a store of value, and shared most of its characteristics. They were homogeneous, reasonably durable, and of convenient size for the smallest or, in packets, for the largest transactions. Incidentally, they could be clipped or sweated by rolling them between the fingers so that tobacco fell out.

Cigarettes were also subject to the working of Gresham's Law. Certain brands were more popular than others as smokes, but for currency purposes a cigarette was a cigarette. Consequently buyers used the poorer qualities and the Shop rarely saw the more popular brands: Cigarettes such as Churchman's No. 1 were rarely used for trading. At one time cigarettes hand rolled from pipe tobacco began to circulate. Pipe tobacco was issued in lieu of cigarettes by the Red Cross at a rate of 25 cigarettes to the ounce and this rate was standard in exchanges, but an ounce would produce 30 homemade cigarettes. Naturally, people with machine-made cigarettes broke them down and rerolled the tobacco, and the real cigarette virtually disappeared from the market. Hand-rolled cigarettes were not homogeneous and prices could no longer be quoted in them with safety: Each cigarette was examined before it was accepted and thin ones were rejected, or extra demanded as a makeweight. For a time we suffered all the inconveniences of a debased currency.

Machine-made cigarettes were always universally acceptable, both for what they would buy and for themselves. It was this intrinsic value which gave rise to their principal disadvantage as currency, a disadvantage which exists, but to a far smaller extent, in the case of metallic currency;—that is, a strong demand for nonmonetary purposes. Consequently our economy was repeatedly subject to deflation and to periods of monetary stringency. While the Red Cross issue of 50 or 25 cigarettes per man per week came in regularly, and while there were fair stocks held, the cigarette currency suited its purpose admirably. But when the issue was interrupted, stocks soon ran out, prices fell, trading declined in volume and became increasingly a matter of barter. This deflationary tendency was periodically offset by the sudden injection of new currency. Private cigarette parcels arrived in a trickle throughout the year, but the big numbers came in quarterly when the Red Cross received its allocation of transport. Several hundred thousand cigarettes might arrive in the space of a fortnight. Prices soared, and then began to fall, slowly at first but with increasing rapidity as stocks ran out, until the next big delivery. Most of our economic troubles could be attributed to this fundamental instability.

PRICE MOVEMENTS

Many factors affected prices, the strongest and most noticeable being the periodical currency inflation and deflation described in the last paragraphs. The periodicity of this price cycle depended on cigarette and, to a far lesser extent, on food deliveries. At one time in the early days, before any private parcels had arrived and when there were no individual stocks, the weekly issue of cigarettes and food parcels occurred on a Monday. The nonmonetary demand for cigarettes was great, and less elastic than the demand for food: Consequently prices fluctuated weekly, falling toward Sunday night and rising sharply on Monday morning. Later, when many people held reserves, the weekly issue had no such effect, being too small a proportion of the total available. Credit allowed people with no reserves to meet their nonmonetary demand over the weekend.

The general price level was affected by other factors. An influx of new prisoners, proverbially hungry, raised it. Heavy air raids in the vicinity of the camp probably increased the nonmonetary demand for cigarettes and accentuated deflation. Good and bad war news certainly had its effect, and the general waves of optimism and pessimism which swept the camp were reflected in prices. Before breakfast one morning in March of this year, a rumor of the arrival of parcels and cigarettes was circulated. Within ten minutes I sold a treacle ration, for four cigarettes (hitherto offered in vain for three), and many similar deals went through. By 10 o'clock the rumor was denied, and treacle that day found no more buyers even at two cigarettes.

More interesting than changes in the general price level were changes in the price structure. Changes in the supply of a commodity, in the German ration scale or in the makeup of Red Cross parcels, would raise the price of one commodity relative to others. Tins of oatmeal, once a rare and much sought after luxury in the parcels, became a commonplace in 1943, and the price fell. In hot weather the demand for cocoa fell and that for soap rose. A new recipe would be reflected in the price level: The discovery that raisins and sugar could be turned into an alcoholic liquor of remarkable potency reacted permanently on the dried fruit market. The invention of electric immersion heaters run off the power points made tea, a drug on the market in Italy, a certain seller in Germany.

In August 1944, the supplies of parcels and cigarettes were both halved. Since both sides of the equation were changed in the same degree, changes in prices were not anticipated. But this was not the case: The nonmonetary demand for cigarettes was less elastic than the demand for food, and food prices fell a little. More important however were the changes in the price structure. German margarine and jam, hitherto valueless owing to adequate supplies of Canadian butter and marmalade, acquired a new value. Chocolate, popular and a certain seller, and sugar fell. Bread rose; several standing contracts of bread for cigarettes were broken, especially when the bread ration was reduced a few weeks later.

In February 1945, the German soldier who drove the ration wagon was found to be willing to exchange loaves of bread at the rate of one loaf for a bar of chocolate. Those in the know began selling bread and buying chocolate, by then almost unsalable in a period of serious deflation. Bread, at about 40, fell slightly; chocolate rose from 15; the supply of bread was not enough for the two commodities to reach parity, but the tendency was unmistakable.

The substitution of German margarine for Canadian butter when parcels were halved naturally affected their relative values, margarine appreciating at the expense of butter. Similarly, two brands of dried milk, hitherto differing in quality and therefore in price by five cigarettes a tin, came together in price as the wider substitution of the cheaper raised its relative value.

Enough has been cited to show that any change in conditions affected both the general price level and the price structure. It was this latter phenomenon which wrecked our planned economy.

PAPER CURRENCY—BULLY MARKS

Around D-Day, food and cigarettes were plentiful, business was brisk and the camp in an optimistic mood. Consequently the Entertainments Committee felt the moment opportune to launch a restaurant, where food and hot drinks were sold while a band and variety turns performed. Earlier experiments, both public and private, had pointed the way, and the scheme was a great success. Food was bought at market prices to provide the meals and the small profits were devoted to a reserve fund and used to bribe Germans to provide greasepaints and other necessities for the camp theatre. Originally meals were sold for cigarettes but this meant that the whole scheme was vulnerable to the periodic deflationary waves, and furthermore heavy smokers were unlikely to attend much. The whole success of the scheme depended on an adequate amount of food being offered for sale in the normal manner.

To increase and facilitate trade, and to stimulate supplies and customers therefore, and secondarily to avoid the worst effects of deflation when it should come, a paper currency was organized by the Restaurant and the Shop. The Shop bought food on behalf of the Restaurant with paper notes and the paper was accepted equally with the cigarettes in the Restaurant or Shop, and passed back to the Shop to purchase more food. The Shop acted as a bank of issue. The paper money was backed 100 per cent by food; hence its name, the Bully Mark. . . . There could be no overissues, as is permissible with a normal bank of issue, since the eventual dispersal of the camp and consequent redemption of all BMk.s was anticipated in the near future.

Originally one BMk. was worth one cigarette and for a short time both circulated freely inside and outside the Restaurant. Prices were quoted in BMk.s and cigarettes with equal freedom—and for a short time the BMk. showed signs of replacing the cigarette as currency. The BMk. was tied to food, but not to cigarettes: As it was issued against food, say 45 for a tin of milk and so on, any reduction in the BMk. prices of food would have meant that there were unbacked BMk.s in circulation. But the price of both food and BMk.s could and did fluctuate with the supply of cigarettes.

While the Restaurant flourished, the scheme was a success: The Restaurant bought heavily, all foods were salable and prices were stable.

In August parcels and cigarettes were halved and the Camp was bombed. The Restaurant closed for a short while and sales of food became difficult. Even when the Restaurant reopened, the food and cigarette shortage became increasingly acute and people were unwilling to convert such valuable goods into paper and to hold them for luxuries like snacks and tea. Less of the right kinds of food for the Restaurant were sold, and the Shop became glutted with dried fruit, chocolate, sugar, etc., which the Restaurant could not buy. The price level and the price structure changed. The BMk. fell to four-fifths of a cigarette and eventually farther still, and it became unacceptable save in the Restaurant. There was a flight from the BMk., no longer convertible into cigarettes or popular foods. The cigarette re-established itself.

But the BMk. was sound! The Restaurant closed in the New Year with a progressive food shortage and the long evenings without lights due to intensified Allied air raids, and BMk.s could only be spent in the Coffee Bar —relict of the Restaurant—or on the few unpopular foods in the Shop, the owners of which were prepared to accept them. In the end all holders of BMk.s were paid in full, in cups of coffee or in prunes. People who had bought BMk.s for cigarettes or valuable jam or biscuits in their heyday were aggrieved that they should have stood the loss involved by their restricted choice, but they suffered no actual loss of market value.

PRICE FIXING

Along with this scheme came a determined attempt at a planned economy, at price fixing. The Medical Officer had long been anxious to control food sales, for fear of some people selling too much, to the detriment of their health. The deflationary waves and their effects on prices were inconvenient to all and would be dangerous to the Restaurant which had to carry stocks. Furthermore, unless the BMk. was convertible into cigarettes at about par, it had little chance of gaining confidence and of succeeding as a currency. As has been explained, the BMk. was tied to food but could not be tied to cigarettes, which fluctuated in value. Hence, while BMk. prices of food were fixed for all time, cigarette prices of food and BMk.s varied.

The Shop, backed by the Senior British Officer, was now in a position to enforce price control both inside and outside its walls. Hitherto a standard price had been fixed for food left for sale in the shop, and prices outside were roughly in conformity with this scale, which was recommended as a "guide" to sellers but fluctuated a good deal around it. Sales in the Shop at recommended prices were apt to be slow though a good price might be obtained: Sales outside could be made more quickly at lower prices. (If sales outside were to be at higher prices, goods were withdrawn from the Shop until the recommended price rose: But the recommended price was sluggish and could not follow the market closely by reason of its very purpose, which was stability.) The Exchange and Mart notice boards came under the control of the Shop: Advertisements which exceeded a 5 per cent departure from the recommended scale were liable to be crossed out by authority; unauthorized sales were discouraged by authority and also by public opinion, strongly in favor of a just and stable price. (Recommended prices were fixed partly from market data, partly on the advice of the M.O.)

At first the recommended scale was a success: The Restaurant, a big buyer, kept prices stable around this level; opinion and the 5 per cent tolerance helped. But when the price level fell with the August cuts and the price structure changed, the recommended scale was too rigid. Unchanged at first, as no deflation was expected, the scale was tardily lowered, but the prices of goods on the new scale remained in the same relation to one another, owing to the BMk., while on the market the price structure had changed. And the modifying influence of the Restaurant had gone. The scale was moved up and down several times, slowly following the inflationary and deflationary waves, but it was rarely adjusted to changes in the price structure. More and more advertisements were crossed off the board, and black market sales at unauthorized prices increased: Eventually public opinion turned against the recommended scale and authority gave up the struggle. In the last few weeks, with unparalleled deflation, prices fell with alarming rapidity, no scales existed, and supply and demand, alone and unmellowed, determined prices.

PUBLIC OPINION

Public opinion on the subject of trading was vocal if confused and changeable, and generalizations as to its direction are difficult and dangerous. A tiny minority held that all trading was undesirable as it engendered an unsavory atmosphere; occasional frauds and sharp practices were cited as proof. Certain forms of trading were more generally condemned; trade with the Germans was criticized by many. Red Cross toilet articles, which were in short supply and only issued in cases of actual need, were excluded from trade by law and opinion working in unshakable harmony. At one time, when there had been several cases of malnutrition reported among the more devoted smokers, no trade in German rations was permitted, as the victims became an additional burden on the depleted food reserves of the Hospital. But while certain activities were condemned as antisocial, trade itself was practiced, and its utility appreciated, by almost everyone in the camp.

More interesting was opinion on middlemen and prices. Taken as a whole, opinion was hostile to the middleman. His function, and his hard work in bringing buyer and seller together, were ignored; profits were not regarded as a reward for labor, but as the result of sharp practices. Despite the fact that his very existence was proof to the contrary, the middleman was held to be redundant in view of the existence of an official Shop and the Exchange and Mart. Appreciation only came his way when he was willing to advance the price of a sugar ration, or to buy goods spot and carry them against a future sale. In these cases the element of risk was obvious to all, and the convenience of the service was felt to merit some reward. Particularly unpopular was the middleman with an element of monopoly, the man who contacted the ration wagon driver, or the man who utilized his knowledge of Urdu. And middlemen as a group were blamed for reducing prices. Opinion notwithstanding, most people dealt with a middleman, whether consciously or unconsciously, at some time or another.

There was a strong feeling that everything had its "just price" in cigarettes. While the assessment of the just price, which incidentally varied between camps, was impossible of explanation, this price was nevertheless pretty closely known. It can best be defined as the price usually fetched by an article in good times when cigarettes were plentiful. The "just price" changed slowly; it was unaffected by short-term variations in supply, and while opinion might be resigned to departures from the "just price," a strong feeling of resentment persisted. A more satisfactory definition of the "just price" is impossible. Everyone knew what it was, though no one could explain why it should be so.

As soon as prices began to fall with a cigarette shortage, a clamor arose, particularly against those who held reserves and who bought at reduced prices. Sellers at cut prices were criticized and their activities referred to as the black market. In every period of dearth the explosive question of "should nonsmokers receive a cigarette ration?" was discussed to profitless length. Unfortunately, it was the nonsmoker, or the light smoker with his reserves, along with the hated middleman, who weathered the storm most easily.

The popularity of the price-fixing scheme, and such success as it enjoyed, were undoubtedly the result of this body of opinion. On several occasions the fall of prices was delayed by the general support given to the recommended scale. The onset of deflation was marked by a period of sluggish trade; prices stayed up but no one bought. Then prices fell on the black market, and the volume of trade revived in that quarter. Even when the recommended scale was revised, the volume of trade in the Shop would remain low. Opinion was always overruled by the hard facts of the market.

Curious arguments were advanced to justify price fixing. The recommended prices were in some way related to the calorific values of the foods offered: Hence some were overvalued and never sold at these prices. One argument ran as follows: Not everyone has private cigarette parcels; thus, when prices were high and trade good in the summer of 1944, only the lucky rich could buy. This was unfair to the man with few cigarettes. When prices fell in the following winter, prices should be pegged high so that the rich, who had enjoyed life in the summer, should put many cigarettes into circulation. The fact that those who sold to the rich in the summer had also enjoyed life then, and the fact that in the winter there was always someone willing to sell at low prices were ignored. Such arguments were hotly debated each night after the approach of Allied aircraft extinguished all lights at 8 P.M. But prices moved with the supply of cigarettes and refused to stay fixed in accordance with a theory of ethics.

CONCLUSION

The economic organization described was both elaborate and smooth-working in the summer of 1944. Then came the August cuts and deflation. Prices fell, rallied with deliveries of cigarette parcels in September and December, and fell again. In January 1945, supplies of Red Cross cigarettes ran out and prices slumped still further: In February the supplies of food parcels were exhausted and the depression became a blizzard. Food, itself scarce, was almost given away in order to meet the nonmonetary demand for cigarettes. Laundries ceased to operate, or worked for £s or RMk.s: Food and cigarettes sold for fancy prices in £s, hitherto unheard of. The Restaurant was a memory and the BMk. a joke. The Shop was empty and the Exchange and Mart notices were full of unaccepted offers for cigarettes. Barter increased in volume, becoming a larger proportion of a smaller volume of trade. This, the first serious and prolonged food shortage in the writer's experience, caused the price structure to change again, partly because German rations were not easily divisible. A margarine ration gradually sank in value until it exchanged directly for a treacle ration. Sugar slumped sadly. Only bread retained its value. Several thousand cigarettes, the capital of the Shop, were distributed without any noticeable effect. A few fractional parcel and cigarette issues, such as one-sixth of a parcel and twelve cigarettes each, led to momentary price recoveries and feverish trade, especially when they coincided with good news from the Western Front, but the general position remained unaltered.

By April 1945, chaos had replaced order in the economic sphere: Sales were difficult, prices lacked stability. Economics has been defined as the science of distributing limited means among unlimited and competing ends. On April 12, with the arrival of elements of the 30th U.S. Infantry Division, the ushering in of an age of plenty demonstrated the hypothesis that with infinite means economic organization and activity would be redundant, as every want could be satisfied without effort.

2

SUPPLY AND DEMAND

This chapter is an introduction to supply and demand, the basic tools of microeconomics, and a preview of the remaining chapters of this book. It is also a summary chapter; once the theories of demand (developed in Chapters 3 and 4) and supply (developed in Chapters 5 and 6) are complete, the two are combined to determine equilibrium values of price and quantity in the markets for goods and services (Chapters 7, 8, and 9). Moreover, income distribution theory (Chapters 10, 11, and 12) is essentially supply–demand analysis concerned with the prices of productive resources. A preview is considered essential at this point to provide a framework for organizing subsequent material. In short, this chapter gives a glimpse of the forest before studying the trees, to provide the reader with a better perspective of microeconomic theory.

CLASSIFICATION OF MARKETS

There are numerous ways in which markets may be classified, and the best classification for any given circumstance depends largely on the problem at hand. For some problems, it may be sufficient to distinguish consumer goods markets from resource markets. In other situations, it might be most useful to classify markets by industrial type, such as agricultural markets as opposed to manufactured goods markets. Again, in other cases, domestic markets may be distinguished from foreign ones.

For purposes of economic theorizing, however, the most important scheme for classifying markets is based on the number of participants on both sides of the market. Economics is concerned with how efficiently a market performs the basic economic functions, and economists have found that one of the most important determinants of market performance is the *number* of buyers and sellers. Table 2–1 shows a three-fold division for the buyer side of markets: (1) many buyers, (2) few buyers, and (3) one buyer, and a similar three-fold division for the seller side which, when combined, produces a very useful taxonomy.

TABLE 2-1 Classification of Markets

	Many Buyers	Few Buyers	One Buyer
Many Sellers	Competition	Oligopsony	Monopsony
Few Sellers	Oligopoly		
One Seller	Monopoly		Bilateral Monopoly

As indicated in the table, various types of markets have been named, based solely upon the numbers of market participants on both sides of the market. For instance, a market dominated by a single buyer with perhaps many sellers is called monopsony, a market we will explore at greater length when we discuss factor pricing. Monopoly, the case of a single seller and many buyers, is familiar to all. Not so familiar, but particularly interesting is the case of bilateral monopoly (one buyer and one seller), which we will study in Chapter 11 when we analyze a market situation in which a single union bargains with a single employer. Oligopoly, which exists when there are a few sellers of a product, is representative of much of American industry, and we will develop models to help explain oligopoly behavior in Chapter 9.

Our objective in this chapter is to describe the basic market mechanism to gain an understanding of how markets perform the basic economic functions. To do this, we single out for study the market structure that has been investigated most by economists, competition. (Competition will be studied in more detail in Chapter 7.)

SUPPLY AND DEMAND—COMPETITION

Market Demand

Assume a market for good X consisting of many buyers and many sellers. Although it is not essential, we can think of market transactions as taking place at a single location, a central marketplace. The product, X, is assumed to have been widely used for some time, so the market is organized and efficient. Information circulates quickly among buyers and sellers, so all are aware of the prices and quantities of X traded. In addition, X is assumed to be a homogeneous or standardized product, so that there are no differences between the units of X sold by one seller or another, and buyers do not care which seller they buy from. Finally, no government restrictions such as price ceilings or floors exist in the market. The government's function is to prevent fraud, misrepresentation, and cheating, and to enforce contract rights.

The *market demand function* for good X relates the total quantity of X purchased in the market within a given time period to the factors which influence consumers' buying plans. These factors include the price of the good, the level of aggregate income, the price of the good relative to other goods, consumers' tastes, and their expectations about the future. Using mathematical symbols we might state the demand function for X as:

$$D_x = f(P_x, P_y, P_z, Y, U_d), \qquad (1)$$

where D_x is the quantity of X consumed in the market per unit time; P_x is the price of the good; P_y and P_z are the prices of related goods; Y is the level of aggregate income of consumers and U_d is a portmanteau variable standing for all other factors influencing the quantity demanded of X.

The *market demand* for X is derived from the demand function by holding constant P_y, P_z, Y, and U_d, and showing the effects of changes in P_x on D_x. The non-price variables affecting the quantity demanded are held constant by the *ceteris paribus* assumption. When the values of P_x and the quantities of X are plotted on a graph, the result is the market *demand curve* for X.

D_x in Figure 2–1 is the graph of a hypothetical demand curve for X.[1] Price is a barrier to buyers and to consumption, so the curve slopes downward to the right, reflecting an increased quantity purchased by buyers when the price barrier is reduced. The market demand curve reflects the willingness and ability of consumers to buy different quantities of the product at different prices, assuming all other variables affecting quantities demanded are held constant. Of course, the only observable point on a demand curve is a point where actual transactions occur. For example, the curve indicates that if price

FIGURE 2–1 Market Demand Curves

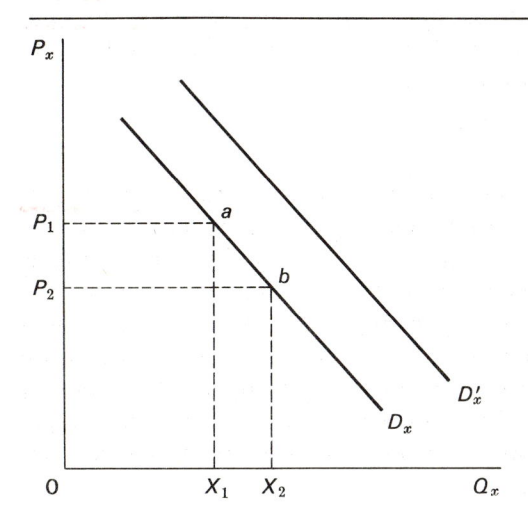

[1] Students often wonder where the curve comes from. For our subsequent discussion in this chapter, we need only a demand curve that is representative of what a demand curve might look like in some market. D_x is simply an arbitrary demand schedule for some hypothetical good X. In Chapters 3 and 4 we will show how a demand curve is developed.

drops from P_1 to P_2, the quantity demanded will increase from X_1 to X_2. Stated another way, people can be induced to buy more units of a commodity only if its price is reduced.

The quantity of X which will be purchased at any given price must be associated with a certain period of time, say a day or a week. And the relevant time period will differ among different commodities. The time period for cups of coffee might be one day; for groceries, a week; and for grand pianos, a generation. Often this time dimension is not explicitly stated and one sometimes makes the statement that the quantity demanded at a certain price will be 60 units or 100 units. A time dimension is always implied, however, even if it is not stated.

If one of the non-price determinants of demand changes, then the demand curve itself shifts. That is, if one of the variables on the right side of (1) changes (other than P_x) then demand is changed. For example, if the incomes of consumers increase, this might cause the demand curve to shift to the right to a new position such as D_x'.[2] While such factors as increased income might shift the curve to the right, other changes in the non-price determinants of demand, such as decreases in prices of goods similar to X, might shift the market demand curve for X to the left. There is, in other words, a separate demand curve for each set of values of the non-price determinants of demand. We must distinguish, therefore, *a change in demand from a change in quantity demanded*. A change in price will cause a change in *quantity demanded* (a movement along demand curve D_x from point *a* to *b* in Figure 2–1), while a change in one of the non-price determinants of demand shifts the *demand curve* itself. A change in the price of X can, from our definitions, have no effect on demand, only the quantity demanded.

Market Supply

Price restricts consumers of a good but encourages suppliers. The higher the price, the greater the incentive for suppliers. Just as purchasers can be induced to *purchase* additional quantities of a good if the price barrier is lowered, so suppliers can be induced to *supply* additional quantities of the good if its price is increased. Referring to Figure 2–2, S_x represents a market *supply curve* for a consumer good. Given this supply curve, an increase in price from P_1 to P_2 would cause an increase in quantity supplied from X_1 to X_2. As in the case of demand, the supply curve is derived from the *supply function* by making the *ceteris paribus* assumption. The supply function can be represented mathematically as:

$$S_x = f(P_x, P_a, P_b, F, U_s), \qquad (2)$$

[2] We will explore at a later point the case where the demand curve is shifted to the left with a rise in income.

FIGURE 2-2 Market Supply

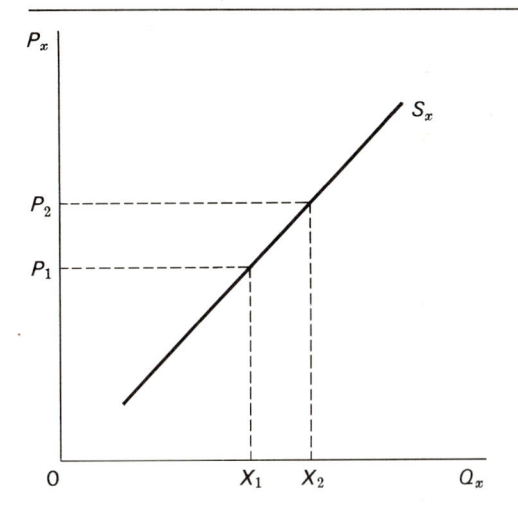

where P_x is the price of the good; P_a and P_b are the prices of resources needed to produce X; and F represents the existing technology for producing X; U_s represents all the other factors influencing suppliers' decisions. One of these factors might be the level of excise taxes applicable to the good in question, and we will investigate later how the imposition of such taxes affects the market supply curve. The *market supply curve*, S_x, in Figure 2-2 represents the quantities of X which will be supplied at different prices by suppliers, assuming the non-price determinants of supply are held constant. Since we are working with a hypothetical good X, the curve is drawn linear for simplicity.

The schedules of market supply and demand represent the *plans or intentions* of the two groups of market participants, so they are called *ex ante* schedules. (*Ex ante* is a Latin phrase meaning "beforehand.") The schedules depict, in the aggregate, what each group will do *if* certain market conditions prevail, that is, what quantities consumers and suppliers plan to demand and supply at various price levels. We observe at any one time, however, only one market price and quantity for a given commodity. In other words, price will be some single value once stability is achieved. But, the fact that market participants have alternative plans ready to be put into effect at other prices insures that this *final* or *recorded* price is not an arbitrary one but represents the interaction of buyers and sellers. The study of the process whereby the plans of buyers and sellers are brought into harmony is *equilibrium analysis*.

Market Equilibrium

The market supply and demand curves for good X are presented together in Figure 2-3. Point *e*, the point of intersection of S_x and D_x, is of special

FIGURE 2-3 The Determination of Equilibrium Price and Quantity

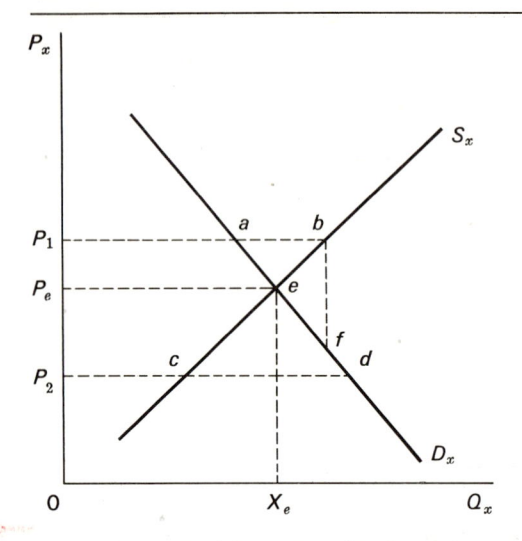

significance, because only at that point are the plans of suppliers in harmony with those of buyers. To illustrate, let us consider the effects of a price higher or lower than that indicated by the intersection of S_x and D_x.

First, suppose price is P_1 and the quantity of X supplied, as a consequence, is equal to the distance P_1b. Referring to the demand curve, quantity P_1b will be demanded only if the price is at a lower level indicated by the price at point f. At price P_1, only P_1a units will be demanded. The plans of buyers and sellers are not in harmony at the originally stated price–quantity combination. Some suppliers will not be able to exchange their supplies at price P_1; e.g., they will not be able to complete their plans. The quantity ab represents an *excess supply* at price P_1. What will happen as a consequence of this excess supply? Those suppliers holding excess supplies will likely offer their holdings to buyers at a lower price. Not all suppliers are able to complete their plans at price P_1, but these individuals are almost certain to communicate to purchasers their willingness to accept a lower price, because otherwise they will be left with excess holdings of X. The existence of an excess supply will tend to bid the price of X down.

Now consider price P_2, which prompts suppliers to offer the quantity P_2c. Since, in the aggregate, the quantity P_2d will be demanded at that price, some buyers will not be able to satisfy their purchase requirements. The quantity cd is defined as the *excess demand* at price P_2. Some unsatisfied buyers will likely offer a higher price to sellers or at least make it known that they would be willing to pay more and this will cause the price to be bid up. The existence of excess demand will cause buyers in effect to advise sellers that they should raise their price.

Only at price P_e is there no excess supply or excess demand and thus no tendency for price to move down or up. We define P_e as the equilibrium price. Given the demand and supply curves, any other price is unstable, for forces are generated at such prices which cause price to move toward P_e. Only when excess supply and excess demand are zero is the market price an equilibrium one, because only then is each buyer and each seller carrying out his plans or intentions. Buyers may feel that the price is too high and sellers that it is too low, but in both cases the market participants are, *at the existing price*, free to offer (or buy) as much or as little X as they wish. When these conditions are satisfied we say the price "clears the market."[3]

THE FUNCTIONS OF PRICE BRIEFLY INTRODUCED

The basic function of price in our market under investigation is very simple: *it is to prevent buyers from consuming too much of the good and sellers from producing too little.* Suppose the price of good X dropped to zero. Buyers would face no barriers to the consumption of X and would, therefore, consume as much of the good as they pleased. Would this be desirable from an economic standpoint? Yes and no. Yes, if the good could be produced at no cost to society. If the product were a free good, it would not matter whether a little or a lot were consumed, because by definition, a "free good" requires no scarce resources to produce, so consumption of such a good would not require that the output and consumption of other goods be curtailed. But most goods are not free; they require resources for their production, which makes it undesirable for them to sell at a zero price. A zero price charged for a good which must be produced with scarce resources would likely cause consumers to consume more of the good than would be desirable, since consumption of good X would occur at the expense of other goods. (If, for some reason, we decided to give away belts, the result might be too few shoes.) Of course, to those consuming the good it seems desirable because they are paying a zero price for the benefits derived. (Barefoot belt-wearers would be pleased.) The point is that resources used to make X could have been used to produce something else, say good Y. So the benefits associated with consuming X are realized at the cost of those benefits that would otherwise have been realized from consuming Y. And possibly good Y would be more desirable to consumers than X, or, more likely, some combination of X and Y would be best. When both X and Y sell for a price, the result is to prevent the consumption of too much of each, yet encourage producers to supply just enough. The prices of the two goods should reflect both the relative costs of producing them and the valuations placed on them by consumers.

[3] The interaction of supply and demand described in this section works most efficiently in the case of competition. As you will see in later chapters, other market structures may distort the interrelationships of buyers and sellers.

One of the objectives of this book is to show that in an economy characterized by competitive markets throughout, equilibrium prices insure that neither too little nor too much of any commodity or service will be produced. This is equivalent to saying that resources are efficiently allocated, because associated with any given output "mix" is a unique pattern of resource allocation. Restated, the principal function of the price system is to allocate the economy's resources, a job that encompasses the determination of what goods will be produced, what techniques will be used in their production, and how they will be distributed. The term efficiency has a special interpretation in economics. The resources of an economy are efficiently allocated when the resulting production achieves a socially optimum combination of output. In other words, it is the well-being of society that is of paramount importance. When we speak of an "inefficient producer," we mean one not using techniques that result in the maximum output possible from his given inputs, or one not producing goods in optimum quantities. Efficiency in economics is determined with respect to social well-being.

The remainder of this book will be concerned with the twin problems of (1) determining how prices are arrived at, not only in competitive output markets, but noncompetitive markets and factor markets as well, and (2) evaluating the economic performance of competitive and noncompetitive markets as a foundation for economic policy.

THE ROLE OF INFORMATION

In our discussion, we have implied that the market behaved as though price signals to producers and consumers are transmitted and received loud and clear. In effect, throughout most of our presentation we treated markets as if their activities were managed by an omniscient auctioneer who received buy and sell bids and posted them immediately for all market participants to see. (The stock market approaches the ideal; purchase and sale prices and quantities are made instantaneously available throughout the central marketplace and via wire communication to brokerage houses throughout the world.) The auctioneer is assumed in our model to be quietly and efficiently at work while the market operates performing the function of transmitting information back and forth between buyers and sellers.

However, in most markets the "auctioneer" is not so efficient. In fact, in many cases, misinformation is promulgated by sellers puffing their wares to make them seem rarer and more valuable than they are. And buyers are sometimes guilty of similar practices. Where market information is slow, spotty, or misleading, we may not get a smooth market adjustment to equilibrium price and quantity. In some instances quantity adjustments will take place faster than price adjustments. Of course, buyers and sellers can, with effort, obtain the information they need to make decisions, but such information is not generally free. Market participants will typically incur costs in the process of obtaining information. We must allow for the effects of information costs in our theory, because they may seriously affect the functioning of markets.

For example, in the absence of an auctioneer to provide information about job markets, a student finishing school must spend potential work time searching out employment opportunities, which often entails explicit costs, such as transportation costs, as well as the implicit costs associated with time and effort expended. And there is no guarantee that the job taken is the best available. As another example, grocery shoppers and car buyers often devote a great deal of time and effort studying ads produced at considerable cost and effort by grocery and car sellers. The list of information costs could be expanded to cover almost every market.

At one extreme society might employ auctioneers to spread information about the availability and cost of supplies in all markets to improve their performance. If nothing is done we might have to depend on a slower, less efficient adjustment of markets, accepting the cost of a certain amount of market inefficiency. However, information is a scarce good and is thereby valuable. We can expect, therefore, that a kind of market will develop for market information itself. There are many illustrations of markets of this sort; for example, brokers, buying agents, buying services, and the like are suppliers in the markets for market information.

In the absence of complete information, the apparent demand for a commodity or for a resource might not be the true demand under certain conditions, so the market might relay false information to participants particularly when price controls or other market imperfections are in existence. An example often cited is the post World War II market for automobiles when prices were kept artificially low. At the going price, which was below equilibrium, many more buyers wanted cars than there were cars available. And most of those buyers made the rounds to several dealers to put in orders, knowing that all the orders but one would be cancelled. As a result, the false, apparent demand for cars as measured by total orders was many times larger than the true demand. Such a situation, where the true demand is obscured, can occur when markets are not free or where market information is incomplete or misleading.

AN APPLICATION OF SUPPLY AND DEMAND ANALYSIS: TAXES

Elementary supply and demand analysis can serve as an efficient tool for analyzing a variety of economic problems. One interesting application of supply–demand theory is that of determining the effect of an excise tax on market price and quantity. Suppose a state is considering imposing a unit

36 Introduction

FIGURE 2–4 The Effects of a Unit Tax on Equilibrium Price and Quantity

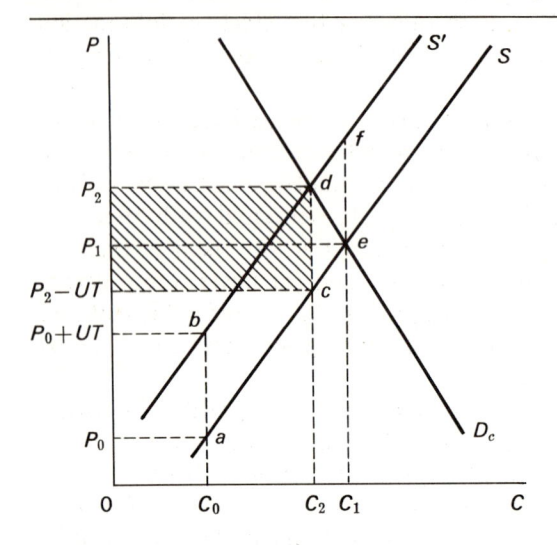

tax on cigarettes, and the policy makers want to predict the effect of the tax on numbers of units consumed, price, and total tax revenues. In Figure 2–4, D_c is assumed to be the market demand for cigarettes. The steepness of the curve reflects the view that the quantity demanded of cigarettes is relatively insensitive to price changes. (In Chapter 3, we will discuss a measure of the degree of price sensitivity called elasticity. For now we will simply indicate that D_c is drawn to reflect price–quantity insensitivity.) The supply schedule, S, applies before the imposition of the tax. The before-tax equilibrium price and quantity are P_1 and C_1, respectively.

The effect of the unit tax is to shift the market supply curve vertically upward by the full amount of the tax. Consider the output level C_0. Curve S at point a indicates that, in the aggregate, suppliers were willing before the tax to supply C_0 units at price P_0. After the imposition of a unit tax, UT, suppliers should be willing to supply C_0 units at a price of $(P_0 + UT)$, because their net proceeds for the sale of C_0 units, after paying UT to the taxing agent, is the same as it would have been at a price of P_0 without the tax. Since the same argument could be made for any output level, the after-tax supply curve S' lies vertically above S by the distance ab, the amount of the unit tax. By operating at any point on S', suppliers can, after paying the cigarette tax, be just as well off as before the tax.

The shift in supply from S to S' causes equilibrium price to rise to P_2 and quantity to fall to C_2; determined at 'd' the point of intersection of S' with D_c. Suppliers will receive a gross price per unit of P_2, but, after paying the tax, will receive a net price of only $(P_2 - UT)$. The total tax receipts of the state are equal to the product of the unit tax, distance cd, and the equilibrium quantity of cigarette packs sold, C_2; this product is the area of the shaded rectangle in Figure 2–4. Because the quantity of cigarettes demanded is relatively insensitive to price, the burden of the tax has fallen largely on the consumer. Equilibrium price has increased from P_1 to P_2. However, the price increase is smaller than the unit tax. If the quantity demanded had been completely insensitive to price (if the demand curve had been vertical), price would have increased from the price indicated at point e to that indicated by point f on S', and buyers would have borne the entire burden of the tax.

CONCLUSION

In this chapter, we have previewed the heart of microeconomic theory—supply and demand. Supply and demand curves both imply that the quantity of any resource or product supplied or demanded is dependent on price. In the case of supply, price and quantity are directly related, a higher price generally implying that a greater quantity will be supplied. In the case of demand, price and quantity are inversely related; a higher price normally means a smaller quantity demanded.

We mentioned the various types of markets with which we will deal in the rest of the book: competition (many buyers and sellers of a homogeneous product), oligopoly (few sellers and many buyers), monopoly (one seller and many buyers), oligopsony (few buyers and many sellers), monopsony (one buyer and many sellers), and bilateral monopoly (one buyer and one seller).

As an introduction to equilibrium analysis, we have shown how supply and demand interact in competitive markets to determine equilibrium values of price and quantity. The existence of excess supply in a market tends to cause price to fall toward equilibrium while an excess demand will tend to cause price to rise. Only when both excess demand and supply are zero will there be a stable or equilibrium price. We noted that the competitive supply–demand model assumes market information is freely available to all participants, and where this assumption is dropped, economic theory must provide for the effects of information costs on the efficiency of the market mechanism.

As an application of supply–demand analysis, we considered the effects of an excise tax on the equilibrium price and the quantity consumed of cigarettes.

PROBLEMS

1. Given the market supply and demand schedules, D_x and S_x:
    (a) The equilibrium price is _____.
    (b) At price OC there is an excess (supply, demand) of _____.

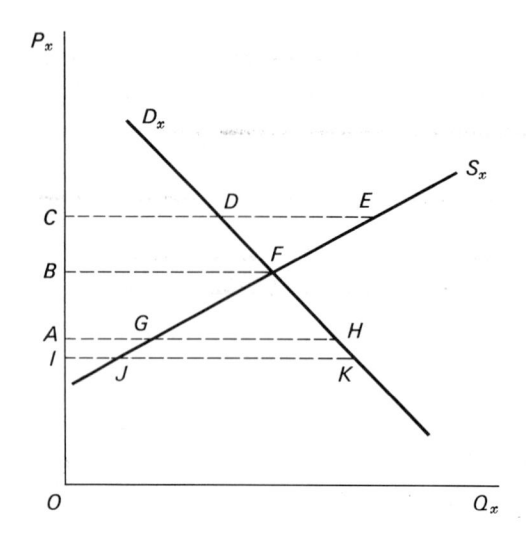

(c) This will cause (suppliers, purchasers) to bid price (up, down).
(d) At price OA there is an excess (supply, demand) of _____.
(e) This will cause (suppliers, purchasers) to bid price (up, down).
(f) Suppose government imposes an absolute ceiling price of OC. This would (raise price, lower price, have no effect).
(g) Suppose government imposes an absolute ceiling of OI. This would cause (surpluses, shortages, neither shortages nor surpluses).

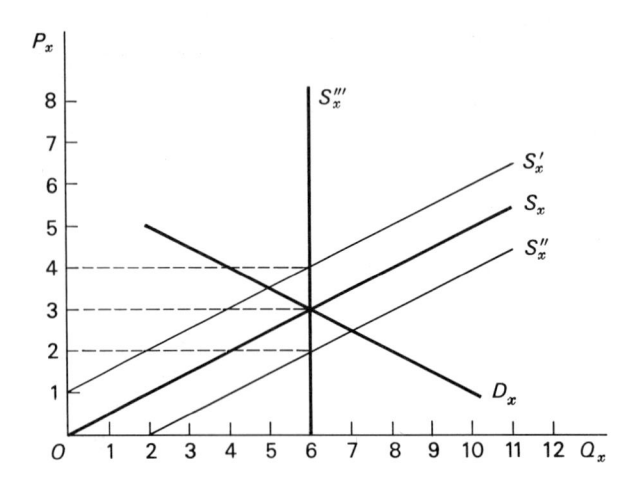

2. In the graph above, let D_x be the market demand for X.
   (a) If S_x is market supply, what is equilibrium price? _____.
   (b) If S_x''' is market supply, what is equilibrium price? _____.

(c) Suppose S_x''' is market supply and the government imposes a $1 unit tax on X. What is the new market price? _____.

(d) Suppose S_x is market supply and the $1 unit tax is imposed. What is the new market price? _____.

(e) Suppose S_x is market supply and the government pays a subsidy to each and every supplier of $1 for each unit produced and sold. What is the new market price? _____.

APPENDIX TO CHAPTER 2

Abundance — Scarcity

FREDERIC BASTIAT

In the following selection, we present a nineteenth-century analysis of the relationship between scarcity, price, and wealth by the French laissez-faire economist Bastiat. The reader will recognize Bastiat's paper as an attack on mercantilist principles and policies. Bastiat uses the sophistic style and elementary supply-demand theory to produce a most interesting and timeless work.

Which is best for man and for society, abundance or scarcity?

What! you exclaim, can that be a question? Has anyone ever asserted, or is it possible to maintain, that scarcity is at the foundation of human well-being?

Yes, this has been asserted, and is maintained every day; and I hesitate not to affirm that the *theory of scarcity* is much the most popular. It is the life of conversation, of the newspapers, of books, and of political oratory; and, strange as it may seem, it is certain that Political Economy will have fulfilled its practical mission when it has established beyond question, and widely disseminated, this very simple proposition: "The wealth of men consists in the abundance of commodities."

Do we not hear it said every day: "The foreigner is about to inundate us with his products"? Then we fear abundance.

Did not M. Saint-Cricq exclaim: "Production is excessive"? Then he feared abundance.

Do workmen break machines? Then they fear excess of production, or abundance.

Has not M. Bugeaud pronounced these words: "Let bread be dear, and agriculturists will get rich"? Now, bread can only be dear because it is scarce. Therefore M. Bugeaud extols scarcity.

From *Economic Sophisms*, by Frederic Bastiat, translated by Patrick James Stirling. T. Fisher Unwin, Ltd. London: Adephi Terrace, pp. 5–15, 1909. The original work *Sophismes Economiques* first appeared in 1845.

Does not M. d'Argout urge as an argument against sugar-growing the very productiveness of that industry? Does he not say: "Beetroot has no future, and its culture cannot be extended, because a few acres devoted to its culture in each department would supply the whole consumption of France"? Then, in his eyes, good lies in sterility, in dearth, and evil in fertility and abundance.

La Presse, Le Commerce, and the greater part of the daily papers, have one or more articles every morning to demonstrate to the Legislative Chamber and the Government that it is sound policy to raise legislatively the price of all things by means of tariffs. And do the Chamber and the Government not obey the injunction? Now tariffs can raise prices only by diminishing the *supply* of commodities in the market! Then the journals, the Chamber, and the Minister put in practice the theory of scarcity, and I am justified in saying that this theory is by far the most popular.

How does it happen that in the eyes of workmen, of publicists, and statesmen abundance should appear a thing to be dreaded and scarcity advantageous? I propose to trace this illusion to its source.

We remark that a man grows richer in proportion to the return yielded by his exertions, that is to say, in proportion as he sells his commodity at a *higher price*. He sells at a higher price in proportion to the rarity, to the scarcity, of the article he produces. We conclude from this that, as far as he is concerned at least, scarcity enriches him. Applying successively the same reasoning to all other producers, we construct the *theory of scarcity*. We next proceed to apply this theory, and, in order to favour producers generally, we raise prices artificially, and cause a scarcity of all commodities, by prohibition, by restriction, by the suppression of machinery, and other analogous means.

The same thing holds of abundance. We observe that when a product is plentiful, it sells at a lower price, and the producer gains less. If all producers are in the same situation, they are all poor. Therefore it is abundance that ruins society. And as theories are soon reduced to practice, we see the law struggling against the abundance of commodities.

This fallacy in its more general form may make little impression, but applied to a particular order of facts, to a certain branch of industry, to a given class of producers, it is extremely specious; and this is easily explained. It forms a syllogism which is not *false*, but *incomplete*. Now, what is *true* in a syllogism is always and necessarily present to the mind. But *incompleteness* is a negative quality, an absent *datum*, which it is very possible, and indeed very easy, to leave out of account.

Man produces in order to consume. He is at once producer and consumer. The reasoning which I have just explained considers him only in the first of these points of view. Had the second been taken into account, it would have led to an opposite conclusion. In effect, may it not be said:

The consumer is richer in proportion as he *purchases* all things cheaper; and he purchases things cheaper in proportion to their abundance; therefore it is abundance which enriches him. This reasoning, extended to all consumers, leads to the *theory of plenty*.

It is the notion of *exchange* imperfectly understood which leads to these illusions. If we consider our personal interest, we recognise distinctly that it is double. As *sellers* we have an interest in dearness, and consequently in scarcity[1]; as *buyers*, in cheapness, or what amounts to the same thing, in the abundance of commodities. We cannot, then, found our reasoning on one or other of these interests before inquiring which of the two coincides and is identified with the general and permanent interest of mankind at large.

If man were a solitary animal, if he laboured exclusively for himself, if he consumed directly the fruit of his labour—in a word, *if he did not exchange*—the theory of scarcity would never have appeared in the world. It is too evident that, in that case, abundance would be advantageous, from whatever quarter it came, whether from the result of his industry, from ingenious tools, from powerful machinery of his invention, or whether due to the fertility of the soil, the liberality of nature, or even to a mysterious *invasion* of products brought by the waves and left by them upon the shore. No solitary man would ever have thought that in order to encourage his labour and render it more productive, it was necessary to break in pieces the instruments which saved it, to neutralize the fertility of the soil, or give back to the sea the good things it had brought to his door. He would perceive at once that labour is not an end, but a means; and that it would be absurd to reject the result for fear of doing injury to the means by which that result was accomplished. He would perceive that if he devotes two hours a day to providing for his wants, any circumstance (machinery, fertility, gratuitous gift, no matter what) which saves him an hour of that labour, the result remaining the same, puts that hour at his disposal, and that he can devote it to increasing his enjoyments; in short, he would see that *to save labour* is nothing else than *progress*.

But *exchange* disturbs our view of a truth so simple. In the social state, and with the separation of employments to which it leads, the production and consumption of a commodity are not mixed up and confounded in the same individual. Each man comes to see in his labour no longer a means but an end. In relation to each commodity, exchange creates two interests, that of the producer and that of the consumer; and these two interests are always directly opposed to each other.

It is essential to analyse them, and examine their nature.

Take the case of any producer whatever, what is his immediate interest? It consists of two things: first, that the fewest possible number of persons should devote themselves to his branch of industry; secondly, that the greatest possible number of persons should be in quest of the article he produces.

[1 Bastiat here means scarcity of supply outside of the seller's own business which would allow him to fix his own price.]

Political economy explains it more succinctly in these terms: Supply very limited, demand very extended; or, in other words still, Competition limited, demand unlimited.

What is the immediate interest of the consumer? That the supply of the product in question should be extended, and the demand restrained.

Seeing, then, that these two interests are in opposition to each other, one of them must necessarily coincide with social interests in general, and the other be antagonistic to them.

But which of them should legislation favour, as identical with the public good—if, indeed, it should favour either?

To discover this, we must inquire what would happen if the secret wishes of men were granted.

In as far as we are producers, it must be allowed that the desire of every one of us is anti-social. Are we vine-dressers? It would give us no great regret if hail should shower down on all the vines in the world except our own: *this is the theory of scarcity*. Are we iron-masters? Our wish is that there should be no other iron in the market but our own, however much the public may be in want of it; and for no other reason than that this want, keenly felt and imperfectly satisfied, shall ensure us a higher price: *this is still the theory of scarcity*. Are we farmers? We say with M. Bugeaud: Let bread be dear, that is to say, scarce, and agriculturists will thrive: always the same theory, *the theory of scarcity*.

Are we physicians? We cannot avoid seeing that certain physical ameliorations, improving the sanitary state of the country, the development of certain moral virtues, such as moderation and temperance, the progress of knowledge tending to enable each man to take better care of his own health, the discovery of certain simple remedies of easy application, would be so many blows to our professional success. In as far as we are physicians, then, our secret wishes would be anti-social. I do not say that physicians form these secret wishes. On the contrary, I believe they would hail with joy the discovery of a universal panacea; but they would not do this as physicians, but as men and as Christians. By a noble abnegation of self, the physician places himself in the consumer's point of view. But as exercising a profession, from which he derives his own and his family's subsistence, his desires, or, if you will, his interests, are anti-social.

Are we manufacturers of cotton stuffs? We desire to sell them at the price most profitable to ourselves. We should consent willingly to an interdict being laid on all rival manufacturers; and if we could venture to give this wish public expression, or hope to realise it with some chance of success, we should attain our end, to some extent, by indirect means; for example, by excluding foreign fabrics, in order to diminish the *supply*, and thus produce, forcibly and to our profit, a *scarcity* of clothing.

In the same way, we might pass in review all other branches of industry, and we should always find that the producers, as such, have anti-social views. "The shopkeeper," says Montaigne, "thrives only by the irregularities of youth; the farmer by the high price of corn, the architect by the destruction of houses, the officers of justice by lawsuits and quarrels. Ministers of religion derive their distinction and employment from our vices and our death. No physician rejoices in the health of his friends, nor soldiers in the peace of their country; and so of the rest."

Hence it follows that if the secret wishes of each producer were realised, the world would retrograde rapidly towards barbarism. The sail would supersede steam, the oar would supersede the sail, and general traffic would be carried on by the carrier's wagon; the latter would be superseded by the mule, and the mule by the pedlar. Wool would exclude cotton, cotton in its turn would exclude wool, and so on until the dearth of all things had caused man himself to disappear from the face of the earth.

Suppose for a moment that the legislative power and the public force were placed at the disposal of Mimeral's committee, and that each member of that association had the privilege of bringing in and sanctioning a favourite law, is it difficult to divine to what sort of industrial code the public would be subjected?

If we now proceed to consider the immediate interest of the consumer, we shall find that it is in perfect harmony with the general interest, with all that the welfare of society calls for. When the purchaser goes to market he desires to find it well stocked. Let the seasons be propitious for all harvests; let inventions, more and more marvellous, bring within reach a greater and greater number of products and enjoyments; let time and labour be saved; let distances be effaced by the perfection and rapidity of transit; let the spirit of justice and of peace allow of a diminished weight of taxation; let barriers of every kind be removed;—in all this the interest of the consumer runs parallel with the public interest. The consumer may push his secret wishes to a chimerical and absurd length, without these wishes becoming antagonistic to the public welfare. He may desire that food and shelter, the hearth and the roof, instruction and morality, security and peace, power and health, should be obtained without exertion and without measure, like the dust of the highways, the water of the brook, the air which we breathe; and yet the realisation of his desires would not be at variance with the good of society.

It may be said that, if these wishes were granted, the work of the producer would become more and more limited, and would end with being stopped for want of aliment. But why? Because, on this extreme supposition, all imaginable wants and desires would be fully satisfied. Man, like Omnipotence, would create all things by a simple act of volition. Well, on this hypothesis, what reason should we have to regret the stoppage of industrial production?

I made the supposition not long ago of the existence of an assembly composed of workmen, each member of which, in his capacity of producer, should have the power of passing a law embodying his *secret wish*, and I said that the code which would emanate from that assembly would be monopoly systematised, the theory of scarcity reduced to practice.

In the same way, a chamber in which each should consult exclusively his own immediate interest as a consumer, would tend to systematise liberty, to suppress all restrictive measures, to overthrow all artificial barriers—in a word, to realise the *theory of plenty*.

Hence it follows:—

That to consult exclusively the immediate interest of the producer, is to consult an interest which is anti-social:

That to take for basis exclusively the immediate interest of the consumer would be to take for basis the general interest.

Let me enlarge on this view of the subject a little, at the risk of being prolix.

A radical antagonism exists between seller and buyer.[2]

The former desires that the subject of the bargain should be scarce, its supply limited, and its price high.

The latter desires that it should be *abundant*, its supply large, and its price low.

The laws, which should be at least neutral, take the part of the seller against the buyer, of the producer against the consumer, of dearness against cheapness, of scarcity against abundance.

They proceed, if not intentionally, at least logically, on this datum: *a nation is rich when it is in want of everything.*

For they say, it is the producer that we must favour by securing him a good market for his product. For this purpose it is necessary to raise the price, and in order to raise the price we must restrict the supply; and to restrict the supply is to create scarcity.

Just let us suppose that at the present moment, when all these laws are in full force, we make a complete inventory, not in value but in weight, measure, volume, quantity, of all the commodities existing in the country, which are fitted to satisfy the wants and tastes of its inhabitants—corn, meat, cloth, fuel, colonial products, etc.

Suppose, again, that next day all the barriers which oppose the introduction of foreign products are removed.

Lastly, suppose that in order to test the result of this reform they proceed three months afterwards to make a new inventory.

Is it not true that there will be found in France more corn, cattle, cloth,

---

[2] The author has rectified the terms of this proposition in a later work.—See *Harmonies Economiques*, ch. xi.—FRENCH EDITOR. [The translation of the passage referred to is as follows: "I have been reproached with reason for having written this phrase—'Between the vendor and purchaser exists a radical antagonism.' The word antagonism, above all with the word radical added, goes far beyond my meaning. It seems to indicate a permanent opposition of interests, and consequently an indestructible social discord; but I only meant to speak of that temporary debate which precedes any bargain and which is inherent in the very idea of the transaction."]

linen, iron, coal, sugar, etc., at the date of the second than at the date of the first inventory?

So true is this that our protective tariffs have no other purpose than to hinder all these things from reaching us, to restrict the supply, and prevent depreciation and abundance.

Now I would ask, Are the people who live under our laws better fed because there is *less* bread, meat, and sugar in the country? Are they better clothed because there is *less* cloth and linen? Better warmed because there is *less* coal? Better assisted in their labour because there are *fewer* tools and *less* iron, copper, and machinery?

But it may be said, If the foreigner *inundates* us with his products he will carry away our money.

And what does it matter? Men are not fed on money. They do not clothe themselves with gold, or warm themselves with silver. What matters it whether there is more or less money in the country if there is more bread on our sideboards, more meat in our larders, more linen in our wardrobes, more firewood in our cellars?

Restrictive laws always land us in this dilemma:

Either you admit that they produce scarcity, or you do not.

If you admit it, you avow by the admission that you inflict on the people all the injury in your power. If you do not admit it, you deny having restricted the supply and raised prices, and consequently you deny having favoured the producer.

What you do is either hurtful or profitless, injurious or ineffectual. It never can be attended with any useful result.[3]

---

[3] See also *Harmonies Economiques*, ch. xi., and also *Abundance*, in the French Collected Edition, vol. v., p. 393.—FRENCH EDITOR.

PART II. THE THEORY OF CONSUMER BEHAVIOR AND DEMAND

3

TWO THEORIES OF CONSUMER BEHAVIOR

In this chapter we focus our attention on the consumer, the principal decision-making unit on the demand side of the product market. We will investigate consumer behavior by presenting two theoretical analogs of the decision-making process employed by a person seeking to make the best possible allocation of his available income. We want to know why consumers buy particular goods and services in the quantities they do. How important are price, income, and expectations? Why are some goods, such as foods, purchased in certain quantities, relative to other goods such as entertainment? In addition, we want to understand why there are changes in consumer buying patterns. For instance, what causes consumers to buy larger cars or smaller houses? What would cause a shift to mobile homes? Or to Caribbean vacations? We seek in this section a thorough understanding of the concept of consumer demand, which, when aggregated and combined with supply, determines the allocation of scarce resources in a market economy.

Equally important, we want to lay a theoretical foundation for welfare economics. Before we can proceed with economic policy we need a measurement scheme for analyzing the effects of alternative policy actions on individual and social well-being. It is essential that we be able to ascertain when social well-being has been improved or worsened in a given situation; otherwise, we cannot evaluate economic policy. The behavioral models developed in this chapter are based upon the individual consumer. These models provide a theoretical framework which is useful for formulating policies to improve social well-being and the criteria for determining their success.

The two theoretical systems for analyzing consumer behavior are *marginal utility theory* and *indifference curve theory*. These theories provide us with a useful set of tools for sorting out the forces which together shape a rational individual's consumption decisions. Both are presented because certain problems are best solved with one approach and other problems are more appropriately treated with the other.

Both theories provide a framework for showing the relationship between the quantity of a good an individual will consume and the most important forces affecting that quantity. The latter include the consumer's income, tastes and preferences, and the price of the product relative to the prices of other goods and services available to him. The models which we develop in this chapter provide us with a logical framework for showing how all these important economic variables interact to determine the consumer's optimum consumption mix. Moreover, we keep the analysis manageable by restricting our study to models which incorporate only two or three of the most important variables at a time.

Although it is probably true that no consumer ever consciously employs the techniques suggested by either marginal utility theory or indifference curve theory, the approach taken in the models is nevertheless analogous to the decision process of a thoughtful consumer. An individual using subjective thought processes in making most economic decisions will arrive at the same result suggested by the theory, if he is goal-oriented and systematic in his attempt to reach his goals. The principal presumption of consumer theory is that the consumer *is* goal-oriented, that he is an optimizer, and that he seeks an optimum adjustment to his environment in a rational manner. What does he optimize? His own well-being.

One of our principal objectives in this chapter is the derivation of an individual's demand for a commodity or service. Once we have completed the theory of individual demand, we develop market demand by aggregating the demands of all consumers. The theory of consumer behavior developed in this chapter therefore provides a foundation for the theory of market demand developed in Chapter 4.

MARGINAL UTILITY THEORY

The theory of marginal utility was developed in the second half of the nineteenth century independently and almost simultaneously by several economists.[1] It has provided economists at once with a theory of consumer behavior and an analytical tool of considerable efficiency. The basic analytical techniques developed by the marginal utility theorists (despite shortcomings which we will consider later) are used by economists today, not only for exposition of economic principles, but also for analyzing, diagnosing, and solving economic problems.

---

[1] They were Hermann Heinrich Gossen of Germany; W. S. Jevons, a British economist who wrote on utility theory while in Australia; Karl Menger of Austria; and Leon Walras of Lausanne, Switzerland. Gossen, who died of tuberculosis in 1858, first published his theory in 1854. Jevons discovered after the publication of the first edition of his own book that his ideas had been anticipated by Gossen and therefore gave him credit in later editions.

The Objectives of Consumers

The theory of consumer behavior assumes that the principal economic goal of each individual is to obtain over his lifetime the largest amount of satisfaction possible, given the individual's limited resources and productive abilities, and the opportunities open to him.[2] In other words, we assume that consumers will seek an optimum adjustment to their economic environment. However, marginal utility theory does not presume that everyone maximizes his lifetime satisfaction or happiness without regard to other considerations. For instance, many individuals consume less than they could over their life span because they want to leave a bequest. In addition, the theory does not presume that consumers will not experiment and make mistakes, and even behave irrationally on occasion. The theory assumes only that "on the whole and as an average" people are conscious of many opportunities for earning income and for consuming products; that they are aware of limitations on their earning capacity and on balance take advantage of their opportunities within the constraints imposed by society.[3]

We emphasize the fact that the individual considers the long-run, as well as the short-run, consequences of his decisions and will not take actions that result in short-run satisfaction if these actions seriously reduce his prospects for future satisfaction. For example, most of us would not quit our jobs just because it is a beautiful spring day and we would like to go fishing, or we probably would not go deeply into debt to purchase a round-the-world vacation, if repayment of the debt would reduce future income and cause serious privation. In Chapter 12, we will investigate how a consumer explicitly incorporates the future in his decision-making when we develop the theory of the interest rate. In particular, we will show how a consumer's current saving rate is related to the rate of interest.

The Nature of Utility

Any willing consumption of goods or services usually produces satisfaction or enjoyment for the consumer. If you purchase and consume a hamburger, onion rings, and a cold drink after Saturday night's football game, you do so because it is pleasurable; it satisfies your hunger and thirst. The satisfaction derived from consumption is called "utility" by economists, and is measured

---

[2] The word "family" or "household" may be substituted for "individual" in this statement.
[3] A different theory of economics would apply to a society subject to different constraints, e.g., in which price-cutting by one firm led to retaliatory bombing by competitors instead of retaliatory price cuts, or where one consumer, about to lose the last box of Valentine's Day candy to another buyer, would attack his rival with a knife instead of offering a higher price or looking in another store for what he wanted. Effective social constraints are the rules of the game and are implicitly assumed throughout the book.

in *utils*. (We will discuss later in the chapter the difficulties associated with measuring utility.) Perhaps consuming the hamburger results in more utils than the after-game meal, especially if your team won. The utility derived from watching the game reminds us that intangible economic goods—or services, such as entertainment and medical services—produce utility just as tangible goods do.[4]

Economists used to distinguish three types of utility: form, time, and place utility. If you are hungry, a hamburger has form utility. But if it is in the next town, it lacks place utility. And if it will not be cooked until tomorrow, it lacks time utility. These distinctions were introduced to stress that economic production involves all the activities necessary to get finished commodities to consumers, including not only manufacturing, but also shipping, storage, and retailing services.

A final note: some goods and services produce utility in a special sense. For example, dental services may not directly add to a consumer's utility but do prevent future disutility which would otherwise result from loss of teeth or pain from cavities. Or, for another example, insurance policies produce utility by allaying fears of future economic losses.

The Concept of Marginal Utility. To illustrate the concept of marginal utility we have developed a simple model in Table 3–1, which shows the

TABLE 3–1

(X) No. of Hamburgers	(TU) Total Utility	(MU) Marginal Utility
0	$TU_b + 0$	
		5
1	$TU_b + 5$	
		6
2	$TU_b + 11$	
		4
3	$TU_b + 15$	
		1
4	$TU_b + 16$	
		−3
5	$TU_b + 13$	

number of *utils* derived by an individual from consuming various quantities of hamburgers. These data and our subject consumer are purely hypothetical; the model is designed simply to present the basic principles of utility theory. The first column indicates the number of hamburgers consumed by the individual in a given, short time period, and the second one shows the resulting

[4] Early classical economists tended to discount the value of services. They called "unproductive" the labor which was devoted to service industries.

utility measured in utils. Column two, labeled "total utility" (TU), shows the total utility derived from consuming different quantities of X. We are making the *ceteris paribus* assumption, holding constant the quantity consumed of all other goods (including football games, drinks, and onion rings), while we consider the effects on total utility of changing only one variable, the quantity of hamburgers consumed. The utility enjoyed from consuming all other goods and services, including, for that matter, the football game, are presumed to produce a level of total utility equal to TU_b. The subscript indicates the level of utility *before* consuming hamburgers. Column three we will explain below.

Marginal utility theory is concerned not so much with the total utility which results from consuming a given quantity of a good, as with changes in the level of utility which occur as an individual consumes successive (additional or marginal) units of the good. The *change* in level of utility as successive units of X are consumed is called marginal utility. Focusing on the effects of marginal changes in the level of consumption of goods on the level of utility was the major innovation of marginal utility theory. We will presently see why this approach has proved so useful.

We define marginal utility as follows:

> Marginal utility *shows at each level of consumption of a good the addition to total utility which occurs when one more unit is consumed.*

In general:

$$MU = \frac{\Delta TU}{\Delta X},$$

where ΔTU is the change in total utility caused by ΔX, assumed to be a one-unit increase in the consumption of the commodity.

What happens to the level of utility enjoyed by an individual who consumes more and more units of a particular economic good? Returning to the after-game snack, suppose not one hamburger is consumed, but two, three, or more, while the amount consumed of onion rings and cold drinks is held constant at one each. Utility theory postulates that, *ceteris paribus*, total utility will rise as more hamburgers are consumed, but after a point, the increases will become smaller and smaller. Eventually the additions to utility may become negative.[5]

---

[5] Will total utility ever *fall* with the consumption of the first units of some commodity? Not if the commodity is an economic good to the consumer in question. If the consumption of a commodity causes total utility to fall, then marginal utility is negative with the first unit consumed and the commodity must be viewed as a "bad" not a "good" to the individual in question. Of course, any given commodity may be a good to one person and a bad to another, for example, a double martini. Bads will not be willingly consumed by a rational individual.

Referring to column 3 of Table 3–1, notice that when the consumer increases his consumption of hamburgers from zero to one unit, this raises his total utility from TU_b to $TU_b + 5$. The marginal utility, MU, of the first unit consumed is five utils. Similarly, the consumption of the second unit adds six utils to total utility, so $MU = 6$. Thereafter, marginal utility declines rapidly, so the fourth unit is barely worth consuming, and the fifth results in an actual decline in total utility. The fifth unit would not be consumed even if it were free since it causes total utility to decline for reasons we are all aware. (Of course, if hamburgers were suddenly to become temporarily free, the individual might obtain more than four units, storing the surplus. But maintaining inventories of consumer goods is a form of production. Utility theory properly applies to the consumption of goods, not to their production, so we ignore the possibility of investment in inventories at this point.)

Our utility schedules in Table 3–1 should be adjusted to indicate net utility. For if most of us consume our fill of hamburgers, onion rings, and cokes, there is a very real delayed disutility: a gain in weight. Again, the consumer will likely take the long view and discount the expected future disutilities by balancing discounted future disutilities off against the immediate utilities. Of course, there may be future positive utilities to discount for some consumers (i.e., in our example, for those who are underweight).

The Principle of Diminishing Marginal Utility. The basic principle referred to earlier can now be stated formally:

> The principle of diminishing marginal utility states that as successive quantities of any one good are consumed per some fixed time period, ceteris paribus, *marginal utility eventually declines.*

Notice, this does not necessarily mean that MU must begin to decline immediately with the consumption of the second unit of a good. In our example, it actually rose from five to six, with the consumption of the second hamburger. The principle of diminishing marginal utility indicates only that MU must eventually start to decline. The inclusion of *ceteris paribus* in the statement is essential since the extra utility associated with consuming an extra hamburger would definitely be affected if we simultaneously increased the quantity consumed of cold drinks or of onion rings.

Subsequently, we will see that the principle of diminishing marginal utility helps explain the downward slope of an individual's demand curve for a commodity.

A Graphical Presentation. The principle of diminishing marginal utility is illustrated graphically in Figure 3–1 for units of a theoretical consumer good labeled X. The figure presents basically the same kind of information as the table; however, the graph gives a visual picture which is for many students more helpful in understanding the relationship between marginal and total

FIGURE 3–1 Total and Marginal Utility Curves for Product X

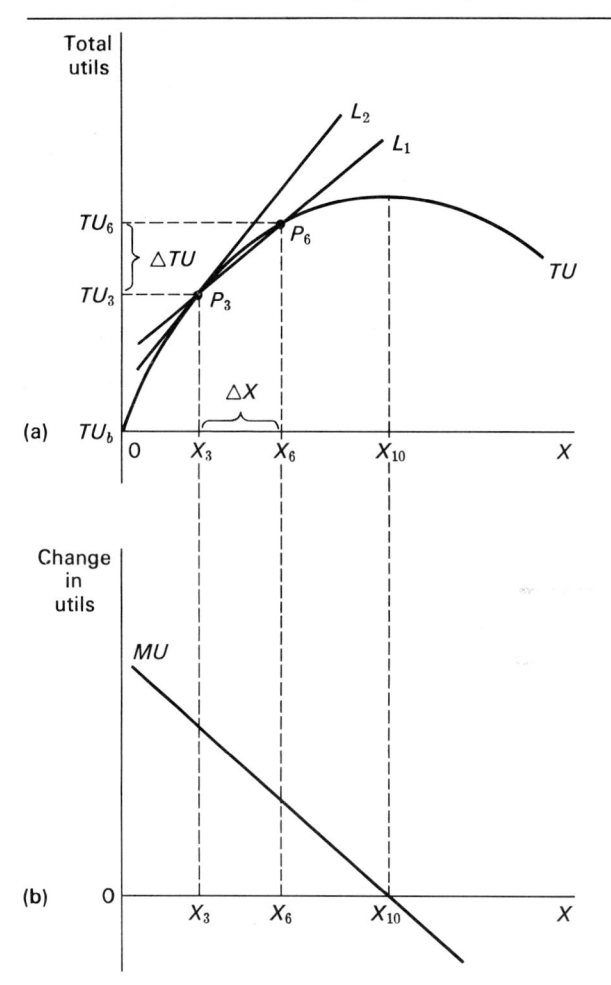

utility than the tabular data. In panel (a) of Figure 3–1, the horizontal axis shows alternative quantities of X which might be consumed by a single individual, while the vertical axis measures total utility in utils. Notice that the horizontal axis begins at zero and includes positive quantities of X consumed, while the vertical axis begins at TU_b, the level of utility enjoyed as a result of consuming given quantities of other goods and services. The curve, *TU*, indicates the total utility derived by our hypothetical individual from consuming various quantities of X, while holding to our *ceteris paribus* assumption. In panel (b), the vertical axis shows marginal utility, while the horizontal axis measures units of X consumed, as in the upper panel. The curve, MU, indicates the marginal utility associated with different levels of consumption of X. MU provides the answer to this question: given that the individual is consuming a certain quantity of the good, what is the marginal utility obtained from consuming one additional unit? From our discussion above, we know that marginal utility will vary with the level of consumption of the good. That is, MU is a function of the level of consumption of X. Using mathematical symbols, we would write:

$$MU = f(X).$$

Some Elementary Mathematical Relationships

The Slope of TU *and* MU. It is important at this point to indicate an elementary mathematical relationship between the slope of the *TU* curve and *MU* at a given output level. Suppose we measure the slope of the *TU* curve in Figure 3–1 between points P_3 and P_6. We must divide the *rise* over the *run* which occurs as we change from the first to the second position on the *TU* curve, where the *rise* is equal to $TU_6 - TU_3$ or ΔTU, and the *run* is $X_6 - X_3$ or ΔX. The slope is then:

$$\text{Slope of } TU = \frac{\Delta TU}{\Delta X},$$

equal to the slope of line L_1 in Figure 3–1. But $\Delta TU/\Delta X$ is equivalent to our definition of marginal utility, if ΔX equaled one. Even though the change from X_3 to X_6 be greater than one, the slope of *TU* between points P_3 and P_6 is the "average" marginal utility for the range $X_3 - X_6$. Thus the slope of *TU* between P_3 and P_6 is equal to the marginal utility associated with the jump in consumption from X_3 to X_6.[6]

Referring again to Figure 3–1, *TU* increases continuously as more and more units of X are consumed, until the consumer reaches X_{10} units. For increases in consumption up to X_{10} units, total utility increases at a decreasing rate. This means that *MU* is positive, although falling, up to the X_{10} level. Total utility is at a maximum at the X_{10} level, indicating that marginal utility and the slope of *TU* are zero and the consumer is satiated with X. If the consumption of X is increased beyond X_{10}, *MU* becomes negative, reflecting a decline in total utility. A negative value for *MU* indicates the consumer has too much

---

[6] If the difference between X_3 and X_6 is very small, then point P_3 is close to point P_6, and the slope between the two points is approximated by the slope of *TU* at point P_3, which equals the slope of line L_2 drawn tangent to the *TU* curve at point P_3. This slope would represent an estimate of marginal utility at the consumption level X_3 for very, very small changes in X. In general, if ΔX is small the slope of the *TU* curve at a point is equal to marginal utility at that point.

of a good and would be better off consuming less, e.g., consumption of fuel in a home kept uncomfortably hot in winter.

Marginal and Total Functions. The relationship between a marginal function and a total function, whether for consumer utility or for some other economic phenomenon, will appear repeatedly in price theory. For this reason, it is worthwhile at this point to summarize the mathematical relationship between total and marginal functions. In each case the principles are identical:

1. The marginal function has a zero value for that value of the total function which is either a maximum or minimum. Referring to Figure 3–2, we have shown a total function in panel (a) which reaches a peak at X_1 units and

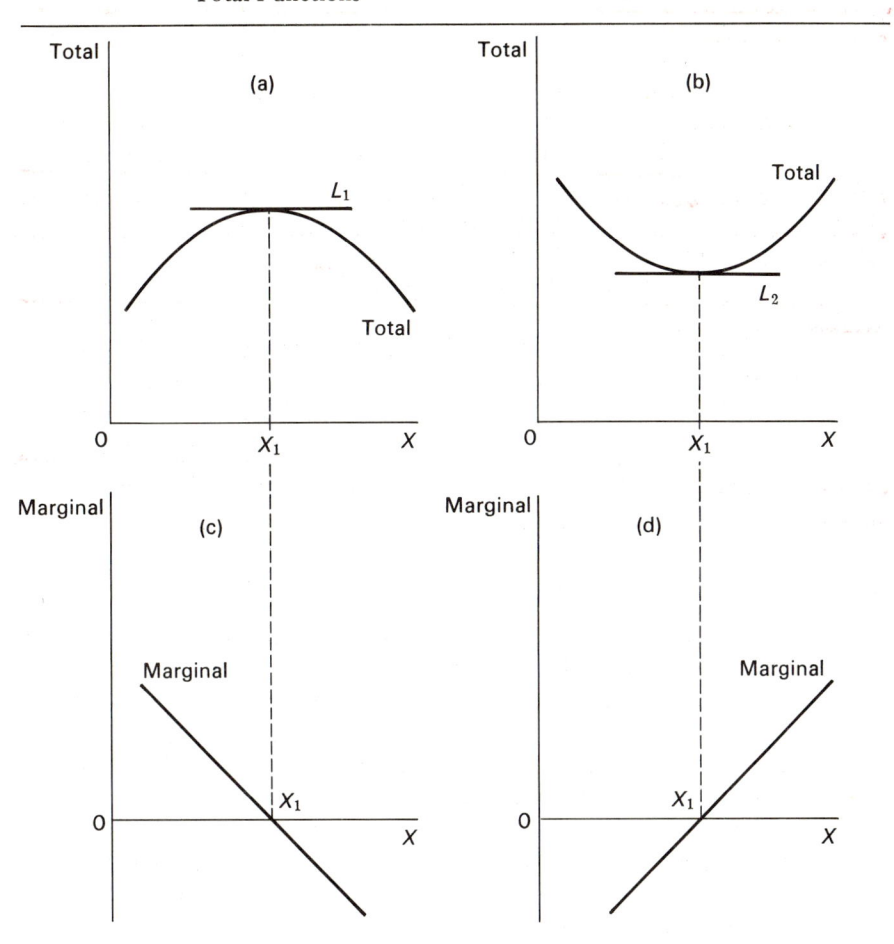

FIGURE 3–2   The Relationship Between Marginal Functions and Total Functions

one in panel (b) which reaches a trough or minimum at X_1. (The total function could be utility, cost, revenue, etc.) Below each of the total functions we have drawn in panels (c) and (d) their respective marginal curves. The marginal value at any level of X is derived by finding the slope of the total curve at that X value. Since at X_1 in either panel (a) or (b), the slope of the total function is zero (e.g., the slopes of lines L_1 and L_2 drawn tangent to the total function are zero), this means both marginal curves must cut across the horizontal axis indicating a zero marginal value at X_1.

2. The value of the total function will increase at a point as long as the value of the marginal function is *positive*, whether the latter is increasing or decreasing. Notice that this statement is reversible: If the value of the marginal function is positive, the value of the total function must be increasing, and if the value of the total function is rising, the value of the marginal function must be positive. For example, in panel (a), the value of the total function rises for values of X between zero and X_1, although the value of the marginal function is declining, while in panel (b), the value of the total function rises for values of X greater than X_1, while the value of the marginal function is rising. The value of the total function will always rise if the marginal is positive. However, if the marginal is positive and rising (panel d), the total increases at an increasing rate, and if the marginal is positive and falling (panel c), the total will rise, but at a decreasing rate.

3. The value of the total function decreases when the value of the marginal function is *negative*, whether the latter value is rising or falling, and vice versa. Again referring to Figure 3–2, the value of the total function declines for values of X greater than X_1 in panel (a) and declines in panel (b) for X values less than X_1, though the marginal curve is declining in the first instance and rising in the latter one. To summarize, the total will always decline if the marginal is negative, though it will fall more rapidly if the marginal is also falling.

The Diamond–Water Paradox

One of the early theoretical problems which received classical economists' attention was the so-called diamond–water paradox. The classical writers were puzzled by the fact that diamonds, which in the aggregate must produce very little total utility in relation to the total utility of water, nevertheless, commanded a high unit price, while water, which produces untold total utility by making life itself possible, commanded a low unit price. Early economists tried to explain the phenomenon by inventing two kinds of value, value in use and value in exchange. Their approach failed to explain the paradox, however, because there is no convincing reason why the two sorts of value should differ. How could market value be above use value? Consumers will not pay a "market value" price to get a good with less "use value."

Marginal utility analysis quickly dispels the paradox. The value of a unit of an economic good is determined, not by the total utility which that good produces for consumers, but by the marginal utility of the last unit consumed. We cannot determine what the marginal utility of the last unit consumed will be, however, unless we know something about the total quantity consumed. For diamonds, the marginal utility of the last unit consumed is very high because the supply of diamonds is restricted relative to the demand for them, though the total utility enjoyed by people from consuming all available diamonds is probably relatively low. In contrast, the marginal utility of the last gallon of water consumed by a typical consumer is very low, evidenced by water's use for washing cars or watering lawns, activities which yield relatively little extra utility to most consumers. So the price of water is about what consumers feel a watered lawn is worth, not what they feel human life is worth. If water were very scarce, it would be restricted to uses which provide more utility, and its price would rise accordingly.

An Equilibrium Model of Consumer Behavior

The Role of Price and Income. If all prices were zero, or if the consumer had an unlimited budget, there would be little difficulty in determining how the individual would maximize utility: one would simply consume that level of each good which maximizes total utility. This consumption level could be determined by consuming successive units of the good until marginal utility fell to zero. There are a few goods for which the constraints are not appreciable for most consumers. The prices of such goods are so low that the consumer's total expenditures on them are an insignificant part of his total budget. Consumption of these goods can be carried to the point of zero marginal utility. Examples are drinking water, salt, tooth-picks, and chewing gum.

However, the prices of most economic goods are appreciable to most consumers and few individuals have unlimited budgets. The typical consumer cannot purchase all goods in the quantities he would like and, indeed, there are some goods he cannot purchase at all. In the typical case, then, the consumer is forced to make choices. He must decide which goods to buy and in what quantities, and he must work within his limited budget. Our task now is to show how these choices will be made, given both the constraints on consumers imposed by budgets and the constraints imposed because goods and services have prices attached to them. We begin with a simple model of consumer behavior.

A Two-Commodity Model of Consumer Behavior. To simplify the presentation of consumer behavior, we make the realistic assumption that the consumer has a budgetary constraint, which sets the limits on what he will purchase, and the unrealistic assumption that he has the option of consuming various amounts of only two commodities, X and Y. Assuming only two

60 The Theory of Consumer Behavior and Demand

commodities makes for a highly simplified model of consumer behavior, but one nevertheless useful.

The budgetary constraint appropriate for a given period may or may not be equal to the consumer's nominal income in that period. We presume the consumer will take the long-run view and will set his budget based not only upon current income but also on future earnings. If future income is expected to rise, the consumer may choose to borrow upon these earnings to augment his current budget. On the other hand, if a decline in future earnings is anticipated, a consumer may choose to save out of current income, in which case the current budget (for expenditures on goods and services) will be less than current income. Even if nominal income is constant from period to period, the consumer will possibly budget more or less than his income in any one period.[7] To simplify the presentation of our basic model, however, we assume the consumer's income is uniform over time and that the current budget for expenditures on goods and services is equal to current income. In summary, our two simplifying assumptions facilitate the presentation of marginal utility theory, without losing the essential features of the mechanism of consumer choice. Despite its disadvantages, we will stick with the simple two-commodity model of consumer behavior.

For our illustration, we will let the prices of commodities X and Y be $1 and $2, respectively, and set the consumer's daily budget to $8.00. In Table 3–2 are

TABLE 3–2

Units of X	$P_x = \$1$ MU_x	MU_x/P_x	Units of Y	$P_y = \$2$ MU_y	MU_y/P_y	$P_y = \$1$ MU_y/P_y
0			0			
	5.5 —	5.5		10 —	5	10
1			1			
	4 —	4		9 —	4.5	9
2			2			
	3 —	3		8 —	4.0	8
3			3			
	2 —	2		7 —	3.5	7
4			4			
	1 —	1		6 —	3.0	6
5			5			
	0 —	0		4 —	2.0	4
6			6			
	−1 —	−1		3 —	1.5	3
7			7			

---

[7] We will investigate in more detail consumer's time preferences for consumption in Chapter 12.

presented our hypothetical consumer's marginal utility schedules for goods X and Y. These schedules are drawn following the assumption that the two goods are independent; the level of consumption of X has no effect on the marginal utility schedule for Y, and vice versa. We will later consider complementary goods, which are used together (e.g., coffee and sugar), and substitute goods, which can be used in place of each other (e.g., coffee and tea).

Since consumers are assumed to be rational economic animals, the main task of our subject consumer is to select that particular combination of goods X and Y which maximizes total utility, subject to his budget constraint. As an aid to the determination of that combination, marginal utility theory provides us with the following rule:

> A consumer maximizes total utility by purchasing that particular combination of X and Y which exhausts his budget and for which the marginal utility per dollar derived from consuming the last X equals the marginal utility per dollar derived from consuming the last Y.

This is where the prices of X and Y come in. To compare the marginal utilities per dollar spent on the two goods, we generate two new columns in Table 3–2, MU_x/P_x and MU_y/P_y (columns 3 and 6), by dividing the marginal utility schedule for each good by its respective price. What we are measuring is the number of utils a consumer gets per dollar expenditure on a good. Once this is established, we can compare the "utility-generating" power of a dollar spent on one good with the "utility-generating" power of a dollar spent on another good. For example, referring to Table 3–2, consumption of the first unit of Y results in a marginal utility of 10 utils. Since the price of Y is $2, we can also say that the consumer gets 10 utils/$2 or five utils per dollar spent on the first Y. A second Y would result in 4.5 utils per dollar spent, while the purchase of the first X would produce 5.5 utils per dollar, and so on. The schedule of MU per dollar for good X, Column 3, is the same as Column 2, since the price of X is $1.

But we still have not determined which combination of X and Y is optimal. To get the answer we begin by supposing the consumer has as yet made no purchases. He begins making purchases following the common-sense rule that he will always choose to buy that good which gives him the most utils per dollar and will continue to make purchases, following this rule, until his budget is exhausted. For the first purchase, the consumer would compare the utils per dollar which he would derive from consuming the initial X with the utils per dollar derived from the first Y. The first X results in 5.5 utils per dollar, the first Y, only 5; thus, the utility-maximizing first purchase will be an X.

We keep track of purchases and expenditures in Table 3–3. After the first

TABLE 3-3

Transaction Number	No. of X's	No. of Y's	Expenditures	Cumulative Expenditures
1	1		$1.00	$ 1.00
2		1	$2.00	$ 3.00
3		1	$2.00	$ 5.00
4	1		$1.00	$ 6.00
5		1	$2.00	$ 8.00
Totals	2	3	$8.00	$23.00

purchase, our subject consumer is consuming one X and zero Y's. If he buys a second X, he gets 4 utils per dollar, while the first Y would result in 5 utils per dollar, so rationally the second purchase would be a Y. Three dollars have now been spent, leaving $5 still available for making purchases. For the third purchase, the individual compares the 4.5 utils per dollar which would be realized with the second purchase of a Y with 4.0 utils per dollar for the second X, and buys a second Y.

Having purchased two Y's and one X, the individual compares the 4 utils per dollar he would gain by purchasing a second X with 4 utils per dollar for a third Y. In this case, the rule does not indicate the proper purchase, since the MU per dollar is identical for both goods. To break the deadlock, suppose the consumer buys another X. Now he has 2 X's and 2 Y's and $2 left to spend. Since the marginal utility per dollar for the third Y, 4.0 utils, is greater than that of a third X, 3.0 utils, the consumer's final purchase will be a Y. Tallying up, the consumer has purchased 2 X's and 3 Y's and has exhausted his $8.00 budget.

The total utility which the consumer enjoys with the combination of 2 X's and 3 Y's is the maximum possible given the prices of X and Y, his budget, and his pattern of preferences for the two goods. With this combination, the consumer is equating the marginal utility per dollar of good X with that of Y:

$$\boxed{\frac{MU_x}{P_x} = \frac{MU_y}{P_y}},$$

or

$$\frac{4 \text{ utils/unit of } X}{\$1 \text{ unit}} = \frac{8 \text{ utils/unit of } Y}{\$2 \text{ unit}},$$

$$\frac{4 \text{ utils}}{\$1_x} = \frac{4 \text{ utils}}{\$1_y},$$

and is exhausting his budget.

If our hypothetical consumer were to alter the 2X − 3Y combination in favor of another Y, he would have to give up 2 X's yielding a total of 9.5 utils (5.5 for the first and 4 with the second) to get the $2 needed to buy the fourth Y, but would gain only 3.5 utils from its consumption. Clearly this is not to his advantage. Similarly, if the individual were to alter the 2X − 3Y combination in favor of another X, he would have to give up one-half of a Y (assuming Y's are divisible), to get the necessary $1 to buy one more X. But another X would only bring 3 utils of utility, while giving up one-half of a Y would cause a loss of about 4 utils (since the marginal utility of the third Y was 8). Thus, the combination of 2 X's and 3 Y's is optimal, because any change would worsen the consumer's situation.

Derivation of Individual Demand

A consumer's *demand function* for good Y relates the quantity of Y which will be consumed by the consumer to the price of Y, the prices of substitutes and complements, the consumer's income, tastes, preferences, and expectations, and any other variables significant to the consumer's decision to purchase Y's. An individual's *demand curve* for Y, on the other hand, relates the various possible prices of Y with the corresponding quantities the consumer is willing and able to buy, holding the non-price determinants of demand constant. To derive the consumer's demand curve for Y, we must determine the various quantities of Y the consumer will consume at different prices while holding to the *ceteris paribus* assumption.

To derive the demand curve for one commodity, say for Y in our two-commodity model, we begin with a $2 price and then drop the price to $1 to see what effect this price change has on the consumer's purchases of Y. We already know that at the $2 Y price the consumer purchases 2 X's and 3 Y's. After the price change, however, the 2X − 3Y combination is no longer optimal because the consumer's marginal utility per dollar spent on Y is no longer equal to the marginal utility per dollar spent on X. In short, the consumer is no longer maximizing utility. To determine the new optimum combination of X's and Y's, we compute in the last column of Table 3–2 a new column showing the marginal utility per dollar spent on Y, reflecting the new price. Following the same procedure used before, the first five purchases would be Y's, the next would be an X, and the final expenditure would be the purchase of both a Y and an X simultaneously. The consumer will have exhausted his budget, purchasing 6 Y's and 2 X's. The decrease in the price of Y has caused an increase from 3 to 6 in the quantity of the good consumed.

If we repeated our experiment by considering other prices of Y, we could derive more price–quantity relationships. However, if we assume for simplicity (only) a linear demand curve, two points are sufficient to determine the curve. Collecting the information about the individual's consumption of Y, we have the following combinations which are plotted in Figure 3–3.

64 The Theory of Consumer Behavior and Demand

P_y	Q_y
$2	3
$1	6

The curve d_y shows the various quantities of Y which will be purchased by the consumer at different prices, assuming that all non-price determinants of demand such as the prices of other goods, the consumer's budget, and his tastes and preferences are held constant.

FIGURE 3-3 The Consumer's Derived Demand for Product Y

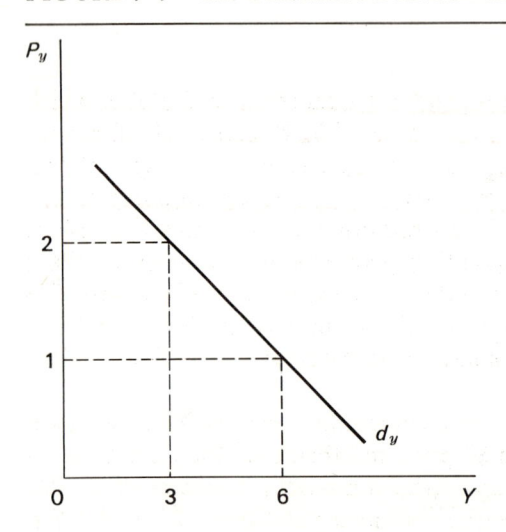

The Notion of Consumer Surplus

An individual's demand curve is a graphical representation of his willingness and ability to purchase a commodity. To consider a different example from the previous model, d_x in panel (a) of Figure 3-4 is a hypothetical consumer's demand curve for product X. This demand curve shows that the maximum price he will pay for one unit of X is $8 as determined by point c on d_x. Suppose we construct a rectangle $8 high and one unit wide with the right-hand side of the base at one unit of X. The area of this rectangle, ABCD, is equal to $8, which is the value of the first unit of X to the consumer, if a dollar is used as the unit of measurement of value. Since the consumer is willing to pay a maximum of $7 for a second unit, the value of that second unit is equal to the area BHGF, and the value of both the first and second units is equal to area ABCD plus area BHGF. The consumer will pay a maximum of $6 for a third unit, which adds to his value received the amount

FIGURE 3-4 The Measurement of Consumer Surplus

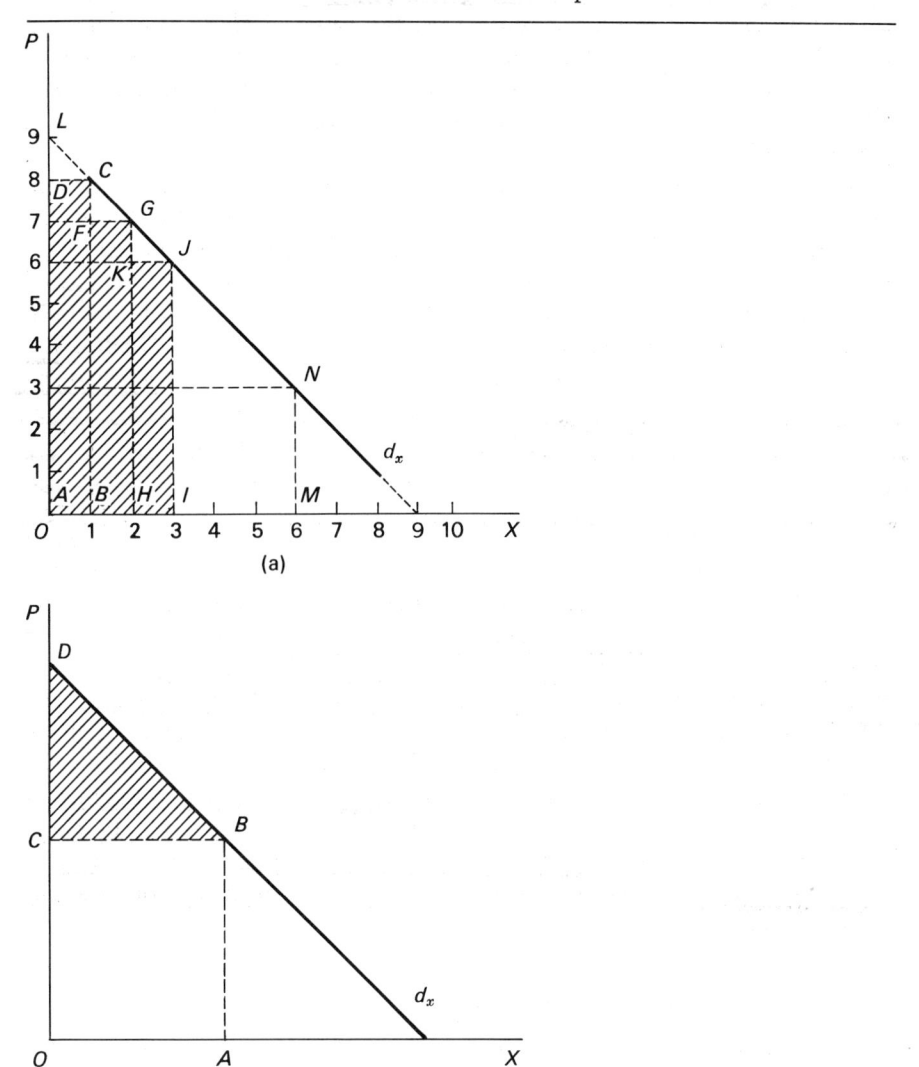

(a)

(b)

HIJK. Therefore, if he is consuming three units, they are worth in value an amount equal to areas *ABCD*, *BHGF*, and *HIJK*. But this latter sum is also equal to the area of the polygon *OIJL*, if we disregard the areas of the little triangles *LDC*, *CFG*, and *GKJ*. In other words, we can measure the value to this consumer of three units of X by the area included under his demand curve out to the three-unit level of X. Polygon *OIJL* also represents the maximum total amount the consumer will pay for three units. As another example, if the consumer consumes six units of X, the value of these units sums to OMNL. The area enclosed by the demand curve is not a direct measure of consumer welfare, since dollars and not utils is our basic unit of measurement, but this area is a reasonable stand-in—probably the best available for most practical problems.

Now refer to panel (b) and presume the price to the consumer is OC and his consumption level, as determined by d_x (his demand curve for X), is OA. The area OABD is the value to the consumer of these units and represents the maximum amount he will pay for them. But if the consumer purchases X in a competitive market, he pays price OC for *all* units purchased. His total outlay for OA units is price OC times quantity OA or the area OABC. We define *consumer surplus* for this consumer as the difference between the maximum he will pay for OA units, which is area OABD, and the amount he in fact pays, which is area OABC. The consumer surplus is the shaded area CBD. The triangle CBD represents a sum the consumer would be willing and able to pay, if forced to do so on an all-or-nothing basis, but which he need not pay.

We can estimate the consumer surplus of all consumers in the market for a given price–quantity combination by computing the difference between the area under the market demand curve and the total expenditures of all consumers. For example, if d_x in panel (b) of Figure 3–4 is the market demand curve and the equilibrium price and quantity are OC and OA, respectively, then area CBD is the sum of the consumer surpluses of all consumers. The inference is at least reasonable that the total utility of all consumers is maximized when we maximize the area under the market demand curve above the market price. That triangular area, representing consumer surplus in the market for commodity X, will be greater, the lower the price and the larger the quantity of X produced and sold; and consumer surplus in the aggregate will be greater, the lower the average price and the larger the quantity consumed of all commodities.

Criticisms of Marginal Utility Theory

The most damaging criticism of marginal utility theory has been leveled at the basic assumption that utility can be measured. A complete theory of marginal utility requires that utility be *cardinally* measurable. Examples of cardinal measuring systems are temperatures, weights, lengths, and volumes. A characteristic of all of these measuring schemes is a zero and a unit of measurement, such as a degree, pound, foot, or cubic centimeter. By contrast, an *ordinal* measuring system employs a ranking scheme, say a beauty contest in which there is a winner, a first runner-up, and a second runner-up. There is no zero and no unit of measurement in an ordinal system. In the latter system, we measure two quantities by saying one is larger or smaller than the other.

Suppose an individual's level of consumption of a good is increased by one unit. He will probably be able to say that his utility level has changed. But can he say how much it has changed? An increase of 6 utils, or 8 utils? More likely he will not be able to say much more than: "It has increased a great deal" or "It has increased a little" or "I'm as well off either way." There is no way to enter the consumer's head and measure the electrical charge or chemical change that occurs to cause utility or satisfaction as consumption takes place. As yet, we do not have a satisfactory technique for cardinally measuring utility, nor can we be certain that one can be developed.

A satisfactory cardinal measure of utility would require a zero level and a unit measure of utility. It is almost impossible to conceive of a zero utility level, and the determination of a unit of measurement, the util, has with one exception, not been accomplished. The one exception is a method developed by Morgenstern and von Neumann for measuring utility under conditions of risk.[8] However, most economic decisions in which prices and utilities are to be compared are associated with zero or minimal risk, so the Morgenstern–von Neumann demonstration is not an altogether satisfactory response to the basic criticism. Perhaps the experiments being conducted by psychiatrists at Tulane and other centers with electrical impulses directed to various brain centers could presage the development of a cardinal utility measure.

The Goals of the Marginal Utility Theorists

The original marginal utility theorists expected that the measurement problem would somehow be resolved, and they continued with their work, using the analytical tools of utility theory to investigate a wide variety of economic problems. Their first aim was to make economics a quantitative science of human welfare, and their principal goal was the maximization of social utility. Economics was to provide the necessary tools for accomplishing this goal through enlightened public policy. First came the development of a theory of the individual consumer, based upon the principles of marginal utility. The next step was expected to be a system for measuring utility for the whole society, where the objective was no less than the development of a social utility function. Such an aggregative measuring scheme, if practicable, would enable the economist to compare the social performance of alternative forms of economic organization. For example, the social utility generated in a free market system might be contrasted with that of a socialistic form of economic organization. If existing systems were found inefficient in one or more respects, it would be the role of economic policy to suggest alternative systems of organizing the society's productive resources, as well as its systems of output distribution, to maximize social utility.

[8] J. von Neumann and O. Morgenstern, *The Theory of Games and Economic Behavior* (Princeton: Princeton University Press, 1947).

The early utility theorists had great hopes that economics would develop into a quantitative science capable of predicting economic behavior with much the same precision that characterizes the physical sciences such as chemistry and physics. The ability to predict accurately the consequences of various actions would, in turn, lead to effective policies to maximize social utility. The expectations of these earlier theorists have not been realized. Economists have had to be content with much less precise analytical tools, and as a consequence, have been forced to make policy recommendations with some uncertainty about their effects on social utility. Probably the main reason for the failure of economics to realize the early expectations of utility theorists is the fact that there is considerably greater variability in the behavior of economic units than is evident in the physical processes of physics and chemistry. That variability renders impossible the development of precise analytical tools and completely reliable predictions of economic behavior.

INDIFFERENCE CURVE THEORY

Two economists, J. R. Hicks and R. G. D. Allen, demonstrated a theoretical model of consumer behavior in the 1930's that was not subject to the basic criticism of marginal utility theory.[9] This was accomplished by incorporating in the behavioral model a measuring scheme which was ordinal rather than cardinal. The main assumption of the new theory was that individuals can distinguish differences in the *level* of utility experienced under different circumstances, though they cannot determine the magnitude of utility, as assumed by the marginalists. The individual asserts his preferences based upon differences in satisfaction enjoyed from consuming one combination of two goods relative to another. For example, a consumer might decide that he prefers combination 1 of goods X and Y over combination 2, because combination 1 produces more utility. He need not know how much utility is associated with 1, only that it is more than he gets from 2. Or, in another instance, a consumer might decide that two different combinations of X and Y give him the same utility, in which case, he would be indifferent if asked to choose between the two combinations.

Indifference Curves and Budget Lines

To facilitate our presentation of indifference curve theory, we retain the simplifications of the previous model: a single consumer with a budgetary constraint has the option of purchasing different quantities of two goods, X and Y, at given prices. We limit ourselves to two commodities for sim-

---

[9] The basic approach was expounded by F. Y. Edgeworth and V. Pareto in the late nineteenth century; however, Hicks and Allen were more successful in popularizing indifference curve theory.

plicity and so that we may illustrate the theory using two-dimensional graphs.

Definition of Indifference Curve. The relationship between various quantities of two goods consumed by a consumer, and the utility which results from their consumption, may be stated using mathematical symbols as:

$$U = f(X, Y),$$

where U is the level of utility enjoyed by the individual and X and Y are the various quantities of the two goods consumed. If we hold the utility level constant, and enumerate all of the various combinations of X and Y which produce that level of utility, we have an indifference curve. In other words, an indifference curve pertains to a single consumer and shows graphically all the various quantities of two goods, X and Y, which provide that consumer with a given or equal amount of utility. In symbols an indifference curve for a utility level of 10 can be written:

$$\overline{U}_{10} = f(X, Y),$$

where the bar over U_{10} indicates that the level of utility is constant, and the subscript indicates an ordinal ranking of 10. The subscript, 10, discloses that the combinations of X and Y along I_{10} generate a level of utility greater than utility level U_9 and less than level U_{11}. It does not signify a utility level of 10 utils, since a util is deemed unmeasurable in indifference curve theory. The subscripts denote a *ranking* of utilities only.

A graph of an indifference curve is presented in Figure 3–5 labeled I_{10}. Any combination of goods X and Y along I_{10}, such as combination A, B, or C, results in the same level of utility for our hypothetical consumer. Thus, the consumer is indifferent between combinations A and B, A and C, and B and C. If he were offered either combination B or C free, he might just as well flip a coin to determine which to accept.

The Marginal Rate of Substitution. Having introduced the indifference curve, what we need now is a measure which will facilitate the presentation of indifference curve characteristics. The *marginal rate of substitution* of Y for X is the amount of Y the consumer is just willing to give up to get an additional unit of X, without changing the level of utility which he enjoys. Using mathematical symbols:

$$MRS_{yx} = -\frac{\Delta Y}{\Delta X},$$

where ΔY is the amount of Y given up, and ΔX is equal to a one-unit increase in the consumption of X. Since ΔY will typically be negative and ΔX positive, the negative sign before the fraction will insure that MRS_{yx} will usually be positive. For example, suppose an individual is initially consuming combination A of goods X and Y along indifference curve I_{10} in Figure 3–5. The marginal rate of substitution, MRS_{yx}, at that point is +3, since the consumer

FIGURE 3–5 A Consumer's Indifference Curve for Goods X and Y

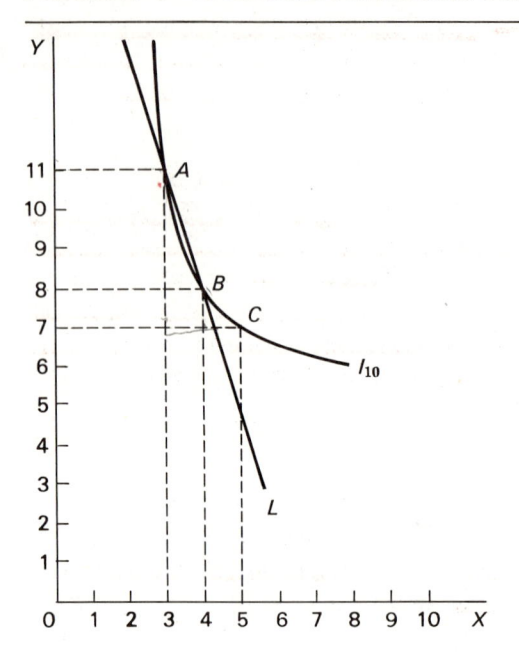

would be willing to switch to combination B, giving up 3 Y's and gaining 1 X ($MRS_{yx} = - -3/1$). At point B, the MRS_{yx} is +1, since the individual will be willing to move from B to C, giving up 1 Y to get another X. The MRS can also be computed for changes in X that are greater or less than 1. If we let ΔX be a number larger than one, $MRS = -\Delta Y/\Delta X$ will give an average MRS over the range chosen. If X is less than one, MRS becomes an estimate of the marginal rate of substitution. For many problems, we simply let MRS equal $-\Delta Y/\Delta X$ and place no restrictions on ΔX.

Now we must investigate the relationship between the slope of an indifference curve and the marginal rate of substitution. Suppose we computed the slope of the line L drawn through the points A and B in Figure 3–5. We would divide the *rise* in moving from point A to point B, which is $(8 - 11)$, by the *run* $(4 - 3)$ to get: slope line $L = (8 - 11)/(4 - 3)$ or -3. But if we take the absolute value of the slope of line L, this equals the MRS_{yx} between points A and B.[10] Therefore, we may conclude that the absolute value of the slope of a straight line drawn between two points on an indifference curve is the MRS between the two points. If the distance between the two points is not great, the slope of the straight line L in Figure 3–5 approximates the

---

[10] The absolute value of a number is its numerical value regardless of sign. For example, the absolute value of -10 is $+10$, and the absolute value of $+10$ is $+10$.

slope of indifference curve I_{10} at point A (and at point B). Of course, the slope of the indifference curve at point A is the slope of a line drawn tangent to I_{10} at A. But if the distance between points A and B becomes smaller and smaller, the slope of a line through the two points becomes a more accurate estimate of the slope of the indifference curve at point A or B. We may describe the MRS at a point as the "instantaneous" rate of substitution of Y for X and further conclude that the MRS at any point on an indifference curve is equal to the absolute value of the slope of the indifference curve at that point. Henceforth, we will consider the MRS at a point and the absolute value of the slope of the indifference curve at that point as equals.

The Characteristics of Indifference Curves. Indifference curves exhibit the following basic characteristics:

1. They are nonintersecting.
2. They have negative slopes.
3. They are convex to the origin.

To prove the first characteristic, we will consider the case where two indifference curves, such as I_1 and I_2 in Figure 3–6, intersect and show why this is not admissible. The combinations of goods X and Y at points P_2 and P_1 in

FIGURE 3–6 The Case of Intersecting Indifference Curves

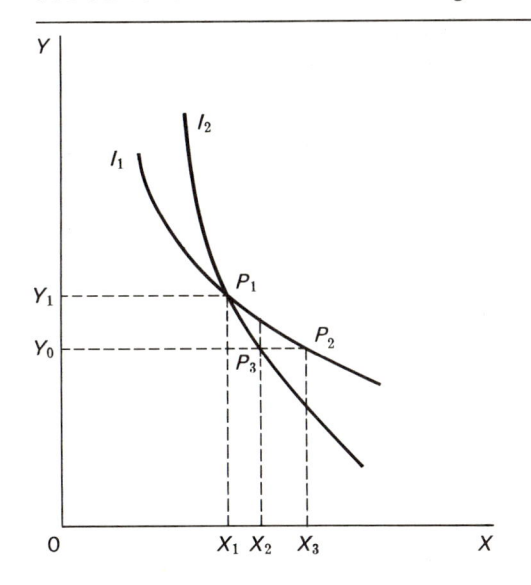

Figure 3–6 produce equal satisfaction, since they lie along indifference curve I_1. Moreover, combinations P_1 and P_3 produce equal satisfaction, since they lie along indifference curve I_2. Finally, combinations P_3 and P_2 must produce

equal utility also, since each is equal in utility to combination P_1. Things equal to the same thing are equal to each other. But combination P_2 contains more units of X than combination P_3, while both P_2 and P_3 contain the same amount of Y. The equality of utility between combinations P_3 and P_2 could only arise if the addition of $(X_3 - X_2)$ units of X to combination P_3 resulted in zero extra utility to the consumer. We will adopt the *nonsatiety assumption* that the individual will always prefer more of a commodity to no more extra units. Following this assumption, the utility of P_2 must be greater than that of P_3, not equal in utility, and the two points cannot lie along a single indifference curve. Thus, by contradiction, we have shown that intersecting curves are not admitted.

The nonsatiety assumption also rules out indifference curves with positive slopes. Consider the case of indifference curve I_1 in Figure 3–7. The combination of goods X and Y at P_2 contains more units of the two goods than combination P_1. Moreover, the slope of the indifference curve is positive in the range from P_1 to P_2. Since both points P_1 and P_2 are on a single indifference curve I_1, the utility associated with each is defined as equal. However, since point P_2 represents more units of the two goods than P_1, it should generate more utility per the nonsatiety assumption. There is an obvious contradiction. The necessary conclusion is that positively sloped indifference curves are ruled out by the nonsatiety assumption.

FIGURE 3–7 A Positively Sloped Indifference Curve

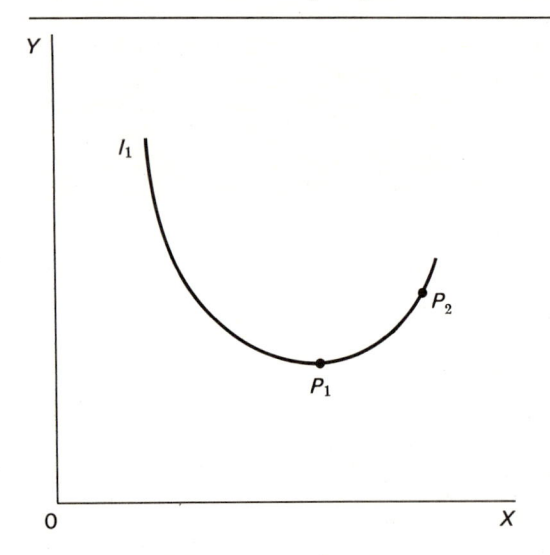

The final characteristic of indifference curves is their convexity to the origin. Suppose you have a great deal of Y and little X, say, Y_4 units of Y and only X_1 units of X in Figure 3–8. Probably, you would trade a large quantity

FIGURE 3–8 A Convex Indifference Curve for Goods X and Y

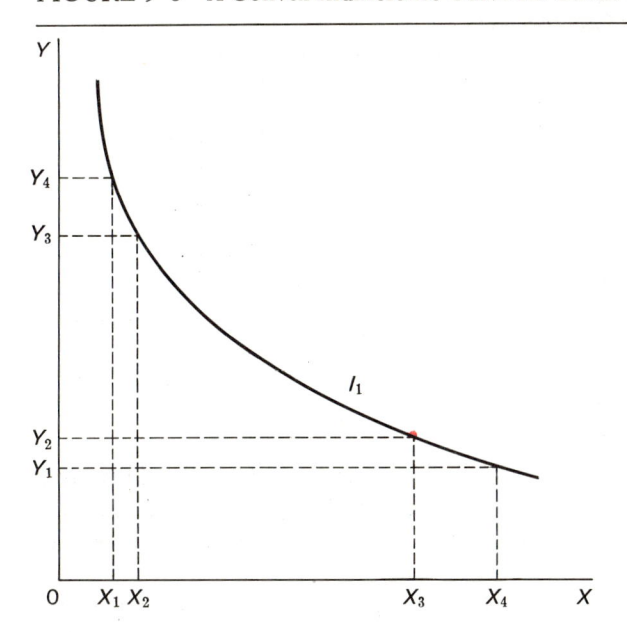

of Y for one additional X under these conditions. An additional X would be valuable to you since you have only a small quantity of it relative to Y, and you would be willing to pay a high Y price for that extra X. In other words, the MRS_{yx} is likely to be high when the ratio of the quantity consumed of Y to X is high. Conversely, if you presently consume X_3 units of X and Y_2 units of Y, it is likely that you would be willing to give up only a small amount of Y to get one more unit of X, since your level of consumption of X is already considerable and your level of consumption of Y is small. This is tantamount to saying the consumer's MRS_{yx} is low. When we shift from high ratios of Y to X to high ratios of X to Y (a movement from the Northwest to the Southeast along I_1 in Figure 3–8), the value of MRS_{yx} falls. Of course, MRS_{yx} is equal to the absolute value of the slope of I_1, which will always be negative according to the nonsatiety assumption. Therefore, the slope of I_1 changes from large negative values to smaller negative values as we move down the curve. This change in slope which occurs as we move along an indifference curve implies the convexity of the curve.

An indifference curve for two goods, X and Y, which are very close substitutes for each other, will look like I_1 in panel (a) of Figure 3–9. The MRS_{yx} changes but little as the ratio of Y to X falls, indicating X is a good substitute for Y even at high levels of consumption of X. To take the limiting case, the indifference curve for two goods which are perfect substitutes would approach a straight line, and the MRS_{yx} would, as a consequence, approach a constant value. For example, if Y were nickels and X dimes (not really consumer

FIGURE 3–9 (a) Close Substitutes (b) Poor Substitutes
(c) Perfect Complements

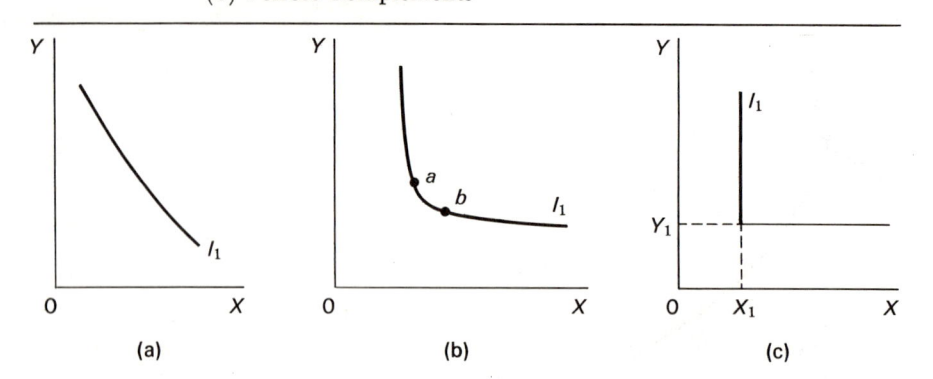

goods), then an indifference curve for, say, $1 worth of utility would exhibit a constant MRS_{yx} of 2.[11] In the case of a constant MRS_{yx} there would be little economic reason for considering the goods as separate or distinct so far as that consumer is concerned.

If two goods are very poor substitutes for each other, the indifference curve might look like I_1 in panel (b) of Figure 3–9. For X–Y combinations along I_1 above point a, Y is such a poor substitute for X that the consumer is willing to give up a large quantity of Y to get an extra X. Or the consumer would require a great deal of Y to compensate him for a small loss in X. In other words, the MRS_{yx} is a very large number. To the right of point b, X becomes a poor substitute for Y and thus the MRS_{yx} is low. Only in the range between points a and b are the two goods reasonably good substitutes for each other. For the extreme case, illustrated by indifference curve I_1 in panel (c), the goods must be used in fixed proportions (Y_1 to X_1), otherwise the MRS is either infinite or zero. This curve illustrates the case of perfect complements, examples being toothbrushes and toothpaste, pen and ink, and so on.[12] Even in the case of apparent perfect complementarity, however, there may be some range, like ab along I_1 in panel (b), for which one good may be substituted for the other at a declining MRS_{yx}.

The Family of Indifference Curves. There exists for each consumer an infinite number or what we can describe as a family of indifference curves, one

---

[11] For higher indifference curves, say for $100, the MRS_{yx} might not be constant. For example, nickels weigh more than dimes, and if this produces an inconvenience, the consumer's MRS_{yx} might be say $100/49$ for points on the indifference curve, where the ratio of Y to X is high. The reader can think of other sources of inconvenience in having all Y's or X's under different circumstances.

[12] The question is left for the reader whether an indifference curve like I_1 in Figure 3–9(c) always implies complementarity.

FIGURE 3–10 A Family of Indifference Curves

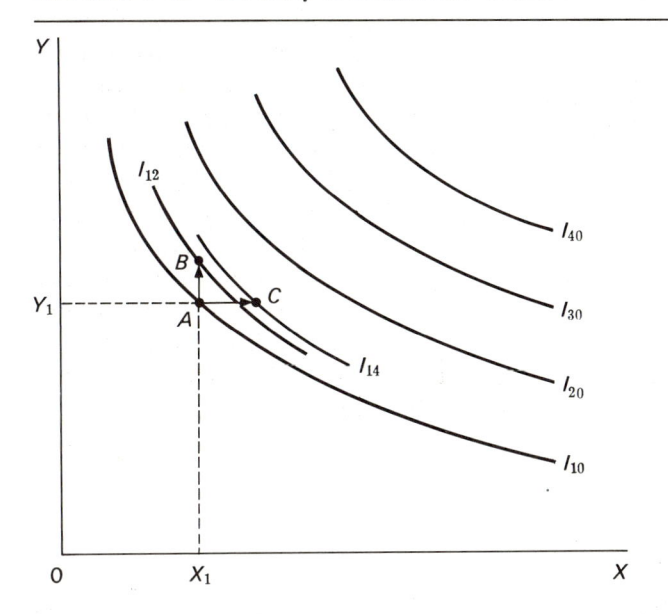

for each possible level of utility. For example, indifference curve I_{30} in Figure 3–10 represents a higher level of utility than either I_{10} or I_{20}. The utility associated with combinations along I_{30} is less than that along I_{40}, and so on. Notice that we are saying nothing about the absolute level of utility, only the relative levels. The utility associated with I_{40} is greater than that associated with I_{30} and I_{20} and I_{10}, or, generalizing, $U_{40} > U_{30} > U_{20} > U_{10}$, where variables U_{40} through U_{10} stand for the respective utility rankings. We do not know how much is the utility associated with I_{40}, only that it is greater than I_{30}. Finally, any upward or rightward movement (or combination of upward and rightward movements) in a field of indifference curves will cut across separate curves. For example, an upward movement from point A on I_{10} in Figure 3–10 brings the consumer to point B on I_{12}, representing more utility, as does the rightward movement from point A on I_{10} to point C on I_{14}.

We have represented a hypothetical consumer's pattern of preferences for two goods, X and Y, by showing in Figure 3–10 only a few of the infinite number of indifference curves that could conceivably be mapped. Any combination of the two goods is represented by one point on a single indifference curve. Any indifference curve in the map indicates both the utility associated with the combinations of X and Y, along the curve, relative to the utility associated with other combinations, and the terms of exchange (MRS_{xy}) of one goods for the other which will leave the consumer's level of utility unchanged. However, we do not yet have a complete theory of consumer behavior. To complete the model, we must introduce the principal constraints, which (1) set the terms at which the two goods can be purchased in the market and (2) prevent the consumer from moving out to an indifference curve with infinite utility. The latter constraint is principally the consumer's budget or income, whereas the former consists in the prices of the two goods X and Y.

The Budget Line or Line of Attainable Combinations. Suppose that our hypothetical consumer sets his daily budget at $16 and that the prices of X and Y are $4 and $2 per unit, respectively. If he were to spend his entire budget on Y's first, and then buy no X's, he could obtain a total of 8 units, since the price per Y is $2 and he has $16 to spend per day. On the other hand, if he buys all X's, he can purchase a total of 4 units, $16/$4 per unit. Another possible combination of X and Y which would exhaust his $16 budget is 2 Y's and 3 X's. In fact, all possible combinations of X and Y which could be purchased with $16 are determined by the equation:

$$\text{Budget} = P_x \cdot X + P_y \cdot Y,$$

or

$$\$16 = \$4 \cdot X + \$2 \cdot Y,$$

where X and Y are the quantities of the two goods purchased, and are restricted to nonnegative values.

The graph of the above equation is the line labeled BL in Figure 3–11, called a *budget line* or *line of attainable combinations*. If we assume that the prices of X and Y remain constant and that fractional amounts of X and Y can be purchased, then BL is an unbroken straight line which shows all combinations of X and Y that will exhaust the consumer's budget of $16 at prices of $4 and $2 for X and Y, respectively.[13] The consumer can purchase quantities of X and Y along BL or at any point to the left of BL. However, the consumer cannot buy X–Y combinations to the right of BL, because such combinations require more than the consumer's budget.

The slope of the budget line, BL, is equal to $-P_x/P_y$, which is determined simply by (1) dividing the vertical intercept, $16/P_y$, by the horizontal intercept, $16/P_x$, giving $16/P_y \div 16/P_x$ or P_x/P_y, and (2) attaching a negative sign. Since $P_x = \$4$ and $P_y = \$2$, the ratio of P_x to P_y is $4/$2 or 2 and the slope of BL is -2. This ratio may be given an economic interpretation. For every 2 Y's which the consumer decides not to purchase, 1 X may be purchased instead. On the other hand, for every X given up (not purchased), 2 Y's may be obtained. In general, the price ratio, P_x/P_y, determines the rate at which one good may be exchanged in the market for the other.

---

[13] Actually, we are assuming that any *real number* quantity of X or Y can be purchased. In addition to integers and fractions, real numbers include irrational numbers like $\sqrt{3}$ and $\sqrt{7}$; the purchase of such quantities is generally a practical impossibility.

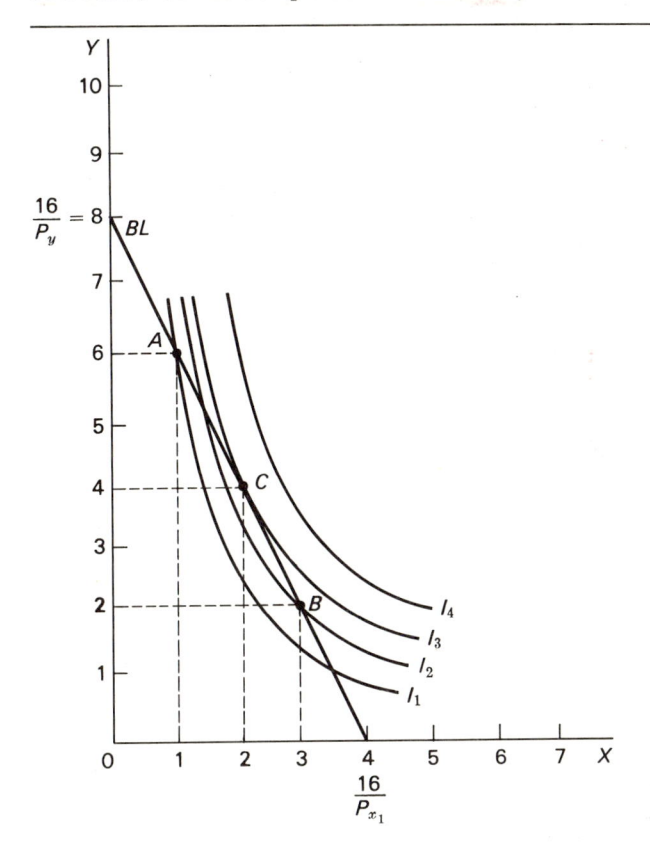

FIGURE 3-11 A Complete Two-Commodity Model of Consumer Behavior

The Equilibrium Combination of X *and* Y. But which of the possible combinations should the consumer buy to maximize his utility? Is combination A (6 Y's and 1 X) in Figure 3-11 optimal? No, since the consumer could switch to combination B (2 Y's and 3 X's) and increase his utility. Combination B would be preferred to A, since point B lies along indifference curve I_2, which represents greater utility than I_1. However, combination B is not optimal either. By switching to combination C, the consumer can increase his utility still more, since combination C is on indifference curve I_3, which represents more utility than either indifference curve I_2 or I_1. Indifference curve I_3 is in fact the highest the consumer can reach and combination C is therefore optimal. For instance, I_4, which would provide more utility than I_3, cannot be reached by the consumer, because any point on I_4 would require a larger expenditure than his limited budget of $16 per day.

At the optimum combination of X and Y, point C, the budget line, BL, just touches the indifference curve I_3 and is, therefore, tangent to I_3. Since BL and I_3 are tangent at combination C, their slopes are equal at that point. Therefore, a necessary condition for the optimal combination of X and Y is:

> The slope of the budget line must equal the slope of an indifference curve.

But since the slope of the budget line is the ratio $-P_x/P_y$ and the slope of any indifference curve at a point is equal to the MRS_{yx} at that point, with a negative sign attached, the equilibrium requirement is:

$$-MRS_{yx} = -\frac{P_x}{P_y},$$

$$MRS_{yx} = \frac{P_x}{P_y}.$$

Restated, the consumer will buy that combination of goods X and Y for which the market rate of exchange equals the rate at which the consumer is willing to substitute the goods to maintain a given level of utility. If the market rate of substitution, P_x/P_y, is less than the consumer's willing rate of substitution, MRS_{yx} (e.g., point A on BL), the consumer will exchange Y for X. On the other hand, if the market rate of substitution is greater than the consumer's minimum acceptable rate of exchange of Y for X (e.g., point B on BL), he will not be willing to exchange Y for X, but will be willing to swap X's for Y's. Only when the two rates of substitution are equal, one rate reflecting market conditions and the other reflecting the consumer's preferences, will the individual be content with his existing combination of the two goods.

Derivation of Demand Curve

The indifference curve model can be used as an analytical tool for deriving the consumer's demand for either X or Y. To illustrate, assume initially that the price of X is P_{x_1} and the price of Y is P_y and that the consumer is initially purchasing Y_1 units of Y and X_1 units of X as shown in panel (a) of Figure 3–12. Now suppose the price of X decreases from P_{x_1} to P_{x_0} ($P_{x_0} < P_{x_1}$). This price change will have no effect on the individual's pattern of preferences for goods X and Y and, thus, will have no effect on the family of indifference curves for the two goods. We assume the goods are not "Veblen goods" or "snob goods" for which the utility enjoyed from consuming the good is partly a function of price.

The budget line will be affected, however. Given the original price of X, the consumer could buy a maximum of B_1/P_{x_1} units, which equals the horizontal axis intercept of the original budget line, BL_1. After the price of X has been

FIGURE 3-12 The Derivation of a Consumer's Demand for Product X

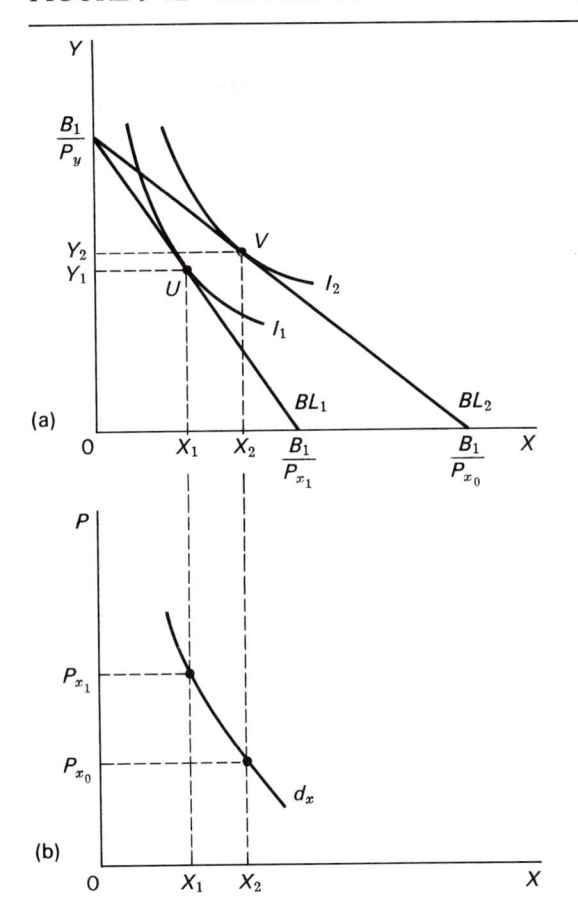

(a)

(b)

reduced to P_{x_0}, the maximum amount of X which can be purchased increases to B_1/P_{x_0}, which equals the horizontal-axis intercept of the new budget line, BL_2 in panel (a) of Figure 3-12. Since the consumer's budget and the price of Y are unchanged, the maximum amount of Y which can be bought remains the same, so the vertical axis intercept of both budget lines is unchanged at B_1/P_y. Generalizing, we may conclude that a decrease in the price of X rotates the budget line counterclockwise about the vertical axis intercept. Conversely, an increase in the price of X, with the price of Y unchanged, will rotate the budget line clockwise about the same point.

When the price of X falls, the equilibrium combination of goods X and Y at point U is no longer optimal. The consumer can now afford the combinations of X and Y along BL_2 and will seek that particular combination which maximizes his total utility. The new optimum combination is found at point V, the point of tangency of BL_2 with indifference curve I_2. The utility-maximizing consumer will now purchase Y_2 units of Y and X_2 units of X, and his budget will once again be exhausted. Since I_2 is to the right of I_1, the consumer's utility has increased as a result of the price decline.

The data provided by the two equilibrium points, U at P_{x1} and V at P_{x2}, allows us to determine two points on the consumer's demand curve for X. When the price of X is P_{x1}, he purchases X_1 units, and if the price of X falls to P_{x2}, ceteris paribus, the quantity purchased rises to X_2. The inclusion of ceteris paribus means that only the price of X is changed; the consumer's budget, his tastes and preferences (as summarized by the family of indifference curves), and the price of Y and the prices of all other goods are held constant. Summarizing this information:

P_x	Q_x
P_{x1}	X_1
P_{x2}	X_2

We have plotted this data in panel (b) of Figure 3–12, and, assuming the experiment is repeated for many different prices of X, we generate the individual's demand curve for X, labeled d_x in panel (b). There d_x shows the various quantities of X, which the consumer will purchase at different prices, assuming all other factors are held constant.

Derivation of Engel Curve

The indifference curve model may be used to show the effects on consumer behavior of changes in the consumer's income as well as changes in price. Referring to Figure 3–13, assume the consumer's income is initially B_1 and the prices of X and Y are P_{x1} and P_{y1}, respectively. The consumer maximizes utility by purchasing X_1 units of X and Y_1 units of Y (point U in Figure 3–13). Now, while holding the prices of X and Y unchanged, conceptually increase the consumer's income so that his budget line increases from B_1 to B_2. The rise in income allows the consumer to purchase larger combinations of both X and Y along budget line BL_2. But since the prices of X and Y are the same as before, the market rate of exchange is unchanged, and the slope of BL_2 equals that of BL_1. The two budget lines are, therefore, parallel. The consumer will now maximize utility by purchasing the combination of X and Y represented by point V, the point of tangency of the new budget line, BL_2, and indifference curve, I_2. With the higher income, the consumer will purchase X_2 units of X and Y_2 units of Y.

Collecting the data on the two budget levels and the corresponding levels of consumption of good X, we get:

Budget	Units of X
B_1	X_1
B_2	X_2

FIGURE 3–13 The Derivation of a Consumer's Engel Curve for Product X

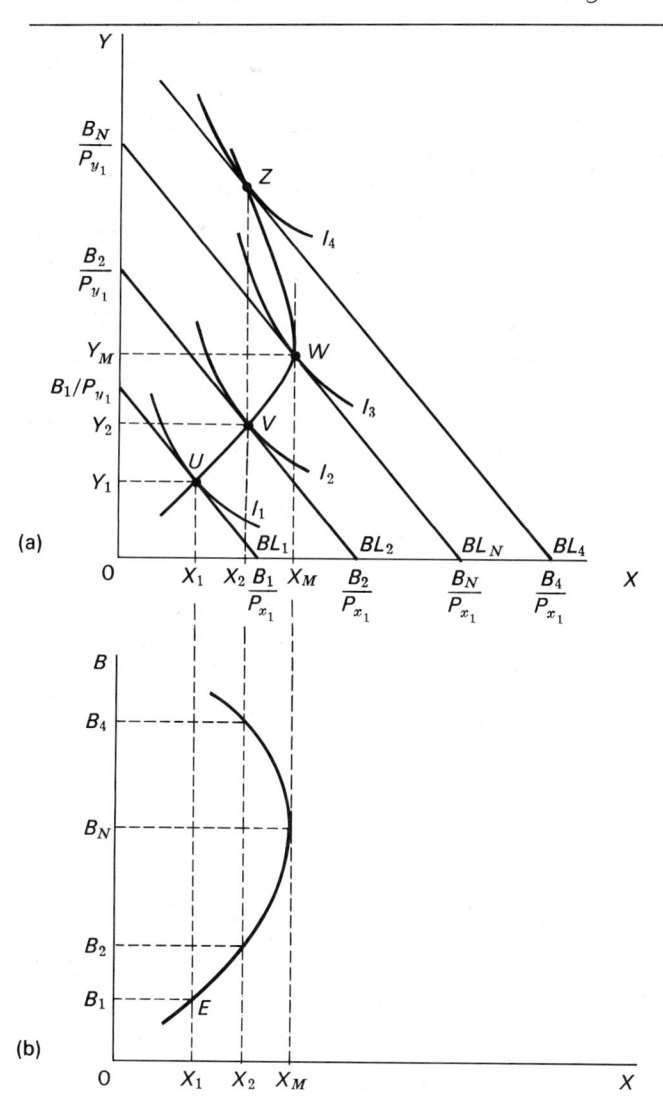

Plotting this data in panel (b), and again assuming the experiment is repeated for values of B between B_1 and B_4, other than B_1 and B_2, we generate the curve labeled E. Note that since the axes in the upper panel of Figure 3–13 are units of Y and X, respectively, we must construct a new graph (panel b) to show the relation of budget levels to quantities of X consumed. Curve E in panel (b) is called an *Engel curve*, named for the nineteenth-century head of the Austrian Bureau of Statistics, Ernst Engel (1821–1895), who was the first to investigate statistically the relationship between income changes and changes in quantities consumed of various goods and services. The Engel curve shows the various amounts of a good which will be consumed by a consumer at different income levels assuming all nonincome determinants of demand remain constant, including the price of the good itself. The Engel curve may be thought of as an income–demand curve, in contrast with a demand curve that is more completely described as a price–demand curve. (One generalization Engel made based on his data, known today as Engel's law, states that as a family's income rises, a smaller proportion of income will be spent for food.)

As a consumer's income rises, he may increase or decrease the quantity he purchases of a given commodity. If the quantity he consumes of a good increases with income increases, it is defined as a *normal* or *superior* good.[14] Examples for a given consumer might be color TV's and sirloin steak. Otherwise, if the quantity consumed of a good decreases when a consumer's income increases, it is an *inferior* good for that consumer. Possible examples might be hamburgers and compact cars. These definitions are reversible, so that if income falls and the quantity consumed of an item declines, it is deemed a normal good. If the quantity of a good consumed rises with a fall in income, the good is inferior.

For any particular consumer, a good may be normal for a given income range and then become an inferior good at higher income levels. Referring to our previous example illustrated in Figure 3–13, X is a normal good for levels of the consumer's income less than B_N and an inferior good for income levels above B_N.

Income and Substitution Effects of a Price Change

Retaining our simplified two-commodity model of consumer behavior, we may now study in more detail the total effects of a change in the price of one of the goods. Suppose the price of X declines, while the price of Y, the consumer's budget, and his tastes and preferences all remain constant. The case is illustrated in Figure 3–14. The decline in the price of X from P_{x_1} to P_{x_0} ($P_{x_1} > P_{x_0}$) causes the consumer's budget line to rotate counterclockwise about B/P_{y_1} from B_{L_1} to B_{L_2}. The decrease in P_x relative to P_y (increase in

---

[14] Some would reserve "superior good" for products whose consumption increases by a greater proportion than the increase in income.

Y's price relative to X's) will cause the consumer to substitute X for Y in consumption, thus increasing his purchases of X as a result of the price change.

However, there is an income effect of the price change, in addition to the substitution effect, caused by the now cheaper price of X relative to Y. After the decline in the price of X, the consumer can buy the original combination of X and Y (X_1 and Y_1) and still have enough of his budget remaining to buy more of X and/or more of Y. Real income is contrasted with nominal income in that the former is the consumer's actual purchasing power as measured by the numbers of units of goods and services that he can purchase with a given dollar or nominal income. So if the index of prices paid for goods and services rises in the same ratio as a person's nominal income, his real income has been unchanged. On the other hand, if a consumer's nominal income is constant from period to period and the prices of goods and services rise, his real income has declined.

In our illustration, the price of X has decreased while all other prices have remained unchanged, so the effect on the real income of the consumer is positive. However, whether the consumer will buy more of X (or Y) as a result of the income effect of the price change depends upon whether X (or Y) is a normal or an inferior good. Suppose X is an inferior good. Then as a result of the consumer's increased real income, less of X will be purchased. But the price of X has fallen (thus causing the increase in real income), so X will tend to be substituted for Y. This latter substitution effect of the price change will tend to increase the quantity of X consumed, whereas the income effect of the price change will tend to decrease the quantity consumed of X, since it is an inferior good. On the other hand, if X is a superior good, the positive income effect of a decline in the price of X will cause more of X to be purchased, and the substitution effect of the price change will be reinforced by the income effect.

The indifference curve model can be used to isolate how much of a given change in the quantity demanded of a commodity after a price change is due to the income effect of the price change, and how much is due to the substitution or price effect of the price change. One reason for separating the income and price effects is that a demand curve by definition relates the various quantities of a commodity that would be purchased at all possible prices, all other things (*including the consumer's income*) remaining constant. If income is understood to mean real income rather than money income, a theoretical demand curve may be defined to include only the substitution effects of price changes. The approach which we will first use to isolate income and substitution effects was originally suggested by J. R. Hicks.

The Hicksian technique for isolating the income and substitution effects of a price change is illustrated in Figure 3–14 and described as follows. First, consider again that the price of X has declined from P_{x_1} to P_{x_0} and, as a result,

84 The Theory of Consumer Behavior and Demand

FIGURE 3–14   Income and Substitution Effects: The Hicks Approach

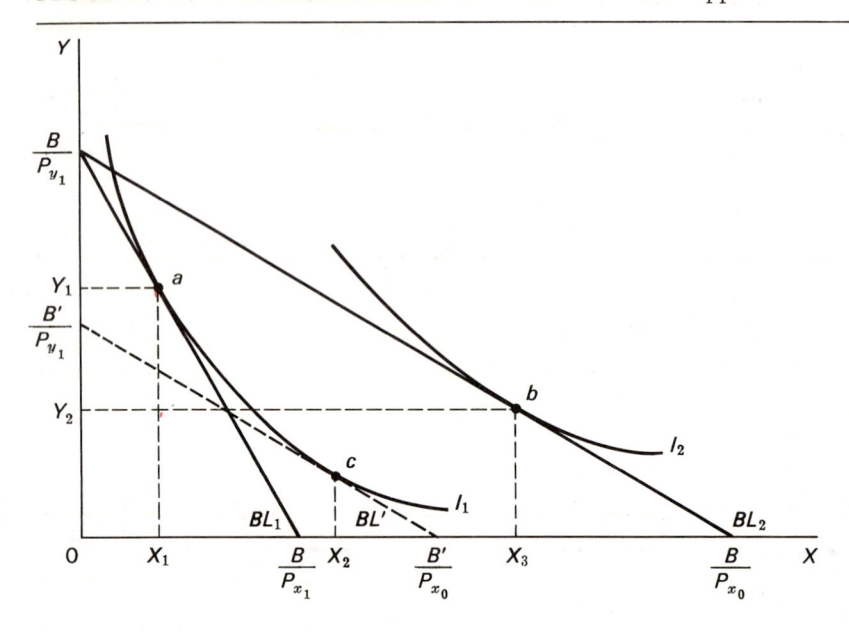

the consumer's optimum quantity of X changes from X_1 to X_3, i.e., point a to point b. Note also that the increase in the quantity of X consumed occurred as a result of both an income and a substitution effect. Now our objective is to cancel the income effect of the price decline. To accomplish this, we shift the budget line BL_2 to the left, so as to restore the consumer to the level of satisfaction he enjoyed before the change in price of X. In other words, we develop a new budget line which is freed of the income effect but retains the substitution effect, and we eliminate the income effect by a leftward, parallel shift from budget line BL_2 until our new budget line becomes tangent to indifference curve I_1 at point c. The new conceptual budget line, the dotted BL', contains a compensating income adjustment to restore the old level of real income (utility) at the new price ratio. By keeping BL' parallel to BL_2, we incorporate in budget line BL' the new price of X. The shift from BL_2 to BL' has presumably removed the income effect of the price decline, because the consumer is now back on indifference curve I_1, the original curve, and is thus restored to the level of utility enjoyed before the price change.

The change in the optimum combination of X and Y from point a to c is what we would expect if the price of X were reduced and the income effect of the price change simultaneously eliminated. Now we can isolate income and price effects. The decline in the price of X causes the equilibrium quantity of X to change from X_1 to X_3, of which $X_1 \rightarrow X_2$ is the substitution effect, and

$X_2 \to X_3$ the income effect. The movement from point a to point c along I_1 would occur as a result of the change in the relative prices of X and Y only. Notice that good X is normal, since the income effect of the price decline has resulted in more X consumed.

Eugen Slutsky has proposed an alternative technique for separating the income and substitution effects of price changes. The Slutsky technique is illustrated in Figure 3–15. Suppose again that the price of X has fallen, so

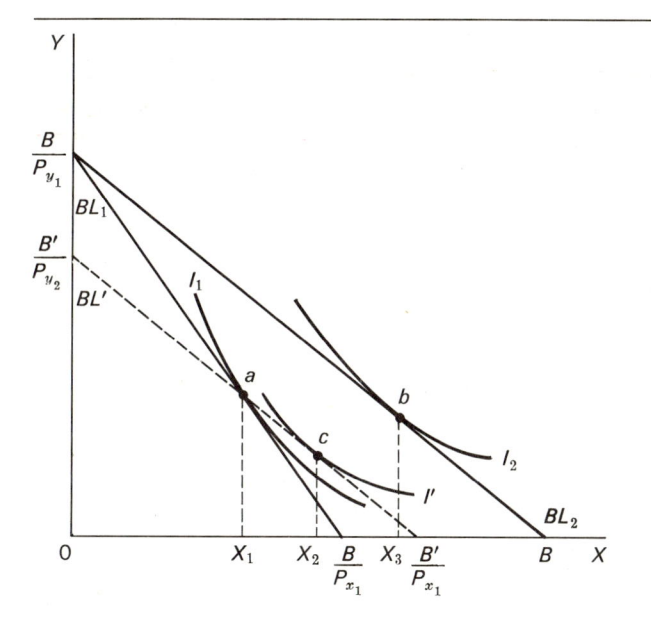

FIGURE 3–15   Income and Substitution Effects: The Slutsky Approach

that the utility-maximizing combination of X and Y changes from point a to point b. Instead of conceptually eliminating the consumer's real income increase by making BL' tangent to I_1 (which is impossible to determine), we shift BL' to the left and thereby reduce income to a level that will just permit the consumer to buy his original combination of the two goods. We draw BL' through point a to restore the original real income, by giving the consumer just enough income to buy the original combination of X and Y at the new price ratio. After the income effect of the price change has been eliminated, the consumer would buy combination c of X and Y. The shift from point a to c occurs as the substitution effect of the price change, whereas the shift from point c to b occurs as a result of the income effect. Slutsky's technique has an advantage over Hicks's, because one can empirically determine how much income the consumer would need to buy the original combination at a, whereas the point of tangency of BL' with I_1 in Figure 3–14 cannot be determined unless we know the shape of the consumer's indifference curves.

We can now derive a consumer's demand curve for X which includes only the price effect (or substitution effect) of a price change, by using $P_{x_1} - X_1$ as one point and $P_{x_0} - X_2$ from Figure 3–14 (per Hicks) or $P_{x_0} - X_2$ from Figure 3–15 (per Slutsky) as the other point. The resulting theoretical demand curve would be useful for proving the law of downward sloping demand. Without this particular conception of a demand curve, the law of downward sloping demand is seemingly less universal, as the following discussion will indicate.

Giffen's Paradox

If a consumer's total expenditure on a good is a small portion of his income, the substitution effect of a price change will likely be greater than the income effect, so that on balance, a price decline will cause a larger quantity of a good to be demanded, whether the good is normal or inferior. However, in some cases, the income effect can dominate the substitution effect. An interesting situation arises when the income effect of a price change is dominant and the good is inferior. In this case, a decrease in the price of the good results in a tendency for it to be substituted for other goods, but the income effect of the price change causes less of the good to be bought, since it is an inferior good. Since the income effect is dominant, a price decrease will, on balance, cause the quantity of the good consumed to decrease. Such goods are called "Giffen goods." Giffen, a nineteenth-century economist, studied the spending patterns of English poor and found that a decrease in the price of wheat would paradoxically induce the consumption of *less* bread instead of more, a seeming contradiction to the law of downward sloping demand. The solution to this paradox is that purchases of food constituted the largest expenditure of many consumers of Giffen's era, and a major part of the food budget went for bread, a decidedly inferior good. As a result, the income effect of cheaper bread would be large, and the one thing a consumer would *not* buy with an increase in real income would be more bread. The additional income would be devoted to other food items, such as meats and vegetables, and to nonfood commodities.

SUMMARY

In this chapter, we have developed two theoretical models for analyzing the choice behavior of a consumer seeking to allocate his available income among aternative uses in a way that is optimal. We have assumed that consumers are basically rational and goal-oriented, so that prediction of their behavior using these models is possible. In addition, we have taken the view that consumers seek to maximize their well-being over their entire lifetime; that is, they consider the future consequences of current decisions.

We described first the marginal utility theory of consumer behavior. Utility is the economists' term for pleasure or satisfaction derived from the consumption of any good, and this satisfaction is measured in utils. The concept of marginal utility, defined as the change in utility that occurs when a consumer consumes an extra unit of some good, is the principal tool of analysis. One of the marginal utility theorists' main postulates was the principle of *diminishing marginal utility*, which states that as successive units of a good are consumed, beyond some point, marginal utility declines. Further, the consumer will maximize his utility by allocating his total purchases, so that the marginal utility per dollar spent on any good equals the marginal utility per dollar spent on every other good. Since a consumer's marginal utility curve decreases with increased consumption of any one good, we may conclude that generally a consumer can be induced to consume more units of a good only if the price of the good decreases. Thus, the law of diminishing marginal utility is an important foundation for the "law" of downward sloping demand.

The principal shortcoming of marginal utility theory lies in its assumption that utility can be measured. Since this has not been established, marginal utility theory must be viewed as inferior to indifference curve theory, which assumes only that utility is *ordinally* measurable, an assumption that many economists are apparently willing to accept. A cardinal measurement scheme is not required for indifference curve theory, only the assumption that consumers can distinguish levels of utility, that is, state preferences for one combination of goods over another. The marginal rate of substitution between two goods (X and Y), MRS_{yx}, is defined as the maximum number of units of one good (Y) that a consumer will be willing to give up to get one unit of the other (X). The consumer will maximize his utility by equating the marginal rate of substitution with the rate of substitution that is permitted in the market, determined by the ratio of the prices of the two goods, P_x and P_y. In symbols, the consumer is consuming an optimum combination of two goods when:

$$MRS_{yx} = \frac{P_x}{P_y}.$$

Should the assumption of cardinal measurement of utility be accepted, indifference curve theory and marginal utility theory may be considered two versions of the same theory.

By varying the price of a good, while holding constant all other factors, such as the consumer's income and the prices of related goods, we have employed the marginal utility model and the indifference curve model to derive the consumer's demand curve for a product. Individual demand curves will serve as the basis for market demand discussed in the next chapter. In addition, by varying the consumer's income, with other factors held constant, we used indifference curve methodology to derive his Engel curve for a good. Finally, we used the indifference curve model to separate the substitution and income effects of a change in price of any good to demonstrate the generality of the notion that consumers will substitute one product for another, when the price of the former decreases relative to the prices of other products.

88 The Theory of Consumer Behavior and Demand

PROBLEMS

1. A Problem in Budget Allocation

Numbers of Units of Commodity	MU of X	MU/ $ of Y	Expenditures on X	MU of Y	MU/ $ of Y	Expenditures on Y
1	56			58		
2	52			52		
3	48			46		
4	44			40		
5	40			34		
6	36			28		
7	32			22		
8	30			16		
9	28			10		
10	26			4		

The budget of the consumer is $30. Initially the price of X is $4 and that of Y, $2.

(a) Complete the table and determine the allocation of the consumer's income between goods X and Y and the amounts of each bought.

(b) Suppose the price of X falls to $2, while the budget and the price of Y remain the same. Find the new allocation of income and amounts of X and Y bought.

(c) What is the quantity of X demanded at prices $4 and $2?

2. The figure presents an indifference curve model for a hypothetical consumer. Answer the following on the basis of the graph.

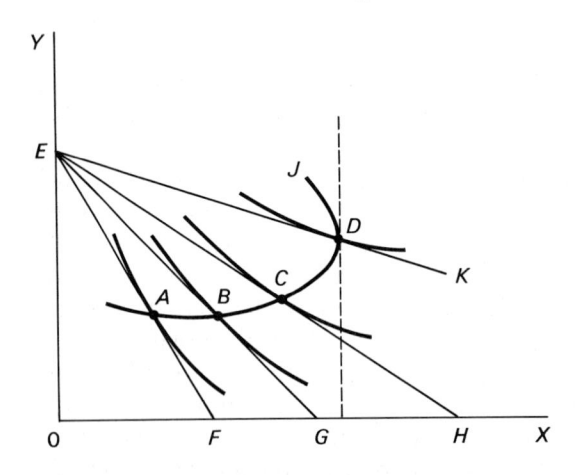

(a) The line segments EF, EG, EH, and EK are called _____.
(b) Line segment EG, as opposed to segment EF, is derived assuming a (lower, equal, higher) price of (Y, X).
(c) Given line segment EK, if the price of X declines, the quantity of X consumed (increases, decreases) indicating a (Giffen, inferior, normal) good.
(d) The (increase, decrease) in price causing the change in the optimal from C to D results in (more, less) of Y consumed. For this to happen, Y must be a (normal, inferior, neutral, cannot be determined) good.

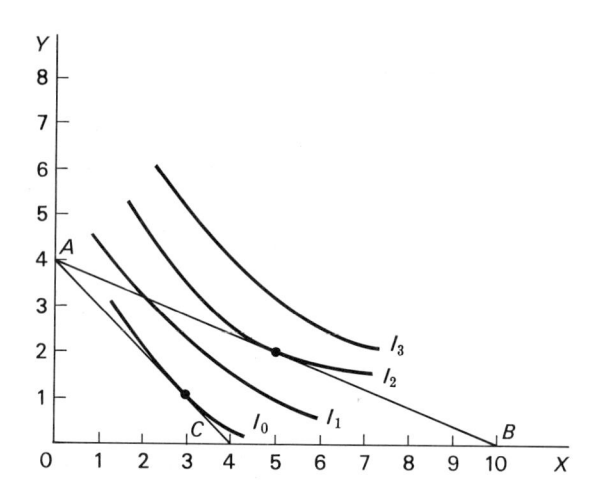

3. (a) Given budget line AB the consumer would purchase _____ X's and _____ Y's.
(b) Given budget line AB, if the price of Y is $2, then the price of X is $_____.
(c) The budget line would rotate to the line AC if the price of (X,Y) (increased, decreased).
(d) Given budget line AC, the consumer would purchase _____ X's and _____ Y's.
(e) If the price of Y is $4 throughout, the price of X has increased from _____ to _____ as the budget line rotated from AB to AC, and the quantity of X consumed has changed from _____ to _____.
(f) Given the two points on the consumer's demand curve derived above, sketch the curve.
(g) Good X (is, is not) a Giffen good.

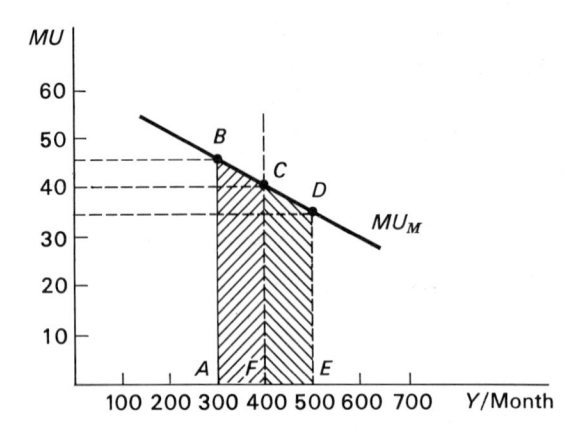

4. In the figure, MU_M is a consumer's marginal utility schedule for money income, showing the extra utility generated by an extra dollar earned per month.
   (a) If income is presently $400 per month, what is the extra utility the consumer would realize if income rises to $500 per month, using symbols _____ and estimated numbers of utils _____?
   (b) Suppose income falls to $300 per month. What is the consumer's loss of utility in symbols _____ and estimated numbers of utils _____?
   (c) If income is $400 per month, would this consumer enter into a wager in which he expects to gain or lose $100 at even odds? If not, why not; if so, why so?
   (d) Would your answer to (c) change if the MU_M schedule were positively sloped?

REFERENCES

Armen, A. Alchian, "The Meaning of Utility Measurement," *American Economic Review* (March 1953), 26–50.

Friedman, Milton, "The 'Welfare' Effects of an Income Tax and an Excise Tax," *Journal of Political Economy*, LX (February 1952), 25–33.

Friedman, Milton, "The Marshallian Demand Curve," *Journal of Political Economy*, LVII (December 1949), 463–495.

Lerner, Aba, "The Analysis of Demand," *American Economic Review*, 52 (September 1962), 783–797.

Mishan, Edward J., "Theories of Consumers' Behavior: A Cynical View," *Economica*, 28 (February 1961), 1–11.

Stigler, George, "The Development of Utility Theory," *Journal of Political Economy* (August 1950).

APPENDIX TO CHAPTER 3

The Experimental Determination of Indifference Curves[1]

K. R. MacCRIMMON and M. TODA

In this paper, MacCrimmon and Toda conduct experiments with University of California undergraduates in an attempt to derive their indifference curves for selected consumer goods. Of particular interest is the experimental technique devised by the authors to obtain the "true" preferences of the subjects. Each participant is motivated to state his preferences correctly by a pay-off procedure which rewards him for accurately drawing his indifference curve. The student will find this paper complementary to the theoretical material in the text and written at a level which should present few difficulties.

I. INTRODUCTION

While indifference curves have been utilized in a large number of theoretical studies, their empirical derivation has received little attention. In this paper we suggest a procedure for experimentally determining indifference curves. Individuals are taught to represent their preferences graphically. They are motivated to give their true preferences by basing the payoff received on the choices made or implied. Techniques for simplifying the number of commodity bundles to be considered are introduced where appropriate.

We present some experimental data to show the ease with which indifference curves can be obtained. Two sets of two commodity bundles were used. In the first experiment the commodities were money and ball point pens—commodities for which it is reasonable to assume that larger amounts are not less preferred than smaller amounts. In the second experiment the commodi-

From the *Review of Economic Studies*, Vol. 34, No. 108 (October 1969). Reprinted by permission.

[1] This work was supported in part by contracts or grant from the Ford Foundation, National Science Foundation, and Office of Naval Research (Contract No. 233 (75)) to the Western Management Science Institute, University of California, Los Angeles. We are grateful to Sid Adelman, David Hitchcock, and Frederick Timson for suggestions on the design of these experiments and for their help in carrying them out. We also wish to acknowledge the helpful comments of Jacob Marschak, John Bassler and Lester Lave.

ties were money and French pastries, and since the pastries had to be eaten on the spot a satiation level might be expected to exist. As we shall see these two different sets of commodities yield quite different indifference curves. We especially focus on the extent to which the curves satisfy the commonly postulated properties of indifference curves.

II. BACKGROUND

In the theory of consumer demand, indifference curves can serve to represent preferences. Pareto first showed that demand functions could be obtained just as readily from indifference curves as from the more restrictive concept of marginal utility. Notable subsequent contributions were made by Slutsky, Hicks and Allen, and Hicks, among others. Even revealed preference, which seeks to obviate indifference curves, has its counterpart in the behaviour lines of Little.

Observation of work in consumer demand theory makes it clear that interest in indifference curves is certainly secondary to interest in demand curves. Economists, however, have generally rejected Cassel's position that we should start with demand functions and leave any study of preferences to the field of psychology. That is, this position has been rejected in theoretical work, but on the empirical side we find many empirical demand studies and hardly any attention devoted to the empirical determination of indifference curves. It is to this imbalance that we direct this paper.

The lack of empirical work in this area is especially unfortunate because indifference curves are not solely of interest in consumer demand theory. In many non-market choice situations, where a demand function is a meaningless concept, it is useful to represent preferences by indifference curves.

Particular properties are generally assumed for indifference curves. One such property is the non-intersection of indifference curves. Intersection would imply intransitivity of the indifference relation and we would generally call such preferences inconsistent. A second property relates to the desirability of the commodities considered. If we assume the commodities are desirable in any amount, then in order to get more of one commodity we would be willing to give up some amount of a second commodity, and hence the indifference curves would have a negative slope. A third property is an empirical matter. The indifference curves are assumed to be convex to the origin. This implies that the marginal rate at which you would give up one commodity for a second decreases as the amount of the second commodity increases, i.e., the marginal rate of substitution diminishes. In a later section we shall discuss each of these properties in the context of our experimental data.

III. PREVIOUS EMPIRICAL STUDIES

Empirical determinations of indifference curves may be based on (1) actual expenditure data, and (2) experimental data. An observation of the expenditures of a single economic unit at a point in time provides a single observation for the indifference map (viz. the relative prices yield the slope of the indifference curve at the quantities taken). In order to build up a reasonable picture of the map, it is necessary to study one economic unit over a long period of time and in a variety of price/income situations (all the while assuming stability of tastes). Or alternatively, one could study a number of economic units at one period of time in a variety of price/income situations and assume that the tastes of all units are the same. More realistically, the studies could be both cross-sectional and temporal.

Actual expenditure studies, though, do not attempt to construct indifference curves. The emphasis is completely on the demand functions and their characteristics. However, from the classic studies of Schultz, and those of Wold with Jureen, Stone *et al.* and others, some characteristics of a composite indifference map can be inferred.

Indifference curves derived from actual expenditures would be much more convincing than those obtained experimentally. The prime reason perhaps is that when the consumer spends his own money to obtain some commodity he wants, we do not have to worry about his motivation for making a careful choice. With experiments, however, motivation can be a serious problem. There are some advantages, though, to an experimental approach. The most obvious one is that the experimenter has control over the environment and can more assuredly hold to *ceteris paribus* conditions. This suggests that experiments may offer some intriguing possibilities for determining indifference curves. We have been able to find only two previous studies, an early one by Thurstone and another by Rousseas and Hart.

The pioneering work on determining indifference curves experimentally was performed by the psychologist Thurstone, stimulated by conversations with Schultz. Thurstone used three different commodities: hats, pairs of shoes, and overcoats. By asking his subject which bundles of hats and shoes she preferred to a reference bundle, he built up two regions—one in which the reference bundle was preferred and the other in which the bundles, represented by the points offered, were preferred. Thurstone then assumed 5 postulates of behaviour in such situations and this allowed him to fit a curve, between the two regions, passing through the reference point. The principal postulate was the equivalent of Fechner's logarithmic law and constrained the indifference curve to be hyperbolic. This hyperbolic curve was fit to the data by considering preference inversions and by using the method of averages. Four such indifference curves were obtained for the hat-shoes commodity bundles. Thurstone used a similar procedure to obtain 4 indifference curves for hats and overcoats. He then attempted to validate his procedures by predicting indifference curves for shoes and overcoats and comparing them to experimentally derived data.

Thurstone's experiment can be criticized on a number of grounds. First, hats, shoes, and overcoats are not the types of commodities a subject (even a female subject) would reasonably acquire a large number of. The maximum number he used of each item was 24, and the average minimum number of one commodity in each bundle was 10. Second, the subject's choice was completely hypothetical—she realized that she was not going to get 16 overcoats and 14 hats, or the like. Third, the problem size is overwhelming: for each curve she was required to make 256 comparisons (between a proposed bundle and the reference bundle). Fourth, Thurstone's assumptions (i.e., postulates) are questionable. It would seem more desirable to observe and not specify such things as the shape of the indifference curve. (In fact, Thurstone may have done this by forming the postulates *ex post.*) Other more minor points such as the desirability for more than one subject, the method of curve fitting, and the assumptions underlying his attempted validation could also be mentioned.

However, the fact that Thurstone was the first to experimentally derive indifference curves should not be lost among the criticisms. He also developed the feature of comparing bundles with a reference bundle, thus building up the preferred and the not preferred spaces vis-à-vis the reference bundle. This seems like a very useful way of having the subject determine the indifference line. In fact we applied this technique quite independently in our experiment and did not learn until after the initial writeup of our results that it had been developed and used by Thurstone more than 35 years earlier.

Rousseas and Hart obtained indifference curves for eggs and bacon. They offered each of 67 subjects 3 alternative bundles of eggs and bacon and requested a ranking of them in order of preference. The top ranked bundle apparently had to be eaten. Each subject made only one such ranking since it was thought that a series of choices would impose too much strain on a single individual. The commodity space considered was from 0 to 5 eggs and 0 to 5 strips of bacon. It was assumed that a saturation point would occur between 2 and 3 eggs and 2 and 3 strips of bacon. By drawing lines at 2·5 eggs and 2·5 strips of bacon, the commodity space was divided into quadrants with a saturation region at a corner of each quadrant. Eighteen commodity bundles were symmetrically chosen in each quadrant but only 60 of these 72 different patterns were presented. Seven choice patterns were duplicated by presenting them to a second subject.

By assuming homogeneity of tastes for these commodities, Rousseas and Hart proceeded to construct indifference curves from these rankings, thus building up a composite indifference map. Their procedure involved forming saturation vectors based on the direction of preference between the first ranked preference and the second and third. Slope vectors were formed based on the direction of the second and third choices. Those saturation and slope vectors consistent with the assumed saturation and convexity, respectively, were used as the basis for constructing the indifference curves. The experiment was rerun one month later with the same subjects.

A main weakness in the Rousseas and Hart experiment was the assumption of homogeneity of tastes. Most of the duplicate rankings in an experiment were not identical, and the listing of ideal combinations of bacon and eggs requested after the second experiment was over, were quite varied. This latter information also makes the particular saturation area assumed somewhat questionable. Another weakness was the degree of arbitrariness in this positioning of the slope vectors and the subsequent construction of indifference curves through these quite arbitrarily placed fragments—even after the anomalous cases had been eliminated.

A very useful aspect of the Rousseas and Hart study, though, was the acquisition of preference data at two distinct time periods. Some exactly duplicated choice alternatives gave information on the stability of preferences. There is also stability data on symmetrically presented choices, but the interpretation of these depends on the particular saturation hypothesis. Another useful aspect of these experiments was the forced consumption of the commodities—a condition that hopefully contributed to a more careful consideration by the subject. Although the use of slope vectors and the subsequent curve fitting procedure is very cumbersome as an experimental method, it does have some properties of the statistical fitting that would be necessary with market data and perhaps serves as a bridge between indifference curves derived from experiments and those derived from actual expenditures.

In a very clear expository article, Wallis and Friedman record their skepticism about the usefulness of indifference curve analysis on empirical data—especially experimental data. After considering the Thurstone experiment, Wallis and Friedman conclude that "it is probably not possible to design a satisfactory experiment for deriving indifference curves from economic stimuli applied to human beings." The basis for this strong statement is the following: (1) hypothetical choices do not elicit actual preferences; (2) a long period of time and many different situations must be observed to obtain preferences; and (3) "economic phenomena are so integral a part of life that effective experimentation would require control of virtually the entire existence of the subject."

While recognizing the issues raised as important, we nevertheless disagree with the conclusion of Wallis and Friedman. The first concern can be handled by the conditions on the commodities considered (e.g., forced consumption) and by the payoff procedure used. We feel that the method we use is particularly effective in this respect. The second point relates to the number of choices the subject can make at a given time. This would seem to be a more serious problem in studies of actual expenditures than with experiments in which the choices to be considered are under the control of the experimenter and can be varied widely. Clearly, if after making a choice the subject receives the commodities immediately, his future preferences will be affected unless we wait some time until his stock is down to the previous level. Such intermittent payoffs, however, do not have to be part of a well-designed experiment, and here too our payoff procedure forces the subject to carefully consider a variety of possible bundles at any given time, even though he knows he will only receive one of them. We also introduce techniques to drastically reduce the number of bundles that must be considered. The third concern of Wallis and Friedman is to some extent covered in the other two but, to the extent that it refers to the *ceteris paribus* question, it too can be handled in experiments. The experimenter cannot only impose some control over the subject's state during the experiment (e.g., by deferring all payoffs until the conclusion), but can also exert some control over the subject's state at the beginning of the experiment by selection procedures, participation prerequisites (e.g., skipping lunch), or even the timing and location of the experiment.

Since we do use procedures to resolve the problems raised, we feel that we have satisfactorily performed an experiment constructing indifference curves. The procedure we use can be readily understood by subjects and obtains continuous indifference curves very efficiently. One issue implicit in the Wallis and Friedman discussion that we do not treat in this paper is the stability of preferences over time and in a variety of situations. This would be a large scale study, a prerequisite to which would be the development of an effective way to measure preferences such as we feel we present here. Let us now describe this procedure in more detail.

IV. INDIFFERENCE CURVE DETERMINATION PROCEDURE

Consider various bundles of two commodities X and Y, represented by the commodity space in Figure 1. Let us consider P_0 as a reference point. We wish to determine the indifference curve passing through P_0. This is equivalent to determining two regions whose common boundary is the indifference curve. These regions are: (1) an *accept* region, abbreviated "A", of all the points to which P_0 is not preferred (i.e., they would be accepted in lieu of P_0), and (2)

FIGURE 1

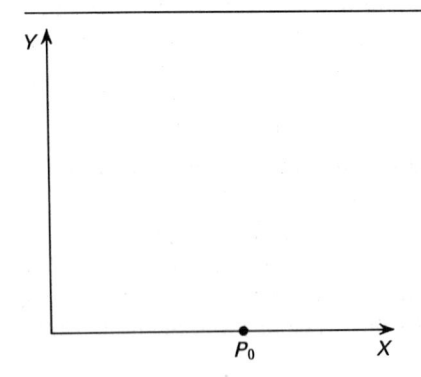

a *reject* region, abbreviated "R", of all the points to which P_0 is preferred (i.e., they would be rejected in favour of P_0). Thus, if we can determine for each point in the commodity space whether it would be taken instead of P_0 (the A region), or whether P_0 would be taken instead of it (the R region), then the boundary separating the two regions is the indifference curve we seek.[2]

There are two major difficulties with this as an experimental procedure. First, what motivation is there for a person to reveal his true preferences? Why should he carefully draw the indifference curve? Second, how can a person be expected to consider every, or even many, points in the commodity space? To obviate these questions we need to develop some procedures that will lead to true preference being exhibited, and will reduce the number of commodity bundles to be considered. We shall examine each of these aspects in turn.

Payoff Procedures

We attempt to motivate a person to reflect his true preferences by making his final outcome (i.e., payoff) contingent on the indifference curve he has drawn. For example, let us assume that he has drawn the curve of Figure 2.

FIGURE 2

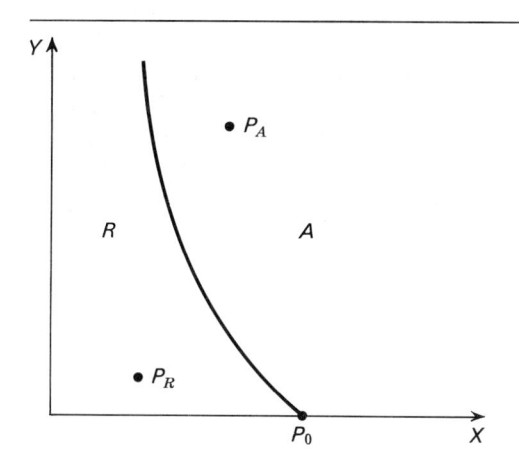

We then tell him that we are prepared to give him P_0—or perhaps something he likes more. We do this by selecting at random a point in the commodity space we are considering. If the point, say P_A, is in the A region, we

---

[2] As we have defined it, the boundary lies within A. Clearly, by modifying the preference definitions we could alternatively locate the points of indifference solely in R, in both A and R, or in neither A nor R. Any of these would suffice; we are only interested in establishing a boundary.

give him P_A instead of P_0 (since he has indicated that he prefers P_A to P_0). If, however, the point, say P_R, is in the R region, we give him P_0 (since he has indicated that he prefers P_0 to P_R). Thus, this payoff method forces him to be sure that he would really prefer P_0 to each possible P_R.

There is, then, the motivation to draw the indifference curve as carefully as he can to mirror his true preferences in each part of the space since he does not know in advance in which part of the space the randomly selected point will fall. A simplified form of this method was used by Becker, DeGroot, and Marschak in measuring the utility of money. A theoretical consideration of various general forms of the method is given in Toda and MacCrimmon.

Complexity Reduction Procedures

In attempting to reduce the number of commodity bundles to be considered we can make use of the knowledge that more of some (not all) commodities can be expected to be preferred to less (or at least is not less preferred). By utilizing this information and by proceeding sequentially, i.e., by making the points examined dependent on previous choices, we can substantially reduce the complexity of the problem.

Let us assume for the moment that for both X and Y, more of the commodity is preferred to less. (As we shall see, not only can this assumption be tested at each point in the process, but procedures can also be developed when it does not hold.)

Again we take P_0 as our reference point, so assuming more of X is preferred to less and more of Y is preferred to less implies that all points above and to the right of P_0 are in the A region. That is, they yield either more X or more Y, or more of both. Let us denote (sub-regions of) the A region by shading, as in Figure 3. Consider now point P_1. The person is asked if he would take

FIGURE 3

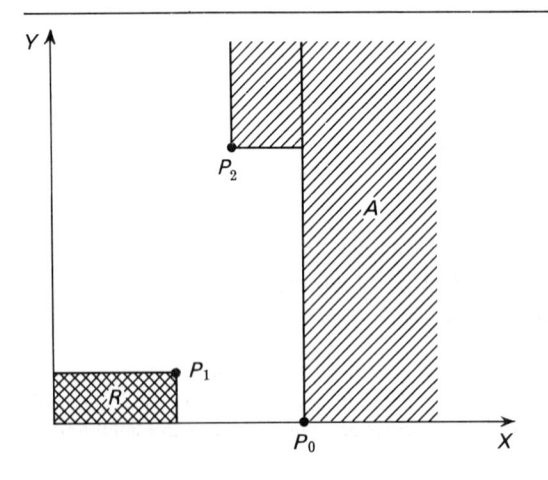

P_1 instead of P_0. If he would not, then P_1 is a point in the R region. We also know, however, that if P_1 is in the R region then any bundle that offers less of X without offering more of Y, or conversely, is also in the R region (in that it is less preferred than P_1). Thus, all points to the left of and below a point in the R region are also in the R region. Let us denote (sub-regions of) the R region by cross-hatching.

Now consider bundle P_2. Suppose that the person prefers P_2 to P_0. Then P_2 and all points above and to the right of it are in the A region. We can proceed in this fashion by asking the person to consider new points not yet in the A or R region. By proceeding sequentially we can build up a number of A and R sub-regions and thus put tighter and tighter constraints on where the indifference curve may lie. Suppose that after considering a number of such points we have developed the A and R regions of Figure 4. At this point it

FIGURE 4

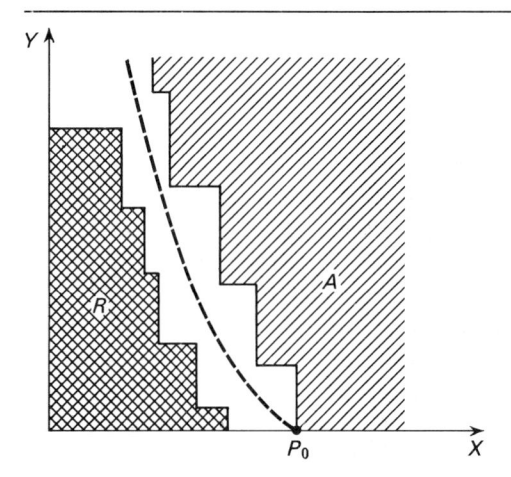

is probably quite clear where the indifference curve lies and the person can probably draw it in directly (say, the dashed line). If he still is not sure of where the curve should lie, he simply considers more points—those not yet in an A or R sub-region.

This method is, of course, particularly effective in reducing problem complexity when we know that more of both X and Y is preferred to less. We can, however, use a less powerful procedure when for only one of the commodities can we assume more is preferred to less. Suppose just X has this property, so that for Y more may even be less preferred than less. That is, a saturation point is reached for Y. In this case instead of drawing A and R *rectangles* above and to the right and below and to the left, respectively, we now draw an A *line* to the right of an A point and an R *line* to the left of an R point. (If the roles of X and Y were interchanged the lines would be drawn vertically.) This also reduces the number of points to be considered with reference to P_0 but not as effectively as the former procedure. After considering a number of points the lines may look as in Figure 5. The indifference curve may then be drawn in directly (say, the dashed line).

FIGURE 5

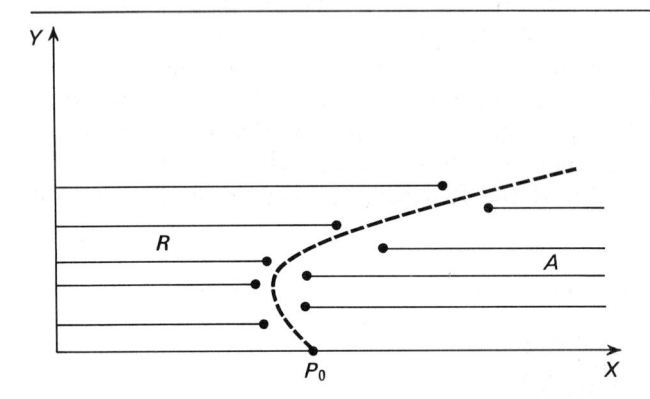

When we cannot assume that more is preferred to less for either commodity then we cannot use a space reduction procedure and must consequently consider a great number of points. If we have knowledge of where the saturation point might occur (as assumed by Rousseas and Hart, for example) we can use a combination of the line and the rectangle procedure up to the saturation level and then past it—but we must be quite sure of the saturation level. Thus, the problem reduction techniques can be used even when both commodities can reach a saturation as long as we know where this occurs.

The procedures described are, of course, not restricted to obtaining only one indifference curve. Reference points other than P_0 can be selected as new reference points and we can obtain a series of indifference curves directly drawn by the individual whose preferences we are studying.

V. EXPERIMENTAL CONDITIONS AND RESULTS

Conditions

We used the procedure described in the previous section to obtain indifference curves for 7 undergraduates in an experiment performed at the University of California, Los Angeles in May 1967. Two of the subjects were female; all had majors in mathematics, engineering, or economics. In recruiting the subjects we specified that each should have had 4 university level courses in mathematics. This was to avoid any concern about the subject's ability to draw and understand graphs. Undoubtedly it was overly cautious, since mathematically naïve subjects can understand the necessary rudiments of drawing the rectangle or lines.

Prior to the regular experiments we had a training session of about 2 hours. During this time the procedure for forming A and R rectangle and lines, selecting points for comparison with P_0, and the payoff method were explained to the subjects.[3] The subjects also practised drawing indifference curves with money and pencils as commodities (to which the rectangle method was applied). The subject first drew an indifference curve through the reference point of $3 (and no pencils) and then on a separate sheet of graph paper drew an indifference curve through the point $5 (and no pencils). Both curves were then given to the subject and he was asked to transfer the 2 curves to a third sheet of graph paper. He was told that he could re-position the lines on the joint sheet if he felt that upon reflection the original position did not reflect his true preferences. The implication of intersecting lines (i.e., in this case the willingness to substitute $5 for $3) was explained, and he was told that if his lines intersected he could redraw them if he wished. After the curves had been drawn on the joint graph to his satisfaction, and after any questions were answered, one of the lines was chosen as a reference line, a random number was selected, and a payoff determination was made. This payoff, along with another one, involved a payment of $6 to each subject.

During the first regular experimental session money and ball point pens were the commodities used. The pens had a retail selling price of $.19. The commodity space considered ran from $0 to $25 and from 0 to 180 pens. We assumed that more of each commodity would be preferred (or indifferent) to less and the rectangle procedure was used; no subject later indicated that this assumption was inappropriate. The following reference points involving only money were presented in the randomized order: $6, $13, $4, $10, $2, $8, and $20. After using the rectangle method and drawing each of the 7 indifference curves on a separate graph, we asked the subject to copy all 7 lines onto one graph. They were allowed to re-position the lines on this joint graph if they intersected or if the subjects had second thoughts about the correct position of the lines. The payoff determination was deferred until after the second session. The sets of indifference curves for the 7 subjects will be discussed below.

In the second session, held on the following day, money and French pastries were the commodities used, with the stipulation that the pastries had to be consumed in the laboratory before the subject received any other payoff. Thus

---

[3] A verbatim account of the instructions and procedures is too long to present here but the authors will gladly send a copy to anyone interested. Let us also note here that slightly more than half of the two hour training session was devoted to training in drawing indifference curves in an equi-probable wager space. This aspect will not be discussed here.

102   The Theory of Consumer Behavior and Demand

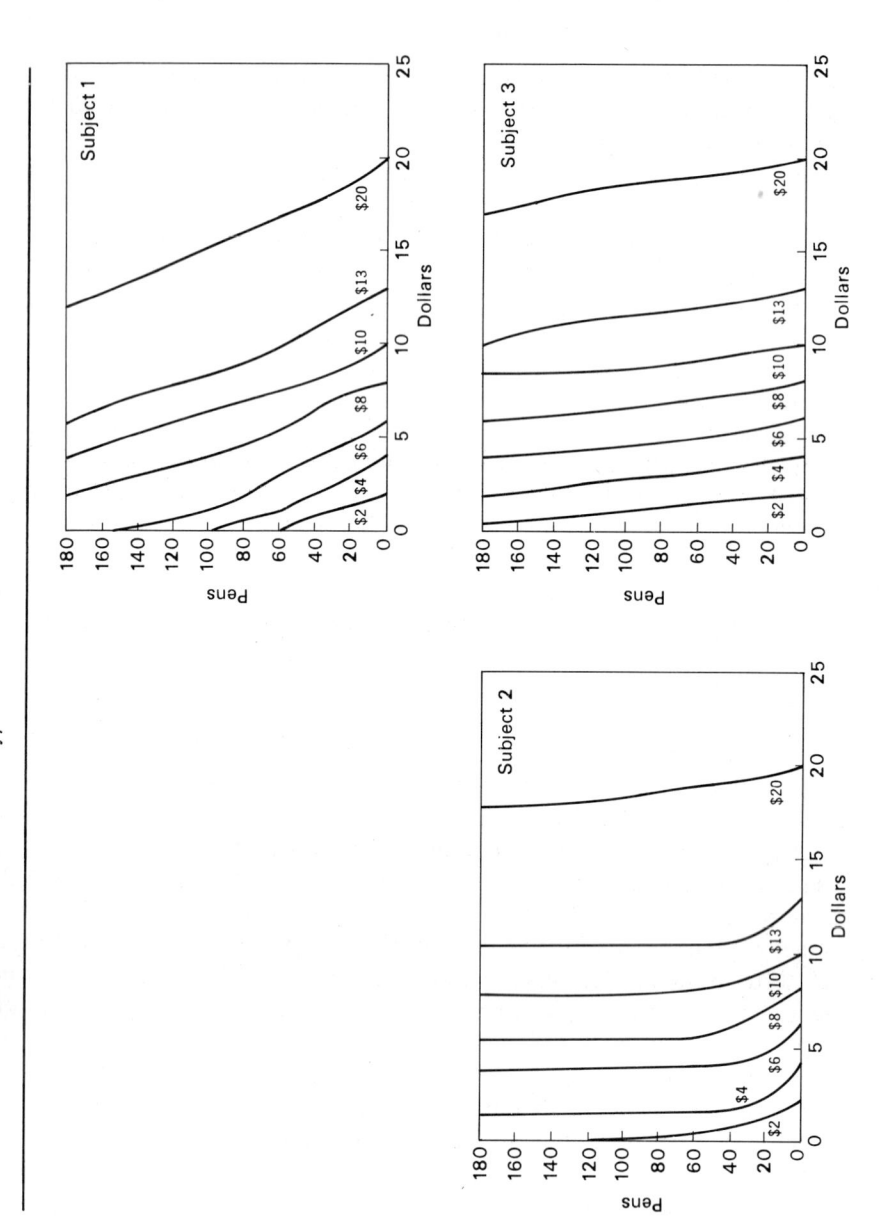

FIGURE 6   Indifference Curves for Money/Pen Bundles

FIGURE 6 (Contd.)

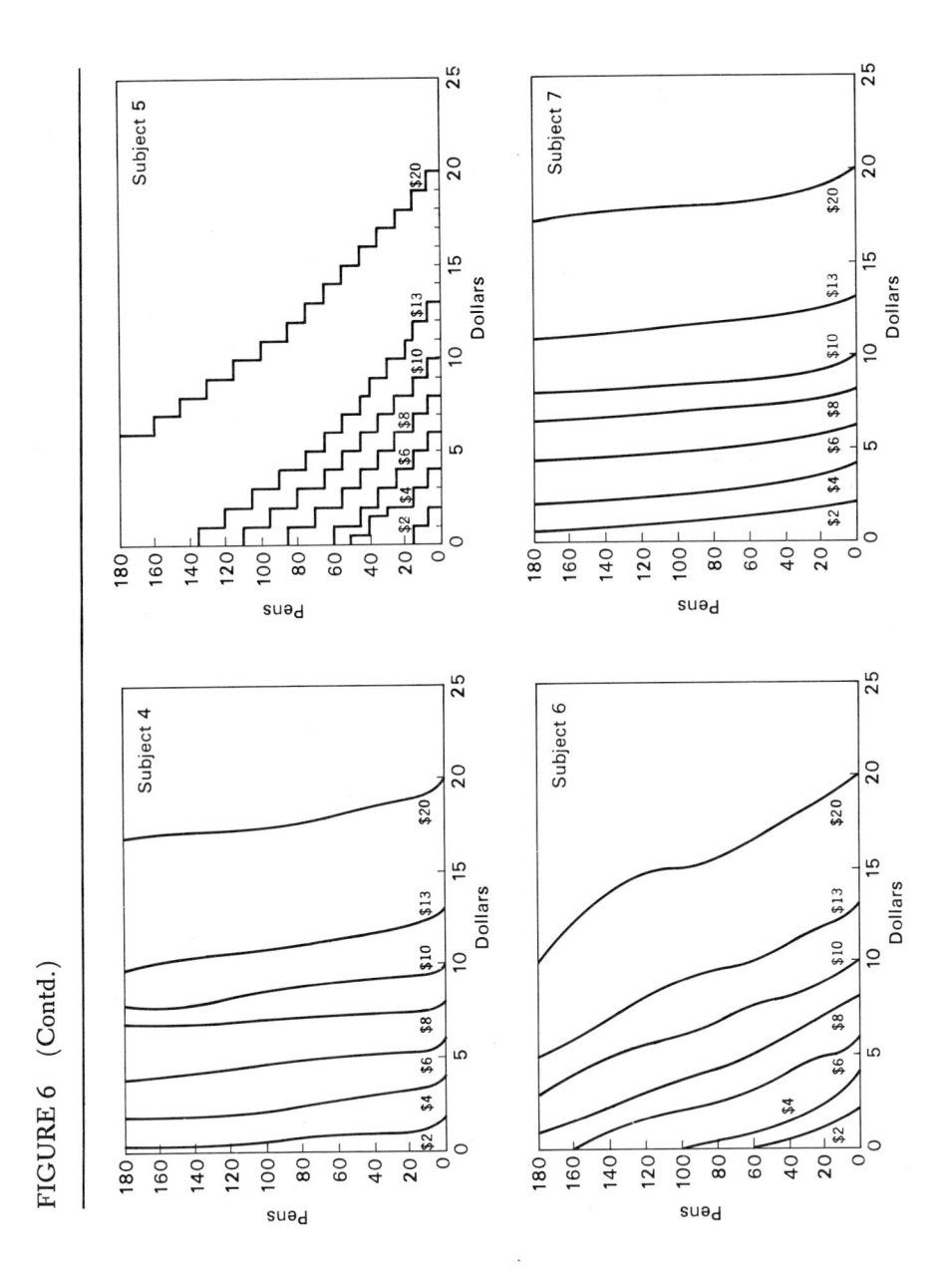

FIGURE 7 Indifference Curves for Money/Pastry Bundles

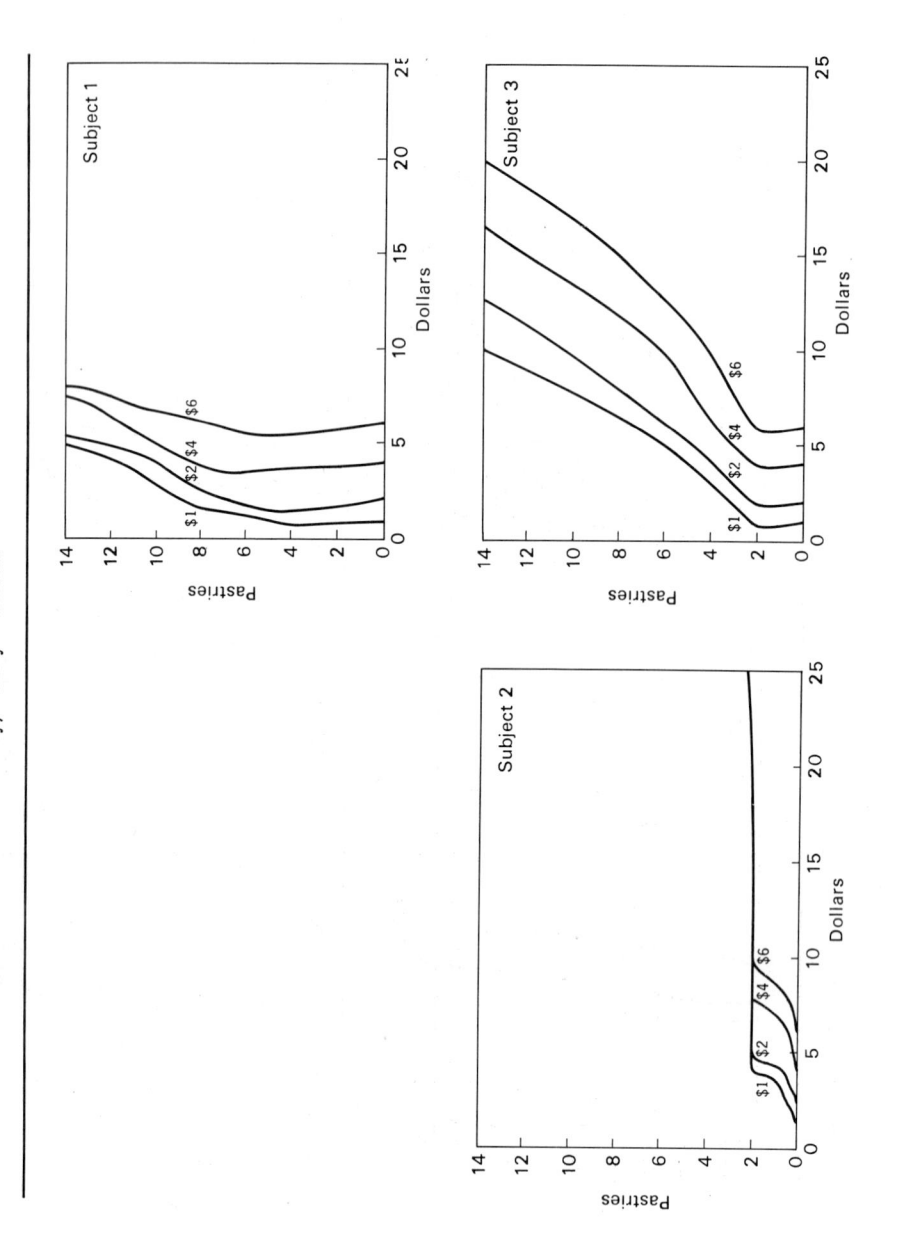

FIGURE 7 (Contd.)

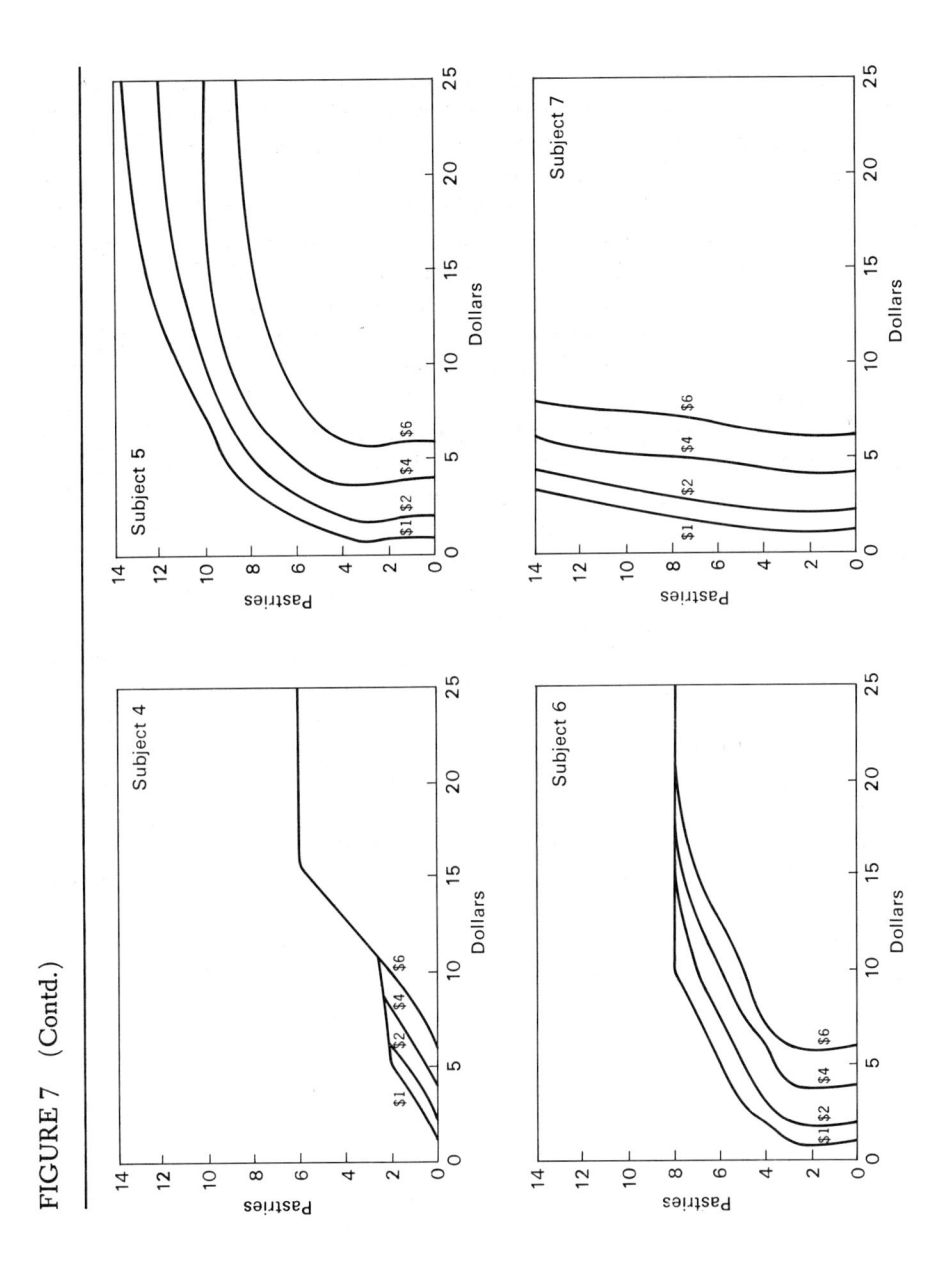

one might expect that more pastries are not necessarily preferred to less, and so the line method, rather than the rectangle method, was used. The commodity space ranged from $0 to $25 and from 0 to 14 pastries. The pastry scale was shown in fifths of a pastry. The reference points were presented in the randomized order: $4, $2, $1, and $6. The same construction procedure as in the first session was followed, that is, all lines were first drawn on separate sheets of graph paper and then later drawn on a joint graph. The sets of indifference curves from this session will also be discussed below.

When the final pastry determination was made, the point selected fell into the A region of 5 of the 7 subjects. Thus, these 5 subjects (the 5 males) had to eat an average of slightly more than 4 whole pastries in addition to receiving money. Not until the pastries were eaten was the money paid. The payoff determination for the dollars and pens case was delayed until this point so that the subjects' preferences with respect to money would not be influenced (by us) during the experiment, and the delayed payoff served as a further incentive for fulfilling the obligation to eat the pastries.

Each experimental session took about 2 hours, but only half this time was devoted to the construction of indifference curves for commodity bundles as described above. The subjects seemed to have no difficulty in drawing the indifference curves and on the whole seemed quite confident in the curves they had drawn. To test their preferences, at the end of both sessions we collected their indifference curve graphs and presented each subject with pairs of commodity bundles written on cards, and requested that he select the one bundle on each card that he preferred. These pairs were obtained individually for each subject by: (1) taking points on each side of an indifference line (about $.50 away from the line) at different levels of the indifference line, and (2) taking points on two adjacent lines. At least one test was made about each line, and when supplemented with points from adjacent lines there were a total of 12 money/pen and 9 money/pastry choices altogether. The results are discussed below under the appropriate commodity pair.

Results

The results of each experiment will be discussed separately. We are especially interested in information on the main properties usually postulated for indifference curves, that is: (1) non-intersection, (2) general negative slope, and (3) convexity to the origin. The sets of indifference curves in Figures 6 and 7 were obtained by tracing the curves exactly as they were drawn by the subjects. Subjects 2 and 4 are female.

The indifference curves for *money/pen* bundles for the seven subjects are given in Figure 6. Note that none of the curves, for a given subject, intersect. When the curves drawn originally on the individual graphs are superimposed on each other, they also do not intersect. Hence the non-intersection is not due to a change made by the subject when he redrew his curves on the joint graph.

All the curves have a general negative slope over their domain. That is, to maintain indifference as the number of pens is decreased the number of dollars must be increased. This relation is true in the strong form just expressed for all subjects except S5 whose curves are step functions ("I assume I can sell them only in units of ten"), but even S5's curves are non-increasing as we move from left to right.

Another commonly postulated property of indifference curves is that they are convex to the origin. This can also be stated as a diminishing marginal rate of substitution of money for pens as one moves to the right. Other than S5's step functions, the only major example of non-convexity is in the $20 line of S6. The upper part of this curve is distinctly concave. This may be due to careless thought about his preferences. Further reflection might have led to a redrawing since an examination of the individual graphs reveals that there was a similar concave region at the top of his $13 line, and this was changed when transferred to the joint graph. Even though these are the only non-convex regions, it should be noted that the degree of convexity is not high, and that most graphs contain long linear segments.

The lack of interest by most subjects in large numbers of pens is evident from examining the slopes of the curves in their upper regions (say above 50 pens). The curves for subjects S2, S3, S4 and S7 are all very steep—the marginal rate of substitution is at least 60 pens per dollar. The retail price of the pens being $.19 gives a price exchange ratio of 5 pens per dollar. These subjects estimated the market price (independently) as $.30, $.19, $.49 and $.10, respectively. Subjects S1, S5 and S6 have less steeply sloped curves, with a marginal rate of substitution of less than 25 pens per dollar in this region. They too, of course, are much higher than the relative price. These subjects estimated the price at $.14, $.20, and $.10, so the relatively higher value they place on large numbers of pens is not due to their perception of a higher retail price (for possible resale) than the other group. Some subjects explicitly stated their disinterest in the pens (S2: "Those pens have ruined 2 dresses of mine.").

One might expect a lower marginal rate of substitution of money for pens, for a fixed number of pens, at higher dollar values. This implies that the rightmost curves might be expected to be more convex at larger money amounts. If this characteristic is true it is not particularly pronounced, and is definitely contradicted by the $20 line of S2.

The inconsistencies between the indifference curves (on the joint graph) and the pairwise comparisons are given for money/pen bundles in the left side of Table I. The table indicates the pairs in which inconsistencies occurred and the line from (or around) which the pairs were constructed. Note that 3 of the seven subjects had inconsistencies—S3 had two inconsistencies. There were only 4 inconsistent pairwise choices in the 84 (7 subjects times 12 pairs

108 The Theory of Consumer Behavior and Demand

TABLE I

Commodity bundle	Money/pens				Money/pastries		
Number of pairs	12				9		
Subject	S1	S3		S5	S2		
Number of inconsistencies	1	2		1	2		
Bundle preferred	($5.50, 100)	($1.80, 20)	($3.60, 25)	($7.50, 40)	($24, 2½)		($3.25, ⅘)
Bundle rejected	($10, 20)	($3.90, 5)	($4.50, 100)	($0, 145)	($7.75, 1)		($5.75, 1⅘)
Corresponding curve(s)	$10	$2, $4	$4, $6	$13	$1, $2, $4	$2	

per subject) pairs presented. The choice of a dominated bundle in the second inconsistency of S3 suggests carelessness in considering the choices.

The indifference curves for *money/pastry* bundles are given in Figure 7. The conditions of the experiment (i.e., forced consumption of pastries) yield the unconventional slopes shown. The curves do not have a general negative slope, and in fact only at the extreme lower part of 5 of the 7 sets of curves is it even close to negative. The curves for S2 and S4, the female subjects, slope positively from the start, meaning that you have to pay them to induce them to eat even a part of a pastry.

The beginning of the positive slope indicates a point of relative satiation; that is, up to this number of pastries the subjects are willing to forego some money to eat the pastries but after this point they will consume more pastries only if they are paid for it. For the 5 male subjects this occurs at about 3 pastries. For four subjects, S2, S4, S5 and S6, a level of absolute satiation is apparently reached in that no more money (in the domain considered) could induce them to eat more pastries (although there does seem to be a slight upward bend at the right end for S2). Thus the indifference curves become horizontal at between 2 and 6 pastries for the females (S2 and S4) and between 8 to 14 for the males (S5 and S6). The curves for S1, S3 and S7, on the other hand, tend to continually increase over the range of pastries offered.

In general the curves are increasing at a decreasing rate. The only regular concavity from the left side is found in the curves for S3 in the whole region of their positive slope, and the curves for S1 at the top. The female subjects both exhibit strong preferences—note the concavity until the satiation level abruptly terminates it in the case of S2, and the concavity introduced by the unusual step-type function for satiation levels in S4. Even though S7's curves are not concave the steep linear slope should be noted. Apparently S1, S3 and S7 are not near any absolute satiation level.

Even though no curves cross for any subject, the intersection of all 4 curves at their right end for S2, S4 and S6 causes obvious problems. By this joining-up of the curves they are implicitly stating their indifference between $1 and $6. It would have been useful to give them pairwise comparisons to bring this out; however, it was not done in this experiment. On the other hand, the joining-up may reflect only an inability to represent graphically the minute differences in preference. On the separate graphs two of the other four subjects had drawn lines that crossed (the $1, $2 and $4 curves crossed each other for S1, and the $4 curve crossed the $2 and $6 curve for S3), but in transposing these curves to the joint graph these subjects modified the regions with the intersections.

Only one subject had inconsistencies between the indifference curves and the pairwise comparisons—S2 had 2 inconsistencies. Note, in Table I, that both inconsistencies involved pastries very close to 2, and so these inconsistencies may indicate carelessly considered preferences—or perhaps an indifference "band"—in this region, since the curves not only merge at 2 pastries but seem to have a slight upward bend.

VI. SUMMARY AND CONCLUSIONS

The primary purpose of this paper is to describe and present some results of a procedure for efficiently obtaining indifference curves. The procedure involves training an individual to draw his own indifference curves for two-commodity bundles, and by basing his payoff on the curves he has drawn he is motivated to represent his true preferences. Making use of the monotonicity of commodity preferences, when appropriate, considerably reduces the complexity of the task. In this section we shall summarize and evaluate the main features of the indifference curve determination procedure and the experimental design—noting some possible areas for improvement in each. In the process some implications of the experimental results will be developed, and we shall consider the uses for various elements of the procedure in different experiments on choices and also nonexperimental decision making situations.

The payoff procedure used is a powerful method for inducing the individual to give his true preferences. After some explanation it was easily understood by the subjects and evidence of its effectiveness comes from three basic sources. First, the indifference curves drawn on the separate graphs are very consistent when superimposed. Second, of the 21 consistency checks given to each subject, and chosen to be difficult (i.e., very close to an indifference line), an average of less than one choice per subject was actually inconsistent with the appropriate indifference curve. Third, none of the subjects seemed to display any post-payoff dissonance when the actual payoffs were made, that is, even though the random points occurred very near an indifference curve for most subjects they did not express regret at not having drawn their indifference curve differently.

It should be noted that this method can be used in many more situations than simply the determination of indifference curves. Most choice situations involve a determination of an equivalence relation, and the method can undoubtedly be adapted to most of these situations. A further discussion of its generality and a theoretical basis for it is given in Toda and MacCrimmon.

Although dominance-based concepts, through the rectangle and line methods, have not been used in the previous experimental determinations of indifference curves (Thurstone, especially, would have found them useful), they are commonly used in many different contexts. Their obviousness does not detract from their usefulness though. The inappropriateness of any particular form (i.e., the rectangle or line) would not cause a problem because it would be discovered by the subject as he made his choices, so there is no danger of forcing an inappropriate exclusion method on him.

Another important feature of our procedure is the emphasis on allowing the subject to carefully consider his choices. The training session at the beginning —a half hour to an hour would suffice—teaches him how to represent his preferences. He is given another opportunity to reflect on his preferences when he is asked to transfer the individually drawn indifference curves to the joint graph. After this the graphs are taken away and he is given a series of pairwise comparisons among bundles on either side of the curves he has drawn. We used these as checks on his consistency, but ideally they would be compared by the subject with the curves he had drawn and he would be allowed to make changes. This procedure could be repeated and perhaps could even be set up as a visual computer display with the consistency checks programmed in and performed on-line in real-time.

We think such opportunities for the subject to reflect on his choices are used all too infrequently in preference, judgment and general choice situations. After all, if we are really trying to obtain the subject's true choices rather than trying to trick him into inconsistencies, he should be given an opportunity to carefully consider those choices. More effective use of training sessions in which the subject is taught to generate the relevant questions can be very efficient both in terms of subsequent experimental time and in obviating the need to prepare elaborate experimental materials.

In the particular experiments we performed we did not force any of the usual properties of indifference curves (as both Thurstone and Rousseas and Hart did). None of the indifference curves actually crossed, but the joining up of the money/pastry curves for 3 subjects is a violation of transitivity. In no case did we ask subjects to redraw intersecting curves, although we did explain the implications of this at the training session. It would have been useful to have asked specific questions of the 3 subjects. There was also no attempt to force the curves to have a negative slope, and the nature of the use of pastries as a commodity in fact led us to expect a positive slope. In the money/pen case the use of the rectangle method does not constrain the curves to slope downward if this is not a true reflection of preferences since if the preferences were such that in some region the subject wanted the curve to slope upward he would discover this by attempting to overlap the A and R regions. Finally, we did not force the curves to be convex, and we do note some concave regions in both commodity pair graphs. It would have been useful to test these regions of non-convexity by presenting the subject with pairwise comparisons of bundles from those regions.

The particular experiments we performed while providing interesting information are by no means definitive. The results give some indication of the preferences of a small group of individuals for particular commodities at one point in time. Let us take up these restrictions one by one.

The sample size could be usefully broadened even for the commodities used. Certainly if we are ultimately interested in market behaviour we cannot confine our attention solely to college students. It also would be worthwhile to sample on the basis of attributes we think might be significant for the commodities used, for example, income level, weight, education, family size, etc. Note that we obtained a significant sex difference for pastries. It should be observed that even with our seven subjects we get diverse preferences that fall into reasonable classes—for example, the strong and mild disinterest in large numbers of pens, and the existence and location of relative and absolute satiation levels for pastries.

In addition to using more subjects, a variety of commodities could be introduced. We have used two quite diverse, and consequently special ones. In one case the consumption of the commodity was forced immediately, while in the second case consumption was not forced at all. Considering each commodity as a representative of a more general class, the former is an example of a situation that we would pay to get out of, while the latter is one in which we personally would consume a small amount but would stock, give away, or resell larger amounts. In addition to representing this larger class of commodities, forced consumption of the pastries hopefully contributed to more careful thought on the part of the subject since he realized he would suffer directly if he misrepresented his preferences. The diversity of shapes of the money/pastry curves should be noted; it certainly seems to question homogeneity of taste assumptions that are commonly made.

In the case of the pens there is reason to believe that no subject was planning to personally use large numbers of pens, rather they were planning to give them to friends or to sell them. This fact should not cast doubt on the curves as the appropriate reflection of their preferences—for after all we are not, in general, concerned with motivations in predicting market behaviour. Whether he uses the commodity himself, gives it away or resells it makes no difference in his indifference curves (although it could have an effect on the total) as long as there is relative stability in his own tastes, his perception of his friends' tastes, and the downward sloping demand schedule he faces for resale. Alternatively, if the long linear segment or possible resale bothers anyone, the region above 10 pens can be cut off and the scale in the lower region can be expanded to get the more convex curves we are accustomed to seeing.

In further experiments a reasonable class of commodities to be represented would be one which lies between the extremes we have considered. That is, the subject would personally consume a large amount at his leisure. One procedure that might be helpful in such cases would be to select the subject on the basis of his known consumption of the commodity to be used. For example, we considered selecting photographers and using rolls of film, smokers and using pipe tobacco or cigarettes, and beer drinkers and using beer and peanuts. Another useful change in future experiments would be to construct commodity bundles in which money was not included as one of the commodities. In such a case one could check for substitutability or complementarity.

An additional modification in our design that could be quite interesting would be to obtain preferences for the same commodity bundles at different points in time. These points might either be chosen randomly or could be chosen to reflect some expected differences in preferences (e.g., for foodstuffs at different times of the day, or for money or many other commodities just before and just after pay-day). Such a study could provide useful information for an important concern of any theory of choice—the stability of preferences over time.

Many other changes in the experimental design could be proposed. It would be desirable to observe the sensitivity of the indifference curve to the particular reference point used. For example, the subject could be given a reference point that fell on an intermediate part of a curve he had previously drawn, and he would be asked to construct the indifference curve through this reference point. If the curves did not coincide, the subject would be shown the divergence and allowed to redraw the curve(s).

Such a sensitivity test is in some sense a type of validation of the curves drawn, but more direct validations could be proposed. The indifference curves obtained could be used to predict choices among commodities not lying on one of these curves. This could be done by simple extrapolation or interpolation. Another possible attempt by validation could be performed if a constant marginal utility of a common commodity could be assumed and two sets of indifference curves would be used to predict the third set, as Thurstone attempted to do.

A more interesting test would be to form pairs of individuals and put them together in a barter situation with some fixed amount of two commodities and allow them to leave with whatever division they agree upon. By putting their indifference curves together into an Edgeworth box one could see how close they come to the contract curve. That is, one would predict that in a one-shot situation they would form a division on the contract curve and the actual division would form a test of the accuracy of the individual indifference curves.

Alternatively, they could be started on the contract curve and any movement away would be noted and would be evidence of the lack of validity of the indifference curves.

Another attempt to validate the indifference curves by direct prediction would be to make the appropriate assumptions to get numerical utilities and then these could be used to predict choices. Any discrepancy though could be attributed to either poor indifference curves or the invalidity of the assumptions made. This topic will be explored in some depth in a forthcoming paper (MacCrimmon and Toda).

Most of the discussion above is directed to determination of indifference curves in situations that an experimenter constructs. However, we might wonder whether these procedures can be used in real world choice situations where preferences could be reflected by indifference curves, for example, the bombs and bombers trade-off of Hitch and McKean. It should be obvious that the emphasis on training, reflection, and checks on consistency could be part of any consideration of preferences. Also, the complexity reduction techniques based on admissibility can easily be used. This, then, only leaves the question of whether the payoff part of the method is useful in real world choices. Note that as we use it in experiments it is particularly effective because the subject will actually receive a commodity bundle based on his positioning of the indifference curve. Clearly there are many situations, not only bombs and bombers, in which we are not prepared to give the individual one of the commodity bundles. This leads to the question of whether the payoff part of the method is of any use when applied hypothetically—for example, "suppose after you draw the indifference curve we randomly select a combination of bombs and bombers, if it is in your accept region we will give you that combination, if it is in your reject region you get the reference bundle." Whether such hypothetical payoffs are effective is an empirical matter, but in any case it is probably as good as any other procedure in these contexts. Since all important decisions involve a representation of preferences in some form or other, it would be useful to explore the possibilities of applying these experimentally based procedures in real world choice situations.

4

THE THEORY OF MARKET DEMAND

PARTIAL EQUILIBRIUM AND *CETERIS PARIBUS*

In the previous chapter we considered the theory of demand from the standpoint of the individual consumer. Now we focus on market or industry demand. Concentrating on one market is an application of partial equilibrium analysis, which isolates for study some particular sector of the economy, for instance, one industry, on the assumption that each industry is partially independent of the remainder of the economy. For example, an industry's behavior at any one time may be quite different from that of the economy as a whole; the economy might be expanding while a particular industry may be contracting.

Market supply and demand are the principal forces governing an industry's behavior. Other forces such as the supply and demand conditions of related products or the prices of resources not directly used in the given industry generally play a less important role. To concentrate on the main forces which determine industry behavior, we make the *ceteris paribus* assumption, which holds constant all of the lesser forces. We can thereby concentrate our attention on the determinants of industry supply and demand and the mechanism which achieves equilibrium, without having to study all the other related but less important factors.

THE NATURE OF AN INDUSTRY OR MARKET

Nearly all consumer products and services are more or less related to each other. For instance, two consumer goods may be close substitutes for one another, such as tea and coffee, or they may be complementary, like automobiles and tires. And even if commodities are neither complements nor substitutes, they are similar in that they provide consumers with utility.

Moreover, each commodity is produced with resources that may be used to produce other goods. So even if the demand for one commodity changes without affecting the demand for other commodities directly, the increased demand for one good will likely affect the prices of resources used, not only by the given industry, but by other industries as well. In summary, all industries in an economy are related to all other industries, either directly, in the output market, or indirectly, via resource markets, or both, so a disturbance in one industry will have repercussions throughout the economy.

At this point, however, we will not emphasize the interdependence among sectors of an economy but rather the possibility that a sector may be distinct and therefore worthy of separate study. The criterion which we employ to determine "distinctness" of an industry is the degree of similarity of the product sold in the output market. In many cases, the degree of interrelatedness between commodities in the product or output market is quite small, perhaps seemingly nonexistent. For example, we might infer that the demand for typewriters is unrelated to the demand for shoes, that these two commodities are neither complements nor substitutes, and, in addition, are produced with dissimilar resources. On the other hand, the markets for lead pencils and mechanical pencils would appear to be very closely connected. We will assume a degree of independence in the behavior of firms within a given industry, where an *industry* is defined to include all firms producing and selling a group of products or services, which are either identical or close substitutes for each other, and to include all actual and potential buyers of the industry's output.

The boundaries of a given industry are established by the characteristics of the product itself, that is, the extent to which the product is distinct from all other products but homogeneous within the industry. Some products are in a category by themselves in this respect. For example, there is little difficulty defining the product of the cigarette industry or the telephone industry. In the case of the electronics industry, however, the product is not so easily defined. For instance, it may not be appropriate to consider the demand for transistor radios in the same category with the demand for television sets (though many domestic manufacturers produce both), since the two products are different and the consumer markets for them are largely segregated. At least the two would be considered distinct markets within the electronics industry. On the other hand, we might be interested in the entire electronics equipment industry, in which case, we would have to include not only the producers of radios and TV's, but also those firms producing stereos, electronic computers, and other industrial equipment. For many analytical problems it is more useful to keep industry classifications narrowly restricted.

THE GEOGRAPHIC MARKET AREA

A second important dimension of product markets is the geographic one. In some instances, firms within an industry market and distribute their products nationally or even internationally, while other industries serve only a limited geographic area. In the United States, the steel, automobile, and aluminum industries sell largely in national markets, while the motion picture industry might be considered international. In other markets, the geographic dimension is regional, local, or even neighborhood. For example, the milk industry serves local markets for the most part, despite national brands and some interstate movement of milk in areas like New England. A more restricted market is the newspaper industry, which typically serves a metropolitan area. In short, markets have a geographic dimension that may be more or less restrictive. The actual geographical shape of such local markets may be gerrymandered by the ease, speed, availability, and cost of transportation. Therefore, it might be convenient to picture industries operating in a sort of "economic space," whose size is a function of the convenience, ease, speed, and cost of marketing firms' output.

In the following discussion, we assume that markets are accurately defined, regarding both their product and geographic dimensions. We generally disregard the effect of geographical boundaries for all industries. In addition, for our initial model of competitive behavior, we assume intra-industry product homogeneity. Together, these simplifying assumptions allow us to concentrate on the basic forces of supply and demand, without burdening ourselves with problems of market definition. Later we will relax the homogeneity assumption when we analyze imperfect competition.

MARKET DEMAND AND ITS MEASUREMENT

The Derivation of Market Demand

In the last chapter, we considered two methods of deriving an individual's demand for a consumer good based on his tastes and preferences, his income, and the prices of other goods. Now we may extend our discussion to the market, for individual demand serves as the basis for deriving market demand.

In general, if we know the demand schedules of all consumers of a given product, we can determine market demand for that product by aggregating the individual demands. To show how individual demand curves are summed to get market demand, consider the case of a market for good X, which has *only two buyers*. The hypothetical demand curves of the two buyers are D_1 and D_2 in Figure 4–1. These curves indicate that for prices above P_m, industry sales will be zero units, since neither consumer will purchase X at such prices. At price P_1, however, the first consumer would buy X_1 units and the second consumer would buy X_2 units, so the total quantity demanded in the industry would be $X_1 + X_2$. Similarly, to obtain the aggregate quantity demanded at any other price, we add up the respective quantities of the two goods purchased by the two participants. If the summation is done for every possible price, we generate the industry demand curve, D_m. Market demand for our two-buyer market is the horizontal summation of the separate demand curves D_1 and D_2. Generalizing, where there are two or more buyers, market demand is found by algebraically adding the quantities demanded by all buyers at each possible price.

The algebraic summation of all the individual demand curves is an accurate

FIGURE 4-1   Market Demand: The Summation of Individual Demands

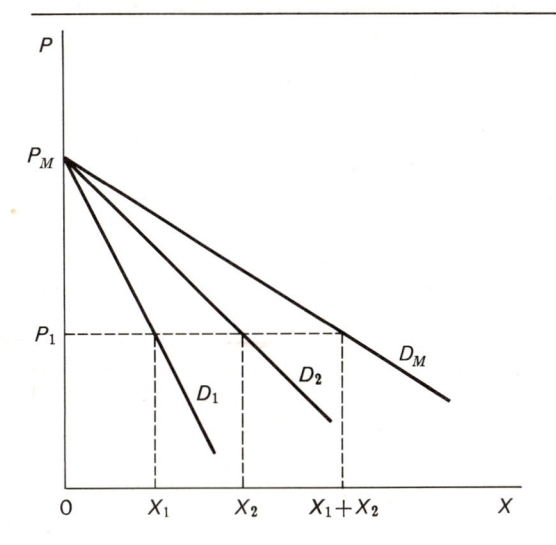

first approximation to industry demand. However, a simple summation disregards one factor which may significantly complicate the analysis—the possibility of interdependence among individual demand curves. In the discussion above, we have implicitly assumed that each consumer's demand schedule is independent of the demand curves of others; if so, we could algebraically sum the separate demand curves, without the summation process affecting any one demand schedule. In deriving individual demand, we made the *ceteris paribus* assumption, which holds constant all non-price variables that might affect the quantity demanded by the consumer; one of these non-price variables may very well be the quantities of the good consumed by others. Now we are questioning whether it is possible to aggregate individual demands while holding to the *ceteris paribus* assumption.

The assumption of no interdependence among individual buyers may be unrealistic in some instances, for an individual's demand for some products may be a function of the quantities of the good consumed by others. For example, a style-conscious individual's demand for new clothes will very likely depend upon consumption of the product by others, especially fashion leaders. If the demand for double-breasted suits generally increases, the style-conscious consumer's demand will also rise. On the other hand, a snob's demand for a luxury consumer good may be an inverse function of the effective demands of others for the good or for similar goods. The snob's demand for a product may decrease if the quantity consumed by others rises; that is, if the good becomes too common. In general, the demand schedules of consumers are often interdependent, so that if one consumer's demand for a product shifts, another's demand might shift, too.

But how does this conclusion affect our summation of demand curves? First, any one demand curve is derived by assuming the consumer has a given understanding of market conditions and has formed an expectation of what other consumers in the market are going to do (the *ceteris paribus* assumption). His demand curve is appropriate for only one set of non-price equilibrium conditions in the market. The summation process violates this assumption, because as soon as we start aggregating, the one consumer will be influenced by the changes of other consumers. If those changes were unanticipated, their effect will cause a shift in the one consumer's demand. The determination of market demand becomes much more complicated when the individual demands are interdependent, because we must now ascertain the reactions of each consumer to the actions of all others. Only if we know how each individual will react to the actions of all others is it possible to derive market demand.[1]

In general, however, the algebraic summation of individual demand curves gives a good approximation to market demand if the degree of interdependence among consumer's demands is not strong.

Measuring the Effect of Price Changes on Quantity

If the price of automobiles drops 20 percent, more will be sold, and if the price of color TV's increases 30 percent, fewer will be sold. But how will the sales of autos increase and the sales of color TV's decrease? The answer depends upon how responsive or sensitive the quantities demanded of TV's and autos are to price changes, and that responsiveness in turn depends on the shapes of the market demand curves for the two goods.

What we need is a measure of how much quantity changes when price changes. One measure sometimes used for this purpose is the slope of the demand curve. Consider two hypothetical demand curves for good X, D_1, and D_2, shown in Figure 4–2. If price falls from P_1 and P_2, the quantity demanded of X increases from X_1 to X_2, referring to demand schedule D_1, and from X_1 to X_3, referring to D_2. Obviously, the quantity demanded of X along D_2 is more sensitive to price changes than the quantity demanded along D_1.

We may be misled if we use the slope of the demand curve as an indication of how responsive quantity is to price changes. If the unit of measurement chosen for the horizontal or vertical axes is changed, the slope of the demand curve changes. For example, if we consider the demand for apples, the slope will change depending on whether quantity is measured in individual apples, pounds, bushels, hundreds of pounds, carloads, or some other measure. To illustrate using different price denominations, refer to demand D_1 in Figure 4–2 and let X_1 equal 10 units and X_2 equal 12 units. If price is measured in

---

[1] See Harvey Leibenstein, "Bandwagon, Snob, and Veblen Effects in the Theory of Consumers' Demand," *Quarterly Journal of Economics*, 64 (May 1950), 183–207.

FIGURE 4-2 Slope as a Measure of Demand

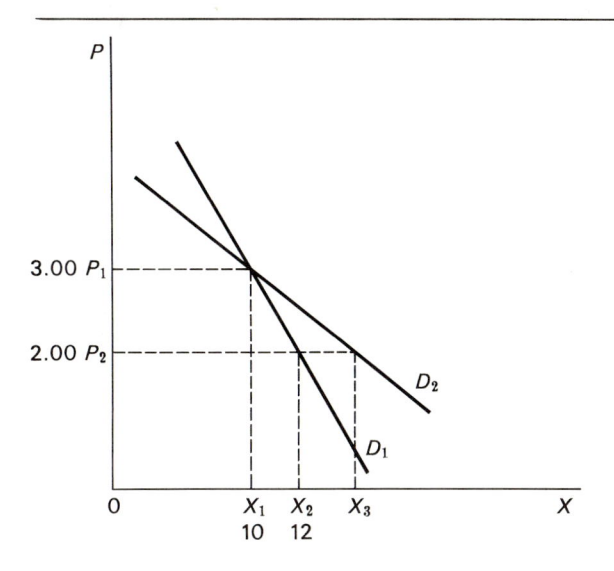

[Figure: Graph with P on vertical axis and X on horizontal axis. Two demand curves D_1 and D_2 intersect. $P_1 = 3.00$ and $P_2 = 2.00$ marked on vertical axis. $X_1 = 10$, $X_2 = 12$, and X_3 marked on horizontal axis.]

dollars per unit, the slope of D_1 between prices P_1 and P_2 is $(3 - 2)/(10 - 12)$ or $-\frac{1}{2}$. On the other hand, if price is measured in cents per unit, the slope changes to $(300 - 200)/(12 - 12)$ or -50. The slope of a demand curve is thus dependent on the unit of measurement used on the price and quantity axes. Clearly, this is an undesirable feature of slope as a measure of price-quantity sensitivity. Comparisons between two or more goods using slope as the measure would be meaningless. Therefore, slope is an inefficient and often inaccurate measure and generally should not be used.

The Concept of Elasticity. The measure which economists mainly use to show the responsiveness of quantity changes to price changes along a demand curve is called the *price elasticity of demand*.

The price elasticity of demand is the ratio of the following two percentages: (1) the percentage change in quantity demanded of a good which occurs as a result of (2) a given percentage change in its price. If the price of a consumer good declines 1 percent and, as a result, the quantity demanded of the good increases 5 percent, the price elasticity of demand (E_a) equals $+5/1$ or $+5$. Notice that price elasticity measures price-quantity sensitivity when price changes from one level to another. And, typically, price elasticity is most useful when the price change is small. In other words, we are talking about small movements *along* a demand curve. Price elasticity of demand is not a measure of the over-all, price-quantity sensitivity of an entire demand curve. We will find that for most consumer goods, price elasticity for an entire demand curve is meaningless, because E_a is different at different price levels.

A problem arises when computing the percentage changes of price and quantity. Referring to the demand curve D_x in Figure 4–3, suppose price falls

FIGURE 4–3 A Hypothetical Demand Curve for Product X

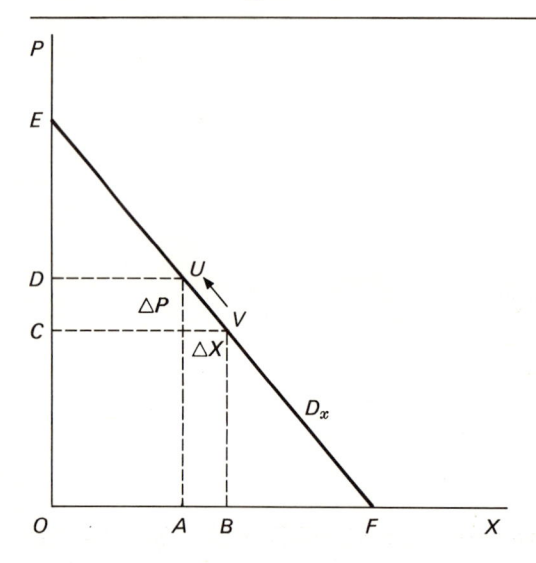

from D to C. What is the percentage change in price? It is the absolute decline $(C - D)$, divided by a base price, or:

$$\frac{\Delta P}{\text{Base } P} = \frac{C - D}{\text{Base } P}.$$

But the base price could be either D or C or some combination of the two prices. The choice of the base price is largely arbitrary. We will take the average, giving:

$$\text{Percentage change in price} = \frac{\Delta P}{(D + C)/2} = \frac{C - D}{(D + C)/2}.$$

Similarly, the percentage change in quantity demanded, which occurs as a result of the decrease in price, is:

$$\left.\begin{array}{l}\text{Percent change in quantity}\\ \text{demanded of } X\end{array}\right\} = \frac{\Delta X}{(A + B)/2} = \frac{B - A}{(A + B)/2}.$$

Now we can define price elasticity, E_a, as:

$$E_a = \frac{\text{Percent change in quantity demanded}}{\text{Percent change in price}},$$

or:

$$E_a = \frac{B - A}{(A + B)/2} \div \frac{C - D}{(D + C)/2},$$

which may be simplified to:

$$E_a = \frac{B - A}{C - D} \cdot \frac{D + C}{A + B},\qquad(1)$$

where $(B - A)$ is ΔX and $(C - D)$ is ΔP. Price elasticity E_a is called *arc elasticity*, because it indicates the sensitivity of quantity changes to price changes along a small segment or arc of a demand curve. An alternate way to present formula (1), which focuses on the initial and subsequent values of price and quantity, is:

$$E_a = -\frac{Q_2 - Q_1}{P_2 - P_1} \cdot \frac{P_1 + P_2}{Q_1 + Q_2},\qquad(2)$$

where P_1 and P_2 are D and C, respectively, and Q_1 and Q_2 are A and B, respectively. Notice that a negative sign has been added to insure that the elasticity formula will give positive values for the coefficients. Since demand curves exhibit an inverse relationship of price to quantity, percentage changes in quantity consumed will typically be opposite in sign to the percentage changes in price. The elasticity formula would yield negative values without the negative sign affixed to the formula. Otherwise, formula (2) is identical to formula (1).

In Table 4–1 we are given information about the market demand for a

TABLE 4–1

P_y	Q_y
$12	100
11	120
10	140
9	165
8	200

hypothetical good, Y. Suppose we wish to know the price elasticity of demand when price changes from $11 to $10. Using formula (2), and letting P_1 and Q_1, the initial price and quantity, be $11 and 120, respectively, we get:

$$E_a = -\frac{Q_2 - Q_1}{P_2 - P_1} \cdot \frac{P_1 + P_2}{Q_1 + Q_2},$$

$$E_a = -\frac{140 - 120}{10 - 11} \cdot \frac{11 + 10}{120 + 140},$$

$$E_a = +\frac{20}{1} \cdot \frac{21}{260},$$

$$E_a = +\frac{21}{13} = +1.62.$$

122 The Theory of Consumer Behavior and Demand

Notice that the result would be identical if the initial price were $10 and we considered a $1 price increase.

The value $E_a = +1.62$ can be interpreted as follows: given an initial price of $11, if price decreases by 9.5 percent $[(\Delta P)/(\text{Base } P) = (+1)/(10.5) = +.095]$, then quantity demanded will increase by 1.62 times 9.5 or 15.4 percent. For this particular example, the given percentage decline in price causes a greater percentage increase in quantity demanded.

Point Elasticity. The price elasticity measure which we just discussed concerned finite price changes and quantity changes. Now suppose we investigated the response of quantity to infinitely small price changes. That measure is called *point elasticity*, because it measures the price–quantity sensitivity at a given point on a demand curve. One of the advantages of point elasticity is that it gives an instantaneous measure of price–quantity sensitivity at each and every price along a demand curve. Arc elasticity, since it concerns a finite range of price, in effect gives an average measure over the range of price. If the range is large enough, arc elasticity may conceal important changes in price–quantity sensitivities at strategic prices. For instance, to measure arc elasticity between the prices $90 and $110 may give misleading information concerning the price–quantity sensitivity at price $99.95. Second, point elasticity is a useful measure for certain statistical procedures (regression techniques) that seek to estimate demand curves from time series data.

Referring to Figure 4–3, suppose the difference between prices D and C becomes very small; that is, let point V on D_x approach closer and closer to point U. Using formula (1) for the arc elasticity coefficient:

$$E_a = \frac{B - A}{C - D} \cdot \frac{D + C}{A + B}$$

As point V approaches point U, C approaches D and B approaches A, thus $D + C$ will approach $2D$, and $A + B$ will approach $2A$. Substituting in the formula just above we get:

$$E_p = \frac{\Delta X}{\Delta P} \cdot \frac{2D}{2A},$$

$$E_p = \frac{\Delta X}{\Delta P} \cdot \frac{D}{A}. \qquad (3)$$

Although both ΔX and ΔP become very small as V approaches U, the ratio $\Delta X/\Delta P$ will not necessarily become small but will approach some constant value.

In fact, since $\Delta P/\Delta X$ is the slope of D_x, $\Delta X/\Delta P$ is simply the inverse of the slope of the demand curve at point U. Moreover, since D_x is linear, its slope is the same at point V as at point U or for any other point on D_x and is:

$$\frac{\Delta P}{\Delta X} = -\frac{OE}{OF},$$

where OE is the vertical intercept of D_x, and OF is its horizontal intercept. The ratio OE/OF is, in turn, equal to AU/AF, because triangle OEF is similar to AUF, all angles of the first being equal to those of the second.

We have seen that:

$$\frac{\Delta P}{\Delta X} = -\frac{OE}{OF} = -\frac{AU}{AF}.$$

Therefore, taking reciprocals, and dropping out the middle portion we get:

$$\frac{\Delta X}{\Delta P} = -\frac{AF}{AU}.$$

Substituting this result in (3) we get:

$$E_p = -\frac{AF}{AU} \cdot \frac{D}{A},$$

and, since D is identical to OD and A to OA, we can write:

$$E_p = -\frac{AF}{AU} \cdot \frac{OD}{OA}.$$

Moreover, since $AU = D = OD$, we can simplify the formula as follows:

$$E_p = -\frac{AF}{OD} \cdot \frac{OD}{OA},$$

$$E_p = -\frac{AF}{OA}.$$

Finally, to insure positive values for the elasticity coefficient, we drop the negative sign, giving:

$$E_p = \frac{AF}{OA}. \tag{4}$$

The distance OA is the quantity demanded at the given price, whereas the quantity AF is the horizontal intercept of the linear demand curve, minus OA. Now, we have a convenient formula for computing point elasticity at different points along a linear demand curve.

In panel (a) of Figure 4–4, we have drawn a linear demand curve, and in panel (b) have plotted the value of E_p for various quantities of X. For instance, using formula (4), at quantity A_2 (equal to $\frac{1}{2}F$), $E_p = +(F - \frac{1}{2}F)/(\frac{1}{2}F)$, which reduces to 1. At quantity A_3, $E_p = +(A_3F)/(OA_3)$, which by inspection is less than 1, since the numerator A_3F is smaller than the denominator OA_3, whereas at quantity A_1, $E_p = (A_1F)/(OA_1)$, which is greater than 1. These values of E_p, as well as values at other output levels, are plotted in panel (b) of Figure 4–4. As price falls toward zero, E_p approaches zero since the numerator of the fraction in formula (4) would become smaller and smaller, while the denominator would become larger. Therefore, moving

124 The Theory of Consumer Behavior and Demand

FIGURE 4-4 Measuring Price Elasticity of Demand Along a Linear Demand Curve

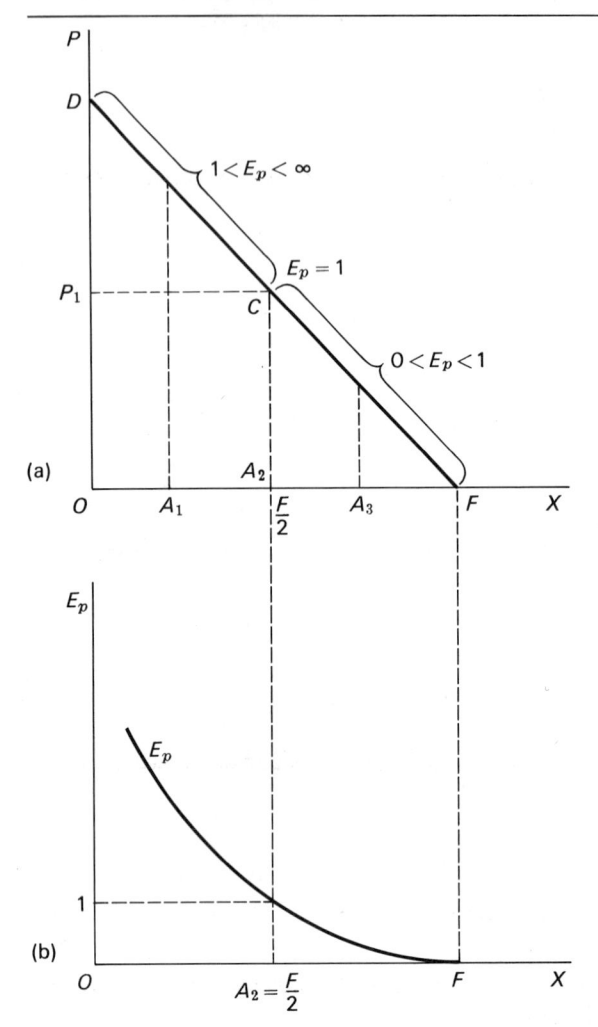

southeast in panel (a) along the demand curve from point C to point F causes E_p to change from 1 to 0. If we move northwestward from point C toward D, E_p becomes increasingly large, because the closer we approach the vertical axis, the larger becomes the numerator of the fraction in formula (4), while the smaller becomes the denominator. As we consider prices ranging from zero to D, the value of E_p changes from zero to ∞.

Note the contrast between these results and the results obtained with our original crude measure of price–quantity sensitivity, the slope of the demand curve. Though the slope of D_x is constant at all points along its length, E_p exhibits a different value for every distinct point on the curve. Referring to

Figure 4-4, for prices between zero and P_1, E_p varies from 0 to 1, while for prices above P_1, E_p varies from 1 to ∞. We will define as *inelastic* that segment of the demand curve below point C, where $0 < E_p < 1$, and as *elastic* the segment of D_x above point C, where $1 < E_p < \infty$. In general, if we are dealing with the elastic portion of the demand curve for a good, a given percentage change in price will cause a greater percentage change in quantity demanded, and on the inelastic portion, a given percentage change in price will cause a smaller percentage change in quantity. If $E_p = 1$, then demand is of unitary elasticity, meaning that a given percentage change in price is exactly matched by the percentage change in the quantity of the good. For the linear demand curve in Figure 4-4, price elasticity is unitary for very small changes in price about P_1.

We can determine point elasticity at any price along a curvilinear demand curve, as well as along a linear one. Referring to D_x in Figure 4-5, suppose we

FIGURE 4-5 Computing Point Elasticity for a Curvilinear Demand Curve

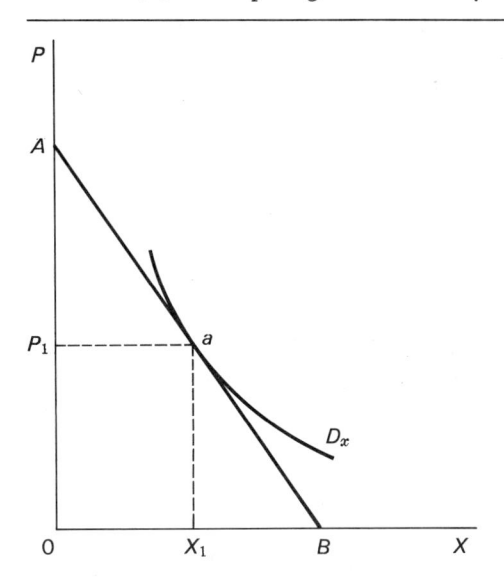

are interested in knowing the point elasticity of demand at a price of P_1. First we construct a straight line, AB, tangent to the demand curve at point a. Line AB has the same slope as the demand curve at point a. To obtain the price elasticity of demand at P_1, we simply compute point elasticity for line AB at the given price. Thus, the point elasticity of demand for X at price P_1 is:

$$E_p = \frac{X_1 B}{0 X_1}.$$

Alternatively, if the slope of D_x at output X_1 is known, its inverse can be substituted into formula (3) and E_p computed directly.

One disadvantage of point elasticity is that its range for prices above P_1 is much greater than its range for prices between zero and P_1. One way to correct for this would be to modify the elasticity formula as follows:

$$E_m = \frac{1}{1 + E_p}, \tag{5}$$

where E_m is a modified elasticity coefficient and E_p is point elasticity using the standard formula. Now when E_p changes from zero to 1 (moving up a linear demand curve like D_x in Figure 4–4 to price P_1), then E_m varies from 1 to ½. As E_p changes from 1 to ∞ (for prices above P_1), E_m declines from ½ to zero. The modified elasticity formula gives a more symmetrical measure of price elasticity for the whole range of possible prices, varying by one-half for prices between zero and P_1 (again refer to Figure 4–4) and by one-half for prices above P_1 to D. Note, however, that changes in E_m are in the opposite direction to changes in E_p.

Demand Elasticity and Total Expenditures. At this point, we wish to illustrate one of the uses of the elasticity measure by showing the relationship between the price elasticity of demand for an industry product and the effects of changes in market price on the total receipts of the industry. (This knowledge is particularly useful in formulating public policy for the agriculture industry. United States farm policy has been directed at maintaining minimum prices for numerous agricultural products. To assess the success of this policy, we must know the effects of changes in agricultural prices on the total receipts of agriculture. We will find that the effects of a change in price on the industry's receipts will depend on the price elasticity of market demand for agricultural output.)

Suppose D_x in Figure 4–6 is the market demand for product X. If the market price were P_1, the industry would sell X_1 units, and consumers' total expenditures would amount to $P_1 \cdot X_1$. Total expenditures by consumers equal the total receipts of the industry. At different prices, the quantity demanded of X changes and so too does the level of total expenditures. In panel (b) of Figure 4–6, total expenditures are plotted for all possible price–quantity combinations along D_x. For example, total expenditures increase from zero (when zero units are purchased) to a maximum of TE_1 as we move down the demand curve from point b, the vertical axis intercept, to point a. Total expenditures fall from TE_1 to zero again as we consider price–quantity combinations along D_x from point a to the horizontal intercept. At the lower extreme, point c, the price of X is zero, so total expenditures by consumers would be zero also.

In panel (c) of Figure 4–6, we have included the curve showing the value of point elasticity at various quantities, so that comparisons can be made between values of E_p and the effects of price changes on total consumer expenditures. Concentrating on the segment of the demand curve between points b and a which is elastic, a decrease (increase) in price causes total expendi-

FIGURE 4–6 Price Changes and Total Expenditure Changes: Their Relationship to Price Elasticity

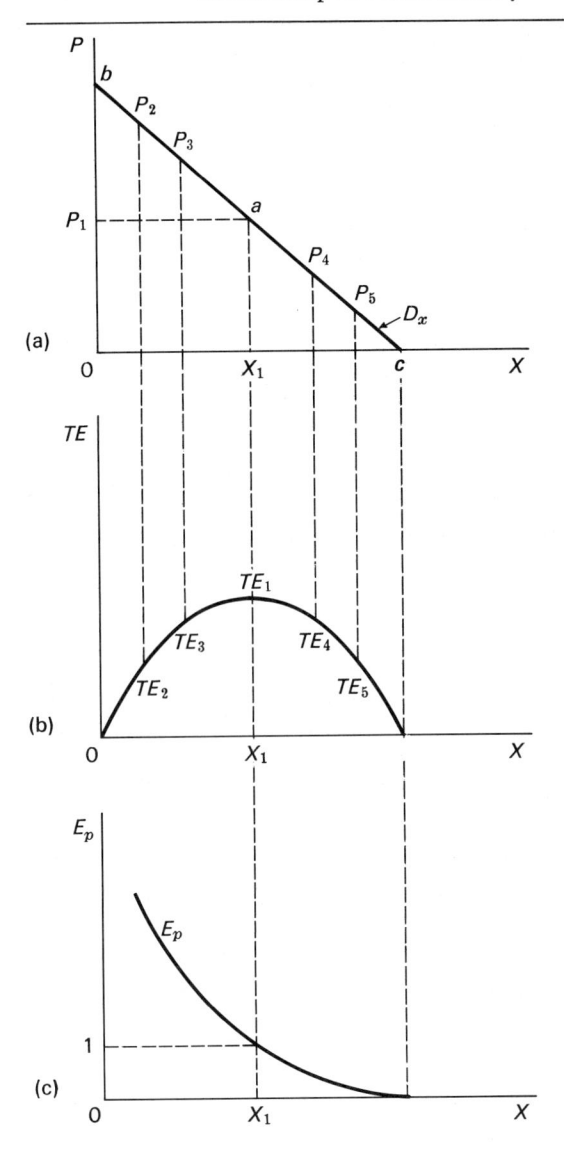

tures to increase (decrease). For example, if price falls from P_2 to P_3, total expenditures by consumers rise from TE_2 to TE_3. In general, an inverse relationship exists between *changes* in price and *changes* in total expenditures, where demand is elastic. On the other hand, for the segment of D_x between points a and c price decreases cause total expenditures to decrease also. For example, if price falls from P_4 to P_5, total expenditures decreases also, from TE_4 to TE_5. Since demand is inelastic in the range ac, we may conclude that price decreases (increases) cause total expenditure decreases (increases), if demand is inelastic. Finally, for very small price changes in the neighborhood of P_1, where demand is of unitary elasticity, total expenditures remain unchanged at the peak, TE_1.

THE MARKET DEMAND CURVE AND THE DEMAND FUNCTION

Shifts in the Demand Curve

At this point, it is necessary to amplify on the distinction we have made between the demand curve for a good and the demand function for the same good. In Chapter 2, we said the demand function relates the quantity of a good consumed to all factors that influence consumers' purchases of the good, including its price, the aggregate level of income, the characteristics of the good relative to other goods, and other forces such as consumers' tastes and their pattern of expectations about the future. In symbols, the market demand function for X is:

$$D_x = f(P_x, P_y, P_z, Y, U_d), \tag{6}$$

where D_x is the quantity of X that will be consumed per unit time; P_x is the price of the good; P_y and P_z are the prices of related goods (complements and substitutes); Y is the aggregate level of income in the economy; and U_d stands for all other factors influencing the quantity of X demanded. The demand curve, or simply, market demand, for X, is the relation between D_x and P_x when all of the non-price determinants of demand are held fixed. The market demand curve has, of course, been our principal concern thus far in this chapter. But now we must expand our discussion to incorporate the non-price determinants of market demand.

Suppose that aggregate income increases and that this income increase is experienced by all purchasers of good X. Before ascertaining the over-all effects of this change, let us first consider the effects on an individual consumer, using indifference curve analysis. In Figure 4-7, we have presented an indifference curve model in which income is measured on the vertical axis and quantity consumed of X on the horizontal axis. The consumer allocates his income between purchases of X and purchases of all other goods. Initially income is OA and, given the price P_{x_1}, the consumer buys X_1 units. Now we show that the increase in income shifts the budget line from BL_1 to BL_2. The new optimum combination occurs at point V, and X_2 units of X are now purchased.

Notice that the amount of X purchased has increased as a result of the income increase, though the price of X has remained unchanged. In effect, this

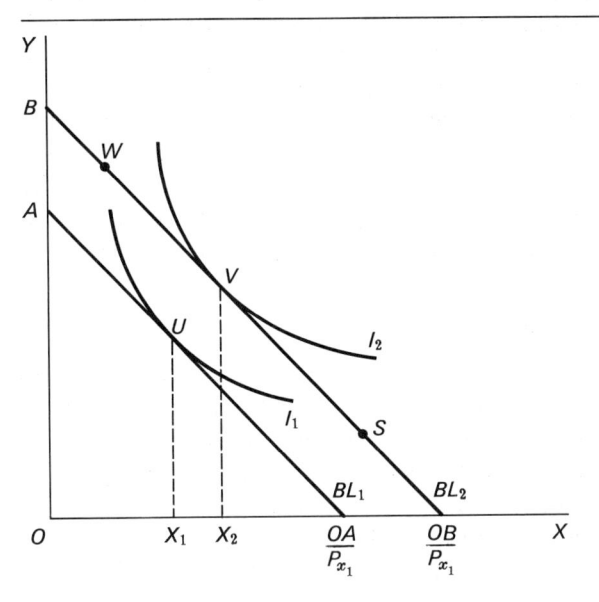

FIGURE 4–7 The Effects of Budget Changes on the Quantity Purchased of Product X

consumer's demand for X has shifted to the right with the income increase. Now, *if* our hypothetical consumer is typical of *all* other purchasers of X, then the market demand curve, which is an aggregation of the demand curves of all the separate purchasers of X, will shift to the right also.

But suppose our hypothetical consumer is not typical. For our consumer, we have indicated the quantity of X increasing as income increases, meaning the good is a normal good for our subject consumer. It is entirely possible, however, that for some other consumer, the shapes of the indifference curves will be different, so that an income increase will result in less of X being consumed, such as an equilibrium at point W on BL_2. The good X is inferior to this second consumer, and his demand curve for X would then shift to the left as his income increases. Given that purchasers of X are heterogeneous, we may expect that some individual's demand curves will shift one way and others will shift in the opposite direction or possibly not shift at all. The effect on the market demand for X of a change in aggregate income will depend therefore on the sum total of the effects on all individual buyers in the market for X. And if higher income shifts market demand to the right, it is not necessarily true that any one individual's demand for X has been affected in the same manner.

We have been discussing the effects on the market demand curve of changes in one of the non-price determinants of market demand, income. Changes in any of the other non-price determinants will also affect the market demand curve, however. For example, an increase in the price of good Y will cause the demand for X to shift to the right, if good Y is a substitute good for all of the consumers of X and Y. Or an increase in the price of good Z will cause market demand to shift to the left, if Z is a complementary good. Finally, any change in the pattern of tastes and preferences for a good will affect market demand for the good, as will purchaser's expectations about the future price of the good. In the following sections, we will discuss in turn the important non-price determinants of demand and show how the elasticity concept can be used to measure the sensitivity of changes in quantity of a good demanded to changes in each of these non-price determinants of demand.

The Market Demand Function and Engel Curves

For some purposes, the most important determinant of the quantity consumed of a consumer good is not the price of the good but income. We have defined an individual's Engel curve for some good as relating the quantity of the good that will be consumed to the individual's income or budget. We now extend the concept to the market and define a market Engel curve for a good as showing the various quantities of the good that will be consumed at various levels of aggregate income. Using symbols, a market Engel curve is defined as:

$$D_x = f(\overline{P}_x, \overline{P}_y, \overline{P}_z, Y, \overline{U}_d), \tag{7}$$

where all of the determinants of quantity demanded on the right-hand side are held constant except Y, the level of aggregate income. Now, if the price of X changes, we may expect a shift in the Engel curve, analogous to a shift in the demand curve caused by a change in income.

The sensitivity of quantity changes to income changes along a market Engel curve, is measured by the coefficient of income elasticity. The income elasticity coefficient is equal to the ratio of the following percentages: (1) the percentage change in the quantity demanded of a good caused by (2) a given percentage change in aggregate income. The formula is:

$$E_y = \frac{X_2 - X_1}{(X_1 + X_2)/2} \div \frac{Y_2 - Y_1}{(Y_2 + Y_1)/2},$$

or, simplifying:

$$E_y = \frac{X_2 - X_1}{Y_2 - Y_1} \cdot \frac{Y_2 + Y_1}{X_2 + X_1}, \tag{8}$$

where X_1 is the quantity consumed when aggregate income is Y_1, and X_2 is the quantity consumed at the Y_2 income level. Consider the market Engel curve pertaining to a consumer good X presented in Figure 4–8. The income elasticity of demand will be positive for the segment *ab* of the Engel curve,

FIGURE 4–8 A Market Engel Curve for Good X

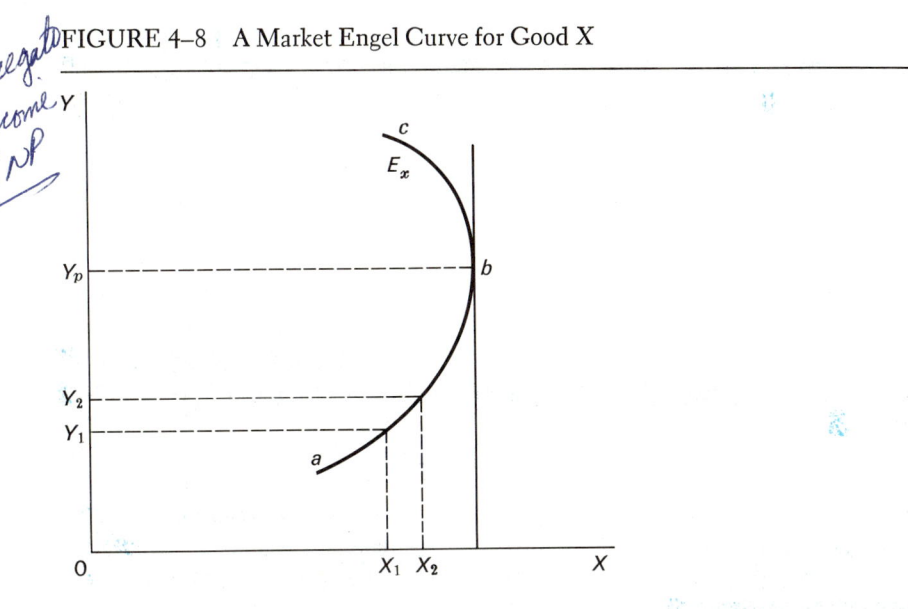

since the percentage changes in both Y and X are of the same sign. Income elasticity will be negative for the segment bc, however, because percentage increases (decreases) in income cause percentage decreases (increases) in quantity consumed. A negative income elasticity indicates the quantity of X consumed in the market will decline with an increase in aggregate income.

A good is defined as normal (or superior) in the aggregate, if the quantity consumed of the good rises with increases in aggregate income, and as *inferior*, if the quantity consumed falls with increases in income.[2] Thus, good X is a normal good for income levels below Y_p, but for income levels above Y_p (the segment bc of the Engel curve), the good is inferior. In general, a positive income elasticity of demand indicates a normal good, and a negative income elasticity of demand indicates an inferior good. Of course, a good may in the aggregate be a normal good with a positive elasticity, even though the good is inferior for a particular purchaser, or inferior in the aggregate and normal for a particular purchaser.

The Role of Substitutes and Complements

Among the determinants of the quantity demanded of good X are the prices of goods that are related to X. Thus, in the demand function (6) we have included the variables P_y and P_z as representing prices of substitute goods and complements. Of course, for any one purchaser, there may be more

---

[2] Some economists reserve the term superior for goods whose consumption increases in a greater proportion than the increase in income.

than one substitute for X and more than one complement. In any case, a change in the price of one of these "related" goods will affect the individual's demand curve. Moreover, market demand for X will also be affected by changes in the prices of related goods. But again we must recognize that although market demand is shifted in one direction as the result of a change in price of say, good Y, the demand curves of some individual purchasers may have shifted in an opposite manner.

The concept of elasticity may be used to investigate the relationship between the quantity consumed of good X and changes in the price of some other good, to show whether, in the aggregate, the two goods may be considered substitutes or complements. In addition, the elasticity measure will allow us to determine the strength of the substitute or complementary relationship. Notice that we are now observing the changes which will occur in the quantity consumed of X due to changes in the price of some good, say, good Y, while holding all other determinants of demand constant, including the price of X and income. The measure used is the *cross elasticity of demand for X*, which is the ratio of (1) the percentage change in quantity demanded of good X which occurs due to (2) a given percentage change in the price of a second good, good Y. The price of X is assumed to be held constant. In symbols:

$$E_{xy} = \frac{\Delta X}{X_{\text{base}}} \div \frac{\Delta P_y}{P_{y\text{base}}},$$

$$E_{xy} = \frac{X_1 - X_2}{(X_1 + X_2)/2} \div \frac{P_{y_1} - P_{y_2}}{(P_{y_1} + P_{y_2})/2},$$

$$E_{xy} = \frac{X_1 - X_2}{P_{y_1} - P_{y_2}} \cdot \frac{P_{y_1} + P_{y_2}}{X_1 + X_2}. \quad (9)$$

The double subscript *xy* indicates that we are varying the price of Y and analyzing the resulting effects on the quantity consumed of X.

Referring to panel (b) of Figure 4–9, suppose the price of Y rises from P_{y_1} to P_{y_2} due to a decrease in the market supply of Y from S_y to S_y'. As a result, suppose the market demand curve for X decreases from D_1 to D_2. The decrease in the demand for X indicates a complementary relationship between X and Y. The cross elasticity of demand will, in this case, be negative, since the first fraction in the formula above is negative. The numerator $(X_1 - X_2)$ is positive, but the denominator $(P_{y_1} - P_{y_2})$ is negative, whereas the second fraction is positive. A negative cross elasticity is associated with complementary goods.[3]

---

[3] We will subsequently qualify this statement to allow for the income effects of price changes.

FIGURE 4-9 The Relationship Between the Price of Y and the Demand for X

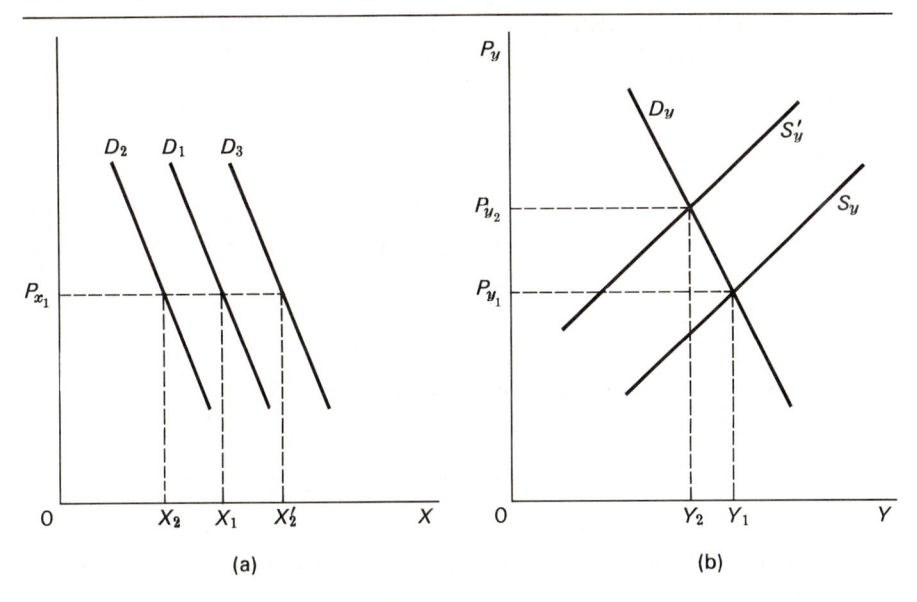

(a)

(b)

In contrast, if the rise in the price of Y had shifted D_1 to D_3, indicating a substitute relationship between X and Y, then the cross elasticity of demand would be positive, since both $(X_1 - X_2)$, the numerator of the first fraction in the formula above, and $(P_{y_1} - P_{y_2})$, the denominator, would be negative, whereas the second fraction remains positive.

In general, a positive cross elasticity of demand indicates a substitute relationship between two goods, and a negative value indicates a complementary relation. Moreover, the numerical value of the cross elasticity of demand indicates the strength of the substitute or complementary relationship between two goods. A large, positive cross elasticity coefficient between two goods would indicate a strong substitute relationship, whereas a decidedly negative cross elasticity would mean a strong complementary relation.

In this analysis of the use of cross elasticity to determine complementary or substitute relationships between two goods, we have ignored the income effects of price changes, because, in most cases, the income effects of the price change will be relatively weak and will not upset our results. It will be worthwhile, however, to investigate these income effects of price changes and their possible relationship to cross elasticity. A higher price for Y results in an income effect which increases or decreases the demand for X, depending upon whether X is an inferior or a normal good. The income effect is in addition to the substitution or complementary effect of the price change. If the relationship between X and Y is a substitute one, then a rise in the price of Y relative to X will cause X to be substituted for Y. However, the income effect of the increase in Y's price will cause the quantity of X consumed to decrease, if X is a normal good, and to increase, if X is an inferior good. If the income effect is appreciable and in the opposite direction from the substitution effect, the cross elasticity coefficient might give an incorrect indication of complementarity or substitutability.

One of the uses of cross elasticity is in defining the theoretical boundaries of different industries. For instance, an industry might be defined to include all products with positive cross elasticities above some arbitrary level. All the included products could then be defined as close enough substitutes that all the firms producing them would be considered part of the same industry.

The Determinants of Price Elasticity of Demand

Now we may consider the factors that determine price elasticity of demand. Why, in the case of some market demand schedules, is a price change accompanied by a large response in quantity? And why are other market demand curves characterized by little response of quantity to price changes? We will find the answer and gain some insight into price–quantity sensitivity by analyzing the non-price determinants of market demand.

Often we find it useful to describe the market demand for some commodity as "very elastic," "elastic," or "inelastic." Strictly, that usage is incorrect, because any given market demand curve may exhibit a range of elasticity from zero to infinity, as our earlier discussion has indicated. For example, this is true for any hypothetical linear demand curve with positive vertical and horizontal axis intercepts. To describe a market demand curve as "elastic" must mean it is elastic for some range of price. Henceforth, we will mean by an elastic demand that price elasticity is elastic for prices close to the "normal" or "typical" price. For instance, if we say an individual's demand for compact cars is elastic, we mean it is elastic at current prices, say around $2,000, not at $10,000 at one extreme or $1 at the other, since these latter prices are not of much practical importance. With this in mind, it is instructive to investigate the determinants of the elasticity of demand.

One of the most important determinants of the price elasticity of an individual's demand for a good is the number of substitutes for the good. Suppose the price of X has risen. If there are a number of close substitutes for X, an individual will be inclined to substitute these goods for X, since the substitutes are now relatively cheaper. If the degree of substitutability is close, then only a small difference in utility exists between the goods, and the individual is partly compensated for substituting by the relatively lower price of the substituted goods. On the other hand, if the price of good X falls, this prompts an individual who previously was consuming substitutes for X to buy more of X, because the price of X is now relatively lower compared with the prices of the substitute goods. For any given change in the price of X, the change in quantity of X demanded will be greater the more substitutes there are. In general, the larger the number of substitutes for a good the greater will be a consumer's elasticity of demand for that good.

A second factor influencing the elasticity of demand for a good is the relative importance of the good in an individual's budget. A given consumer's demand for a product will tend to be less elastic the smaller the consumer's total expenditure on the item relative to his income. Consider an extreme case, where the consumer spends an insignificant percentage of his income on a good. Some examples, for most consumers, are commodities such as toothpicks, salt and pepper, pocket combs, and lifesavers. A price increase for such items will have little effect on the consumer's total expenditure for the item relative to his income, even if he purchases the same quantity as before. The individual might decide to disregard the prices of such goods, as well as any changes in their prices, and consume enough of each to maximize total utility. His demand for such goods would then be perfectly inelastic. On the other hand, if a consumer spends an appreciable proportion of his income on one good, he will be more sensitive to price changes, so his demand for that good will be more elastic. Generalizing, the smaller a consumer's total expenditure for a commodity, the lower will be his elasticity of demand for the good.

The elasticity of aggregate demand for a consumer good will depend upon the factors discussed above; however, qualifications must be made to allow for differences among consumers. For example, one individual with one pattern of tastes and preferences may recognize many substitutes for a given commodity, whereas another consumer with different tastes may recognize few if any substitutes for the same good. The demand of the first will be more elastic than that of the second. Moreover, demand elasticity may vary among individuals because one individual's expenditures on a good may represent a larger percentage of his income than those of another individual, because the latter's income may be larger.

We must allow for the effects on price elasticity of aggregating demand curves. Market demands exhibit greater elasticity the more buyers there are in the market. For example, suppose market demand for a good is the sum of individual demands D_1 and D_2 in Figure 4-10. So long as price is above P_1, the good will not be used in the first sector at all (Demand D_1). If the price falls below P_1, however, the good will begin to be used in the first sector, and price elasticity will increase abruptly. If we include a large number of potential demands, so that decreases in price entice a broader use of the product, elasticity will increase with the number of potential demands. Aluminum, though more a resource than a consumer good, nevertheless provides a good example. At an earlier period, when the technology for producing aluminum was very costly, the price of aluminum was very high and the metal found

FIGURE 4–10 The Elasticity of Market Demand Versus Individual Demand

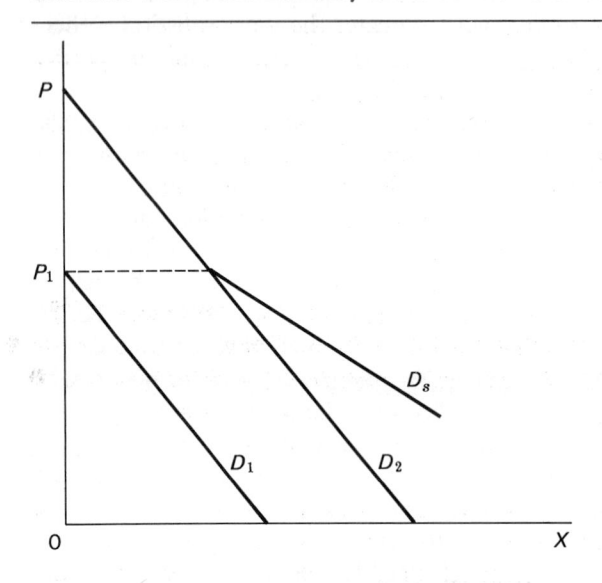

very few applications. Napoleon is said to have preferred a set of aluminum tablewear to platinum, and by the 1880's aluminum still cost as much as $5 per pound. However, with the discovery of the electrolytic process of manufacture, and with cheap electrical power, aluminum prices have fallen considerably relative to other metals. By 1900, the cost of manufacture had dropped to less than $.50 a pound. The fall in aluminum prices resulted in widespread use of the metal in manufacturing. Uses of aluminum formerly ruled out by high price are now commonplace. In conclusion, the price elasticity of demand for aluminum is high because of the existence of a large number of actual and potential aluminum users and uses.

Elasticity of Expectations

We have reserved for last our consideration of the portmanteau variable among the determinants of demand for X, U_d, a stand-in for the tastes and preferences of consumers and all other factors that might influence the quantity of X demanded in the market. One of the most important factors in this category is the expectations of consumers concerning the future behavior of the price of a good, and possibly expectations about other economic phenomena.

Again, we may use the basic elasticity concept to measure consumer's expectations about the future pattern of factors such as price, income, and interest rates. One measure which accomplishes this task is the *elasticity of expectations* (EOE) about price changes, the ratio of (1) the percentage change in the *expected* price of a good to (2) the percentage change in the *current* price.[4] For example, if the previous rate of increase in the price of a good has been 1 percent, and the experience of increasing prices leads to the expectation of a 5 percent rate of increase in the future, then the EOE is +5, and so would be decidedly elastic. If the 1 percent price rise leads to the expectation of a future 1 percent rise, then the EOE is +1, or unitary. If the EOE is zero and prices have been constant, then people would expect prices to be unchanged in the future. As a final example, if a 1 percent rise in price leads to an expectation of a 0.5 percent future rise, then EOE is +0.5, which is inelastic.

In addition to these three cases, in which previous price changes lead to expectations of further price changes in the same direction (elastic, unitary, and inelastic), there are three additional cases where previous price increases are associated with expectations of future price decreases. The coefficient of elasticity of expectation will be negative in the latter three cases. For example, if the experience of a 1 percent price increase leads to expectations of a future 1 percent price decrease, the elasticity of expectations is −1 (unitary). The reader will probably agree that where the elasticity of expectations is very negative (elastic), some factor or factors other than the immediate pattern of past price behavior must be influencing expectations. It could be individuals feel the price of a good has risen too far and must now decline. Consumers might feel the price of the good is at the top of a cycle and will therefore begin to turn down. Finally, we could just as well have been talking about past price decreases leading to an EOE that might be positive or negative, and elastic, inelastic, or of unitary elasticity. There is no particular reason for working out all of the cases, however.

When we have drawn the consumer's demand curve for a particular good or service, we have assumed that all non-price determinants of demand have been held constant, among them consumer's expectation of the future pattern of the price of the good demanded and all other goods as well. If an individual's expectations change, as well they might if he is suddenly provided with new market information, then his demand schedule will shift too. For example, suppose an individual's elasticity of expectations for good X changes from positive to negative. If prices have been rising, now the individual expects them to fall. That expectation would tend to decrease his demand for X, shifting the demand curve to the left, as he waits for the lower price to develop. In contrast, a shift from negatively elastic expectations to positively elastic expectations would tend to shift the curve to the right, because it would seem the product would be better bought immediately, in advance of the price increase. Very often the case which is of most interest is that of positive, unitary elasticity of expectations. In any event, we may generally conclude that any shift in market expectations will affect the market demand curve.

[4] J. R. Hicks, *Value and Capital*, 2nd ed. (Oxford, England: The Clarendon Press, 1946).

Price Expectations and General Inflation

Many economists believe that price expectations played an important role in the inflation which began in 1965 and continued into the 1970's. The basic argument runs something like this: Once an inflation gets under way, people anticipate that it will continue in the near term future. That anticipation means that the elasticity of expectation regarding the over-all level of prices becomes positive. Some people may hold very elastic expectations about future prices, whereas others may hold unitary elastic expectations. In any case, an individual or firm having a positive EOE, developed during a period of inflation, will adjust his behavior to maximize his utility if a consumer, or maximize long-run profits if a firm, based upon expected higher future prices. For example, a firm contemplating a capital investment would be more inclined to purchase now, if its EOE were positive, rather than wait, since it would expect to have to pay a higher price later. Consumers with positive EOE's might also increase their current expenditures, particularly for investment-type goods such as homes or autos, as well as for other consumer durables, rather than pay the expected higher prices in the future.[5] On the supply side, workers with positive EOE's will press harder for wage increases and, if they do not already have them, escalator clauses in labor contracts. But the effects of such actions by both buyers and sellers will tend to raise price in the immediate upcoming period. In other words, the very existence of positive EOE's will help cause inflation to develop. A prophecy of inflation can be self-fulfilling, if enough people believe it.

The argument suggests that an economy in which consumers and firms have positive and elastic price expectations may be somewhat unstable. In the short run, this observation may be true, and the latter part of the 1960's could be offered as evidence. If we examine a long period of time in the United States, however, we do not find any inherent tendency for the level of prices to accelerate or decelerate uncontrollably as a result of expectations alone. Thus, the level of prices may rise as a result of elastic expectations, but it is unlikely that the process will continue for long unless accompanied by other changes, such as increases in the money supply, to sustain the increase.

SUMMARY

In this chapter, we have indicated the rationale for consideration of separate industries in an economy. We have then described market or industry demand as an aggregation of individuals' demands, being careful to distinguish the market demand *curve* from the market demand *function*. The market demand function, using mathematical symbols, is $D_x = f(P_x, P_y, P_z, Y, U_d)$,

---

[5] It is easy to overestimate the strength of this inducement, however. See Gerald Sirkin, *Introduction to Macroeconomic Theory* (Homewood, Ill.: Richard D. Irwin, Inc., 1970), pp. 72–74.

which indicates the quantity demanded of a good (X) is a function of all of the forces affecting that quantity. The demand curve relates D_x to P_x when all of the other variables are held constant. On the other hand, an Engel curve relates D_x to Y when all other variables are held constant. An analysis of substitute and complementary relationships between good X and other goods is accomplished by examining the relation of D_x to P_y and P_z and the prices of any other goods that might be important. Finally, U_d is a stand-in variable for all other factors affecting D_x. We chose to look at one of these forces, that of consumers' expectations about the expected future behavior of price, and concluded that changes in people's expectations about the future price of X will affect the present consumption of X by shifting the market demand curve.

To measure the effects of changes in the determinants of market demand on the quantity demanded of X, we have introduced the concept of elasticity. The most important elasticity measure, the price elasticity of demand, indicates the response of quantity changes to price changes, with all other variables held constant. The income elasticity of market demand shows the response of the quantity consumed of X to changes in aggregate income, i.e., quantity–income elasticity along an Engel curve. Cross elasticities of demand measure the effects on the quantity of a good demanded to changes in the prices of related goods such as complementary goods and substitute goods. This measure will generally be positive for goods that are substitutes and negative for complementary goods. Finally, the elasticity of expectations, EOE, provides one measure of the strength of people's expectations about the future behavior of price.

PROBLEMS

1. The price elasticity of demand for automobiles has been estimated at about +1.5. What will be the effect of a $50 per unit price increase on the quantity of automobiles demanded by consumers? Assume a ten million unit equilibrium quantity initially and an initial price of $3,000 for all automobiles. Ignore all other factors such as differences in the quality of automobiles.
2. In the following graph, given demand curve D_x:
    (a) What is point elasticity at a price of $4?_____.
    (b) What is arc elasticity between prices $4 and $2? _____.
    (c) At what price is point elasticity of demand unitary?_____.
    (d) Suppose demand shifts to D_x'; what is point elasticity at price $4?

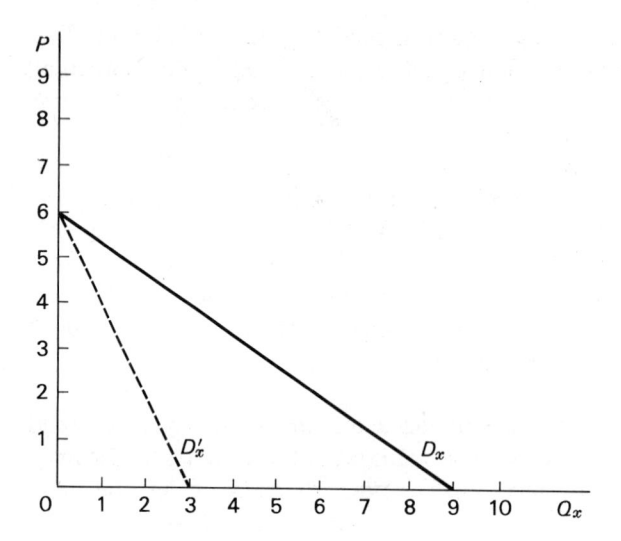

[Graph showing demand curves D_x and D'_x with price on vertical axis (0-9) and Q_x on horizontal axis (0-10). D_x goes from P=6 at Q=0 to Q=9 at P=0. D'_x is a steeper dashed line from P=6 at Q=0 to approximately Q=3.]

3. The Florida Citrus Commission reports that anticipated higher crop yields in the upcoming year will reduce the industry's revenues by 10 percent. What is the Commission's estimate of the price elasticity of demand for citrus products (elastic, unitary elastic, inelastic)?

4. D_1 and D_2 are the demand curves of the only two purchasers of good X.

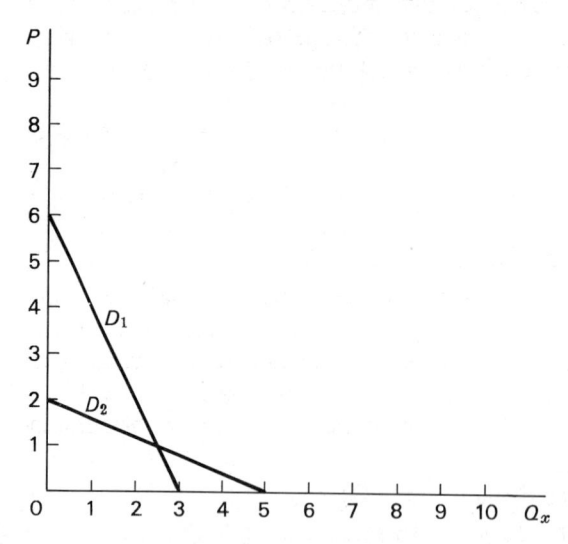

[Graph showing demand curves D_1 and D_2 with price on vertical axis (0-9) and Q_x on horizontal axis (0-10). D_1 goes from P=6 at Q=0 to Q=7 at P=0. D_2 goes from P=2 at Q=0 to Q=3 at P=0.]

(a) Sum the two separate demands to get market demand.
(b) Given market demand, what is the point elasticity at price $1?_____.
(c) What is the point elasticity at price $1 for D_1?_____.

5. Suppose the supply of X's is perfectly elastic at a price of $6 and the cross elasticity of demand between goods X and Y $[(E_{xy} = (\%\Delta Q_x)/(\%\Delta P_x)]$ is -3. If the original quantity of X consumed is 100 units, what will be the quantity consumed of X, if the price of Y increases from $3.00 to $4.50? (Illustrate by drawing the supply and demand schedules for both X and Y.)

6. Draw the Engel curve for good X if the income elasticity of demand for X is $+2$ for all levels of X consumed up to income level $500/week, and -2 for all income levels above $500/week. At what level of consumption of X does the good change from a normal to an inferior good?

7. If an individual's elasticity of expectations regarding the price of new housing changes from unitary elastic to $+5$, this would tend to (increase, decrease) his demand for new housing.

REFERENCES

BAILEY, MARTIN J., "The Marshallian Demand Curve," *Journal of Political Economy*, 62 (1954), 255–261.

LEIBENSTEIN, HARVEY, "Bandwagon, Snob, and Veblen Effects in the Theory of Consumers' Demand," *Quarterly Journal of Economics*, 64 (May 1950), 183–207.

MISHAN, EDWARD J., "Theories of Consumers' Behaviour: A Cynical View," in David R. Kamerschen, *Readings in Microeconomics*. New York: The World Publishing Company, 1967, 82–94.

MORRISON, H., "Supply and Demand on Broadway," Chapter 21 in P. A. Samuelson, R. L. Bishop, and J. R. Coleman, *Readings in Economics*, 3rd ed. New York: McGraw–Hill Book Company, Inc., 1958.

STIGLER, G. J., "The Limitations of Statistical Demand Curves," *Journal of the American Statistical Association*, XXXIV (September 1939), 469–481.

SUITS, DANIEL B., "The Demand for New Automobiles in the U.S., 1929–1956," *Review of Economics and Statistics*, 40 (August 1958), 273–280.

WOLD, HERMAN O. A., with JUREEN, LARS, *Demand Analysis*. New York: John Wiley and Sons, 1953.

WORKING E., "What Do Statistical Demand Curves Show?" in G. J. Stigler and K. E. Boulding (eds.), *Readings in Price Theory*. Chicago: Richard D. Irwin, Inc., 1952.

APPENDIX TO CHAPTER 4

The Pope and the Price of Fish

FREDERICK W. BELL*

In 1966, Pope Paul VI issued a decree which led to the termination of obligatory meatless Fridays for Catholics. Bell briefly examines the effects of this decree on the demand function for fish in the northeastern United States and on the commercial fishing industry.

For over one thousand years, the Catholic Church required its members to abstain from meat on Friday in the spirit of penance. This obligatory abstinence from meat has helped maintain the sagging U.S. commercial fishing industry. However, Pope Paul VI in February of 1966 issued an apostolic decree, "Poenitemini," relaxing the rules on fasting and abstinence during Lent. As part of the decree, the Pope delegated power to national conferences of local Bishops to decide whether to continue the rule of Friday abstinence. Having this authority, the Catholic Bishops of the United States terminated obligatory meatless Fridays, except during Lent. Starting in December 1966, Catholics were no longer bound to abstain from meat eating on non-Lent Fridays (i.e., approximately 46 Fridays during the year).

The actions of Pope Paul VI and the U.S. Bishops have come in the wake of government efforts to arrest the decline in commercial fishing through the 1964 Fishing Fleet Improvement Act. On a broader scale, the reaction of the world's 584 million Roman Catholics may seriously damage commercial fish-

From the *American Economic Review*, Vol. LVIII, No. 5, part I (December 1968). Reprinted by permission of the author and publisher. Copyrighted by the American Economic Association.

* This article was written while the author was on leave from the Federal Reserve Bank of Boston as associate professor of economics, Clark University. Presently, the author is chief of economic research, Bureau of Commercial Fisheries. He would like to thank Linda Kreuger, Ellen Temple, Penny Dyson, and Ted Baker for their assistance as well as Walter Sullivan, Neil Murphy, and Harlan Lampe for their comments on this article. Errors are the responsibility of the author.

ing in many countries. The purpose of this article is to assess the short-run economic impact of the Papal-Bishop decree.[1] For New England, the test area, it will be demonstrated that during the nine-month period following the P-B decree the demand curve for fish has shifted downward resulting in a 12.5 percent fall in landing prices.

I. THE DEMAND FUNCTION FOR FISH

To evaluate the impact of the P-B decree on fish prices, all other factors which affect prices must be held constant. The following log-linear demand function for the i'th species of fish was specified:

$$P = KQ^a\ Y^b\ S^c\ I^d\ C^e\ L^f\ Z^g\ (P-B)^h, \qquad (1)$$

where

P = Ex-vessel or landing price in New England for the i'th species (cents per pound),
Q = Quantity landed of the i'th species in New England (thousands of pounds),
Y = Aggregate personal income in 1957–59 dollars for the Northeastern United States (tenths of millions),[2]
S = Cold storage holdings of the i'th species at the beginning of the month in New England (thousands of pounds),
I = Imports of the i'th species into New England (thousands of pounds),
C = Consumer price index for meat and poultry; 1957–59 = 100,
L = Lenten demand: 1 for non-Lent months; 10 for Lenten months,[3]
Z = Weighted ex-vessel price for competing New England fish products landed (cents per pound),
$(P\text{-}B)$ = P-B decree: 1 for all months prior to the decree; 10 for all months in which decree is in effect.

A log-linear demand function was specified since a substantially better statistical fit was obtained through the use of a logarithmic as compared to a simple linear function and the unexplained residuals were more uniform over

---

[1] Since Pope Paul VI authorized the national Bishops to make the meatless Friday decree, we shall refer to the two decrees as the Papal-Bishop decree. The abbreviation P-B will be used throughout the remainder of this note.
[2] Northeast is defined as Maine, New Hampshire, Vermont, Massachusetts, Connecticut, Rhode Island, New York, Pennsylvania, and New Jersey. Most of the species landed in New England are marketed as fresh fish in the Northeast.
[3] When 1 and 10 are converted to common logarithms, the dummy variable becomes 0 and 1 in the log-linear equation.

the range of independent variables when expressed in percentages rather than absolute terms. Most of the variables included in the demand function are self-explanatory. Of special importance, the quantity landed is functionally related to the movement of fish populations and the weather. There is little attempt by fishermen to influence landing prices by deliberate variation in quantity landed. In the short run, the supply function is completely inelastic and shifts in this function should "trace-out" the demand curve. And, since we are using monthly observations, the period is approximately the short run. Therefore, no identification problem is present since quantity landed is exogenous. Cold storage holdings may have two different effects on price. The first is negative or stock adjustment of inventory effect. The second is positive since buyers may purchase when prices are falling (i.e., in the summer months) and sell (i.e., in the winter months) when prices are rising. This latter speculative behavior has been pointed out by Brennan. (P-B) should have a negative parameter if Catholics switch from fish to meat on Fridays. An estimate of "h" will allow us to compute the percentage shift in the demand curve after the November 1966 P-B decree.

II. STATISTICAL ANALYSIS AND RESULTS

The Northeast United States is an excellent area to analyze the impact of the P-B decree on the demand curve for fish. Large quantities of fresh fish are landed at many New England ports and are mainly distributed throughout the Northeast. In addition, the last Census of Religion revealed that 45.1 percent of the population in the Northeast were Catholics, more than double the percentage in any other U.S. region. Seven species of fish were selected for this study (see Table 1). There are two time periods under consideration: (1) a 10-year period (monthly observations) before the P-B decree, January 1957 to November 1966[4] and (2) the period after the decree, December 1966 to August 1967, but excluding February and March. These two months were excluded because Catholics are still obliged to abstain from meat on Lenten Fridays.

After logarithmic transformation, the parameters of Equation (1) were estimated using least-squares.[5] The parameters and t-values (in parentheses) are shown in Table 1. Quantity landed displayed a negative sign while income showed a positive sign in six out of seven species. The expansion in aggregate personal income has a positive impact on price due, primarily, to population

---
[4] The Lenten months for 1966 were excluded from the first period due to the possible influence of the Papal decree alone on these observations.

[5] Two other versions of equation (1) were estimated where the variables were first deflated by the consumer price index for all items and then this index was included in the equation as a separate variable. This procedure yielded approximately the same results as shown in Table 1. However the fact that meat, poultry, and fish prices are contained in the consumer price index for all items introduces an unnecessary bias. Hence, these versions were not used.

TABLE 1 Regression Results: A Test of the Papal-Bishop Decree Impact, Monthly Data, 1957–67 (Landing Price (P) is Dependent Variable)

Species	Constant	Q	Y	S	I	C	L	Z	(P-B)	N	R_2	D-W	Percent Change in Price Due to (P-B)
Sea Scallops	1.667 (1.540)	−.653 (−9.888)	.395 (1.874)	−.154 (−6.068)	.014 (.759)	.461 (1.700)	−.004 (−.217)	−.260 (−3.900)	−.082 (−3.019)	123	.696	.709	−17
Yellowtail Flounder	−5.678 (−4.766)	−.436 (−13.732)	.861 (3.090)	.182 (5.179)	−.054[a] (−1.097)	1.749[a] (5.417)	.089 (4.791)	.259 (4.511)	−.064 (−1.961)	123	.789	1.164	−14
Large Haddock	−.237 (−.135)	−.460 (−12.431)	.212 (.816)	−.019 (−.513)	−.001 (−.366)	.878 (3.554)	.010 (.721)	.388 (9.314)	−.108 (−4.650)	123	.853	.781	−21
Small Haddock (Scrod)	−1.748 (−1.517)	−.456 (−12.861)	−.152 (−.542)	.057 (1.845)	.042 (1.047)	2.231 (8.569)	.039 (2.412)	.202 (3.745)	−.009 (−.367)	123	.802	.660	−2
Cod	−2.552 (−2.896)	−.317 (−8.859)	.031 (.155)	.117 (4.232)	.028 (.714)	1.784 (7.081)	.031 (2.060)	.307 (6.477)	−.047 (−2.003)	123	.780	.978	−10
Ocean Perch	.383 (.509)	.004 (.182)	.003 (.018)	−.012 (−.605)	.063 (2.465)	−.076 (−.392)	.013 (1.250)	.176 (3.666)	−.045 (−2.630)	123	.309	.513	−10
Whiting	−9.909 (−5.047)	−.045 (−4.961)	1.442 (3.167)	−.058 (−2.189)	−.154 (−2.384)	2.127 (4.296)	.103 (3.665)	.558 (3.360)	−.104 (−2.205)	115	.682	1.352	−20

[a] Lagged one month. t values in parentheses.

increase. The per capita consumption of most species considered in this study has remained relatively constant over the 1957–67 period, indicating that fish is not an inferior good. Cold storage holdings seemed to conform to a stock adjustment hypothesis for sea scallops, large haddock, ocean perch, and whiting and to a speculative hypothesis for flounder, scrod, and cod. Imports show a mixture of signs: four positive and three negative.[6] Meat and poultry prices, Lenten demand, and the price of competing fish products have a positive impact on price in six out of seven cases. In general, the parameters seem to conform to a priori theory for all variables except imports.

The (P-B) decree dummy variable exhibited a negative sign for all seven species which is consistent with the hypothesis that the demand curve for fish shifted downward after the P-B decree. For the seven species combined, prices fell approximately 12.5 percent when weighted by landings. The decline in monthly prices ranged from approximately 21 percent for large haddock to 2 percent for scrod as shown in Table 1.

Unfortunately, little can be concluded about the statistical significance of the parameters of Equation (1) due to positive autocorrelation in the residuals as evidenced by the Durbin-Watson statistic. However, the estimates remain unbiased and consistent and also agree in direction of sign with a few surveys made of Catholic reaction to the P-B decree. Equation (1) was converted to first-differences in logarithms and the parameters estimated. This procedure eliminated the autocorrelation. However, first-differencing the (P-B) dummy variable yields only *one* observation which shifts the demand function rather than seven when levels are used (i.e., seven months of the P-B decree). Signs for the (P-B) remained negative for all seven species, but the standard errors were as large as the coefficients. Hence, first-differencing of dummy variables is not a satisfactory procedure even though it reduces autocorrelation.[7]

---

[6] There are two possible reasons for the poor showing of imports in explaining variation in domestic landing prices. First, there may be an identification problem. That is, higher imports will depress the price, but a higher price will attract more imports. This two-way flow may explain the half-and-half mixture of positive and negative regression signs. Second, fish imports are almost exclusively frozen while domestic landing prices refer to the fresh fish market. New England landed fish usually are marketed to fresh fish outlets such as restaurants and institutions. Hence, there are really two different fish products (fresh and frozen), each not highly price-sensitive to the other. The second explanation is probably the fundamental reason for the weak relation between domestic landing prices and foreign imports. Therefore, the parameters for quantity landed (fresh) and quantity imported (frozen) would markedly differ as indicated in Table 1.

[7] Under certain circumstances, it might be feasible to posit two regimens, with the first performing one way, and yielding one set of coefficients, before the decree, and another, presumably significantly different, thereafter. Unfortunately, the model cannot be applied to the period after the decree due to the lack of degrees of freedom (i.e., at the time of this study seven observations were available after the decree while the demand equation contains seven independent variables).

In light of these results, it would appear that the P-B decree had a negative influence on fish prices and therefore industry revenues. If losses in revenue persist, an attrition of both capital and labor from domestic commercial fishing may be produced since wages and the rate of return on capital are already at low levels. This may create economic problems for many small communities along the coastal United States.

Change and Innovation in the Technology of Consumption

KELVIN LANCASTER

Lancaster discusses a topic which may appear novel to the reader, and that is the technology of consumption. Economists often terminate their study of production and consumption at the point when purchasers purchase goods. But Lancaster points out that consumption itself is a process in which economic goods are the inputs and the characteristics of the goods enjoyed by consumers are the outputs. It should be possible, therefore, to analyze this input–output process using a variant of production theory.

We typically think of technology as applying to production rather than consumption, and my first task is to establish just what I mean by the technology of consumption.

I am drawing on ideas which have been set out in some detail in another paper of mine which is to be, but unfortunately has not yet been, published elsewhere.[1] This paper, "A New Approach to Consumer Theory," sets out a model of consumption and the consumer with certain features which provide the basis for the present explorations. I must necessarily start with a brief description of those features.

"A New Approach . . ." presents the following view of consumption. Goods, as such, are not the immediate objects of preference or utility or welfare, but have associated with them characteristics which are directly relevant to the consumer. The term "characteristics" was chosen for its normative neutrality; in my earliest draft of this idea I called them "satisfactions," but that has too many connotations. The consumer is assumed to have a preference ordering over the set of all possible characteristics vectors, and his aim is to attain his most desired bundle of characteristics subject to the constraints of the situation. The consumer's demand for goods arises from the fact that goods are required to obtain characteristics and is a derived demand.

From the *American Economic Review*, Vol. 56, No. 2 (May 1966). Reprinted by permission of the author and publisher. Copyrighted by the American Economic Association.

[1] In the *J.P.E.*, Apr., 1966.

An analogy to production theory is starting to appear. We are viewing goods as inputs into a process in which these characteristics are the outputs. The structure of consumption activities is, however, typically different from the structure of production activities. In the typical production activity we have joint inputs and a single output, while we shall regard the typical consumption activity as having a single input (a good) and joint outputs (a bundle of characteristics). Some consumption activities may require several goods, or even other inputs. For example, the activity driving a car requires the use of a consumer capital good, the using up of other goods (gas and oil), and the labor of the consumer to give the bundle of characteristics associated with the activity. If we were discussing the theory of consumer durables, we would pursue this example further, but, in the present context, we shall think of the typical consumption activity as using up a unit of some good and deriving the bundle of joint characteristics from it.

The jointness of the characteristics is really the core of the whole approach. If we eat an apple, we are enjoying a bundle of characteristics—flavor, texture, juiciness. Another apple may have the same flavor but associated with a different texture, or be more or less juicy. A single good may have more than one characteristic, and a single characteristic may be obtainable from more than one good. Goods which share a common characteristic may have their other characteristics qualitatively different, or they may give the same characteristics but in a quantitatively different combination. If the relationship between goods and characteristics was merely one-to-one in both directions, so that the only characteristic of an apple was appleness and the only source of appleness was an apple, then there would be no operational difference between the traditional approach to consumer theory and that being portrayed here.

It will be assumed that characteristics are, in principle, intrinsic and objective properties of consumption activities. Given arbitrary units, each consumption activity is defined by its inputs (most often assumed to be a unit of a single good) and by the vector of characteristics which forms its output. It will further be assumed that the activities are linearly homogeneous, so that doubling the goods input gives double the characteristics. Essentially psychological effects, such as the consumer's relative interest in different characteristics or effects similar to diminishing marginal utility, are assumed to make their appearance in the preference ordering of the characteristics vectors, not in the relationship between goods and characteristics.

The set of all possible consumption activities forms the consumption technology. In a highly developed economy, with many different goods and product variants, the technology will be complex; in a less developed economy, the technology will be simpler. In a country like the U.S.S.R. we may have a complex production technology combined with a relatively simpler consumption technology.

The consumption technology will relate goods on the one hand with characteristics on the other. In general, there is no reason why the number of characteristics and the number of goods should be related to each other (any more than the number of goods and the number of factors should be related in the production technology), and I shall make the working hypothesis that the number of goods in a complex consumption technology like that of the U.S. will probably exceed the number of operationally distinguishable characteristics. There may well be several combinations of goods which give rise to the same bundle of characteristics, and this gives rise to a very important distinction between the present and traditional approaches to consumer theory.

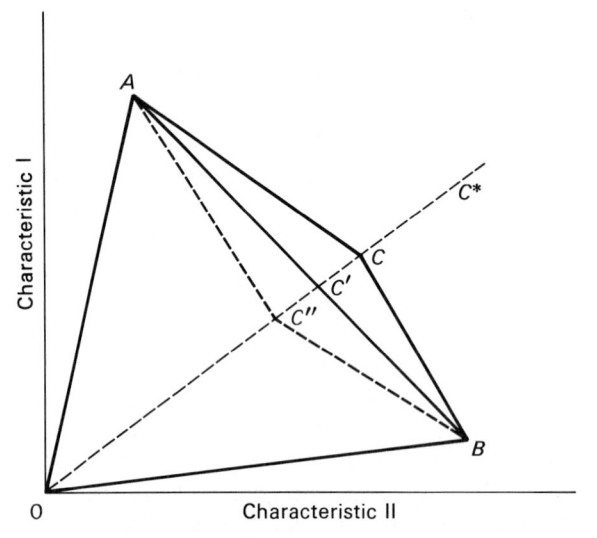

Consider a simple example of a consumer in a world of two characteristics and three goods. Each good gives rise to a vector of the two characteristics, and the consumption technology consists of the activities, consuming each of the goods separately, and consuming them in linear combination. If we impose a budget constraint on the goods, we can explore the characteristics vectors attainable by the consumer. The attached diagram shows the two-dimensional characteristics space and the points A, B represent the characteristics attainable if the whole budget is spent on goods A, B, respectively. By spending the whole budget on combinations of A and B, characteristics vectors represented by points along the line AB can be attained. Now consider the third good, C, which gives rise to the characteristics in proportions represented by the line OC^*. The price of C will determine how far out along OC^* the consumer can get by spending all his income on C. If this price is low enough, this point might be represented by C. All the attainable bundles of characteristics for the given price–income situation are given by the points A, B, C and their linear combinations, which are the points in and on the triangle ABC.

The consumer chooses his preferred characteristics bundle from the attainable set. Note that efficiency considerations arise—a radical departure from traditional theory—since, for any bundle of characteristics attainable by combinations of A and B, a larger bundle with the same proportions can be attained by C or by combinations of A and C or B and C. An efficient consumer will choose combinations on ACB, the efficiency frontier for characteristics. Just which point he chooses will depend entirely on his preferences. If consumers have well-distributed preferences and are efficient, we can expect to find that all three goods are sold, but that no single consumer consumes both A and B.

In this model, the consumer faces a double choice. He makes an efficiency choice in rejecting goods combinations which do not enable him to reach the efficiency frontier and a private choice in finding his preferred point on the frontier. If the markets are competitive so that all consumers face the same prices, and given the linearity of the consumption activities, the shape of the efficiency frontier is the same for all individuals. Income differences appear only as scalar enlargements or reductions of the typical frontier. Thus efficient choice is objective and common to all individuals in a given price situation.

The efficiency frontier changes with relative prices, however. In the example given, if the price of C should rise so that the characteristics vector attainable by spending the whole income on that good moved to C'', AB would now be the efficiency frontier. No combination using C would be efficient and C would no longer have any buyers at that price. Price changes may give rise to a substitution effect between goods rising wholly from efficiency effects and unrelated to any convexity of the preference structure. This efficiency substitution effect has been discussed in detail in "A New Approach. . . ."

The general nature of the consumption technology has now been established, and the remainder of the paper will be devoted to answering the question, can we have change, innovation, and technical progress in consumption technology, just as we have in production?

In the case of production technology, considered in activity analysis form, changes in that technology can be regarded in one or more of the following ways: (1) "Magic wand" effects, in which a particular input combination that gave a certain output in 1965 gives a greater output in 1966. (2) Shifts from actual capabilities, or the upgrading in efficiency of those firms whose productivity is below the known technological potential. Strictly speaking, this is not a change in technology but it will manifest itself in aggregate data in a similar way. (3) An identified technical change arising from the introduction of specified new activities. (4) A change in the nature of inputs such as the introduction of new capital goods, new labor or management skills.

In analyzing production technology, output can be measured with relative ease, as can the input of broadly defined factors. This places much emphasis on magic wand effects, such as unexplained residuals. On the other hand, information concerning the detailed nature of inputs is more difficult to discover, so that the effects of changes in the nature of inputs are less emphasized. In consumption technology the situation is reversed; we have information concerning the changes in the goods which form the inputs, but little information concerning the outputs. We have no interest, therefore, in magic wand effects, but the other three effects can be important.

Since our model of consumer behavior provides scope for efficient choice and hence for the possibility that not all consumers are efficient, there is scope for technical progress in the special sense of increased consumption efficiency, even with no change in the nature of goods or consumption activities.

In consumption, as in production, the prime reasons for inefficient use of the existing technology are ignorance and lack of managerial skill. The consumer may not be aware that a certain good possesses certain characteristics or that certain goods may be used in a particular combination to give a specified bundle of characteristics. Producers or sellers may use advertising to ensure that no characteristics of their product regarded as particularly desirable should go unnoticed by consumers. They will go to less pains to ensure that consumers are aware of some other characteristics of their product.

Organizations such as the Consumers Union exist to provide more objective information on the characteristics of goods than is easily available elsewhere. Some consumers are willing to pay for information which assists in attaining efficient points on their characteristics possibility sets and, on the model presented here, are rational to do so. However, since efficient choices are the same for all consumers, there is a clear argument in favor of public information on these matters and in favor of legal requirements, such as composition and contents labeling, designed to increase knowledge of the available consumption technology.

We can use our model to demolish the old argument, favored by sellers of established products, that, since consumers "reveal" their preference for the product already, labeling laws are unnecessary. Traditional theory may seem to lend some weight to this argument, but the present theory does not, since actual choice by consumers can no longer be regarded as revealing their preferences for characteristics—they may merely be making an inefficient choice.

The consumption technology, in a society like that of the United States, is very complex. Efficient consumption, even in the presence of adequate information concerning the technology, involves some managerial skills. As any social worker will testify, many households are noticeably deficient in this skill. Conventional consumer theory leads to a presumption that the family which spends its income on an eccentric collection of goods is simply revealing its preferences for that collection. Of course, this might be true, but it may also be that the family is consuming inefficiently. If the consumer's desired characteristics collection could be ascertained even in a very general way, some type of advising might lead to more efficient consumption.

A crucial difference between the production and consumption sectors is that the market mechanism does not tend to guarantee efficiency in consumption in the same way it does in production. In a society at subsistence level, the inefficient consumer may not survive. In a more affluent society he will survive, but will remain at a lower welfare level than that potentially available to him. Again, this leads to the presumption that public consumer education would be socially valuable.

A relatively static technology, in consumption as in production, will, if coupled with stable relative prices, probably lead to a situation in which the efficient activities become generally known and traditional. Traditional consumption patterns will be efficient only within a relatively unchanging choice situation and only optimal for consumers whose preferences on characteristics approximate the society mode. Tradition will be less useful when the technology is changing rapidly, when relative prices are changing considerably, or when the consumer's preferences diverge from the mode. Furthermore, the typical consumer will inherit his traditions from his social background, and they may not serve him at a radically different income level. We are all aware that the *nouveau riche* may consume differently from persons already established in the higher income group. This analysis suggests that it is at least possible that the desired characteristics of the new and old rich need not be different: the newcomers may be less efficient in achieving their aims. The same considerations may work in reverse; so that a consumer suddenly thrust from a wage income to welfare payments may take some time to discover efficient methods at the new income level, although at this level efficiency may be crucial.

One suspects that there may be great scope for increasing consumption efficiency in the kind of changing situations outlined above. These include the transition from peasant to market economies and from rural to urban societies in developing countries and, within countries, among social groups migrating from one region to another or from one income level to another.

Because the market system does not place pressure on consumers to be efficient, this aspect of technical progress has been stressed more than it might be in discussing production. But innovation in the true sense occurs in the consumption technology, and this takes place primarily through the introduction of new goods or new variants and product differentiation.

Traditional consumer theory is at its most unenlightening when confronted by the problem of new goods. Introduction of a new good requires either that the preference function defined on n goods is thrown away, and with it all the knowledge of behavior based on it, and replaced by a brand new function defined on $n + 1$ goods, or the fiction that the consumer has a potential preference function for all goods present and future and that a new good can be treated as the fall in that good's price from infinity to its market level. Neither approach gets us very far.

In the present model, it may be that the good is so revolutionary that its characteristics are not possessed by any existing goods. We are no better off, in this case, than in the traditional one. But most new goods can be regarded as simply giving rise to existing characteristics in new proportions, and we have available an operationally meaningful way of approaching the problem. A new good of this kind—and this probably covers nearly all new goods and certainly all product variants—adds a new activity to the technology and is, in the proper sense of the word, an innovation in that technology. Whether the innovation is efficient depends entirely on the price of the new product. If the price is too high, its characteristics correspond to a point within the efficiency frontier and it will not be purchased by efficient consumers, except perhaps initial experimentation to discover whether it is efficient or not. If the price is sufficiently low, however, the new good will push part of the efficiency frontier forward and will enter the efficient technology. Unless that particular part of the frontier happens to contain no consumer's preferred characteristic collection, the new good will sell. Furthermore, the introduction of a successful new good will result in an increase in welfare, if other prices are unchanged.

It may not always be clear whether we should classify a new good as an innovation on the production or the consumption side, but it certainly seems most useful to regard a variant of an existing product, involving no fundamental change in the technical nature of the production process, as an innovation in consumption technology. In terms of our model of consumption, the difference between a new product and a product variant is only the degree to which the characteristics mix of the new product differs from that of existing products. We have, in this model, a satisfactory technique for analyzing product differentiation.

Consider a simple model with two characteristics, derivable in different proportions from two goods. We can use the same diagram as before and suppose A, B to represent the two goods. If the goods are divisible and can be used in combination, the attainable characteristics collections for a consumer, given the budget constraint, correspond to the line AB. The introduction of a third good, C, whose characteristics vector lies between those of A and B, can be regarded as a product variant, and this good will sell if its price is low enough to bring the characteristics vector to point C' or beyond in the diagram. Given this product variant, further variants lying between A and C, and C and B would, if suitably priced, expand the efficiency frontier and therefore be sold. If the relationships between the technical properties of the product variants and their relative prices is such as to give a convex frontier with every variant represented by a corner of the frontier, then all variants will be in demand, provided consumers' preferences are well distributed.

If we consider the situation from the production end and look through the consumption technology, we see that a producer is ultimately selling characteristics collections rather than goods. The degree of product differentiation will depend on the possibilities, at the production end, of producing variants with characteristics, and at prices, that give a convex frontier.

A producer with some monopoly power (and we might note that the theory of product differentiation presented here does not require imperfect competition as a prerequisite) will seek the profit maximizing price and differentiation policy. A theory of imperfectly competitive behavior can be built up by pursuing the above analysis, but it is not proposed to do this here.

If products cannot be utilized in combination, the analysis of product differentiation is somewhat different. Consider a highly simplified model of automobiles as consumption activities, expressed in terms of two characteristics, transportation per dollar of gas and comfort. Let two variants, Cadillacs and Volkswagens, be represented by A and B in the diagram. Now one cannot obtain a combination of these characteristics by taking half a Cadillac and half a Volkswagen, so that, although the points A and B are on the frontier, points on AB are not. Then a variant priced to give point C'' might be preferred by some consumers to either A or B, and the convexity of the price–characteristics relationship is not a necessary condition for marketability in this case.

New goods and differentiated products may not simply add to the spectrum of consumption activities; they may replace previous goods. This replacement will occur when the characteristics and price properties of the new product push the frontier forward in such a way that some existing good is no longer part of the efficient set. This will, of course, happen if the new good, for the same outlay, gives more of all characteristics in approximately the same proportions as the old. Such a change seems to correspond to what is often meant by an "overall improvement in quality." In other cases a quality improvement may correspond rather to an increase in some characteristics, with the others unchanged.

Although the introduction of a new product or a new variant can be expected to increase welfare in the simple Paretian sense if the new product is actually purchased and if the existing product is still available at the old price, this may not be the case if the seller takes the old product off the market as he puts the new one on. If the new product, however much of some characteristics it may offer per dollar of outlay, offers less of some other characteristic than the old, then some consumer may be deprived of part of the efficient technology relevant to his particular tastes.

The distinction between the technology of production and that of consumption is a great convenience in analysis but is not based on an absolute criterion of any kind. The ultimate constraints on the system are resources; the ultimate products are characteristics. Some resources may be used to first produce goods which are all intermediate goods in the final analysis, and these goods may then be used in the consumption technology to produce characteristics. But some resources may directly enter the consumption technology without the production of goods as intermediates. As the technologies of both production and consumption change, activities may move back and forth between the consumption and production sectors. This is particularly true of the service and distribution phases of production.

Ultimately the supply of resources, particularly labor, is determined by characteristics. A particular job will have associated with it several characteristics: some will be, in relation to characteristics derived from goods, of a negative kind, but some may well be of a positive kind. The traditional idea of "nonmonetary advantages" has been an attempt to face this obvious fact. We can expand the idea of the consumption technology to include the activities associated with the consumer's sale of labor or other resources. Since labor as an activity may have some characteristics associated with it that are shared by goods, the particular work a consumer performs may partly determine his choice of goods. A taxi driver may spend less of his budget on taking weekend drives than the social norm; yet traditional theory would find no connection between his consumption and his occupation.

New occupations and even new work conditions can be considered as changes in consumption technology. They may also lead to changes in production technology, but this is not necessarily the case.

It would be possible to follow through the kind of analysis we have been making here at very much greater length than is available, but I think the point has been made. There is a technology of consumption. It is the subject of continual change and innovation, just as is the production technology. This change does lead to increased welfare, but the direction from which change comes, the incentives for change, and the analysis and measurement of change differ considerably between production and consumption.

PART III. A THEORY OF PRODUCER BEHAVIOR

5

THE THEORY OF PRODUCTION: MARGINAL PRODUCTIVITY ANALYSIS

Output and price in a competitive industry are determined by the interaction of demand and supply in the industry. The preceding two chapters have presented one-half of the theory of price determination—the theory of market demand. In this chapter and the following one, we present two versions of the theory of production, the basis for the second half of the theory of price determination—the theory of supply. To see why production theory is fundamental, we outline below the steps involved in the development of supply theory:

1. We first determine the firm's input requirements for efficient production at various levels of output.
2. Production information is then used to derive the firm's cost functions, that is, the firm's cost of producing different output levels.
3. Given the firm's cost data and objectives, we can complete the theory of firm supply.
4. Finally, market supply is determined by aggregating the supply functions of all firms in a given industry.

The two approaches to production theory which we will consider are (1) the marginal productivity approach, in this chapter, and (2) the isoquant–isocost approach, presented in Chapter 6. The two approaches are complementary and are, in effect, two versions of one general theory. Both lead to the same basic conclusions about production and costs. The reason for considering both theories is that each approach has its own special uses and applications. For example, marginal productivity theory is useful in analyzing short-run decision making by the firm, while isoquant–isocost analysis is useful for analyzing long-run firm production adjustments. In addition, isoquant–

isocost analysis serves as the basis for linear programming, a highly useful, practical decision-making device described in Chapter 6. The differences between the analytical techniques of marginal productivity theory and isoquant–isocost analysis parallel the differences between marginal utility theory and indifference curves. In fact, the student will soon see that a marginal product curve looks much like a marginal utility curve, and isoquant and isocost curves (also developed in Chapter 6) look like a consumer's indifference curve and budget line, respectively.

THE THEORY OF PRODUCTION

Firms, Plants, and Industries

The suppliers of goods and services are called *firms*. All firms, whether small proprietorships or giant industrial corporations, share a common characteristic: they are owned and controlled as a unit. A plant, in contrast, is a capital asset used by a firm in production, and a single firm may own one plant or many. To develop a theory of supply, we focus our analysis on the firm, because firms make the basic decisions that determine industry output levels, costs, and profits; firms are the principal decision-making units on the supply side of the market, just as consumers are on the demand side. Of course, the market itself makes no decisions at all but generates equilibrium values of economic variables through the interaction of firms and consumers.

An *industry* is composed of all firms (one or more) producing the same, or similar, products or services. We have noted problems which arise in defining industry boundaries when two or more firms produce products which are similar, though not identical. For example, some industries, such as the automobile industry, are relatively easy to define (but even here we might need to distinguish the luxury car industry from the economy car industry). Others, however, such as the construction industry, present special problems in defining boundaries; does the construction industry include both residential and industrial construction? To avoid problems of industry definition, we will assume that industry boundaries can be clearly established.

For simplicity, it is convenient to assume that each firm operates one plant and produces one product. Although in reality many firms operate several plants and produce diversified product lines, the simplifying assumption of single-plant, single-product firms is a good starting place, because it greatly facilitates exposition of the theory of production.

Firms As Input–Output Devices

Just as the consumer's goal is to maximize utility, firms seek to earn profits, to grow, or, in some cases, merely to survive. Whatever their goals, to be successful, firms must acquire the necessary resources, or inputs, such as labor, machinery, and raw materials to produce products and services, or outputs, which consumers desire. Firms are, therefore, input–output devices, and the process of converting inputs into salable outputs is called production. We must investigate this input–output relationship at some length to illustrate the basic principles of production, for these principles are the foundation upon which the theory of firm supply is built. One warning: although we tend to think of production in terms of manufacturing hard goods, production encompasses the output of firms such as retailers, realtors, wholesalers, accountants, doctors, and the like. In other words, firms produce services as well as goods.

The Production Function

The *production function* expresses the physical relationship between various quantities of resource inputs used by the firm and the resulting levels of output. As generally interpreted, the production function does not state *all* possible input–output relationships, only the most efficient ones, those relationships which produce the maximum possible output from each combination of inputs (or, alternatively, the minimum inputs for each level of output; although this latter definition is subject to certain difficulties, as we shall note later).[1] A general statement of this input–output relationship, using mathematical notation, is:

$$X = f(a, b, c),$$

where X is the number of physical units of output produced, and a, b, and c represent the respective quantities of three resources needed to produce X. A given maximum level of output, say 10 units of X, may result when 2 units of a, 1 unit of b, and 3 units of c are employed. Likewise, 1 unit of a, 1 unit of b, and 4 units of c may be just sufficient to produce 10 units of X. Moreover, the level of output may be increased, to say 15 units of X, if more resources are employed. The production function is a generalized expression which summarizes all of these efficient input–output relationships.

Suppose technique number 1 employs 2 a's, 3 b's, and 4 c's to produce a maximum of 12 X's, while technique number 2 uses 3 a's, 3 b's, and 4 c's to produce a maximum of 12 X's. Technique 2 is apparently inferior to 1, since it requires more resources to produce the same output. We will describe technique 2 as *technically inefficient* relative to 1. The production function indicates the maximum output associated with different input combinations and is therefore concerned with technically efficient combinations only, since we follow the assumption that management always uses the best production techniques available. Inefficient combinations might, however, be of importance in special circumstances which prevent management from using the best technique.

---

[1] A function relating *all* possible combinations and all possible resulting outputs could be constructed. Such a function is known as a *resource transformation function*.

The Short-Run Production Function, with Capital Indivisible and Adaptable

The Short Run for an Industry. Many of the firm's decisions about output levels must be made for a period of time so short that one or more of the inputs to production must be treated as fixed in quantity. For example, inputs of new plant facilities or heavy machinery and equipment may be fixed in the short run and added to the production process only after allowing sufficient time for planning, letting contracts, installation, and adjustments. If a time period is so short that one or more inputs cannot be increased or decreased by a firm, it is designated a *short-run period*.[2] The short run is not a certain time period, such as six months or two years, which applies to all industries, but varies from industry to industry. For some industries, such as service industries and light manufacturing, the short run may be quite short, while for other industries, such as steel or electrical power production, the short run is much longer.

The Short-Run Production Function Defined. The relationship between maximum output levels possible with given input quantities, when one or more resources is fixed in amount, is expressed by the *short-run production function*. Assuming for simplicity that only resources a and b are necessary to produce X, then the short-run production function can be stated symbolically as:

$$X = f(a, \bar{b}),$$

where X is units of output, and a and b are inputs. The bar over b indicates that its quantity is fixed, while the quantity of a is variable. The short-run production function shows how output changes as different quantities of a are employed along with the fixed amount of b. Realistically, there may be more than one fixed and more than one variable resource. But even when there are many resources involved, if at least one of them is fixed in amount, the principles of short-run production are applicable. Our two-input model is an oversimplification but, nevertheless, illustrates the basic principles of short-run production. Therefore, we employ the model throughout the remainder of this chapter.

A Numerical Illustration. To illustrate the basic principles of production, we have developed a numerical example of a short-run production function. Table 5–1 shows the various quantities of output, X, which can be produced with different amounts of labor, a, assuming that capital, b, is fixed in quantity. The data in the table are derived from a purely hypothetical production function for a firm. Following our initial assumption of a two-input production model, labor and capital (labeled a and b, respectively, in the table), are the only resources needed to produce X.

---

[2] A time period so short that no inputs can be varied is called "the very short run."

We are making two additional assumptions about the inputs *a* and *b*. The first is that capital is *indivisible* but *adaptable* to units of *a*. By indivisible, we mean that we cannot divide up the fixed quantity of *b* into a large number of units and employ successive amounts of *a* with successive "batches" of capital. By *adaptable*, on the other hand, we mean that the fixed amount of *b* will adapt to successive units of *a*; *a* and *b* do not have to be employed in fixed proportions. Adaptable capital is like a plant facility with a continuous production line, and unadaptable capital is like a shovel that can only be used by one worker, or like a plant with many identical machines, each combining with a unit of labor in fixed proportions to produce the finished output. We will consider the case of unadaptable capital later in the chapter.

The second assumption, which we will retain throughout, is that the variable input *a* is homogeneous. Each unit of *a* is indistinguishable (of equal productivity) from every other unit of *a*.

In our numerical example shown in Table 5–1, *total product* (*TP*), labeled

TABLE 5–1

(1) Capital	(2) Labor	(3) Total Product	(4) Average Product	(5) Marginal Product
b	a	X	AP	MP
1	0	0		
				1
1	1	1	1	
				2
1	2	3	1.5	
				3
1	3	6	2.0	
				3
1	4	9	2.25	
				2
1	5	11	2.20	
				1
1	6	12	2.00	
				0
1	7	12	1.71	
				−1
1	8	11	1.38	

X in column 3, increases from zero to a maximum of 12 per unit of time, as more and more labor is added to the fixed amount of capital. To reveal more concerning the productivity of the variable resource, we will require more information than that provided by total product alone. Two of the most useful measures are average product and marginal product.

164 A Theory of Producer Behavior

Average product (AP) is defined as total product divided by the number of units of the variable factor. AP is computed by dividing column 3 by column 2 and is presented in column 4. In general:

$$AP = \frac{TP}{a} \quad \text{or} \quad \frac{X}{a}.$$

AP is output per unit of the variable factor. For example, in Table 5–1, where we assume capital inputs are fixed and labor variable, the average product of labor, AP, is 2 when 3 units of *a* are employed and 1.38 when 8 units of *a* are employed.

Marginal product (MP) is defined as the change in total product occasioned by the employment of one additional unit of *a*. In general, MP is the ratio of the change in $TP(\Delta TP)$ to the change in inputs of resource *a* (Δa) which caused the output change. In symbols:

$$MP = \frac{\Delta TP}{\Delta a}.$$

The values for marginal product are presented midway between the quantity value in column 5 of Table 5–1. For example, the third unit of *a* employed causes output to increase from 3 to 6, so $\Delta TP = 3$. Since $a = 3 - 2 = 1$, MP is equal to 3/1 or 3; the marginal product of the third unit of *a* is 3. To give another example, the marginal product of the fifth unit of *a* is 2, since the fifth unit of *a* employed causes the output of X to increase from 9 to 11. Notice that marginal product is different for different values of *a*.

A Graphical Illustration. A graphical presentation of the short-run production function is often easier to comprehend than data such as that shown in Table 5–1. Figure 5–1 is a graphical model of the input–output relationships shown in Table 5–1. The data in columns 3, 4, and 5 in Table 5–1, plotted on the vertical axes, against the data in column 2, on the horizontal axes, give the total, average, and marginal product curves in Figure 5–1. The relationships among the three product curves are fairly well illustrated by the data in Table 5–1 or in Figure 5–1. However, arithmetic examples share one shortcoming: Because they are measured in discrete, one-unit increments, they do not give results which precisely agree with the pure theory that assumes that inputs and outputs can be varied in very (infinitely) small increments.

Figure 5–2 is a generalized statement of the relationships among the typical total, average, and marginal product curves. It is based on the assumption that the variable input, *a*, and output, X, are continuously variable, that *a* and X can take on fractional values so that the functions can be drawn as smooth, unbroken curves.[3] In both panels of Figure 5–2, the horizontal axis shows different quantities of variable resource *a* (labor) employed per unit of time. However, the vertical axis in panel (a) is designed to show total output of X,

---

[3] More precisely, *a* and X can be any real number.

FIGURE 5–1 Short-Run Total, Marginal, and Average Product Curves Derived from Table 5–1

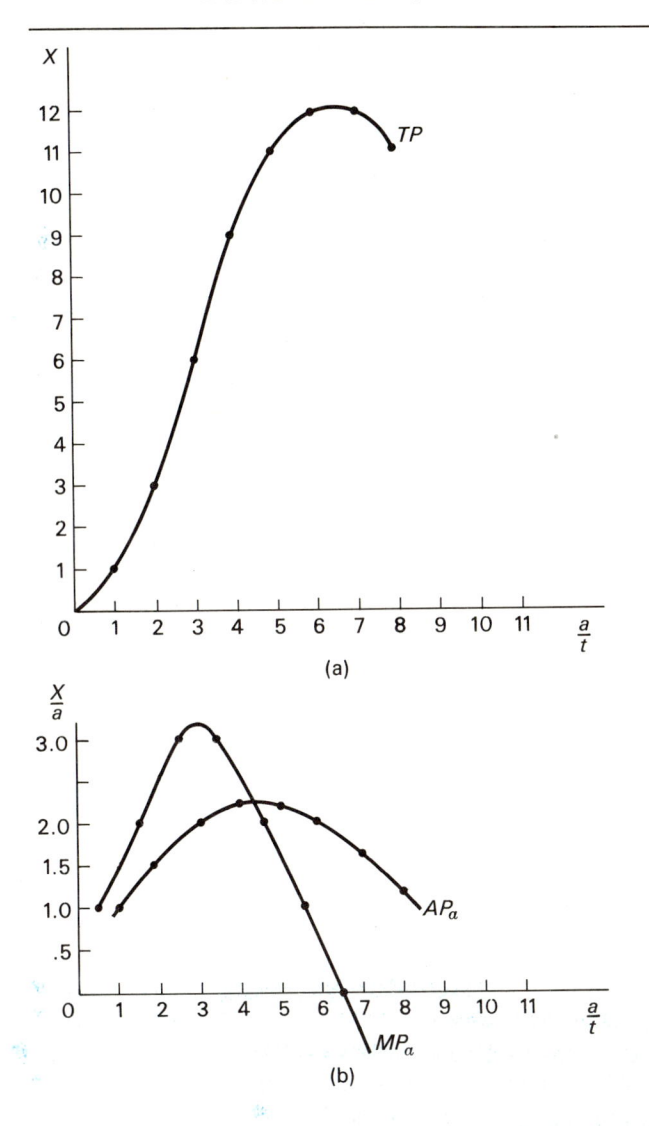

and the TP curve indicates total output at different values of a, whereas in panel (b), the vertical axis is designed to measure AP and MP, with the curves relating AP and MP to different values of a. We could have shown all three production curves on one graph, but it is helpful to use a different scale to measure AP and MP to show their interrelationship more clearly. (Also, TP is stated in terms of X, and AP and MP in terms of X per unit of a.)

FIGURE 5–2 Short-Run Production Curves Illustrating the Three Stages of Production

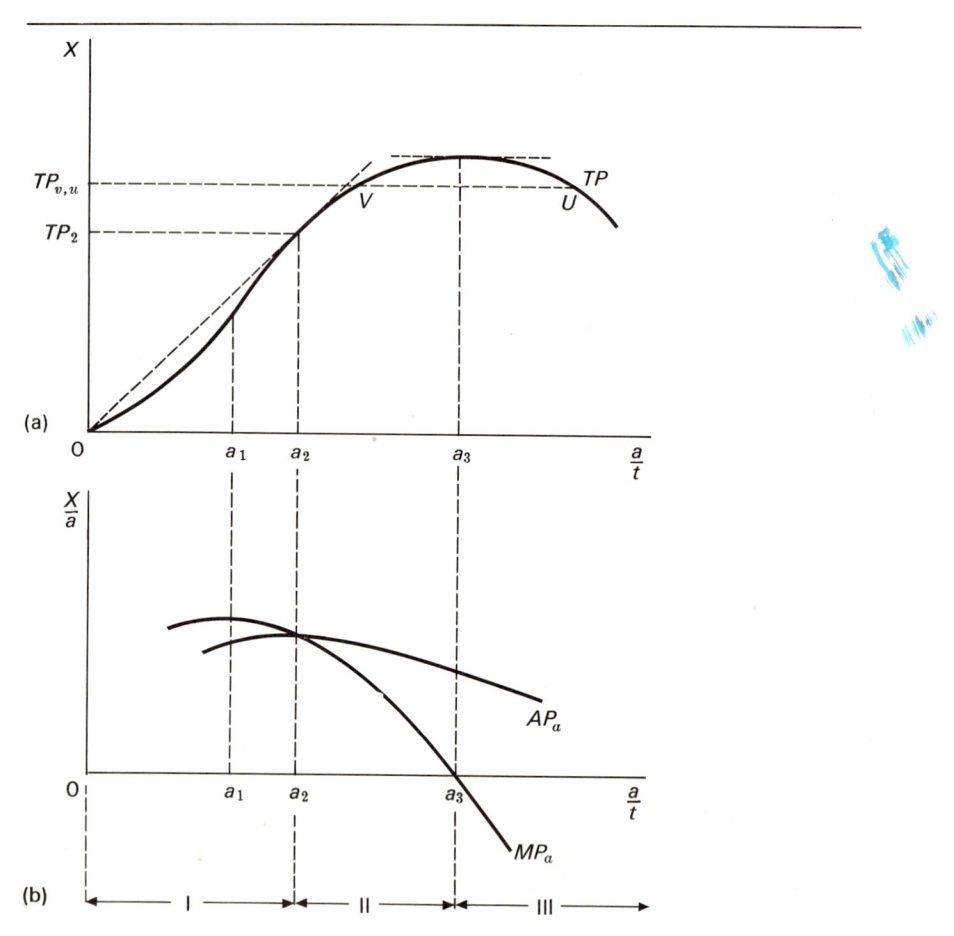

The Law of Diminishing Returns. The law of diminishing returns, applicable to all short-run production processes, states that as successive amounts of a resource are added to a production process per unit of time, with at least one of the resources held fixed in amount, total output will increase, but beyond some point, the increases will become smaller and smaller.

Referring to Figure 5–2, the law of diminishing returns requires that the marginal product of input a (MP_a) must eventually decline as more and more a is employed with the fixed amount of b. MP_a reaches a peak just as a_1 units of a are employed. This is the point of diminishing returns. Beyond a_1, as additional units of a are added to the production process, output increases, but at a decreasing rate, which means MP_a is decreasing. Consequently, the rate of change in output, which is measured by the slope of TP, increases for values of a up to a_1 and then decreases. When employment of a increases to a_3, TP becomes horizontal, so the slope of TP is zero. Since the slope of a line is its rate of change, MP simply measures the slope of TP. Referring to Table 5–1, diminishing returns set in just as the fifth unit of a is employed, since MP_a drops (for the first time) from 3 to 2.

As the first few units of a are employed, it is possible that MP_a will initially increase, as shown in Figure 5–2 for values less than a_1. To illustrate increasing returns, suppose we add successive units of labor to a fixed plant facility with a continuous production line. The first worker employed will spend most of his time moving from one work station to another. It is likely, therefore, that the MP of the initial worker in a plant with a continuous production line will be very low and possibly zero. However, as a second and third worker are added, the separate tasks can be divided up between them more effectively, cutting down on time lost moving around and enabling each worker to specialize in a particular activity. As a consequence, TP increases at a faster rate when the second and third workers are hired. In other words, MP_a increases. The initial low value for the marginal product of labor is basically due to the indivisibility of resources. The fixed plant and equipment of an assembly line cannot be divided up into small units, each unit manned by successive units of a. Neither can the single worker be divided up simultaneously among all stations on the assembly line. Only a full complement of workers will allow each work station to be manned.

Marginal product cannot continue increasing forever, however. As more and more labor is added to the production process, the law of diminishing returns must eventually take hold, and MP will begin to decrease. Once a full complement of workers is employed and all the principal work stations are occupied, additional workers must be assigned less productive tasks such as cleaning up and running errands. As a consequence, the employment of these workers adds less to total output than laborers hired earlier. Marginal product declines.

Furthermore, MP may eventually fall to zero and even below. As more and more workers are employed, marginal workers begin to interfere with production because of overcrowding. Their contribution to output is perverse. Total output, TP, will then decline, and marginal product will, as a consequence, become negative.[4] In Figure 5–2, total output begins to decline after a_3 units of a are added to the production process. Simultaneously, MP_a cuts the horizontal axis, as its value changes from positive to negative.

---

[4] We may assume that, realistically, production will not be allowed to fall absolutely, simply because management is effective and tells redundant workers to keep out of the way. However, that is to assume that the excessive workers hired are not actually employed in production.

The Stages of Production

To help reveal technically efficient and inefficient combinations of resources a and b, the production process is divided into three stages. Remember that when we speak of different combinations of a and b, only the number of units of a vary; the quantity of resource b is fixed.

> Stage I includes all combinations of a and b for which AP is rising, and MP is greater than AP. This means values of a from zero to a_2 in Figure 5-2.
> Stage II includes all combinations of a and b for which AP is declining but MP is still positive, that is, between a_2 and a_3 units of a.
> Stage III includes the combinations of a and b for which the marginal product of the variable factor is negative, that is, more than a_3 units of a applied to the fixed amount of b.

Stage III combinations are inefficient because the input of a is so great relative to the fixed amount of b that the marginal product of a is negative. Even if a were free,[5] no more than a_3 units should be used with the fixed quantity of b, because total output would actually decline as a result. Consider the combination of a and b at point U in Figure 5-2. The output which results, TP_3, could be produced with the resource combination at point V, which requires fewer units of a. The combination U in Stage III is thus technically inferior to combination V. Therefore, the firm would never rationally operate in Stage III if a is a variable input.

Stage I includes combinations of a and b which are not technically inefficient in the short-run period assumed, but which would be considered technically inefficient if resource b were variable rather than fixed. Consider those combinations of a and the fixed quantity of b in Stage I. Because the number of units of a is small relative to b, resource b cannot be employed efficiently. The quantity of the fixed resource b is excessive relative to a (just the reverse of Stage III). Of course, inputs of b are fixed in the short run. But the ratio of b to a is a relatively large number in Stage I, because the quantity of a used is small. The ratio of b to a is so great in Stage I that if b could be increased (which is not possible in the short run since b is fixed) total output would decline. Consequently, as we increase the ratio of a to b in Stage I, by increasing the quantity of a, the AP of a increases. The increase in AP_a is caused by the excessive ratio of b to a in Stage I.[6]

---

[5] E.g., the air which must be mixed with gasoline for internal combustion engines is a freely available variable productive resource. We must combine air and gasoline in the right proportions, however, or output (horsepower) suffers. If too much air is used relative to gasoline, output declines; too much gasoline relative to air, and output again suffers.
[6] An imperfectly competitive firm may find it necessary to operate in Stage I in the short

Combinations of *a* and *b* in Stage II are technically efficient ones, whether we are restricted to the short run or not. MP_a, though decreasing, is positive throughout the second stage. As a consequence, total output increases as *a* is added to *b*, indicating the ratio of *a* to *b* is not excessive. Moreover, since AP_a is declining throughout Stage II, neither is the ratio of *b* to *a* excessive. Neither resource is used to excess relative to the other for the combinations of *a* and *b* between a_2 and a_3 in Figure 5-2.

The firm's exact level of short-run output using Stage II combinations of *a* and *b* depends on the prices of the inputs *a* and *b*, as well as on output prices and the firm's objectives. A determination of the firm's optimal output level must be deferred, therefore, until Chapter 7, when we combine cost and revenue curves.

The Short-Run Production Function, with Capital Divisible and Unadaptable

It is possible that marginal product will behave somewhat differently than depicted with the traditional production curves of Figure 5-2. To illustrate a different case, we will assume that the fixed factor of production, *b*, though divisible, is completely unadaptable to the variable factor *a*. Instead of a plant with a continuous production line, suppose output is produced using units of labor, *a*, and units of capital, *b*, in fixed proportions. Unadaptability means that *a* and *b* must be used in a fixed ratio, say one unit of *a* for each unit of *b*, one shovel to one worker. If you try to add more *a*'s to the unit of *b*, output stays the same. The production line, in other words, consists of a single step. For illustration purposes, we assume that the fixed capital includes a plant facility with one thousand machines and that one unit of *a* combines with one machine to produce 5 units of output. It is clear that marginal product will not look like the typical, inverted MP curve (such as MP_a in Figure 5-2). As successive amounts of *a* are added to the fixed capital, they will be assigned to successive machines, e.g., the first *a* with the first machine, the second *a* with the second machine, and so on. The marginal product of the first *a* is 5, as illustrated in panel (*b*) of Figure 5-3, but so is the marginal product of the second. In fact, marginal product would have a constant value of 5 for all inputs of *a* up to one thousand units, and total product, illustrated in panel (a) of Figure 5-3, would as a consequence rise at a constant rate until reaching 5,000. Total product would be linear over the range of *a* from zero to 1,000. In addition, average product would equal marginal product over the same range.

---

run, even though too much *b* is employed relative to *a*. For example, if the firm wishes to produce less than TP_2 units of output in the short run, and *b* is indivisible, the firm will be forced to use a high ratio of *b* to *a*. For this reason, we have declined to identify Stage I combinations of *a* and *b* as technically inefficient in the short run.

170 A Theory of Producer Behavior

FIGURE 5-3 Total and Marginal Product Schedules: Divisible but Unadaptable Capital

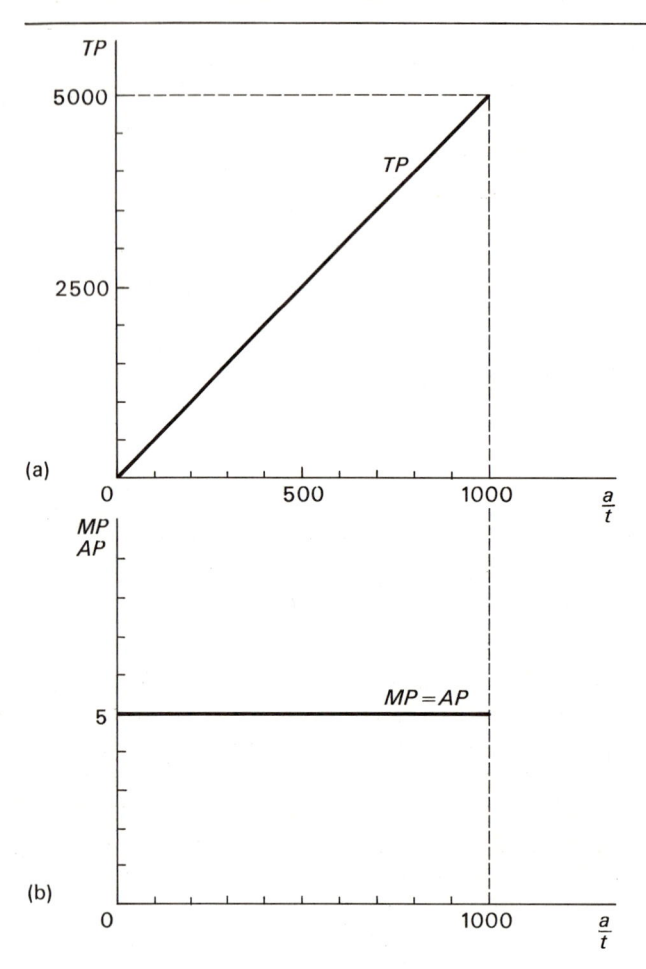

(a)

TP graph: TP rises linearly from 0 through (1000, 5000); 2500 marked on vertical axis, 500 and 1000 on horizontal axis $\frac{a}{t}$.

(b)

MP/AP graph: horizontal line at 5 labeled MP = AP, extending to 1000 on horizontal axis $\frac{a}{t}$.

Although the illustration in Figure 5-3 contrasts markedly with the previous one, it does not violate the law of diminishing returns. The law of diminishing returns requires only that MP must *eventually* decline. As units of a are added to the production process beyond one thousand, marginal product must certainly decline in our example (perhaps to zero), since there are no more machines for additional units of a to work with. Their marginal products might nevertheless be positive; e.g., extra units of labor could be used for maintenance or for "spelling" workers. Summarizing, marginal product might be constant over a wide range before it falls. Furthermore, a number of additional cases might be considered which result in marginal product curves of still different shapes.[7]

COST CURVES

Short-Run Costs

Firms must know the costs of production, as well as the quantities of inputs needed to produce different levels of output, because firms must base their decisions not only on revenues, but also on the costs incurred in generating those revenues. Only when both revenue and cost information is known can the firm determine the effects of its operation on profits and net worth. To determine the costs of producing alternative output levels, we must combine the production data already developed with information on the prices of resources. As a first step, we assume that the price of the fixed factor, b, is given, and that the price of the variable factor, P_a, is equal to $10, regardless of how much a the firm employs. The supply of resource a to the firm is then perfectly elastic.

In Figure 5–4, we have reproduced a total product curve like that developed in Figure 5–2, and we have constructed a new scale along the horizontal axis of the diagram by multiplying the number of units of a (the horizontal scale in Figure 5–1) by the price of a, assumed to be $10 per unit. P_a times a is *total variable cost*. In symbols:

$$TVC = a \cdot P_a.$$

By relating the total product curve to the new horizontal axis in Figure 5–4, we can determine the total variable cost of producing various output levels. For example, two units of a costing a total of $20 (two units times $10 per unit), employed with the fixed quantity of b, will produce an output of 60 units. Turning the statement around, the TVC for 60 units of output is $20. Notice that, although the price of a is fixed at $10 per unit, the total expenditure on a is variable, since the firm can increase or decrease the number of units of a it employs. Of course, when the number of units of a increases, total output increases, unless the firm is operating in Stage III. The TVC curve shows the total variable cost associated with all possible short-run output levels. The shape of TVC is determined by the shape of the total product curve and the price of a, reflecting the fact that output costs are a function of the prices and productivity of resources a and b.

[7] See George Stigler, "Production and Distribution in the Short Run," *Readings in the Theory of Income Distribution* (Homewood, Ill.: Richard D. Irwin, Inc., 1951).

172 A Theory of Producer Behavior

FIGURE 5-4 The Derivation of the Total Variable Cost Curve

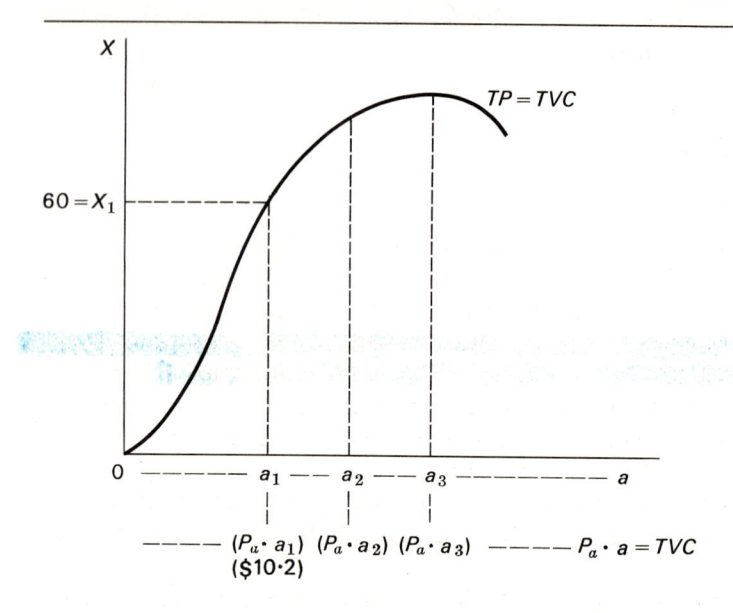

[Figure 5-4: Graph with X on vertical axis, showing TP = TVC curve. $60 = X_1$ marked on vertical axis. Along horizontal axis: a_1, a_2, a_3, a. Below: $(P_a \cdot a_1)$ ($10 \cdot 2$), $(P_a \cdot a_2)$, $(P_a \cdot a_3)$ ---- $P_a \cdot a = TVC$]

Cost curves are typically graphed with the output level on the horizontal axis and costs on the vertical axis. TVC in Figure 5-4 can be presented in the conventional way, simply by reorienting the horizontal and vertical axes. The resulting cost curve is TVC in Figure 5-5.

FIGURE 5-5 Total Cost: The Sum of Total Variable and Total Fixed Cost

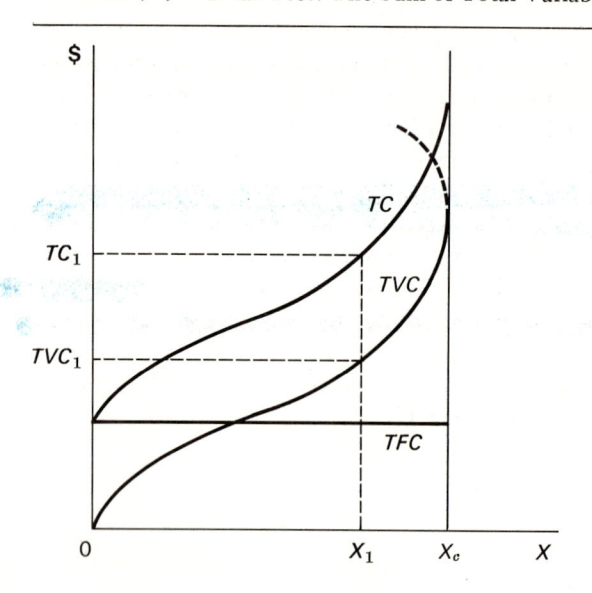

[Figure 5-5: Graph with $ on vertical axis and X on horizontal axis. Shows TC, TVC, and TFC curves. TC_1 and TVC_1 marked on vertical axis, X_1 and X_c marked on horizontal axis.]

Notice that the *TVC* curve shows the minimum total cost of producing any output in the short run. There can be only one *TVC* for any output, and that is the least cost possible. The combination of *a* and *b* that produces a given output at least cost is referred to as *economically efficient*. (Therefore, we disregard the resource combinations which result in the downsloping part of the *TP* curve in Figure 5–4 and the dashed part of *TVC* in Figure 5–5.)

The total cost of operating in the short run includes both variable and fixed costs. *Fixed costs* are those costs or outlays which do not vary when output varies. In our simple two-input production model, the fixed cost is the total outlay for the fixed factor, or $b \cdot P_b$. Since in the short run, the quantity of b is fixed, the firm incurs the cost of b whether output is zero units or a positive amount. In Table 5–1, one unit of b is the fixed input of b regardless of how much a is employed and how much X produced; the firm is obligated to pay the cost of 1 b in any case. In effect, the firm cannot buy more units of b than the fixed quantity, but is forced to make a minimum outlay sufficient to pay for the fixed quantity of b, whether it uses this input or not. An illustration would be a firm's interest payments on its outstanding bonded indebtedness. The firm's total fixed cost curve (*TFC*) is therefore drawn perfectly horizontal in Figure 5–5.

To obtain the total cost curve, total fixed cost is added vertically to total variable cost at every possible output level. The resulting total cost curve is labeled *TC* in Figure 5–5. For example, when X_1 units of output are produced, total variable cost is TVC_1, total fixed cost is *TFC* and total cost is $TC_1 = TVC_1 + TFC$. The total cost curves increase rapidly as they approach the vertical line at X_c.[8] This output level corresponds to the peak of the total product curve in Figure 5–4 and is the short-run capacity output of the firm. At the other extreme, *TC* is equal to *TFC* as output falls to zero. Like the *TVC* curve, *TC* derives its shape from the total product curve and the price of *a*. The price of *b* determines the height of the curve.

SHORT-RUN UNIT COSTS

Average Cost Curves. For many purposes, it is more convenient to work with average costs rather than total costs; for example, in comparing the cost of higher education at a state university and a private college, it may be more revealing to examine the cost per student at each school (average cost) than to compare the total budgets of the two schools.

Average cost information is computed from the total cost data in Figure 5–5 and presented in Figure 5–6. Since there are three separate total cost

---

[8] The vertical distance between *TVC* and *TC* is the same at all output levels, despite the fact that the two curves *seem* to get closer together as capacity output is approached and the two cost curves turn vertical.

174 A Theory of Producer Behavior

FIGURE 5–6 The Short-Run Unit Cost Curves of a Firm

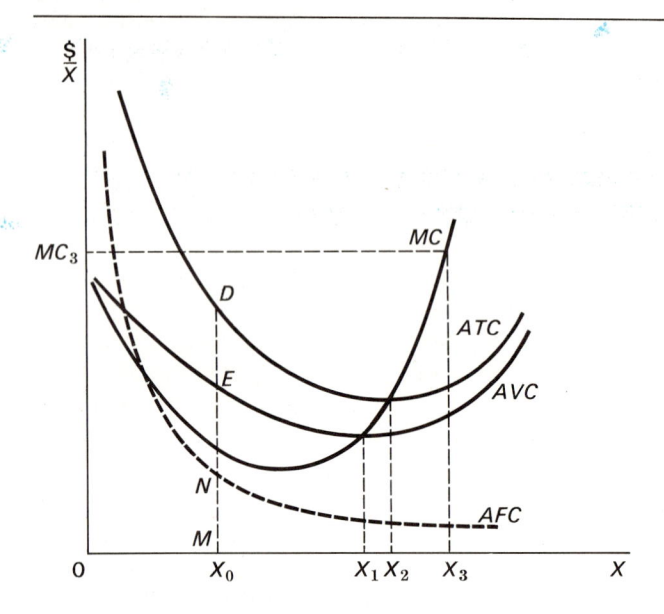

curves in Figure 5–4, we will be able to compute three different "average" curves. The *average total cost* curve (ATC) is derived by dividing total cost at each possible level of output by the corresponding quantity of output, and plotting the resulting points on a graph. In symbols:

$$ATC = \frac{TC}{X},$$

where X is any given level of output. Average variable cost (AVC) is determined in a similar manner, symbolically:

$$AVC = \frac{TVC}{X}.$$

Finally, average fixed cost (AFC) is determined by dividing total fixed cost by each output level or:

$$AFC = \frac{TFC}{X}.$$

As output increases, AFC steadily falls. This reflects the effects of "spreading" the fixed cost over increased numbers of units. The AFC curve has the shape of a rectangular hyperbola with the left-hand portion (the portion which would otherwise appear in Quadrant III) eliminated.[9]

---

[9] A rectangular hyperbola is given by the equation $y = k/x$, where k is a constant.

To help understand why AVC behaves as it does, we will develop a simple mathematical relationship between AVC and the firm's AP curve, which will serve as a useful tool of analysis. First, we note that total variable cost is defined as:

$$TVC = P_a \cdot a.$$

Then average variable cost can be obtained from this equation by dividing TVC by the number of units of output X.ABividing both sides of the equation we get:

$$\frac{TVC}{X} = \frac{P_a \cdot a}{X}.$$

Rearranging the right-hand portion and writing AVC for TVC/X, we get:

$$AVC = \frac{P_a}{X/a}.$$

But X/a or TP/a (X is the same as TP) is average product, AP, so, in the case of a short-run, two-input model where $X = f(a, b)$, AVC may be written as:[10]

$$AVC = \frac{P_a}{AP_a}. \qquad (1)$$

In words, the average variable cost associated with any output level is directly proportional to the price of the variable factor of production and inversely proportional to its average product at the given output level. Referring to Figure 5–6, average variable cost declines steadily as output increases to X_1 units and increases for output levels above X_1. Now, with the aid of Equation (1) above, we can investigate why AVC behaves as it does. As the initial quantities of a are added to b, average product increases because the firm is operating in Stage I. (Refer to Figure 5–2.) Therefore, as output increases in Stage I, the denominator of Equation (1) increases, and since P_a is constant, AVC decreases. Then, as the quantity of a relative to b rises still further, AP declines, as we proceed from Stage I to Stage II combinations.

Referring again to Equation (1), AP_a and AVC are inversely related, so the *minimum* point on the AVC curve corresponds to the *maximum* point on the average product curve; the combination of a and b that makes AP a maximum also results in AVC reaching a minimum. In other words, the greatest degree of productivity per unit of a variable resource corresponds to the lowest cost per level of output of that resource.

Now we turn our attention to the pattern of movement of average total cost, which is simply the sum of AVC and AFC at each output level. For example, in Figure 5–6 at output X_0, MN, the AFC at X_0, plus ME, the AVC

---

[10] AVC can also be defined where more than one input is variable.

at X_0, gives the distance MD, which is ATC at that output. Distance MN is then equal to ED. At each output level, the ATC curve lies above AVC by the amount of the AFC. Moreover, the shape of the ATC curve is determined by the shapes of its component curves AVC and AFC. Average total cost will be very large for values of X close to the vertical axis, since AFC is large for small values of X. For higher output levels, however, AFC becomes smaller and ATC looks more like AVC. The minimum point on ATC lies to the right of that of AVC, since ATC is the vertical sum of two curves, one of which is continuously falling. For instance, if output is increased just beyond X_1 units (the minimum point for AVC), AVC rises but AFC falls. The fall in AFC tends to pull ATC down, whereas the rise in AVC tends to make ATC go up. The net result of the two conflicting forces is that ATC initially falls. But if output is increased above X_2 units, the effect on ATC of an increasing AVC overcomes the effect of a declining AFC, thus ATC is at a minimum and starts to rise. (Remember AFC falls at a decreasing rate and AVC rises at an increasing rate.) The difference between the two minimum points (X_1 and X_2) will be greater the larger the fixed cost is relative to variable cost. Therefore, if the fixed cost were zero, the two points would coincide.

A final note: each of the unit costs, average total, average variable, and average fixed, is a *function* of the output level. That is, the value for, say, average total cost depends upon the output level and is different for different levels of output. It would make no sense to say average total cost is $6, unless we know what output level results in a $6 unit cost.

Marginal Cost. One of the most theoretically useful measures of cost is marginal cost. Marginal cost provides information on the effects of *changes* in the firm's output on its cost. Marginal cost information provides answers to such questions as, "What happens to costs if the firm expands output?" "What are the incremental costs associated with a given decision?" Whereas marginal product measures the change in output that occurs when an additional unit of the variable factor is added to the production process, marginal cost measures the addition to total cost that occurs when one more unit of output is produced by the firm. In symbols:

$$MC = \frac{\Delta TC}{\Delta X},$$

where ΔX is equal to 1.[11] For example, in Figure 5–6, if X_3 units of output are currently being produced, output can be increased one unit by an additional expenditure of MC_3; i.e., total costs rise by the amount MC_3 due to the one-unit increase in output above X_3. It may take many or only a few additional units of the variable factor of production to produce the additional unit

---

[11] Even if ΔX increases by more or less than one, the formula will give an average value for MC over the range of output considered.

of X. The number of units of a needed depends on the marginal product of a. Marginal cost is determined by both the marginal product and the price of the variable factor as we shall see.

There is a mathematical relationship between marginal product and marginal cost for our two-input production model, just as there is a relationship between AP and AVC. We have defined marginal cost as:

$$MC = \frac{\Delta TC}{\Delta X}.$$

But any change in TC is equal to the change in TVC, since TFC is constant. Thus:

$$MC = \frac{\Delta TVC}{\Delta X}.$$

But TVC is $P_a \cdot a$, so:

$$MC = \frac{\Delta(P_a \cdot a)}{\Delta X}.$$

Since P_a is constant:

$$MC = \frac{P_a \cdot \Delta a}{\Delta X}.$$

Rearranging, we get:

$$MC = \frac{P_a}{\Delta X/\Delta a}.$$

And, since $\Delta X/\Delta a$ is marginal product, we may restate marginal cost as:

$$MC = \frac{P_a}{MP_a}. \tag{2}$$

In words, marginal cost is directly proportional to the price of the variable factor and inversely proportional to its marginal product.

Equation (2) can now be used to explain the movement of MC in Figure 5–6. As the ratio of a to b is increased, we find that marginal product initially increases, assuming the fixed factor is indivisible but adaptable. But, looking at (2), as MP_a rises, MC falls. However, because of the law of diminishing returns, marginal product eventually declines as the ratio of a to b increases, and thus marginal cost must eventually rise. The minimum point on the marginal cost curve in Figure 5–5, therefore, corresponds to the maximum point on the marginal product curve. When the marginal productivity of the variable factor is greatest, the additional cost associated with increased output is least.

The marginal cost curve in Figure 5–6 intersects the minimum points of both the ATC and AVC curves. This is a general characteristic of all average and marginal functions. To demonstrate, we make use of the graph of total variable cost in Figure 5–7. At any point on TVC, say point A, AVC is equal

FIGURE 5–7 The Total Variable Cost Curve of a Firm

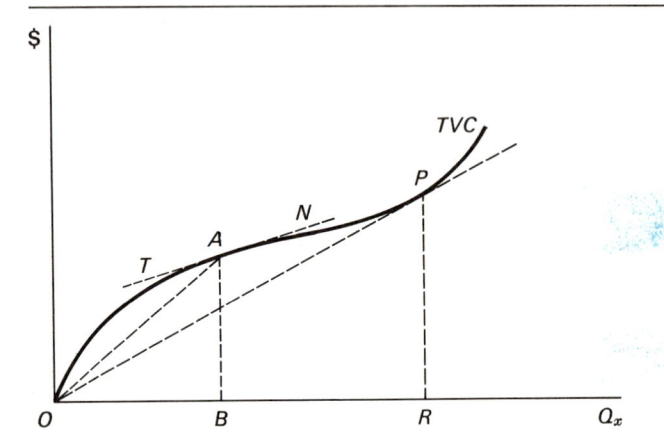

to TVC (BA) divided by the quantity of X (OB). That is, AVC = BA/OB. But BA/OB also equals the slope of the dotted line, OA. MC at point A, on the other hand, is the ratio of the change in TVC to the change in X, $\Delta TVC/\Delta X$, which equals the slope of the TVC curve at that point. The slope of TVC at point A is equal to the slope of the line labeled TAN drawn tangent at point A. Since line OA is steeper than line TAN, AVC is greater than MC at output OB.

If more lines are drawn from the origin to points to the right of point A along the TVC curve, they will become successively less steep until line OP, which is the flattest line that can possibly be drawn from the origin and still make contact with TVC. Therefore, at output OR, RP/OR is the lowest possible value for AVC. But line OP is also tangent to TVC at point P, so the slope of OP equals both the AVC and MC at that output level. Thus, MC equals AVC when AVC reaches its lowest possible value.

For any point along TVC to the right of point P, the slope of TVC (which is MC) is steeper than the slope of a line drawn from the origin to the point (which is AVC). So to the right of point P, MC is greater than AVC.

We can now summarize the foregoing discussion with three general statements:

1. MC < AVC, when AVC is falling.
2. MC = AVC, when AVC is at its minimum.
3. MC > AVC, when AVC is rising.

These same relationships hold between MC and ATC, and this can be proved in a manner similar to that employed to show the relationship between MC and AVC.

The cost curves which we have developed in this section provide the basis for understanding short-run decision-making by the firm. A firm must know its costs of operating at different output levels before it can rationally adjust to a given set of market circumstances. It does not matter whether the firm seeks to maximize sales, growth, or some other variable; knowledge of costs is essential, because almost every key variable is affected by costs. But knowledge of costs alone is not enough to make a decision. The firm must combine cost information with information on revenue before an optimal decision is possible. In Chapter 7, we will put the two together in a complete model of short-run firm behavior.

LONG-RUN COSTS

In the short run just discussed, at least one input was fixed, but given sufficient time, the firm can alter the quantities of all inputs used in production; a time period long enough to allow all inputs to be varied is designated the *long run*. In the long run, a firm can enter the industry if there are no barriers to entry, or an existing firm can exit the industry if it is advantageous to do so. Leaving an industry may take some time, for a firm likely has contractual obligations which cannot be broken immediately, such as interest on indebtedness, lease agreements, and the like. The long run is a period of time which allows the firm to dispose of assets and leave the industry. In addition, the long run encompasses a period of time sufficient for the firm to plan, construct, and bring into operation a plant facility of any size. What is the best combination of resources for any output level if all inputs may be varied? The best combination will be the one that results in the least possible cost for any given output. Our task now is to determine the least cost for all output levels, given the absence of input restrictions. We begin by distinguishing constant, increasing, and decreasing return to scale.

Constant Returns to Scale

Suppose the firm is operating at output level X_1 in Figure 5–8, employing a_1 units of a and b_1 units of b. Now assume that a_1 and b_1 is the least costly combination of a and b that could be used to produce X_1 units when both a and b can be varied. The average cost, X_1Z at output X_1, is defined as the long-run average cost (*LRAC*) at that output, since this is the least possible unit cost of producing X_1 units, given that the firm can vary the quantities of both a and b. There can be only one *LRAC* at a given output level, and that is the least possible unit cost obtainable by selecting the least costly combination of resources. Now suppose the quantities of a and b are both doubled to

FIGURE 5–8 The Long-Run Average and Marginal Cost Curves: Constant Returns to Scale

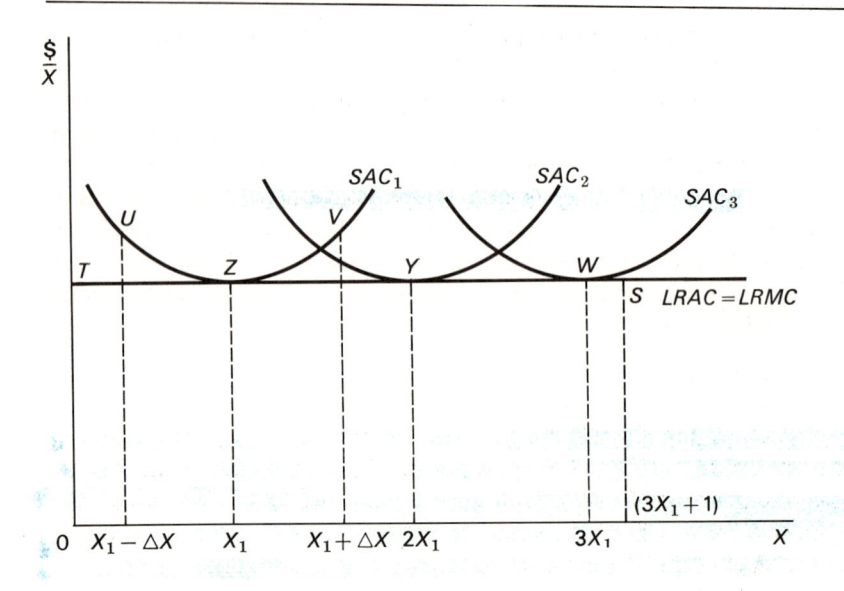

$2a_1$ and $2b_1$. It is perfectly plausible to presume that output will also double, a case of constant returns to scale.

> Constant returns to scale characterize a production function if a given proportional change in all inputs results in an identical proportional change in output.

If the prices of a and b remain constant, then doubling the quantity of a and b will cause total costs to double, but since both output and total costs have doubled, long-run average cost will remain the same.[12] Thus, at output $2X_1$, LRAC is found at point Y. For a threefold increase in output from X_1 to $3X_1$, the unit cost will again stay the same at point W. Moreover, if we consider intermediate output levels, and assume that any percentage increase in a and b causes output to increase in the same proportion, even if the percentages are fractions, then we would generate the horizontal LRAC curve in Figure 5–8. To summarize, a constant returns to scale production function results in a horizontal LRAC curve, assuming fixed factor prices.

Now consider again the output level, X_1, in Figure 5–8. If the firm increases output by ΔX to $X_1 + \Delta X$ by holding the quantity of b fixed at b_1 and increas-

---

[12] We will investigate later the effects on LRAC of changes in the prices of a and b caused by increased quantities purchased by the firm. Now we assume the supply curves for resources a and b are perfectly elastic to the firm.

ing the number of units of a (a short-run adjustment), then unit costs will rise to point V on SAC_1. SAC_1 is the short-run unit cost curve associated with b_1 units of b. Or, if output is reduced in the short run to $X_1 - \Delta X$, then unit costs rise to point U on SAC_1. In both cases, the unit costs after the output change are higher than what they would have been if the firm had made a long-run adjustment (increased or decreased both b and a) to outputs $X_1 + \Delta X$ and $X_1 - \Delta X$. In other words, a long-run adjustment will be more economically efficient (less costly) than a short-run adjustment. This conclusion is in agreement with the common sense notion that a production adjustment, where there are no input restrictions, will generally be more efficient than one where there are restrictions.

We can summarize the above by saying that if the firm operating at X_1 makes a short-run adjustment in production, then the appropriate cost curve is the short-run cost curve, SAC_1 in Figure 5-8. Otherwise, the appropriate cost curve is the horizontal LRAC curve. Moreover, since a short-run adjustment in production must be less economically efficient then a long-run adjustment, SAC must be above LRAC at every output level except X_1, where the short-run and long-run unit costs are equal. Now suppose the firm makes a long-run adjustment to output level $3X_1$, producing this output at a unit cost of $3X_1W$, using $3b_1$ units of b. Any subsequent short-run changes in output would entail changes in unit costs measured along curve SAC_3. SAC_3, like SAC_1 and SAC_2, contributes only one point (point W) to the LRAC curve. The three SAC curves in Figure 5-8 are representative of the infinitude of potential short-run cost curves that exist (one for each possible quantity of the fixed factor b), and each potential short-run cost curve contributes a single point to LRAC. LRAC is often described as an envelope of the short-run cost curves.

We define the long-run marginal cost of a firm as follows:

> Long-run marginal cost measures the increment to total cost occasioned by the production of one more unit of output, providing that the firm has sufficient time to vary all inputs to the production process.

For the case of constant returns to scale (and constant factor prices), the long-run marginal cost (LRMC) curve is identical to the LRAC curve, because the incremental cost of producing one more unit is constant and equal to the average cost of producing all units. Consider again Figure 5-8 and suppose the firm expends output from $3X_1$ to $3X_1 + 1$. What is the long-run marginal cost of the firm's expansion? First, we can measure the total cost of producing $3X_1$ units as the area $03X_1WT$, and the total cost of producing $(3X_1 + 1)$ units as $0(3X_1 + 1)ST$. The change in cost is then the area of the narrow rectangle, $3X_1(3X_1 + 1)SW$. But this area is equal to the long-run average cost $3X_1W$, since the base of the rectangle is 1. Therefore, the LRMC at output $3X_1$ and any other output is equal to the LRAC.

Increasing Returns to Scale

Now let us consider the possibility that a doubling of all inputs to a production process will more than double output.

> Increasing returns to scale exist when a proportional increase in inputs a and b causes output to increase in greater proportion.

Consider output X_1 in Figure 5–9, which is produced with inputs a_1 and b_1, and assume this is the least costly combination of a and b for that output. This means X_1Z is the long-run unit cost of producing X_1 units. Now if a and b are doubled to $2a_1$ and $2b_1$, and there are increasing returns to scale, output will increase by more than two-fold, say to X_2, where $X_2 > 2X_1$. Assuming again that the prices of a and b are constant, total cost will double, since the firm is purchasing twice as much of a and b. But since total output has more than doubled, average cost will fall. Thus, LRAC falls from point Z to W as output is increased to X_2 units. In general, increasing returns to scale will cause long-run unit costs to decline with increases in output.

FIGURE 5–9 The Long-Run Average and Marginal Cost Curves: Increasing Returns to Scale

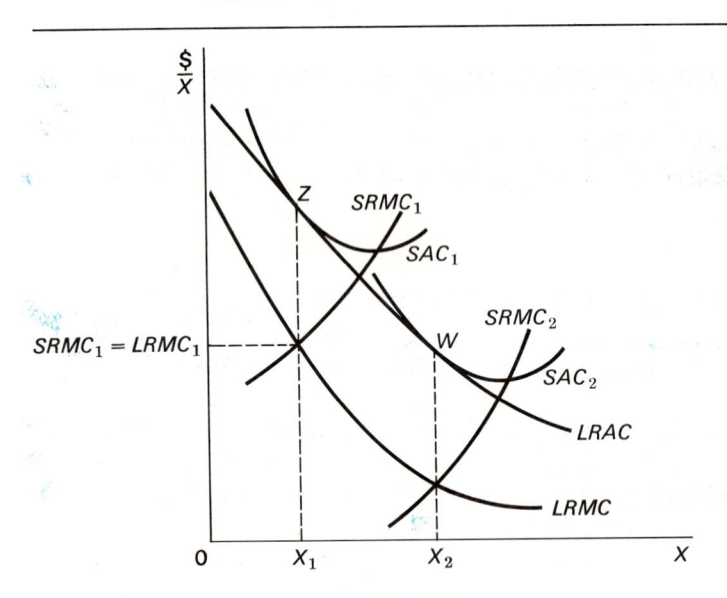

With LRAC declining, the relationship between LRAC and the short-run cost curves appears more complicated. If at output level X_1, the firm makes a short-run production adjustment, unit costs will vary along the short-run unit cost curve SAC_1. For output levels just below or just above X_1, SAC must be greater than *LRAC*, for the same reasons outlined above; consequently, SAC_1 contributes only one point, Z, to *LRAC*. Continuing, since at X_1, *SAC* equals *LRAC*, then short-run total cost must equal long-run total cost, and since SAC_1 is tangent to *LRAC* at Z, the two *total* cost curves (not shown) would be tangent also. But if the total cost curves are tangent at X_1, their respective slopes, *LRMC* and *SRMC*, are equal. Thus, as indicated in Figure 5–9, $SRMC_1$ intersects *LRMC* at output X_1. Similarly, at output X_2, $SRMC_2$ will equal *LRMC*, though *LRAC* is falling. Notice that for those outputs for which *LRAC* declines, *LRMC* must be below *LRAC*. *LRMC* will lie below *LRAC*, given increasing returns to scale and constant resource prices.

Decreasing Returns to Scale

The case of *decreasing returns to scale* is illustrated in Figure 5–10, where *LRAC* rises as output increases, because a proportional increase in inputs and thus costs causes a less than proportional output increase. The arguments supporting the fact that *LRAC* increases (analogous to those presented above) are left for the student to work out.

FIGURE 5–10 The Long-Run Average and Marginal Cost Curves: Decreasing Returns to Scale

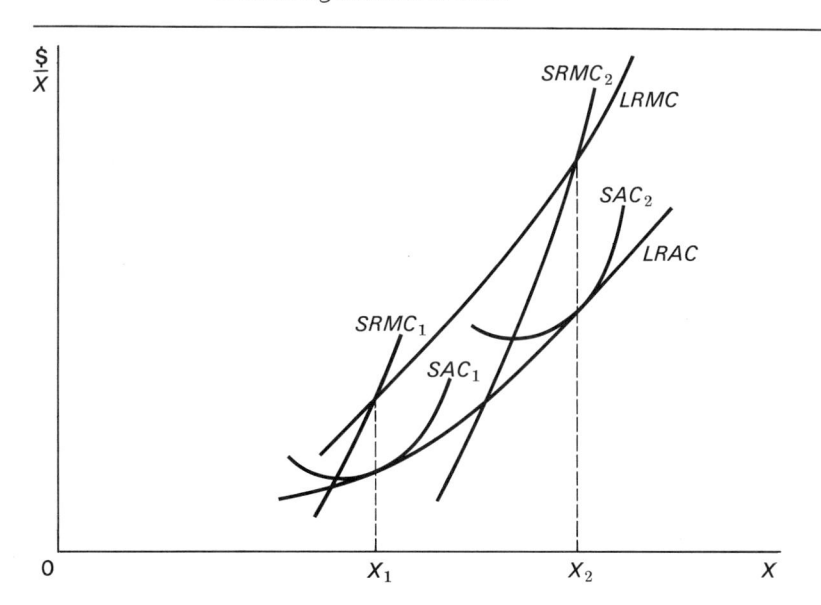

Increasing and Decreasing Returns to Scale

Figure 5–11 demonstrates the case which many feel is typical of many businesses: increasing returns and decreasing unit costs at first, and then

FIGURE 5–11 The Long-Run Average and Marginal Cost Curves: Increasing, then Decreasing Economies of Scale

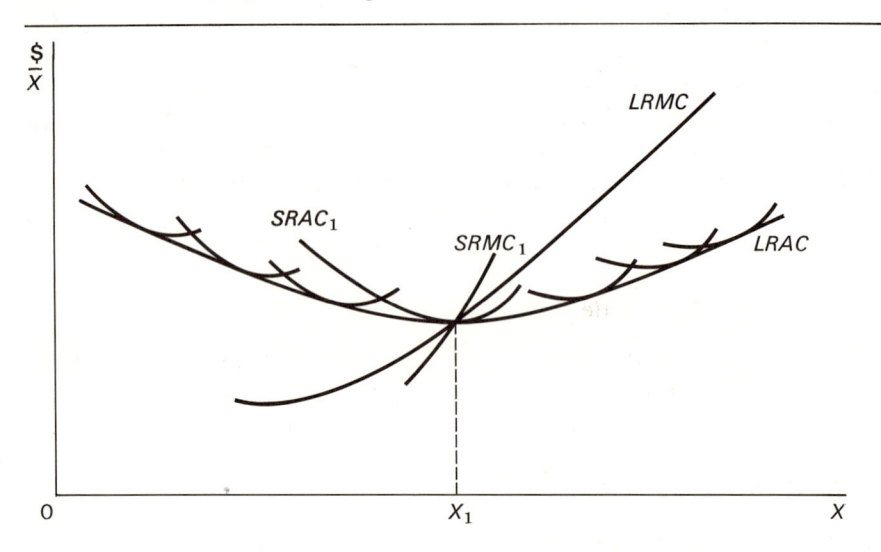

decreasing returns and increasing costs after the firm expands beyond the short-run capacity, represented by $SRAC_1$. The result is a U-shaped long-run average cost curve configured much like the short-run average cost curve. This long-run average cost curve, developed by Jacob Viner,[13] is called an *envelope curve*, since the long-run curve envelopes a great number of tangent short-run functions. Note that all the short-run curves to the left of $SRAC_1$ are tangent to the long-run curve to the left of their low point, while all the short-run curves to the right of $SRAC_1$ are tangent to the long-run function to the right of their low point. So only the one short-run curve, $SRAC_1$, is tangent to the U-shaped long-run curve at the low point, because at the minimum point the slopes of $SRAC_1$ and $LRAC$ are equal, and both are horizontal.

If we assume that the firm will expand along $LRAC$, we can construct a Long-Run Marginal Cost curve, $LRMC$, which relates to $LRAC$ just as any marginal and average cost curves are related. However, the concept has been criticized, because in fact, the firm may not follow $LRAC$, but may expand at least to the low point on each $SRAC$ curve before expanding its capacity. Therefore, in fact, the firm's $LRMC$ curve will be a discontinuous function,[14]

[13] Jacob Viner, "Cost Curves and Supply Curves," *Zeitschrift für Nationalökonomie*, III (September 1931), pp. 23–46.
[14] The mathematically inclined may prefer "first derivative of the $LRAC$" to "$LRMC$ curve."

since the firm's actual expansion will require that it follow a scalloped pattern.

However, that criticism can be disregarded if we simply use the long-run average and marginal cost curves as convenient devices for planning purposes. The long-run average and marginal cost curves exist as theoretical constructs, and are valid as such. So, if we grant the existence of both the long-run and short-run average and marginal cost curves, we find that the four curves are all equal at one point: the low point on the long- and short-run average cost curves, the point at which the two are equal—at the point of tangency of LRAC and SRAC, in Figure 5-11. The long-run least-cost output is X_1.

Now, let us consider what could cause LRAC to fall first and then to rise as output increases. To illustrate, first, increasing returns to scale, consider the case of a firm which provides warehouse facilities. To increase the plant capacity of the firm by a given proportion may require less than a proportional increase in additional materials. If the walls of the plant are doubled in length, say from 50 feet to 100 feet each, the plant area (and volume) is quadrupled, from 2500 square feet to 10,000 square feet. This one component of the inputs, the walls, therefore, increases much less in proportion to plant capacity, as measured by square feet (or volume) of plant space. The existence of increasing returns to scale would result in a declining LRAC curve for warehouse services.

In addition, increasing returns to scale may be explained by the indivisibility of resources. Certain types of machinery and equipment are not available (even for rent) in small units. Such machinery is efficiently used only when the volume of output is large. Moreover, the physical size of the unit of output often dictates a minimum size for some of the inputs. The indivisibility of labor also causes inefficiencies when the scale of a production process is small. Thus, we typically find small firms employing one person to perform two or more separate functions. But one person cannot be divided up among a number of tasks without losing advantages of specialization. It is difficult for one individual to become expert in more than one field. One can be a "Jack of all trades and master of none." On the other hand, as the scale of production increases, greater specialization of labor is possible. For instance, the firm can hire specialists in personnel management, industrial relations, plant layout, and so on. In summary, many resources are characterized by indivisibilities of one sort or another, which makes small-scale production economically inefficient relative to large-scale production.

Decreasing returns to scale are usually associated with growing shortages of one or more resources, such as qualified management. As an enterprise grows very large, it becomes increasingly difficult for management to coordinate efficiently all its activities, particularly for geographically dispersed firms with diversified product lines. Effective managerial talent is scarce, and the best techniques of production may not be used, either because they are unknown or the requisite management for using them is not available. Moreover, there is a tendency for large institutions to develop bureaucratic solutions to problems of management, and this often contributes to administrative inefficiency. However, the development of large-scale computers has greatly reduced the problems of administering a large enterprise, by reducing laborious clerical chores and speeding the flow and quality of information within the organization. In addition, management science has developed management techniques that help overcome the disadvantages of size; for example, the divisional structure, such as that used by General Motors. Such developments suggest that an organization may become very large before decreasing returns become very important.

Economies and Diseconomies of Scale

As we have seen, the long-run average cost curve is affected by increasing or decreasing returns to scale. But long-run costs are also influenced by economies and diseconomies of scale. At this point, we must draw a distinction between increasing or decreasing returns to scale and a related term, economies or diseconomies of scale: Increasing or decreasing returns to scale apply exclusively to the effects of changes in the scale of the physical production process on output. Economies and diseconomies of scale, on the other hand, incorporate the role of cost. Long-run unit costs may decrease (increase) with output increases, for reasons apart from the effects of increased (decreased) returns to scale, already discussed.

> *In general, if long-run average cost decreases with output, either for internal reasons (increasing returns to scale) or external reasons (such as decreases in factor prices), the firm is said to experience economies of scale. If LRAC rises, the firm experiences diseconomies of scale.*

Some effects are external to the firm. Thus, even if returns to scale are constant, the firm's long-run unit costs might decrease with output. As an illustration, output expansion might enable the firm to obtain resources at reduced prices. Thus, the firm supplying the given firm with inputs may experience economies that allow price to fall when quantities are increased, e.g., quantity discounts. As another example, a machine with twice the productivity of another machine will possibly cost appreciably less than twice the smaller machine.

Empirical Studies of Cost Functions

Many studies of cost functions have been completed in recent years, producing a number of interesting, and in some cases unexpected, results. With respect to short-run cost functions, some studies have indicated that marginal cost in some industries is constant over a wide range of output.[15] This conclusion is in apparent agreement with many businessmen who seem to operate as though short-run marginal costs are constant. There is no necessary conflict with this observation and short-run production principles. The law of diminishing returns states only that marginal product must eventually decline and that marginal cost, as a result, must eventually increase. It is quite possible that marginal product will be constant over a wide range of output, in which case short-run marginal cost will be constant as well. Earlier we considered just this possibility, that is, the case of a divisible but unadaptable fixed resource. Using our basic equation relating MP to MC, $MC = P_a/MP_a$; if MP is constant as a is increased holding b constant, then MC will be constant also, since P_a is constant. Once the firm approaches short-run capacity output, however, marginal product must fall, and marginal cost will, as a consequence, increase.

Studies of scale economies and diseconomies in American industry have produced equally interesting conclusions. Some studies have implied that long-run average and marginal costs are constant over a wide range of output in many industries.[16] These studies indicate that economies of scale are realized for low levels of output, say up to X_1 units in Figure 5–12, followed by constant returns over a wide range of output, between X_1 and X_2. Diseconomies occur only when output becomes quite large. Referring to the graph, diseconomies occur for output levels above X_2 units of output, so LRAC begins to increase. In addition, considering X_1 units of output the *minimum optimum output level*, the studies indicate this output level is typically small relative to the total output in most industries in the United States.[17] In other words, most industries in the United States seem capable of supporting many firms, all operating at the minimum optimum level of production.

Opportunity Cost

The best measure of the cost of any action is the opportunities that must be given up because of that action. For example, suppose you decide to keep $1000 in your checking account at a bank. What is the cost of doing so? Some would argue that there is no cost, since the bank imposes no charge for providing this service (until checks are written on the account). However, there is

---

[15] For a critical survey of the earlier literature, see Hans Apel, "Marginal Cost Constancy and Its Implications," *American Economic Review* (December 1948), pp. 870–885.

[16] See, for example, John R. Moroney, "Cobb–Douglas Production Functions and Returns to Scale in U.S. Manufacturing Industry," *Western Economic Journal*, Vol. VI, No. 1 (December 1967), pp. 39–51.

[17] See Joe Bain, *Industrial Organization*. 2d ed. New York: John Wiley and Sons, Inc., 1968.

FIGURE 5–12 Increasing, Constant, and Decreasing Economies of Scale

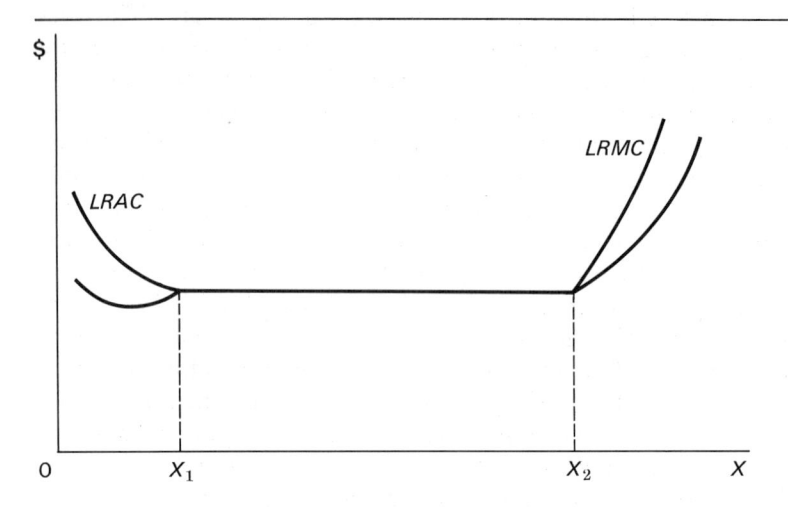

a cost associated with keeping funds in the checking account, which is measured by the return that could be earned if the funds were placed elsewhere. This cost is called *opportunity cost*.

> The opportunity cost of using a resource is measured by the highest return the resource could earn in its best alternative employment.

In other words, the $1000 could be used to buy a security or a share account in a savings and loan which would earn $50 a year if the interest rate is 5 percent. So the opportunity cost of keeping $1000 in the checking account is $50 per year.

From the viewpoint of society, the real cost of using resources in one firm is the value of the goods and services which these resources could have produced in their best alternative employment. The actual or explicit payment of the firm to the unit of labor may or may not be equal to the opportunity cost. For example, the firm may pay less than the opportunity cost if market imperfections prevent a worker from changing to a new job with a higher wage rate. One such imperfection may be the worker's ignorance of the better paying job. On the other hand, the firm may be ignorant of the market wage rate and pay more than the worker's opportunity cost. The real cost of using resources is their opportunity cost, regardless of the money payments made for the use of the resources. Because economics is a social science concerned with social welfare, its cost accounting must be social, not private.

To illustrate the contrast between social and private cost accounting, consider a small, owner-managed firm, and assume that the owner of the firm furnishes resources in the form of money capital and the owner's own labor.

Very possibly, the money payment to these resources will not accurately reflect their real cost. Suppose the firm has total sales in one year of $25,000, and the cost of goods sold is $15,000. Allowing a salary for the proprietor of $5000, profits are computed at $5000. It is likely that profits are much less. Since the proprietor uses his own funds for working capital during the year, there is an implicit cost attached to their use measured by the opportunity cost. Moreover, the salary of the proprietor, equal to $5000, may be considerably less than the maximum salary the proprietor could command in his best alternative employment. Assuming the proprietor could have earned $10,000 working for someone else and $500 on his capital, then the year's operation produced economic losses, not profits. Thus, accounting profits may overstate profits, because they do not include the implicit as well as the explicit costs of operation. (However, many owners receive "psychic income" or non-monetary rewards, such as pride or independence, from operating their own businesses. Such psychic income is a negative opportunity cost, and its value —however figured—should be added back into profits.)

Since economics is a social science concerned principally with the efficient utilization of all resources in the economy, the opportunity cost concept underlies all of microeconomics. However, economists must be prepared to study the economy as it exists, and this often means analyzing firm behavior under circumstances where the firms make decisions on the basis of cost as the firm experiences cost, which may not be the social opportunity cost. The owners' perceptions of the costs and benefits may differ from society's perception. Air and water pollution illustrate the divergence between the costs and benefits as perceived by owners and managers, and by society. In other words, we must distinguish between normative and positive economic models. The latter models will have to measure costs as they are perceived by the firm, whereas the former would be based on social opportunity costs alone. In the following chapters, in which we develop models of firm behavior, we will assume that the firm's decision costs are identical with social opportunity costs. In Chapter 13, we will investigate cases in which the firm's decision costs are not synonymous with social opportunity costs, and the possible implications of the disparity for public policy.

PROBLEMS

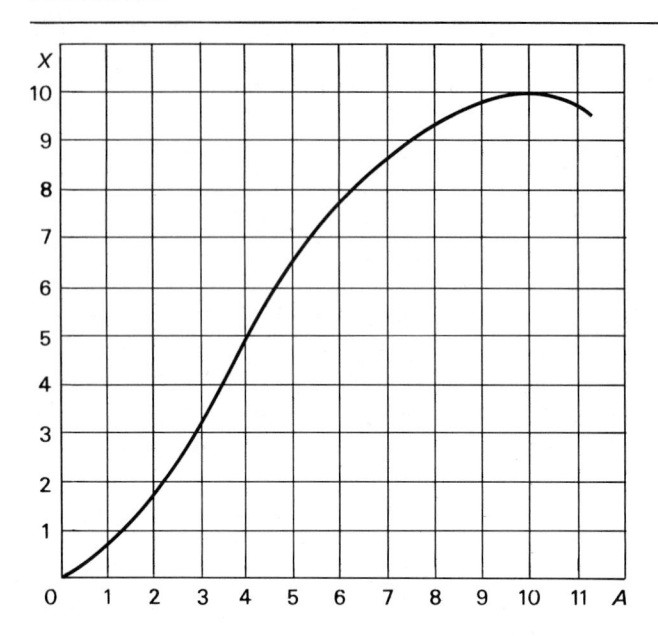

1. The accompanying graph shows a firm's total product function. Using the data in this graph, construct the firm's total cost curve in the empty graph below, assuming that the variable factor, a, costs $1 per unit and the fixed factor, b, costs $10.

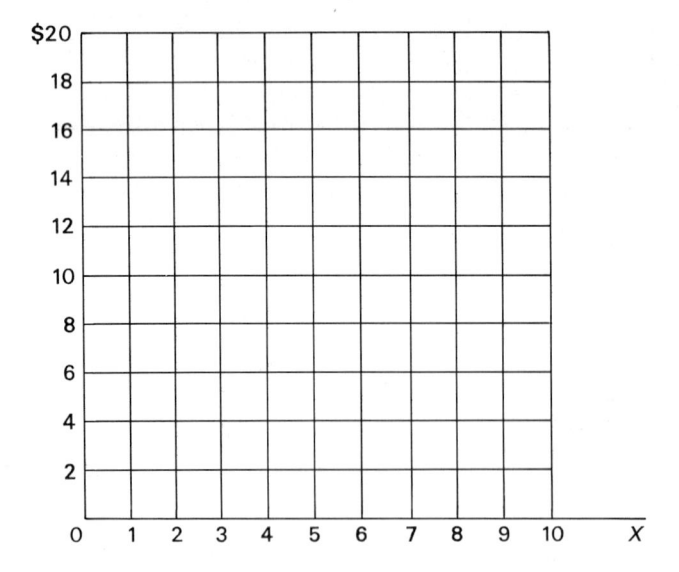

2. Use the total cost curve you constructed in the second graph to work out the following cost schedules:

X	AFC	AVC	ATC	MC
1				
2				
3				
4				
5				
6				
7				
8				
9				
10				

3. What is the AFC when output is .5X? Or .25X? In general, what shape does AFC have?
4. Assuming capital is the fixed resource, what would the effect on AFC be if capital were not adaptable?
5. Assume that you work for a cotton compress which bales farmers' cotton using one truck, two hydraulic presses, one building, burlap wrapping material, steel bands, and green cardboard tags to be pinned to each bale for identification purposes. How would you categorize each input as a fixed or variable resource?

REFERENCES

Casels, J. M., "On the Law of Variable Proportions," *Explorations in Economics.* New York: McGraw-Hill Book Company, Inc., 1936. Pp. 223–236.

Forobotn, Eink G., "The Orthodox Production Function and the Adaptability of Capital," *Western Economic Journal*, 3 (Summer 1965), 288–300.

Leibenstein, Harvey, "The Proportionality Controversy and the Theory of Production," *The Quarterly Journal of Economics* (November 1955), 619–625.

Machlup, Fritz, "On the Meaning of the Marginal Product," *Explorations in Economics.* New York: McGraw-Hill Book Company, Inc., 1936.

Stigler, George J., "The Division of Labor Is Limited by the Extent of the Market," *Journal of Political Economy* (June 1951), 185–193.

APPENDIX TO CHAPTER 5

A Long-Run Cost Function for the Local Service Airline Industry: An Experiment in Non-Linear Estimation

GEORGE EADS, MARC NERLOVE, and WILLIAM RADUCHEL

In the selected reading for this chapter, the authors attempt to derive the long-run cost curve for the local service airline industry. The reading is recommended for two reasons. First, the student will be made aware of the many conceptual and technical problems which arise in attempting an empirical investigation of cost curves. Second, he will be introduced to the statistical procedures used to go from theoretical cost curves to estimated real-world cost curves. The reader may prefer to skip the detailed statistical and mathematical explanations in section III, since these require a rather thorough knowledge of multiple regression techniques. The authors' conclusions can nevertheless be grasped with little loss in continuity.

> ...a hoarse voice spoke next. "Change engines—" it said, and there it choked and was obliged to leave off.
> —*Through the Looking Glass*

In this study we formulate and estimate a cost function for the United States local service airline industry. Section I discusses certain characteristics of the industry and its regulation by the Civil Aeronautics Board (CAB) which influence the form of the cost function and the method of estimation chosen. The model is outlined in section II. The data available and the method of estimation are discussed in section III. Some tentative conclusions are presented in section IV.

I. LOCAL SERVICE AIRLINE INDUSTRY

Although in most cases the local service airlines now fly longer routes with larger aircraft than they did when they were founded immediately after World

Review of Economics and Statistics, Vol. 51, No. 3 (August 1969). Reprinted by permission.

War II, there is evidence that these carriers still constitute a meaningful unit for separate analysis.[1] Even in 1966 the average aircraft flown by the local service carriers was only one-half the size of that flown by the trunks, and the average local service flight flew only one-fourth as far as the average trunk flight.

The local service airline industry initially adopted the 21 to 28-seat DC–3 as a readily available interim aircraft.[2] However, as average passenger loads began to increase and as the local service carriers began to acquire longer and denser routes from the trunk carriers, carrier interest turned to larger aircraft. A few twin-turboprop aircraft of 36 to 40-seat capacity were purchased; most carriers, however, added larger piston engine aircraft seating 36 to 52 passengers, both to replace many of their DC–3's and to increase total capacity. These larger piston engine aircraft had been designed in accordance with the specifications of the trunklines, rather than for local service operations. They were purchased primarily because of their low initial price.

Recently the local service carriers have been disposing of their remaining DC–3 aircraft and have been either buying new turboprop aircraft or converting their larger piston engine aircraft to turboprop power.[3] They have also been purchasing large numbers of "small" jets seating from 70 to 100 passengers. Although there are many local service routes on which traffic is so great that even aircraft twice the size of the DC–3 might be too small, and although the average passenger load for local service carriers rose from 8.3 in 1952 to 21.2 in 1966, a substantial number of routes remain on which the DC–3 is a much larger aircraft than traffic warrants.[4]

Since certain equipment changes now being undertaken by the local service

---

[1] The following official Civil Aeronautics Board carrier designations are the ones which we shall use:

Local Service Carriers		*Trunk Carriers*	
Allegheny	Ozark	American	Northeast
Bonanza	Pacific	Braniff	Northwest
Central	Piedmont	Continental	TWA
Frontier	Southern	Delta	United
Lake Central	Trans Texas	Eastern	Western
Mohawk	West Coast	National	
North Central			

[2] In 1953, 150 of the 152 aircraft in the local service airlines' fleets were DC–3's.

[3] Conversion kits are manufactured by the Allison Division of General Motors and by Rolls-Royce/Convair.

[4] In 1963, the Systems Analysis and Research Corporation (SARC) performed a study of the potential market for smaller transport aircraft for the Federal Aviation Agency, which concluded: ". . . in 1975 [projecting 1963 traffic growth rates] there should be more widespread use of smaller aircraft than is presently made of the DC–3. Current [1963] DC–3 operations of the local service carriers account for some 45.5 per cent of total routings operated by the local service carriers, whereas in 1975, even with the greater traffic volumes which are forecast, 61 per cent of the local industry routings will most economically be operated with aircraft of less than 40-seat capacity."

carriers may be unwarranted, given both current and projected traffic levels, the impact of these changes on local service airline industry costs is of obvious interest. We have attempted to formulate our cost function to shed light on this issue.

Since the end of 1966, three mergers involving seven of the thirteen local service carriers have been consummated. These mergers have been encouraged by the CAB. A cost function such as the one we are proposing may illuminate the extent of returns to scale and thus the possible consequences of mergers for efficiency.

The local service airlines are subject to detailed economic regulation by the CAB. Generally they are not allowed to compete against each other, but recently they have been permitted to compete with trunk carriers on a limited basis. Obtaining Board permission to initiate or terminate service on a route is usually an expensive and time-consuming process. Furthermore, minimal service amounting to at least two flights per day is required on authorized routes provided traffic stays above certain specified levels.[5] Since about 1960, the CAB's method of subsidy compensation has included a limitation on the maximum number of flights per day to be subsidized, but this number has not remained constant. The Board has extremely limited powers to control the size of aircraft used through its subsidy formulae.

It may be concluded that the CAB has effective control over the number of stations served by the local service carriers and substantial, but not complete, control over the total number of aircraft miles flown. However, it has little effective control over the aircraft mix used by the carriers to fly these aircraft miles. To the extent that the measure of output adopted below depends on the aircraft mix, it cannot be considered fully exogenous.

II. COST MODEL FOR THE UNITED STATES LOCAL SERVICE AIRLINE INDUSTRY

In his study of the costs of thermal electric power generation, Nerlove estimated a cost function which was a reduced form of a Cobb-Douglas production function assuming that output and factor prices are exogenous and that the firms in the industry minimize costs. We shall employ a version of this approach but shall modify it for the following reasons:[6]

One major problem with the use of the approach just outlined is that, except by chance, one never observes a firm on the long-run total cost function but instead observes it on a short-run total cost function. The firm is unable in

---

[5] In 1967 *Flight Magazine* reported that ". . . in eleven years of Use-It-Or-Lose-It conditions, 101 points have suffered a suspension of service." The same source reported that in 1966, forty-one stations not meeting the standard were still receiving service.
[6] A synthetic cost function approach similar to that employed by Caves, Straszheim, and the Systems Analysis and Research Corporation was rejected for reasons outlined in Eads.

the short run to adjust all of its factors of production to the optimum level for the output level it is given to produce.[7] Furthermore, it is not possible to predict a priori the direction of the bias that might result from the estimation of a long-run cost function from a scatter of points generated by observations on a family of short-run cost functions. Meyer and Kraft suggest that such bias may be eliminated by averaging observations over several time periods and performing a regression on the averaged data. This technique appears to be highly arbitrary. In an industry such as the one we are studying, moreover, it is not feasible because of the small number of firms. We estimate a family of short-run cost functions in a way that enables us to derive the parameters of the underlying long-run function.

The relationship between the long-run cost function and the associated family of short-run cost functions is well-known and available in a number of locations.[8] Consider a production function,

$$y = f(x_1, \ldots, x_n), \tag{1}$$

where y represents output and $x_1, \ldots, x_n$ represents inputs, x_n being the quantity of the fixed factor. The short-run cost function obtained from (1), assuming prices exogenous and cost minimization by the firm, can be written,

$$c_s = \phi(y, p_1, \ldots, p_{n-1}, x_n) + p_n x_n, \tag{2}$$

where $p_1, \ldots, p_n$ are prices. This equation states nothing more than that short-run total costs are the sum of short-run variable costs and fixed costs. Writing (2) as an implicit function we obtain

$$c_s - \phi(y, p_1, \ldots, p_{n-1}, x_n) - p_n x_n = G(y, p_1, \ldots, p_n, x_n) = 0. \tag{3}$$

The condition existing at each point of tangency between a short-run cost function and the long-run cost function is

$$\partial G/\partial x_n = 0. \tag{4}$$

---

[7] Borts contends that the firm will not even be on its short-run cost function but on some hybrid function. Reasons are advanced in Eads for believing that this is not the case for firms in the local service airline industry.

[8] See, for example, Henderson and Quandt. Two works in which the relationship between the short-run and the long-run cost functions has been used are Bressler's 1952 study of city milk distribution and the study of the costs of electricity generation reported in Johnston. In both of these studies, plant size was included as a variable in the cost function. The short-run cost function was obtained by holding plant size constant and varying output. The long-run cost function was obtained by allowing plant size to vary and tracing out a number of short-run cost curves. The long-run cost function was then constructed graphically as the envelope of the short-run functions. We are aware of no instance prior to Eads in which the short-run, long-run relationship has been utilized as it is here. For possible reasons, see Eads.

Solving (4) for x_n and substituting the result into (3), we obtain the long-run cost function,

$$H(y, p_1, \ldots, p_n) = 0, \tag{5}$$

which is a function only of output and the input prices.

This suggests an indirect method of estimating the parameters of the unobservable long-run cost function; one could estimate the parameters of a family of short-run cost functions and use the above relationship to determine the parameters of the long-run cost function.

A second problem in applying the methods of the electric power study is defining output for the local service airline industry. A single dimension does not suffice, but using a multidimensional output definition raises problems of a theoretical nature. Klein faced a similar problem in connection with his rail cost study; he defined output for the railroads as consisting of freight ton miles and passenger miles. However, when two or more such variables are incorporated directly in a log-linear production function, the implied product transformation loci are convex rather than concave; thus the second-order conditions for profit maximization cannot be satisfied. Klein argued that this was irrelevant, since the regulated nature of the industry precluded substitution among different outputs, i.e., railroads were not free to vary the mix of passenger and freight services offered. Unfortunately, the choice of a particular relationship among the output levels may affect the statistical relationship of the input levels both among themselves and to the output levels. To avoid the possibility of such misspecification, it seems preferable to adopt a theoretically more defensible form.

Consider the family of functions given by

$$y^n = \tau_1 a_1{}^n + \tau_2 a_2{}^n + \cdots + \tau_m a_m{}^n, \tag{6}$$

where $1 < n < \infty$. Interpret the a_i's as various measures of airline output such as the number of stations served or the number of seat miles flown. The τ_i are weights to be estimated. Defining output, y, as the nth root of the right-hand side of (6) produces product transformation curves of the proper shape. If $n = 2$ and $\tau_1 = \tau_2 = \ldots = \tau_m$, the product transformation locus is an m-dimensional hypersphere. If $\tau_1 \neq \tau_2 \neq \ldots \neq \tau_m$, it is an m-dimensional hyperellipse.[9]

In view of the questions to which the cost function is relevant, it is desirable that the output measure adopted incorporate some measure of aircraft choice. Let us assume that there are k aircraft types. Let a_i be the ith output component defined in (6), and let

$$a_i = \epsilon_1 a_{i1} + \epsilon_2 a_{i2} + \cdots + \epsilon_k a_{ik}, \tag{7}$$

---

[9] If $2 < n < \infty$, the transformation locus becomes an m-dimensional supersphere on superhyperellipse.

where a_{ij} represents the output measure i flown by aircraft type j and ϵ_j represents a weight to be determined.[10]

A final reason for modification of the methodology is that one factor of production, fuel, appears to be used in fixed proportions; that is, fuel costs appear to be determined only by the price of fuel and by output and not by the prices of other factors of production. The use of a cost function derived from a Cobb-Douglas production function implies that the elasticities of substitution between factors of production are equal and equal to one. The use of a CES production function removes the restriction of unitary elasticity of substitution but still implies equality. It is possible, however, to derive a cost function having an underlying production function which permits different elasticities of substitution between different pairs of factors. Irrespective of the underlying production functions, the relationship between the long- and short-run cost functions examined above holds.

We propose a cost model of the following form:

$$c_f = p_f f \text{ (fuel cost equation)} \tag{8}$$

$$c^*_{ao(s)} = (c_{ao(s)} - p_2 x_2)$$
$$= k p_1 y^{1/a_1} x_2^{-a_2/a_1} \tag{9}$$

(short-run variable non-fuel cost equation)

$$c_{ao(l)} = k' y^{1/r} p_1^{a_1/r} p_2^{a_2/r} \tag{10}$$

(all other non-fuel costs, long run)

$$c_t = c_{ao(l)} + c_f \tag{11}$$

(long-run total costs);

where

$$y = \text{output} = [\tau_1(\epsilon_1 a_{11} + \epsilon_2 a_{12} + \cdots + \epsilon_k a_{1k})^2 + \tau_2 a_2^2]^{1/2}, \tag{12}$$

and where

$$r = a_1 + a_2,$$
$$k = a_o^{-1a/1},$$
$$k' = r[a_0 a_1^{a_1} a_2^{a_2}]^{-1/r}$$
$$= r[(a_1/k)^{a_1} a_2^{a_2}]^{-1/r},$$
$$a_0, a_1, a_2 = \text{parameters to be estimated,}$$
$$c_f = \text{fuel costs,}$$

---

[10] Since all carriers do not fly all aircraft types, zero observations will appear. This raises a serious problem in a log-linear output formulation, since the logarithm of zero is undefined. The problem has sometimes been treated by adding a constant to each observation of each output measure, thus assuring that no zeros appear. However, this introduces a bias, since a constant added to a small number results in a larger percentage increase than does the same constant added to a larger number.

Zeros cause no problems of this sort when an output formulation such as (7) is adopted.

198 A Theory of Producer Behavior

$$\begin{aligned}
p_f &= \text{price of fuel, piston } (PFP)^{11} \text{ and turbine } (PFT), \\
f &= \text{gallons of fuel used } (GFP \text{ (piston fuel) and } GFT \text{ (turbine fuel))}, \\
C_{ao(s)} &= \text{total costs except fuel, short run,} \\
C_{ao(l)} &= \text{total costs except fuel, long run,} \\
C^*_{ao(s)} &= \text{short-run variable non-fuel costs } (COST), \\
p_1 &= \text{price of labor less pilots and copilots } (PLNP), \\
p_2 &= \text{price of pilots and copilots } (PPILOT), \\
x_2 &= \text{stock of pilots and copilots } (PCP), \\
c_t &= \text{total long-run costs,} \\
a_{11}, \ldots, a_{1k} &= \text{number of aircraft miles flown by aircraft type (or group) } 1, \ldots, k \ (ACMA, \ldots, ACMK), \\
a_2 &= \text{number of stations served, } (STA), \text{ and} \\
\tau_1, \tau_2, \epsilon_1, \ldots, \epsilon_k &= \text{parameters to be estimated, normalized so that } \tau_1 + \tau_2 = 1 \text{ and } \epsilon_1 + \cdots + \epsilon_k = 1.
\end{aligned}$$

The reader will note that this cost function is derived in part from a Cobb-Douglas production function. The short-run elasticity of substitution between all factors of production is zero while the long-run elasticity of substitution is zero between fuel and the two other factors of production (pilots and copilots and labor other than pilots and copilots), while it is equal to one between the latter two factors of production. The stock of pilots and copilots is assumed to be the factor whose input is fixed in the short run.

Choice of the Fixed Factor

To assume a labor factor as fixed in the short run is somewhat unconventional and requires explanation. To contend that the stock of pilots and copilots is a proper measure of the flow of fixed factor services, it is necessary to argue that short-run changes in the stock of pilots and copilots are at least as difficult to make as short-run changes in the stock of aircraft. We also argue that short-run changes in the utilization of the stock of pilots and copilots are not significant, thus eliminating the problem that arises from using a stock to measure a flow. The argument requires a brief description of the markets for aircraft and pilots and the ways in which an airline might be able to vary its input of each of these services in the short run.

Local service airlines purchase aircraft in two markets—the new aircraft market and the used aircraft market. Until the advent of the pure jets, the

---

[11] The acronyms presented are for the convenience of the reader in interpreting the results shown below. An appendix outlining the procedures used to construct the variables and listing the data sources is available from Eads upon request.

only aircraft purchased only in the new aircraft market was the F–27; virtually all of the large piston and DC–3 aircraft purchased were used aircraft. New aircraft are seldom available for immediate delivery. At the time of his order the purchaser is usually assigned a position in a delivery queue, and actual delivery does not take place for several months or, in some cases, for several years.

The used aircraft market works differently. There usually exists a small pool of used aircraft of various types which are available for purchase on relatively short notice. Such purchases are arranged through aircraft brokers, and the carrier may acquire the aircraft from almost any point in the world. Because of safety regulations, the buyer of used aircraft is aware of the condition of any aircraft in which he may be interested. The market is highly competitive, and the price reflects the condition of the aircraft. Thus, if an airline is willing to acquire used aircraft, it is possible for it to obtain them on relatively short notice without paying a substantial premium for early delivery.

If purchases of new or used aircraft were the only two ways in which a carrier might increase the supply of aircraft services, it would be necessary to consider the stock of aircraft as fixed to the industry as a whole, at least in a period as short as a quarter. This would introduce some complication in the treatment of aircraft services as variable for the individual air carriers.

Fortunately, two other sources exist. First, there is a world market for the leasing of aircraft by one carrier from another. A carrier with temporary over-capacity can reduce it and a carrier needing additional capacity on a short-run basis can obtain it rapidly. Unlike the used aircraft market, the market for leased aircraft is not limited to older types of aircraft, but short-term leasing may be relatively expensive.

Second, the utilization rates of existing fleets of aircraft may be varied in the short run. Though limited by maintenance requirements set by law, significant short-run changes in fleet utilization are possible and are, in fact, widely observed. The cost of maintaining a small number of fully depreciated aircraft in order to be able to provide short-run increases in capacity is not large and airlines are known to maintain such hedging stocks. (Note that such stocks result in difficulties in using the stock of aircraft to measure services from the fixed factor.)

In contrast, the stock of pilots and copilots cannot be varied so easily as the stock of aircraft. To be sure, there usually exists a pool of trained and licensed pilots who may be hired by an airline, but in many cases newly-hired or promoted pilots and copilots must be trained and certified to fly the particular types of aircraft the airline owns. This is time consuming, and the problem is exacerbated by the large variety of aircraft flown by the local service carriers.

Furthermore, even if pilots certified to fly the particular types of aircraft possessed by the airline are available, they cannot be put to work immediately upon being hired, because they must be thoroughly familiarized with the routes over which they will be flying before they can operate with paying passengers. Route familiarization requires the use of flight time of senior pilots, which is obviously in short supply when an airline is faced with an unplanned increase in its output. Differences in operational procedures among airlines and pilot seniority rules also serve to hamper carrier flexibility in the acquisition and termination of pilots in response to short-run fluctuations in demand.

Utilization of the stock of pilots and copilots also cannot be varied easily. Airlines are discouraged from maintaining a stock of pilots in excess of normal requirements by union agreements which require that a large portion of a pilot's salary be paid regardless of whether or not he flies. The maximum amount of time a pilot can fly during a month and at one continuous stretch is regulated by the Federal Aviation Administration. Collective bargaining agreements concerning pilot and copilot scheduling restrict actual utilization to considerably below these limits.

The airline strike of 1966 provides, perhaps, the best example illustrating that the stock of pilots and copilots, rather than the stock of aircraft, is the fixed factor in the short run. The local service carriers which served areas also served by the struck trunk carriers were faced with an unexpected and massive increase in demand and were able to take advantage of this increase only to a limited extent. This was partly because of a limited stock of aircraft and pressure on ground facilities, but the major difficulty mentioned in reports during the strike was the problem of obtaining sufficient pilot time to fly the aircraft the local airlines had, at the rates of aircraft utilization they were able to achieve.[12]

The choice of the number of pilots and copilots as a measure of services from the fixed factor appears justified.[13]

III. DATA AND ESTIMATION

The Data

The data used in this study consist of quarterly observations on twelve of the thirteen local service carriers over a nine-year period from the first quarter of 1958 through the fourth quarter of 1966, virtually the entire period of transition from use of the DC–3 to use of larger aircraft. At the end of 1957, ten of the thirteen local service carriers were operating all DC–3 fleets. The first of the turboprop aircraft, the F–27, was introduced in 1958. Extension of the

---

[12] For example, Mohawk Airlines reported near the end of July that it would have to suspend operations for the last three days of the month unless the pilot's union allowed it to waive portions of the union contract dealing with pilot scheduling. Other carriers saved pilot time by skipping low-density stops and concentrating on the larger markets. Aircraft capacity was seldom mentioned as a major constraint.

[13] Our confidence in this choice was increased by the highly unsatisfactory results obtained when measures of aircraft services were used.

period of observation prior to 1958 in order to cover the entire equipment transition was precluded by a major change in the CAB accounting system which took effect in 1957, as well as difficulty of access to earlier data.

Aircraft Classes

The local service airlines have used several aircraft types. Table 1 contains a list of all the aircraft types that were operated up to the end of 1966 with the exception of small single engine and twin engine aircraft, most of which had been replaced by DC-3's by the early 1950's. Table 1 also illustrates the similarity among a number of these aircraft types and suggests that a suitable grouping of similar types would not result in the loss of a great deal of information.

Another reason for grouping is that a costing method such as the one proposed here should not find significant differences in cost behavior among closely similar aircraft types. Since each carrier tends to operate only one of the aircraft from each of the groups (e.g., either Martin 202's or Convair 240's, but not both), if differences in cost behavior between two similar aircraft were found by the model, it might show the existence of interfirm differences in the method of operation rather than true significant differences in aircraft cost characteristics. Conversely, by adjusting the sample to remove all firm effects, some of the variance due to the different types of aircraft operated by the firms might be simultaneously removed.

Group A consists of the DC-3 and the Nord 262. Although the Nord 262 is turbine powered and might be conceivably placed in Group C with the other turboprop aircraft, its similarity in size and power to the DC-3, plus the limited experience in its operation, dictate the chosen grouping. Only one airline, Lake Central, has purchased the Nord, and it began Nord operations only late in 1965. Furthermore, the Nord was grounded for a substantial period of time due to in-flight engine failures which have since been corrected.

The case for grouping aircraft types is most obvious among the large piston aircraft which are referred to as Aircraft Group B: the Convair 240, 340, and 440 and the Martin 202 and 404. They are all of virtually the same size and seating capacity; their cruising speeds are similar; they are powered by modifications of the same Pratt & Whitney engine, the R-2800. The major difference among the aircraft in this group is that the Convair 240 and the Martin 202 are not pressurized, while the other aircraft are.

Aircraft Group C consists of all turboprop aircraft excluding the Nord 262. On the basis of power alone, it might appear that the turboprop aircraft should be divided into two classes: (1) the F-27 and FH-227, and (2) the turboprop Convair conversions. However, since the turboprop Convairs did not begin significant operations until the very end of our sample period, there are insufficient observations on their operations to justify grouping them separately.

TABLE 1 Selected Specifications of Aircraft Used by the Local Service Airlines

Aircraft Group	Aircraft Type	Crew	Passengers	Gross Weight[a]	Speed[b]	Engine Characteristics
A	DC-3	2	21–28	25,000	167	2, piston, 1275 hp.[c]
	Nord 262	2	27–29	22,930	224	2, turboprop, 1065 eshp.[d]
B	Convair 240	2	40	41,790	265	2, piston, 1800 hp.
	Convair 340	2	44	47,000	284	2, piston, 1800 hp.
	Convair 440	2	44–52	49,100	289	2, piston, 1800 hp.
	Martin 202	2	36–40	39,900	286	2, piston, 1800 hp.
	Martin 404	2	40	43,000	280	2, piston, 1800 hp.
C	F-27A	2	36–48	42,000	293	2, turboprop, 2020 eshp.
	FH-227	2	44–52	43,500	293	2, turboprop, 2230 eshp.
	Convair 540	2	48–52	50,670[e]	322	2, turboprop, 3500 eshp.
	Convair 580	2	52	50,670[e]	342	2, turboprop, 3750 eshp.
	Convair 600	2	46	45,000	312	2, turboprop, 3025 eshp.
D	DC-9-10	2	90	77,700	559	2, turbofan, 14000 lbs.[f]
	BAC 111-200	2	69	78,500	550	2, turbofan, 10410 lbs.
	Boeing 727	3	70–131	161,000	520	3, turbofan, 14000 lbs.

[a] Normal gross weight in pounds.
[b] Best cruise speed in miles per hour.
[c] Brake horsepower.
[d] Equivalent shaft horsepower.
[e] Maximum landing weight.
[f] Pounds thrust.

Group D consists of pure jet aircraft. Local service airline experience with these aircraft is also quite limited, the first having been put into service by Mohawk in 1965. Towards the end of the sample period, however, their use was becoming quite widespread. The major lack of homogeneity in this group involves the Boeing 727. This aircraft has three engines, as compared with two for the BAC 111 and the DC–9, and it carries a flight crew of three, instead of the usual two. Only two local service airlines, Pacific and Frontier, use this aircraft, and they each acquired it in mid-1966.

Estimation of the Fuel Equations

Separate equations were estimated for turbine and piston fuel. Estimation of a single equation requires a single fuel price, but a single price index is not meaningful, since it depends solely upon the relative weights given to the prices of piston and turbine fuel. Furthermore, the use of a single equation implies the possibility of substitution between turbine and piston fuel, and this is not possible once a choice of aircraft has been made.

The entire sample was used to estimate the piston fuel equation. A smaller, nine-carrier, seven-quarter sample was used to estimate the turbine fuel equation. The shorter period encompassed all significant turbine operations for most carriers with the exception of those few which bought F–27's in 1958 and 1959. The equations were estimated in natural units, not logarithms, and were forced through the origin on the assumption that if no aircraft miles were flown and no aircraft departures were made, no fuel was used.

The method of estimation used was the two-round procedure developed by Balestra and Nerlove. In their procedure it is assumed that the residual disturbance term can be divided into two stochastically independent parts, a time-invariant firm effect and a remainder. The ratio of the contribution to total variance of the time-invariant effect to the total variance is denoted by ρ. It is also possible to include a firm-invariant time effect. This was not done for reasons of computational simplicity and because the need for it in this case was not readily apparent. An estimate of the disturbance variance-covariance matrix was obtained in the first round and used in the second round to obtain the coefficient estimates by means of generalized least squares.

The estimates are shown in Table 2.[14] The relative magnitudes and signs of the coefficients are as expected. The multicollinearity tests suggested by Farrar and Glauber indicate that there is significant collinearity present. As would be expected, the diagnostic section of the tests indicates that important collinearity exists between the aircraft mile and aircraft departure variables for each aircraft type. Consequently, a second equation for each fuel type was estimated using only the aircraft mile variables in each case. The results are

---

[14] Each coefficient can be interpreted as the number of gallons of fuel required for flying one aircraft mile or for performing one takeoff and landing using aircraft of the appropriate group, everything else being held constant.

TABLE 2 Fuel Equations

I. $GFP = 0.595\ ACMA + 1.093\ ACMB + 8.639\ ACDA + 17.283\ ACDB$ $R^2 = 0.9930$[a]
         (0.041)   (0.033)   (3.408)   (3.675) $\rho = 0.2793$

II. $GFP = 0.679\ ACMA + 1.241\ ACMB$ $R^2 = 0.9915$[a]
         (0.009)   (0.006) $\rho = 0.3758$

III. $GFT = 1.222\ ACMC + 2.842\ ACMD + 40.825\ ACDC + 94.723\ ACDD$ $R^2 = 0.9874$[a]
         (0.201)   (0.374)   (27.245)   (69.432) $\rho = 0.3487$

IV. $GFT = 1.517\ ACMC + 3.369\ ACMD$ $R^2 = 0.9847$[a]
         (0.027)   (0.090) $\rho = 0.3855$

[a] The R^2's shown in Tables 2 and 3 are the ratios of the explained variance of the original dependent variable (denoted $u'\ u$) to the total variance of the original dependent variable (denoted $y'\ y$); i.e., $R^2 = (y'\ y - u'\ u)/y'\ y$.

The explained variance calculated from the second round estimates of the two-round Balestra-Nerlove procedures is the explained variance of the *transformed* dependent variable (denoted $u^*\ 'u^*$). The following equation gives the relationship between $u'\ u$ and $u^*\ 'u^*$,

$$u'u = [(1 - \rho + T\rho)/(1 - T\rho)]\, u^*\, 'u^*,$$

where ρ is as defined in footnote 16 and T is the number of time periods in the sample.

also shown in Table 2. Note that the estimated values of ρ are much closer for regressions II and IV than for I and III.

Estimation of the "All Other Costs, Short Run" Equation

This equation was estimated in two parts. It was not found possible in earlier estimation attempts to obtain simultaneous estimates of the fixed factor coefficient, a_2/a_1 and ρ, the ratio of the variance of the firm "effect" to the total residual variance. A possible reason for this difficulty is that the factor does vary, albeit slowly, over time and that its level reflects interfirm differences to some extent. The method adopted was to obtain an independent estimate of the fixed factor coefficient from a derived demand equation for pilots and copilots. The equation estimated was of the form:

$$x_2 = k'' y^{1/r} (p_2/p_1)^{-a_1/r} v, \tag{13}$$

where

$k'' = a_2(a_0 a_1^{a_1} a_2^{a_2})^{-1/r}$.
$x_2 = $ number of pilots and copilots (PCP).
$y = $ output ($ACMT$).
$p_1 = $ price of labor net of pilots and copilots ($PLNP$).
$p_2 = $ price of pilots and copilots ($PPILOT$).
$v = $ an error term whose logarithm is assumed to have the properties outlined in Balestra and Nerlove.

Total aircraft miles (unweighted) was used as a simple proxy for output in this equation.[15]

This equation is a long-run derived demand equation for pilots and copilots; therefore, a way must be found to deal with the disturbing influences of short-run demand fluctuations. Ideally, we should formulate a distributed lag structure and estimate it as part of the equation. For simplicity, however, we took eight-quarter moving averages of the price and output variables, centered on the fourth quarter. In doing so, a specific lag distribution of exceptionally simple form was imposed. The simple output definition and the arbitrary distribution assumed are perhaps the weakest links in our estimation procedure and more work is clearly needed in this connection. For this reason we use this equation only to determine the necessary adjustment to costs in the short-run cost equation.

The results of the estimation of the derived demand equation for pilots and copilots are shown in Table 3. The estimates were obtained using the two-round Balestra–Nerlove procedure previously described. The signs of the coefficients are all as expected and the level of significance is high.

From Table 3 we see that $-a_1/r = -0.3624$ and $1/r = 0.7840$. From these

---

[15] The correlation between the price ratio and total aircraft miles was not significantly different from zero.

TABLE 3 Derived Demand Equation for Pilots

$$\log PCP = 0.2712 + 0.7840 \log ACMT$$
$$(0.2265) \quad (0.0207)$$
$$- 0.3624 \log (PPILOT/PLNP)$$
$$(0.1458)$$

$R^2 = 0.882$[a]
$\rho = 0.397$

[a] See footnote a, Table 2.

we obtain $r = 1.2755$, $a_1 = 0.4622$, and, by utilizing the definition of r, $a_2 = 0.8133$. Finally we obtain the estimate we are seeking, $a_2/a_1 = 1.7596$. This value multiplied by the logarithm of the number of pilots and copilots was added to the logarithm of the dependent variable for each observation. This "adjusted" variable was then used as the dependent variable in the equation explaining short-run costs less fuel costs.

In estimating the equation for short-run costs less fuel costs, we employed a maximum-likelihood approach rather than the two-round procedure used for the previous five equations. The two-round procedure was ruled out by the highly nonlinear definition of output (see Equation (12)). As will appear, our results are reasonable economically, which was not the case in the earlier study of Balestra and Nerlove, when the maximum-likelihood approach was attempted in a similar context.

The likelihood function to be maximized is of the form,

$$L(\psi, \rho, \sigma^2) = -NT/2 \log 2\pi - 1/2 \log |\Omega|$$
$$- 1/2 u'\Omega^{-1} u, \quad (14)$$

where N is the number of firms in the sample; T is the number of time periods; Ω, ρ, and σ^2 are defined exactly as in Balestra and Nerlove,[16] ψ stands

[16] That is,
let
σ^2 = the variance of the time-invariant firm effect,
σ^2_u = the variance of the remaining disturbance,
$\sigma^2_v = \sigma^2_u + \sigma^2_v$,
$\rho = \sigma^2_u/\sigma^2$,
and

$$\Omega = \sigma^2 \begin{Bmatrix} A & 0 & \cdots & 0 \\ 0 & A & \cdots & 0 \\ \vdots & \vdots & & \vdots \\ 0 & 0 & \cdots & A \end{Bmatrix}, \quad (NT \times NT),$$

and

$$A = \begin{Bmatrix} 1 & \rho & \rho & \cdots & \rho \\ \rho & 1 & \rho & \cdots & \rho \\ \vdots & & & & \vdots \\ \rho & \rho & \rho & \cdots & 1 \end{Bmatrix}, \quad (T \times T).$$

for the parameters of u, and u is defined as follows:

$$u = c' - \log k - \kappa/2 \log [\tau_1(\epsilon_1 ACMA + \epsilon_2 ACMB + \epsilon_3 ACMC + \epsilon_4 ACMD)^2 + \tau_2(STA)^2], \tag{15}$$

where κ is the short-run elasticity of all costs excluding fuel costs with respect to changes in output, $c' = \log COST + a_2/a_1 \log PCP$, k is the constant term of Equation (9), and a_2/a_1 is the estimate obtained from the derived demand equation presented in Table 3.

Balestra and Nerlove show that (14) can be rewritten as:

$$\hat{L}(\psi, \xi, \eta) = -\frac{NT}{2} \log 2\pi - \frac{N}{2} \log \xi - \frac{N(T-1)}{2} \log \eta - \frac{1}{2} \left\{ \frac{M_1(\psi)}{\xi} + \frac{M_2(\psi)}{\eta} \right\}, \tag{16}$$

where

$$\xi = \sigma^2 [(1-\rho) + T_p];$$
$$\eta = \sigma^2 (1-\rho),$$

$$M_1(\psi) = 1/T \sum_{n=1}^{N} \sum_{t=1}^{T} \sum_{t'=1}^{T} u_{nt} u_{nt'};$$

and

$$M_2(\psi) = \sum_{n=1}^{N} \left\{ \sum_{t=1}^{T} u^2_{nt} - \frac{\left(\sum_{t=1}^{T} u_{nt}\right)^2}{T} \right\}.$$

The calculations may be simplified by maximizing (16) partially with respect to certain of the parameters and then using a computer algorithm to maximize the partially maximized, or concentrated, likelihood function with respect to the remaining parameters.[17, 18] The maximum-likelihood estimates for ξ and η can be written as:

$$\text{est } \xi = \frac{M_1(\psi)}{N} \quad \text{and est } \eta = \frac{M_2(\psi)}{N(T-1)}. \tag{17}$$

---

[17] The computer algorithm used was developed in Fletcher and Powell and modified by William Raduchel.
[18] The important principle of stepwise maximization is discussed in Hood and Koopmans.

208 A Theory of Producer Behavior

Substituting these definitions for ξ and η into (15) and simplifying, we obtain:

$$\hat{L}(\psi) = -\frac{NT}{2}(\log 2\pi + 1) - \frac{N}{2}\log\frac{M_1(\psi)}{2}$$
$$- \frac{N(T-1)}{2}\log\frac{M_2(\psi)}{N(T-1)}. \tag{18}$$

This expression is a function only of ψ. Once the values of the parameters which maximize $L(\psi)$ have been found, the corresponding values for ρ and σ^2 can be calculated:

$$\rho = \frac{(T-1)M_1(\psi) - M_2(\psi)}{(T-1)[M_1(\psi) + M_2(\psi)]}, \tag{19}$$

and

$$\sigma^2 = \frac{M_1(\psi) + M_2(\psi)}{NT}. \tag{20}$$

The u which was used in maximizing (18) was not the one defined in Equation (15), but was

$$u = c' - \kappa/2 \log[(\Upsilon_1 ACMA + \Upsilon_2 ACMB + \Upsilon_3 ACMC + \Upsilon_4 ACMD)^2 + \chi(STA)^2]. \tag{21}$$

A maximum for the likelihood function was found within the theoretically admissible range for ρ (est $\rho = 0.619$). Instead of estimating Y_i and χ directly, we estimated their square roots in order to ensure that the estimates themselves would be positive. The resulting constrained estimates were then normalized to obtain estimates of the cost function parameters:

$$\epsilon_i = \frac{\Upsilon_i}{\Sigma \Upsilon_i}, \tag{22}$$

$$\tau_1 = \frac{(\Sigma \Upsilon_i)^2}{(\Sigma \Upsilon_i)^2 + \chi}, \tag{23}$$

$$\tau_2 = \frac{\chi}{(\Sigma \Upsilon_i)^2 + \chi}, \tag{24}$$

and

$$\log k = \kappa/2 \log[(\Sigma \Upsilon_i)^2 + \chi]. \tag{25}$$

Using the normalized parameter estimates, the equation for short-run variable costs (less fuel costs), $c^*_{ao(s)}$, can be written as:

$$c^*_{ao(s)} = 279.81\,[0.102\,(0.197\,ACMA$$
$$+ 0.242\,ACMB + 0.202\,ACMC$$
$$+ 0.359\,ACMD)^2$$
$$+ 0.898\,(STA)^2]^{2.125} \cdot PCP^{-1.759}$$
$$\text{est } \sigma^2 = 0.0205. \tag{26}$$

The ratio of the "explained" variance of costs to the total variance was extremely high ($R^2 = 0.93$). No attempt was made to estimate the asymptotic variance-covariance matrix for the parameter estimates because of the complexity of the calculations required.[19] Direct observation of the paths of the parameter estimates, their derivatives, and the values of the likelihood function during the course of maximization convinced us that the estimates of both the aircraft group relative weights and the elasticity with respect to output of short-run variable costs less fuel costs were indeed good ones. . . . We feel that less confidence can be attached to the estimates of the relative weights of the aircraft mile and stations served variables inasmuch as the likelihood function is quite flat with respect to variations in their coefficients. Additional maximization attempts utilizing different starting points and further experimentation with the likelihood function only served to confirm these conclusions.

Long-Run Total Cost Function for the Local Service Airline Industry

The results developed in section II may now be used to derive the long-run total cost function from the short-run variable cost function. From Equation (26), $1/a_1 = 2.125$ and $a_1 = 0.471$. Note that this estimate of a_1 is remarkably close to the corresponding estimate from the derived demand equation for pilots, thus giving increased confidence in the reliability of the estimate. From the derived demand equation for pilots and copilots (Table 3), we have already obtained $a_2/a_1 = 1.759$, which implies that $a_2 = 0.770$.[20] From these results, we can obtain the long-run cost elasticity with respect to changes in the price of pilots, $a_2/r = 0.638$, and the long-run cost elasticity with respect to changes in the price of labor net of pilots, $a_1/r = 0.362$. The constant term for the long-run cost equation, k', is obtained as

$$k' = r\left[\left(\frac{a_1}{k}\right)^{a_1} a_2^{a_2}\right]^{-1/r} = 14.79. \qquad (27)$$

Combining these results with the fuel equations shown in Table 2, we obtain the long-run total cost equation:

---

[19] It is known that the maximum-likelihood estimates are, under general circumstances, distributed with asymptotic variance-covariance matrix given by the inverse of the matrix of second partial derivatives evaluated at the estimated parameter values.

[20] To the extent that output is in fact endogenous the estimate obtained for r is biased. For example, if a positive correlation between output and the disturbance of the production function existed, then there would be a negative correlation between output and the disturbance in the cost function (since v, the disturbance in the cost function, equals $1/u$, where u is the disturbance in the production function). This means that the estimate of $1/r$ may be biased downward; that is, there may be a bias in the direction of increasing returns to scale.

$$\begin{aligned}c_t = 14.79\ [&0.102\ (0.197\ ACMA\\&+ 0.242\ ACMB + 0.202\ ACMC\\&+ 0.359\ ACMD)^2\\&+ 0.898\ (STA)^2]^{0.770} \cdot PLNP^{0.362}\\&PPILOT^{0.638} + PFP\ (0.679\ ACMA\\&+ 1.241\ ACMB) + PFT\ (1.517\ ACMC\\&+ 3.369\ ACMD).\end{aligned} \quad (28)$$

It is this equation which may be used to answer questions such as those raised at the end of the first section of the paper.

IV. CONCLUSIONS

Although our model has certain weaknesses that can only be remedied by further work, the following conclusions appear to be justified:

1. No evidence has been discovered that the local service airline industry is subject to substantial increasing returns to scale. . . . Although an estimate of the degree of returns to scale cannot be read directly from Equation (27), it is likely to be quite close to (but certainly less than) 1.3, the reciprocal of the long-run elasticity of all costs less fuel costs.[21] Since "output" as defined above, may not be strictly exogenous, there is reason to suspect a possible bias in the direction of increasing returns to scale. If this is the case, it should be concluded that the industry is subject only to slightly increasing returns to scale.

Evidence in support of such a conclusion is provided by the results of the three mergers mentioned in section I. The industry's smallest carriers were absorbed by the largest; yet, no significant cost economies have been encountered to date. In fact, in at least one case, the surviving carrier has encountered significant diseconomies attributable to the merger, though this may prove to be only a short-run phenomenon.

2. In contrast to a priori expectations, Group C aircraft (the turboprops and turboprop conversions) compared favorably on a total cost basis to Group A aircraft (primarily the DC–3's).[22] Total operating expenses per aircraft mile

---

[21] The degree of returns to scale is not equal to 1.3 because this figure does not take into account the elasticity of fuel costs with respect to output. The degree of returns to scale will be *less than* 1.3 because, although a 1 per cent increase in aircraft miles flown will result in a 1 per cent increase in fuel costs, a 1 per cent increase in aircraft miles flown results in greater than a 1 per cent increase in output as it has been defined in Equation (12). However, the difference from 1.3 will not be great because the true estimate of the degree of returns to scale will be a weighted average of 1.3 and the reciprocal of the elasticity of fuel costs with respect to changes in output, and fuel costs constitute a relatively small share of total operating costs.

[22] This result does not appear to be due to our exclusion from short-run variable costs of aircraft depreciation expenses as recorded by the carriers. When these expenses were included in short-run variable costs, and Equation (26) was re-estimated, there was no apparent tendency for the relative aircraft weights to deviate from those shown in the paper.

for Group C aircraft are estimated as being only three per cent greater than for Group A aircraft. It appears, therefore, that the cost consequences of DC-3 replacement are not great, *provided* these aircraft are replaced by Group C aircraft. Only a relatively minor increase in traffic in response to the improved quality of service offered by the Group C aircraft would be required to offset their higher operating costs.

3. Group B aircraft (the 36 to 52-seat piston engine aircraft acquired secondhand from the trunklines) have been surprisingly expensive to operate. Equation (27) indicates that total operating expense per aircraft mile for operating these aircraft is 23 per cent above that of the DC-3's they have replaced. Consequently, to the extent that these aircraft have been used on routes better suited to DC-3's, substantial unnecessary costs have been incurred by the carriers.[23] A more interesting question is why the local service carriers delayed so long in converting their Group B aircraft to turboprop power or failed to purchase Group C aircraft in the first place.[24] Did the fault lie with the CAB regulatory policy? To what extent is the severe credit rationing claimed by the local service carriers responsible and how might it have been overcome? These are questions which we are currently investigating.

4. As expected, Group D aircraft (pure jets) are very expensive to operate. Their total operating cost per aircraft mile is 82 per cent greater than the DC-3. These aircraft are very productive, however, and, if used on routes of relatively high density, quite profitable. Our results make it clear, though, that such aircraft should not be used on low-density routes. Any route with a traffic density sufficient to require a jet is not a proper route to receive Federal subsidy. In this regard the recent CAB action requiring carriers to separate costs incurred on subsidized and nonsubsidized routes is encouraging, though the Board should recognize both the problem involved in allocating costs jointly incurred on subsidized and nonsubsidized routes and the incentive created to allocate as large a share of these joint costs as possible to the subsidized operations.

The only changes were in the weight of the aircraft mile variable relative to the stations served variable and, of course, in the constant term.

[23] From results presented elsewhere it can be estimated that in 1966 the unnecessary costs incurred by the use of Group B aircraft where Group A aircraft were better suited may have been about 18 million dollars.

[24] It is apparent from trade publications that the turboprop conversions were commercially available as early as 1958. By 1962 one carrier, Bonanza, had acquired a fleet that was completely turbine powered. If it can be assumed that *all* carriers could have replaced their Group B aircraft with Group C aircraft by 1962, it is possible to estimate the unnecessary costs incurred due to the operation of Group B rather than Group C aircraft over the 1962–1966 period as approximately 250 million dollars. In contrast, the total Federal subsidy payments to the local service carriers during the Fiscal 1962–1966 period amounted to approximately 350 million dollars.

6

ISOQUANT–ISOCOST ANALYSIS AND LINEAR PROGRAMMING

An isoquant–isocost model is a theoretical tool used to determine which combinations of inputs minimize the cost of producing alternative levels of output. The theory is a close parallel in production to indifference curves and budget constraint lines in consumption. Think of each indifference curve as an *iso-utility function* and of the budget restraint as an *iso-outlay function*, and notice the similarities as you read this chapter. (The prefix *iso* means *constant*.) One of the main differences between an isoquant–isocost production model and the marginal productivity model of the previous chapter is that the latter is most efficient in analyzing short-run problems, whereas the former is more efficient in studying long-run production problems. That is, it is useful for analyzing production given the absence of restrictions on the quantities of resources *a* and *b*, and thus is employed to analyze changes in the scale of a production process. The marginal productivity model cannot be as efficiently used to analyze scale adjustments, since a principal assumption of the model is that one factor is fixed in quantity. For this reason, it is helpful to explore this second approach to the theory of production. In addition, the isoquant–isocost model has a special application, linear programming, which we will explore at the end of this chapter.

ISOQUANT–ISOCOST FUNCTIONS

The Nature of Isoquants

To simplify our presentation of isoquants, we retain our two-input production model throughout this chapter. However, we relax the short-run assumption that inputs of *b* are fixed. The two-factor production function can be described symbolically as:

$$X = f(a, b),$$

where X, a, and b are total output and units of the two inputs labor and capital, respectively. The short-run production function, discussed in the previous chapter, shows the various quantities of X produced when a is varied, holding b fixed. By contrast:

> An isoquant shows all of the alternative combinations of resources a and b which can be used to produce a fixed quantity of X.[1]

The isoquant can be stated in mathematical symbols as:

$$\overline{X}_i = f(a, b).$$

The bar over X_i indicates that the output level is fixed, while the number of units of resources a and b is variable. The subscript i denotes the output level. For example, I_{100} in Figure 6-1 is the isoquant curve for 100 units of X, where the number of units of resources b and a are plotted on the vertical and horizontal axes, respectively. The combinations of a and b represented by points C, E, F, D, or G, as well as all other points along I_{100}, result in the production of exactly 100 X's.

The isoquant I_{100} in Figure 6-1 indicates that a very large number of different combinations of a and b can be employed to produce the same quantity of output. The reason is that each input, within limits, is presumed a substitute for the other; that is, labor can be substituted for capital and vice versa.[2] For instance, the isoquant indicates that either 10 b's and 3 a's (combination

FIGURE 6-1 An Isoquant for 100 Units of Output

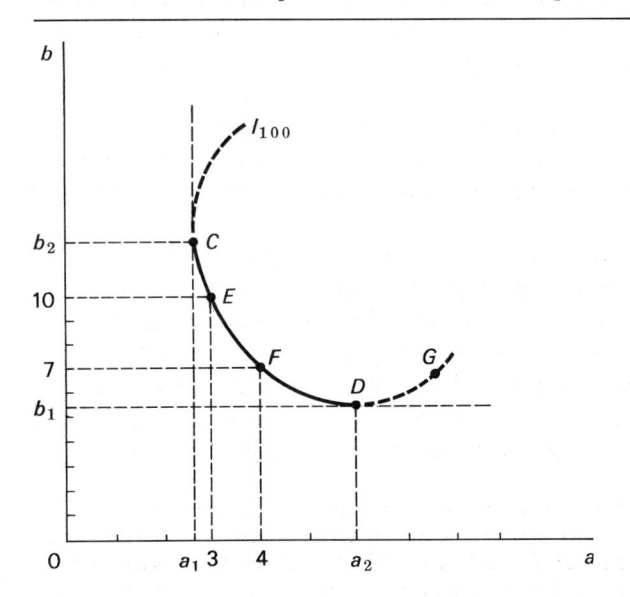

[1] Occasionally an isoquant is called an isoproduct curve.
[2] Production functions may also describe limited or no resource substitutability. We will explore these cases later in the chapter.

E) or 7 b's and 4 a's (combination F) is capable of producing 100 units of output. If combination E is employed initially, then rejected in favor of combination F, one extra unit of a must be added to the production process, whereas the number of units of b can be decreased by a maximum of three and still maintain the given output level. Combination C on I_{100} has a special characteristic: it represents the minimum input of resource a needed to produce 100 units of X; e.g., the minimum amount of a needed is a_1 units. Similarly, combination D represents the minimum amount of b needed to produce 100 X's. If less than a_1 units of a or b_1 units of b are available, output would be reduced below 100 X's.

The Marginal Rate of Substitution. What we need is a measure of the ability of one resource to substitute for another in production. This measure is provided by the marginal rate of substitution.

> The marginal rate of substitution of resource a for b, MRS_{ab}, measures the maximum amount of b that one additional unit of a can replace in production, without changing the output level.[3]

Symbolically:

$$MRS_{ab} = -\frac{\Delta b}{\Delta a},$$

where the changes in a and b are not just any changes; Δa and Δb must leave output unaffected, i.e., a movement along an isoquant. Since Δb will typically be negative and Δa positive (a is increased while b is decreased), the negative sign before the fraction $\Delta b/\Delta a$ will generally result in a positive value for MRS_{ab}.

To illustrate: given the initial combination of a and b at point E on I_{100} in Figure 6–1, the MRS_{ab} is 3, because a maximum of 3 units of b can be replaced by one unit of a by switching to combination F, without affecting the output level.

The equality of the MRS_{ab} between two points along an isoquant and the absolute value of the slope of the isoquant between the same two points is analogous to the equality of the MRS_{xy} and the absolute value of the slope of an indifference curve, as discussed in Chapter 3. Thus, the value of the MRS_{ab}, 3, between points E and F in Figure 6–1, also measures the slope of a straight line between these points (disregarding the negative sign of the slope). Moreover, if point E approaches point F, the MRS_{ab} between the two

---

[3] The marginal rate of substitution in indifference curve analysis is distinguished from the marginal rate of substitution of resources by the subscripts; e.g., MRS_{xy} pertains to a consumer's indifference curve for goods X and Y while MRS_{ab} pertains to an isoquant for a given level of output of a commodity that requires the resources a and b for its production. The two concepts may also be distinguished by calling the MRS in production the "marginal rate of technical substitution," to stress the relationship to the techniques of production.

points approximates the absolute value of the slope of the isoquant at point F. Conversely, the absolute value of the slope of the isoquant at point F measures the marginal rate of substitution, MRS_{ab}, at that point. In general, we will consider equal the absolute value of the slope of an isoquant at a point and the MRS_{ab} at that point.

The Characteristics of Isoquants. Isoquants exhibit the following basic characteristics:

1. They are negatively sloped.
2. They are convex to the origin.
3. They are nonintersecting.

Characteristics 1 and 2 follow from the partial substitutability of resources (assumed), and characteristic 3 follows from the assumption that firms always employ resources efficiently, so the employment of one quantity of resources cannot lead to less output than the employment of a larger quantity; i.e., we rule out technically inefficient resource combinations.

Resource combinations on the positively sloped section of an isoquant are inefficient and generally may be disregarded. Only the negatively sloped portion of the isoquant is relevant to the firm in most circumstances. Consider again the isoquant I_{100}, in Figure 6–1. The section with positive slope, DG, indicates that, although both resources a and b increase, output remains unchanged. Resource a is being used to such excess relative to b (the ratio of a to b is so high), that any additional employment of a *reduces* output unless b is simultaneously increased to keep the proportion of a to b from rising further. Combinations of a and b to the right of point D along I_{100}, therefore, will be avoided by the firm and are in fact technically inefficient combinations.[4] The reader will recognize that combinations of a and b to the right of point D are Stage III combinations for a, i.e., combinations of a and b for which the ratio of a to b is so high that the marginal product of a is negative. Similarly, resource combinations above point C on I_{100} are inefficient since these are Stage I combinations for a where the quantity of b is excessive relative to a, such that the marginal product of b is negative.

The second characteristic of isoquants, their convexity to the origin, derives from the nature of resource substitution. Two resources, say capital and labor, are not perfect substitutes for each other in production; if they were, there would be no economic reason for considering them different resources. Imagine a production process using labor and capital, in which labor is successively substituted for capital. The situation is depicted graphically by a southeast-

---

[4] Notice again that a resource combination may be technically inefficient in the long run (all resources variable) but may not be so considered in the short run. A firm might operate a plant at a very low percent of capacity in the short run (a high b to a ratio), simply because a small output is desired and the fixed input cannot be reduced. This would place the firm on the positively sloped portion of the isoquant for that output.

ward movement along isoquant I_{100} in Figure 6–1, where labor is resource a and capital is resource b. As the ratio of labor to capital rises, labor will become a poorer and poorer substitute for capital. To hold output constant while reducing the quantity of b employed, more and more labor must be added to production to compensate for the successive reduction in the number of units of capital employed. The result is a steady decrease in the marginal rate of substitution of labor for capital. MRS_{ab} declines as the ratio of a to b rises, and eventually MRS_{ab} will fall to zero. For example, at point D on I_{100} in Figure 6–1, a is employed to such excess relative to b that a ceases to be a substitute for b, and the MRS_{ab} as a consequence is equal to zero at that point. Similarly, at point C on I_{100}, b is used to such excess relative to a, that b can no longer be substituted for a. At point C, the MRS_{ab} is infinite, since b at that point will no longer substitute for a. The steady fall in the MRS_{ab} between points C and D means the slope of the isoquant changes from a large negative number to zero. This change in slope results in the convexity of the isoquant.

The third characteristic follows from the definition of isoquants and the assumption that firms will not use inefficient production methods. If isoquants should intersect, this would indicate that two different resource combinations, one containing more units of both resources (or more of one and the same quantity of the other), would produce the same output. Referring to Figure 6–2, suppose isoquants I_1 and I_2 intersected. The resource combinations at Z and W result in the same output since they lie along indifference curve I_2. Also, combinations of a and b at Z and S result in the same output, since they lie along I_1. Presumably, then, combinations at W and S would result in the same output, since the output of each is equal to the output obtained with Z. But combination W contains more units of b than S, whereas both indicate a like quantity of a. Firms will generally produce the highest output from any

FIGURE 6–2 Intersecting Isoquants

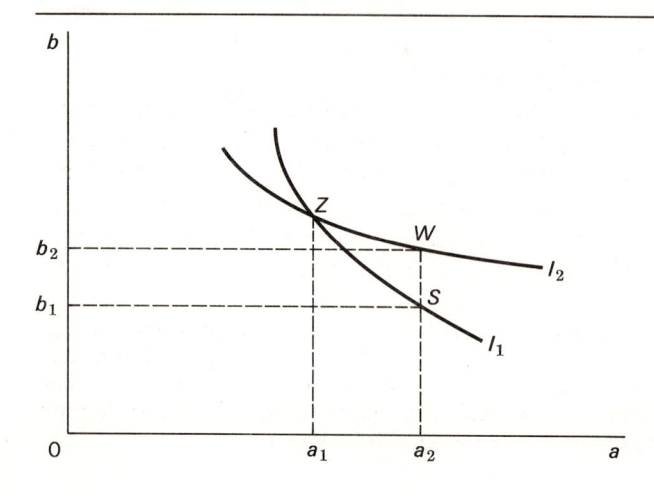

given combination of inputs used, and the combination of inputs with the larger quantity of b (combination W) will always result in more output if the firm is using efficient combinations of the two resources, i.e., Stage II combinations. Therefore, intersecting isoquants are not permitted. The firm will not settle for the output produced with combination W, when the same output can be produced with combination S.

The Family of Isoquants. Of course, output levels other than 100 are pos-

FIGURE 6–3   A Family of Isoquants

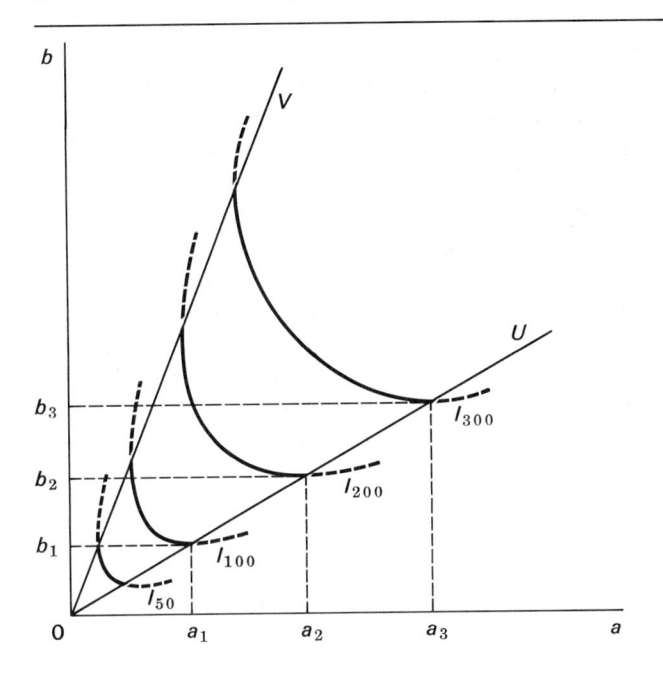

sible. In Figure 6–3, we have drawn to the right and above I_{100}, isoquants I_{200} and I_{300}, which represent outputs of 200 and 300 units, while I_{50}, to the left, is the isoquant for 50 units. Line V, called a *ridge line*, connects up the points on all isoquants where the slopes or marginal rates of substitution of the isoquants become infinite. Similarly, ridge line U connects the points along all isoquants where the slopes or marginal rates of substitution become zero. These ridge lines enclose the long-run, technically efficient combinations of a and b, excluding all technically inefficient input combinations (again long-run ones) below and to the right of U and above and to the left of V, where the addition of one of the inputs lowers production. Although only four isoquants are shown in Figure 6–3, there are an infinite number, a *family*, of such curves, each representing a different level of output. The isoquants in Figure 6–3 are derived from a production function characterized by constant returns to scale.

Fixed Versus Variable Input Coefficients. It is not always possible to substitute one resource for another in production, as we assumed when we discussed the convexity of isoquants. Some products and some techniques require that inputs be used in rigid proportions. For example, the production of some chemical products, like house paint, requires that ingredients be combined in fixed proportions. None of the separate ingredients can be substituted for the others (except possibly to a very minor extent), if tolerances for the final product are to be maintained. As another illustration, say ice production requires two inputs, water and capital, and neglect all other inputs, such as labor. Generally, it will not be possible to substitute to any extent capital for water or water for capital to produce a unit of the finished product. An isoquant for a production process with completely rigid input requirements would have sides radiating horizontally and vertically from a point which defines the required combination of the two resources needed for the given quantity of output. All combinations of a and b along the sides of the isoquant would be inefficient except at the point of their intersection.

In those cases where inputs must be used in fixed proportions, the isoquant is not particularly useful. But most production processes allow for some substitutability among the different inputs, giving firms some discretion over input combinations. And where resource substitution is possible, the firm must choose among all possible input combinations for each output level. The firm's choice of inputs for any output level will rationally be governed by the criteria of cost minimization. This brings us to the subject of isocosts.

Isocost Curves

An *isocost curve* indicates the maximum quantities of two inputs which can be purchased with a given dollar outlay. All of the possible combinations for an outlay of C_1 are determined by the equation:

$$\overline{C}_1 = \overline{P}_a \cdot a + \overline{P}_a \cdot b,$$

where P_a and P_b are the prices of inputs a and b, respectively. The bars over P_a and P_b, as well as C_1, indicate that these are constant to the firm. P_a and P_b are constant because they are market-determined prices over which the firm has no control. C_1 is constant in the sense of a predetermined outlay. Because there are only two variables, the equation is linear, and the graph of the equation is a straight-line isocost curve, illustrated by IC_1 in Figure 6-4. The prices of a and b determine the slope of the curve, and the size of the outlay determines its position. The vertical axis intercept of IC_1 is C_1/P_b, which represents the maximum amount of b that can be purchased with the given outlay without buying any a, and the horizontal axis intercept, C_1/P_a, shows the maximum amount of a which can be acquired, assuming zero units of b are purchased. All other combinations of a and b that would exhaust the C_1 dollars are along isocost curve IC_1, for example, combinations at points A, B,

FIGURE 6–4 A Complete Isoquant–Isocost Model

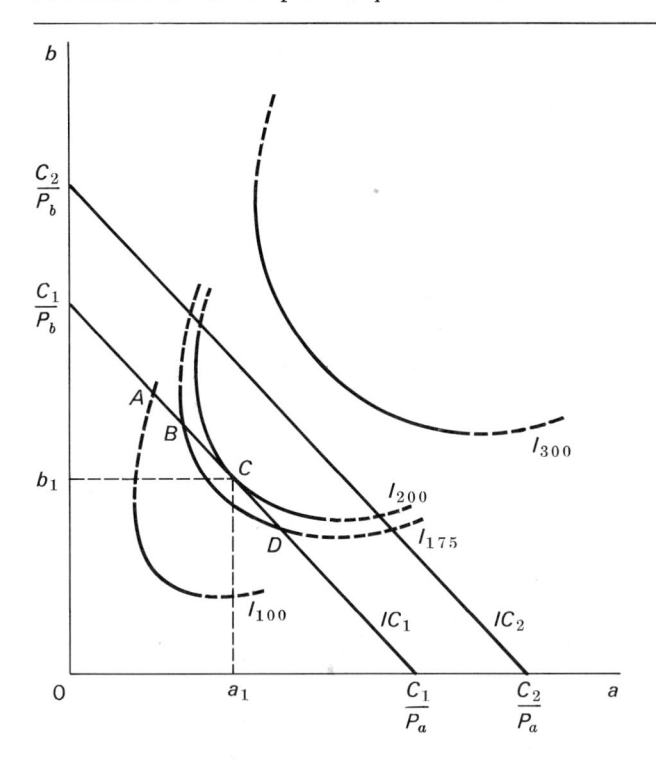

C, and D. To illustrate using numerical values, if the total outlay C_1 is $1000, the price of b, $2, and that of a, $4, then either a maximum of 500 b's or a maximum of 250 a's can be bought. All combinations of a and b that could be purchased with a $1000 outlay are determined by the equation: $1000 = 4a + 2b$.

A different isocost curve is associated with each possible dollar outlay. The isocost curves for outlays greater than C_1 would be to the right of IC_1; for example, IC_2 in Figure 6–4 is the isocost curve for an outlay of C_2, where $C_2 > C_1$. For smaller outlays, the isocost curves will be to the left of IC_1. We may conclude that there is a whole family of isocost curves, a different curve for each possible value of C.

The slope of the isocost curve IC_1 in Figure 6–4 is equal to $-P_a/P_b$, which is calculated by dividing the vertical intercept of IC_1, C_1/P_b (the rise) by the horizontal intercept, C_1/P_a (the run), and attaching a negative sign. Barring a change in the price of a or b, the slopes of all isocost curves will be the same, so all are parallel.

The ratio of P_a to P_b also measures the market rate of substitution of a for b. For example, suppose the market price of b is $2 and the price of a $4. Then the ratio $+$4/$2 or $+2$ indicates that for each unit of a the firm gives up (or, more accurately, decides not to purchase), 2 units of b may be obtained without affecting total outlay, or, looking at it from another angle, if the firm acquires an extra unit of a, it must give up 2 units of b to hold total cost unchanged.

Least-Cost Combination of Resources

To find the least-cost combination of resources for any output level requires information about both the productivity and costs of inputs. The isoquant provides information about the productivity of inputs a and b, whereas the isocost curve summarizes their relative cost. Now it is time to put the two together to determine the optimum input combination.

For a moment, assume the firm has decided to produce the maximum output possible with an outlay of C_1. This outlay allows the firm to purchase at a maximum any combination of a and b along IC_1 in Figure 6–4, such as the combinations at points A, B, C, and D. (The firm could, of course, purchase any combination to the left of IC_1, but we restrict it to the line IC_1, which means the firm spends its entire budget.) But which combination of a and b along IC_1 will the firm select? Obviously, the one producing the greatest output for the given outlay. Point A is certainly not the best; by switching to the combination at point B, output increases from 100 to 175 as indicated by isoquants I_{100} and I_{175}, respectively. Moreover, point D is no better than point B from the standpoint of either cost or output. In fact, the combination at point C would be selected because it produces the largest possible output. Since IC_1 is tangent to I_{200} at point C, I_{200} is the highest isoquant that can be reached for the given outlay of C_1. Combinations of a and b just above point C or to the right of C would result in a greater output, but such combinations would require an outlay greater than C_1. Combination C is optimal, therefore, for the given outlay. Notice also that the statement: "Two hundred units of output is the maximum possible given on outlay C_1" can be reversed to read: "The least possible cost of producing 200 units of output is C_1." The argument for the latter statement is left to the student.

Note that the labeling of isoquants has a meaning in terms of a cardinal, measurable increase in output. In contrast, the labeling of indifference curves indicates an ordinal measure of utility only.

We can conclude that a necessary condition for an optimum combination of resources a and b, given any outlay, is that the isocost curve associated with that outlay be tangent to an isoquant function. For the two curves to be tangent, the slopes of the isocost and isoquant curves must be equal, and since the slope of IC_1 is $-P_a/P_b$ and the slope of I_{200} is $-MRS_{ab}$, the necessary condition for the least-cost combination of a and b can be stated in mathematical symbols as:

$$-MRS_{ab} = -\frac{P_a}{P_b},$$

or

$$MRS_{ab} = \frac{P_a}{P_b}.$$

A firm may have an infinite number of potential isoquant and isocost curves, so there exist an infinite number of points of tangency where $MRS_{ab} = P_a/P_b$. By requiring that a given outlay be exhausted (or that a given output be produced), we limit our analysis to one particular equilibrium.

THE DETERMINATION OF FIRM COSTS

Now we can use the isoquant–isocost model to determine the effects on the firm's costs of adjustments in the scale of the production process. To illustrate, we have presented in panel (a) of Figure 6–5 a number of isoquants derived from a production function which exhibits constant returns to scale. Neglecting costs for the time being, suppose the firm increases the quantity of a and b employed in production, as depicted by a left-to-right movement along the straight line L_1. One of the important results of moving along a straight-line segment which passes through the origin, such as L_1, is that the two inputs a and b are thereby changed in the same proportion. That is, a jump from one point on line L_1, to another, indicates a scale adjustment in which the ratio a to b remains constant. This can only mean that the percentage change in one input equals that of the other. Line L_1 can be thought of as one of many possible *expansion paths* the firm might take, since any rightward movement along L_1 represents an increase in the over-all *scale* of production. Notice the ease of representing scale adjustments using isoquant–isocost analysis, as compared with marginal productivity models. With the latter, we have to draw up new total product curves every time the quantity of b changes.

As the firm changes from combination A to combination B, in panel (a) of Figure 6–5, doubling the input combination $a_1 - b_1$ to $2a_1 - 2b_1$, output increases from 100 to 200, since we have assumed constant returns to scale. Doubling the quantities of both inputs is the same as doubling the scale of production. Moreover, if the input combination is raised to $3a_1 - 3b_1$ (point C), output increases to 300. Similar results would be obtained, that is, percentage increases in output which equal percentage increases in both inputs, if the input combination were changed to a higher or lower ratio of a to b (switch to a new line segment such as L_2) and the scale increased. For instance, notice that although the input ratio a to b associated with a northeast movement along L_2 is lower than for L_1, in both cases the ratio of the change in the scale of production to the resulting change in output is equal to one. For instance, expansion along line L_2, using the input ratio represented by the coordinates of point Z, would give similar results as obtained by expansion along L_1; e.g., a doubling of inputs would double output.

By contrast, we have drawn in panel (b) of Figure 6–5 isoquants which

222 A Theory of Producer Behavior

FIGURE 6–5 (a) Constant Returns to Scale
(b) Decreasing Returns to Scale

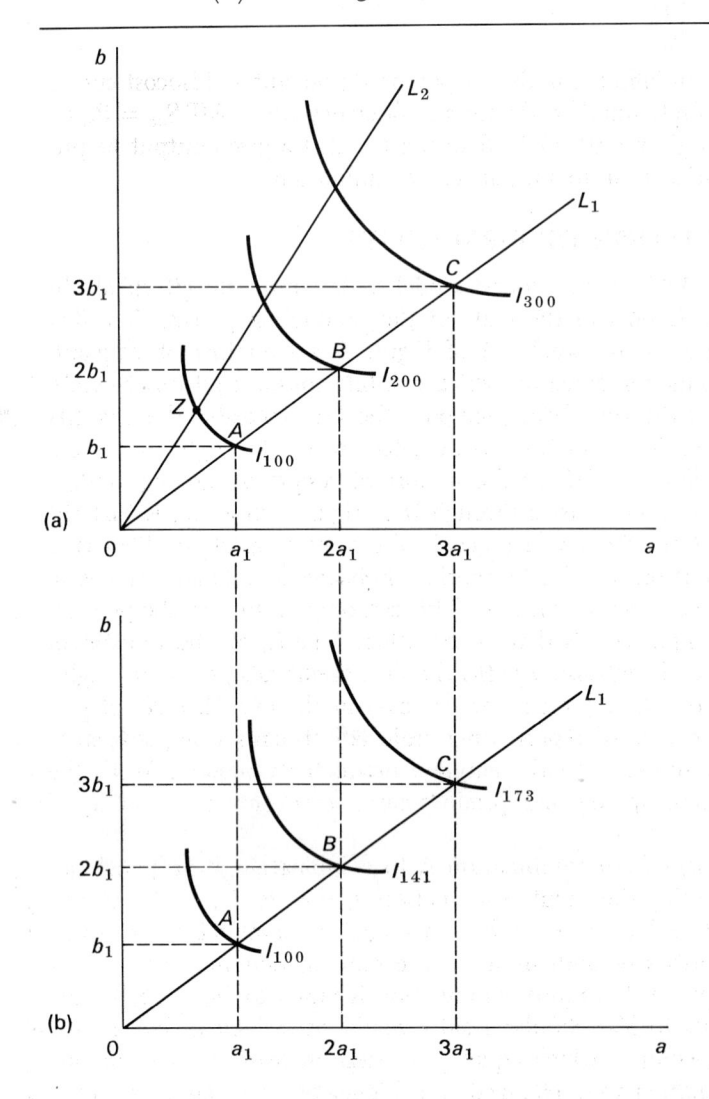

illustrate a production function characterized by *decreasing returns to scale*. As the quantity of inputs a and b is increased along line L_1 in panel (b) (with the same input ratio as L_1 in panel (a)), output increases, but the percentage increase in output is less than the proportionate increase in the scale of production. For example, as the input ratio doubles from $a_1 - b_1$ to $2a_1 - 2b_1$, output increases from 100 to 141, not to 200 as in panel (a), and a three-fold increase in inputs raises output to 173 units as shown by I_{173}, not to 300 units as in panel (a).[5] In other words, the isoquants for successive output increases of 100 units become increasingly spread out as we move further out along the expansion path.

The final possibility is, of course, that a production function may exhibit *increasing returns to scale*. If so, a given percentage increase in the quantity used of a and b would cause output to increase by a *greater* percentage. For instance, if the scale of production is doubled, and output goes up two-and-a-half times, the production function shows increasing returns to scale. In the case of increasing returns to scale, the isoquants showing successive output increases of 100 units would become closer together as we move along the expansion path.

The Optimum Long-Run Expansion Path

Given the production function (whether constant, increasing, or decreasing returns) and the prices of a and b, which expansion path will the firm in fact choose? The answer is to expand output so as to minimize costs at every output level, which means for any outlay, MRS_{ab} must equal P_a/P_b. Given the prices of a and b set at P_a and P_b, the optimum expansion path is illustrated for a production function with constant returns to scale in Figure 6–6. The isocost curves for outlays C_1, C_2, and C_3 are IC_1, IC_2, and IC_3, respectively, where C_2 is twice C_1, and C_3 is thrice C_1. The optimum combination for outlay C_1 is determined at point A where IC_1 is tangent to I_{100}. As the firm's outlay is successively increased by an amount equal to C_1, the optimum combination changes from point A to B, then to C. Thus line L_1 describes the *optimum expansion path* for the firm, given the ratios of the two input prices and the production function.

The cost curve in panel (b) of Figure 6–6 is derived from the cost–output data shown in panel (a); TC indicates the total cost associated with outputs between 100 and 300 units. For example, the optimum combination at point A in panel (a) indicates that an output of 100 units is produced at a minimum cost of C_1. These cost and output data, as well as the cost and output combinations determined at points B and C in panel (a), are plotted in panel (b) to generate the firm's total cost curve, TC. Since output increases in the same proportion as the scale of the production process (constant returns to scale), total cost increases in the same proportion as output if resource prices remain unchanged. Under these conditions the TC curve, which shows cost as a function of output, increases at a constant rate. Long-run marginal and average cost would under such circumstances be constant for all output levels and equal to $(C_2 - C_1)/(200 - 100)$. The TC curve in Figure 6–6 is the firm's *long-run* total cost curve.

---

[5] Decreasing returns exist if output increases in smaller proportion to the increase in scale. The choice of numbers here is merely illustrative.

FIGURE 6–6 The Derivation of Long-Run Total Cost: Constant Returns to Scale

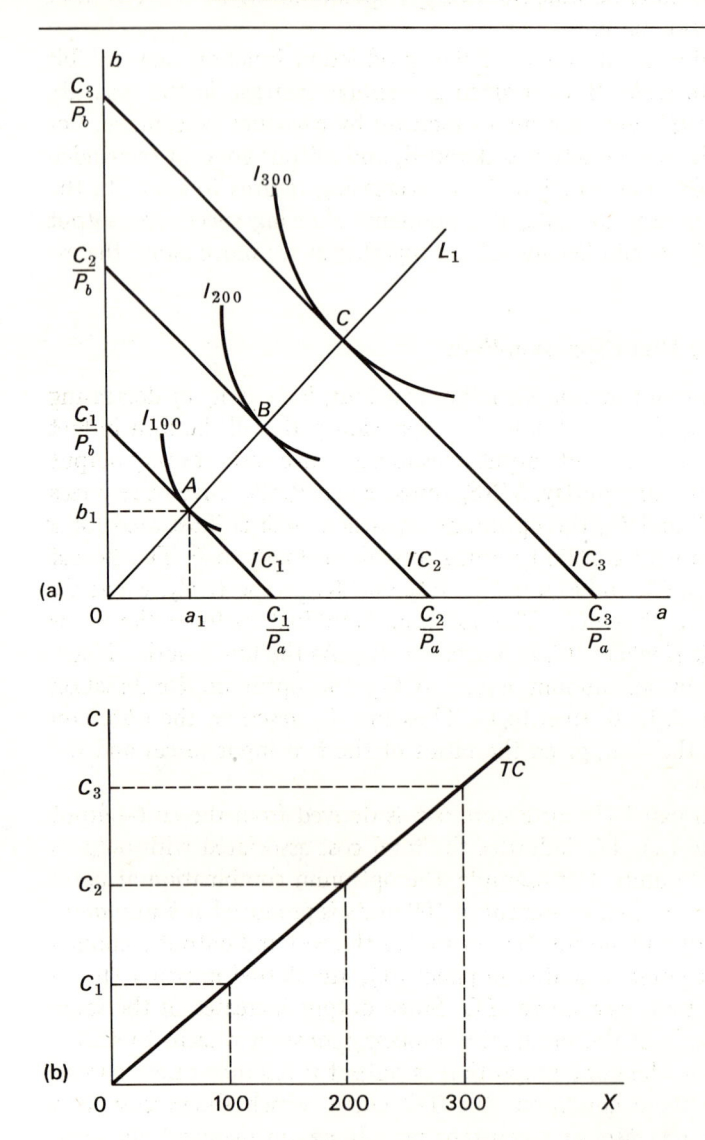

In contrast, in Figure 6–7 we have developed the firm's total cost curve for the case of decreasing returns to scale. As in the preceding case, C_2 is twice C_1, and C_3 is thrice C_1. However, in the case of decreasing returns to scale, successive equal increases in outlay result in successive output increases which decline. Given the ratio of the input prices, the optimum expansion path is along line L_1. Thus, output rises from 100 to 141, less than a doubling, though the increase in outlay from C_1 to C_2 results in a two-fold increase in the quantities employed of inputs a and b, e.g., the change from point A to B. In addition, the optimum output for an outlay of C_3 is 173, which is still less than twice the output associated with an outlay of C_1, though the input combination at C is three times that at A. In panel (b) of Figure 6–7, we have

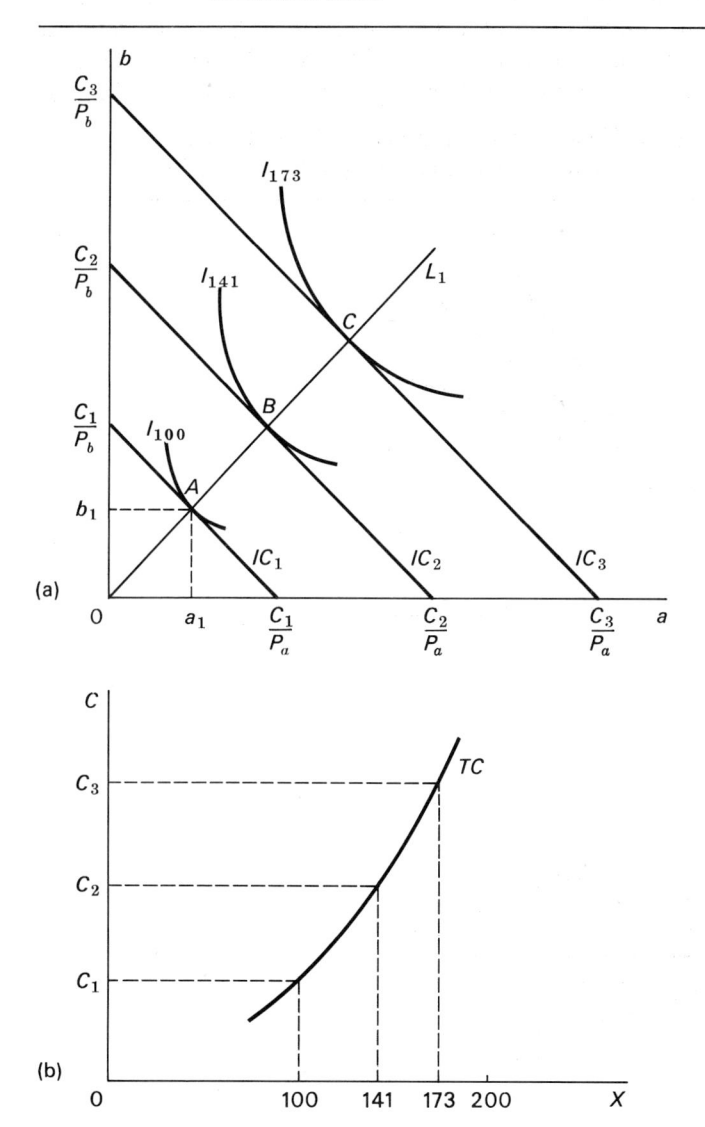

FIGURE 6–7   The Derivation of Long-Run Total Cost: Decreasing Returns to Scale

plotted the firm's total costs associated with outputs 100, 141, and 173. If we considered all possible outlays, we would get the unbroken total cost curve, TC, in panel (b). In general, where the firm experiences decreasing returns to scale and faces constant factor prices, its long-run total cost curve increases at an increasing rate. This will result in a rising AC curve and a MC curve which is everywhere above AC.

Finally, if the firm experiences increasing rather than decreasing returns to scale, its long-run total cost curve would increase as output increases, but the increases in total cost would occur at a decreasing rate. This would result in both declining average and marginal costs. So MC would be everywhere below AC in this case. To illustrate, panel (a) of Figure 6–8 shows the long-run

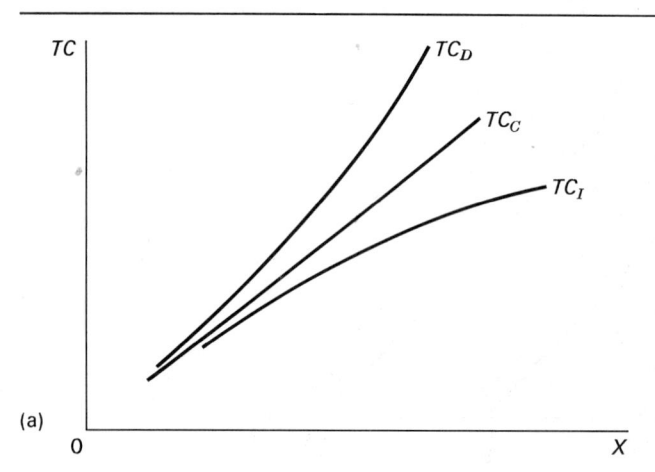

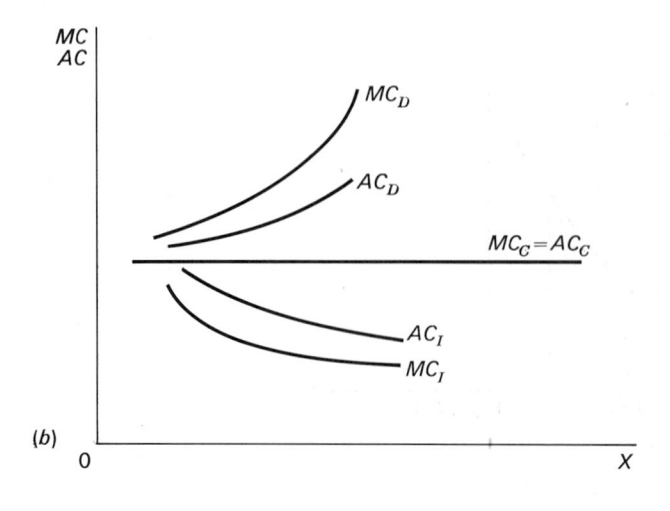

FIGURE 6–8 Long-Run Total, Average, and Marginal Cost Curves: Increasing, Constant, and Decreasing Returns to Scale

total cost curves associated with constant, increasing, and decreasing returns to scale and panel (b) shows the associated marginal and average curves. The subscripts D, C, and I indicate decreasing, constant, and increasing returns, respectively.

Short-Run Adjustments

The isoquant model may be used not only to investigate long-run or scale adjustments in production but short-run adjustments in output as well. For example, suppose the firm can obtain no more than b_1 units of input b and, therefore, can vary output only by changing the quantity of a employed. The case is illustrated in panel (a) of Figure 6–9. Assuming that resource b is indivisible but adaptable, the firm can increase short-run output by employing increasing amounts of a with the fixed b, described by a rightward movement along the horizontal line, L_1. When a_1 units of a are employed with b_1 units of b (point A on isoquant I_{400}), total output is 400 units. If the number of a's used in production rises to a_2, output increases to 500 units, and if the number of a's is increased again to a_3 units, output rises to 600 units. Notice that to get successive output increases of 100 units, the amount of a employed must be increased in ever greater amounts; e.g., $a_m - a_4$ is greater than $a_4 - a_3$, which is greater than $a_3 - a_2$. As we know, output cannot be increased indefinitely in the short run. Once a_m units of a are employed with the fixed quantity of b, any further employment of a will not raise output. In panel (b) of Figure 6–9 are plotted the various outputs associated with a_1 through a_m units of a. Assuming the experiment is repeated for all values of a between a_1 and a_m (holding the quantity of b fixed at b_1), we get a smooth curve which is the firm's short-run total product curve.

The production function which we are using to illustrate short-run firm adjustments assumes constant returns to scale and an adaptable but indivisible fixed factor, b. Moreover, we are principally concerned with adjustments to input ratios within the ridge lines R_1 and R_N. Thus, the combination of a and b represented by point Z in panel (a) of Figure 6–9 is not considered, since it is to the left of the ridge line, i.e., on the positively sloped portion of the isoquant, I_{300}. If the firm decided to produce 300 units in the short run, it would operate at Z, if b is indivisible.[6] However, since we are considering only those combinations of a and b within the ridge lines, the total product curve we have drawn increases at a decreasing rate throughout its length, and, as a consequence, marginal product and average product (not shown) decline throughout.

By combining the firm's short-run product curve with resource price data,

---

[6] We will discuss in Chapter 7 the principle that a profit-maximizing competitive firm will never rationally operate at such combinations, though a monopolistic firm might do so.

228 A Theory of Producer Behavior

we can derive short-run cost curves just as we did in the previous chapter, so the isoquant model is adaptable to studying short-run production adjustments as well as scale changes.

FIGURE 6–9 The Derivation of the Short-Run Total Product Curve Using Isoquants

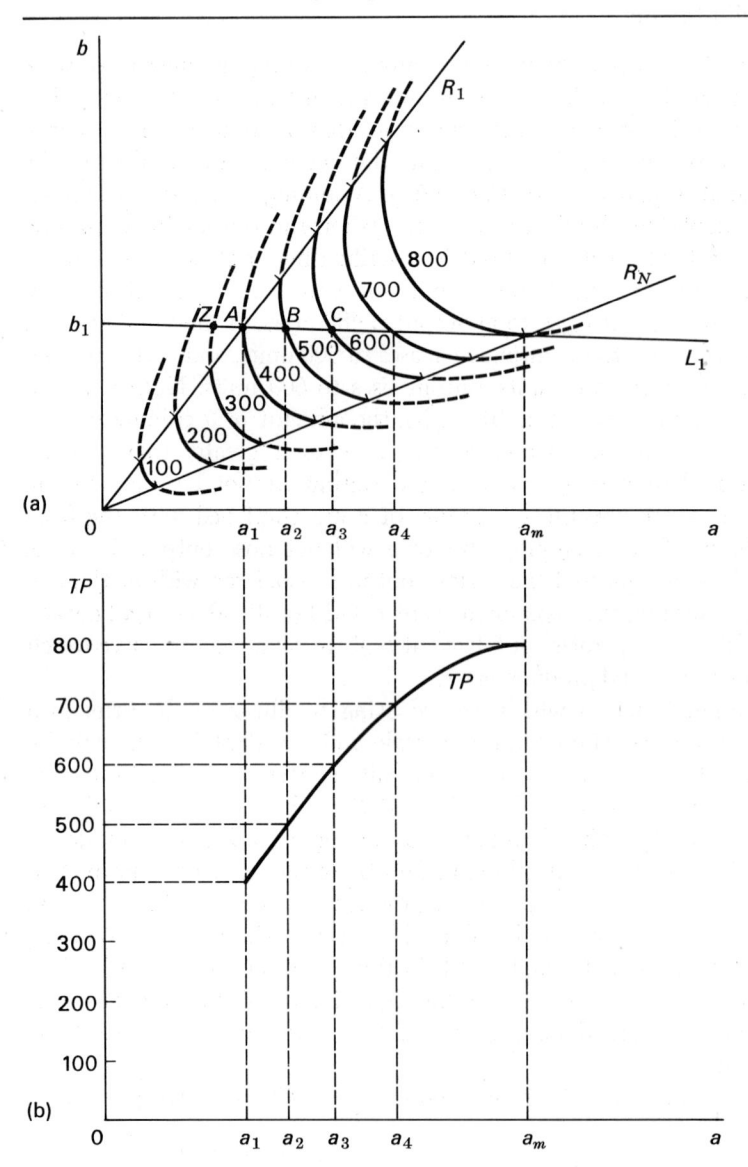

The Isocost as a Restraint

Though the point is often neglected, perhaps because firms usually have better sources of financing than consumers have, the isocost curve may constrain the firm, just as the budget line constrains consumer behavior. If a firm is to expand output in the long run by moving out its optimum expansion path, it must secure the necessary funds for expansion. For many firms, especially new, small, or unprofitable firms, expansion entails financial problems. Funds for expansion may not be available on favorable terms. New firms typically do not have ready access to capital markets and must resort to borrowed or internally generated funds for expansion. The latter source of financing can be very slow, and the former may be very costly, especially in periods of restricted credit.

LINEAR PROGRAMMING

Linear programming (LP) has developed into one of the most successfully used planning tools in industry. It is a mathematical technique for determining how a linear function with two or more independent variables can be maximized or minimized subject to certain constraints on the values of the variables. The applications of linear programming are numerous: the maximization of output, subject to the constraint imposed by limited resources; the maximization of profits subject to resource limitations and market constraints, and the minimization of costs of production subject to a minimum output level constraint. Two simple examples will illustrate linear programming techniques and indicate the types of problems for which linear programming is useful. We start with a maximization problem, followed by the application of LP to problems of cost minimization. The latter application is particularly relevant to the rest of the material in this chapter.

To illustrate a simple linear programming problem, suppose a firm produces two products, X and Y, and in the next short-run period wishes to produce that combination of the two goods which maximizes profit. The profits per unit for X and Y are assumed to be $40 and $30, respectively. The price of the product and the firm's costs per unit are constant, so that the profit per unit figures are constant no matter how many X's or Y's are produced. The firm's total profits will equal $40X + $30Y, where X is the number of units produced of the first good and Y the second. Thus, the firm's principal objective is the maximization of:

$$\pi = \$40X + \$30Y,$$

where π is defined in the linear programming problem as the *objective function*.

What prevents the firm from producing an infinite amount of X and Y, thereby making total profits infinite? The answer is that the firm can produce only a limited amount of X and Y in the following period because of certain limitations on the time and materials needed to produce the two products. Suppose there are two processes involved in making the two goods. As shown in Table 6–1 there are 600 hours available for process 1. Only Y's are processed

TABLE 6–1

	Time Required for an X	Time Required for a Y	Time Available
Process 1	0	100 hours/unit	600 hours
Process 2	40 hours/unit	20 hours/unit	320 hours

in process 1, each Y requiring 100 hours. On the other hand, there are 320 hours available for process 2, and both products must be processed. Each X requires 40 hours, whereas each Y requires 20 hours for processing in the latter process.

The *constraint* imposed by the limited time in process 1 may be stated algebraically:

$$0 \cdot X + 100Y \leq 600,$$

or

$$0 \cdot X + Y \leq 6. \tag{1}$$

As far as the first process is concerned, the maximum number of Y's that can be made is 6, whereas there is no constraint on the number of X's.

By the same reasoning, we can state algebraically the constraint imposed by the second process as:

$$40X + 20Y \leq 320,$$

or

$$2X + Y \leq 16. \tag{2}$$

Any combination of X and Y can be processed through the second process, so long as inequality (2) is not violated. For instance, we could process a maximum of 16 Y's (no X's) or a maximum of 8 X's (no Y's) in process 2, or we could process 2 X's and 12 Y's. For our illustration, we assume two inputs, A and B, are required to produce X's and Y's and only 100 units of A and 140 units of B are available for the next period. The materials requirements for X's and Y's are summarized in Table 6–2, and from this information we can develop

TABLE 6–2

	Requirements for X	Requirements for Y	Amount Available
Material A	10/unit	10/unit	100 units
Material B	20/unit	0/unit	140 units

the following materials constraints:

$$10X + 10Y \le 100,$$
$$20X + 0Y \le 140,$$

which simplify to:

$$X + Y \le 10, \tag{3}$$
$$X + 0Y \le 7. \tag{4}$$

Now we can put all the pieces together and state the linear programming problem algebraically:

Maximize: $\pi = 40X + 30Y$;

Subject to:
(1) $0X + Y \le 6$,
(2) $2X + Y \le 16$,
(3) $X + Y \le 10$,
(4) $X + 0Y \le 7$,

$$X, Y \ge 0.$$

All maximization problems in linear programming are set up in this general form. An objective function of two or more independent variables is to be maximized subject to one or more constraints which place limitations on the values of the independent variables. Typically the constraints take the form of inequalities (though there may be constraints which appear as equations). In addition, we add the constraints, $X \ge 0$ and $Y \ge 0$, since negative values of the independent variables in a linear programming problem are generally impossible; e.g., we cannot make -3 units of X.

Our illustrative linear programming problem has been purposely limited to two variables, X and Y, so we can use graphical techniques to illustrate the solution. For example, to illustrate the first constraint, we graph the equation $Y = 6$, giving line R_1 in panel (a) of Figure 6–10. Since Y must be ≤ 6, any combination of X and Y *on* or *below* line R_1 in Quadrant I stays within the first constraint. In other words, as far as the first constraint is concerned, any combination of X and Y can be produced which is not above line R_1.

232 A Theory of Producer Behavior

FIGURE 6–10 Graphical Solution of a Linear Programming Problem

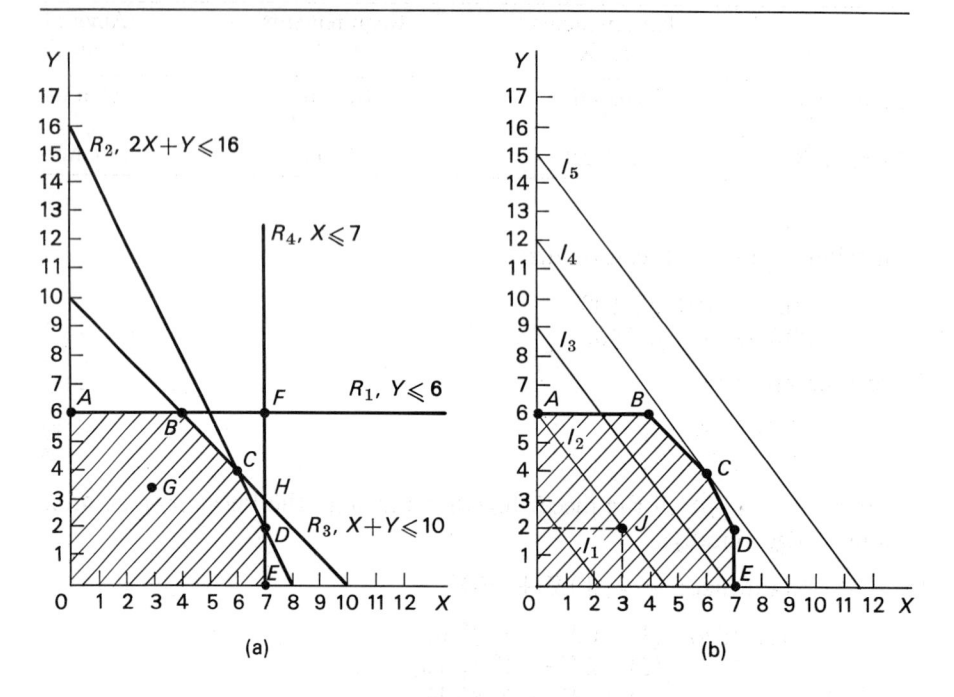

However, the first constraint is not the only one. Considering the last constraint, $X \leq 7$, no combination of X and Y to the right of line R_4 is permissible. Thus, considering for a moment constraints 1 and 4 only, the permissible combinations are confined to those within the rectangle OEFA or along one of its borders; e.g., it would be permitted to operate along line segments OA, AF, FE, or EO.

The two additional constraints, 2 and 3, restrict combinations of X and Y to the left or along lines R_2 and R_3, respectively. Thus, line R_2 is the graph of the equation $2X + Y = 16$, and all combinations of X and Y on or to the left of R_2 satisfy the inequality $2X + Y \leq 16$ and do not exhaust the limited time available in process number 2. Finally, R_3 is the graph of $X + Y = 10$. All combinations of X and Y along and to the left of line R_3 satisfy the third constraint. Considering all four constraint lines, the permissible combinations of X and Y are restricted to those within the shaded polygon OABCDEO or along one of the borders. For example, combination G within the polygon is permitted since it does not violate any of the principal constraints and those combinations at points A, B, C, D, and E along the border are permitted for the same reasons. Notice that combination H, though it does not violate either constraints 1, 3, or 4, does violate constraint 2, since it is to the right of line R_2. Point H must, therefore, be ruled out as not permitted. Summarizing, all combinations of X and Y within or along the sides of the polygon OABCDEO represent a *feasible solution* to the linear programming problem, because none violates any of the constraints.

Having determined the feasible solutions to the problem, our task now is to determine which of the feasible solutions is optimal, i.e., maximizes the objective function. A fundamental theorem of linear programming aids in this task:

> An optimal solution to a linear programming problem will occur at one of the "corners" of the feasible region.

An optimal solution *will* appear at either O, A, B, C, D, or E. Our task is now greatly simplified. All we have to do is compute the value of the objective function for each of the combinations of X and Y at these corner points and choose the one which is optimal.

As an alternative approach to determining the optimal combination, consider the graph of the objective function for a value of π of $180, that is, I_2 in panel (b) of Figure 6–10. I_2 has the characteristic that, given the profit per unit of $40 for each X and $30 for each Y, the sale of any combination of X and Y along I_2 results in a total profit of $180. Thus, the horizontal intercept, 4.5 units of X (zero Y's) times $40/unit of X gives $180, or the vertical intercept 6.0 units of Y times $30/unit of Y gives $180. Or at point J, 3 X's at $40/unit plus 2 Y's at $30/unit gives the same total profit of $180.

> Line I_2 is called an isoprofit line since it shows the various combinations of X and Y that yield the same profit.

Moreover, there are an infinite number of such lines, one for each profit level. Those to the right of I_2 indicate a larger profit, those to the left, a smaller profit. All isoprofit lines have the same slope equal to minus the profit per unit of X, divided by the profit per unit of Y. The isoprofit line is analogous to the isocost curve described earlier in the chapter.

Now the process of determining the optimal solution can be pictured as that of finding the highest (furthest to the right) isoprofit line which satisfies all of the constraints. I_1 and I_2 have the characteristic that all combinations of X and Y along their lengths are within the feasible region. They are not optimal, however, since by switching to I_3, the firm raises profit (I_3 is to the right of I_2 and I_1). Note that the firm cannot operate above AB along I_3. I_3 is not optimal either, since the firm can "push out" all the way to the corner solution at C, realizing the profit associated with I_4. Since the firm would violate one or more of the constraints if it moved either above or to the right of C, higher isoprofit curves to the right of I_4, such as I_5, cannot be reached. Therefore, point C represents the optimal solution. The firm will maximize its

234 A Theory of Producer Behavior

profits by producing 6 X's and 4 Y's. The value of π for this combination is $360, which is the maximum possible given the existing constraints. This completes the graphical solution of the maximization problem.

An Illustration of a Minimization Problem

Suppose a firm wished to minimize the total cost of producing 100 units of output, X, where two resources, a and b, are required to produce X. Total cost is:

$$C = P_a \cdot a + P_b \cdot b,$$

and the prices P_a and P_b are assumed constant to the firm. If we set the problem up as a linear programming problem, the cost equation is the objective function, and its value, C, is to be minimized by appropriate choice of quantities of a and b. The graph of C is, of course, an isocost curve. The principal decision facing the firm is which production process to employ, a decision which determines how much of a and b to purchase to minimize cost, and the principal constraint is that the quantities of a and b chosen must produce no less than 100 units of output.

The isoquant I_{100} in Figure 6–11 represents the principal constraint. All combinations of a and b enclosed by I_{100}, as well as along the curve, are feasible solutions to the problem (though not necessarily optimal), since employing these combinations will satisfy the requirement that at least 100

FIGURE 6–11   A Minimization Problem

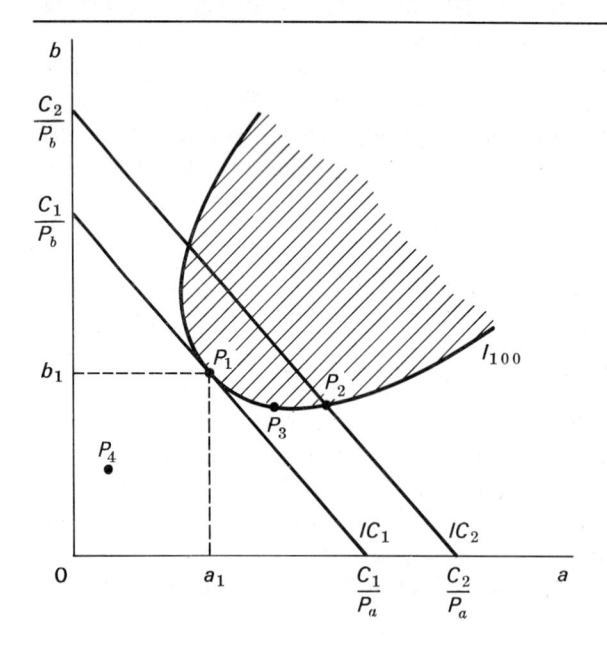

units of X be produced. No combination of a and b to the left or below the shaded area enclosed by I_{100} is a feasible solution, since less than 100 units of output would be produced if such combinations were employed. The constraint precludes the firm from minimizing cost by producing less than 100 units of output. To illustrate, the combination of a and b shown by point P_2 is a feasible solution, because it does not violate the constraint. However, the combination at point P_4 is not permitted, since this point would lie on an isoquant for a lower output.

Although the combination of a and b represented by point P_2 is a feasible solution to the LP problem, it is not the optimal solution, since the cost, C_2, is greater than the cost that would result by selecting other resource combinations to the left along I_{100}; e.g., the point P_3 would lie on an isocost curve representing a smaller outlay. The optimal solution to the problem is the combination a_1 and b_1, since the point of tangency between isoquant I_{100} and isocost IC_1 determines the optimum combination of the two inputs, using a graphical technique, which is by now familiar to the reader.

Linear programming, as the name implies, requires the assumption of only straight-line functions. In the preceding example, there is no difficulty with the objective function, for it is linear. However, the principal constraint, the isoquant, is a curvilinear function and, as a consequence, linear programming techniques will not work. If the isoquant were defined by a set of linear equations, rather than by a single nonlinear one, then linear programming could be used. As the following discussion will establish, straight-line-segment isoquants are not only a possible way of presenting isoquants, but they are probably more realistic than curvilinear functions.

Linear Isoquants

Suppose, initially, there are only two different processes for producing units of X, each requiring that inputs a and b be used in a fixed proportion.[7] For instance, the first process uses 2 b's and 1 a for every X. In Figure 6–12, the combination of inputs at point P'_1 would result in 1 unit of output. The combination at P_1, using 4 times the number of both inputs a and b would result in 4 units of output, using process number 1, if we assume that the level of output is directly proportional to the scale of process number one, i.e., assuming constant returns to scale. Movement from left to right along L_1 would mean a proportionate increase in both the scale of production and output, using the first process.

Now consider the second process. Process number 2 uses 1 b and 3 a's to produce one unit of X. Point P'_2 in Figure 6–12 shows the input requirements for one unit of output, and point P_2 indicates the combination of a and b for

---

[7] If b is the fixed resource in the short run, we can conclude that this input is completely unadaptable to a.

FIGURE 6-12   The Derivation of Linear Isoquants

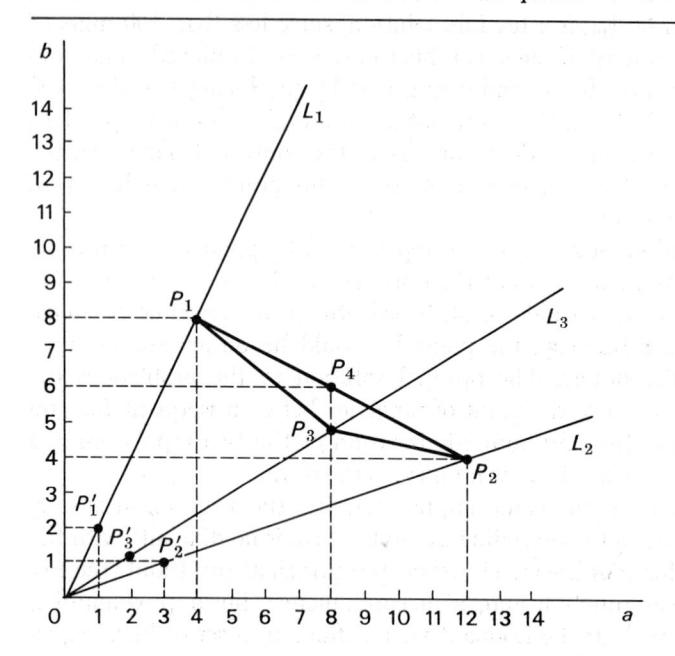

4 units of X, using the second process, and again assuming constant returns to scale. A left-to-right movement along L_2 indicates an increase in the scale of production and output using process 2.

Suppose for a moment that the firm has decided that output must be 4 units. Then, either combination P_1 (8 b's and 4 a's) or combination P_2 (4 b's and 12 a's) will just produce this output, using process 1 or 2, respectively. These two combinations of inputs do not exhaust the possibilities, however. Consider the combination at point P_4 using 6 b's and 8 a's. It is possible to produce 2 units of X, using process number 1, requiring 4 b's and 2 a's, and 2 units of X, using process 2 with the remaining 2 b's and 6 a's, i.e., to operate both processes simultaneously. Moreover, if resources a and b are divisible, then any combination of the two inputs along a line between points P_1 and P_2, by combining processes 1 and 2, will produce 4 units of output. The line P_1P_2, is, therefore, the isoquant for an output of 4 units of X.

A third production process is now introduced, which requires 1.25 units of b and 2 units of a to produce 1 X. Point P'_3 indicates the input requirements for 1 X using process 3 only. The production of 4 X's would require 5 b's and 8 a's, again assuming constant returns to scale. The input requirement for 4 units of output is represented by point P_3. The existence of the third process means that the combination of a and b at P_4, using processes 1 and 2, is now inferior to the combination at P_3, which uses only the third process, since the latter combination of inputs uses the same amount of a, but less b, to produce the same output. Moreover, an output level of 4 units can now be produced by combining processes 1 and 3 and by combining processes 3 and 2. The combinations of a and b along line segment P_3P_2 result from combining the latter two processes, while combining processes 3 and 1 requires combinations of a and b along line segment P_1P_3. The combinations of the two inputs along the combined line segment $P_1P_3P_2$ now render all of the combinations of inputs along P_1P_2 inferior. With only the three separate processes, line $P_1P_3P_2$ is the isoquant for 4 units of output.

As the number of separate processes increases, the number of linear segments increases and their length decreases, and the isoquant approaches a curve like I_{100} in Figure 6–13. I_{100} is the isoquant for an output of 100, developed in the manner described above, assuming 6 separate processes, A through F, for producing the final product. Linear combinations of these separate processes produce the isoquant ABCDEF.

FIGURE 6–13 The Graphical Solution of a Cost Minimization Problem

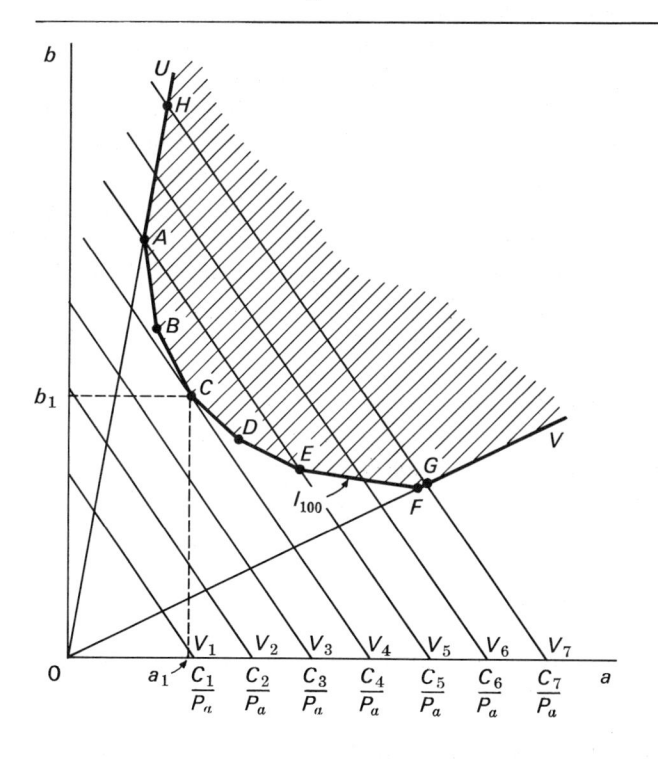

The Complete Linear Programming Model—Minimization

The basic requirements for a linear programming problem are now met. The firm wants to minimize cost, subject to the constraints which require that no less than 100 units of output be produced. Since I_{100} in Figure 6–13 is made up of linear segments, it can be described by a set of linear equations, satisfying the linearity requirement. A linear inequality ($\geq$) is developed for each of the segments AB, BC, CD, DE, and EF which restricts the feasible solution to those combinations of a and b which are to the right of the line segment, e.g., those combinations producing no less than the required output. In addition, the firm could satisfy the basic requirement by operating anywhere on line segment AU, or to the right of AU and along line segment FV or above FV. If the firm did so, it would be operating on an isoquant other than I_{100} but, nevertheless, producing *at least* 100 units. For example, at point H, output would be greater than 100. Such combinations are therefore feasible, and we would need two more inequalities for the segments AH and FV. Finally, the shaded area of Figure 6–13 includes all the feasible solutions to the problem, since any combination within the shaded area results in the production of not less than 100 units of output.

Curves V_1 through V_7 are possible isocost curves for different values of the objective function $C = P_a \cdot a + P_b \cdot b$. The firm's objective is to operate on that isocost curve representing the least outlay, while producing a minimum of 100 units of output. Isocost curves to the southwest, closer to the origin, are associated with a smaller outlay than those to the northeast. However, no combination of a and b along V_1 through V_3 is a feasible solution to the linear programming problem, since each isocost lies completely outside the constraint area, i.e., results in less than 100 units of output. Combinations of a and b between points H and G along V_7 are feasible solutions, since they satisfy the constraint that not less than 100 units be produced. These are not optimum combinations, however, since a number of combinations along V_6, with less cost, are feasible also. The problem is to find the combination of a and b that minimizes cost yet satisfies the constraint inequalities. By inspection, the corner combination at C is the optimum one. Any southwest movement away from point C would reduce the firm's outlay but would result in a combination of a and b outside the feasible region, and in less output than the required minimum. The firm will use a_1 and b_1 units, respectively, of the two inputs resulting in total cost, C_4, which is the least possible cost of producing the given output.

SUMMARY AND CONCLUSION

In this chapter, we have outlined the theory of isoquant–isocost analysis and have used the model to study firms' short-run and long-run production adjustments. We derived firms' long-run cost curves assuming constant, increasing, and decreasing returns to scale, and demonstrated how short-run product curves can be derived.

An isoquant or constant output function is analogous to the indifference or isoutility curve of Chapter 3, and an isocost or constant outlay function is somewhat analogous to the consumer's budget restraint. The similarities between isoquant–isocost analysis and indifference curve–budget restraint analysis go farther. Just as the indifference or ordinal utility model complements marginal utility theory, so does the isoquant–isocost analysis complement marginal productivity theory.

Both isoquant–isocost analysis and an adaptation, linear programming, can be used to find the optimum combination of resources for each level of the firm's output or for each total outlay. The isoquant–isocost model is a theoretical tool of analysis, whereas linear programming is a practical tool which has been extensively used and proven.

The appendix to this chapter presents an introduction to the simplex technique for solving linear programming problems. The simplex technique is an algebraic method which is not restricted to two dimensions as in the graphical technique.

PROBLEMS

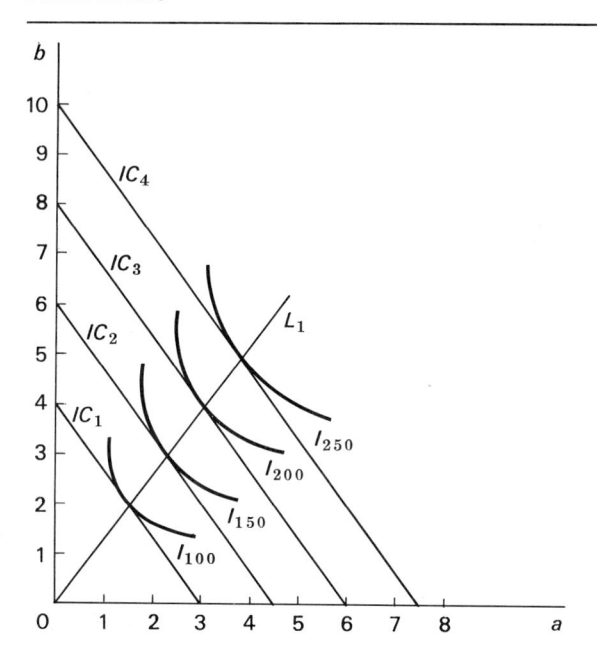

1. Answer the following with reference to the graph:
   (a) The production function with isoquants I_{100} through I_{250} in the figure exhibits (constant, increasing, decreasing) returns to scale.
   (b) The line L_1 is called a (ridge line, optimum expansion path, Engel line).

240 A Theory of Producer Behavior

(c) If the cost associated with IC_1 is $240, then the price of a is _____, the price of b is _____. The total cost of producing 200 units is _____.

(d) If the cost associated with IC_1 is $24, what are LRAC and LRMC? _____

2. Suppose an isoquant is linear throughout, with slope equal to that of the isocost curves. What would this imply?

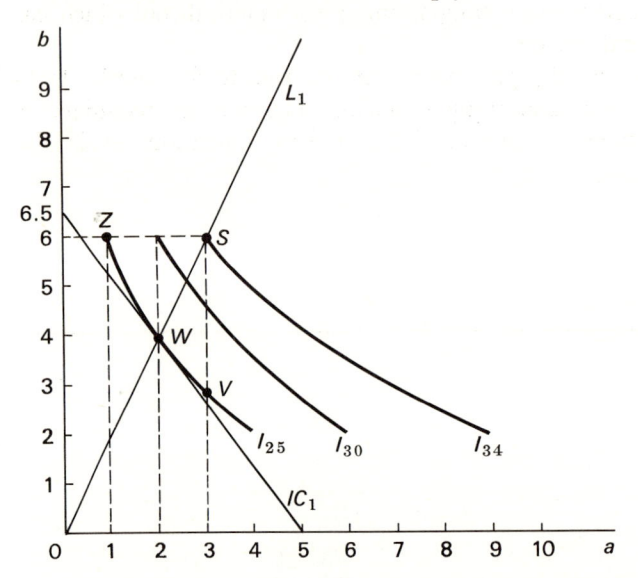

3. Answer the following based upon the graph:
   (a) If b is fixed at 6 units, the MP of the 2nd a is _____, of the 3rd a is _____.
   (b) The MRS_{ab} between points Z and W is _____.
   (c) The MRS_{ab} at point W is _____.
   (d) The MRS_{ab} between W and V is _____.
   (e) The scale of the production process increases _____ fold in moving from point W to S on L_1. Output increases _____ fold.

4. Complete the following:
   (a) If $P_a = \$2$, and $P_b = \$1$, draw the isocost curves for $C_1 = \$40$, $C_2 = \$60$, $C_3 = \$80$, $C_4 = \$100$.
   (b) Assuming the ratio of b to a is 2 : 1 along the optimum expansion path, sketch the isoquants tangent to isocosts already drawn.
   (c) If the first isoquant is for 10 units, label all the others, assuming constant returns to scale.
   (d) What is LRAC?

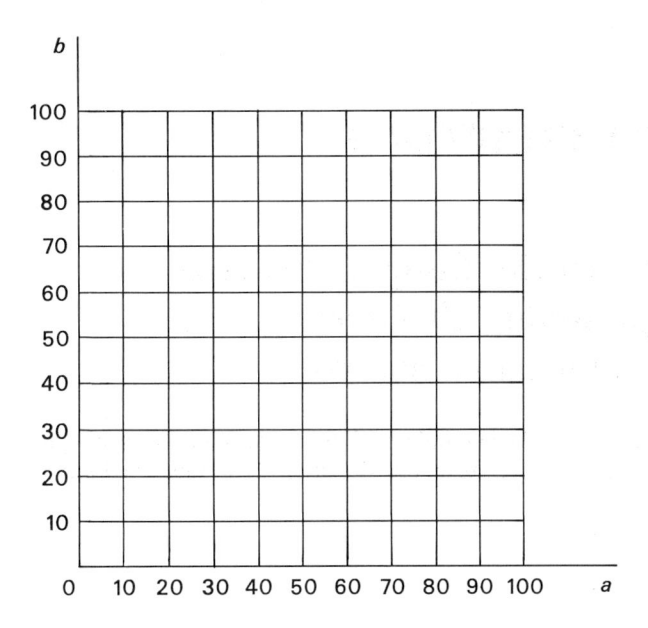

REFERENCES

Dorfman, Robert, "Mathematical or 'Linear' Programming: A Non-Mathematical Exposition," *American Economic Review*, 43 (December 1953), 797–825.

Gass, Saul I., *Linear Programming: Methods and Applications*, 2nd ed. New York: McGraw-Hill Book Co., Inc., 1964.

Hall, R. L., and Hitch, C. J., "Price Theory and Business Behavior," Oxford Economic Papers, 2 (1939).

Johnston, J., *Statistical Cost Analysis*. New York: McGraw-Hill Book Co., Inc., 1960.

Moore, F. T., "Economics of Scale—Some Statistical Evidence," *Quarterly Journal of Economics*, 73 (May 1959), 232–245.

Robinson, Joan, "The Production Function," *Economic Journal*, 65 (1955), 67–71.

Spivey, W. Allen, *Linear Programming: An Introduction*. New York: The Macmillan Co., 1963.

Stigler, J. George, "The Economies of Scale," *Journal of Law and Economics*, I (October 1958), 54–71.

Viner, Jacob, "Cost Curves and Supply Curves," *Zeitschrift für Nationalökonomie*, III (September 1931), 23–46.

Wu, Yuan–Li, and Kwang, Ching–Wen, "An Analytical Comparison of Marginal Analysis and Mathematical Programming in the Theory of the Firm," in Kenneth E. Boulding and W. Allen Spivey (eds.), *Linear Programming and the Theory of the Firm*. New York: McGraw-Hill Book Co., Inc., 1960, 94–157.

APPENDIX TO CHAPTER 6

An Introduction to the Simplex Solution to Linear Programming Problems

E. WARREN SHOWS and ROBERT H. BURTON

The following illustration of one widely employed linear programming technique is offered for the student who wishes to study the subject in somewhat more depth.

INTRODUCTION

Finding the solution to a linear programming problem is relatively simple when there are only two variable inputs. The corners and the selection of the optimum corner can be done graphically. With three variables, however, the graphical method becomes much more difficult to use, and with more than three variables, it breaks down altogether. The Simplex Method, or variations of this method, is probably the most widely used technique for solving linear programming problems involving variables. In contrast to the graphical method we have used, the Simplex Technique is an algebraic one and is thus not subject to restrictions on the number of variables that may be introduced.

AN ALGEBRAIC APPROACH TO LINEAR PROGRAMMING

In this section, we discuss an algebraic technique for solving LP problems, which serves as the basis for understanding the Simplex procedure. To illustrate the algebraic solution we have devised the following problem:

$$\text{Maximize:} \quad 7X_1 + 8X_2;$$

$$\text{Subject to:} \quad 3X_1 + 2X_2 \leq 18, \quad (1)$$
$$3X_1 + 4X_2 \leq 24, \quad (2)$$
$$X_1 \geq 0, \; X_2 \geq 0.$$

We will assume profits are to be maximized by producing two products X_1 and X_2, yielding \$7 and \$8 profit per unit, respectively. The first constraint indicates labor hours are limited to 18 per day, and each X_1 requires 3 hours and

FIGURE 1 Graphical Solution of a Profit Maximization Problem

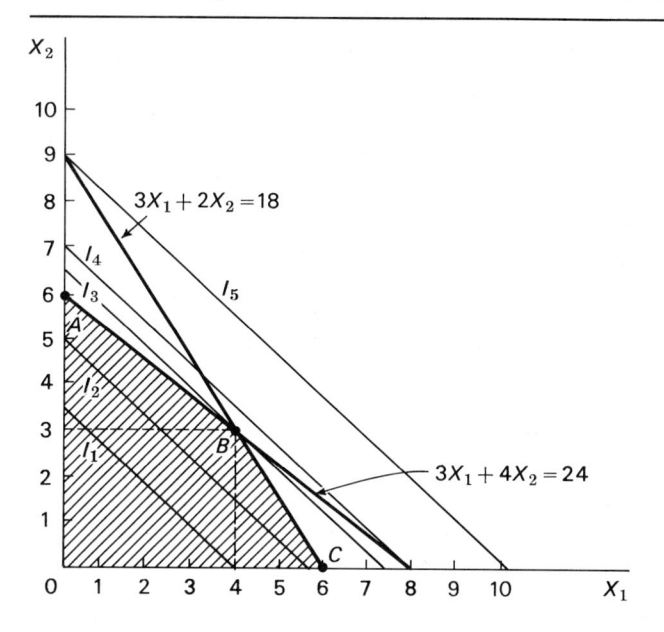

each X_2, 2 hours. The second constraint is on machine hours; 24 hours are available, each X_1 requiring 3 and each X_2, 4 hours for completion. Finally, as a further aid in explaining the algebraic method, we have presented the graphical solution to the problem in Figure 1.

Before we can solve this *LP* problem algebraically, we must convert constraints (1) and (2) from inequalities into equations. This is done by adding a slack variable, S_1 and S_2, respectively, to each equation, giving:

$$3X_1 + 2X_2 + S_1 = 18, \tag{3}$$
$$3X_1 + 4X_2 + S_2 = 24. \tag{4}$$

If a feasible solution to the problem uses less than the full 18 labor hours available, then S_1 will be a positive number equal to the amount of slack time in that department. For example, as far as constraint (1) is concerned, 1 X_1 and 2 X_2's may be produced. But this would require $3 \cdot 1 + 2 \cdot 2 = 7$ labor hours, leaving 11 hours unused; S_1 would then equal 11. Similarly, slack variable S_2 is added to the machine hours constraint, so that it can be stated as Equation (4) above. So that both variables will appear in both equations, we add S_1 to (4) with a zero coefficient and S_2 to Equation (3) with a zero coefficient. After these two changes, we have the constraints in equation form:

$$3X_1 + 2X_2 + S_1 + OS_2 = 18, \tag{5}$$
$$3X_1 + 4X_2 + OS_1 + S_2 = 24. \tag{6}$$

What results do we get if we attempt to solve these equations simultaneously?

Since there are two equations and 4 unknowns, there is no unique solution to (5) and (6). In fact, there is an infinite number of solutions.

As a general rule, given a system of linear equations in 'n' unknowns, there must be 'n' independent equations to generate a unique solution to the system. Since we have only two equations (5) and (6), we can determine a unique solution only by setting two of the unknowns to zero and solving for the other two. For example, if X_2 and S_2 are set to zero, and the system is solved for X_1 and S_1, the solution is 8 and -6, respectively. On the other hand, if X_2 and S_1 are set to zero, and the system is solved for X_1 and S_2, the solution is $X_1 = 6$, and $S_2 = 6$. The production of six units of X_1 exhausts the available 18 hours of the first constraint; therefore, there would be no slack time in the labor section and S_1 would be zero. The time available in the second department, however, is not exhausted, so S_2 is 6. The complete solution is $X_1 = 6$, $X_2 = 0$, $S_1 = 0$ and $S_2 = 6$, which is represented by point C in Figure 1, a feasible corner solution to the LP program.

Now we set the slack variables S_1 and S_2 to zero and solve for X_1 and X_2 and get: $X_1 = 4$, and $X_2 = 3$. This solution is represented by point B in Figure 1. Finally, setting X_1 and S_2 to zero and solving, we get: $X_2 = 6$, and $S_1 = 6$, represented by point A in Figure 1.

> As a general rule, by setting to zero (n − m) unknowns, where n is the total number of variables, and m is the number of constraints in an LP problem (converted to equation form), we can locate the "corners" of the constraint inequalities by solving the resulting equations.

Some of the solutions we generate by the procedure above will not be corner solutions; e.g., when we set X_2 and S_2 to zero the solutions were: $X_1 = 8$, and $S_1 = -6$. Since negative values of either X_1, X_2, or the slack variables are not possible, we may disregard any solution with a negative answer.

The final step in determining the optimum solution is to compute the value of the objective function for each corner solution:

    At corner C, $7 \cdot 6 + 8 \cdot 0 = \$42$.
    At corner B, $7 \cdot 4 + 8 \cdot 3 = \$52$.
    At corner A, $7 \cdot 0 + 8 \cdot 6 = \$48$.

Obviously, the solution at B is the optimum one. The firm should produce 4 X_1's and 3 X_2's, earning \$52 in total profits, the largest possible given the constraints. I_3 is the highest isoprofit line reachable.

THE SIMPLEX METHOD

The Simplex Method employs an algebraic procedure basically like that described above, except that it is streamlined to a number of definite steps, that is, made into a "cookbook" procedure. Moreover, the procedure is designed so as to minimize the number of steps required to arrive at an optimum solution. The Simplex Method does not require that all of the "corner" of the constraint inequalities be investigated. The Simplex procedure in effect "zeros in" on the optimum solution, by systematically testing the corners of the constraint inequalities, one at a time, until one is found which is optimal.

We begin by describing the *initial tableau* in an LP maximization problem:

$$\begin{array}{|ccc|} \hline A & I & b \\ \hline -c & 0 & 0 \\ \hline \end{array},$$

where A is the array (called a matrix) of the coefficients of the variables of the constraint inequalities, before the slack variables have been introduced. From our example, A is the array of numbers

$$\begin{pmatrix} 3 & 2 \\ 3 & 4 \end{pmatrix}.$$

I is the array of coefficients of the slack variables taken from the constraint equations, giving

$$\begin{pmatrix} 1 & 0 \\ 0 & 1 \end{pmatrix}$$

for our example. The column of constraints on the right-hand side of the constraint equations are inserted for b in the tableau giving

$$\begin{pmatrix} 18 \\ 24 \end{pmatrix}.$$

Finally, c is a row of numbers which are the coefficients of the independent variables in the objective function, taken one at a time, with a negative sign attached to each. For our illustration, $-c$ equals $(-7 \quad -8)$. Now putting all of the parts together and inserting zeros in the two lower right-hand cells, we get the initial tableau for our illustration:

	X_1	X_2	S_1	S_2	b
S_1	3	2	1	0	18
S_2	3	4	0	1	24
π	-7	-8	0	0	0
	Indicators				

Note the symmetry between the initial tableau and the constraint equations (5) and (6), and also the addition of labels.

The tableau above is called the *initial basic feasible solution* (IBFS) to the LP problem. The left-hand labels S_1 and S_2 and π refer to the numbers in the b column. For the IBFS, the values of the slacks are 18 and 24, respectively. Since 18 labor hours and 24 machine hours are all the time available for labor and machine production, respectively, then output must be zero, and so too will be the value of the objective function indicated by the zero in the lower right corner of the tableau. In effect, we are beginning at the corner of the feasible region represented by the origin in Figure 1.

The operation of the tableau is governed by the following steps:
1. Select the column with the largest negative indicator, the negative number with the largest absolute value. This is the *pivot column*.
2. Divide each of the numbers in the pivot column into the number in the same row in the b column. Select the quotient that is smallest. The *pivot number* is the number in the pivot column that was used to obtain the smallest quotient.
3. Divide the entire row in which the pivot number appears by the pivot number and insert the new row, called a *pivot row*, into a new tableau in the same position. Label this row with the label of the pivot column.
4. For each of the *remaining rows* of the original tableau:
   a. Multiply the number in the pivot column of the first remaining row times each of the numbers of the pivot row and subtract the result from the first remaining row.
   b. Insert the row calculated by *a* above into the new tableau in the corresponding position.
   c. Continue with *a* above (substituting second, third, etc. for first remaining row) until the rows of the new tableau are filled.
5. If there are any negative indicators remaining, return to step 1.

The First Iteration

To illustrate the steps, we have rewritten the *initial basic feasible solution* below:

	X_1	X_2	S_1	S_2		
S_1	3	2	1	0	18	
S_2	3	④	0	1	24	T_1
	−7	−8	0	0	0	

The second column is the pivot column, since −8 is larger (greater absolute value) than −7. Following step 2, we divide 2 into 18, giving 9, and 4 into 24, giving 6. The second quotient is smallest, so 4 (circled in T_1 above) is the pivot number. Dividing the second row by 4, we get

$$(\tfrac{3}{4} \quad 1 \quad 0 \quad \tfrac{1}{4} \quad 6),$$

which is inserted into T_2, and the label X_2 attached.

	X_1	X_2	S_1	S_2		
S_1	6/4	0	1	−2/4	6	
X_2	3/4	1	0	1/4	6	T_2
	−1	0	0	2	48	

Now we must operate on the 1st and 3rd rows of T_1, beginning with row 1. First, we multiply the second row of T_2, the pivot row, by 2 (the number in the pivot column position of the first row) to get

$$2(3/4 \quad 1 \quad 0 \quad 1/4 \quad 6) = (6/4 \quad 2 \quad 0 \quad 2/4 \quad 12).$$

Second, we subtract this result from row 1 of T_1, giving:

$$\begin{array}{r}(3 \quad 2 \quad 1 \quad 0 \quad 18) \\ -(6/4 \quad 2 \quad 0 \quad 2/4 \quad 12) \\ \hline (6/4 \quad 0 \quad 1 \quad -2/4 \quad 6),\end{array}$$

which is inserted in row 1 of T_2.

The second row of T_2 is now multiplied by -8 (the number in the pivot column position of the third row) and the result subtracted from row 3 of T_1. The calculations are:

$$-8(3/4 \quad 1 \quad 0 \quad 1/4 \quad 6) = (-6 \quad -8 \quad 0 \quad -2 \quad -48),$$

which is subtracted from row 3 of T_1, giving:

$$\begin{array}{r}(-7 \quad -8 \quad 0 \quad 0 \quad 0) \\ -(-6 \quad -8 \quad 0 \quad -2 \quad -48) \\ \hline (-1 \quad 0 \quad 0 \quad 2 \quad 48),\end{array}$$

which is inserted into the final row of T_2. Notice that there is a 1 in the position of the pivot number and zeros in the remaining positions in that column. If this were not true, an error would be indicated.

Since there are negative indicators in T_2, we must return to step 1 and repeat the entire process.

The Second Iteration

Since there is only one negative indicator in T_2, column 1 is the pivot column. To determine the pivot number, we divide 6/4 into 6, giving 4, and 3/4 into 6, giving 8. The first quotient is smaller, and thus 6/4 is the pivot number. The first row of T_2 is now divided by 6/4, giving

$$(1 \quad 0 \quad 4/6 \quad -1/3 \quad 4),$$

248 A Theory of Producer Behavior

which is inserted into T_3 with the proper label.

	X_1	X_2	S_1	S_2		
X_1	1	0	$4/6$	$-1/3$	4	
X_2	0	1	$-1/2$	0	3	T_3
π	0	0	$4/6$	$5/3$	52	

To complete the second row of T_3, we multiply $3/4$ (the number in the pivot column position of row 2 in T_2) times row 1 of T_3 and subtract the result from row 2 of T_2. The calculations are:

$$
\begin{array}{r}
(3/4 \quad 1 \quad\quad 0 \quad\quad 1/4 \quad 6) \\
-(3/4 \quad 0 \quad\quad 1/2 \quad -1/4 \quad 3) \\ \hline
(0 \quad 1 \quad -1/2 \quad\quad 0 \quad 3)
\end{array}
$$

The result of these calculations is inserted into the second row of T_3.

Finally, the last row of T_3 is determined by multiplying -1 (the number in the pivot column position of row 3 in T_2) by the pivot row in T_3, giving

$$(-1 \quad 0 \quad -4/6 \quad 1/3 \quad -4)$$

and subtracting the result from row 3 of T_2. The calculations are:

$$
\begin{array}{r}
(-1 \quad 0 \quad\quad 0 \quad 2 \quad 48) \\
-(-1 \quad 0 \quad -4/6 \quad 1/3 \quad -4) \\ \hline
(\ 0 \quad 0 \quad\quad 4/6 \quad 5/3 \quad 52)
\end{array}
$$

which is inserted in the last row of T_3.

Since there are no more negative indicators in the completed tableau T_3, we have an optimum solution to the program. The labels indicate that 4 units of X_1 and 3 units of X_2 are to be produced. Moreover, the optimum value of the objective function, π, in the lower right-hand cell is \$52. The results of the Simplex solution agree with the graphical solution in Figure 1.

Economies of Scale in High School Operation
JOHN RIEW*

The following selection is a straightforward study of scale economies in high schools, demonstrating that the theory of production is applicable to nonprofit service industries as well as profit-maximizing manufacturers. Riew concludes that scale economies were very significant for his sample of senior high schools in Wisconsin.

In the school year 1963–1964, according to the National Education Association, the total expenditures to educate 41.7 million pupils of the Nation's public schools exceeded 21 billion dollars. This expenditure figure shows a significant increase from 15.6 billion dollars in 1959–1960 and 5.8 billion dollars in 1949–1950 which were spent, respectively, for 34.2 million and 24.1 million pupils. In view of the magnitude of the resources involved and the rapid growth of their amounts, inquiry into scale economies in public education has not received adequate treatment by researchers.

The main reasons for this seem to be (1) the difficulty of determining the quality of various schools, and (2) varying opinions regarding the importance of the implications of such a study. The cost per pupil may reflect differences in the quality of education among schools, unless this quality differential is somehow taken into account. Then, if a study indicates an economic advantage for large size schools, there is a question of how this fact should affect policy decisions when there are other factors to be considered.

The United States Office of Education, for many years, has been making surveys of public school costs in cities of varying sizes. Their results in general show higher per-pupil costs for schools in larger cities. In the year 1958–1959, the cost per pupil in cities with a population of less than 10,000 was 312 dollars. The cost in cities with populations ranging from 10,000 to 24,999 was 305 dollars. In cities with populations from 25,000 to 99,999, it was 321

From the *Review of Economics and Statistics*, Vol. XLVIII, No. 3 (August 1966). Reprinted by permission.

* I am indebted for many valuable suggestions to Professor Martin Bronfenbrenner, Harold M. Groves, Werner Z. Hirsch, Thomas Iwand, and Peter O. Steiner. The assistance from the Social Systems Research Institute of the University of Wisconsin is also gratefully acknowledged.

dollars, and in cities of over 100,000 people, 361 dollars.[1] In 1939–1940, the equivalent figures were 80 dollars, 87 dollars, 102 dollars, and 127 dollars, respectively.[2]

The surveys obviously were not intended for analysis of economies of scale in school operation. Although large schools are typically in large cities and small ones in smaller cities, city population is hardly a suitable index of school size. Also these surveys do not account for differences in the quality of schools among size classes.

The first serious inquiry on the subject was made recently by Werner Z. Hirsch.[3] In his analysis, which employs multiple correlation and regression techniques and uses an elaborate device to distinguish quality differences among schools, he finds no significant economies of scale. He thus concludes that consolidation is unlikely to solve the fiscal problems of public schools. Hirsch uses a school district as the unit of observation. A study based on school districts undoubtedly has its merits, but schools, by and large, operate independently within a district. Thus, a more meaningful analysis of the size-cost relation, as Hirsch also implies, should be based on *individual schools*. Of the 27 St. Louis public school systems included in his study, all but six had enrollments of more than 1,500. To test the validity of a conjecture that significant scale economies exist over a relatively low size-range into which the nation's great majority of schools fall,[4] we need a sample with a larger number of smaller units.

Schmandt and Stephens, in a rank order correlation analysis, offer the conclusion that there is a significant negative relation between school size and per pupil current expenditures.[5] They too attempt to consider quality variation among schools, but for the measure of quality they use the number of subfunctions performed in each school. As the authors admit, this fails to differentiate the quality of each subfunction and gives equal weight to all such func-

---

[1] Gerald Kahn, *Current Expenditures Per Pupil in Public School Systems: 1958–59* (Washington, D.C.: U.S. Office of Education, Circular No. 645, Government Printing Office, 1961), 6.

[2] Lester B. Herlihy and Walter Deffenbaugh, *Statistics of City School Systems, 1939–40 and 1941–42* (Washington, D.C.: U.S. Office of Education, Government Printing Office, 1945), 15. (For this earlier year, the second and the third size classes were divided at 30,000 instead of 25,000.)

[3] See Werner Z. Hirsch, "Expenditure Implications of Metropolitan Growth and Consolidation," this REVIEW, XLI (Aug. 1959), 232–240 (especially 239–240); and "Determinants of Public Education Expenditures," *National Tax Journal*, XIII (March 1960), 29–40.

[4] Of 37,019 public school districts that existed in the United States in 1961–1962, 84.2 per cent had enrollments of less than 1,200 and 75.7 per cent had less than 600. United States Office of Education, *Digest of Educational Statistics* (Washington, D.C.: U.S. Government Printing Office, 1963), 29.

[5] Henry J. Schmandt and G. Ross Stephens, "Measuring Municipal Output," *National Tax Journal*, III (Dec. 1960), 369–375.

tions. Their study was based on 18 "school district areas" of Milwaukee County, the district areas again taken as the basis of analysis.[6]

In these previous studies,[7] elementary and secondary schools are combined into individual units. Elementary schools operate differently from secondary schools. Most important, the secondary schools call for a higher degree of specialization in the teaching staff and for more facilities than do the elementary schools. Thus, these two levels of public schools should be considered as two distinct industries, and a joint treatment results in mixing two possibly dissimilar tendencies.

THE APPROACH AND THE DATA

The present study, in analyzing the relationship between school size and cost, concentrates on public high school systems and approaches the subject on the basis of individual schools rather than school districts. This study deals exclusively with the senior high schools, comprising grades nine to 12 and ten to 12. Junior high and combined high schools of grades seven to 12 were not included because of the probable cost variation associated with the differences in organization.

Wisconsin high schools were chosen as the object of the study because the state offers unusually good sources of information for the purpose. In Wisconsin, the State Department of Public Instruction, actively committed to aid for public education, secures quite a thorough annual report from each school district. The report contains a school census and detailed information on revenues and expenditures for all elementary schools and for all high schools in the district separately. However, neither the annual report nor the district files give separate accounts for individual schools. Thus, for this study, districts were selected which had only one high school. Many larger schools are in larger school districts and eliminating these districts which have more than one high school reduces the number of large schools in the sample. There is, however, a sufficient number of districts with one high school of larger size for the purposes of this study.

[6] Of the 18 school district areas, only 13 provide both elementary and secondary schools. Each of the remaining five is a combination of an elementary district and the secondary district to which they send their pupils. Thus, all 18 units are made to cover grades one to 12 or kindergarten to 12 for the sake of comparability, but when some units are a multiple of districts while the others are single districts the meaning of the analysis becomes more doubtful.

[7] There is also a recent study by the Committee for Economic Development which stresses the advantage of a larger school system. It suggests that educational advantages continue to accrue until a combined school system (kindergarten to 12 or one to 12 years) has "perhaps 25,000 students" and that there are financial advantages of many kinds in even larger units. The Committee for Economic Development, *Paying for Better Public Schools* (New York, Dec. 1959), 64.

All told, there were 430 public senior high schools in the state in 1960–1961. We observe in Table 1 that more than half of these schools had an

TABLE 1 Distribution by Enrollment —Wisconsin Public High Schools 1960–1961

Pupils in Average Daily Attendance	Number of Schools
200 or less	134
201–300	93
301–500	86
500 or more	117
Total	430

SOURCE: Wisconsin Department of Public Instruction, *The Summary of High School Preliminary Reports* (1960–1961).

enrollment of less than 300 and only about one-quarter had an enrollment of more than 500. Undoubtedly, educational programs and qualities among these schools vary and it will be futile to attempt an inquiry into size-cost relations without taking into account these variations.

As a partial measure of quality, for this analysis, a step was first taken to select only those schools which were accredited by the North-Central Association. In 1960–1961, there were 152 accredited public high schools, of which 142 encompassed grades nine to 12 or ten to 12. The elimination of districts with more than one high school reduced the sample size by 26. To further narrow differences in standards, schools which appeared to rank considerably above the majority were excluded. This was done by eliminating schools where the 1960–1961 average teacher salary exceeded $6,500. This produced an additional loss of seven schools (several schools paying high teacher salaries were already excluded when large districts with two or more high schools were left out).[8]

We have, thus, 109 schools (92 four-year and 17 three-year high schools) which survived the tests of accreditation and "non-exceptionality" and are by and large comparable in organization. In setting a floor based on the judgment of the North-Central Association and arbitrarily setting a ceiling based on average teacher salary, the intent was to reduce variations in the standard

[8] There is no great significance to this particular figure. It was observed that $6,000 was not very far above average salaries for the majority and using that figure would have eliminated too many schools. On the other hand, $7,000 was too far up in the salary scale. The mean of the average salaries for the 109 schools was $5,662. Teacher salaries alone certainly cannot be an adequate measure of the standard of a school. It was assumed, however, that salaries are in general significantly associated with the quality of teachers and often even with other provisions offered in a school.

of schools and analyze the size-cost relation with minimum interference from these variations.

In Table 2, schools are grouped by size, and average per pupil expenditures are related to various size classes. Additional information is then provided for respective size classes concerning (1) average teacher's salary, (2) ratio of teachers holding a master's degree, (3) average years of teacher experiences, (4) average pupil–teacher ratio, (5) number of credit units offered, and (6) average number of courses taught by a teacher. The first three are assumed to reflect teacher qualifications, the fourth class size, the fifth breadth of school programs, and the last the degree of specialization in instruction. While the foregoing aspects are not all that may be relevant in judging a school they do constitute important ingredients of school qualities.[9] The size-cost relation, then, can be observed along with those measures which indicate the nature and direction of quality biases that may be associated with size.

The expenditure figures in Table 2 relate to operational items only; neither capital outlays nor debt services are included. Of the operational expenditures, those for transportation, auxiliary services, and other minor items are excluded. The per pupil costs of transportation often vary more with population density, and the distance a school bus has to travel, than with the size of a school, which may or may not reflect population density. As for auxiliary services, which include school lunch, pupil recreation and health programs, a comparison of costs is made difficult because some schools, especially larger ones, do not have lunch programs.

Thus, included in our analysis are outlays for *administration, teacher's salaries, other instruction* (salaries for clerical assistants to the teaching staff, text books, library books, and other instructional supplies), *operation* (salaries and wages of the custodial staff, fuel, utilities, etc.), and *maintenance* (staff salary, supplies, and contract services related to property maintenance). For high schools of Wisconsin as a whole, these items in 1960–1961 comprised 92.1 per cent of total operating expenditures (the total excluding costs of transportation) and 63.0 per cent of all school expenditures.[10]

Table 2 provides a fairly comprehensive picture and may be considered highly informative. We shall first examine the table and then, for further insights, we shall turn to a more rigorous statistical analysis.

---

[9] These are largely input measures. An ideal approach to the measurement of school quality would be to consider *output* rather than *input* inasmuch as our prime concern in education is not with what we invest in schools but with what we get out of them. However, unavailability of output measures (not to mention difficulties in agreeing upon output substances) and variation in intelligence and socio-economic background among pupils make such a project extremely difficult.

[10] All school expenditures include both operational and capital outlays, but not debt services, since including the latter would be a double counting for loan-financed capital outlays. The percentage figures are computed from the data available in the *1960–61 Summary of Annual Reports of School Districts* (Wisconsin Department of Public Instruction), 9–10.

TABLE 2 Averages of Operating Expenditures and Characteristics of Teachers in 109 Accredited High Schools of Wisconsin Grouped by Size, 1960–1961

Number of Schools	Pupils in Average Daily Attendance	Operating[a] Expenditure Per Pupil	Average Teacher's Salary	Percentage Teachers Holding Master's Degree	Average[b] Years Taught	Pupil-[c] Teacher Ratio	Credit[d] Units Offered	Average[e] Course Load Per Teacher
6	143–200	$531.9	$5,305	18.1	6.3	17.3	34.7	3.8
12	201–300	480.8	5,187	15.1	6.1	18.2	36.9	2.9
19	301–400	446.3	5,265	18.8	6.3	20.0	39.6	2.5
17	401–500	426.9	5,401	18.5	7.4	20.9	44.0	2.3
14	501–600	442.6	5,574	23.5	7.5	20.7	46.5	1.9
13	601–700	413.1	5,411	22.5	6.8	20.9	45.3	1.7
9	701–900	374.3	5,543	22.3	7.1	24.1	46.4	1.8
6	901–1100	433.2	5,939	34.0	7.3	21.4	57.7	1.6
6	1101–1600	407.3	5,976	36.5	11.9	24.4	63.4	1.6
7	1601–2400	405.6	6,230	54.5	11.2	24.2	80.3	1.6

[a] The figures represent the sum of current operating expenditures on administration, teachers' salaries, other instruction, operation, and maintenance. Expenditures on transportation, auxiliary services (school lunch, pupil recreation and health programs) and other minor items are not included.

[b] The mean of median years taught in individual schools within each size class. (For other variables, the average was the mean of mean values for individual schools in each size class.)

[c] Number of pupils in average daily attendance divided by number of teachers, the latter being the full-time equivalent of staff members devoted to teaching only.

[d] A two-semester course meeting five times weekly is counted as one credit unit. For smaller schools, the number of credit units relate to a two-year program because in these schools some courses are offered only in alternate years.

[e] Total credit units divided by number of teachers. In determining the number of teachers, multiple counting is avoided. If, for instance, because of large enrollment, several teachers teach the same course, they are counted as one. When a teacher devotes part of his time, say two-fifths, for a course taught by others, only that fraction is subtracted.

FINDINGS AND EVALUATIONS

1. The per-pupil expenditures decline fairly steadily from $531 to $374 as enrollment rises from less than 200 to 701–900. Within the above range of enrollment, (a) smaller schools have lower average pupil-teacher ratios, (b) larger schools, on the other hand, have relatively more teachers with advanced degrees on their faculty, and, more important perhaps, (c) larger schools offer a broader curriculum and more specialized instruction.[11] The of credit units, an indication of the breadth of curriculum (see note d to Table 2), ranges from 34.7 for schools with less than 200 pupils to 46.4 for those with 701–900 pupils. The average number of courses taught per teacher varies from 3.8 for the smallest schools to 1.8 for those with 701–900 pupils.[12]

2. The per-pupil expenditures, after a fairly consistent fall, rise from $374 to $433 as enrollment increases from 701–900 to the next size-class of 901–1,100. However, this rise in expenditures accompanies a notable rise in the proportion of teachers with a master's degree and a considerable broadening of the school curriculum. It appears that, with enrollment in the vicinity of one thousand, the demand for advanced courses and for teachers with advanced training rises and becomes more effective.[13]

3. As enrollment rises from 901–1,100 to 1,101–1,600, the per-pupil expenditures fall again, from $433 to $407. Then, with a further increase to 1,601–2,400, the expenditures remain stable while the ratio of master's degrees in the faculty and the number of credit units continue to rise.

[11] James B. Conant, in his noted study of American high schools, emphasizes the need for more diversified high school programs. He strongly recommends that students be provided with adequate elective programs in mathematics, languages, science, English, and social studies and that a seven- or eight-period school day be organized to allow students more flexibility in taking these courses. See James B. Conant, *The American High School Today* (McGraw-Hill, 1959), 41–76.

[12] As was noted in Table 2, the number of credit units for smaller schools was related to programs covering a two-year period. In these schools, some courses are offered only in alternate years. To the extent that these two-year arrangements limit the alternatives available for pupils, comparison of the figures shown here does not fully account for their differences.

[13] The fall in pupil-teacher ratio from 24.1 to one to 21.4 to one suggests also that a rise in enrollment at this level introduces more advanced courses where class sizes are typically small until a further increase in enrollment gives the teachers a fuller load.

Sources for Table 2: For information on accreditation, *The North Central Association Quarterly*, XXXVI (Summer 1961), 123–127; for teacher degrees, credit units, number of pupils, and number of teachers, Wisconsin Department of Public Instruction, *High School Preliminary Report* (1960–1961); for operating expenditures, teachers' salaries, and years of teacher experience, Wisconsin Education Association, *Expenditure Per Pupil in City Schools* (1960–1961), *Expenditures Per Pupil in Village Schools* (1960–1961), *Salaries in City Schools* (1960–1961), and *Salaries in Schools Under Supervising Principals* (1960–1961). (The data in these Wisconsin Education Association bulletins are abstracted mostly from the Annual Report of School District and High School Preliminary Report to the State Superintendent of Public Instruction.)

The average pupil–teacher ratio varies rather moderately from 17 to one for schools with less than 200 pupils, 20 to one for those with 301–700 pupils, and about 24 to one for most of the larger schools. The pupil–teacher ratios for schools observed here are all relatively low and differences in pupil–teacher ratios do not seem crucial (none of the individual schools included in the present study had an average ratio of more than 27 to one).

The significance of the pupil–teacher ratio has been challenged for some time and more so recently. Past studies of class-size provide little evidence that large classes materially affect the academic efficiency of the class. After reviewing a great number of class-size studies conducted in the past, Otto and von Bergersrode conclude that ". . . mere size of class has little significant influence on educational efficiency as measured by achievement in the academic subjects . . . ," and that ". . . although experimental evidence does not provide a clear-cut answer to the class-size issue, the general trend of the evidence places the burden of proof squarely upon the proponents of small classes."[14]

Within the range of enrollment of less than 200 to 701–900, then, advantages of a larger school may be considered overwhelming. A larger school not only spends considerably less per pupil but has decisive advantages in curriculum and in teacher specialization.

Whether schools with an enrollment of more than 701–900 provide additional economies depends on one's appraisal of the cost differential as against the differences in what the schools offer. With enrollment of 1,101–1,600 or 1,601–2,400, the per-pupil expenditures are $407 or $406 as compared with $374 for schools with 701–900 pupils. However, these larger schools distinguish themselves with broader curricula (63.4 or 80.3 credit units against 46.4), higher proportions of faculty holding advanced degrees (36.5 or 54.5 per cent against 22.3) and teachers with more experience (11.9 or 11.3 years against 7.1). If one believes these improvements in standards more than compensate for the differences in expenditures this then may be construed as an economy.

One may make an evaluation by direct examination of Table 2 which provides comprehensive information on the subject. Judging school qualities involves subjective values. Given the size, the cost, and variables that are considered relevant to school qualities, one could make his own appraisal and final judgment.

Nevertheless, this approach leaves some important questions unanswered. If, for instance, we agree that there are economies of scale and that cost per pupil decreases with an increase in the size of enrollment, we would want to

---

[14] Henry J. Otto and Fred von Bergersrode, "Class Size," in Walter S. Monroe (ed.), *Encyclopedia of Educational Research* (New York: Macmillan, 1950), 212–216. The authors, however, feel that for elementary schools smaller classes are still preferable to larger classes. See also John I. Goodland, "Room to Live and Learn: Class Size and Room Space as Factors in the Learning–Teaching Process," *Childhood Education*, 30 (Apr. 1954), 355–361; and Herbert F. Spitzer, "Class Size and Pupil Achievement in Elementary Schools," *The Elementary School Journal*, 55 (Oct. 1954), 82–86.

have estimations on such decreases in cost and on their statistical significance. It should be noted also that the figures shown in our table are average values for each size class and tend to conceal variations within classes.

In the estimation of possible cost savings, we seek to isolate the influence of size upon cost. For this we would need to consider other factors which are expected to affect the cost. Presumably, the most important of such factors is school quality. Regardless of the method of analysis, we must make certain assumptions as to what constitute school qualities and our conclusions necessarily must be evaluated with reference to the manner in which qualities are taken into account. Besides quality differences, there are other conditions to account for variations in input requirements and thus in average costs among schools.

The method employed here to approximate the net relationship between school size and per-pupil cost is least-squares multiple regression analysis. The analysis is based on the 109 selected high schools which are included in Table 2. Using largely the factors already introduced in the table, our regression equation includes the following variables:

X_1—Operating expenditures per pupil in average daily attendance.
X_2—Enrollment (number of pupils in average daily attendance).
X_3—Average teacher's salary.
X_4—Number of credit units offered (a two-semester course meeting five times a week is counted as one unit).
X_5—Average number of courses taught per teacher.
X_6—Change in enrollment between 1957 and 1960 (the 1960 enrollment is taken as a percentage of the 1957 enrollment).
X_7—Percentage of classrooms built after 1950.

Used here as our quality variables are average teacher's salary (X_3), number of credit units offered (X_4), and average number of courses taught per teacher (X_5), which may be considered to represent, respectively, teacher qualifications, the breadth of curriculum, and the degree of specialization in instruction. The pupil–teacher ratio is left out in view of the controversies as to how the ratio is associated with classroom efficiency and of the fact that the pupil–teacher ratios observed in the present study are all relatively low. A preliminary result, furthermore, indicated high correlation between average teacher's salary and teacher status with respect to degree and experience; thus, these two were also eliminated.[15]

[15] Of a number of conceivable variables, the teacher's salary seems preferable as an indicator of teacher qualifications, even to the composite of academic degree and experience. Two persons with the same degree and years of experience can be rated differently as teachers and such differences are likely to be reflected in their salaries. It may be argued that living costs are higher in larger cities where there are more larger schools and a part of the salary differential between large and small schools may be considered a corrective of local price variation. Most of the schools included here, however, are in places of less than 50,000 in population, and price variation, if any, cannot be significant.

Changes in enrollment over a period of a few years (X_6) may indicate the pace at which demand for school services changed and thus possibly reflect some lagging adjustments in cost. The last variable, the proportion of new classrooms (X_7), was included because costs of maintenance and operation may vary by the ages of school properties.

In this statistical test, we assume a parabolic relationship between per pupil cost and enrollment. The relations between the cost and the other independent variables were all assumed to be linear. The following results are then obtained:

$$X_1 = 10.31 - \underline{.402 X_2} + \underline{.00012 X_2{}^2} + \underline{.107 X_3}$$
$$(.063)(.000023)\phantom{X_2{}^2}(.013)$$

$$+ .985 X_4 - 15.62 X_5 + .613 X_6 - .102 X_7 .$$
$$(.640)(11.95)(.189)(.109)$$

The figures in parentheses are standard errors of the net regression and the statistically significant coefficients (at a probability level of .01) are underlined. The coefficient of multiple determination adjusted for degrees of freedom lost, R^{*2}, is .557 and is highly significant at a probability level of .01.

Thus, about 56 per cent of the variation in average per pupil operating expenditures among the 109 high schools in 1960–1961 was accounted for by the six independent variables of which average teacher's salary, enrollment, and changes in enrollment were statistically significant.[16] The partial correlation coefficients of these variables are:

$$r_{12.2^2 34567} = .539, \qquad r_{13.22^2 4567} = .648, \text{ and}$$
$$r_{12^2 .234567} = .465, \qquad r_{16.22^2 3457} = .307.$$

When school enrollment (variables X_2 and $X_2{}^2$) is eliminated from our multiple regression analysis, R^{*2} is reduced from .557 to .374. Holding constant the effects of changes in the other five variables, then, 18.3 per cent of the variation in per pupil operating expenditures is explainable in terms of variation in enrollment.

Our regression equation suggests, further, that an enrollment increase of one pupil, holding the other variables constant, lowers average per pupil operating expenditures by $[40.2 - 2(.012 X_2)]$ cents at X_2 level of enrollment until X_2

---

[16] Obviously, some of the unexplained portion of the variation in average per pupil expenditures is attributable to other causal forces not included in the analysis and perhaps, to some degree, to deficiencies of the variables included. Our assumption of linear functional relationships (between per pupil cost and variables other than size) and possible errors and arbitrariness in the reporting of data would undoubtedly have some effects also.

finally reaches 1.675.[17] Thus, a school with an enrollment of 200, for instance, if it behaves in "average fashion," will reduce its per pupil operating expenditures 35.4 cents by having one more pupil. For a school with 500 pupils, adding one pupil would reduce per pupil expenditures by 28.2 cents and for one with 1,000 pupils, by 15.8 cents. Increase in the enrollment of a school from 200 to 500, the other independent variables held constant, would thus mean a saving of $95.45 in average per-pupil operating expenditures.[18] With an increase in enrollment of from 500 to 1,000 the expected saving in per-pupil expenditures would be $111.00, and from 1,000 to 1,675 the expected saving would be $54.67.

These figures of course provide only approximations and are subject to error limitations. However, if we are concerned with an "average" school and our assumptions on school qualities are acceptable, they may be considered as meaningful estimates.[19] That the coefficient of X_6 (the change in enrollment) is significantly positive may deserve some attention. It suggests that under conditions of rapid expansion, the school operates on a short-run cost curve above the level that is achievable under a full long-run adjustment to increased enrollment levels.

A larger school may mean an added transportation cost, especially in a thinly populated area. This additional cost and perhaps the nonmonetary costs (of fatigue, time, parental concern, etc.) would have to be subtracted from the "saving" referred to above. This point, however, should not be overly stressed. There are indications that in the great majority of instances a small enrollment is simply a reflection of a small size of the school district rather than population sparsity. "In only 19 states," a C.E.D. study points out, ". . . is the average geographic area covered by a school system as much as 225 square miles—equivalent to an area 15 miles square. In 21 states it is less than 49 square miles."[20]

---

[17] From our regression equation,

$$\frac{\partial X_1}{\partial X_2} = -.402 + 2(.00012 X_2).$$

Thus, when

$$\frac{\partial X_1}{\partial X_2} = 0, \quad X_2 = \frac{.402}{.00024} = 1{,}675.$$

[18] From our equation, the change in the average per-pupil operating expenditures (X_1) to result from the change in enrollment (X_2) from 200 to 500 would be:

$$\Delta X_1 = [-.402(500) + .00012(500^2)]$$
$$\quad - [-.402(200) + .00012(200^2)]$$
$$= -95.40.$$

[19] The concept of returns to scale deals with a given technology. Thus, in using the present analysis as the basis for future projection, we must assume that the educational methods and policies remain largely unchanged.

[20] The Committee for Economic Development, *op. cit.*, 6.

A recent study conducted by the Wisconsin Department of Public Instruction reveals, furthermore, that differences in average transportation costs between rural and urban areas and between districts covering large areas and those covering small areas are considerably less than commonly believed. In the 1961–1962 academic year, the average of per-pupil transportation expenditures in the most thickly populated counties of Milwaukee, Racine, Kenosha, and Winnebago (each with population density of more than 200 per square mile) was $54.16 as compared with $65.10 for the most thinly populated counties of Sawyer, Bayfield, Florence, and Forest (each with the density of less than ten per square mile) where school districts are much larger in area.[21] This may in part be accounted for by differences in service qualities. The better explanation, however, is that in school transportation the fixed costs (depreciation, driver salary, insurance, garage rental, etc.) comprise such an important part that differences in the mileage of operation, in many cases, affect the total transportation cost much less than is often anticipated.[22]

In the present analysis capital outlays are excluded as they generally fluctuate widely over time. When they are taken into account, greater variation in per-pupil costs among size groups may be expected. Physical education programs and a library, for instance, require many provisions which a school of any size should not lack. For a satisfactory high school program, various equipment and provisions for science laboratories, language, music, and vocational training are basic and essential. For these items, smaller schools bear larger overhead costs. As general standards of high schools continue to improve with increasing investment in capital items, the issue will become even more important.

CONCLUSION

Differentiating educational qualities among individual schools is a difficult task, but based on what may be considered as reasonable assumptions, the study of Wisconsin high schools suggests that economies of scale at this level of public education are very significant.

---

[21] Wisconsin Department of Public Instruction, *Transportation Facts 1962–63* (Madison, Wisconsin, March 1963). The figures are computed from the data available on pages 12–13.

[22] *Ibid.*, 11. The study presents the following illustration of a typical contract for a bus with a daily mileage of 60 miles: Fixed charge per day for:

Depreciation	$4.50	Variable charge per bus mile for gas,	
Driver Salary	6.25	oil, grease, repairs, maintenance, etc.	
Insurance	.50	10¢ (per mile) × 60	$ 6.00
Garage Rental	.75	Total charge per day	$18.00
	$12.00		

Taking the high schools as a whole, capital outlays in recent years comprised roughly a quarter of the total expenditures. Their inclusion in the analysis would most likely have strengthened the present conclusion. This would have increased cost variation among schools, the higher overhead costs being expected to fall on smaller schools.

A sample with a larger number of schools, especially of the upper size classes, and with its size range extended beyond the present limit of 2,400 pupils would have been more informative. The virtue of "that little red schoolhouse" may be of more than an emotional nature. But whatever the merits, they ought to be considered negotiable. When better informed of the opportunity costs, one may wish to reexamine his traditional preference.

Economies of Scale, Expansion Path, and Growth of Plants

T. Y. SHEN*

This reading is a study of scale economies in a number of American manufacturing industries. Shen is concerned with the real-world observation that, at points in time, plants of varying sizes exist simultaneously in many industries, and that there does not seem to be any tendency for all of them to gravitate to one standard, optimum size. He introduces the concept of an expansion path to investigate this phenomenon in a dynamic growth setting.

Casual observation reveals that plants of different sizes exist and have always existed with little tendency to become more concentrated in any particular size class. This can only mean that plants are not operating under conditions of long-run static equilibrium,[1] and that the concept of "optimal" scale cannot be used to explain the actual size distribution or the growth patterns of plants.[2] Some writers have suggested the idea of an "optimal distribution,"

From the *Review of Economics and Statistics*, Vol. XLVII, No. 4 (November 1965). Reprinted by permission.

* I would like to thank Frank Child and John Harsanyi for their helpful comments, Joseph King for providing me with empirical materials, and the National Science Foundation for financial support.

[1] Hymer and Pashigian have argued convincingly that the dispersion of firms cannot be attributed to constant returns to scale. Stephen Hymer and Peter Pashigian, "Firm Size and Rate of Growth," *Journal of Political Economy*, LXX (1962), 556–569. In this paper, we are concerned with the behavior of plants. However, much of the discussion pertaining to the size of firm in the literature is equally applicable to the size of plant.

[2] Some realism is introduced if Gibrat's Law is made the starting point. Gibrat, Hart, Prais and others have discovered that in a large number of industries the size distribution of firms is approximately lognormal, and the law of proportionate effect—that the average growth rate is approximately the same for firms of different sizes—was generally adopted to explain the distribution. Since this results in a continuing divergence of plant distribution over time, it was further proposed that a process of regression is at work, that is, that "the firms in any given size class at time t would still be distributed lognormally at $t + 1$, but their mean size would be nearer to the mean size of all firms." P. E. Hart and S. J. Prais, "The Analysis of Business Concentration: A Statistical Approach," *Journal of the Royal Statistical Society*, Series A, Part II (1956), 150–191. The idea implies that there is some

presumably based on the stochastic nature of human ability and human foresight.[3] Mathematically, the optimal distribution may be related to the stationary distribution corresponding to some stochastic process describing the growth of plants. This growth in turn is explained by such factors as economies of scale, economies of growth,[4] profit margin variations,[5] and other dynamic factors.

The appropriate frame of reference for the optimal distribution is the expansion path, or scale path. The path may be regarded as representing the basic manufacturing activity of an industry. Plants cluster around this path, and their sizes are given by their positions on the path. The size distribution of plants is therefore defined with respect to this path. Similarly, from one period to the next, the growth of plants is given by their movements along the path.[6] It is reasonable to assume that this path is characterized by fixed elasticities (rather than fixed proportions) among the input and output variables, since plants become more capital intensive as they grow.

The present paper investigates (1) the extent of economies of scale along the expansion path for each of the manufacturing industries, and (2) the relationship between economies of scale and the growth pattern of plants. Our principal hypothesis is that with a given expansion path—or given returns to scale—*all* the plants tend to expand at the same rate. In this case, a strict form of Gibrat's Law would apply and it is possible to speak of an equilibrium lognormal distribution of plants with constant dispersion. When a shift of the expansion path takes place, there is also a change in returns to scale along the path. Our hypothesis states that there should be a systematic relationship between changes in returns to scale and changes in the dispersion of plants. The changes in returns to scale result in a differential rate of growth for plants of different sizes, until a new equilibrium lognormal distribution is established. The dispersion of this new distribution will then remain constant if no further change in economies of scale takes place. The empirical results presented in this paper demonstrate that the hypothesis is consistent with the actual behavior of plants.

The paper is divided into three sections. In the first section, we show that

---

optimal firm size, and plants tend to move towards that optimum. However, it is difficult to argue that the optimal size is the mean size, because there is little reason for a firm to expand beyond an optimal size.

[3] See, for example, Milton Friedman's comment on Caleb Smith's paper in *Business Concentration and Price Policy* (Princeton University Press, 1955).

[4] Edith Penrose, *The Theory of the Growth of the Firm* (New York, 1959).

[5] Joseph Steindl, *Small and Big Business* (Oxford Institute of Statistics, Monograph No. 1, 1946).

[6] If the plant is not on the path, its size is determined by the position of its projection on the path. Of course, technological change and substitution also take place from one period to another, resulting in a shift of the expansion path. This is discussed in a later section in the paper.

the distributions of capital, labor, and output are approximately lognormal. It is therefore possible to discuss the changes in these variables under three headings: the changes in the mean of these distributions, the changes in the dispersion of these distributions, and "shuffle," that is, interchange of individual plant positions along the expansion path while leaving the distribution undisturbed. The first two of these are discussed, within the framework of the expansion path, in sections II and III. In section II, the mechanism that relates economies of scale to plant growth is demonstrated. In section III the hypothesis on the relationship between returns to scale and the dispersion of plants is tested. Shuffle, an important phenomenon in the dynamic process of competition, will be the subject of a separate paper.

I. DISTRIBUTION OF PLANTS

Since 1885, a census of manufacturing establishments has been conducted annually by the Department of Labor and Industries of Massachusetts.[7] The Census covers some 10,000 manufacturing plants, or approximately the whole universe of manufacturing plants in the state. For the present study, we have selected a list of cities and towns. All the manufacturing establishments in these localities—nearly 4,000 plants in each of the years from 1935 to 1959—make up our sample. The geographical sampling is an attempt to minimize the sampling bias with respect to scale, technology, or substitution.[8] The plants are then grouped into 14 two-digit industries.[9]

For each of the plants, data are available for capital, labor, and output.[10] As expected, the density distributions of the input and the output variables are highly skewed. A lognormal distribution, selected because of its simplicity, is fitted to each of the variables.[11] Table 1 presents the result of a crude

---

[7] Massachusetts is the only state in the United States to conduct an annual census of manufacturers. All the manufacturing establishments in the state are required by law to return the questionnaire each year.

[8] Obviously, some bias remains because rural areas have been excluded. The peculiar industry mix in Massachusetts also taints the data.

[9] A Massachusetts industrial classification, broadly parallel to the SIC, is used. There are 15 two-digit industries in the Massachusetts classification. One of the industries, petroleum and coal, is excluded because, in our sample, the number of plants in this industry is very small.

[10] The procedures used in deriving a constant-price output figure and a constant-price gross capital figure are described in a paper available on request from the author. The data suffer from the usual conceptual difficulties and measurement errors.

[11] The lognormal distribution has been found to give a good fit to the size distribution of firms by many writers. See Hart and Prais, *op. cit.*; H. A. Simon and C. P. Bonini, "The Size Distribution of Business Firms," *American Economic Review*, XLVIII (1958), 607–617; and Edwin Mansfield, "Entry, Gibrat's Law, Innovation and the Growth of Firms," *American Economic Review*, LII (Dec. 1962), 1023–1051.

TABLE 1   Test of Lognormality: Correlation of Actual and Theoretical Frequencies

Industry	(1935–1959) Output	Capital	Labor
Food	.995	.999	.996
Textiles	.999	1.000	.999
Forest Products	.999	1.000	.999
Paper	.999	.998	.999
Printing and Publishing	.998	.999	.998
Chemicals	.999	1.000	.997
Rubber Products	.996	.992	.995
Leather Products	.998	.999	.999
Stone, Clay, and Glass	.998	1.000	.998
Ferrous Metals	1.000	1.000	.999
Non-ferrous Metals	.999	1.000	.999
Machinery	.996	.998	.997
Transportation Equipment	.997	.996	.997
Miscellaneous	.997	1.000	.998

test of the fit. The actual cumulative frequency of the observations in 43 quantiles is correlated with the expected frequency of a lognormal distribution in the same quantiles.[12] As the table shows, the correlation coefficients have values between .99 and 1.00, and, in 35 out of 42 cases, the coefficient is at least .997. The finding is interesting because our sample is different from the sample used by others. Our sample is more complete with respect to size since it includes unincorporated establishments. Our sample is also more directly related to technology since the basic unit is the plant rather than the firm.

There is no theory that relates these correlation coefficients to the statistical confidence level for rejecting the null hypothesis concerning the goodness of fit of the lognormal distribution.[13] The results do show that for descriptive purposes the lognormal distribution is a satisfactory approximation to the actual distribution. On the other hand, the question of whether the lognormal distribution and its theoretical justification are more acceptable than some alternative distribution and explanation must remain open.

[12] Let x be one of the input-output variables. If $\hat{x}$ follows the lognormal distribution exactly, let it be denoted as $\hat{x}$. Then the points $(Vq_i, \log \hat{x})$ lie on a straight line, where Vq_i is the quantile of order q_i in the corresponding normal distribution $N(0,1)$, and q_i the proportion of sample values smaller than or equal to $\hat{x}$. The correlation tests the extent of deviations of the actual observations from this line. Since the intercept and the slope of the line can only be estimated from the sample, some sampling bias is introduced. See J. Aitchison and J. A. C. Brown, *The Lognormal Distribution* (Cambridge, 1963), 31.

[13] There is no decisive advantage in using the Chi-square test, since it too ignores the sign and the pattern of the differences between the observed and the theoretical distributions.

The application of the Geary and Pearson tests indicate that in a majority of cases the distribution of the variables (after logarithmic transformation) exhibits a significant skewness and kurtosis even at the one per cent level. Scatter diagrams show that in such cases there are invariably too few plants in the first decile (the size class to which the smallest plants belong) and in the last two deciles when the actual distribution is compared to the theoretical distribution. This systematic bias may be partially accounted for by the fact that plants with an output of less than $5,000 in value are not included in our sample. In addition, if the firm had been used as the basic unit of observation, the reduction of all the plants in a multi-plant firm to a single observation would also reduce the bias.

Accepting the lognormal distribution of the input and output variables for descriptive purposes, we may summarize their behavior by three sets of parameters: the geometric means of their distributions,[14] the dispersions, and the "shuffle" parameters measuring the extent of interchange of positions by the plants over time while leaving the distributions undisturbed. In the next two sections we will discuss the relationships between the first two sets of these parameters and economies of scale.

II. ECONOMIES OF SCALE AND INDUSTRY PERFORMANCE

In this section, we estimate the expansion paths for each industry and discuss the causal relationship between economies of scale and the growth of plants along these paths. Our estimates indicate that these paths shift over time, reflecting increases in economies of scale. We demonstrate that these increases provide an additional spur to the growth of plants. Finally, we measure the proportion of improvement in industry performance, as defined below, that can be accounted for by the growth of plants.

The expansion path may be estimated from the data on input and output variables. Let Q be output, K capital, and L labor. After logarithmic transformation, the variables are further standardized by setting their means at zero and their standard deviations at 1.[15] Let the new variables be q, k, and l. The expansion path, s, is fitted by weighted regression:

$$s = a_1 q + a_2 k + a_3 l. \tag{1}$$

By our standardization procedure, the variances of the input and output vari-

---

[14] For a lognormal distribution the arithmetic mean involves both the location and the dispersion parameters and is hence less preferable to the geometric mean (which is equal to the median). See Aitchison and Brown, *op. cit.*, 111.

[15] Logarithmic transformation is made because we assume that expansion paths are characterized by fixed elasticities between input and output variables. Standardization is based on the assumption that, to the decision maker for a plant, capital, labor, and output are equally "important."

ables are given the same weight, and s maximizes the total variances that are explained.

Equation (1) was fitted to the pooled annual plant observations for each of the periods mentioned before. As Table 2 shows, at least 87 per cent of the variances in the input and output variables are accounted for by s. In other words, difference in size appears to be the principal factor accounting for the dispersion of plants, and our assumption that there exists a basic manufacturing activity in each industry appears to be supported by the empirical data.

Table 2 also presents the estimated *a* coefficients. In nearly every instance, there are increasing returns to scale for labor and decreasing returns to scale for capital *along the expansion path*. In the food industry, for example, an increase of output by ten per cent along the expansion path would be accompanied by an increase of capital of 12.8 per cent and an increase of labor of 8.9 per cent during the first period.[16] The table also reveals that, in most industries, the expansion path has shifted in such a way that there is a continuous improvement in returns to scale. Again, using the food industry for illustration, during the last period an increase in output of ten per cent by a plant along the new expansion path required only an increase of capital of 10.8 per cent and an increase of labor of 8.8 per cent. In all, from the first period to the last period, an improvement in returns to scale for both capital and labor took place in eight industries, for capital alone in two industries, for labor alone in three industries, while in only one industry was there little improvement.

It is convenient to analyze the implication of these empirical findings with a model provided by Steindl.[17] If we let the rate of profit be π, cost C, value of output Q, capital K, and the scale of operation S, then a simple model might be:

$$\pi = \frac{(Q - C)}{K}. \qquad (2)$$

If it is further assumed that cost per dollar of output and capital per dollar of output are both functions of S:

$$\frac{C}{Q} = F(S),$$

$$\frac{K}{Q} = \emptyset(S).$$

Then evidently,

$$\pi = \frac{1 - F(S)}{\emptyset(S)} \qquad (3)$$

[16] These figures are reciprocals of the figures given in Table 2.
[17] Joseph Steindl, *Small and Big Business* (Oxford Institute of Statistics Monograph No. 1, 1946), 26.

or:
$$\log \pi = \log [1 - F(S)] - \log \emptyset(S).$$

Upon differentiations,

$$\frac{d\pi}{dS} \frac{1}{\pi} = -\frac{F'(S)}{1 - F(S)} - \frac{\emptyset'(S)}{\emptyset(S)}. \quad (4)$$

TABLE 2 Returns to Scale Along the Expansion Path

Industry	Year	No. of observations	% increase in output if capital increases by 1%	% increase in output if labor increases by 1%	% of total variance "explained" by the expansion path
Food	1935–41	2068	.78	1.12	89
	1942–46	1117	.92	1.08	90
	1947–53	1522	.92	1.13	90
	1954–59	993	.92	1.13	92
Textiles	1935–41	1772	.80	1.01	89
	1942–46	1370	.85	1.09	89
	1947–53	1907	.86	1.09	89
	1954–59	1138	.87	1.13	87
Forest Products	1935–41	701	.77	.94	89
	1942–46	513	.89	1.03	92
	1947–53	694	.95	1.07	94
	1954–59	412	.95	1.09	94
Paper	1935–41	279	.96	1.13	94
	1942–46	237	.90	1.21	93
	1947–53	342	.91	1.22	94
	1954–59	258	.98	1.28	95
Printing and Publishing	1935–41	1602	.86	1.06	93
	1942–46	982	.86	1.10	94
	1947–53	1407	.89	1.16	95
	1954–59	1109	.89	1.16	95
Chemicals	1935–41	546	.94	1.10	92
	1942–46	405	.95	1.14	93
	1947–53	476	.94	1.17	94
	1954–59	298	.95	1.22	93
Rubber Products	1935–41	64	.84	1.01	97
	1942–46	58	.92	.96	98
	1947–53	80	1.08	1.07	98
	1954–59	52	1.08	1.01	98

From (4) it is easy to see that the profit associated with growth along the expansion path depends on F and $\emptyset$, as well as on the "profit margin" $1\text{-}F(S)$. Steindl in fact argued strongly that large firms stop growing because they enjoy too large a profit margin.

Our empirical results indicate that there are strong counter forces. The greater capital intensity of larger plants along the expansion path means that

TABLE 2 Returns to Scale Along the Expansion Path (Cont'd)

Industry	Year	No. of observations	% increase in output if capital increases by 1%	% increase in output if labor increases by 1%	% of total variance "explained" by the expansion path
Leather Products	1935–41	644	.96	1.09	88
	1942–46	490	.98	1.09	90
	1947–53	696	.97	1.09	93
	1954–59	428	.93	1.10	95
Stone, Clay, and Glass	1935–41	392	.87	1.00	84
	1942–46	240	.96	1.11	88
	1947–53	373	.95	1.16	90
	1954–59	254	.93	1.15	91
Ferrous Metals	1935–41	611	.84	1.03	92
	1942–46	443	1.01	1.05	96
	1947–53	638	.94	1.09	96
	1954–59	453	.94	1.13	95
Non-ferrous Metals	1935–41	543	.86	1.12	90
	1942–46	386	.97	1.21	92
	1947–53	588	.95	1.23	93
	1954–59	416	.95	1.23	94
Machinery	1935–41	1154	.86	1.04	95
	1942–46	775	.97	1.05	96
	1947–53	974	1.00	1.07	97
	1954–59	702	1.01	1.09	97
Transportation Equipment	1935–41	165	.99	1.03	95
	1942–46	104	1.16	1.03	96
	1947–53	122	1.14	1.03	97
	1954–59	93	1.14	1.07	98
Miscellaneous	1935–41	1099	.80	.98	91
	1942–46	614	.87	1.03	94
	1947–53	695	.88	1.06	95
	1954–59	482	.88	1.11	96

as labor becomes relatively more expensive a large plant will acquire a relative advantage over the smaller plants. This means a reduction of $F''(S)$. Furthermore, the general improvements in returns to scale also would reduce $F''(S)/F(S)$, while the specific improvements in returns to scale with respect to capital reduce $\emptyset'(S)/\emptyset(S)$. Consequently, the profit associated with increases in the scale of operation must have increased, and, in order to maximize their profit, plants should continue to move ahead along the expansion path.

The growth of plants along the expansion path is consistent with the observed industry performance. The performance of an industry can be described by the change of labor, capital, and output of the median plant over time.[18] From 1935 to 1959, the median plants in almost all the industries became larger and more capital intensive while their labor became more productive. An obvious question is how much of this observed behavior may be explained by the movement of the median plants along the (base-period) expansion paths. The results are presented in Table 3.[19] Evidently, the industry performances

DIAGRAM 1

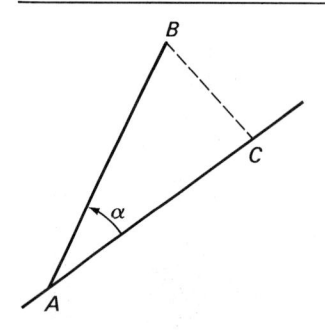

---

from the first period to the second were largely accounted for by movements along the expansion path. In the immediate postwar years the role of expansion appeared to be less significant. However, a careful examination of the results indicates that the low percentages in Table 3 are generally associated with declining output, suggesting that growth along the expansion paths is irreversible.[20] As the plants resumed their growth after the end of postwar

---

[18] More specifically, the median plant in the size distribution of plants with respect to the expansion path.

[19] In Diagram 1, A lies on the base period expansion path and represents the position of the median plant in an industry. During the following period, the plant has moved to B in the input-output space. We draw BC perpendicular to the expansion path. The percentages given in Table 3 are the ratios AB^2/AC^2 and are also equal to $\cos^2 a$.

[20] The negative signs in Table 3 refer to declines in the scale of operation as determined by the position with reference to the expansion path. Occasionally, a median plant suffers a decline in output but still manages to move forward along the expansion path on the strength of its capital or labor increases.

adjustments, movements along the expansion path again became an important factor in explaining the industry performance.

TABLE 3 Industry Performance Explained by Movement Along the Expansion Path

	Per Cent of Median Plant Movement Explained		
Industry	1935–41 to 1942–46	1942–46 to 1947–53	1947–53 to 1954–59
Food	96	17	81
Textiles	53	31	(−) 3
Forest Products	92	58	81
Paper	92	2	85
Printing and Publishing	100	98	56
Chemicals	76	29	67
Rubber Products	90	(−) 3	98
Leather Products	72	(−) 14	67
Stone, Clay, and Glass	49	100	1
Ferrous Metals	88	(−) 38	25
Non-ferrous Metals	90	(−) 3	50
Machinery	94	27	26
Transportation Equipment	85	(−) 3	88
Miscellaneous	85	90	72

III. DISPERSION AND ECONOMIES OF SCALE

If plant growth along the expansion path is related to economies of scale, it is natural to ask whether the dispersion of plants along the expansion path is also related to economies of scale. In the past, several models, utilizing Gibrat's Law, have been proposed to demonstrate the connection between growth rate of plants and their size distribution. In a recent paper, another model was also proposed, involving a growth process in which ". . . the expected growth rates of individual firms are assumed proportional to . . . the time discounted sums of previous increments in size."[21] These models generate the observed skewed distribution of plants, but the economic theory underlying the models has not been made clear.

A different tack is possible. In the last section we argued that a change in factor price ratio or an improvement in economies of scale increases the profits associated with growth. If such profits are termed "dynamic profits," then there exists a dynamic profit function relating dynamic profits to various rates of growth. With constant elasticities among the inputs and outputs along the expansion path, the conjecture is that, other things being equal, the optimal rate is the same for plants of different sizes. Furthermore, as long as these

[21] Yuji Ijiri and H. A. Simon, "Business Firm Growth and Size," *American Economic Review*, LIV (March 1964), 79.

elasticities remain the same (and if the rate of change in relative factor prices does not change drastically), then the rate of growth will also remain the same. There would be no change in the dispersion of plants along the expansion path. This is a case where Gibrat's Law would apply and it is possible to speak of an equilibrium distribution of plants with changing median but constant dispersion.[22]

We can carry the conjecture further. It is also likely that there is a systematic relationship between *changes* in returns to scale and *changes* in dispersion. An improvement in returns to scale may be regarded as the result of technological innovations undertaken by large plants. Such innovations affect both returns to scale and dispersion. For example, if the innovation by a large plant is labor saving, the dispersion of output relative to the dispersion of labor for the industry as a whole would increase. In addition, the relation between the dispersions would also be affected if the large plant chooses to grow more rapidly to take advantage of its innovation. On the other hand, as the small plants increase in size, they will also employ the new technology. This establishes a new expansion path with greater economies of scale. It seems reasonable to assume that the two effects—changes in returns to scale along the expansion path and changes in dispersion—should bear some systematic relationship to each other.

These conjectures may be formulated more precisely for empirical testing. Since we still wish to exclude the short-run and cyclical factors, the data will still be pooled into the four periods mentioned before. This reduces severely the degrees of freedom so that only the simplest hypothesis—that the relationship between returns to scale and dispersion is proportional—will be tested.[23]

More specifically, returns to scale may be expressed as:

$$r_k = a_k D_k, \tag{5}$$

where r_k is returns to scale with respect to capital along the expansion path, a_k an "error" term, and D_k a measure of dispersion to be discussed below.[24] If a_k remains constant over time, then a proportionate relationship between returns

---

[22] The equilibrium distribution is characterized by a constant growth rate for all the plants and, therefore, a constant dispersion for all the input and output variable distributions. Let X be an input or output variable, and ε its rate of growth:

let
$$X_{t+1} = \varepsilon X_t.$$

then
$$x = \log(X),$$

since
$$x_{t+1} = \varepsilon' + x_t, V(x_{t+1}) = V(x_t) + \sigma^2_{\varepsilon'},$$

$$\sigma^2_{\varepsilon'} = 0, V(X_{t+1}) = V(x_t).$$

[23] It should be noted, however, that the test is being applied to all industries separately. If the evidence is consistent with our hypothesis in *each* industry, the result of the test would be significant.

[24] The same arguments will apply also to the case of returns to scale with respect to labor.

to scale and dispersion is indicated. All other factors affecting dispersion (or differences in the growth rate among plants of different sizes) are either insignificant, offsetting, or directly related to returns to scale.

One method of estimating a_k at a given time is to return to Equation (1):

$$S = a_1 q + a_2 k + a_3 l.$$

Clearly the a's are the direction cosines of the expansion path, and, by definition:[25]

$$\frac{a_1}{a_2} = \frac{q}{k} = \frac{\dfrac{lnQ - \overline{lnQ}}{\sigma lnQ}}{\dfrac{lnK - \overline{lnK}}{\sigma lnK}} = \frac{\sigma lnK}{\sigma lnQ} \cdot \frac{lnQ - \overline{lnQ}}{lnK - \overline{lnK}}$$

$$a_2 \sigma_{lnK} lnQ = a_2 \sigma_{lnK} \overline{lnQ} - a_1 \sigma_{lnQ} \overline{lnK} + a_1 \sigma_{lnQ} lnK.$$

During any period, $\overline{lnQ}$, $\overline{lnK}$, σ_{lnQ} and σ_{lnK} are given, hence we can write:

$$Q = cK^{a_1 \sigma lnQ / a_2 \sigma lnK}. \tag{6}$$

In terms of unstandardized variables Q and K, returns to scale (along the expansion path) have turned out to be $a_1 \sigma_{lnQ}/a_2 \sigma_{lnK}$. In other words, the "error term" a_k in (5) can be expressed as the ratio of direction cosines of the expansion path after the variables have been standardized, and the dispersion parameter D_k as the ratio of the dispersion parameters of the lognormal distributions of Q and K.

The question is whether a_k is a constant over time. But first we need to examine more closely the meaning of D_k, or the relative dispersion of $ln(Q)$ and $ln(K)$. There is a relationship between the output–capital ratio of plants of different sizes and D_k. The dispersion of $ln(Q)$ and the dispersion of $ln(K)$ are, respectively, monotonic functions of the coefficient of variation of Q and the coefficient of variation of K, since Q and K are both lognormally distributed. An increase in the relative dispersion of $ln(Q)$ to $ln(K)$ therefore implies an increase of σ_Q/σ_K relative to $\overline{Q}/\overline{K}$. This in turn implies that the distribution of Q has become relatively more skewed than the distribution of K, and that the output–capital ratio has increased at a greater rate for large plants than for small plants.

The difference in the rates of change of the output–capital ratio for plants of different sizes is in turn related to their rates of growth. If returns to scale for capital improve, at a given level of capital input the output–capital ratio will generally rise. This rise is greater for larger plants. Hence, the output–capital ratio for larger plants tends to increase relative to that for smaller

[25] Remembering that q, k, and l are defined as
$$\frac{lnQ - \overline{lnQ}}{\sigma lnQ}, \frac{lnK - \overline{lnK}}{\sigma lnK}, \text{ and } \frac{lnL - \overline{lnL}}{\sigma lnL},$$
respectively.

274 A Theory of Producer Behavior

plants. On the other hand, because of the prevalence of diminishing returns to scale for capital along the expansion path, any expansion of capital input by a plant leads to a decline in the output–capital ratio. Hence, if large plants expand more rapidly than small plants, the gap between the increase of the output–capital ratio for large plants and that for small plants would narrow, and even disappear altogether.

In short, any improvement in returns to scale for capital tends to increase the output–capital ratio of large plants relative to that of small plants and thus increase D_k. This tendency is countered by a decline in the same relative ratio if large plants expand their capital input more rapidly than small plants. A stable a_k indicates a "balance" between the two tendencies; a balance which is maintained for varying degrees of improvement in returns to scale.

TABLE 4 Returns to Scale and Dispersion
(Plants in Operation in 1935)

		r_k	a_k	D_k	r_l	a_l	D_l
Food	1935–41	.78	1.05	.74	1.12	1.02	1.10
	1942–46	.92	1.05	.88	1.08	1.02	1.06
	1947–53	.92	1.04	.88	1.13	1.01	1.12
	1954–59	.92	1.04	.88	1.13	1.02	1.11
Textiles	1935–41	.80	1.04	.77	1.01	1.05	.96
	1942–46	.85	1.03	.83	1.09	1.07	1.02
	1947–53	.86	1.04	.83	1.09	1.07	1.02
	1954–59	.87	1.05	.83	1.13	1.09	1.04
Forest Products	1935–41	.77	1.05	.73	.94	1.02	.92
	1942–46	.89	1.03	.86	1.03	1.01	1.02
	1947–53	.95	1.02	.93	1.07	1.00	1.07
	1954–59	.95	1.02	.93	1.09	1.00	1.09
Paper	1935–41	.96	1.02	.94	1.13	1.02	1.11
	1942–46	.90	1.02	.88	1.21	1.03	1.17
	1947–53	.91	1.01	.90	1.22	1.02	1.20
	1954–59	.98	1.01	.97	1.28	1.01	1.25
Printing and Publishing	1935–41	.86	1.04	.83	1.06	1.01	1.05
	1942–46	.86	1.02	.84	1.10	1.01	1.09
	1947–53	.89	1.02	.87	1.16	1.01	1.15
	1954–59	.89	1.02	.87	1.16	1.02	1.14
Chemicals	1935–41	.94	1.02	.92	1.10	1.01	1.09
	1942–46	.95	1.02	.93	1.14	1.02	1.12
	1947–53	.94	1.02	.92	1.17	1.02	1.15
	1954–59	.95	1.01	.94	1.22	1.01	1.21
Rubber Products	1935–41	.84	1.01	.83	1.01	1.02	.99
	1942–46	.92	1.01	.91	.96	1.01	.95
	1947–53	1.08	1.01	1.07	1.07	1.00	1.07
	1954–59	1.08	1.01	1.07	1.01	1.00	1.01

The empirical results are presented in Table 4. The parameter a_k was calculated from the statistically estimated a_1 and a_2 in (1), and the parameter D_k directly from the sample data. With one exception (stone, clay, and glass), a_k exhibits great stability over the four periods, while r_k and D_k are much more variable. Furthermore, where r_k remains more or less constant, a_k has also remained constant—as in the case of the chemicals industry. This suggests the absence of independent factors in the determination of dispersion, and the presence of a "dynamic equilibrium"—an equilibrium where, if returns to scale are given, all the plants expand their capital and output at the same rate so that the relative dispersion of output to capital remains undisturbed.[26]

[26] The rate of expansion may be zero or negative.

TABLE 4 Returns to Scale and Dispersion (Cont'd)
(Plants in Operation in 1935)

		r_k	a_k	D_k	r_l	a_l	D_l
Leather	1935–41	.96	1.04	.92	1.09	1.04	1.05
Products	1942–46	.98	1.02	.96	1.09	1.02	1.07
	1947–53	.97	1.02	.95	1.09	1.03	1.06
	1954–59	.93	1.01	.92	1.10	1.01	1.09
Stone, Clay,	1935–41	.87	1.10	.79	1.00	1.01	.99
and Glass	1942–46	.96	1.05	.91	1.11	1.02	1.10
	1947–53	.95	1.04	.91	1.16	1.01	1.15
	1954–59	.93	1.01	.92	1.15	1.01	1.14
Ferrous Metals	1935–41	.84	1.03	.82	1.03	1.02	1.01
	1942–46	1.01	1.02	.99	1.05	1.01	1.04
	1947–53	.94	1.02	.92	1.09	1.01	1.08
	1954–59	.94	1.02	.92	1.13	1.02	1.11
Non-ferrous	1935–41	.86	1.02	.84	1.12	1.02	1.10
Metals	1942–46	.97	1.01	.96	1.21	1.02	1.19
	1947–53	.95	1.01	.94	1.23	1.02	1.21
	1954–59	.95	1.02	.93	1.23	1.02	1.21
Machinery	1935–41	.86	1.02	.84	1.04	1.00	1.04
	1942–46	.97	1.02	.95	1.05	1.01	1.04
	1947–53	1.00	1.02	.98	1.07	1.01	1.06
	1954–59	1.01	1.02	.99	1.09	1.01	1.08
Transportation	1935–41	.99	1.03	.96	1.03	1.00	1.03
Equipment	1942–46	1.16	1.02	1.13	1.03	1.00	1.03
	1947–53	1.14	1.02	1.12	1.03	1.01	1.02
	1954–59	1.14	1.01	1.13	1.07	1.00	1.07
Miscellaneous	1935–41	.80	1.04	.77	.98	1.01	.97
	1942–46	.87	1.02	.85	1.03	1.02	1.01
	1947–53	.88	1.02	.86	1.06	1.01	1.05
	1954–59	.88	1.01	.87	1.11	1.01	1.10

For the relationship between output and labor, the corresponding parameters are a_l, D_l, and r_l. Their interpretation is basically analogous, although in one aspect there is an asymmetry. Since r_l is nearly always greater than one, the two factors affecting the output–labor ratio now work in the same direction. An improvement in returns to scale for labor leads to a direct increase in the output–labor ratio if a plant chooses to employ the same labor input as before, and a further increase in the output–labor ratio if the plant expands its labor input. Once more, the increase in the output–labor ratio is greater for large plants for a given improvement in returns to scale, and this discrepancy is widened if large plants also expand their labor input at a greater rate than the small plants. The stability of the *a* coefficients suggests again that there is a stable response by plants of different sizes to different changes in returns to scale.

These ideas may be illustrated by a numerical example in which the unit of measurement has been standardized so that the "small plant" has 100 units of capital, labor, and output:

	in t_1	in t_2	% change, t_1 to t_2	in t_3	% change, t_2 to t_3
Small plant					
Capital	100	105.75	5.75	111.83	5.75
Labor	100	103.50	3.50	107.12	3.50
Output	100	105.00	5.00	110.25	5.00
Large plant					
Capital	230	235.00	2.20	248.51	5.75
Labor	174	173.50	−.30	179.50	3.50
Output	200	220.00	10.00	242.00	5.00

In this example, during the initial period t_1 both the small plant and the large plant lie on an expansion path. Along this expansion path a five per cent increase in output is accompanied by a six per cent increase in capital and a four per cent increase in labor. Between t_1 and t_2 an improvement in returns to scale took place, and in t_2 the two plants lie on a new expansion path. Along this new expansion path an increase in output of five per cent is accompanied by an increase in capital of 5.75 per cent and an increase in labor of 3.5 per cent.

Due to its innovation (which is responsible for the shift of the expansion path), the large plant can produce the same output in t_2 as in t_1 with greatly reduced capital and labor. In our illustration, the large plant in fact takes advantage of this and expands its output by ten per cent in contrast to the five per cent expansion registered by the small plant.[27] This expansion of output is

[27] The difference between the rate of growth of output for the large plant and that for the small plant is not arbitrary. The stability of the *a* coefficients suggests that the rate

accomplished by a small increase in capital input and a reduction of labor. The "gaps" of capital and labor between the large plant and the small plant are now reduced, while the gap of output is increased. In other words, the relative dispersions of output to capital and of output to labor have both increased in response to the improvements in returns to scale.

There is no change in returns to scale from t_2 to t_3 in our illustration. Both the large plant and the small plant expand along the new expansion path at the same rate which demonstrates another implication of the stability of the a coefficients. The relative dispersions of output to capital and of output to labor therefore remain constant. Such proportionate rate of growth (or contraction) by all plants in each of the variables will continue until a new improvement in returns to scale takes place.

The numerical example is meant to illustrate the type of historical development that had taken place. We have already noted that, between the first and the last periods under study, most improvements in returns to scale were accompanied by increases in the relative dispersions of outputs to inputs. We have also noted that without improvements in returns to scale the relative dispersions have remained largely constant. With $r_k \neq 1$ and $r_l \neq 1$, this is possible only if all the plants expand at the same rate. One more point may be added. During the span from 1935–1941 to 1954–1959, σ_{lnQ} increased by five per cent or more in 11 out of 14 industries, σ_{lnK} in five industries, and σ_{lnL} in six industries. This indicates that large plants tend to react to an improvement in returns to scale by a rather modest increase in output while keeping their capital and labor down to a rate of growth less than that of the small plants. An explanation may be found in the engineering constraints on the total amount of inputs that may be effectively organized in one plant. Improvements in returns to scale can then be seen as a way to transcend these constraints so that more output can be turned out without adding the inputs.

---

of expansion of output (and input) for plants of different sizes must be such that the relationship between relative dispersion and the improvement in returns to scale remains approximately proportional.

7

THE THEORY OF COMPETITION: THE FIRM AND THE INDUSTRY

In this chapter, we employ the concepts of supply and demand developed in the first six chapters to construct a model of industry and firm behavior under perfectly competitive conditions. Perfect competition and monopoly, which we consider in the next chapter, are considered at the outset because they represent the two theoretical limits on the size of industries: perfect competition requires a very large number of firms; monopoly, only one firm. Perfect competition may be considered synonymous with free enterprise, the popular term used to describe an industry in which a large number of small purchasers and suppliers pursue their plans free from official coercion or interference. Private ownership of resources and freedom of entry and exit of firms are important characteristics of such a system. Of course, buyers and sellers are not completely unconstrained, for all operate within the constraints of the market and the existing social environment, and all must obey the laws governing civil behavior, especially the laws of contract.

THE RATIONALE FOR A COMPETITIVE MODEL

The theory of perfect competition examines firm and industry behavior under a set of assumed conditions which are narrowly specified and highly artificial. As a consequence, the theory is both simplistic and unrealistic. Few industries in the United States come even close to fitting the perfect competition mold. But simplicity is the theory's principal advantage. A more realistic model must include more variables, which would make it unwieldy. And complete realism is impossible. The theory of perfect competition is useful for two main reasons: (1) it describes the behavior of firms under specified market conditions and serves, therefore, as a standard to be used in examining other industry structures, and (2) in those industries where competition can exist, it may serve as a normative model. In such cases, comparisons can be made between real-world industries and perfect competition. If the comparison reveals serious discrepancies between the real and the normative, public policy may be employed to improve upon economic performance. As an illustration of one such attempt, at the close of World War II the United States disposed of government-owned aluminum plants by sale to two new aluminum manufacturers, Kaiser and Reynolds. The government's aim was to break the fifty-year monopoly of Alcoa and establish more competitive conditions.

The competitive model is also useful as a pedagogical device because it introduces the student to economic reasoning under controlled conditions. By studying perfect competition, the student becomes familiar with the analytical apparatus of economic theory and the use of this apparatus to solve elementary economic problems. Since most of the "answers" have already been worked out by economists for the competitive model, the student is provided with a standard for comparing the results of his own work. In other words, the student learns to reason like an economist. The noncompetitive models which we study in subsequent chapters, monopoly, oligopoly, and monopolistic competition, use the same analytical apparatus; only the underlying conditions are different. So perfect competition is a convenient foundation for the study of all microeconomic models of firm and industry behavior.

THE CHARACTERISTICS OF THE COMPETITIVE MODEL

Our methodology in this chapter is partial equilibrium analysis of a perfectly competitive industry. The theory is a partial equilibrium model because we incorporate only those factors which are assumed to have an important and direct effect on firms, and we partially exclude factors which apparently have only an indirect or weak influence. These latter, secondary forces provide the background or market environment in which the firm and the industry operate, and by the *ceteris paribus* assumption, are assumed to remain constant. One technique which we use throughout the chapter is to assume a given industry situation, say a given market price, and observe a single firm's adjustments to that market situation. This technique allows us to focus on the optimizing behavior of the firm, the principal decision-making unit of the industry.

Characteristics of Perfect Competition

We have already given a general description of a perfectly competitive industry. Now we must be more precise. Below is a list of prerequisites for perfect competition:

1. There must be a large number of buyers and sellers.
2. The product must be homogeneous.

3. The factors of production, including firms, must be mobile.
4. Neither buyers nor sellers may organize to control prices or output.
5. Buyers and sellers must have complete market knowledge.

First, competition requires a large number of suppliers. How many? Enough so that each firm is so small relative to the market that no one firm can noticeably affect price, whether it sells all of its output or none of it. In other words, each firm's output is an insignificant portion of market supply. The King Ranch in Texas, though a huge beef producer, is relatively small compared with the total market for beef in the United States, and the largest cotton farms add only a few thousand bales to a total crop of many millions of bales. Even these large producers could not single-handedly have much effect on the price of beef or cotton. There must likewise be a large number of buyers of the competitive industry's output, large enough to insure that no single buyer can influence market price by increasing or decreasing his purchases. Any buyer stands in the same relationship to the market as does any seller; both are "price takers"—neither may be "price makers." Perfect competition is sometimes called "atomistic competition," since each market participant is relatively insignificant vis-à-vis the market.

Second, perfect competition requires that each firm's output be indistinguishable from that of every other firm, e.g., a homogeneous product. If all suppliers sell a like product, buyers will be indifferent whether they purchase from firm A, firm B, or any other firm in the industry. Since buyers will prefer paying a lower price to a higher one for a given homogeneous product, no firm can charge a price higher than any other firm, so long as all buyers are well informed of existing prices. Moreover, since no firm would rationally offer its product for a price lower than the market price, and cannot obtain a higher price, each must accept the market price. This leads to the general conclusion that prices will be uniform throughout the industry. No buyer or seller can get a better price than any other. (We are ignoring price differences which might arise due to transportation costs between manufacturing points and different market areas.) Examples of homogeneous products may be found in agriculture, for instance, a given variety of wheat, eggs of a certain size and grade, or cotton of a certain grade and staple.

The third requirement for perfect competition is complete factor mobility. There must be neither nonmarket restrictions on flows of resources to and from firms in a competitive industry nor any restrictions on the entry or exit of firms from the industry. A competitive firm is free to increase or decrease its purchases of all resources at the market prices for these resources, and its purchases have no effect on these prices. In effect, the supply curve the firm faces for each factor of production is assumed perfectly elastic at market prices. Resource ownership, therefore, must be decentralized, and there must be no organization of resource buyers or sellers with the power to affect resource prices. Entrepreneurship is another "factor" that must be completely mobile. Entrepreneurs must be free to start up new firms and enter profitable industries if given sufficient time to obtain and organize resources. Finally, factor mobility implies that firms reducing their output must be free in the short run to release redundant resources and, in the long run, to dispose of all their assets and withdraw from a competitive industry entirely, if this best serves their interests.

The fourth requirement, no collusion between buyers or sellers, means that the market price is to be an equilibrium one in which there is no excess supply or demand. At the equilibrium price, every buyer can purchase whatever quantity he wants, and every seller can supply whatever quantity he chooses. And price must be free to fluctuate in response to changes in supply and demand without nonmarket interference. Buyer or seller collusion of any kind on price or output is assumed nonexistent, ruling out buyer's cooperatives and seller arrangements designed to limit production. Such institutions are characteristic of imperfectly competitive markets.

Finally, buyers and sellers are assumed to be completely informed of market conditions at all points in time and to be free to act on the basis of this knowledge. In effect, we are assuming market knowledge is produced at zero cost and is freely available to all suppliers and purchasers. This assures that price will be uniform for all. If all of the requisites for competition are present but this latter one, the market is described as *purely* competitive rather than *perfectly* competitive.[1]

The effect of most of the characteristics of perfect competition listed above is to insure that no buyer or seller can appreciably affect either price or quantity in a competitive market. In other words, all participants must be price takers rather than price makers. The essence of perfect competition is decentralized decision-making. Each participant in the market, whether buyer or seller, responds to the opportunities open to him to achieve his own objectives. The determination of aggregate output levels, prices, and a number of other important economic magnitudes is made through the free interaction of these buyers and sellers in the market. The market itself is completely impersonal, and its basic adjustment mechanisms are spontaneous and without central direction or control. Nevertheless, a perfectly competitive market made up of small autonomous units, each acting in its own self-interest, will efficiently perform most of the basic economic functions outlined in the first chapter. In the rest of this chapter, we will examine why this is true.

---

[1] Unfortunately, authors differ in their definitions of perfect versus pure competition. Some make perfect competition more exclusive than the definition given here by requiring perfect foresight as well as perfect knowledge of existing market conditions.

Short-Run Revenue Curves of the Individual Firm

No competitive firm controls the price of its product. It must accept the going market price and is therefore a *price taker*. The firm does decide, however, how much to produce at the market price, and, if rational, will choose its output level to achieve its basic objectives. The firm's principal objective may be maximum profits, fast growth, a large share of the market, maximum sales, or any one of a number of things. Some firms seek only to survive. However, we assume at this point that the firm's principal objective is to realize maximum profits in both the short and long run. In a later chapter, we will discuss the conditions that might make alternative objectives more appropriate, and we will assess the effects of these objectives on the firm's behavior.

The competitive firm's short-run profits are equal to the difference between its total revenues, TR, and total costs, TC. Letting PR signify profits:

$$PR = TR - SRTC.$$

Profits are a function of the firm's output level, which determines its costs, and market price, which determines its total revenues for any output. Then for any given market price, profits can be stated as a function of the firm's output alone. In Chapter 5, we examined the relationship between firms' short-run output levels and costs. Now we investigate how a competitive firm's revenues vary with output.

Panel (b) of Figure 7–1 shows the market demand and supply schedules for a competitive industry, and panel (a) presents the average revenue curves appropriate for a single firm. This is a convention we will follow throughout the chapter: *market schedules on the right and the firm's schedules on the left*. The left-hand schedules may be considered representative of any one firm in the industry. The horizontal axis of panel (a) is labeled with a lower case x to indicate that the firm's output level is a very small percentage of quantities supplied in the market, whereas market output levels are represented by the use of a capital X on the horizontal axis in panel (b). Suppose the equilibrium market quantity and price are initially X_1 and P_1, determined by the intersection of D and S in panel (b). Since the competitive firm can sell any quantity it wishes at price P_1, the horizontal line labeled $AR_1 = P_1 = MR_1$ in panel (a) is its average revenue curve. In effect, AR_1 is the demand curve the firm faces for its output, and since it is horizontal, it is perfectly elastic.

The firm's total revenue at any given output equals average revenue (price) times the quantity of X sold. The total revenue curve shows the total revenue for all possible quantities of X which might be sold. Of course, alternative revenue–quantity combinations are mutually exclusive—only one total revenue value can exist for an upcoming period of time. The schedules are there-

FIGURE 7-1 The Derivation of a Competitive Firm's AR, MR, and TR Schedules

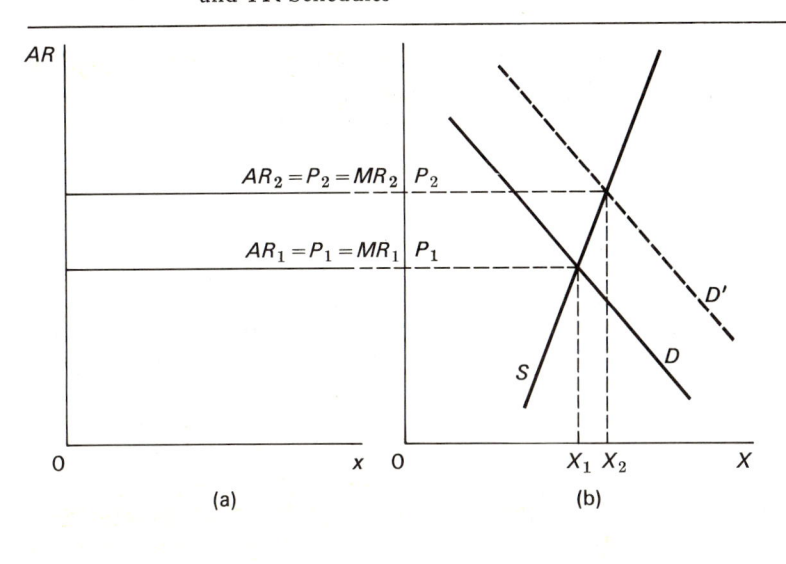

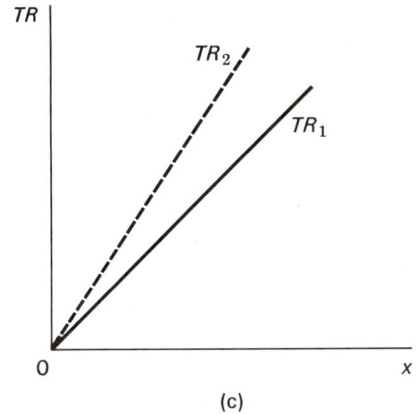

fore *ex ante*, meaning they are prospective rather than retrospective. Given market price, P_1, the firm's total revenue function is:

$$TR_1 = AR_1 \cdot x$$

or

$$TR_1 = P_1 \cdot x,$$

where AR_1 is constant and X, of course, variable. TR_1 is plotted in panel (c); it is a linear function radiating out from the origin with a constant slope equal to AR_1. Should market demand shift to D', price will rise to P_2, and the firm's revenue curves in panels (a) and (c) would shift up to AR_2 and TR_2, respectively.

Marginal revenue is defined as the addition to a firm's total revenue which occurs when it sells one additional unit of output. Marginal revenue is a concept akin to marginal cost, except the latter indicates the addition to *total cost* when an extra unit of output is produced. In symbols, marginal revenue may be defined as:

$$MR = \frac{\Delta TR}{\Delta X},$$

where ΔTR is the change in TR caused by ΔX. If a competitive firm sells 100 units of output per time period at $10 each, total revenue is $1000; if it then sells one more unit at the same price, total revenue increases to $101 \cdot \$10 = \$1010$. Then, ΔTR is $10; ΔX is 1; and MR is $\Delta TR/\Delta X = \$10$. By definition, a perfectly competitive firm can always sell additional units of product at the existing market price. No matter how many units it happens to be selling, by selling one more unit, it adds to its total revenue an amount equal to the market price of the good. In other words, the competitive firm's marginal revenue equals market price. In panel (a) of Figure 7-1, the horizontal line MR_1, equal to AR_1, is the competitive firm's marginal revenue curve at market price P_1. Like the AR curve, MR is perfectly elastic at the market determined price, P_1, and since MR_1 is $\Delta TR/\Delta X$, it is equal to the slope of TR_1.

Short-Run Profit-Maximizing Output

Now we are ready to combine the firm's revenue and cost curves. In panel (a) of Figure 7-2 is presented the firm's TR curve, assuming a market price of P_1. Superimposed on the same graph is the firm's short-run total cost curve, $SRTC$. $SRTC$ is derived from a short-run production function characterized by indivisible but adaptable capital and thus has the characteristic inverted-S shape. By subtracting short-run total cost from total revenue, we can derive the firm's total profit or loss for each level of output. For example, at output X_1, there is a loss equal to $X_1e - X_1f$, whereas at output levels X_2 and X_4, total revenue and cost are equal, so profits are zero. Finally, TR exceeds TC at output level X_m, so the firm would realize total profits measured by the distance ba.

In panel (b) of Figure 7-2 is a graph of the firm's total profit, PR. This curve is a plot of the vertical difference between TR and $SRTC$ at every possible short-run output level. For those output levels less than X_2, or greater than X_4, PR indicates losses, whereas output levels between X_2 and X_4 units result in positive profits. Inspection of panel (b) of Figure 7-2 shows that PR

FIGURE 7-2 Determining the Profit-Maximizing Output for a Competitive Firm Using *TC–TR* Approach

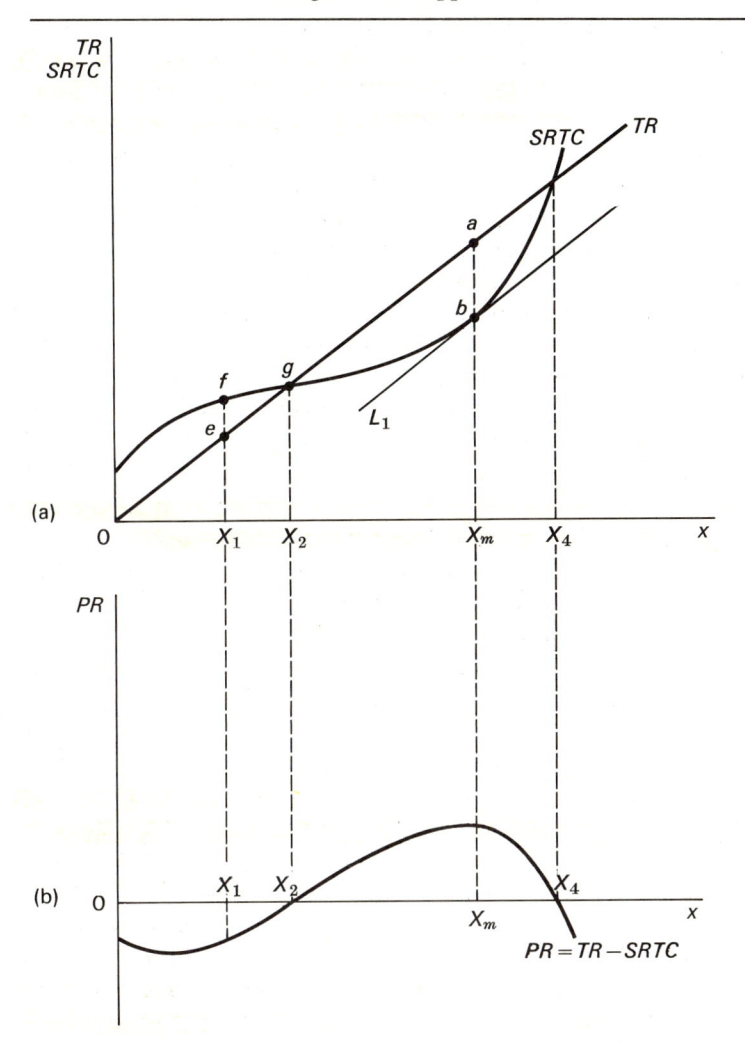

is at a peak at output level X_m. This means that the vertical distance between TR and SRTC, distance ba in panel (a), is the maximum profit obtainable.

> Basic mathematical principles tell us that the vertical distance between TR and SRTC is at a maximum at X_m only if the slope of TR equals the slope of SRTC at that output level.

Thus, at X_m, the slope of TR, which is constant, must equal the slope of $SRTC$, which is the slope of line L_1 drawn tangent to $SRTC$. But the slope of $SRTC$ is equal to short-run marginal cost, and the slope of TR is marginal revenue. Therefore, to say that the slopes of TR and $SRTC$ must be equal where profits are maximized is to propose that a necessary condition for profit maximization is that marginal revenue, MR, must equal marginal cost, MC.

Suppose output is increased to a level above X_m. At the greater output, the slope of $SRTC$ increases, while the slope of TR remains constant. Since the slopes were previously equal, the slope of $SRTC$ must now be greater than that of TR, which means marginal cost is greater than marginal revenue. A rightward movement causes a greater addition to costs than to revenues, thus profits decline. If output is reduced below X_m, this would mean the slope of $SRTC$ is decreased below that of TR. Marginal revenue would exceed marginal cost. The leftward movement therefore causes TR to fall more than total costs and profit again would decline. Notice that MR and MC must be carefully interpreted for a contraction: The contraction in output causes total revenue and total cost to fall, though marginal revenue and marginal cost are positive. We may conclude that only at X_m, where the slope of $SRTC$, which is MC, equals the slope of TR, which is MR, are profits maximized.

Now we can determine the profit-maximizing output level for a competitive firm using MR and MC schedules. In Figure 7–3, the firm's MR and MC curves are presented in panel (a) and profits, PR, in panel (b). Now consider the competitive firm's decision-making process, supposing it is initially producing X_0 units. If the firm expands output by ΔX, it adds to total revenues an amount greater than the addition to costs occasioned by the production of the ΔX extra units, since $MR_1 > MC_1$. So a decision to expand short-run output from X_0 to $X_0 + \Delta X$ increases profits. In general, short-run increases in output will be profitable as long as marginal revenue is greater than marginal cost. Output expansion is profitable only up to X_m. Beyond X_m, TR increases less than TC, so profits fall. For example, if production is increased from X_m to $X_m + \Delta X$, the addition to cost is larger than the addition to total revenue, $MC_2 > MR_1$, indicating that the additional output would be worth less to the firm than the extra cost of producing it. The point of intersection of MC and MR at X_m is the competitive firm's short-run profit-maximizing output level.

Notice that $MC = MR$ is only a necessary condition and not a *sufficient* condition for achieving the maximum profit level. There may be more than one point of equality of MC and MR. Referring to Figure 7–3, marginal cost equals marginal revenue at output X_0 as well as X_m. However, profits are negative at X_0. How can the firm determine which output level, X_0 or X_m, results in maximum profits? One approach is simply to compare profits at X_0 and X_m and to select the output with the largest positive profit (or the smaller loss). Another is to stipulate that not only must MC equal MR, but MC must be

FIGURE 7-3 Determining the Profit-Maximizing Output Using
$MC = MR$ Approach

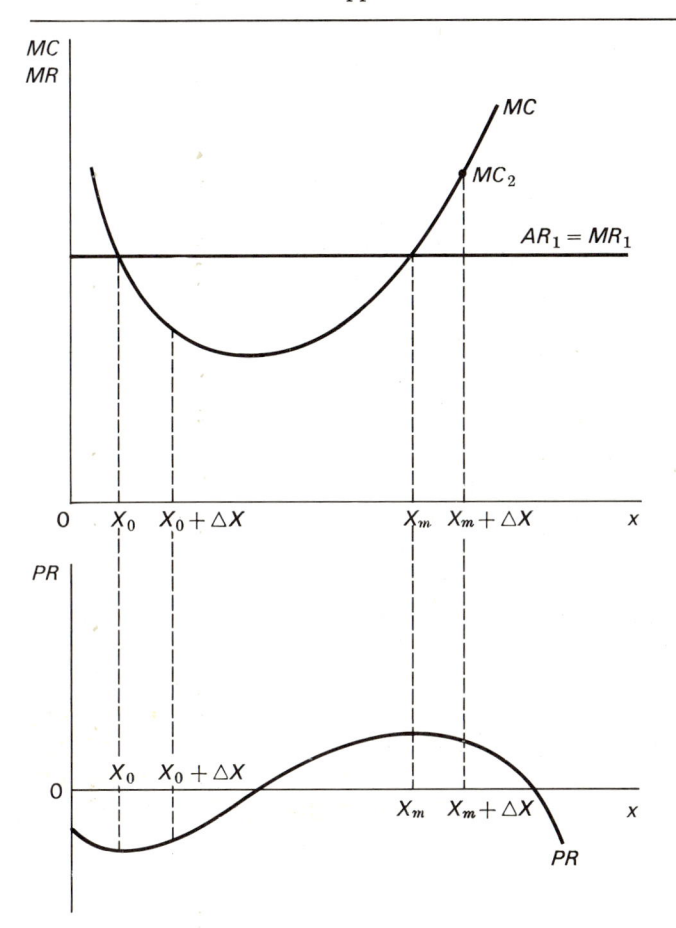

rising. (There are exceptions to this rule, such as the possibility that MR is rising faster than MC, but such cases are rare.) For most situations, this modification to the $MC = MR$ rule will provide us with both the *necessary* and *sufficient* conditions for profit maximization. Since MC is falling at X_0, this output level is ruled out, but MC is rising at X_m, and MR is constant; thus the equality of MC with MR at X_m serves as a necessary and sufficient condition for profit maximization. At output X_0, *losses* are in fact at a maximum relative to output levels slightly larger or smaller than X_0.

All of the competitive firm's short-run unit-cost and revenue curves are combined in Figure 7-4. The firm maximizes short-run profit by equating

288 A Theory of Producer Behavior

FIGURE 7–4 Short-Run Profit Maximization for a Competitive Firm

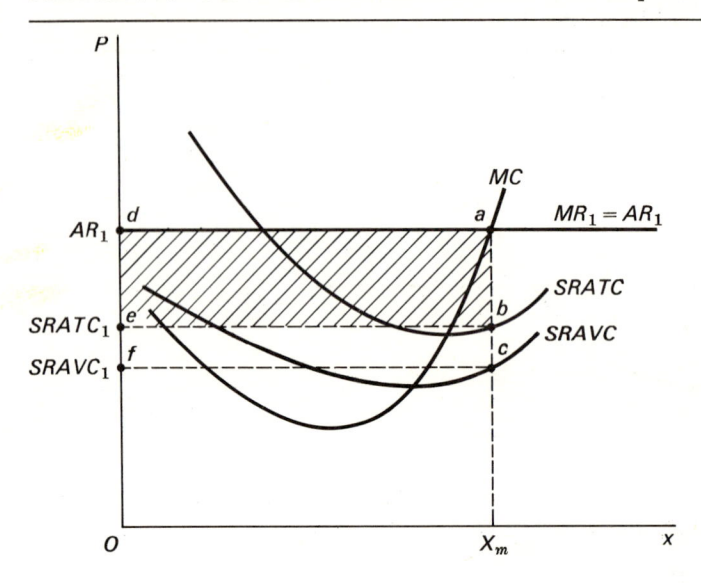

MR_1 with MC, at X_m units as before. At the profit-maximizing output, X_m, total revenue, TR_1, equals $AR_1 \cdot X_m$, the area of rectangle OX_mad. Short-run total cost at the profit-maximizing output is equal to the area of rectangle OX_mbe, which is $SRATC_1$ multiplied by X_m. $SRAVC_1$ multiplied by X_m equals short-run total variable cost, the area of rectangle OX_mcf. Finally, by subtracting the area representing total cost from that of total revenue (the area of rectangle OX_mad minus the area of rectangle OX_mbe), we obtain the competitive firm's short-run total profits, the shaded area, $ebad$.

Short-Run Firm Supply

Now that we have seen how a competitive firm adjusts its output to a given market price, we are ready to see how it will adjust to different prices. Suppose market demand is D_3 and short-run industry supply is S, as illustrated in panel (b) of Figure 7–5. Equilibrium industry output is X_3 and market price P_3. The cost and revenue curves of a representative firm in the industry are depicted in panel (a) of Figure 7–5, and they indicate that the firm has made a short-run adjustment to the market situation by producing x_3 units. Since AR_3 equals $SRATC$, the firm's profits are zero. It will nevertheless find it advantageous to operate at x_3, since its only other realistic option is not to operate at all. Its short-run loss from producing zero output is the amount of its fixed costs, since it must pay its fixed costs in any event. So at price P_3, the firm would supply x_3 units of output and just cover all costs, including a normal return on its capital but no economic profits.

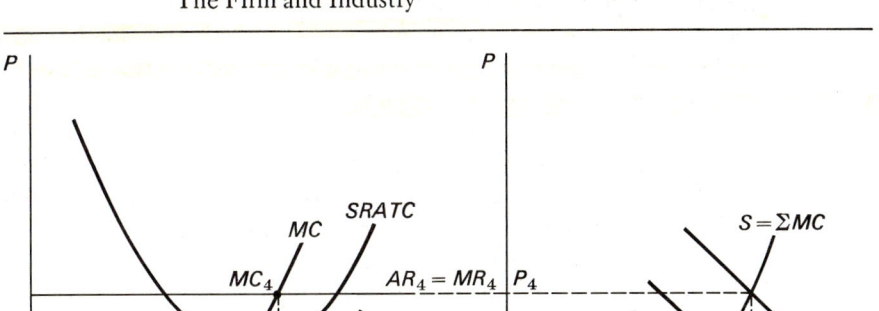

FIGURE 7-5 Derivation of Short-Run Competitive Supply: The Firm and Industry

Now suppose market demand increases from D_3 to D_4. Short-run supply and demand schedules in panel (b) indicate an increase in price from P_3 to P_4, which raises the representative firm's average revenue schedule to $AR_4 = MR_4$. Now MR_4 is greater than MC at output x_3, so the firm would expand output until marginal revenue and marginal cost are brought back into equality at output x_4.[2] At this output, AR is above ATC, so the firm will realize positive economic profits. The increase in market price from P_3 to P_4 causes the representative firm to respond to the potential for economic profits by raising its output from x_3 to x_4.

If market demand falls from D_4 to D_2, price will drop to P_2. At output level x_4, the firm's MC is above MR_2, which induces it to contract output to x_2 units, at which MR_2 is equal to MC_2. However, since AR_2 is less than SRATC, the firm would incur losses if it produced at x_2. Now it must decide whether the loss it realizes by producing x_2 units is less than the loss it would realize from not producing. The latter is, of course, its total fixed cost. Should the firm produce or not? The decision criterion is simple: which option results in the smaller loss? We obtain the answer by comparing average revenue with average variable cost. Since average revenue, AR_2, is greater than average variable cost at output level x_2, then total revenue will be greater than total vari-

---

[2] We are looking at our representative firm in isolation at this point. Actually, market price rises to P_4 as *all* firms increase the quantity supplied in the market.

able cost. This means that after covering all *variable* costs of operating at x_2, the firm will have some revenue remaining which may be applied against its fixed cost. A loss will be incurred if the firm operates at x_2, but this loss will be less than the loss from producing zero output. So at price P_2, the firm minimizes its short-run losses by producing x_2 units.

The minimum price at which the firm will supply output in the short run is P_1. To illustrate, suppose market demand falls to D_1, bringing price down to P_1 and the firm's average revenue curve to AR_1. Here, x_1 is the indicated profit-maximizing output level. But at x_1, AR_1 equals AVC_1, which means total revenue equals total variable cost. Since profits are equal to $TR - (TVC + TFC)$, the firm would realize a loss exactly equal to its fixed cost. It might just as well produce zero units as x_1 units at price P_1, since the loss in either case would be the same. Of course, if market price dropped below P_1, the firm would minimize its losses by ceasing production rather than produce at the output indicated by $MC = MR$. Now we must add a further qualification to the $MC = MR$ rule for maximum profits or minimum losses: AR must be above AVC. Otherwise, the firm will minimize losses by ceasing production.

Taken together, the price–quantity combinations, P_1-X_1 through P_4-X_4, show the quantities of output the firm will supply at different prices, and are therefore points on the firm's short-run supply curve. A glance at Figure 7–5 shows that these points lie along the firm's MC curve. In fact, the firm's MC curve is also its short-run supply curve. There is one qualification: the firm's supply is that portion of its MC curve which lies above AVC, since the firm will produce zero units of output if average revenue falls below average variable cost. In general, a competitive firm's MC curve above AVC is its supply curve in the short run.

Short-Run Industry Supply

Having determined the firm's short-run supply schedule, we now focus our attention on market supply. As a general proposition:

> Short-run competitive supply is the horizontal aggregation of all the short-run supply schedules of individual firms in the industry.

The reader will recall that when we summed demand schedules in Chapter 5, we had to allow for the possible effects of the summation process on individual demand curves. We have to be aware of the same problems when summing *individual* firms' supply curves. In deriving firms' marginal cost curves, we assumed that resource prices were constant, and it is perhaps realistic to expect that expansion by a single firm will leave resource prices unaffected. But if the *industry* expands, it is possible that resource prices will rise, and, if so, this would cause firms' cost curves to shift. So the above general proposition is valid only if expansion by the competitive industry has no effect on resource prices—which implies that the supply of resources to the industry is perfectly elastic. This assumption may be called the *small industry assumption*. Adopting the small industry assumption, we can now easily derive industry supply. Referring to panel (b) of Figure 7–5, S is shown as ΣMC, the sum of all firms' supply curves.

If a competitive industry is an appreciable buyer of any productive resources, ΣMC is no longer short-run supply. For then if the industry expands output, its increased demand for resources raises their prices, causing firms' cost curves to rise, including marginal cost. For simplicity, however, we will retain the small industry assumption, which allows us to treat market supply as ΣMC. (The comic book industry probably can expand or contract its aggregate output with negligible impact on the price of ink or paper.)

We now have a complete theory of short-run price in a perfectly competitive market. The theory of market demand was developed in Chapter 4, based upon consumer theory presented in Chapter 3, and short-run market supply has been developed in this chapter based upon the theory of the firm and the principles of production presented in Chapters 5 and 6. Combining the two aggregate schedules determines equilibrium market price in a competitive industry in the short run.

Long-Run Firm Equilibrium

Given enough time, the firm can vary the production process in any way that is technically feasible. It can not only increase or decrease the intensity of utilization of its existing plant facilities, but it can also expand or contract plant capacity or, if necessary, go out of business altogether. A period of time long enough for the firm to make any desired production changes we have defined as the long run. The reader will recognize that this concept of long run is identical to that used in Chapters 5 and 6 to derive long-run cost curves. Of course, the firm must expect a given market situation to be long lasting before it would make a long-run adjustment based upon that situation. But if it does, then short-run cost curves are no longer appropriate. The relevant cost curves for planning long-run adjustments are, as their name implies, the firm's long-run cost curves.

Industry–Firm Equilibrium: Blocked Entry. To simplify the presentation of long-run equilibrium analysis, we retain our assumption that the representative firm serves as a proxy for all other firms in the industry, and we add an additional assumption that the number of competitive firms in the industry is fixed. In other words, entry into the industry is blocked and exit from the industry prohibited.[3] This assumption, which we will presently relax, allows us

---

[3] Notice that this violates one of the requisites for perfect competition.

292   A Theory of Producer Behavior

to focus first on the long-run equilibrium adjustments of firms within a competitive industry, without considering simultaneously the possibility of entry of new firms and exit of existing firms.

In order to illustrate the relationship between short- and long-run production adjustments by a competitive firm, we turn to a simple problem of comparative statics. We begin with the equilibrium conditions illustrated in Figure 7–6, where short-run market supply schedule, S, and demand schedule, D, result in an initial equilibrium price, P_1. Correspondingly, the demand curve for the representative firm's output is AR_1 in panel (a). To maximize profits in the long run, the firm equates long-run marginal cost with marginal revenue at point b and output x_1.[4] Since the firm is making an optimum long-run adjustment to price P_1, it must also be making an optimum short-run adjustment, so $SRMC_1$ must also equal MR at output x_1. It would be a contradiction to say that the firm has made an optimum long-run adjustment to the market situation but not an optimum short-run adjustment. The first implies the second, though the converse is not necessarily true, as we shall see.

If market demand increases to D', short-run price will rise to P_2, determined by the point of intersection of D' with the industry's short-run supply curve, S. In the short run, the representative firm will adjust to the new price by expanding output to x_2 units, determined by the point of intersection of

FIGURE 7–6 Short-Run and Long-Run Competitive Behavior—
Blocked Entry

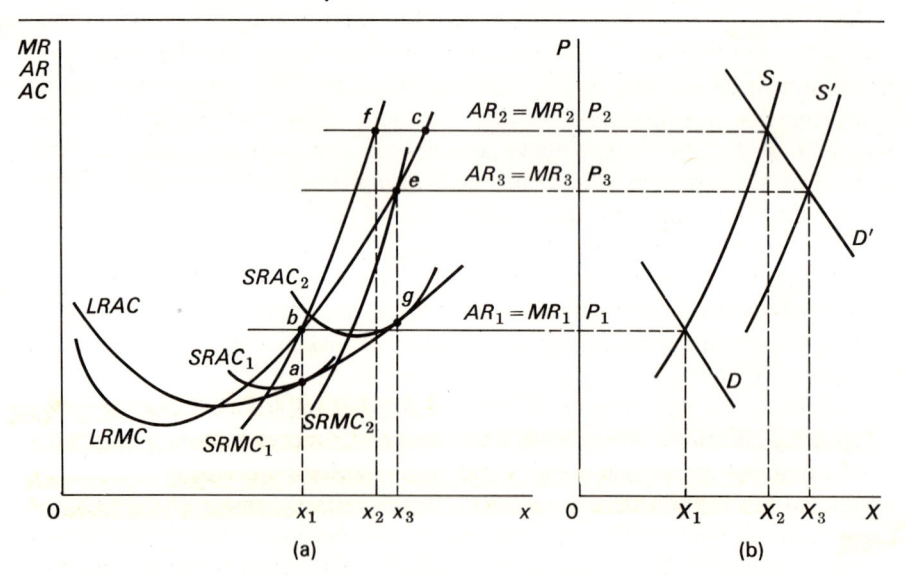

[4] We are, in effect, assuming all other firms except the representative firm have made a long-run adjustment to price P_1. Otherwise, if all firms began expanding output, price would fall below P_1 because of increased supply.

$SRMC_1$ and MR_2 (point f). Short-run equilibrium is achieved once market price and quantity stabilize at P_2 and X_2.

But what will be the firm's and the industry's long-run adjustment to the new market situation? A first reaction is to expect the competitive firm to expand in the long run to the output level at which MR_2 equals $LRMC$ (point c). A moment's reflection will reveal that this will not be the case, however, for as the representative firm and all others in the industry expand plant capacity, their $SRMC$ curves will shift to the right and, as a consequence, so will short-run market supply. (Remember that industry supply is the sum of firms' MC curves.) As all the competitive firms in the industry begin making a long-run adjustment to D', market price will fall. The process of adjustment will stop when market price falls enough and firms' long-run marginal cost rises enough to bring about equality between the two. As shown in Figure 7–6, equilibrium is restored for the representative firm and all others in the industry at price P_3.[5] Short-run supply is now S', the sum of all firms' new short-run MC curves. The new long-run equilibrium price is above the original price, P_1, but below P_2, and since AR_3 is above $LRAC$, the representative firm realizes profits at the new equilibrium level, x_3, which will be greater than the profits realized before the increase in market demand.[6] Thus, where entry is blocked, an increase in demand enhances the profit opportunities of all firms in the industry.

Industry Equilibrium with Free Entry and Exit. To determine the effects of free entry and exit of firms on long-run equilibrium in a competitive industry, we remove the condition of blocked entry and exit. To begin, assume the conditions for a competitive firm and industry are those illustrated in Figure 7–7. Short-run market supply and demand are initially S_1 and D, resulting in equilibrium price P_1. The representative firm equates $LRMC$ with MR_1 at x_1 units. At this output, profit per unit, ab, multiplied by the quantity produced, x_1, gives the total profits of the firm. Since our firm is representative, we may conclude that all firms in the industry realize economic profits.

---

[5] One of the chief disadvantages of comparative statics is that it does not show how the system adjusts from one situation to another. In our example, the model indicates that the initial market equilibrium, P_1 and X_1, will be replaced with equilibrium market price P_3 and quantity X_3, if firms are given enough time to adjust to demand D' and if the market is inherently stable. What we cannot show are the details of how firms adjust from the initial equilibrium condition to the subsequent one. Are a few firms first to expand plant capacity, or do they all react simultaneously? Does price change smoothly from one price to another, or is there a possibility of "overshooting" the equilibrium price in one direction and then in the other? Is there any assurance that price will ever reach equilibrium? Comparative statics does not provide the answers to all of these questions that pertain to the dynamics of the adjustment process, though we can usually determine the conditions which will insure stability (the tendency to move more or less smoothly toward equilibrium values), and can predict the equilibrium values of price and quantity under different situations, once the principal forces of disequilibrium have worked themselves out.

[6] We assume that the representative firm's costs are unaffected by the industry's expansion.

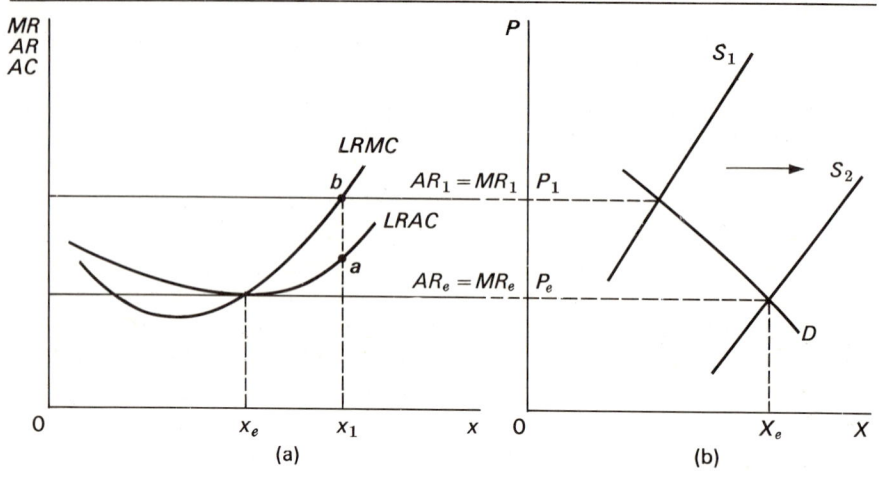

FIGURE 7-7 Long-Run Competitive Behavior—Free Entry

The existence of economic profits will attract new firms into the industry, if time is allowed for them to organize, build plant facilities, and hire the other resources needed to set up production. The entrance of new firms will cause short-run industry supply to shift to the right which, in turn, will cause price to decrease and market quantity to increase. With market price falling, firms will find their profits falling, too. But so long as profits are positive, there will be an incentive for firms to enter the industry, since economic profits represent a surplus over *all* economic costs, including the opportunity cost of the capital invested by owners.

The entry of new firms will cease and industry supply will stop increasing when price has fallen to a level which eliminates all economic profits. At the intersection of S_2 with D in Figure 7-7, price is P_e, and the representative firm's demand is AR_e. Since AR_e just equals $LRAC$ at the profit-maximizing output level, X_e, profits of the representative firm are eliminated. There is no longer any incentive for new firms to enter the industry. On the other hand, since zero profits include a normal return for each firm's owners, there is no incentive for existing firms to exit the industry.

In general, the long-run equilibrium condition for firms in a competitive industry is summarized by the mathematical statement:

$$LRAC_e = AR_e = MR_e = LRMC_e = P_e.$$

We will explore later in the chapter the possibility of using these long-run equilibrium characteristics as a standard for comparing the performance of firms in noncompetitive markets.

There are few real-world industries for which resources flow smoothly to and fro in response to economic profits and losses as we have described in our model. However, one illustration might provide us with a reasonable approximation to such resource fluidity, and that is the restaurant industry in a metropolitan area. Suppose the area is experiencing rapid population and economic growth, which raises the demand for restaurant services. This will increase the profitability of existing restaurants—which will induce other persons to start up new ones. Since the capital requirements for a new restaurant are not prohibitive, and the time delay in obtaining the needed facilities is reasonably short, there are few restrictions on would-be firms. We might expect that the industry will expand fairly rapidly in response to the profit incentive, as we have described in our model. If growth in the metropolitan area suddenly stops, then the industry will likely stabilize eventually at a given number of firms, each earning little more than a normal return on its capital. On the other hand, if the area declines, economic losses will force some firms out of the industry as it contracts in response to diminished market demand.

In the appendix to this chapter we have included a reading which attempts to develop a competitive theory of the housing industry.

Long-Run Supply—Constant Cost Industry

In this section, our task is to derive the long-run supply curve for a perfectly competitive industry. We will find that the shape of the supply curve will depend upon whether the industry is an increasing, decreasing, or constant cost industry. We will illustrate first a *constant cost industry*, in which industry expansion or contraction has no effect on either resource prices or productivity. In other words, the supply curves of resources to a constant cost industry are perfectly elastic, so growth or decline of the industry has no effect on individual firms' long-run or short-run cost curves.

Suppose long-run equilibrium conditions prevail in a competitive industry, as illustrated in Figure 7–8, with short-run market supply and demand schedules, S and D, resulting in price P_1 and output X_1. The representative firm's output is x_1 and, since P_1 equals $LRAC$ at its low point, profits are zero for the firm and all others in the industry. There is no incentive for new firms to enter or for existing firms to leave the industry. Now let us disturb this equilibrium by letting market demand increase from D to D', due perhaps to a shift in consumer preferences. (D could be the demand for "hot pants" in 1969 and D' the demand in 1971.) The shift causes price to rise in the short run from P_1 to P_2. The representative firm will equate MR_2 with $SRMC_1$ at point b and increase production from x_1 to x_2 units. Profits will rise from zero to a positive amount equal to ab, profit per unit, times X_2, the number of units produced.

The existence of economic profits causes new firms to enter the industry in the long run. (To keep the analysis simple, we will assume that *existing* firms in the industry do not attempt to make a long-run adjustment to the market

FIGURE 7–8 Derivation of Long-Run Supply—Constant Cost Competitive Industry

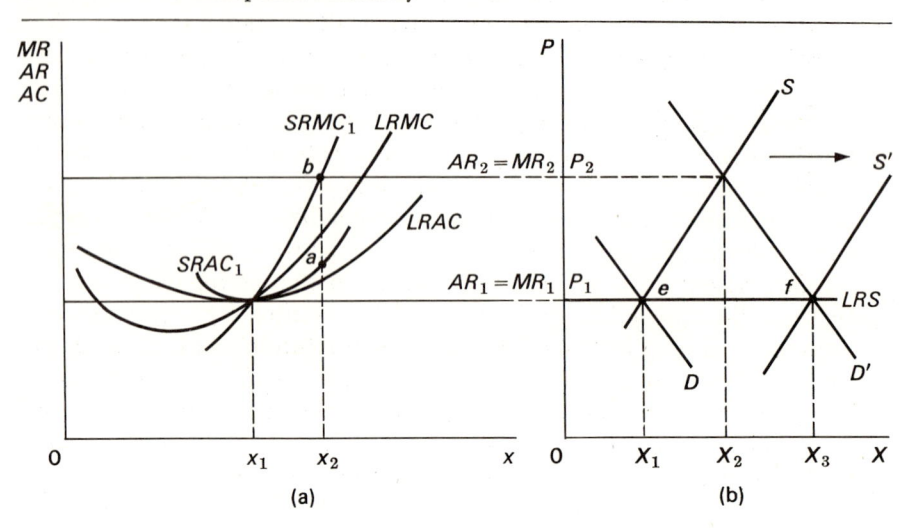

situation.) The entry of new firms increases short-run supply and decreases market price, which, in turn, causes each firm's profits to decline. However, growth will continue until cconomic profits fall to zero, for only then would there be no further inducement for firms to enter the industry. In panel (b) of Figure 7–8, the new long-run equilibrium market price and quantity are shown as P_1 and X_3, determined by the intersection of the new short-run supply curve S' and market demand D'. Equilibrium price again equals the representative firm's LRAC, eliminating all economic profits in the industry.

Because of our assumption of a constant cost industry, the LRAC curves of the representative firm and all others have not been affected by the industry's expansion. The industry initially supplied X_1 units at price P_1; then in long-run response to increased demand, supplied X_3 units at the same price. Therefore, the two points $P_1 - X_1$ (point e) and $P_1 - X_3$ (point f) in panel (b) of Figure 7–8 must lie along the industry's long-run supply curve. By collecting all such points, we generate the long-run supply curve, LRS. The LRS curve is perfectly elastic at price P_1, the minimum value of LRAC of the representative firm. The increase in the long-run quantity supplied ($X_2 - X_1$) has been accomplished by an increase in the number of firms in the industry, each operating the optimum size plant facility.

Our assumption that the entry of new firms leaves long-run average costs unchanged implies that resource prices are unaffected by the industry's increased demand for resources.[7] Under what conditions will the supply of a

---
[7] If resource prices do rise when new firms enter the industry, it is still possible for LRAC curves to remain unchanged. This can occur if industry expansion causes an increase in resource productivity which offsets any rise in resource prices.

resource to an industry be perfectly elastic? This is possible if the industry is a relatively small user of the resource. The competitive industry must stand in about the same relationship to the resource market as the buyer in a perfectly competitive product market. The purchases of each are so small relative to the market that they have no effect on market price; as an illustration, any one of the retail trades industries is likely to be a relatively small user of clerical labor.

Long-Run Supply—Increasing Costs

Increasing costs associated with industry expansion may be caused by a rise in resource prices, by decreased productivities of resources, or by a combination of both. The derivation of long-run supply for an increasing cost industry is illustrated in Figure 7–9. We begin with market demand and short-run supply schedules D and S, which result in equilibrium market price and quantity, P_1 and X_1. The representative firm has made a long-run adjustment to the market price by equating MR_1 with $LRMC$ at output x_1. Since AR_1 equals $LRAC$ at that output, profits are zero for the representative firm and all others. Now suppose market demand increases from D to D', causing short-run market price to rise from P_1 to P_2. In the short run, the representative firm will adjust to the higher price by equating $SRMC$ with MR_2 at point b and output x_2.[8] Industry output rises from X_1 to X_2 as all firms increase short-run output. Profits of the representative firm are equal to ab multiplied by x_2 units of output.

FIGURE 7–9 Derivation of Long-Run Supply—Increasing Cost Competitive Industry

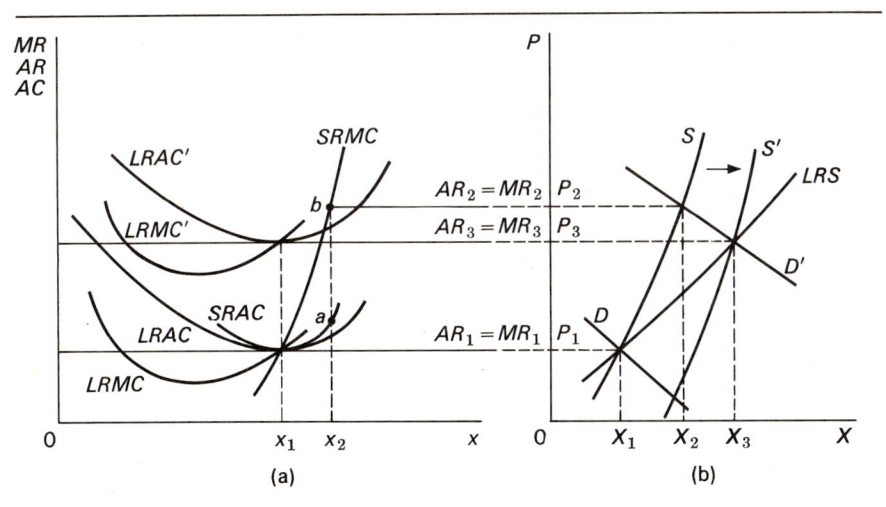

[8] We are assuming that the increasing cost effects of industry expansion are important for long-run industry adjustments only.

The existence of short-run economic profits induces new firms to enter the industry in the long run, just as in the previous illustration, and this increases market supply and decreases price. Firms' profits are therefore reduced. The principal difference between the previous case of a constant cost industry and the present case of an increasing cost industry is that the entry of new firms, and the consequent industry expansion, causes *resource* prices to rise which, in turn, causes the cost curves of all firms to shift upward. Profits decline more rapidly than under constant costs, because they are squeezed in two ways: (1) Short-run supply increases as new firms start producing, so market price falls, and (2) industry expansion causes factor prices to increase, so costs rise.

Firms will stop entering the competitive industry when costs have risen enough, and product price has fallen enough, to eliminate economic profits. Referring to Figure 7-9, the new long-run equilibrium price and output are P_3 and X_3. Short-run supply has shifted to S', and the representative firms' LRAC curve has risen to $LRAC'$. The firm equates $LRMC'$ with MR_3 at output x_1 and, since LRAC equals AR_3, profits are again zero. We have assumed that industry expansion has increased all resource prices in the same proportion, so $LRAC'$ lies vertically above LRAC, making the optimum output level the same for LRAC as for $LRAC'$. In other words, the long-run, most efficient plant size and output are the same after the rise in resource prices as before. Once again, the expansion in industry output has been accomplished by the entry of new firms.

Collecting all the possible long-run equilibrium combinations of price and quantity which would be generated if we considered alternative market demand curves, including $P_1 - X_1$ and $P_3 - X_3$, we obtain the industry's long-run supply curve, LRS in Figure 7-9. The curve slopes upward, indicating that the industry can supply larger quantities only at higher prices.

Long-Run Supply—Decreasing Cost Industry

The derivation of long-run supply for a decreasing cost industry is illustrated in Figure 7-10. The competitive industry is initially in long-run equilibrium with price P_1 and quantity X_1, as determined by the intersection of market demand, D, and short-run industry supply, S. Then demand increases from D to D', causing market price to rise in the short run from P_1 to P_2. In response to the higher market price, the representative firm increases its short-run output to x_2 units and realizes positive profits.

The existence of economic profits induces new firms to enter the industry, which shifts short-run supply to the right, lowering output price. But in the case of a decreasing cost industry, long-run industry expansion also causes firms' LRAC curves to shift *downward*. Both market price and firms' costs decline with industry expansion. Equilibrium will be restored when the falling

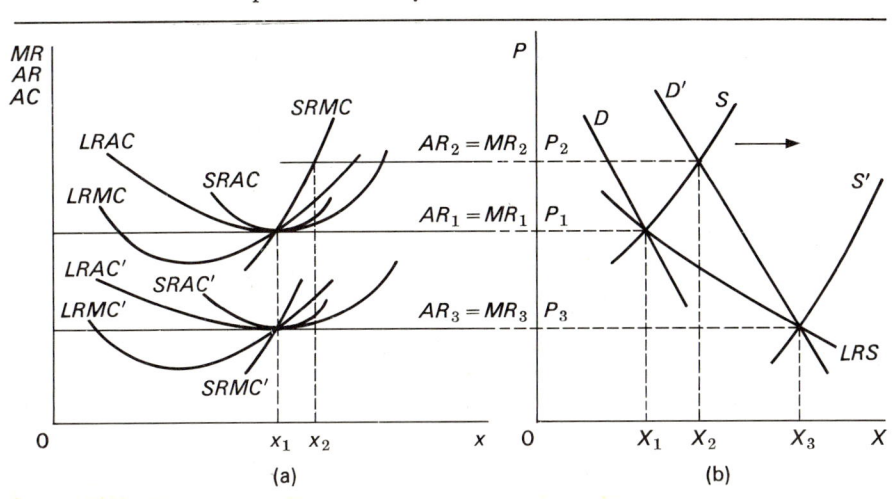

FIGURE 7–10 Derivation of Long-Run Supply—Decreasing Cost Competitive Industry

output price overtakes declining unit costs, so that profits are again reduced to zero.[9] In Figure 7–10, the new long-run unit cost curve of the firm has declined to LRAC′ and, since AR$_3$ equals LRAC′ at x$_1$, profits are eliminated. The representative firm equates LRMC′ with MR$_3$ at output X$_1$, the original output level. We have again assumed that industry expansion causes all resource prices to change in the same proportion, so LRAC′ is vertically *below* LRAC.

Collecting the two long-run equilibrium combinations of price and quantity, $P_1 - X_1$ and $P_3 - X_3$, as well as all other possible price–quantity combinations which would be generated with alternative demand curves, we obtain the industry's long-run supply curve, labeled LRS in Figure 7–10. Because industry expansion results in lower unit costs, LRS is negatively sloped, indicating the industry will respond to a permanent increase in market demand by increasing quantity supplied *at a lower price*.

The case of decreasing costs is not often encountered in industrially developed economies, but it does appear in young, developing ones. For example, the textile industry probably enjoyed decreasing costs in the early period following its introduction into the United States economy, as did other manufacturing activities introduced later. In many cases, decreasing costs occur because of external production economies arising from improved transportation and communication facilities. The latter are apt to be in rudimentary condition in the early stages of an economy, but improve with industrial growth.

---

[9] We assume that the industry is inherently stable, so that a new equilibrium price and output will be achieved.

This lowers costs for all. In other words, there may be economies of industry size just as there are firm economies, so that as an industry grows, its costs go down. But these effects are external so far as the firm is concerned, and are sometimes called *external economies* to distinguish them from internal economies of scale.

CONCLUSION: LONG-RUN EQUILIBRIUM OUTPUT UNDER PERFECT COMPETITION

We indicated at the beginning of this chapter that one of the most important uses of perfect competition theory is as a standard for measuring the performance of other industries. That standard is most important when considering, as we do in the next three chapters, the long-run performance of the noncompetitive industry structures, monopoly, monopolistic competition, and oligopoly. Our remaining task in this chapter is to see what is unique about the competitive model.

Long-run equilibrium for a perfectly competitive firm and industry is presented in Figure 7–11. One of the main characteristics of the model is that industry profits are zero. Freedom of entry and exit assures zero profits in the long run, because positive profits will induce new firms to enter the industry, which drives down prices and possibly increases costs until profits are eliminated; and losses cause firms to leave a competitive industry, which raises output prices and possibly reduces costs until zero-profit equilibrium has been restored.

The tendency of perfect competition to eliminate economic profits and losses has two advantages: one relating to the dynamic aspects of the adjustment process and the other relating to the static characteristics.

1. The existence of economic profits in an industry generally serves as a signal that the output of the industry is too low. Consider the case of a competitive industry where *entry is blocked*. Now let demand increase, raising price and the economic profits of all firms in the industry. (We considered this case at the beginning of our discussion of long-run adjustments.) Remember that the existence of economic profits means the industry's total receipts are in excess of the opportunity costs of all resources used in production. The existence of industry profits means, therefore, that consumers' expenditures would cover the economic cost of producing a *larger* output, and unless consumers were completely satiated, an increase in output would increase social utility. That consumers are not satiated with the good is evidenced by their willingness to pay a positive price. Therefore, if price is above unit costs, giving rise to economic profits, an expansion of industry output would in general be efficient. On the other hand, industry losses mean consumers' aggregate expenditures do not equal total production costs, a condition which signals an excess of resources in the given activity. If society is not willing to pay the opportunity cost of using these resources in the given

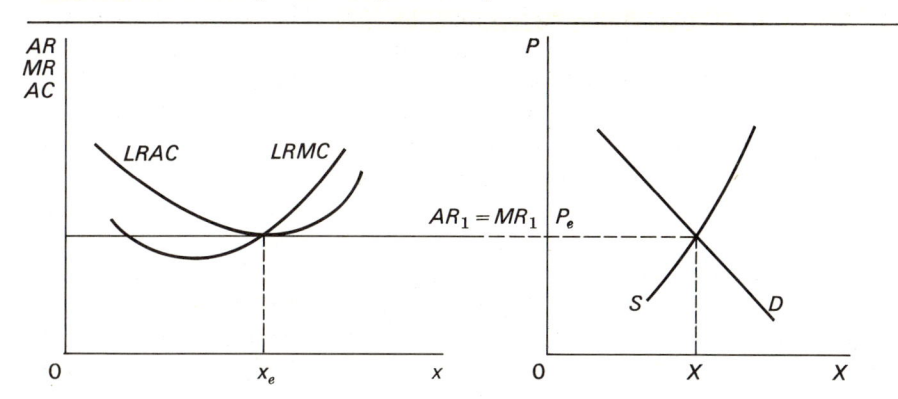

FIGURE 7-11 Long-Run Competitive Equilibrium

industry, it would be more efficient for it to contract production, so resources can be released to other industries where consumers *are* willing to pay their opportunity costs. In other words, if price is below average cost, a contraction in output in general would increase economic efficiency.

From our knowledge of the competitive model, we can state the following general conclusion:

> Where economic profits (losses) exist in a competitive industry, there is a tendency for the industry to expand (contract) output until these profits are reduced to zero.

In other words, a perfectly competitive industry responds to changes in demand in a way that is economically efficient.

2. Zero long-run profits may also be said to imply an efficient income distribution. To see why, consider the case where profits are positive. The existence of positive economic profits indicates a firm is receiving total revenues greater than the opportunity costs of the resources it uses. This excess is a pure surplus which accrues to the firm's owners. There is no justification for it on grounds of economic efficiency. On the other hand, economic losses would mean resources are receiving less than they could earn in an alternative employment, and this would be inefficient, also. (None of this is to imply that the payment of wages or other factor payments according to opportunity cost are necessarily *ethically* correct—just that such factor payments are economically *efficient*. Ethics cannot be proved or disproved, but efficiency can.)

From our knowledge of competitive markets we may conclude that:

> In the long run, a competitive industry and all the firms within the industry receive a return which just covers their opportunity cost and no more.

Long-run equilibrium in a competitive industry is therefore consistent with the notion of an efficient distribution of income.

3. Finally, we conclude that long-run competitive equilibrium implies equality of output price and long-run marginal cost. This is a necessary condition for an efficient distribution of resources and assures that neither too much nor too little of the product is produced. Suppose output price, P_1, is above marginal cost, MC_1. Then consumers' valuation of the last unit produced, measured by P_1, is greater than the opportunity cost or opportunity value of the resources needed to produce the last unit, as measured by MC_1. In other words, consumers value more highly the use of these resources in the given activity than in any other economic activity they might engage in. Under these circumstances, the production of the given product should be expanded until the value to consumers of the last unit produced is equal to that of the resources required for its production. On the other hand, if marginal cost, MC_2, is in excess of price, P_2, at a given level of industry production, then output should be reduced. For if $MC_2 > P_2$, the opportunity value of the resources needed to produce the marginal unit is greater than the value consumers place on the last unit produced. Some of these resources should be diverted to the activities for which their opportunity value is greater. In summary, where $MC < P$, output should be increased, and where $MC > P$, it should be decreased to achieve an efficient allocation of resources. Again, the condition is satisfied in the long run under perfect competition.

In Chapter 13 we will expand upon these notions of economic efficiency when we develop a general equilibrium model of an economy.

SUMMARY

Perfect competition exists when a large number of buyers and sellers exchange a homogeneous product, in a market free of arbitrary restrictions on price or the mobility of resources, and when market information is perfect. The theory of perfect competition, though both simplistic and unrealistic, is nevertheless a useful construction, because it serves as a standard for making comparisons with other industry structures.

Our first model of output determination begins by deriving the competitive firm's short-run supply curve, which we found to be identical to the firm's MC curve above AVC. The firm equates MC with price to determine its short-run profit-maximizing output. When the MC curves of all firms in a competitive industry are aggregated, we derive short-run industry supply which, coupled with market demand, determines both short-run market price and output. Competitive firms may earn zero, positive, or negative profits in the short run. But the existence of short-run profits causes long-run growth in a competitive industry which lowers price and perhaps increases costs until profits are eliminated. And negative profits force a long-run industry contraction which raises price and perhaps lowers costs until losses are eliminated. We found that long-run supply in a competitive industry will be upsloping if industry expansion raises firm's costs, a characteristic of an increasing cost industry and downward sloping in a decreasing cost industry. If industry growth neither raises nor lowers firms' costs, the industry is a constant cost industry, and its long-run supply curve will be perfectly elastic at the minimum point on firms' LRAC curves.

The long-run behavior of a perfectly competitive industry is consistent with the notion of economic efficiency. The behavior of firms within a competitive industry is motivated by profits; the existence of positive economic profits causes the industry to grow until profits are eliminated. This constitutes an efficient response, since profits are a sign that people want—and will pay for—an expansion in a given activity. On the other hand, losses will cause a competitive industry to contract in the long run, as firms attempt to avoid them. This is an economically efficient response, since losses signal an excess amount of resources in a given activity. Finally, long-run competitive equilibrium is characterized by the equality $P = MR = LRMC = LRAC$, which indicates that every consumer pays for every unit of the product he buys no more than the long-run marginal cost of producing the last unit. And since price equals firms' average cost, consumers pay no more than the economic costs of producing the long-run output. Together these characteristics are consistent with an efficient use of society's resources.

PROBLEMS

1. Answer the following based on the accompanying graph.
    (a) If market price is P_4, the competitive firm will supply _____ units and earn (profits, losses) equal to the area _____.

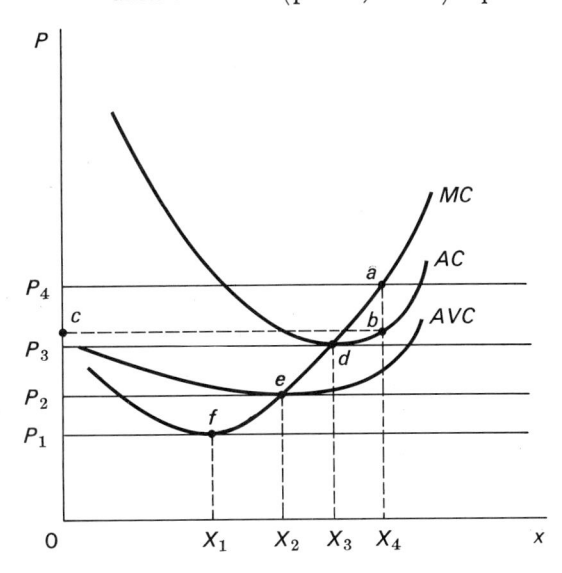

(b) If market price is below P_2, the competitive firm will supply _____ units and earn (profits, losses) equal to _____.
(c) If market price is P_1 and the firm produces X_1 units, its (profit, loss) will be (greater than, less than) its total fixed cost.
(d) At price P_3, the competitive firm earns (negative, zero, positive) profits and produces _____ units.
(e) The firm's supply curve is that section of (MC, AVC, AC) above point (f, e, d, a).

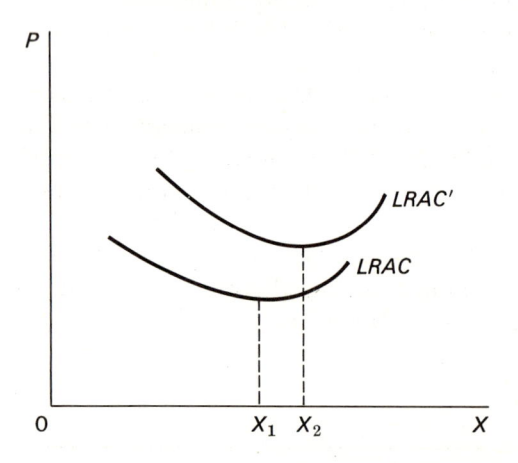

2. Suppose in an increasing cost industry, expansion causes firms' LRAC curves to shift from LRAC to LRAC' in the figure above. Have the prices of the short-run fixed factors increased more or less relative to the variable factors?
3. Answer the following on the basis of the following figure. Assume a constant cost industry.
   (a) If market price is P_3, we may expect a long-run (contraction, stability, expansion) in industry output.
   (b) If market price is P_2, we may expect a long-run (contraction, stability, expansion) in industry output.
   (c) If market price is P_1, we may expect a long-run (contraction, stability, expansion) in industry output.

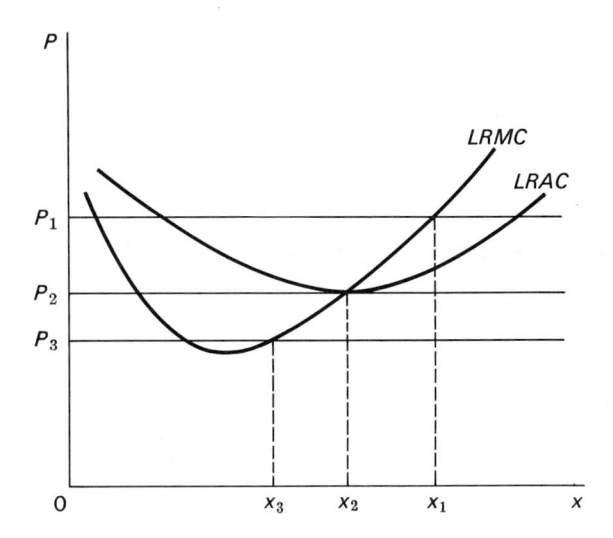

REFERENCES

Baumol, William J., "The Theory of Expansion of the Firm," *American Economic Review,* 52 (December 1962).

Buchanan, N. S., "A Reconsideration of the Cobweb Theorem," *Journal of Political Economy,* 47 (February 1939), 67–81.

Clark, John Maurice, *Competition as a Dynamic Process.* Washington, D.C.: Brookings, 1961.

Greenhut, Melvin L., "A General Theory of Maximum Profit," *Southern Economic Journal,* 28 (1962), 278–285.

Scitovsky, Tibor, "A Note on Profit Maximization and Its Implications," *Review of Economic Studies,* 11 (1943). Reprinted in A.E.A. *Readings in Price Theory.* Homewood, Ill.: Richard D. Irwin, 1952.

Simon, Herbert A., "New Developments in the Theory of the Firm," A.E.A. *Papers and Proceedings,* 52 (1962), 1–15.

Stigler, G. J., "Production and Distribution in the Short Run," *Journal of Political Economy,* XLVII (1939), 305–327. Reprinted in *Readings in the Theory of Income Distribution.* Philadelphia: The Blakiston Co., 1949, 119–142.

APPENDIX TO CHAPTER 7

A Competitive Theory of the Housing Market

EDGAR O. OLSEN*

When we look for examples of competitive industries, we typically turn to agriculture. For in agriculture the assumptions of competition, including homogeneity of product, large number of buyers and sellers, and so on, are most closely met. Below, however, we have presented an attempt by Edgar Olsen to construct a competitive theory of the housing market. Though houses are heterogeneous, Olsen postulates homogeneity of housing *services* and includes all of the other standard assumptions to arrive at a competitive model. Olsen uses his model to define and/or investigate four areas: dwelling unit, slum, shortage, and filtering. His aim is to incorporate microeconomic theory into housing analysis, with emphasis on problems of housing policy.

In his article on the demand for nonfarm housing, Richard Muth rigorously developed a competitive theory of the housing market.[1] Muth used this theory

Reprinted from the *American Economic Review*, Vol. LIX (September 1969), 612–22, by permission of the American Economic Association and the author.

* The author is on the staff of the RAND Corporation. However, this paper was written while he was a postdoctoral fellow in The Institute for Applied Urban Economics at Indiana University. He is indebted for helpful criticisms of earlier drafts to H. James Brown, David Greytak, W. David Maxwell, J. W. Milliman, Richard F. Muth, and R. L. Pfister. The author is also grateful to Resources for the Future for the grant which financed his postdoctoral fellowship.

[1] There are clearly two housing markets. There is a demand for and supply of a consumer good which we shall call housing service. There is also a derived demand for and supply of an investment good which we shall call housing stock. These two markets are integrally related. Indeed, Muth defines one unit of housing service to be that quantity of service yielded by one unit of housing stock per unit of time. Thus, he assumes that housing stock is the only input in the production of housing service. Although all buyers of housing stock are also sellers of housing service, there are many people who participate in one market but not in the other. Consumers who occupy rental housing are not typically in the market for housing stock. They are not buyers or sellers of this capital asset. Builders who construct housing for sale are sellers of housing stock but not of housing service. This

in the statistical estimation of the demand function for housing service and of the speed of adjustment to long run equilibrium in this market. His theory also makes possible the translation of some of the idiosyncratic concepts used by housing specialists into the familiar terms of microeconomic theory. A secondary purpose of this article is to make these translations. More importantly, this theory has implications for a number of crucial issues in government housing policy. The primary purpose of this article is to derive these implications, and use them to suggest additional tests of the competitive theory of the housing market. In order to achieve these purposes, it is first necessary to explain the crucial simplifying assumption which makes it possible to view the market for housing service as a competitive market in which a homogeneous good is sold.

I. THE ASSUMPTIONS

Let us assume that the following conditions are satisfied in markets for housing service: (1) both buyers and sellers of housing service are numerous, (2) the sales or purchases of each individual unit are small in relation to the aggregate volume of transactions, (3) neither buyers nor sellers collude, (4) entry into and exit from the market are free for both producers and consumers, (5) both producers and consumers possess perfect knowledge about the prevailing price and current bids, and they take advantage of every opportunity to increase profits and utility respectively, (6) no artificial restrictions are placed on demands for, supplies of, and prices of housing service and the resources used to produce housing service, and (7) housing service is a homogeneous commodity.

This set of conditions is nothing other than a conventional statement of one set of conditions sufficient for a perfectly competitive market.[2] While objections to all of these assumptions can be found in the housing literature, most scholars would probably find (7) to be the least plausible assumption. Noting the great variations among residential structures as to size, type of construction, and other characteristics to which consumers attach value, many presume that a very heterogeneous good is traded in the housing market. This paper presents a theory with a very different view of the good being traded. An understanding of this theory of the housing market requires an elaboration

---

paper will focus primarily on the market for housing service. Finally, it must be emphasized at the outset that this paper abstracts from consideration of the land on which dwelling units stand.

[2] This set is a composite taken from three standard price theory textbooks by Richard Leftwich, George Stigler, and James Henderson and Richard Quandt. As Stigler clearly explains, this is by no means the weakest set of assumptions sufficient for perfect competition. A strong set of assumptions is used in order to obtain clear-cut implications of the competitive theory.

on its conception of housing. Therefore, we will now focus our attention on this crucial simplifying assumption.

In order to view the housing market as one in which a homogeneous commodity is bought and sold, an unobservable theoretical entity called housing service is introduced.[3] Each dwelling (or housing) unit is presumed to yield some quantity of this good during each time period. It is assumed to be the only thing in a dwelling unit to which consumers attach value. Consequently, in this theory there is no distinction between the quantity and quality of a dwelling unit as these terms are customarily used.

This conception of housing is bound to raise objections. It will be argued that housing is a complex bundle of technically independent attributes. However, since housing service is not observable directly, it is not possible to argue for or against this assumption directly.[4] Hence, it is not possible to test this theory other than by reference to its implications. The competitive theory of the housing market does contain bridge principles which relate housing service to observable phenomena and it does have testable implications in terms of these phenomena. Muth has already tested some of these implications. Other implications will be derived in this paper. Eyesight is not a satisfactory judge of the question of homogeneity. The assumption of a homogeneous good called housing service can only be rejected if theories of the housing market without this assumption have greater explanatory power.

II. THE TRANSLATION OF CONCEPTS

Based on the assumptions of the preceding section, four concepts—dwelling unit, slum, filtering, and shortage—traditionally used in housing market analysis, can be translated into the jargon of conventional microeconomic theory.

What is a dwelling unit? A *dwelling unit* is a package composed of a certain quantity of a capital asset called housing stock. Some dwelling units will contain 10 units of housing stock, other dwelling units will contain 20 units of housing stock. By definition, these dwelling units will be said to yield 10 and 20 units of housing service per time period respectively.[5] In long run competitive equilibrium only one price per unit applies to all units of housing stock and another price to all units of housing service regardless of the size of the

---

[3] Carl Hempel gives an elementary but lucid explanation of the role of unobservable theoretical entities in scientific theories.

[4] Intuitively, it does seem more reasonable to conceive of the difference between an apartment renting for $50 and one renting for $100 in the same city as more akin to the difference between $50 and $100 worth of oranges than to the difference between $50 worth of oranges and $100 worth of golf balls. However, arguments of this sort are not scientific.

[5] Dwelling unit means the same thing as housing unit. Therefore, a housing unit is quite different from a unit of housing stock or housing service. The term dwelling unit is used throughout this paper to avoid this natural confusion.

package in which these goods come. Hence, if we observe that one dwelling unit sells for twice the amount of another dwelling unit in the same market, then we say that the more expensive unit contains twice the quantity of housing stock and, hence, involves twice the total expenditure. This distinction between price, quantity, and total expenditure is not usually made in housing market analysis where it is simply said that the price of the one dwelling unit is twice that of the other dwelling unit. Similarly, if we observe that one dwelling unit rents for twice the amount of another dwelling unit, then we say that the more expensive dwelling unit yields twice the quantity of housing service per time period and, hence, involves twice the total expenditure per time period. Here again, traditional housing market analysis uses a price theory concept, in this case "rent," in a way far removed from its original meaning. Despite the fact that housing service and housing stock are not directly observable, the competitive theory of the housing market contains bridge principles which permit us to compare the relative amounts of housing service yielded by different dwelling units.

What is a slum dwelling unit? A *slum dwelling unit* is one which yields less than some arbitrary quantity of housing service per time period. Using the relationship established between total expenditure and quantity, we might decide to call all dwelling units in a particular locality renting for less than $60 per month slum dwelling units. What is a slum area? A *slum area* is a contiguous area which contains a high (but arbitrary) percentage of slum dwelling units.

It would be possible to give the word "slum" a welfare economics definition in which a slum dwelling unit would necessarily represent suboptimal resource allocation. Otto Davis and Andrew Whinston have provided such a definition. At least one other distinctly different definition of this sort is possible.[6] However, the definition provided above is more in keeping with the use of this word in both popular and scholarly writings.

What is a housing shortage? The most frequently used unit of quantity for housing market analysis has been the dwelling unit. As a result, a housing shortage has usually been defined as a situation in which everyone who is willing to pay the market price for a separate dwelling unit is not able to obtain a separate dwelling unit. This is an unnecessarily narrow definition of a shortage which results from the acceptance of the dwelling unit as the unit of quantity. The unit of quantity introduced by Muth allows us to take a broader view of a housing shortage. To be precise, a *short run housing shortage* is said to exist if, and only if, the quantity of housing service demanded at

[6] Some people care about the housing occupied by low income families for altruistic and more selfish reasons. The market will not properly account for these preferences and, hence, low income families may consume too little housing service by the criterion of efficiency. We might call the dwelling units occupied by these low income families slum dwelling units. Clearly, with this definition slumness is not a characteristic of the housing alone.

the existing market price is greater than the quantity of housing service supplied. Short run shortages will be eliminated by a rise in the price of housing service for bundles of the size which are in excess demand initially. A *long run housing shortage* is said to exist if, and only if, the quantity of housing service demanded at the long run equilibrium price is greater than the quantity of housing service supplied. Long run shortages are eliminated by maintenance, repairs, alterations, and additions as well as by new construction. Clearly, a housing shortage can exist by these definitions even if everyone who wants to occupy a separate dwelling unit at the relevant price is doing so because everyone may want to occupy better housing (i.e., to consume a greater quantity of housing service) at this price than they presently occupy and none may be available.

Although the concept of filtering has been used in housing economics for many years, a rigorous definition of this term has only recently been proposed. Ira Lowry defines filtering as ". . . a change in the real value (price in constant dollars) of an existing dwelling unit." Lowry uses this definition together with a theory of the housing market to demonstrate that filtering is not a process which necessarily results in all families occupying housing above certain minimum standards. With the competitive theory of the housing market, it is possible to define filtering slightly more rigorously and in a manner which significantly clarifies the meaning of the concept and the method of detecting the process. Using this new definition and a competitive theory of the housing market, it is easy to demonstrate the result which Lowry showed with great difficulty.

A dwelling unit has *filtered* if, and only if the quantity of housing stock contained in this unit has changed. A dwelling unit has *filtered up* if, and only if the quantity of housing stock contained in this unit has increased. A dwelling unit has *filtered down* if, and only if, the quantity of housing stock contained in this unit has decreased.[7] Within the theory presented in this paper, Lowry's definition is the same as the new definition if he intended to deflate money values by the cost of construction. This is true because in a perfectly competitive housing market in long run equilibrium the price per unit of housing stock equals the minimum long run average cost of production and, hence, the quantity of housing stock contained in a particular dwelling unit is equal to the market value of this dwelling unit divided by the cost of production.[8] For example, if the cost-of-construction index was 100 in 1960 and 110 in 1962 and if a particular dwelling unit sold for $6000 in 1960 and $6050

---

[7] In these definitions, "housing stock contained in" could be replaced by "housing service yielded per time period by." These definitions are stated in stock terms to facilitate the comparison with Lowry's definition.

[8] Lowry does not say what he intends to use as a deflator.

in 1962, then we would say that this particular unit has filtered down between 1960 and 1962 because our index of quantity of housing stock fell from 60 to 55.[9]

To determine whether particular dwelling units have filtered is of far less importance than understanding the function of filtering in the operation of the housing market. In essence, Lowry set out to demonstrate that filtering is not a process that insures that all consumers will purchase greater than an arbitrarily chosen quantity of housing service per time period. If the housing market is perfectly competitive, then this result is trivial since there is nothing in the operation of such a market which insures that all individuals will consume greater than an arbitrary quantity of the good.[10] As will be shown in the next section, filtering is a process by which the quantity of housing service yielded by particular dwelling units is adjusted to conform to the pattern of consumer demand. The profit incentive leads producers to make these adjustments.

None of the definitions in this section corresponds exactly with previous usage of the terms. No simple definitions could. These definitions have been offered in order to bring housing market analysis within the realm of standard microeconomic theory where advantage can be taken of the accumulated knowledge in this field. The value of this transformation should be strongly emphasized. Even as eminent a price theorist as Milton Friedman [in his *Capitalism and Freedom*] reaches an undoubtedly fallacious conclusion about public housing simply because he did not apply the conventional distinction between the very short run and the long run to the housing market.[11]

---

[9] This method abstracts from changes in the price paid for a particular structure attributable to changes in the relative desirability of its location. Since I do not want to include these changes in my concept of filtering, the market value of the land must be subtracted from the total price of structure and land in determining whether a dwelling unit has filtered. Practically, this might be done by observing the sale price per square foot of nearby vacant land and assuming that the land containing the structure of interest has the same market value per square foot.

[10] For any given positive quantity, there exists a set of admissible indifference curves, relative prices, and income such that the consumer associated with these will choose less than the given quantity.

[11] Friedman concludes that ". . . far from improving the housing of the poor, as its proponents expected, public housing has done just the reverse. The number of dwelling units destroyed in the course of erecting public housing projects has been far larger than the number of new units constructed." Aside from the factual question of whether far more units have been destroyed than constructed and aside from Friedman's use of numbers of gainers and losers rather than the values of gains and losses, Friedman ignores the fact that the displaced families will lose over a few years while housed families will gain over the much longer physical life of the project. As will be demonstrated in Section V, in long run equilibrium the displaced families will occupy the same type of housing and pay the same rent as prior to the public housing project. According to Muth the market for housing

III. THE WORKINGS OF THE MARKET

The workings of the market for housing service under the set of assumptions introduced in Section I can best be illustrated by beginning from a situation in which the price per unit of housing service for bundles of all sizes but one is equal to the long run average cost of production. For the one bundle size, the price is assumed to be greater than the long run average cost. In this situation, producers will be making profits (i.e., they will be making more than a normal rate of return on capital) only on this one size bundle of housing service.

Owners of housing stock can change the quantity of housing stock contained in and, hence, the quantity of housing service yielded by their dwelling units through maintenance, repair, alteration, and addition.[12] In the absence of maintenance, dwelling units deteriorate with use and over time which means that they yield smaller and smaller quantities of housing service per time period. Normally, producers of housing service find it profitable to invest in maintenance (although not enough to halt deterioration completely). If bundles of some particular size become more profitable than bundles of other sizes, then some producers with larger bundles of housing service will allow their housing units to deteriorate more than they would otherwise. That is, they will allow their dwelling units to filter down to the bundle size which is most profitable. This is accomplished by following a lower maintenance policy than would have been followed had all bundle sizes been equally profitable. By the same token, some producers of smaller bundles of housing services will follow a higher maintenance policy than otherwise, resulting in a filtering up of their dwelling units.

The supply of the most profitable size bundle having increased, the price per unit of housing service for bundles of this size will decrease. Since initially there were zero profits for bundles of housing service slightly greater and slightly less than the profitable size bundle, the filtering down of large bundles and the filtering up of smaller bundles will create short run shortages, higher prices, and profits for bundles of these sizes. This will result in filtering down of the larger bundles and filtering up of smaller bundles. Eventually the

---

service adjusts at a rate of one-third of the difference between the present situation and long run equilibrium each year. Hence, there is a 90 percent adjustment in six years. By comparison, the physical life of public housing projects is likely to be far in excess of 50 years. From Edgar Olsen's calculations it can be estimated that the average public housing tenant received benefits from public housing which he valued at $263 in 1965. This benefit would be received each year by some poor family during the entire physical life of the project.

[12] In the remainder of this paper, the word "maintenance" will be used to denote all four of these phenomena.

process will require bundles of sizes which can be provided by the construction of new dwelling units. This new construction will continue until there are no profits to be made on bundles of any size. This requires the price per unit of housing service for bundles of all sizes to be the same.

IV. THE POOR-PAY-MORE HYPOTHESIS

A popular claim in current policy discussions is that the poor pay more for many goods including housing. If the housing markets are perfectly competitive and if it is neither more costly to provide small quantities of housing service nor to provide housing service to low income families, then the poor will not pay more for housing service. It is instructive of the workings of a perfectly competitive housing market to demonstrate this result.

We begin by interpreting the poor-pay-more hypothesis in terms of the theory presented in this article. For some reason the price per unit of housing service is greater for dwelling units yielding small quantities of housing service than for dwelling units yielding large quantities. This price difference is not attributable to differences in cost.[13] For large bundles of housing service, the market works efficiently. The price of housing service tends towards the minimum long run average cost of production of housing service. Consequently, the price per unit of housing service for small bundles exceeds the minimum average cost. As a result, owners of dwelling units yielding small quantities of housing service make economic profits. For some reason, these profits do not stimulate an increase in the supply of these small bundles of housing service. As a result, the consumers of these small bundles (i.e., primarily the poor) consume a smaller quantity of housing service than required for efficient resource allocation.

Participants in a competitive housing market would not allow this situation to persist. Suppose that owners of bundles of housing stock yielding quantities of housing service less than x received a higher price per unit for their production than owners of bundles which yield greater than x units of housing service. These slum landlords would be making higher profits per dollar invested than other landlords. In this case, some owners of dwelling units yielding slightly more than x units will follow a lower maintenance policy than otherwise, allowing the quantity of housing service yielded by their units per time period to fall below x. The supply of dwelling units yielding less than x units of housing service per time period will increase and the price per unit

---

[13] If the price difference is solely attributable to differences in cost, then no market imperfection is involved and government action on grounds of efficiency is not required. A recent study by the U.S. Bureau of Labor Statistics has shown that the poor do pay more for food, but that this difference is fully explained by difference in cost. The poor tend to shop in small areas where merchandising cost per unit is high.

for these small bundles will fall. Eventually, new construction will be induced. Only when the price per unit of housing service for bundles of all sizes is equal to the minimum long run average cost of production will there be no incentive for change.

If we actually observe that the poor consistently pay more per unit of housing service than the rich and that it is not more expensive per unit to provide small packages of housing service or to provide housing service to low income families, then we have evidence contrary to the assumption that the housing market is competitive. This is one of the testable implications of the competitive theory.[14]

V. WILL SLUM CLEARANCE AND URBAN RENEWAL RESULT IN A NET REDUCTION IN SLUMS?

Slum clearance is the destruction of slum dwelling units by government with or without compensation to the owner. It is required by the Housing Act of 1937 as part of the public housing program. It is undertaken independently by many local governments. Finally, slum clearance is the first stage of urban renewal. Slum clearance and urban renewal have been premised in large part on the naive belief that the physical destruction of slum dwelling units results in a net reduction in the number of families occupying such units. Many writers have questioned this presumption and have suggested that slum clearance merely results in the transfer of slums from one location to another. Indeed, this argument should suggest itself to all economists since slum clearance does not increase the incomes of or decrease the prices of any goods to the former residents of the cleared areas. If the market for housing service is perfectly competitive, then his argument can be made completely rigorous.

We have defined a slum dwelling unit as a dwelling unit yielding a flow of less than x units of housing service. Starting from a situation of long run equilibrium in the housing market with normal vacancy rates, the immediate

[14] A recent study by the BLS has shown that the quality of housing occupied by richer families is superior to that occupied by poorer people in the same rent range. Unfortunately, it is almost certainly true that within each rent range the higher the income range, the higher the average rent. The higher rent may completely explain the differences in quality. This author is trying to obtain the BLS data to check this possibility with regression analysis. Finally, the BLS study does not consider the possibility that it is more costly per unit of housing service either to provide small bundles or to sell to low-income families. For example, it is reputed to be much more difficult to collect rents from low income tenants. This involves extra costs in time and nonpayment. Furthermore, the existence and enforcement of building and occupancy codes with penalties for violations increase the long run equilibrium price of low quantity housing in a competitive market because there exist some products and consumers who will have an incentive to violate the code. (I owe this point to Richard Muth.)

effect of slum clearance is to decrease the supply of slum dwelling units. Some of the former residents of the destroyed dwelling units will move into vacant dwelling units providing the same quantity of housing service. Others will have to move into dwelling units which provide slightly more or slightly less housing service than they prefer to buy at the long run equilibrium price. The owners of slum dwelling units will realize that they can both charge higher prices and have lower vacancy rates than before slum clearance. They will take advantage of the short run shortage to raise prices in order to increase their profits. This, however, is only the very short run impact of slum clearance.

In the long run the owners of slightly better than slum dwelling units will allow their dwelling units to filter down to the level of slum dwelling units in order to take advantage of the profits to be made on such units. This adjustment will continue until the rate of return on capital invested in bundles of housing stock of all sizes is the same. In long run equilibrium the price per unit of housing service must be the same for bundles of all sizes. Since neither slum clearance nor urban renewal subsidizes housing consumption by low income families, and since neither results in a lower cost of production of housing service, therefore neither results in a lower price of housing service to the former residents of slum clearance or urban renewal sites in the long run. Neither slum clearance nor urban renewal results in change in the incomes of, or the prices paid for nonhousing goods by the former residents. Consequently, the former residents of the cleared area will, in long run equilibrium consume exactly the same quantity of housing service as before slum clearance or urban renewal. Slum clearance and urban renewal do not result in a net reduction in the occupancy of slums in the long run.

This implication of the competitive theory is testable. To conduct this test, we might observe the characteristics of the housing occupied by former residents of slum clearance sites and their incomes just prior to slum clearance and for six years afterwards. With respect to each characteristic, we shall probably observe that the percentage of families occupying housing with that characteristic is different immediately after slum clearance from what it was immediately before. For example, the percentage of families in dilapidated dwelling units might have been 90 percent before slum clearance and 50 percent afterwards. The competitive theory suggests that in long run equilibrium we will again find 90 percent of these families in dilapidated dwelling units if these families experience no change in real income. Therefore, if we determine the percentage of families occupying dwelling units with that particular characteristic by income groups, then we should observe that within each income group the percentage of families occupying housing having the particular characteristic should, over time, approach the before slum clearance percentage. This convergence provides a weak test of the competitive hypothesis. As mentioned before, Muth estimates that we get a 90 percent adjustment in the housing market in six years.[15] Consequently, we expect that the difference between the percentage at the end of six years and the percentage immediately after slum clearance will be roughly 90 percent of the difference between the percentage immediately before slum clearance and the percentage immediately afterwards. A test of the statistical significance of the difference between these two variables is a strong test of the competitive theory.[16]

There have been, and continue to be, many instances of slum clearance, especially associated with urban renewal. It is quite feasible to conduct studies of displaced families at least partly for the purpose of testing this implication of the competitive theory of the housing market. Since the nature of the housing market is very relevant to the choice of government housing policies, these data might reasonably be collected by the U.S. Department of Housing and Urban Development in conjunction with urban renewal and public housing.

If the housing market is perfectly competitive, then slum clearance and urban renewal result only in a shift in the location of slums rather than in a net reduction in slums. Consequently, we should expect neither urban renewal nor slum clearance to lead to a reduction in the social costs of slum living or to net beneficial spillover effects for properties not on the slum clearance site. Cost-benefit analyses of urban renewal typically find that measured benefits are far less than measured costs. The authors of these studies usually do not attempt to calculate the alleged benefits from these two sources, but they claim that the benefits from the reduction in social costs of slums and the net beneficial spillover effects on neighboring properties might well overcome the excess of measured costs over measured benefits. If the housing market were perfectly competitive, then the expected value of these alleged benefits would be zero and, hence, almost all slum clearance and urban renewal projects would be extremely wasteful.

VI. THE EFFECT OF RENT CERTIFICATES ON THE HOUSING OCCUPIED BY THEIR RECIPIENTS

If it is desired either to decrease the number of occupied slum dwelling units or to improve the housing occupied by low income families and if the housing market is competitive, then slum clearance and urban renewal are

---

[15] Specifically, Muth's estimates indicate that individuals seek to add about one-third of the difference between desired and actual stock during a year, which implies that for the adjustment of the actual housing stocks to be 90 percent completed, six years are required.
[16] If there is much variation in the speed of adjustment among the housing markets in the United States, then it would be desirable to estimate Muth's equation with data from the particular local housing market to obtain the speed of adjustment for that market and to use this estimate for our test.

not the answers. They would have neither of these effects. The most direct ways of obtaining these results are to tax (or prohibit) the occupation of slum dwelling units or to subsidize the housing of low income families. The former method would make the occupants of slum dwelling units worse off as they judge their own well-being. Consequently, to the extent that the desire to decrease the amount of slum housing and to increase the housing consumption of low income families is motivated by a desire to help these people, to that extent the tax (or prohibition) alternative can be dropped from consideration.

Probably the most efficient method of subsidizing the housing of low income families is to allow these families to buy certificates which they could use to pay the rent or make mortgage payments up to an amount equal to the face value of the certificate.[17] The low income family would purchase this certificate for an amount less than the face value.[18] These certificates would be redeemed by the government from sellers of housing service. It would be illegal to exchange these certificates for other than housing service.

Given the amount of public money likely to be spent for such a program and the amount that might be reasonably charged for these certificates, the face values of rent certificates will not be large enough to induce many low income families to move to newly produced housing because new housing typically comes in relatively large bundles of housing stock. Since a rent certificate plan does not directly increase the supply of newly constructed housing and since few of the recipients are likely to demand new housing, many people wonder how a rent certificate plan could result in an increase in the total quantity of housing stock. They suggest that since there will be no increase in housing stock, the only result of the increase in demand stemming from the rent certificate plan will be higher prices for housing service purchased by the low income families who use rent certificates.

By now it should be clear that if the market or housing service is perfectly competitive, then this is only the very short run effect of a rent certificate plan.[19] In the long run, the owners of the smallest bundles of housing stock will either increase their maintenance expenditures (and thereby increase the quantity of housing service yielded by their units) or convert their build-

---

[17] Olsen has made estimates which strongly suggest the rent certificate plan to be significantly more efficient than public housing.

[18] Under the principle of benefit taxation, each recipient should be charged an amount equal to average expenditure on housing service prior to the program by families of the same size and with the same income. . . . This result follows primarily from Muth's finding that the price elasticity of demand for housing service is roughly constant and unitary.

[19] Indeed, since a rent certificate plan would undoubtedly be discussed by Congress for some time before passage, it would be anticipated by sellers of housing service who would find it profitable to adjust their maintenance policy in advance of passage. Consequently, there might be little price inflation immediately after implementation.

ings to other uses. There would no longer be any demand for dwelling units which provide less housing service than can be purchased with rent certificates of the smallest face values.

Some owners of dwelling units presently providing bundles of housing service larger than could be purchased with rent certificates of the highest face value will allow their units to filter down to the relatively more profitable sectors initially affected by rent certificates. As a result, there will be shortages and, hence, economic profits for these larger bundles of housing service. Owners of dwelling units yielding still larger quantities of housing service will allow their units to filter down. Eventually shortages will result for bundles of housing stock which can be provided by new construction. Construction of new dwelling units will continue until there are no more excess profits in the market for housing service. In long run competitive equilibrium all consumers must pay the same price per unit of housing service. Consequently, purchasers of rent certificates with a face value of x dollars per month should be able to consume the same quantity of housing service as individuals who spent this much per month for housing service prior to the program.

This result leads to yet another testable implication of the competitive theory of the housing market. If the competitive theory is correct, then we should observe that the buyers of rent certificates with a face value of x dollars will occupy housing as good as the housing which rented for x dollars price to the rent certificate plan.[20] This is the long run equilibrium situation. The adjustment of this equilibrium will take several years. As already pointed out, Muth's evidence suggests a 90 percent adjustment in six years. Hence, we should observe that the characteristics of the housing occupied by recipients (e.g., whether the dwelling unit has hot and cold running water) should approach the characteristics of the housing occupied by individuals who spent the same amount on housing prior to the program.

It should not be necessary to wait until a national rent certificate plan is adopted to test this implication. According to Meyerson, Terrett, and Wheaton, ". . . welfare agencies in many states in this country do issue rent certificates to families on relief. During the Depression, millions of families received such payments." There may already be data from these experiences to test this implication of the competitive theory of the housing market. Given the demonstrated inefficiency of urban renewal and public housing, it would also seem reasonable for a city to propose and the Federal Government to accept a rent certificate plan in place of the two other programs on a demonstration basis. The experience of the buyers of rent certificates in this city could be used to test the competitive theory.

[20] It would be necessary to correct for changes in the general price level, but we should not expect the relative price of housing to rise in the long run because of the increase in the total demand for housing service, which is a result of the rent certificate plan. Muth finds the supply curve to be perfectly elastic.

VII. CONCLUSION

In this article, the assumptions of Muth's competitive theory of the housing market are stated and the nature of the good called housing service is elaborated upon. This theory is used to translate four familiar terms of housing market analysis—dwelling unit, slum, shortage, and filtering—into the standard concepts of microeconomic theory. If the housing market is perfectly competitive and if it is not more costly per unit to provide housing to low-income families or to provide small packages of housing service, then (1) the poor would not pay more per unit for housing, (2) slum clearance and urban renewal would not result in a net reduction in the number of occupied substandard units, and (3) the recipients of rent certificates would enjoy housing just as good as the housing occupied by others who spent as much on housing as the face value of the certificates. These results and their implications for government policy are deduced. In each of the three cases, testable implications of the assumptions are derived and the nature of the test made explicit. It is hoped that this article will serve to bring housing market analysis within the realm of conventional economic theory and to suggest additional tests of one particular conventional economic theory of markets.

8

MONOPOLY

In this chapter, we hope to accomplish three basic objectives: First, we seek a workable definition of monopoly and a theory which explains how a profit-maximizing monopolist will behave in the short and long run. We will investigate also the behavior of a monopoly firm which has other than profit-maximizing objectives.

Second, we want to use the basic monopoly model to show the effects of price regulation on the price–output decisions of those firms designated as public utilities.

Finally, we want to compare the behavior of the monopoly firm with that of competitive firms, using the criteria of economic efficiency discussed in the previous chapter.

Economists have a long tradition of antipathy for monopoly (dating at least from Adam Smith's denunciation of it) and a preference for competition, based upon the expected efficiencies of the two market structures. Our task is to explore the basis for the traditional view and to indicate those circumstances under which it is in error. After presenting the theory of monopoly, we use the model to suggest alternative economic policies to regulate the behavior of monopoly firms, thereby achieving greater economic efficiency.

A DEFINITION OF MONOPOLY

At first blush, monopoly appears easy to define: *a monopoly exists when a firm is the sole supplier in an industry.* However, as we have seen earlier, difficulties arise when we attempt to define what an industry is. Basically, we have defined an industry as including all of the firms producing a commodity or service for which there are no close substitutes. But there are few products, if any, for which there are no substitutes. This means an industry's boundaries must be defined more or less arbitrarily. One industry definition might include one firm and another might include many, so the determination of whether a monopoly exists is partly dependent upon one's definition of industry.

To illustrate the importance of industry definitions: In a landmark decision, the United States Supreme Court dismissed an antitrust suit against the DuPont Company based upon the Court's concept of industry. DuPont was accused by the antitrust department in 1947 of monopolizing cellophane manufacture, an allegation it could not deny. The company successfully argued, however, that although the firm, along with Sylvania Industrial Corporation, did monopolize the manufacture of cellophane, it did not monopolize the soft packaging industry. The Court agreed that the market for all flexible wrapping materials such as paper, aluminum foil, and the like was the relevant industry, and since DuPont did not monopolize the latter, as defined, the antitrust suit was dismissed.

If an industry is so tightly defined that substitute products are nonexistent, and if the industry is dominated by one firm, then it is a *pure monopoly*. The pure monopolist faces no competition from rival firms, in contrast with the competitive firm which faces competition from a multitude of rivals. Since rarely do we find a firm completely insulated from competition, the occurrence of pure monopoly in the United States economy is rare. Even a single firm producing electrical power in a given locality, a so-called natural monopoly, faces competition in certain uses from other power sources such as natural gas suppliers and coal producers. Because of its rarity, economists have often resorted to hypothetical examples of pure monopoly. One is a firm selling bottled mineral water having unique medicinal properties available from only one natural spring, which the firm owns.

IMPORTANCE OF MONOPOLY THEORY

Despite the difficulties involved in its definition and the rarity of pure monopoly in the economy, the theory of monopoly is important for several reasons:

1. Monopoly is the lower limit to the size of industries (size meaning number of firms), just as perfect competition represents an upper limit, and the limiting cases of any theory are significant even though almost all industries in the United States fall somewhere between the two extremes of perfect competition and pure monopoly.
2. Most firms have some small degree of monopoly power, their own brand, product design, or market area, and the analytical tools developed for pure monopoly can be employed in many situations which, though not purely monopolistic, are something less than perfectly competitive. The term "monopoly"—or "monopolistic"—is sometimes used in any market situation that is not perfectly competitive. In

other words, any market not competitive might be described as monopolistic, though a careful examination would reveal whether the structure is oligopolistic, monopolistically competitive, or purely monopolistic.
3. The model of pure monopoly has proven very useful for analyzing the effects of regulation on the behavior of those monopolies which we have designated as public utilities. For example, the model indicates the effects of price ceilings on the output level and profits of a public utility and allows us to compare the effects of alternative ceilings on the firm's behavior.
4. From the beginning of the United States, we have through our patent laws granted a certain amount of monopoly power to firms as a means of rewarding and thereby encouraging research and development. Also, governments often establish monopolies for one reason or another by granting exclusive franchises to selected firms. We need to know the over-all economic costs of granting such monopoly power, including possible inefficiencies and distribution inequalities, before we can decide if the long-term social benefits received from research and development activities and franchises outweigh the disadvantages.

THE THEORY OF PURE MONOPOLY

We retain for the time being the assumption of the previous chapter that the firm's basic objective is to maximize profits. Later in the chapter, we will consider the effects on monopoly behavior of goals other than profit maximization, such as sales maximization and risk minimization. But first we will develop the standard monopoly model of profit maximization.

The monopolist's profits (PR) are defined as the difference between his total revenue (TR) and total cost (TC), or

$$PR = TR - TC,$$

and like the competitive firm, TR and TC are functions of the monopolist's output level. Just as was true for the competitive firm, we can determine the profit-maximizing (or loss-minimizing) level of output for the monopoly firm in two ways: The total revenue–total cost approach and the marginal revenue–marginal cost approach. We will describe the total revenue–total cost approach first, beginning with an analysis of the monopolist's revenue curves.

Short-Run Monopoly Behavior

The Monopolist's Revenue Curves. As sole supplier, a monopolist faces the industry or market demand curve for his output. The industry demand curve will generally be downward sloping, which means that if the monopolist wants to sell more units of output, he must reduce his price, and conversely, if he raises his price, he must expect to sell a smaller quantity. This introduces a new dimension to the firm's decision-making since it must decide upon a price–output policy, in contrast to the competitive firm, which must decide upon an output policy alone.

A set of hypothetical revenue functions for a monopolist producing the single product, X, is shown in Figure 8–1. The monopolist's demand curve, $D = AR$, in panel (a), indicates the maximum price (or average revenue) which the monopolist can charge at each level of output and is, of course, industry demand. It is assumed linear for simplicity. The curve in panel (b), (TR), indicates the total revenue which the monopolist will receive at each level of output, computed by multiplying price times quantity. For instance, at 3 units of output, total revenue equals price, $80, times quantity, 3 units, or $240. Notice that the distance from point c to point b in panel (b), which is total revenue at an output of 3 units, equals the area of the included rectangle $OTSR$ in panel (a).

The firm's marginal revenue curve, MR, in panel (a) of Figure 8–1, indicates the rate of change of total revenue with respect to output. Using mathematical symbols:

$$MR = \Delta TR/\Delta X.$$

When AR is downsloping, MR is everywhere below AR (except for price–output combinations very close to the vertical axis). The explanation is simple: To sell an additional unit of X, the monopolist must lower price enough to induce some customer to buy that extra unit, and the sale of this extra unit produces a revenue-increasing effect equal to its sale price. But the lower price will, in the absence of price discrimination, apply to *all* the monopolist's customers and *all* units sold. The monopolist will receive a reduced price on all of the previous units sold, and this will result in a revenue-decreasing effect. The result must be an addition to total revenue that is less than average revenue. For example, suppose a telephone company receives $1.50 per 3-minute, long-distance call between city A and city B. At this price, 20,000 calls are made weekly. Assume that if it drops its price to $1.00, the number of weekly calls jumps to 30,000. An extra 10,000 calls at $1.00 each produces a revenue-*increasing* effect of $10,000. But the 20,000 calls previously priced at $1.50 are now priced at $1.00, which produces a revenue-*decreasing* effect of $.50 times 20,000 or $10,000. Summing the two effects, we find that MR is zero; i.e., $MR = \Delta TR/\Delta X = (\$30,000 - 30,000)/10,000 = 0$. Remember, too, that a marginal function will always lie below its corresponding average function, when the latter is declining.

The total and marginal revenue curves associated with any straight-line demand curve with positive vertical and horizontal intercepts have several im-

324 A Theory of Producer Behavior

FIGURE 8–1 The Relationship of a Monopolist's AR, MR, and TR Schedules to Price Elasticity of Demand

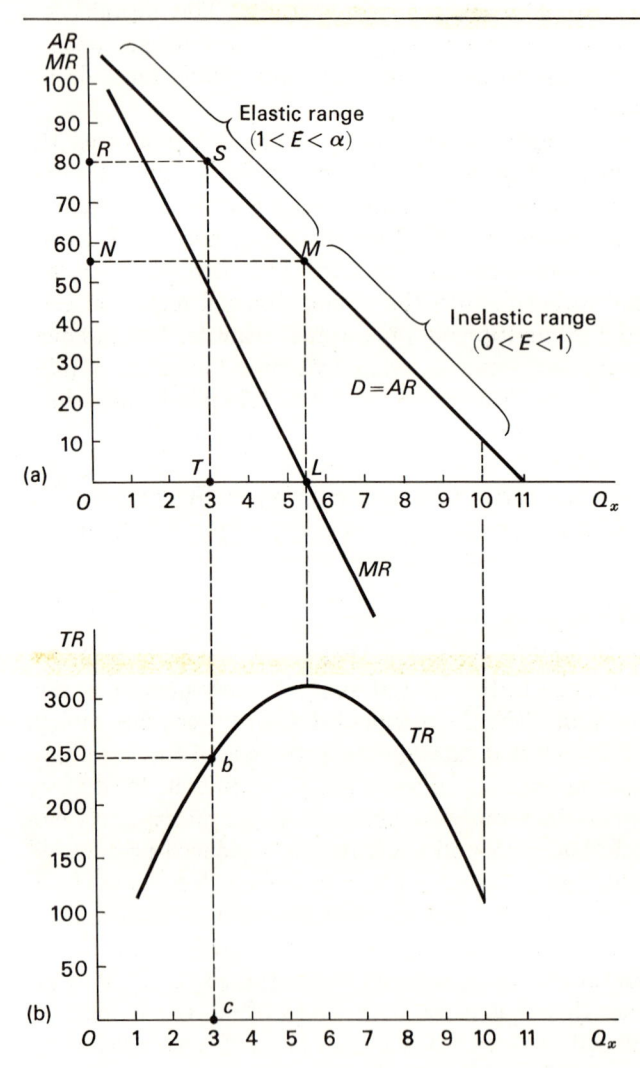

portant characteristics, which were initially described in Chapter 4. Referring to the revenue curves in Figure 8–1, it is well to briefly review these characteristics:

> 1. The demand curve is *elastic* for the range of price–output combinations along D, above point M. Consequently, as price decreases

along the upper half of the demand curve, TR increases, and as price increases, TR decreases. Marginal revenue, MR, is positive (though decreasing) throughout the elastic upper portion of the demand curve.
2. The demand curve is *inelastic* for the range of price–output combinations below point M. Total revenue decreases with price decreases in this range of the demand curve and, conversely, TR increases with price increases. Marginal revenue is negative throughout this range.
3. The demand curve is of *unitary* elasticity at output level OL (5.5 units), which is midway between the vertical axis and the horizontal intercept of the demand curve. A perpendicular line drawn through the midpoint of the demand curve at point M intersects TR at its peak and intersects MR at its zero value.

From revenue information alone, we may conclude that the profit-maximizing monopolist will not operate along the inelastic portion of the demand curve, since marginal revenue is negative and total revenue is declining for price–output combinations in this range. Even if his costs of operation were zero, the monopolist would not set a price lower than ON.

The Monopolist's Short-Run Cost Curves. The monopolist's costs of production will be governed by the same principles that determine the cost curves for competitive firms; therefore, the monopolist's short-run total cost curve will quite possibly have the same inverted-S shape as that of the competitive firm. In any case, the monopolist's short-run cost curves will be subject to the law of diminishing returns, which dictates that in the short run, marginal cost must eventually rise. The cost curves of the monopoly firm and the competitive firm are therefore similar and need not be contrasted, as was true of their revenue curves. It is the differing characteristics of their respective revenue curves which distinguish the two.

Total Costs and Total Revenues. Given the monopolist's total cost and total revenue curves, we can determine his profit-maximizing output level and price by combining the two in one graph, as shown in Figure 8–2. TR and TC are equal at the two breakeven or zero profit points, a and b. Monopoly profit is negative to the left of a and to the right of b. Between points a and b are included all the output levels resulting in positive profits. To maximize profit, the monopolist must determine the one price–output combination within this range for which TR exceeds TC by the greatest amount. In the last chapter, we found that if the vertical distance between TR and TC is at a maximum at a given output level, then the slope of TR equals the slope of TC. Referring to Figure 8–2, line L_r, drawn tangent to total revenue at point e (output level X_1) is parallel to line L_c drawn tangent to the total cost curve at

FIGURE 8–2 Determining the Short-Run Profit-Maximizing Output of a Monopolist (TC–TR Approach)

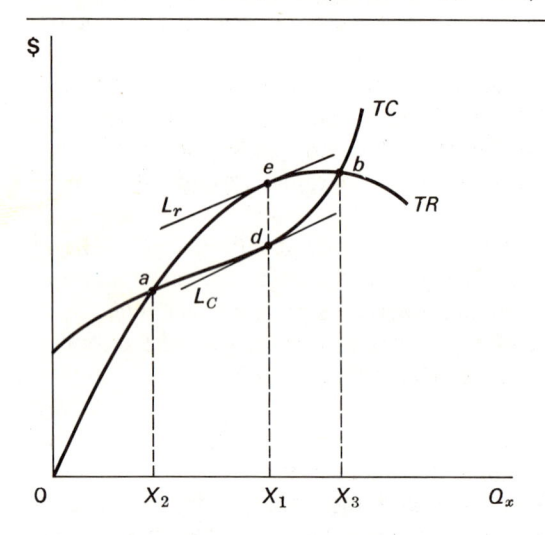

point d. The equality of the slopes of L_r and L_c means, of course, that the slopes of TR at e and TC at d are equal. Total profit at output X_1, $(X_1e - X_1d)$, is therefore at a maximum.

The Marginal Revenue–Marginal Cost Approach. Since the slope of TR in Figure 8–2 is equal to marginal revenue, MR, and the slope of TC is equal to marginal cost, MC, a necessary condition for profit maximization for the monopoly firm is

$$MC = MR,$$

just as was true for a competitive firm. The profit-maximizing behavior of the monopolist can be described, therefore, using unit cost and unit revenue data rather than total cost and total revenue schedules. To illustrate, we have drawn in Figure 8–3 a monopolist's unit cost and revenue curves, including the MR and MC curves. The profit-maximizing output level is indicated by the point of intersection of MC and MR at point e.[1] The short-run, profit-maximizing output is therefore X_1 and the profit-maximizing price, P_1. The firm's profit per unit of output at X_1 is the difference between average revenue and average cost at that output, which is the distance ba. Profit per unit, ba, multiplied by the number of units produced and sold, X_1, equals total profits,

---

[1] Where there are multiple intersection points of MC and MR, the firm will compare the profits at each and choose the output–price combination associated with the largest profit. We will discuss in Chapter 9 the technique for finding maximum profit output if there are no intersection points of MC and MR.

FIGURE 8–3 The Short-Run Profit-Maximizing Output and Price ($MC = MR$ Approach)

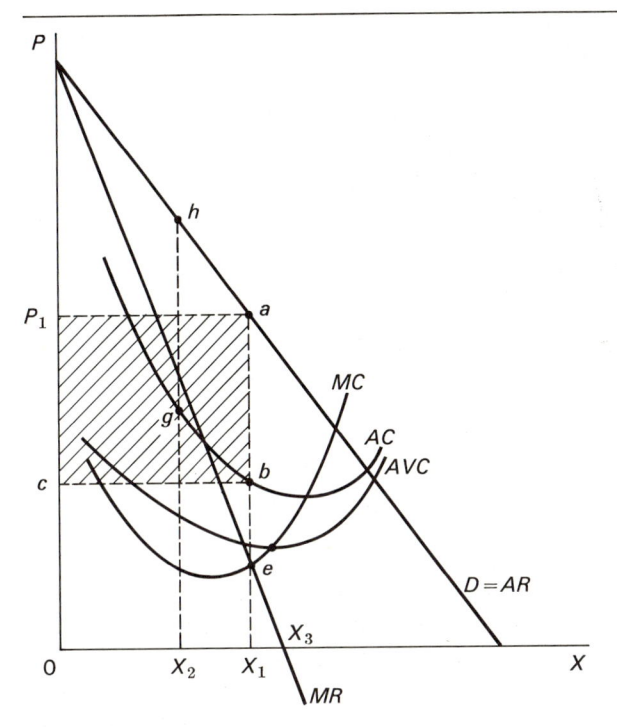

the area of shaded rectangle P_1abc. Notice that profit per unit at X_1, ba, is not at a maximum (profit per unit at X_2, gh, is greater) though *total* profits are maximized at X_2.

We may use the short-run monopoly model just developed to investigate the common but unfounded belief that monopolists always realize profits. In fact, a monopolist may realize short-run losses, and we will investigate in the appendix of this chapter the behavior of the Chesapeake Bay Bridge and Tunnel Commission, which has incurred losses since its formation. To demonstrate short-run losses, suppose a monopolist has been operating in a declining industry for which market demand has shifted so far to the left that average revenue is less than average cost at every output level. The case is illustrated in Figure 8–4. Since AC is above AR at every output, the firm cannot possibly realize an economic profit or break even under these market conditions. The firm will, nevertheless, seek to make the best possible adjustment to the market circumstances, which, in this case, means to minimize losses. To determine the loss-minimizing price–output combination, the firm will first determine the output for which MC equals MR. Referring to Figure 8–4, $MC = MR$ at point b and output X_1. The total loss incurred from operating at this output

FIGURE 8-4 Short-Run Loss Minimization

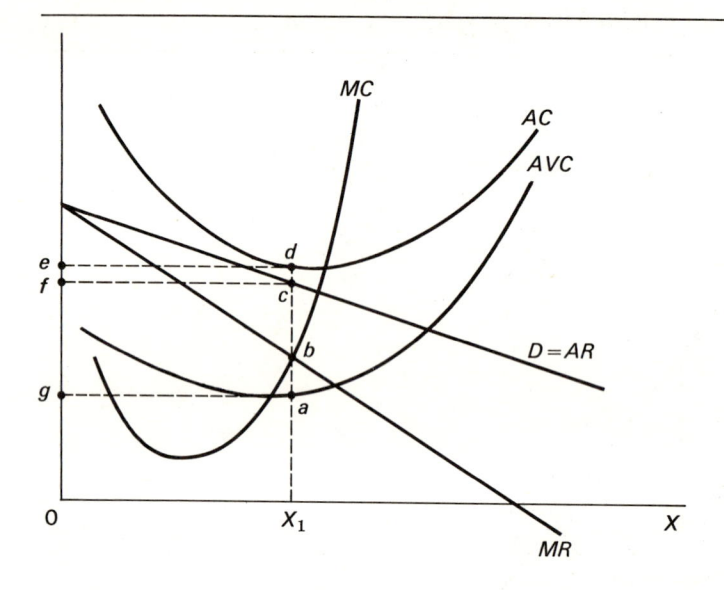

level is cd, the loss per unit, times X_1, the number of units produced, or the area of rectangle $edcf$. The firm should produce the output level indicated by the $MC = MR$ rule if this loss is smaller than the loss incurred if it ceases production. Since at any output the distance between AC and AVC is AFC at that output, ad is average fixed cost at output X_1. If ad is multiplied by X_1, the result is total fixed cost. Therefore, the area of rectangle $adeg$ measures total fixed cost, the firm's loss if it produced zero units. By inspection, area $edcf$ is less than area $adeg$, so the firm minimizes losses by producing X_1 units in the short run.

In general, to minimize losses, the firm compares AVC with AR at the output for which $MC = MR$. If AR exceeds AVC, the firm would minimize losses by producing. If AVC exceeds AR, the firm should cease production. The basic criterion is that *variable costs must be completely covered by revenues* if the firm is to produce a positive output in the short run. The amount of the fixed cost does not influence the firm's short-run decision-making.

Long-Run Monopoly Behavior

Given sufficient time, the monopolist, as well as the competitive firm, will make the best possible long-run adjustment to the market situation it faces. Unlike the competitive firm, however, the revenue curves facing the monopolist may remain relatively stable in the long run, so long as the entry of potential rivals is blocked. The monopolist would therefore maximize profits in the long run by equating LRMC with MR. To illustrate, refer to Figure 8-5,

FIGURE 8-5 Determining Long-Run Price and Output under Monopoly

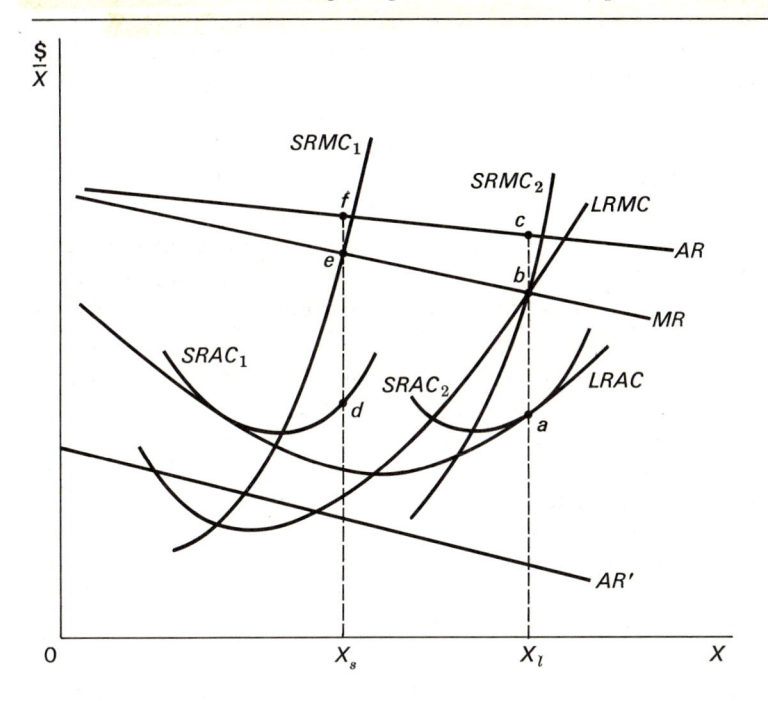

and assume initially that the firm is maximizing short-run profits by equating $SRMC_1$ with MR at point e and output X_s. Total profits are equal to profit per unit, df, multiplied by X_s, the number of units produced. However df times X_s is not the maximum *long-run* profits, because at output X_s, MR is in excess of LRMC. *Maximization of short-run profits does not imply maximization of long-run profits.* The monopolist would expand output in the long run to X_L, determined by the intersection of LRMC with MR at point b. At the new output level, total profits are equal to profit per unit, ac, multiplied by X_L. This is the maximum profit possible, given that the monopolist has enough time to vary all inputs. Notice that maximization of long-run profits *does* imply maximization of short-run profits. To demonstrate this, we have drawn in the short-run cost curves, $SRAC_2$ and $SRMC_2$, associated with point a on the LRAC curve. $SRMC_2$ intersects MR at point b, just as LRMC does, indicating X_L is not only the long-run, profit-maximizing output but also the short-run, profit-maximizing output for the new, larger plant.

A monopolist will leave the industry if AR is below LRAC at all output levels. For instance, referring to Figure 8-5, if the monopolist with cost curves LRAC and LRMC faced the average revenue schedule AR', he would exit the industry in the long run rather than produce at a loss. A possible exception to this conclusion will be discussed later in the chapter, when we consider price discrimination.

To summarize, a monopolist, like a pure competitor, will drop out of an industry in the long run if AR is less than LRAC at every output level. However, unlike the pure competitor, the monopolist may earn profits indefinitely if market demand is stable or increasing, and the firm successfully blocks other firms from entering the industry.

So far we have presented a theory of monopoly behavior, but have not explored the ways in which monopolies come into existence. There are several possible explanations. For one, a firm might be the first and only firm to establish a new industry. The formation of Comsat is a recent example. The first firm in an industry would enjoy the advantage of the innovator, an advantage which might be long lasting or transitory. On the other hand, the last firm in a declining industry, e.g., the last quill pen manufacturer or the last windmill manufacturer, might come to hold a monopoly. As another possibility, a monopoly firm might own the only source of one or more raw materials needed to manufacture a product, giving it the power to block the entry of potential rivals, or the firm may own patent rights to the manufacturing process, which allow it to accomplish the same result. The Aluminum Company of America held a monopoly before World War II, largely because it obtained a patent on the electrolytic process of manufacturing aluminum. And, as we have already noted, monopoly may exist by public decree, as in the case of one or more of the major airlines receiving exclusive franchises to carry passenger traffic between two cities.

Finally, the existence of significant economies of scale might mean that only one firm can efficiently supply a market. Such situations are often described by economists as "natural monopolies," a phenomenon we explore at greater length below.

Natural Monopolies

A *natural monopoly* exists in an industry when a single firm can produce enough output to supply the entire market at a lower unit cost than two or more firms. One firm may realize such scale economies that it can produce the market's requirements at an average cost less than could two firms operating smaller scale processes. Most of our natural monopolies occur in transportation, communications, and the utilities industries such as water, electrical power, and the like.

Because of the scale economies involved in providing phone services, the telephone industry is often cited as a prime example of a natural monopoly. Competition in the telephone industry is deemed socially undesirable because of the inefficiencies associated with many small-scale producers: a large number of firms would almost certainly result in needless duplication of capital equipment. If a large number of firms provide phone services in a given market, there arise monumental problems of connecting up every subscriber to every other subscriber. There would always be an incentive for competing firms to merge because of the efficiencies involved in combining subscription lists. For this reason, competition in such an industry would be unstable, for there would be a tendency for competition to be replaced by oligopoly or monopoly. Mexico City at one time experimented with a degree of competition in its telephone industry. The city had two rival telephone companies whose lines did not interconnect. As a consequence, an individual needed two phones to call others who subscribed to only one service, since some subscribed to the first and others to the second, only. The cost of telephone service was, of course, increased by having to subscribe to two phone companies. To this day, one answers the telephone in Mexico City with a loud *bueno*, not signifying "good morning" or "good evening" but "good connection."

Regulated Enterprise—Public Utilities

The traditional approach of public policy to the "natural monopolies" has been to grant an exclusive franchise to one firm, on the one hand, but to closely regulate its price–output policies on the other. Such regulated enterprises are known as "public utilities," though the term defies precise definition, since all firms provide utility to the public and, except for partnerships and proprietorships, receive their charters from state or national government agencies. Attempts to define a completely acceptable set of specifications for public utilities ultimately break down or degenerate into mere lists of the types of firms which have historically been treated as public utilities. Although we cannot unequivocally establish specifications for designating public utilities, we can use the basic monopoly model developed in this chapter to assess the effects of rate regulation on the behavior of firms so designated.

Suppose a monopolist faces the market demand curve, $P_M CD$, and the associated marginal revenue curve, $P_M EMR$, in Figure 8–6. Now suppose a ceiling price of P_c is imposed by the regulatory authority. What effect does this have on the firm's revenue curves? Since prices above P_c are prohibited, the dashed portions of the market demand and marginal revenue curves, $P_M C$ and $P_M E$, respectively, are now inappropriate. The firm's effective average revenue curve *after the ceiling is imposed* is $P_c CD$. The firm can sell between zero and Q_c units of output at the ceiling price, but if it wishes to sell more, price must be dropped below the ceiling, along segment CD. The effect of the ceiling is to produce a kink in the monopolist's average revenue curve at point C, which in turn means the marginal revenue curve will be composed of two segments. For output levels less than Q_c, marginal revenue is constant and equal to average revenue, so for outputs up to Q_c, marginal revenue is line segment $P_c C$. For output levels greater than Q_c, marginal revenue is the line segment EMR, which is derived from the market demand schedule for levels of output beyond Q_c. Marginal revenue can be readily determined for output levels above and below Q_c, but not at Q_c; it is said to be discontinuous at Q_c.

If the monopolist's marginal cost curve intersects the left-hand section of

FIGURE 8–6 Determining the Effects of a Price Ceiling on Monopoly Behavior

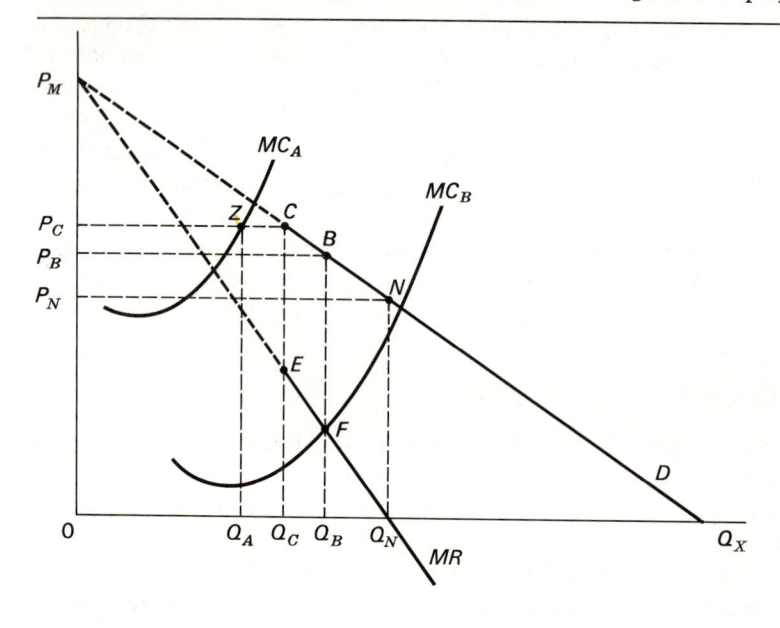

marginal revenue, the firm will maximize profits by producing the quantity indicated at the ceiling price. For instance, if marginal cost is MC_a, the firm would equate MC and MR at point Z and produce and sell Q_a units at the ceiling price, P_c. We assume that producing Q_a is more profitable, or entails smaller losses, than ceasing production. Notice that with marginal cost MC_a, the monopolist supplies only Q_a units, though Q_c units are demanded at the ceiling price; there is an excess demand of $Q_c - Q_a$ units. Some buyers will be unable to satisfy their purchase requirements at price P_c, which means the Q_a units produced will likely be rationed on some non-price basis, perhaps first come–first served. As an example, a few years back, misguided Brazilian policy prescribed very low ceiling rates for telephone service. As a result there was a very large excess demand for phone service, with no efficient method of rationing the service. A customer might wait years for installation of a phone and then wait an hour or more for a dial tone.

If the firm's marginal cost curve were MC_b and the ceiling price P_c, it would maximize profits by producing output Q_b at price P_b, indicated by the intersection of marginal cost and marginal revenue at point F. The ceiling price in this case is ineffective.

Even if the regulatory authority has accurate information regarding a monopolist's cost and revenue functions, the task of determining a price ceiling which will bring about a socially optimal performance is formidable. To illustrate, AR in Figure 8–7 is assumed to be the market demand for a monopolist's product and MR the corresponding marginal revenue curve. If

FIGURE 8-7 Comparing Alternative Ceilings on Monopoly Behavior

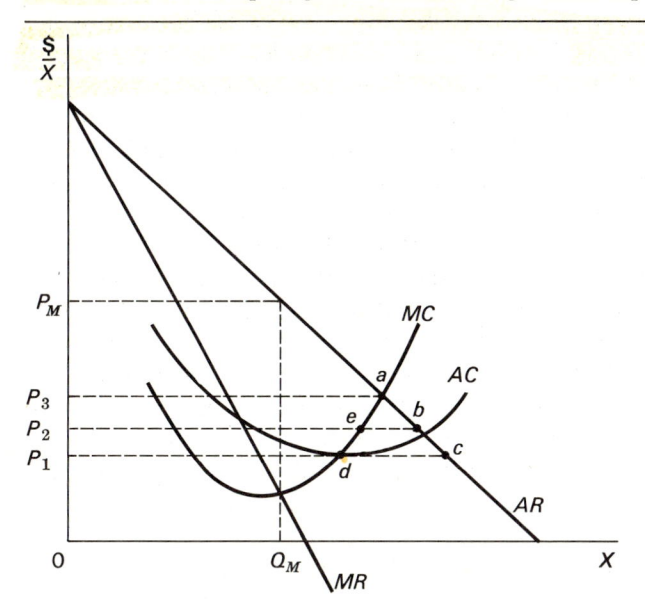

unregulated, the monopolist will set price P_M and produce output Q_M to maximize profits. Now let us consider the possible ceiling prices which a regulatory body might establish. A ceiling price of P_3 would cause the monopolist to produce at the price–output combination shown by point a. This combination has two desirable features: (1) the monopolist will equate MC with AR, and (2) there is no excess demand. However, since average revenue at ceiling price P_3 is above average cost, the monopolist would realize an economic profit. Now let us consider ceiling price P_1, which would cause the monopolist to produce at the price–output combination, point d. This combination has the desirable feature that economic profits are zero, and MC and price are equal. However, since the firm would produce only $P_1 d$ units at price P_1, whereas the quantity demanded is $P_1 c$, there is an excess demand for the product of dc. Some consumers are unable to buy the product, even though they are ready and willing to pay the ceiling price. There will have to be some nonmarket, perhaps arbitrary, allocation of the monopolist's output, analogous to the problem in the Brazilian telephone industry. As a final illustration, a ceiling price set at P_2 eliminates some excess demand; however, it would result in some positive profits. We may summarize by saying that it is often impossible to set a ceiling price which is optimal on all counts, one giving a result comparable to long-run equilibrium in a competitive industry.

We have seen that there are difficulties in setting price ceilings when information is complete. The job of the regulatory authority is compounded when information is incomplete.

Typically, public regulatory commissions set ceiling prices to allow a monopolist a "normal" return on his capital, where the capital invested in the firm is called the *rate base*. A ceiling price is set which will result in just enough revenue to cover operating costs and provide a normal return on the monopolist's capital. Referring to Figure 8–7, the ceiling price might be set at P_1, which would allow the firm to just cover its costs, which include the opportunity cost of the capital invested in the firm. Considerable difficulties arise, however, in determining what constitutes a normal return for capital invested in an activity that is monopolized. Without this information, we cannot ascertain the shape and position of the AC curve of the monopolist and the ceiling price which reduces economic profits to zero. Since the firm is a monopoly, there are no other firms that can be used as a guide to determine the monopolist's cost of capital. Often a comparison is made between the rate currently earned by the regulated firm and the earnings of unregulated firms in similar industries. But since regulated firms have a protected market, such a comparison is not really valid. Presumably, protected monopoly firms should not expect to realize a return as great as an unprotected firm facing greater markets risks.

Additional difficulties arise in determining the rate base or capitalization of a firm. Since a regulated monopolist can maximize his over-all dollar return by maximizing the size of the rate base, there will be a tendency to overstate his capital investment. There are many ways to accomplish this. For instance, some expenditures, like those for research and development, might be counted as either current costs or investment. The firm might find it to its advantage to capitalize such expenditures. In addition, there is the problem of determining the value of capital goods. Do you value machinery at its purchase price or at its replacement cost? To the extent that resource substitution is possible, a tendency may exist for regulated firms to employ more capital and less labor and raw materials than they would if unregulated. There exists also an unfortunate tendency for some regulated firms to overstate the size of their capital plant by such devices as identifying old, outmoded equipment as "standby capacity" and carrying it on their books rather than just scrapping it. Also, the firm might even find it advantageous to pay higher prices for newly purchased equipment. To the extent that such devices convince regulatory commissions that the firm's AC curve is higher than it might be, they result in higher ceiling prices for consumers and disguised economic profits for the monopolist.

Price Discrimination

Price discrimination exists when a seller sells the same product to different buyers at different prices or to a single buyer at different prices for successive units purchased. For example, a monopolist practices price discrimination if he sells at a higher price in one market than in another. Price discrimination can only be practiced by a seller with a degree of monopoly power, because in perfectly competitive markets all units of the same commodity sell for one price. An attempt by a competitive firm to obtain a higher price from certain buyers will fail because these buyers can easily obtain the product from another firm at the market price. Therefore, price discrimination is properly considered in conjunction with monopoly, although a firm does not have to be a pure monopolist to practice price discrimination. In addition, effective price discrimination requires that the firm be able to divide its market into separate segments. Otherwise, resale among buyers (arbitrage) and "crossing over" between markets would eliminate the price difference. In some cases, market segregation exists because the product cannot be resold, for example, medical services. Also, legal and geographical barriers may permit price discrimination. For example, price discrimination among customers in different countries is often possible because of import–export policies which prevent international arbitrage.

First- and Second-Degree Price Discrimination. First-degree or perfect price discrimination exists when a seller can sell each successive unit of his output for the maximum price which that unit of output will fetch, assuming the seller can deal in isolation with the buyer of that unit and force him to pay the maximum price he is willing and able to pay. To illustrate, suppose the step function, D, in Figure 8–8 is the demand curve a monopolist faces in the

FIGURE 8–8   The Derivation of MR (Assuming Perfect Price Discrimination)

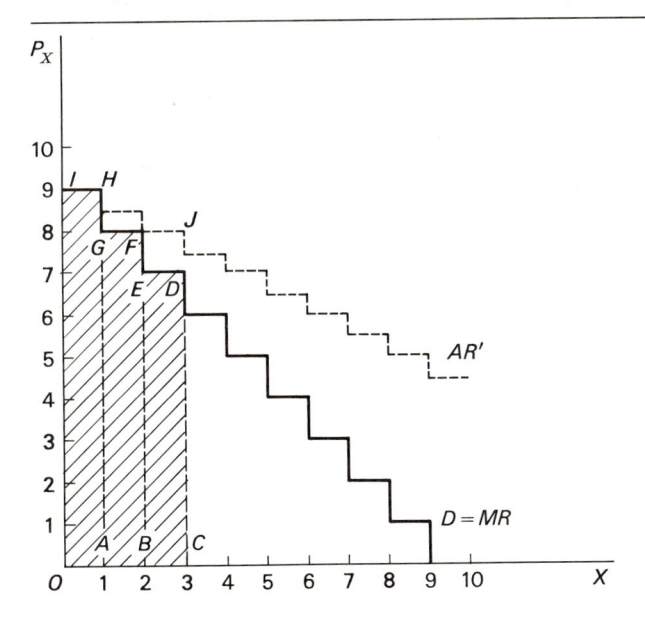

output market, and assume the monopolist is able to practice perfect price discrimination as he sells successive units of X. The first unit would be sold for $9 to one of the monopolist's customers, increasing the firm's total revenue from zero to $9. The second unit would then be sold for $8, either to the same or a different customer, all the while the first unit continues to sell for $9. This second unit adds $8 to total revenue. A third unit would be sold for $7, raising total revenue to $24. The monopolist's total revenue for 3 units is found by summing the three narrow, shaded rectangles, OAHI, ABFG, and BCDE. Notice that if we plot the firm's marginal revenue generated with successive unit sales, we get an MR curve which lies right on the firm's demand curve. Marginal revenue does not fall as it otherwise would, because the firm can sell marginal units of output without dropping the price on all previous units sold. Thus, perfect price discrimination means the firm's demand and marginal revenue curves are the same.

With the sale of 3 units of X, the firm realizes total revenue equal to $24. Its revenue per unit sold is, therefore, $24/3 or $8, plotted above the demand schedule in Figure 8–8 as a horizontal dotted line from point F to J. Notice that this is not the average revenue for each of the three units sold. The first unit sells for more and the third sells for less; the $8 is simply TR/X. If we plot TR/X for every output level, we will generate the dashed curve AR', which is the firm's average revenue curve. AR' is revenue per unit, while D is the price which can be charged for the marginal unit sold. The two curves diverge given price discrimination, but are identical in its absence.

In Figure 8–9, we have drawn a linear demand curve, D, equal to MR for a firm assuming it is a perfect price discriminator. The difference between the revenue curves in Figure 8–8 and the ones in Figure 8–9 is that the latter assume complete divisibility of price and quantity. The profit-maximizing monopolist will equate MC and D = MR at point B and OA units of X. The price of the last unit sold is AB, and revenue per unit is AD. The firm's cost curves are AC and MC. Total revenue, area OADF, less total cost, area OACE, equals total profit, area ECDF. Note that total revenue could also be measured by the area of trapezoid OABG.

Suppose for a moment the monopolist produced OA units for sale *without discrimination*. He would obtain price AB for each, and his total revenue would be equal to area OABH. Consumers would enjoy a consumer surplus equal to the area of triangle HBG. On the other hand, if he is able to discriminate perfectly, as we assumed above, then the firm would obtain with the same unit sales, total revenue equal to area OABG, which is greater by the amount HBG. The shaded area HBG is the consumer surplus the monopolist captures by discriminating, and represents a distribution of income favorable to the firm and unfavorable to consumers.

Assuming for a moment that the monopolist could not discriminate on price and that his long-run average cost curve in Figure 8–9 was AC' rather than AC, he would choose to shut down rather than operate at a loss, since

FIGURE 8–9 The Profit-Maximizing Output of a Monopolist: Degree Price Discrimination

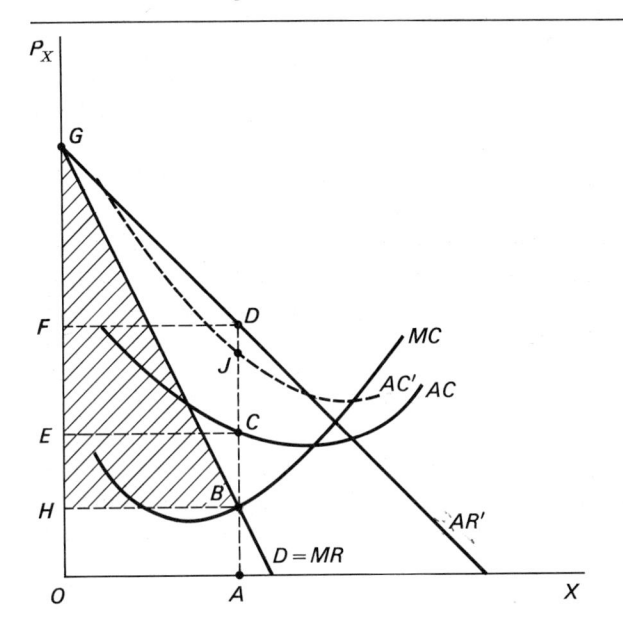

AC' is above D at all outputs. However, if he could practice first-degree price discrimination, his average revenue curve would become AR' and the firm would realize maximum profits at an output of OA units. In this case, the existence of first-degree price discrimination results in a positive output which would not be forthcoming without discrimination.

First-degree price discrimination is unlikely to exist in the real world for several reasons: (1) There is no practical way to determine the maximum price obtainable from each buyer for each unit of a commodity he purchases. (2) Arbitrage between buyers, where possible, will help prevent price discrimination. (3) Even where arbitrage is not possible, the seller will find it difficult to discriminate in the price charged for different units sold to the same buyer. (4) Finally, prices cannot realistically be set with infinitely small differences between them as is required for perfect discrimination. For all of these reasons, perfect price discrimination is useful principally as a model of the upper limit to price discrimination. This does not mean that price discrimination does not exist. It does, but it likely will take different forms. For example, a monopolist might sell to a customer the first 10 units of a product at one price, the next 10 at a lower price, and all additional units at a still lower price. Such discrimination is called *second-degree* price discrimination, since the firm captures some, but not all, of the consumer's surplus.

On the other hand, price discrimination might take the form of separate prices charged for the same commodity in say, two distinct market segments, called *third-degree* price discrimination. For example, a department store might sell the same product for $10 in its upstairs career shop and for $6.98 in its bargain basement; or an accountant may charge a high fee for preparing a wealthy client's tax return and a low fee for a poor client. As another illustration, in 1953, Champion Spark Plugs was charged by the Federal Trade Commission with (third-degree) price discrimination. Champion was selling spark plugs for 6 cents for new car use and for 21 cents and 31 cents for replacement use. This extreme price differential could hardly be explained by marketing economies alone.[2]

Third-Degree Price Discrimination. Third-degree price discrimination may be practiced either with homogeneous products, as in the case of an agricultural product sold in two or more countries, or with nonhomogeneous products, as in the case of first-class versus tourist travel on the same airplane. In the latter illustration, we would test for price discrimination by seeing if the price difference is or is not a reflection of the relative marginal costs of producing the closely similar products. To simplify our model of price discrimination, we will assume a homogeneous product that is sold in two separate markets which are isolated from each other so that arbitrage is impossible. D_1 and MR_1 in Figure 8–10 are the respective demand and marginal revenue

FIGURE 8–10 Third-Degree Price Discrimination: Two Separate Markets

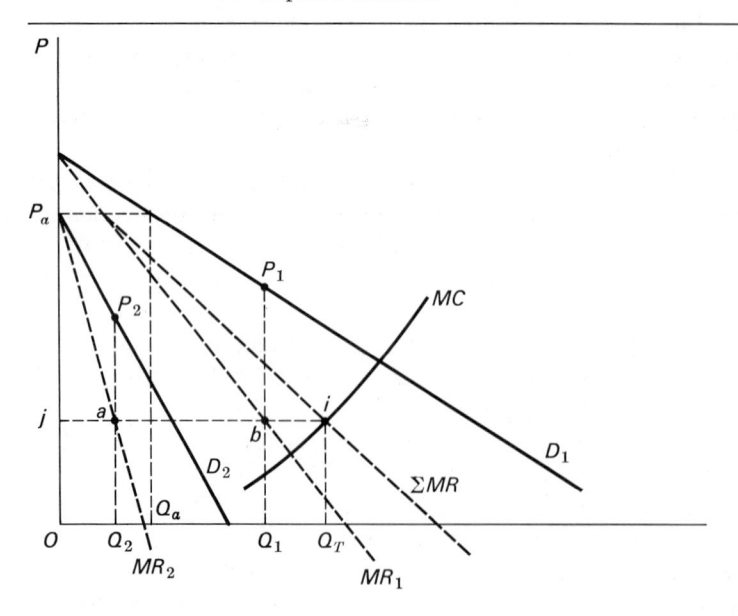

[2] Walter Adams, *The Structure of American Industry*, 3d ed. New York: The Macmillan Company, 1965, 352.

curves for sector 1; and D_2 and MR_2 are the respective demand and marginal revenue schedules for sector 2. MC needs no special explanation; it is simply the firm's marginal cost curve. However, the ΣMR schedule does require explanation. We will show in the next paragraph that we can derive the firm's appropriate marginal revenue schedule for profit maximization by horizontally summing the two separate MR schedules.

The profit-maximizing monopolist will always sell a marginal unit of his output in that market which brings in the largest increment to his total revenue. Referring to Figure 8–10, if the firm's unit sales are to be very small, the firm will sell in market 1 only, since MR is initially higher in market 1 than in 2. For a larger level of unit sales, however, the firm will sell in both markets. When selling in both markets, the firm will always allocate its unit sales so as to equate the marginal revenue it derives in one market with the marginal revenue it derives in the other. If $MR_1 > MR_2$, for any level of unit sales, the firm will reallocate output from market 2 to 1 because total revenue will increase thereby. Since marginal revenue must be identical in the two markets for any level of unit sales, the appropriate MR curve for decision-making purposes is obtained by summing horizontally the two separate MR's.

The profit-maximizing output of the price discriminator is determined by equating ΣMR with MC, which occurs at point i and output Q_T in Figure 8–10. To determine the number of units to sell in each market, we must find the level of unit sales in each market for which marginal revenue equals the value of ΣMR at the equilibrium point i. A horizontal line, ij, is drawn leftward from the point of intersection of MC and ΣMR to the vertical axis. Point a, where line ij crosses MR_2, determines the profit-maximizing price and quantity for the second market, and point b, where ij intersects MR_1, determines the price–quantity combination appropriate for market 1. The prices to charge in the two markets are P_2 and P_1, respectively. Finally, the sum of Q_1, the quantity sold in market 1, and Q_2, the quantity sold in market 2, equals Q_T, the profit-maximizing output of the firm. By charging different prices in the two markets, the firm realizes total profits which are greater than those it would realize if it charged one price to all.

If it should develop that D_1 and D_2 exhibited identical price elasticities, profit maximization would indicate that P_1 should equal P_2, and price discrimination would not improve the firm's profits. So an additional requirement for price discrimination is that the demand curves in the separate markets have different coefficients of elasticity.

NONPROFIT-MAXIMIZING BEHAVIOR

One of the most significant developments in American business in the twentieth century has been the separation of ownership and control in large corporations. Today, control over large incorporated enterprises is typically vested in an elite corps of professional managers who may own little or none of the stock of the firms they manage. Presumably, the managers are hired to manage the firm so as to achieve the goals of the stockholders, the owners. Stockholders will likely seek maximum profits or maximum capital appreciation or, perhaps, some combination of both. But often the stock of the firm is so diversified among owners that they are rendered impotent. In such cases, the stockholders exercise only nominal control over management, leaving managers considerable leeway to pursue their own goals. Under these circumstances, managers' goals may conflict with stockholders' goals. Our purpose in this section is to suggest the possible effects of this development on the objective function of corporate enterprise and show how the analytical tools we have developed may be used to study firm behavior, assuming other than profit-maximizing goals.

We may presume that the principal goals of professional managers will include the maximization of their own remuneration and maximum security from dismissal or loss of power. Since managers will receive only a small portion of the profits they generate if their ownership share is small, they may have little incentive to maximize the profits of the firm. And where stockholders exercise little or no control over the management of "their" firms, they may not succeed in persuading the corps of hired managers that maximum profits constitute the most desirable goal. Professional managers may conclude that their salaries and other forms of remuneration, as well as their personal security, are more closely tied to company size and growth rates than to profits and may favor a price policy which maximizes the firm's sales and a dividend policy which plows back the earnings of the firm into new capital investment.

Up to now, we have assumed that the single goal of both competitive and monopolistic firms is profit maximization and that the firm sets its short-run and long-run price and output policies accordingly. The separation of ownership and control in large corporations suggests, however, that the objective function of these firms may be much more complex then we first assumed. Profit maximization may be only one such goal and possibly not the most important one to the firm at that. Our task now is to investigate firm behavior assuming nonprofit-maximizing goals. As an illustration of the flexibility of our models, we will first consider the behavior of a monopolist who seeks some optimal combination of both *high profits and large sales volume*.

The Maximization of Sales and Profits

As a first step in constructing a profits–sales maximization model, we must determine the combinations of profits and dollar sales which can be achieved, given the nature of the firm's demand and its production costs. The TR and TC curves for our hypothetical monopolist, as well as his total profit curve, PR, are presented in panels (a) and (b) of Figure 8–11. The firm's break-

Monopoly 341

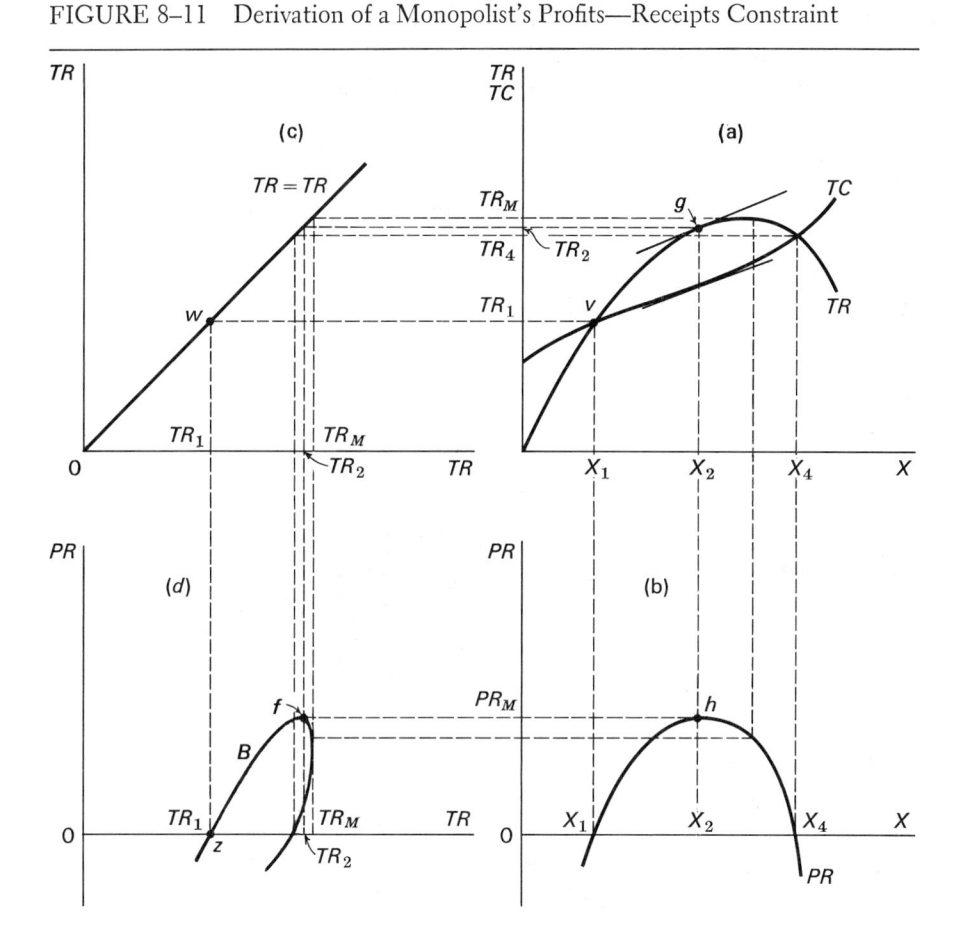

FIGURE 8-11 Derivation of a Monopolist's Profits—Receipts Constraint

even points occur at outputs X_1 and X_4, and positive profits are realized between these two output levels. Maximum profits occur at X_2 units of output. To develop a relationship between profits and levels of total receipts, we make use of panels (c) and (d). Notice that at output level X_1 in panel (a), total receipts are TR_1 and in panel (b), that profits are zero. Now follow the horizontal dashed line from point v in panel (a) over to the $TR = TR$ line in panel (c) (point w) down to point z in panel (d). From panel (b) we know that profits are zero at X_1, and from panel (a) that receipts are TR_1. Point z in panel (d) indicates, therefore, the combination of zero profits and total receipts of TR_1. At the profit-maximizing output, X_2, total receipts equal TR_2. Following the horizontal dotted line from point g in panel (a) over to the $TR = TR$ line, then down to point f in panel (d), we get the combination of total receipts, TR_2, and maximum profits, PR_M. Notice that another dotted line has been drawn from the peak of PR in panel (b), point h, to point f in panel (d), to give the value of profits corresponding to TR_2. If this procedure is repeated for all possible combinations of profit and total receipts we will generate the curve labeled B in panel (d) of Figure 8–11. This curve discloses all combinations of total sales and profits which management can achieve, given the demand curve for its product and the cost curves of the firm.

To show curve B more clearly and to complete our model, we have reproduced it, using an expanded scale, in Figure 8–12.

FIGURE 8–12 Determining Management's Optimum Combination of Revenues and Profits

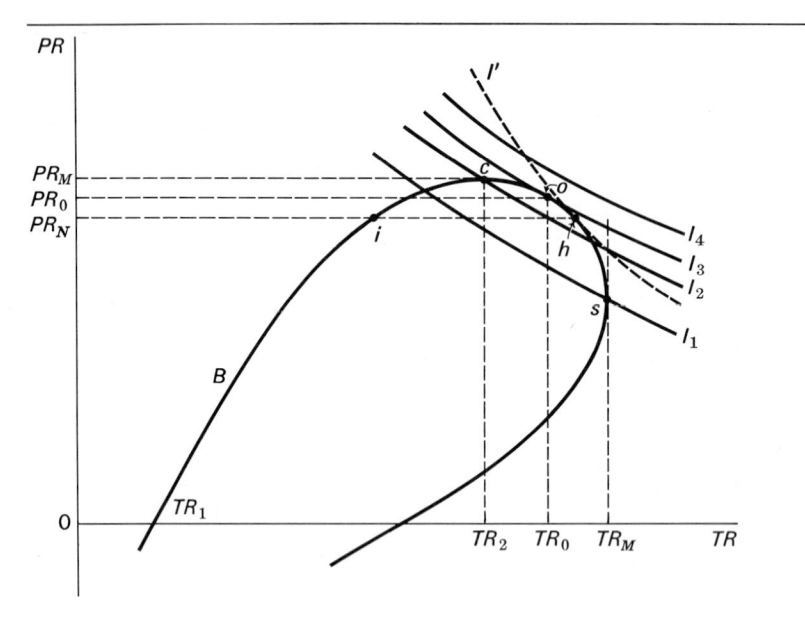

Since managers perceive their long-term level of remuneration as an increasing function of both profits and size, as measured by the firm's dollar receipts, we may infer that management gains utility from both increased profits and increased dollar sales. We may conceive then of a family of indifference curves which reflect management's preferences for profits vis-à-vis sales. The curves labeled I_1 through I_4 in Figure 8–12 are four such curves. They slope down and to the right, reflecting the fact that both profits and dollar-sales volume result in utility for management. Management will give up one only if compensated by an increase in the other. Now we may think of curve B as analogous to a budget line or line of attainable combinations, since it shows all the possible combinations of total profits and dollar sales which the firm may choose. Our problem is to find which combination along B is optimal. If the firm were to operate with the combination of profits and dollar sales at point c, it would be maximizing profits, and at point s it would be maximizing total dollar sales. Point c would be preferred to point s since I_2, through point c, represents greater utility than I_1 through point s. But the combination at point o represents greater utility than either points s or c. In fact, indifference curve I_3, tangent at point o, is the highest the firm can reach, given the restriction to profit–sales combinations along B. For instance, I_4 represents more utility than I_3 but is unattainable given the existing constraints. Management would maximize its utility by selecting the price–output combination which generates profits of PR_0 and total receipts of TR_0.

Several other theories of nonprofit-maximizing behavior have been proposed similar to the one above. One of them, suggested by William Baumol,[3] proposes that so long as profits are above some minimum level acceptable to stockholders, the firm will pursue some other goal, such as increased sales volume, maximum market share, or rapid growth (of capital plant or number of employees or whatever measure of the firm's growth appeals most to management.) To illustrate using the model in Figure 8–12, if PR_N is the minimum profit needed, the budget constraint becomes restricted to the line segment *icoh*. If management has a decided preference for greater sales over higher profits, it might push dollar sales out to the highest level possible without violating the minimum profit requirement. This would be the sales–profit combination at point h. This means management's indifference curves would look like the dotted line, *I′*, drawn tangent to segment *icoh* at the "corner point," h. At h, the firm maximizes sales subject to the minimum profit constraint.

Despite any apparent differences among them, the point of all the theories of nonprofit-maximizing behavior is that managers, who are not owners of their firms, have personal objectives which may differ from owner's objectives in many cases. Managers' rewards include direct and indirect remuneration such as salaries, bonuses, appreciation of stock prices, and nonmonetary benefits such as job satisfaction, security, and so on. Profits are only one source of reward. However, since profits are included in the utility-optimizing criteria of most managers, we have assumed profit maximization in most of our models of firm behavior. We must be prepared, however, to modify our basic assumption in many cases.

Risk and Uncertainty

The definitions of risk and uncertainty which we will use are derived largely from Frank Knight.[4] *Uncertainty* exists when a number of outcomes are possible in a decision, and assigning probabilities to these outcomes in

---

[3] William J. Baumol first suggested a sales maximization theory subject to a profit constraint. See especially W. J. Baumol, *Economics Theory and Operations Analysis*, 2nd ed. (Englewood Cliffs, N.J.: Prentice-Hall, Inc., 1965).
[4] Frank H. Knight, *Risk, Uncertainty, and Profit*. Boston: Houghton Mifflin Co., 1921.

advance is impossible because they depend on forces outside the control of the firm or, perhaps, because little or no experience has been culled upon which to base probabilities. For example, when Ford invested millions of dollars in the Edsel, its management was uncertain about the prospects for its acceptance and market success. We will find that most investment decisions by firms involve a degree of uncertainty. *Risk*, on the other hand, pertains to a decision-making situation in which: (1) there are a number of known outcomes to a given decision and (2) the probability of occurrence of each outcome can be assigned objective probabilities. A gambler at a roulette wheel is an example of a risk situation. If $100 is placed on the red, we can objectively determine the probabilities of winning and losing, along with the dollar amounts in either case. In other words, we distinguish between those future events whose possible occurrence can be predicted by a probability distribution—which is risk—and those events whose possible occurrence cannot be assigned probabilities—which is uncertainty. Of course, for decision-making to have any economic relevance, there must be a potential for economic gain or loss, whether there is uncertainty or risk. Note that it is those events which can be predicted with probability distributions that are capable of being insured against, such as the risk that the firm's plant facility will burn down. The uncertainty whether consumer demand for the firm's product will increase, decrease, or remain stable is uninsurable, however, because there is no way to accurately devise a probability distribution for all of the possible outcomes.

Having introduced the notions of uncertainty and risk, we must further qualify our simplistic assumption about firms' behavior. In reality, all firms are forced to operate in a world fraught with risk and uncertainty, and we may expect they will seek its minimization. In fact, firms may choose to minimize risk and uncertainty in preference to maximizing profit. Or, if there exists the possibility of a trade-off, the firm may exchange some of its anticipated profits for reduced risk.

Suppose a firm is making an investment decision, which involves risk, but no uncertainty, and that its managers are risk averters. By risk averter, we mean a decision maker who prefers less risk to more. Managers who are risk averters will likely give up some anticipated profits in exchange for less risk. Or, turning the statement around, the firm will accept greater risk only if compensated by the prospect of greater returns. Our first step is to establish the combinations of return and risk that are possible, given management's investment opportunities. Assume management has a given sum of money to invest in various productive activities or combinations of such activities, each yielding a unique combination of risks and expected return.

Since we are concerned with an investment decision involving a given sum of money, we can generally conclude that a higher expected rate of return on that investment will be associated with greater risk.

The opportunity curve or line of attainable combinations D_1 in Figure 8-13 is drawn to indicate all possible combinations of risk and expected return that are open to the firm given its alternative investment possibilities and a given level of investment. For simplicity (only) the curve is drawn as a straight line. The firm's expected return on investment is measured along the vertical axis and risk along the horizontal axis. For any given investment selected, the firm may incur losses, or it may realize a large return, or something in between. We will use the weighted mean or average of the possible profit-and-loss levels as the *expected* profit or return, where the weights are derived from the probabilities of occurrence of each profit level. In addition, the expected return is expressed as a percentage, computed by dividing the expected dollar return by the firm's dollar investment. But how can risk be measured? First, to take an extreme case, suppose there is only one possible outcome of the firm's decision to invest a given amount of money, and this outcome is known with certainty. Then the probability of its occurrence is one, and there is zero risk. Now suppose there are several possible outcomes to this investment (e.g., several possible levels of profit or loss which could be realized), each associated with a given probability of occurrence and a return or loss ranging from a large possible profit to a large possible loss. How do we measure risk in this case? One measure often used is the dispersion or variation in the distribution of benefits and losses to the firm, and a typically employed measure of dispersion is the standard deviation, which we shall use.

Indifference curves I_1 and I_2 in Figure 8-13 show the various combinations of risk and expected return which give equal utility to management. Since the firm is assumed to be a risk averter, these curves are positively sloped, indicating that management will accept greater risk only if it is accompanied by higher expected profits.

FIGURE 8-13   The Optimum Combination of Risk and Return

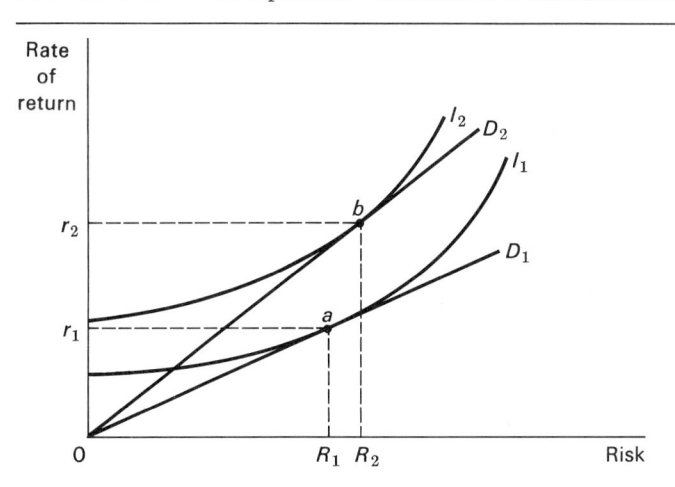

The utility-maximizing combination of risk and return is indicated by the point of tangency of the opportunity curve, D_1, with the highest achievable indifference curve, I_1 in this case. The firm's managers will maximize utility by accepting risks equal to R_1 in order to earn an expected return of r_1. Now suppose the firm's investment opportunities increase to D_2. Then management will accept increased risk (from R_1 to R_2) in order to operate at the equilibrium point b, doubling its expected earnings from r_1 to r_2.

Consider again for a moment that the firm's risk–return opportunities are represented by D_2 and an optimum combination is obtained at point b. To achieve the expected return of r_2 at a risk of R_2, the firm may invest a portion of its available funds in projects characterized by low expected yields, with small risk, and another part of its funds in projects with high expected returns and considerable risk. Or its available funds may be distributed over a wide range of projects from low to high expected yields, to get the over-all r_2–R_2 combination. In any case, projects with high expected returns and high risk will receive less of the firm's available funds than would be true if the risk were lower. In general, we conclude that the existence of risk reduces the amount of resources which will be allocated to an activity, and thereby lessens economic efficiency.

SUMMARY

Now that we have presented the basic theory of competition and monopoly, we are in a position to conclude with a comparison of the economic performance of the two types of industry structures.

We found that where perfect competition can exist, long-run equilibrium in an industry will mean:

1. Each firm realizes zero economic profits.
2. Production occurs at the low point on the long-run average cost curve of each firm.
3. The market price of the product will equal the marginal cost of production.

In sharp contrast, an unregulated monopolist in long-run equilibrium:

1. May realize pure profits.
2. Does not produce at the low point on his long-run average cost curve—except by coincidence.
3. Sells his output for a price which is greater than the marginal cost of production.

So, as a first approximation, we may conclude that perfect competition is socially preferable to pure monopoly on all counts and, by inference, we may expect that any tendency away from perfect competition in the direction of monopoly is economically inefficient.[5] (In the next chapter, we consider those deviations from perfect competition which stop short of monopoly, that is, the market structures of monopolist competition and oligopoly.)

To compare the economic performance of competition with that of monopoly, we make use of the model presented in Figure 8–14. The curve

FIGURE 8–14 A Price–Output Comparison of Monopoly and Competition

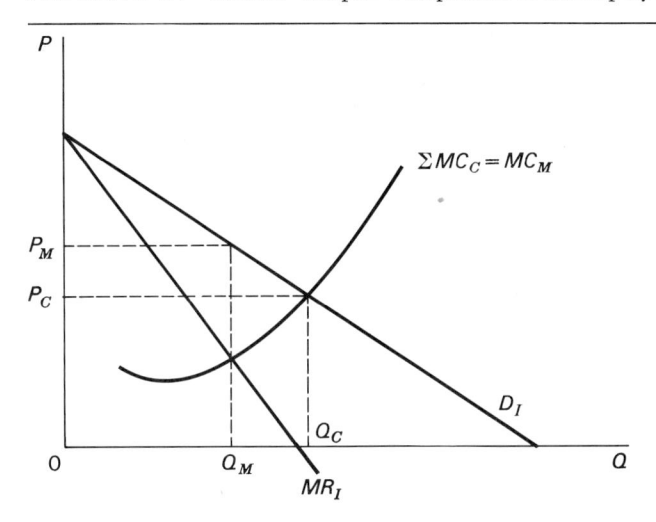

ΣMC_c is the summation of all competitive firms' short-run marginal cost curves, and so may be considered the competitive industry supply curve. If the industry were competitive, the equilibrium price would be P_c and equilibrium output Q_c. Now presume the industry is converted to a monopoly which takes over the plant facilities of all competitive firms. If no scale economies or diseconomies are realized in the conversion to monopoly, then the short-run marginal cost curve of the monopoly, MC_M, will be identical to the summation of the short-run marginal cost curves of all the competitive firms, the short-run competitive supply, ΣMC_c. Referring to Figure 8–14, the profit-maximizing monopolist will produce output Q_M at price P_M. Comparing this

---

[5] The conclusion that more monopoly is worse than less monopoly is not certain, however. The second best theorem indicates that under some circumstances, a partial application of welfare criterion will make matters worse rather than better. (See Chapter 13.)

result with that of competition, we find that the existence of monopoly will result in a price which is greater than the otherwise competitive price, by $P_M - P_C$, and an output which is less than the competitive industry output, by $Q_C - Q_M$. Also, under monopoly conditions, AR is greater than MC. We may conclude that when the industry is monopolized, resources are likely to be inefficiently utilized and there will likely occur a distribution of income to the monopolist not justified by factor costs.

It must be carefully noted that the above comparison is valid only for those industries which can be efficiently made competitive. It is possible that for a given industry, monopoly is preferable to competition. That is, the shortcomings of monopoly may be offset, at least in part, if significant economies of scale exist in the industry. Under these conditions, a monopolist may produce at unit costs well below those of a competitive firm, and the monopolist's price may be lower than the competitive price for this reason.

The effects of price discrimination cannot be easily summed. Price discrimination will lead a monopolist to charge a higher price to some customers than a nondiscriminating monopolist would charge to all. So price discrimination results in the reduction of consumer surplus. However, price discrimination will possibly cause a monopolist to increase his output beyond the level of a nondiscriminating monopolist, and in the limiting case of perfect price discrimination, will cause the firm to equate marginal cost and the price charged for the last unit sold. Therefore, the monopolist practicing perfect price discrimination might produce as much output as a competitive industry would.

When firms pursue goals other than maximum profits, comparisons of market performance are still more difficult to make. There is no assurance that a monopolist's pursuit of goals other than profit maximization will be economically efficient, but it is possible that sales-maximizing monopolists will produce more output and sell for a lower price than profit maximizers. However, the pursuit of nonprofit goals by competitive firms is likely to cause a less than socially optimum result, since long-run competitive equilibrium assuming profit maximization is characterized by $AR = AC = MC$.

Finally, the existence of risk and uncertainty might lead to a greater difference between the monopolist's price and the competitive equilibrium price, and a greater difference in output. Monopoly firms may raise price and reduce output when faced with risk and uncertainty, and then may be sluggish to change their price–output policies. On the other hand, a large monopolist might realize sizable benefits by "pooling" its risks, a possibility not open to the small competitive firm. By pooling risks, the over-all level of risk can be reduced and the monopolist might then have an advantage similar to the advantages of scale economies. In general, we may conclude that the existence of risk and uncertainty tends to lessen the efficiency of both competitive and monopolistic industries.

PROBLEMS

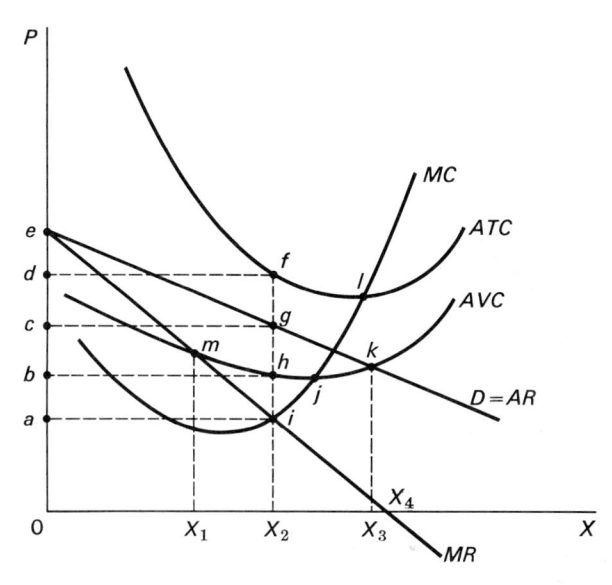

1. Answer the following based on the accompanying graph.
   (a) The profit-maximizing price and output are _____ and _____, respectively.
   (b) Average fixed cost at the profit-maximizing output is _____.
   (c) Average variable cost at the profit-maximizing output is _____.
   (d) The monopolist's (profit, loss) *per unit* is _____.
   (e) The monopolist's total (profit, loss) is equal to the area of rectangle _____.
   (f) Assuming no price discrimination, consumers' surplus is equal to the area _____.

2. Assume a monopolist with cost curves AC and MC faces market demand, D, as shown in the following graph.
   (a) If unregulated, the firm will produce output _____ at price _____.
   (b) If a ceiling price of oc is set by a regulatory authority, the monopolist will maximize profits by producing output _____. Total profits will be equal to the area of rectangle _____.
   (c) If a ceiling price is set at ob, the monopolist will maximize profits by producing output _____. Excess demand at the ceiling price ob will be _____.
   (d) If a ceiling price is set at oa, the monopolist will maximize profits by producing output _____. Excess demand will be _____.

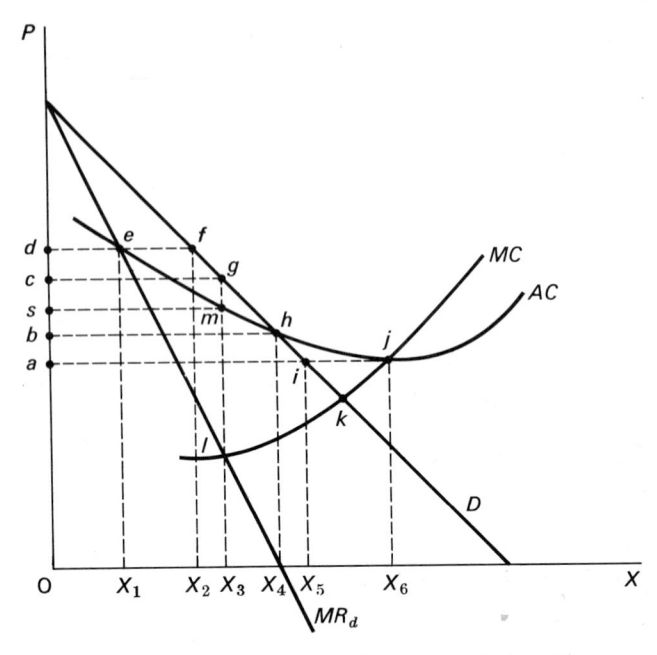

3. Answer the following on the basis of the diagram for this problem. D_1, to the right, is a monopolist's demand in one market and D_2, to the left, is the demand in another. The two markets are kept separate by the monopolist, allowing him to practice price discrimination.

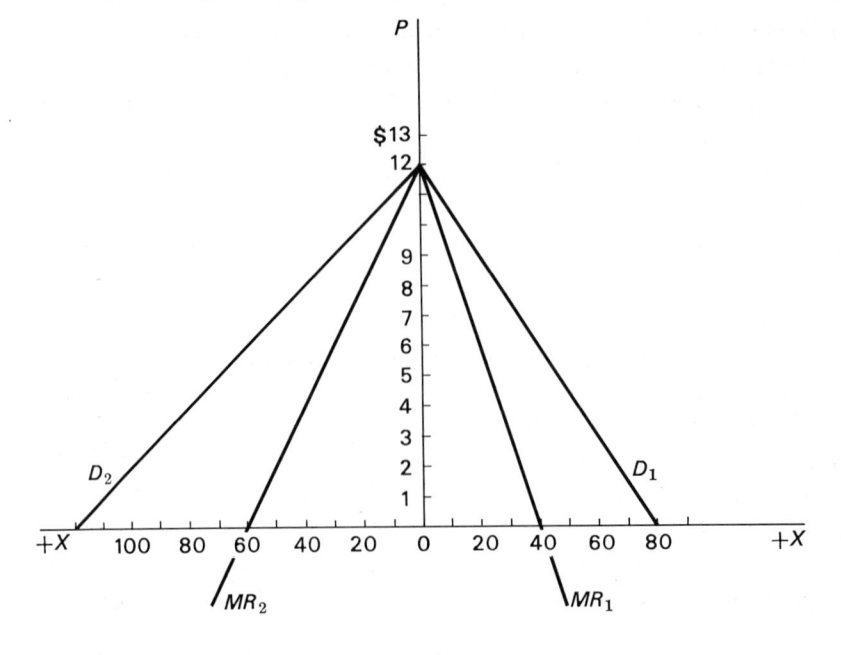

(a) Ignoring costs, if the firm is selling 30 units of X in market 1 and 20 units in market 2, it should (increase, decrease) its unit sales in market (1, 2) and (increase, decrease) its unit sales in market (1, 2).
(b) Price elasticity of demand is unitary at a price of _____ in market 1 and _____ in market 2.
(c) If the monopolist's marginal cost of production is constant at $6, he should produce at a total output of _____ and sell _____ units in market 1 and _____ units in market 2.
(d) If the monopolist's marginal cost is zero, he should produce a total output of _____ and sell _____ units in market 1 and _____ units in market 2.

4. Suppose a monopolist faces a demand schedule that is unit elastic throughout. If his marginal cost and average cost curves are constant at $5, what is the profit-maximizing output?

REFERENCES

ADAMS, WALTER, and GRAY, H. H., *Monopoly in America: The Government as Promoter.* New York: The Macmillan Co., 1955.

BAIN, JOE S., "A Note on Pricing in Monopoly and Oligopoly," *American Economic Review,* 39 (1949), 448–467.

CLEMENS, E. W., "Price Discrimination and the Multi-Product Firm," *Review of Economic Studies,* 19 (1951–1952), 1–11.

CYERT, R. M., and MARCH, J. G., *A Behavioral Theory of the Firm.* Englewood Cliffs, N.J.: Prentice-Hall, Inc., 1963.

HARBERGER, ARNOLD C., "Monopoly and Resource Allocation," *American Economic Review,* 44 (May 1954), 2.

HURVIEZ, L., "The Theory of Economic Behavior." Reprinted in A.E.A. *Readings in Price Theory.* Chicago, Ill.: Richard D. Irwin, 1952.

MACHLUP, FRITZ, *The Political Economy of Monopoly.* Baltimore: The Johns Hopkins Press, 1952, 12–23.

SCHWARTZMAN, D., "The Effect of Monopoly on Price," *Journal of Political Economy,* 67 (August 1959), 352–362.

SCITOVSKY, TIBOR, "A Note on Profit Maximisation and Its Implications," *Review of Economic Studies,* Vol. XI, 1943.

SIMON, HERBERT A., "Theories of Decision-Making in Economics and Behavioral Science," *American Economic Review,* Vol. XLIX, No. 3 (June 1959), 253–283.

WORCHESTER, DEAN A., JR., *Monopoly, Big Business, and Welfare in the Postwar United States.* Seattle: University of Washington Press, 1967.

APPENDIX TO CHAPTER 8

A Case Study in Monopoly Price Setting: The Chesapeake Bay Bridge and Tunnel Commission

E. WARREN SHOWS and ROBERT H. BURTON

The Chesapeake Bay Bridge and Tunnel Commission was organized by Virginia to build and operate the seventeen and one-half mile bridge–tunnel crossing between Chesapeake Beach near Norfolk and the southern tip of the Eastern Shore at Cape Charles. Although the Commission is not a profit-maximizing private firm, its operation of the bridge–tunnel can be analyzed with the tools of monopoly theory, since the Commission is the only seller of a service with no close substitutes.

Here are the principal facts:

1. The Commission raised $200,000,000 in capital by floating a bond issue; $140,000,000 of the funds were used to build the bridge which was opened for traffic in 1964. The remaining funds were held as a reserve to pay interest until revenues from traffic were sufficient to cover payments on both interest and debt.

2. Traffic on the bridge has been approximately one-half of the original estimates, so revenues have not been sufficient to cover the interest payments.

3. Interest payments had about exhausted the Commission's reserve fund by 1970.

In Figure 1 is a model of the monopolist's situation. Interest payments are the main component of average cost; operating costs represent only a small percentage of the total. Assuming operating costs are constant and interest payments are fixed, the Commission's average and marginal cost curves are AC and MC, respectively. Since the greater part of total cost is the fixed component, average cost declines continuously as output (traffic) increases. Marginal cost, determined as the costs associated with providing toll takers, maintenance, insurance, and the like, is modeled as constant, though realistically there are some increasing components, and the curve may in fact slope upward. In any case, operating costs run only about 10 percent of interest payments.

The monopolist equates MR and MC at output V_1, realizing a loss per

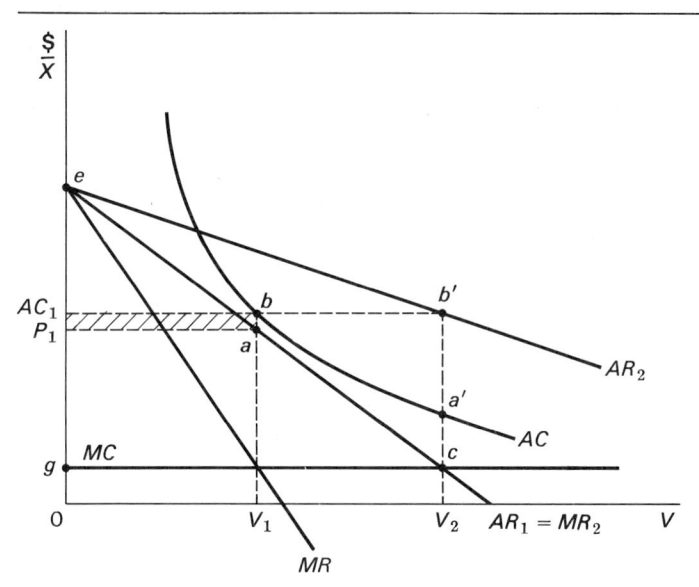

FIGURE 1 Hypothetical Revenue and Cost Curves for the Chesapeake Bay Bridge and Tunnel Commission

unit of ab or total losses equal to the area of rectangle P_1abAC_1. Notice that since the equilibrium value of MR is close to the horizontal axis, the price elasticity of demand is close to unitary, and thus the total revenue curve would be close to its maximum. For a monopolist with low marginal cost and continuously declining unit cost, profit maximization is virtually synonymous with total revenue maximization. Moreover, since the long run for the Commission is a very long period of time (the bridge–tunnel complex might last fifty years or more), the monopoly must expect to realize losses for quite some time.

The promoters of this project had expected the demand for the bridge–tunnel route would be about double what it turned out to be. Referring to the graph, they expected a demand curve at AR_2 rather than AR_1. If AR_2 is simply twice AR_1, then the curve AR_1 serves as the marginal revenue for AR_2. Thus, if the original forecasts had been accurate, the profit-maximizing output level would have been V_2 at approximately the same toll. Profits then would have been positive, and the Commission would have been able to meet interest payments and retire the outstanding debt early.

From the standpoint of economic efficiency, what would be the best public policy? If a ceiling price were set equal to or just above the MC curve in Figure 1 (the demand curve being AR_1), the Commission would be motivated to expand output to V_2. This would mean a lower price for consumers than

P_1 and a more intensive utilization of the bridge facility. Consumer surplus would rise by the area $gcaP_1$. The Commission might then be given a subsidy to pay a portion of the interest payments on the outstanding indebtedness. The subsidy probably should not cover the entire interest liability of the Commission, since the investors in the project would then be completely relieved of their capital losses. Probably the investors should be made to bear at least a portion of these losses, since they originally undertook the risk of loss as well as the potential for profit.

This case is a real-world illustration of several things: (1) It shows that a monopoly, despite its market power, might earn negative profits over a long period of time. (2) Most monopolists do not have a complete or absolute monopoly; for instance, travelers have several alternate routes other than the Chesapeake Bay Bridge–Tunnel. (3) In the real world, firms do not always know exactly what the shapes of revenue functions are and must make decisions in the face of uncertainty. Such decisions may be dead wrong, as in this case. (4) A thorough feasibility study to determine the strength of demand can sometimes reduce the level of risk and uncertainty. (5) Public regulation can sometimes bring about a better utilization of the scarce resources of a monopolist than no regulation at all.

Allocative Efficiency vs. "X-Efficiency"
HARVEY LEIBENSTEIN

We have concluded that monopoly results in an inefficient allocation of a society's resources. What is the magnitude of the welfare loss due to monopoly? Harvey Leibenstein surveys the existing estimates and concludes that the loss due to misallocation is trivial based upon conservative assumptions.

Leibenstein hypothesizes a different kind of efficiency, called X-efficiency, which he believes is a significant cause of increased output and lower costs of firms. X-efficiency arises when inputs are effectively motivated by management to use the best technology to produce the most output, and the motivation is highest when competitive pressures are greatest. Leibenstein says that firms and other organizations will tend to operate *within* their production frontiers rather than on them (as standard economic theory assumes), trading the disutilities of extra work for less output. If pushed or forced by competitive pressures, however, management will increase X-efficiency by more efficiently using existing technology and resources.

At the core of economics is the concept of efficiency. Microeconomic theory is concerned with allocative efficiency. Empirical evidence has been accumulating that suggests that the problem of allocative efficiency is trivial. Yet it is hard to escape the notion that efficiency in some broad sense is significant. In this paper I want to review the empirical evidence briefly and to consider some of the possible implications of the findings, especially as they relate to the theory of the firm and to the explanation of economic growth. The essence of the argument is that microeconomic theory focuses on allocative efficiency to the exclusion of other types of efficiencies that, in fact, are much more significant in many instances. Furthermore, improvement in "nonallocative efficiency" is an important aspect of the process of growth.

In Section I the empirical evidence on allocative efficiency is presented. In this section we also consider the reasons why allocation inefficiency is frequently of small magnitude. Most of the evidence on allocative inefficiency deals with either monopoly or international trade. However, monopoly and trade are not the focus of this paper. Our primary concern is with the broader

From the *American Economic Review*, Vol. LVI (1966). Reprinted by permission of the author and publisher. Copyrighted by the American Economic Association.

issue of allocative efficiency versus an initially undefined type of efficiency that we shall refer to as "X-efficiency." The magnitude and nature of this type of efficiency is examined in Sections II and III. Although a major element of "X-efficiency" is motivation, it is not the only element, and hence the terms "motivation efficiency" or "incentive efficiency" have not been employed.

As he proceeds, the reader is especially invited to keep in mind the sharp contrast in the magnitudes involved between Tables 1 and 2.

I. ALLOCATIVE INEFFICIENCY: EMPIRICAL EVIDENCE

The studies that are of interest in assessing the importance of allocative efficiency are summarized in Table 1. These are of two types. On the one side we have the studies of Harberger and Schwartzman on the "social welfare cost" of monopoly. On the other side we have a number of studies, among them those by Johnson, Scitovsky, Wemelsfelder, Janssen, and others, on the benefits of reducing or eliminating restrictions to trade. In both cases the computed benefits attributed to the reallocation of resources turn out to be exceedingly small.

TABLE 1 Calculated "Welfare Loss" as Percentage of Gross or Net National Product Attributed to Misallocation of Resources

Study	Source	Country	Cause	Loss
A. C. Harberger	A.E.R. 1954	U.S.A. 1929	Monopoly	.07 per cent
D. Schwartzman	J.P.E. 1960	U.S.A. 1954	Monopoly	.01 per cent
T. Scitovsky	(1)	Common Market 1952	Tariffs	.05 per cent
J. Wemelsfelder	E.J. 1960	Germany 1958	Tariffs	.18 per cent
L. H. Janssen	(2)	Italy 1960	Tariffs	max. .1 per cent
H. G. Johnson	Manchester School 1958	U.K. 1970	Tariffs	max. 1.0 per cent
A. Singh	(3)	Montevideo Treaty Countries	Tariffs	max. .0075 per cent

Sources:
(1) T. Scitovsky, *Economic Theory and Western European Integration*, Stanford, 1958.
(2) L. H. Janssen, *Free Trade, Protection and Customs Union*, Leiden, 1961, p. 132.
(3) Unpublished calculation made by A. Singh based on data found in A. A. Faraq, *Economic Integration: A Theoretical, Empirical Study*, University of Michigan, Ph.D. Thesis, 1963.

Let us look at some of the findings. In the original Harberger study the benefits for eliminating monopoly in the United States would raise income no more than $\frac{1}{13}$ of 1 per cent. Schwartzman's study which recomputes the benefits of eliminating monopoly by comparing Canadian monopolized industries as against counterpart competitive U.S. industries, and vice versa in order to determine the excess price attributable to monopoly, ends up with a similar result. Similarly, the benefits attributed to superior resource allocation as a consequence of the Common Market or a European Free Trade Area are also minute—usually much less than 1 per cent.

The calculations made by Scitovsky of the benefits to the Common Market (based on Verdoorn's data) led him to the conclusion that

> . . . the most striking feature of these estimates is their smallness. The one that is really important (for reasons to appear presently), the gain from increased specialization . . . which is less than one-twentieth of one per cent of the gross social product of the countries involved. This is ridiculously small . . .

J. Wemelsfelder has calculated that the welfare gain of reducing import duties and increasing imports and exports accordingly amounts to .18 of 1 per cent of national income. Harry Johnson in an article on England's gain in joining a Free Trade Area calculates the net gain from trade at less than 1 per cent. That is, Johnson arrives at the conclusion that 1 per cent of the national income would be the absolute maximum gain for Britain from entering the European Free Trade Area.

A recent study by L. H. Janssen calculates that the gains from increased specialization for the different countries of the European Economic Community would be largest for Italy, but even here the amount is only $\frac{1}{10}$ of 1 per cent of total production.[1] Janssen points out that, if the production gain for Italy due to specialization were calculated by Scitovsky's method, which he believes involves an overestimation, "the production gain in the most extreme case is still less than .4 per cent." Janssen concludes, as have others, that the welfare effects of a customs union based on the superior allocation of resources are likely to be trivial. He does, however, point to the possibility "that the mere prospect of the frontiers opening would infuse fresh energy into entrepreneurs." He recognizes that certain qualitative factors may be highly

---

[1] R. A. Mundell in a review of Janssen's book appears to reach a similar conclusion to the point made in this paper when he speculates that:
> . . . there have appeared in recent years studies purporting to demonstrate that the welfare loss due to monopoly is small, that the welfare importance of efficiency and production is exaggerated, and that gains from trade and the welfare gains from tariff are almost negligible. Unless there is a thorough theoretical re-examination of the validity of the tools on which these studies are founded, and especially of the revitalized concepts of producers' and consumers' surplus, some one inevitably will draw the conclusion that economics has ceased to be important!

important and that the consequences of growth are certainly more significant than those of allocative welfare.

My research assistant, A. Singh, has calculated the gains from trade (following the Scitovsky method) for the Montevideo Treaty Countries[2] (Argentina, Brazil, Chile, Mexico, Paraguay, Peru, and Uruguay) and found it to be less than $1/150$ of 1 per cent of their combined GNP. Even if we double or triple this result to allow for such factors as the effect of failing to take account of quantitative restrictions in the analysis, the outcome is still trivial.

Harberger's study on Chile which involves the reallocation of both labor and capital yields a relatively large estimate. Harberger intends to obtain as large an estimate as possible of the consequences of reallocating resources by using what I believe to be (and what he admits to be) rather extreme assumptions in order to obtain maximum outer bounds. Despite this he comes up with a number that is between 9 and 15 per cent. However, no actual data are employed. What are used are outer-bound estimates based on personal impressions. I expect that a careful study similar to the Verdoorn-Scitovsky study would probably come up with numbers that would be no larger than 1 or 2 per cent.

The empirical evidence, while far from exhaustive, certainly suggests that the welfare gains that can be achieved by increasing *only* allocative efficiency are usually exceedingly small, at least in capitalist economies. In all but one of the cases considered all of the gains are likely to be made up in one month's growth. They hardly seem worth worrying about.

Let us see briefly why these gains are usually small. We cannot prove that we would expect them to be small on purely theoretical grounds. If we combine our theory with what we could agree are probably reasonable estimates of some of the basic magnitudes, then it appears likely that in many cases (but certainly not all *possible* cases) the welfare loss of allocative inefficiency is of trivial significance. The idea could be developed with the aid of the diagram employed by Harberger. (See Figure 1). In Figure 1 we assume that costs are constant within the relevant range. D is the demand function. Under competition price and quantity are determined at the intersection C. The monopoly price is above the competitive price equal to AB in the figure. The monopoly output is determined at the point A. The welfare loss due to monopoly, which is the same as the welfare gain if we shifted to competition, is equal to the triangle ABC. We obtain an approximation to this amount by multiplying the price differential AB by the quantity differential BC by one-half and multiplying this by the proportion of national income in industries involving the misallocation.

---

[2] Based on data found in A. A. Faraq, *Economic Integration: A Theoretical, Empirical Study*. Unpublished doctoral dissertation, University of Michigan, 1963.

FIGURE 1

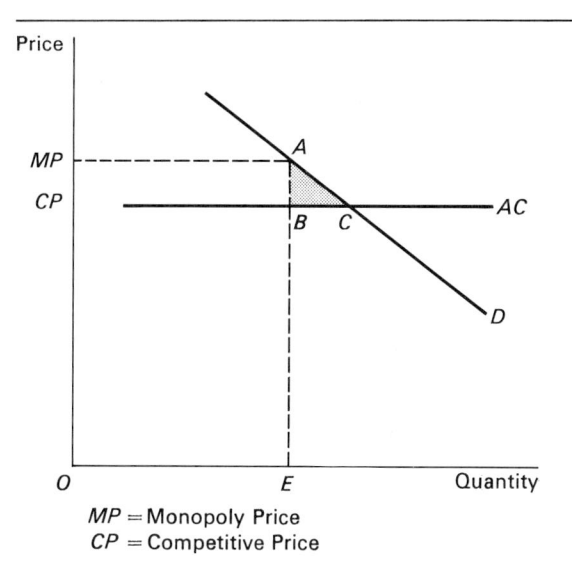

Price

MP - - - - - - - - - A
CP ─────────────── AC
         B   C
                    D

0   E   Quantity

MP = Monopoly Price
CP = Competitive Price

Let us play around with some numbers and see the kind of results we get as a consequence of this formulation. Suppose that half of the national output is produced in monopolized industries and that the price differential is 20 per cent and that the average elasticity of demand is 1.5. Now the outcome will turn out to be 1½ per cent. But we really used enormous figures for the misallocation. And yet the result is small. Monopoly prices, according to estimates, appear to be only about 8 per cent on the average above competitive prices. We can substitute some reason other than monopoly for the misallocation and still come out with similar results.[3]

Consider the cases of subsidized industries under some sort of governmental inducements to growth; and that of governmentally run industries. In the subsidy case the calculation would be similar. Suppose that as much as 50 per cent of the industries are subsidized to the extent of a 20 per cent difference

---

[3] For the sake of completeness we should take the income effect into account in our estimation of consumer surplus. It may readily be seen that this magnitude is likely to be exceedingly small. Suppose that the initial effect of a superior allocation is 1 per cent; then the income effect for a noninferior good will be to shift the demand function to the right by 1 per cent on the average. Thus, the addition to consumers' surplus will be 1 per cent, and the consumers' surplus foregone will be roughly 1 per cent of 1 per cent. If we consider all consequent effects in a similar vein, then the estimated welfare loss will be .010101 . . . < .0102. The actual magnitude will, of course, be smaller because the demand will shift to the left in the case of inferior goods. For an excellent discussion of these matters see A. P. Lerner.

in cost and that the output point on the demand function is where elasticity is unity. This last point may be reasonable since the operators of subsidized industries might want gross revenue to be as large as possible. If, on the other hand, we assume that they are profit maximizers and restrict output to a greater extent, then we might assume a price elasticity of two. This latter, however, is unlikely because monopoly profits are inconsistent with subsidized industries. Those who receive the subsidy would have the legitimate fear that the subsidy would be lowered if unusual profits were earned. Hence, behavior in the direction of revenue maximization appears reasonable and the calculated welfare loss is less than 2 per cent.

A similar result could be achieved in the case in which the government runs industries that affect 50 per cent of the national income of an economy. In all the cases we have considered, the magnitudes chosen appear to be on the large side and the outcome is on the small side.

Of course, it is possible that the magnitude of allocative inefficiency would be large if there are large discontinuities in productivity between those industries where inputs are located and those industries to which the same inputs could be moved. This, in effect, is the basic assumption that Harberger made in his study of Chile. But if it turns out that there is a reasonable degree of continuity in productivity, and that the only way shifts could be made is by simultaneously increasing either social overhead capital or direct capital in order to make the shifts involved, then, of course, a great deal of the presumed gains would be eaten up by the capital costs and the net marginal gains would turn out to be rather small. My general impression is that this is likely to be the case in a great many underdeveloped countries where differential productivities appear to exist between the agricultural sector and the industrial sector. One cannot go beyond stating vague impressions since there is a lack of hard statistical evidence on this matter.

Why are the welfare effects of reallocation so small? Allocational inefficiency involves only the net marginal effects. The basic assumption is that every firm *purchases and utilizes* all of its inputs "efficiently." Thus, what is left is simply the consequences of price and quantity distortions. While some specific price distortions might be large it seems unlikely that all relative price distortions are exceptionally large. This implies that most quantity distortions must also be relatively small since for a given aggregate output a significant distortion in one commodity will be counterbalanced by a large number of small distortions in the opposite direction in quantities elsewhere. While it is possible to *assume* relative price distortions and quantity distortions that would be exceedingly high, it would be difficult to believe that, without intent, the sum of such distortions should be high. However, it is not *necessarily* so on purely *a priori* grounds.

There is one important type of distortion that cannot easily be handled by existing microeconomic theory. This has to do with the allocation of managers.

It is conceivable that in practice a situation would arise in which managers are exceedingly poor, that is, others are available who do not obtain management posts, and who would be very much superior. Managers determine not only their own productivity but the productivity of all cooperating units in the organization. It is therefore possible that the actual loss due to such a misallocation might be large. But the theory does not allow us to examine this matter because firms are presumed to exist as entities that make optimal input decisions, apart from the decisions of their managers. This is obviously a contradiction and therefore cannot be handled.

II. X-EFFICIENCY: THE EMPIRICAL EVIDENCE

We have seen that the welfare loss due to allocational inefficiency is frequently no more than $1/10$ of 1 per cent. Is it conceivable that the value of X-inefficiency would be larger than that? One way of looking at it is to return to the problem of the welfare loss due to monopoly. Suppose that one-third of the industries are in the monopolized sector. Is it possible that the lack of competitive pressure of operating in monopolized industries would lead to a cost $3/10$ of a per cent higher than would be the case under competition? This magnitude seems to be very small, and hence it certainly seems to be a possibility. The question essentially, is whether we can visualize managers bestirring themselves sufficiently, if the environment forced them to do so, in order to reduce costs by more than $3/10$ of 1 per cent. Some of the empirical evidence available suggests that not only is this a possibility, but that the magnitudes involved are very much larger. As we shall see, the spotty evidence on this subject does not prove the case but it does seem to be sufficiently persuasive to suggest the possibility that X-efficiency exists, and that it frequently is much more significant than allocational efficiency.

Professor Eric Lundberg in his studies of Swedish industries points to the case of the steel plant at Horndal that was left to operate without any new capital investment or *technological change,* and furthermore maintenance and replacement were kept at a minimum, and yet output per man hour rose by 2 per cent per annum. Professor Lundberg asserts that according to his interviews with industrialists and technicians "sub-optimal disequilibrium in regard to technology and utilization of existing capital stock is a profoundly important aspect of the situation at any time." (This according to Gorin Ohlin's summary of Lundberg's findings.) If a suboptimal disequilibrium exists at any time, then it would seem reasonable that under the proper motivations managers and workers could bestir themselves to produce closer to optimality, and that under other conditions they may be motivated to move farther away from optimality.

Frederick Harbison reports visiting two petroleum refineries in Egypt less than one-half mile apart.

The labor productivity of one had been nearly double that in the other for many years. But recently, under completely new management, the inefficient refinery was beginning to make quite spectacular improvements in efficiency with the same labor force.

We may inquire why the management was changed only recently whereas the difference in labor productivity existed for many years. It is quite possible that had the motivation existed in sufficient strength, this change could have taken place earlier.

In a recent book on the firm, Neil Chamberlain visualizes his firms reacting to variances between forecasted revenues and expenditures and actual. He quotes from the president of a corporation:

> Actual sales revenue for the fiscal year varied one per cent from the original forecast. Expenditures varied 30 per cent. The reasons were practically entirely due to manufacturing problems of inefficiency and quality. . . . The only actions specifically taken were in attempted changes in methods of production . . . [and] the use of an engineering consulting firm. . . .

One would have thought that the cost-reducing activities mentioned could be carried out irrespective of the variance. Nevertheless, the quotation clearly implies that, in fact, they would not have been motivated to attempt the changes were it not that they were stimulated by the variance.

Before proceeding to present more empirical evidence on the possible magnitude of X-efficiency it is of importance to say something about the nature of the data. The empirical evidence does not present many unambiguous cases. Most of the evidence has to do with specific terms or, at best, industries, and not for the economy as a whole. In the evidence presented on allocative efficiency the entire economy was considered. It is quite possible that the cases considered are entirely atypical and could not be duplicated in large segments of the economy. In addition, the cases do not always deal with X-efficiency in a pure sense. Some additional inputs or reallocations are sometimes involved. Also uncertainty elements and accidental variations play a role. Nevertheless, it seems that the magnitudes involved are so large that they suggest that the conjecture that X-efficiency is frequently more significant than allocative efficiency must be taken seriously.

Now let us turn to Tables 1 and 2. In contrast to Table 1 where the misallocation effects are small, we see in Table 2 that the X-efficiency effects, at least for specific firms, are usually large. Table 2 abstracts (in the interest of conserving space) from a much more comprehensive table developed by Kilby that summarizes the results of a number of ILO productivity missions. (I usually picked for each country the first three and the last items contained in Kilby's table.) It is to be observed that the cost-reducing methods used do not involve additional capital nor, as far as one can tell, any increase in depreciation or obsolescence of existing capital. The methods usually involve some

TABLE 2 ILO Productivity Mission Results

Factory or Operation	Method*	Increase in Labor Productivity %	Impact on the Firm (Unit Cost Reduction) Labor Savings %	Capital† Savings %
India				
Seven textile mills	n.a.	5-to-250	5–71	5–71
Engineering firms				
All operations	F, B	102	50	50
One operation	F	385	79	79
One operation	F	500	83	83
Burma				
Molding railroad brake shoes	A, F, B	100	50	50
Smithy	A	40	29	29
Chair assembly	A, B	100	50	50
Match manufacture	A, F	24	19	—
Indonesia				
Knitting	A, B	15	13	—
Radio assembly	A, F	40	29	29
Printing	A, F	30	23	—
Enamelware	F	30	23	—
Malaya				
Furniture	A, D	10	9	9
Engineering workshop	A, D	10	9	9
Pottery	A, B	20	17	17
Thailand				
Locomotive maintenance	A, F	44	31	31
Saucepan polishing	E, D	50	33	—
Saucepan assembly	B, F	42	30	—
Cigarettes	A, B	5	5	—
Pakistan				
Textile plants	C, H, G			
Weaving		50	33	33
Weaving		10	9	9
Bleaching		59	37	37
Weaving		141	29	29
Israel				
Locomotive repair	F, B, G	30	23	23
Diamond cutting and polishing	C, B, G	45	31	—
Refrigerator assembly	F, B, G	75	43	43
Orange picking	F	91	47	—

* A = plant layout reorganized
  B = machine utilization and flow
  C = simple technical alterations
  D = materials handling
  E = waste control
  F = work method
  G = payment by results
  H = workers training and supervision
† Limited to plant and equipment, excluding increased depreciation costs.
Source: P. Kilby, "Organization and Productivity in Backward Economies," *Quarterly Journal of Economics*, May 1962, 76, 303–10.

simple reorganizations of the production process, e.g., plant-layout reorganization, materials handling, waste controls, work methods, and payments by results. It is of interest that the cost reductions are frequently above 25 per cent and that this result is true for a technically advanced country such as Israel as well as for the developing countries considered in other parts of the table. If the firms and/or operations considered are representative, then it would appear that the contrast in significance between X-efficiency and allocative efficiency is indeed startling. Representativeness has not been established. However, the reports of the productivity missions do not suggest that they went out of their way to work only on cases where large savings in costs could be obtained. By comparative standards (with other productivity missions) some of the results were modest, and in some cases Kilby reports that when some members of the missions returned to some of the firms they had worked on previously (e.g., in Pakistan) they found a reversion to previous methods and productivities.

There are of course a number of other studies, in addition to those by Lundberg and Harbison just mentioned which present results similar to the ILO reports. L. Rostas in his study of comparative productivity in British and American industry points to the finding that differences in amount and quality of machinery per worker and the rates of utilization and replacement do not account for the entire difference in output per worker in the two countries. He further states that

> ... in a number of industries (or firms) where the equipment is very largely identical in the U.S. or U.K., eggs, boots and shoes, tobacco, strip steel (or in firms producing both in the U.K. and U.S. ...), there are still substantial differences in output per worker in the U.K. and the U.S.

Clearly there is more to the determination of output than the obviously observable inputs. The nature of the management, the environment in which it operates, and the incentives employed are significant.

That changes in incentives will change productivity per man (and cost per unit of output) is demonstrated clearly by a wide variety of studies on the effects of introducing payments by results schemes. Davison, Florence, Gray, and Ross review the literature in this area for British industry, survey the results for a number of manufacturing operations, and present illustrative examples of their findings from a number of firms. The summary of their findings follows:

> The change in output per worker was found to vary among the different operations all the way from an increase of 7.5 per cent to one of 291 per cent, about half the cases falling between 43 per cent and 76 per cent. Such increases in output, most of them large, from our "first-line" case histories, and from additional evidence, were found not to be just a "flash in the pan" but were sustained over the whole period of study.

Roughly similar findings were obtained for the consequences of introducing payments by results in Australia, Belgium, India, the Netherlands, and the United States. In Victoria it was found that "soundly designed and properly operated incentive plans have in practice increased production rate in the reporting firms from 20 to 50 per cent." In the Netherlands labor efficiency increases of 36.5 per cent were reported. It seems clear that with the same type of equipment the working tempo varies considerably both between different workers and different departments. Appropriate incentives can obviously change such tempos considerably and reduce costs, without any changes in purchasable inputs per unit.

The now-famous Hawthorne Studies suggest that the mere fact that management shows a special interest in a certain group of workers can increase output. That is, management's greater interest in the group on whom the experiments were tried, both when working conditions were improved and when they were worsened, created a positive motivation among the workers. (The magnitudes were from 13 to 30 per cent.) In one of the ILO missions to Pakistan an improvement in labor relations in a textile mill in Lyallpur resulted in a productivity increase of 30 per cent. Nothing else was changed except that labor turnover was reduced by one-fifth.

Individual variations in worker proficiency are probably larger than plant differences. Frequently the variation between the best to poorest worker is as much as four to one. Certainly improved worker selection could improve productivity at the plant level. To the extent that people are not working at what they are most proficient at, productivity should rise as a consequence of superior selection methods.

Although there is a large literature on the importance of psychological factors on productivity, it is usually quite difficult to assess this literature because many psychologists work on the basis of high- and low-productivity groups but do not report the actual numerical differences. In general, it seems that some of the psychological factors studied in terms of small-group theory can account for differences in productivity of from 7 to 18 per cent. The discoveries include such findings as (1) up to a point smaller working units are more productive than larger ones; (2) working units made up of friends are more productive than those made up of nonfriends; (3) units that are generally supervised are more efficient than those that are closely supervised; and (4) units that are given more information about the importance of their work are more proficient than those given less information. A partial reason for these observed differences is probably the likelihood that individual motivation towards work is differently affected under the different circumstances mentioned.

The shorter-hours movement in Western Europe and in the United States, especially up to World War I, has some interesting lessons for productivity differentials without capital changes. Economists frequently assume that for a given capital stock and quality of work force, output will be proportional to number of hours worked. Experiments during World War I and later showed that not only was the proportionality law untrue, but that frequently *absolute* output actually increased with reductions in hours—say from a ten-hour day to an eight-hour day. It was also found that with longer hours a disproportionate amount of time was lost from increased absenteeism, industrial accidents, and so on. In many cases it would obviously have been to a firm's interest to reduce hours below that of the rest of the industry. Firms could have investigated these relations and taken advantage of the findings. For the most part, governments sponsored the necessary research on the economics of fatigue and unrest under the stimulus of the war effort, when productivity in some sectors of the economy was believed to be crucial. The actual reduction of hours that took place was a consequence of the pressure of labor unions and national legislation.

In this connection it is of interest to note that Carter and Williams in their study of investment in innovations found that a high proportion (over 40 per cent) was of a "passive" character—i.e., either in response to the "direct pressure of competition" or "force of example of firms (etc.) other than immediate rivals." Unfortunately it is difficult to find data that would represent the obverse side of the coin; namely, data that would suggest the degree to which firms do not innovate for lack of a sufficient motivating force, such as a lack of competitive pressure. However, there is a great deal of evidence that the delay time between invention and innovation is often exceedingly long (sometimes more than 50 years), and the lag time between the use of new methods in the "best practice" firms in an industry and other firms is also a matter of years. Salter in his study on *Productivity and Technical Change* points to the following striking example. "In the United States copper mines, electric locomotives allow a cost saving of 67 per cent yet although first used in the mid-twenties, by 1940 less than a third of locomotives in use were electric."[4] Other similar examples are mentioned by Salter and others. A survey of industrial research undertaken by 77 companies showed that one-third were carrying on research for "aggressive purposes," but that two-thirds were "forced into research for defensive purposes."

The relation between the "cost" of advice or consulting services and the return obtained has not been worked out for the ILO productivity missions as a

---

[4] See especially Appendix to Chapter 7, "Evidence Relating to the Delay in the Utilization of New Techniques." It seems to me that Salter did not quite draw the only possible conclusion from his Table 11. Plants with no significant changes in equipment, method, and plant layout had quite startling changes in output per man-hour, especially if we consider the fact demonstrated in the table that output per man-hour frequently falls under such circumstances. The range of variation in the changes (24 per cent) is larger for the plants without significant changes in equipment, etc., than for those with significant improvements. This is not to argue against the thesis that changes in techniques are important, but to suggest that significant variations in production can and do occur without such changes.

whole. In one case (in Pakistan) the savings effected in three textile mills as a consequence of the work of the mission during the year that the mission was there "represented about 20 times the entire cost of the mission in that year." While the study does not indicate how representative this result was, the impression one gets is that rates of return of rather large magnitudes are not entirely unusual.

J. Johnston studied the return to consulting services in Great Britain. For the class of jobs where it was possible to make a quantitative assessment of the results (600 jobs were involved), it was found that on the average the rate of return was about 200 per cent on consulting fees. Johnston's study is of special interest for our purposes because (a) it is a very careful study, and (b) the magnitudes of increases in productivity are of the same order (although the variations are less extreme) as those obtained in underdeveloped countries. The nature of the consulting work was not too dissimilar to that carried out by the ILO teams. On the whole they involved improvements in general management, plant layout, personnel, production procedures, selling organization, management and budgeting and accounting systems. For the consulting jobs whose consequences were quantitatively assessed, the average increase in productivity was 53 per cent, the lowest quartile showed an increase of 30 per cent, and the highest quartile 70 per cent.

The studies mentioned deal with examples that are more or less of a microeconomic nature. In recent years we have had a number of studies that are their *macro*economic complements. The work of Solow, Aukrust, Denison, and others show that only a small proportion of increase in GNP is accounted for by increases in inputs of labor or capital. The "unexplained residual" covers about 50 per cent to 80 per cent of growth in advanced countries. The residual comprehends a greater range of "noninput" growth factors (e.g., technological change, education of the labor force) than was covered in the examples we considered, but the motivational efficiency elements may account for some fraction of the residual. (E.g., Johnston estimates that one quarter of the annual increase in product is accounted for by consulting services.)

What conclusions can we draw from all of this? First, the data suggest that there is a great deal of possible variation in output for similar amounts of capital and labor and for similar techniques, in the broad sense, to the extent that technique is determined by similar types of equipment. However, in most of the studies the nature of the influences involved are mixed, and in some cases not all of them are clear to the analyst. In many instances there appears to have been an attempt to impart knowledge, at least of a managerial variety, which accounts for *some* of the increase in output. But should this knowledge be looked upon as an increase in inputs of production in all instances? Although the first reaction might be that such attempts involve inputs similar to inputs of capital or labor, I will want to argue that in many instances this is not the case.

It is obvious that not every change in technique implies a change in knowledge. The knowledge may have been there already, and a change in circumstances induced the change in technique. In addition, knowledge may not be used to capacity just as capital or labor may be underutilized. More important, a good deal of our knowledge is vague. A man may have nothing more than a sense of its existence, and yet this may be the critical element. Given a sufficient inducement, he can then search out its nature in detail and get it to a stage where he can use it. People normally operate within the bounds of a great deal of intellectual slack. Unlike underutilized capital, this is an element that is very difficult to observe. As a result, occasions of genuine additions to knowledge become rather difficult to distinguish from those circumstances in which no new knowledge has been added, but in which existing knowledge is being utilized to greater capacity.

Experience in U.S. industry suggests that adversity frequently stimulates cost-reducing attempts, some of which are successful, within the bounds of existing knowledge. In any event, some of the studies suggest that motivational aspects are involved entirely apart from additional knowledge. The difficulty of assessment arises because these elements are frequently so intertwined that it is difficult to separate them.

Let us now consider types of instances in which the motivational aspect appears fairly clearly to play a role. The ILO studies discuss a number of cases in which there had been a reversion to previous less efficient techniques when demonstration projects were revisited after a year or more. This seems to have occurred both in India and in Pakistan. Clearly, the new knowledge, if there were such knowledge, was given to the management by the productivity mission at the outset, and the new management methods were installed at least for the period during which the productivity mission was on hand, but there was not a sufficient motivational force for the management to maintain the new methods. The "Hawthorne Effects" are of a more clear-cut nature. Here an intentional reversion to previous methods still led to some increases in output simply because the motivational aspects were more important than the changes in the work methods. The ILO mission reports also mention with regret the fact that techniques applied in one portion of a plant, which led to fairly large increases in productivity, were not taken over by the management and applied to other aspects of the production process, although they could quite easily have done so. In a sense we may argue that the knowledge was available to the management, but that somehow it was not motivated to transfer techniques from one portion of a plant to another.

Studies which showed increases in output as a consequence of introducing payment by results clearly involve motivational elements. For the men subjected to the new payment scheme economic motivations are involved. For the management the situation is less clear. It is possible that in many instances the firms were not aware of the possible advantages of payment by results until they obtained the new knowledge that led to the introduction of the scheme. However, it seems most likely that this scheme is so well known that this is not the case in all, or in many instances. Management quite likely had to be motivated to introduce the scheme by some factors either within the firm or within the industry. In any event, these studies clearly suggest that for some aspects of production, motivational elements are significant.

Both the ILO studies and the Johnston study speak of the need to get the acceptance of top management for the idea of obtaining and implementing consulting advice. In addition, the ILO studies make the point that low productivity is frequently caused by top management's concern with the commercial and financial affairs of the firm rather than with the running of the factory. The latter was frequently treated as a very subordinate task. Whether this last aspect involves a lack of knowledge or a lack of motivation is difficult to determine. However, it seems hard to believe that if some top-management people in some of the firms in a given industry were to become concerned with factory management and achieve desirable results thereby, some of the others would not follow suit. Johnston makes the point that, "without the willing cooperation of management the consultant is unlikely to be called in the first instance or to stay for long if he does come in." The ILO missions make similar remarks.

It is quite clear that consulting services are not only profitable to consultants but also highly profitable to many of the firms that employ them. But it is rather surprising that more of these services are not called for. Part of the answer may be that managements of firms are not motivated to hire consultants if things appear to be going "in any reasonably satisfactory rate." There are, of course, numerous personal resistances to calling for outside advice. If the motivation is strong enough, e.g., the threat of failure of the firm, then it is likely that such resistances would be overcome. But these are simply different aspects of the motivational elements involved.

III. THE RESIDUAL AND X-EFFICIENCY: AN INTERPRETATION

The main burden of these findings is that X-inefficiency exists, and that improvement in X-efficiency is a significant source of increased output. In general, we may specify three elements as significant in determining what we have called X-efficiency: (1) intra-plant motivational efficiency, (2) external motivational efficiency, and (3) nonmarket input efficiency.

The simple fact is that neither individuals nor firms work as hard, nor do they search for information as effectively, as they could. The importance of motivation and its association with degree of effort and search arises because the relation between inputs and outputs is *not* a determinate one. There are four reasons why given inputs cannot be transformed into predetermined outputs: (a) contracts for labor are incomplete, (b) not all factors of production are marketed, (c) the production function is not completely specified or known, and (d) interdependence and uncertainty lead competing firms to cooperate tacitly with each other in some respects, and to imitate each other with respect to technique, to some degree.

The conventional theoretical assumption, although it is rarely stated, is that inputs have a fixed specification and yield a fixed performance. This ignores other likely possibilities. Inputs may have a fixed specification that yields a variable performance, or they may be of a variable specification and yield a variable performance. Some types of complex machinery may have fixed specifications, but their performance may be variable depending on the exact nature of their employment. The most common case is that of labor services of various kinds that have variable specifications and variable performance—although markets sometimes operate as if much of the labor of a given class has a fixed specification. Moreover, it is exceedingly rare for all elements of performance in a labor contract to be spelled out. A good deal is left to custom, authority, and whatever motivational techniques are available to management as well as to individual discretion and judgment.

Similarly, the production function is neither completely specified nor known. There is always an experimental element involved so that something may be known about the current state; say the existing relation between inputs and outputs, but not what will happen given changes in the input ratios. In addition, important inputs are frequently not marketed or, if they are traded, they are not equally accessible (or accessible on equal terms) to all potential buyers. This is especially true of management knowledge. In many areas of the world managers may not be available in well-organized markets. But even when they are available, their capacities may not be known. One of the important capacities of management may be the degree to which managers can obtain factors of production that in fact are not marketed in well-organized markets or on a universalistic basis. In underdeveloped countries the capacity to obtain finance may depend on family connections. Trustworthiness may be similarly determined. Some types of market information may be available to some individuals but not purchasable in the market. For these and other reasons it seems clear that it is one thing to purchase or hire inputs in a given combination; it is something else to get a predetermined output out of them.

Another possible interpretation of the data presented is in connection with the "residual" in economic growth analysis. The residual manifests itself in three basic ways: (1) through cost reduction in the production of existing commodities without inventions or innovations; (2) the introduction of innovations in processes of production; and (3) the introduction of new commodities or, what is the same thing, quality improvements in consumer goods or inputs. We have ignored the introduction of new commodities, but the other two elements are pertinent here. The data suggest that cost reduction that is essentially a result of improvement in X-efficiency is likely to be an important component of the observed residual in economic growth. In addition, there is no doubt that, in some of the cases of reduced cost, new knowledge was conveyed to the firms involved, and this too is part of the residual. It is of special interest that such new knowledge involves knowledge dissemination rather than invention. The detailed studies suggest that the magnitudes are large, and hence a significant part of the residual does not depend on the types of considerations that have been prominent in the literature in recent years, such as those that are *embodied* in capital accumulation or in invention. We have considered the problem in terms of decreasing real costs per unit of output. It is clear that for a given set of resources, if real costs per unit of output are decreased, then total output will grow, and output per unit of input will also rise. Such efforts to reduce cost are part of the contribution of the residual to economic growth.

Both competition and adversity create some pressure for change. Even if knowledge is vague, if the incentive is strong enough there will be an attempt to augment information so that it becomes less vague and possibly useful. Where consulting advice is available it is significant that relatively few firms buy it. Clearly, motivations play a role in determining the degree that consulting advice is sought. The other side of the coin is that, where the motivation is weak, firm managements will permit a considerable degree of slack in their operations and will not seek cost-improving methods. Cyert and March point to cases in which costs per unit are allowed to rise when profits are high. In the previous sections we have cited cases in which there was a reversion to less efficient methods after the consultants left the scene. Thus we have instances where competitive pressures from other firms or adversity lead to efforts toward cost reduction, and the absence of such pressures tends to cause costs to rise.

Some of the essential points made in the previous paragraphs can be illustrated diagrammatically, if (in the interest of simplicity) we allow for abstraction from some of the realities of the situation. The main ideas to be illustrated are as follows: (1) Some firms operate under conditions of nonminimum costs, and it is possible for an industry to have a nonminimal cost equilibrium. (2) Improvements in X-efficiency are part of the process of development, and probably a significant proportion of the "residual." In what follows we assume that there are many firms, and that each firm's output is sufficiently small so as not to affect the output, costs, or prices set by other firms. For simplicity we also assume that for each firm there is an average total unit cost (ATUC) curve that has a significant horizontal segment at its trough, and that the output selected will be on that segment. When we visualize a firm's costs reacting to competitive conditions in the industry we imply that the entire ATUC curve moves up or down. Some firms are presumed to react to changes in the

372 A Theory of Producer Behavior

unit cost of production of the industry as a whole, i.e., to the weighted average of the unit costs of all the firms, in which each firm's weight is in proportion to its contribution to the output of the industry. Here we posit a one-period lag relation. Each firm's expectations of current industry unit costs depend on actual industry unit costs in the previous period. If we choose sufficiently small periods, then this seems to be reasonable relation.

In Figure 2 each curve represents the "reaction cost line" of a firm. The

FIGURE 2

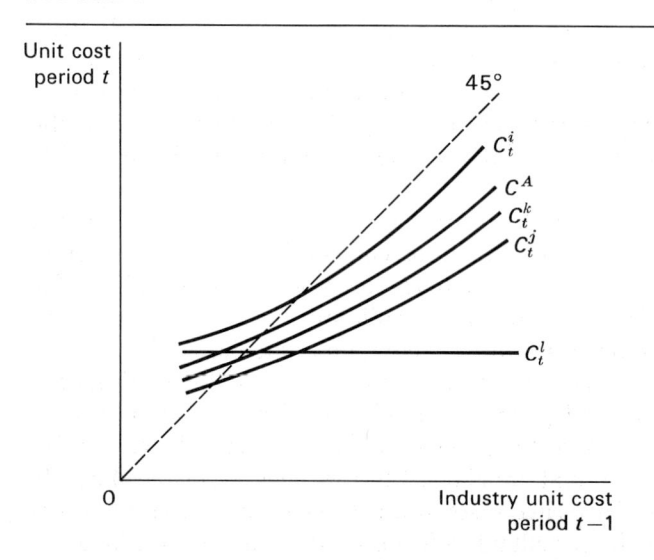

[Figure: Graph with "Unit cost period t" on the ordinate and "Industry unit cost period $t-1$" on the abscissa. A 45° dashed line is shown, along with curves labeled C_t^i, C^A, C_t^k, C_t^j, and C_t^l.]

ordinate shows the actual cost of any firm determined by that firm's reaction to what it believes or expects to be the unit cost performance of the industry as a whole. The alternate expected unit cost performance of the industry is shown on the abscissa. Thus each point on line C_t^i associates the unit cost for firm i in period t, given the average unit cost in the industry in period t-1. The lines are drawn in such a way that they reflect the idea that if the unit cost that is the average for the industry is higher, then the firm's unit cost will also be higher. As average industry unit costs fall, some firms are motivated to reduce these unit costs accordingly. The higher the industry unit cost, the easier it is for any firm to search and successfully find means for reducing its own cost. Therefore, for a given incentive toward cost reduction, the firm is likely to find more successful ways of reducing its cost when industry costs are high compared to what they might find when they are low. As a consequence the typical reaction unit cost lines are more steeply sloped where industry unit costs are high compared to when they are low. Indeed, at very low industry unit costs the firm reaction cost lines approach an asymptote. It is not necessary for our analysis to assume that all firms are nonminimizers. Therefore some firms may have reaction cost lines that are horizontal.

The curve C^A is the average of the unit costs of all the firms in question, where the weight for any firm's cost is the proportion of its output to the total industry output. C^A is the average reaction cost line for all the firms. The basic assumption is that a firm's costs will be higher if the average industry costs are expected to be higher, and vice versa. Beyond some point, where expected average industry costs are very low, every reaction cost line will be above the 45° line.

In Figure 3 the line P is a locus of equilibrium prices. Each point on the line

FIGURE 3

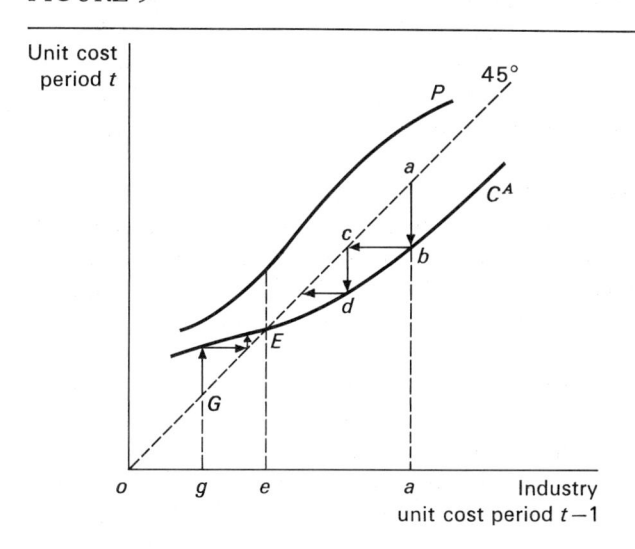

associates an equilibrium price with a level of industry unit cost in the previous period, which in turn determines the unit costs level of the various firms in the current period. Thus, given the industry unit cost in period t-1, this determines the unit cost level for each firm in period t. Each firm in turn will pick that output that maximizes its profits. The sum of all the outputs determines the industry output, and given the demand function for the product, the industry output determines the price. The price will be an equilibrium price if at that price no additional firms are induced to enter the industry or to withdraw from it. Thus the price for each industry unit cost is determined in accordance with conventional price theory considerations. If the price at the outset is above equilibrium price, then the entry of firms will bring that price down toward equilibrium, and if the price is below equilibrium, marginal firms will be forced to leave the industry, which in turn will cause the price to rise. Thus at every level of industry unit cost in period t-1 there is a determinate number of firms, that number consistent with the associated equilibrium price.

The point E in Figure 3, the intersection between curve C^A and the 45° line, is an equilibrium point for all the firms. The process envisioned is that each firm sets its cost in period t in accordance with its expectation of the industry cost, which by assumption is what the industry cost was in period t-1. This is a one-period lag relation. Each firm finds out what all of its competitors were doing as a group in terms of cost and reacts accordingly in the next period. If the industry cost is equal to oe then in the subsequent period each firm would set its cost so that the weighted average unit cost of all the firms would be equal to oe. Hence E is an equilibrium point.[5]

But suppose that the initial industry cost were equal to oa. We want to show that this sets up a movement that leads eventually to the point E. The firms' unit costs will average out at ab, which generates a process shown by the set of arrows $abcd$, etc., toward the point E. In a similar fashion, if we start with an industry cost of og, a process is set in motion so that costs move from G toward the point E. Clearly E is a stable equilibrium point. It is to be noted that every point on curve C^A need not presume that the same number of firms exist in the industry. At higher costs more firms exist, but as costs decline, some firms are forced out and fewer firms exist. In terms of the weighted average indicated by the points on the curve C^A, this simply means that some of the outputs will be zero for some of the firms as we get to lower and lower industry costs.

Figure 4 is intended to illustrate the cost reduction aspect of the residual in growth. When we begin the process the average reaction cost line is C_1^A. Firms start at point a and reduce costs along the arrow shown by ab. At this point additional information is introduced into the industry which is reflected in the diagram by the shift in the reaction cost line from C_1^A to C_2^A. Once firms are on C_2^A they then proceed with the cost reduction process as shown by the arrow cd. This illustrates two basic elements involved in the residual, the process of cost reduction in response to the motivation created by competitive pressures, as well as that part of cost reduction that is reflected in actual innovations, and is illustrated by downward shifts in the reaction cost lines.

[5] In essence the existence of an equilibrium can be shown on the basis of Brouwer's fixed-point theorem. (Point E in Figure 3 can be interpreted as a fixed point.) It would be possible to develop a much more general theory along the same lines based on less restrictive assumptions and achieve essentially the same result. For instance the one-period lag in the reaction unit cost relation can readily be eliminated. Similarly, the unique relation between the firm's unit cost and the industry unit cost level can be relaxed. . . . However the essence of the theory would remain the same. To conserve space and in the interest of simplicity I present the more restrictive version.

FIGURE 4

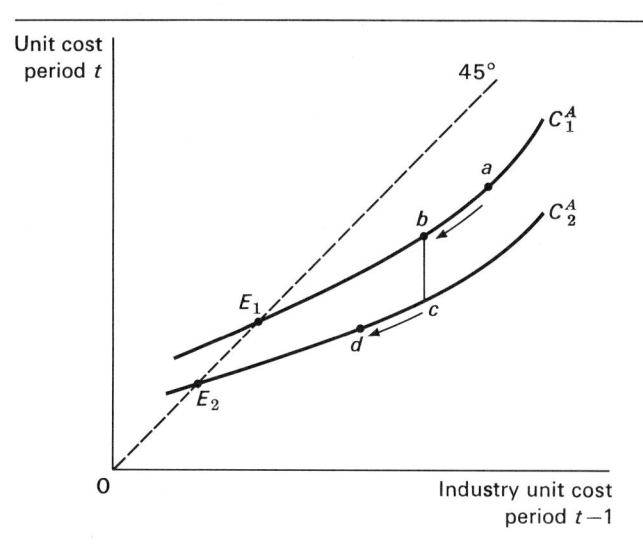

[Figure 4: Graph with axes "Unit cost period t" (vertical) and "Industry unit cost period t−1" (horizontal). Two curves C_1^A and C_2^A shown with a 45° line. Points E_1, E_2 on the 45° line; points a, b, c, d marked on the curves with arrows indicating movement from a to b, b to c, and c to d.]

IV. CONCLUSIONS

We have suggested three reasons for X-inefficiency connected with the possibility of variable performance for given units of the inputs. These are (a) contracts for labor are incomplete, (b) the production function is not completely specified or known, and (c) not all inputs are marketed or, if marketed, are not available on equal terms to all buyers. These facts lead us to suggest an approach to the theory of the firm that does not depend on the assumption of cost-minimization by all firms. The level of unit cost depends in some measure on the degree of X-efficiency, which in turn depends on the degree of competitive pressure, as well as on other motivational factors. The responses to such pressures, whether in the nature of effort, search, or the utilization of new information, is a significant part of the residual in economic growth.

One idea that emerges from this study is that firms and economies do not operate on an outer-bound production possibility surface consistent with their resources. Rather they actually work on a production surface that is well within that outer bound. This means that for a variety of reasons people and organizations normally work neither as hard nor as effectively as they could. In situations where competitive pressure is light, many people will trade the disutility of greater effort, of search, and the control of other people's activities for the utility of feeling less pressure and of better interpersonal relations. But in situations where competitive pressures are high, and hence the costs of such trades are also high, they will exchange less of the disutility of effort for the utility of freedom from pressure, etc. Two general types of movements are possible. One is along a production surface towards greater allocative efficiency and the other is from a lower surface to a higher one that involves greater degrees of X-efficiency. The data suggest that in a great many instances the amount to be gained by increasing allocative efficiency is trivial while the amount to be gained by increasing X-efficiency is frequently significant.

9

IMPERFECT COMPETITION: MONOPOLISTIC COMPETITION AND OLIGOPOLY

During the 1930's economic theory underwent three revolutions: (1) the restoration of aggregate economies by J. M. Keynes, (2) the rationalization of international trade theory by Bertil Ohlin, and (3) the development of the theory of imperfect competition by Joan Robinson[1] and Edward Chamberlin.[2] We are concerned in this chapter with the third of those developments, because until the 1930's economists pictured the economy as containing industry structures which were either perfectly competitive or purely monopolistic. Economists of that era seemed to regard all industries where entry was not blocked as potentially competitive, because firms could enter these industries whenever profits became excessive. However, Mrs. Robinson in England and Professor Chamberlin in the United States proposed that most real-world industry structures fit somewhere between the two extremes of perfect competition and pure monopoly. Moreover, they postulated that no inherent tendency may exist for such industries to become purely monopolistic or perfectly competitive, as economists before them might have expected. They set out, therefore, to develop a theory of imperfectly competitive industry structures to explain their observations and virtually completed the theory of monopolistic competition. In addition, their work spearheaded the development of oligopoly theory. Our task now is to present the theory of imperfect competition, beginning with monopolistic competition.

---

[1] Joan Robinson, *The Economics of Imperfect Competition* (London: Macmillan and Co., 1933).
[2] Edward H. Chamberlin, *The Theory of Monopolistic Competition* (Cambridge, Mass.: Harvard University Press, 1933).

MONOPOLISTIC COMPETITION

Monopolistic competition exists when an industry consists of a large number of firms producing and selling products which are differentiated but which are good substitutes for each other. The noun *competition* is the more important word in *monopolistic competition;* the adjective *monopolistic* implies a tendency away from perfect competition in the direction of monopoly, *but the movement is slight.* A monopolistically competitive industry is much more competitive than it is monopolistic, because it presupposes a large number of firms, which are free to enter and exit the industry, much as in the competitive model.

The main distinction between perfect competition and monopolistic competition is that each monopolistically competitive firm produces a product that is slightly differentiated from other firms' products. The firms, nevertheless, constitute an industry because their products are close substitutes. The essence of monopolistic competition is the existence of many firms producing similar but differentiated products.

Because of product differentiation, the demand curve for each monopolistically competitive firm's output is not perfectly elastic, as it is for the competitive firm. Instead, each firm has some control over the price it charges for its product; consequently it is not simply a price taker, as the competitive firm is. Some customers prefer the firm's product to that of others because of its particular style, brand identification, or unique features. These customers will continue to buy the product, even if the firm raises its price. In effect, each monopolistically competitive firm enjoys a small degree of monopoly power. Examples of monopolistically competitive industries are found in light manufacturing and in the retail trades industries such as restaurants, laundries, and so on.

The monopolistically competitive firm's control over price is definitely circumscribed. It cannot raise its price very much because more and more of its customers would switch to the close substitutes produced by other firms in the industry. Since there are a large number of monopolistically competitive firms in the industry, there exists a wide assortment of close substitutes for the output of any one firm. For example, a men's suit manufacturer such as Brooks Brothers faces competition from hundreds of other manufacturers. The monopolistically competitive firm will therefore face a demand curve that is highly (though not perfectly) elastic over the appropriate price range.

Short-Run Equilibrium

An apparent anomaly exists in that monopolistic competition is closest to perfect competition, but the graphical illustration of the basic features of the short-run equilibrium model for a monopolistically competitive firm is much the same as for a pure monopoly. The reason for the similarity of the graphical models of monopoly and monopolistic competition is that both incorporate a degree of inelasticity in the demand curves of the firms. To illustrate, cost and revenue functions for a hypothetical, monopolistically competitive firm are presented in Figure 9–1. The firm realizes positive profits for output levels between points b and c because average revenue exceeds average cost everywhere between these points. The profit-maximizing output level is Q_e, and the corresponding price P_e, as indicated by the intersection of marginal cost and marginal revenue at point a.

FIGURE 9–1 Short-Run Profit Maximization: Monopolistic Competition

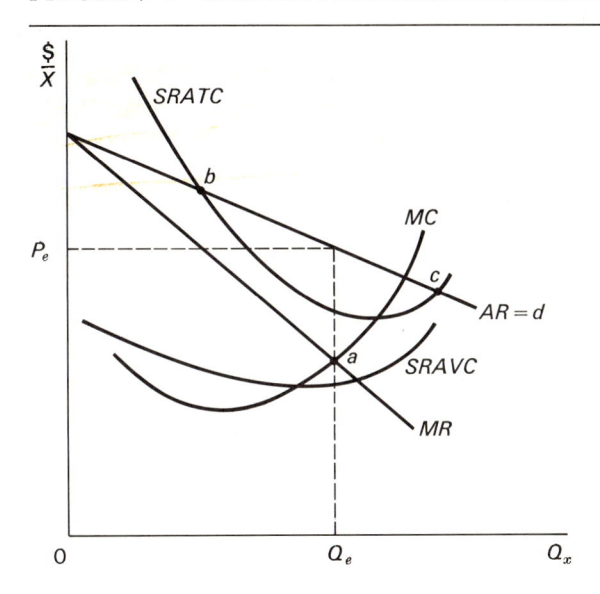

Our illustration indicates positive profits, but a monopolistically competitive firm may realize either profits or losses in the short run. If the firm's AR schedule is below SRATC at every output level, it will realize losses. But in either case, to maximize its profits (or to minimize its losses), the firm will determine the output for which MC equals MR and produce that output if AR exceeds AVC. If AR is below AVC at every output level, the firm will minimize losses by producing zero units of output. Thus, like the competitive firm and the monopolist in the short run, the monopolistically competitive firm may earn positive or negative economic profits. At any rate, from the standpoint of efficiency, comparison among different industry structures should realistically involve comparisons of long-run equilibrium, to which we now turn.

Long-Run Equilibrium

In the absence of artificial barriers, new firms are free to enter and old ones to exit a monopolistically competitive industry if given enough time to make a long-run adjustment to market conditions. If existing firms in a monopolistically competitive industry are earning an economic profit, this induces new firms to enter the industry. As new firms enter, the industry supply will increase and market price will fall.[3] This causes a leftward shift in the demand curve facing each firm and makes it more elastic. Each firm's share of the market will fall as more and more firms enter the industry, so that at any given price a firm will sell less after the new rivals enter the industry than before.

When will new firms stop entering the industry and the long-run adjustment process cease? Each firm's demand curve will continue to shift to the left as long as new firms enter the industry, and new firms will continue to enter the industry until all economic profits are eliminated. To illustrate, refer to Figure 9-2, which shows the long-run equilibrium situation for a monopolistically competitive firm. We assume that the firm depicted in the figure is representative of other firms in the industry, though each firm will likely have somewhat different cost and demand curves. The firm's demand, D, has shifted

FIGURE 9-2 Long-Run Equilibrium: Monopolistic Competition

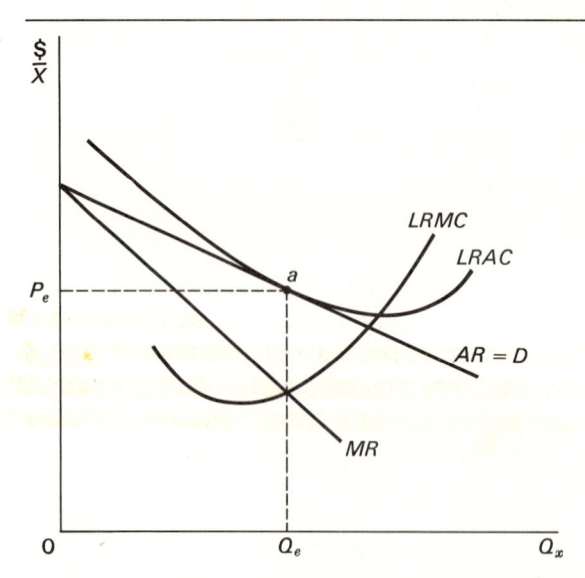

---

[3] The industry price is in fact a "cluster" of prices, since each firm will likely set a different price. However, each firm's price will be close to the price of others in the industry, because all the products are close substitutes.

leftward until it has become tangent to the long-run average total cost curve at point *a*. With LRAC equal to AR, economic profits are zero. Losses would occur if the firm produced an output either to the left or right of Q_e, because average cost exceeds average revenue everywhere except at the tangency point, *a*. Marginal revenue must therefore equal marginal cost at Q_e.

The existence of economic losses in a monopolistically competitive industry would force some marginal firms, presumably those with the greatest losses or weakest financial resources, to leave the industry in the long run. The exit of these firms would cause a rightward shift in the demand curves facing the surviving firms. As the demand curve facing a firm shifted to the right, its losses would be reduced. The exit of firms would cease when firms' demand curves had shifted enough to the right to eliminate losses and restore an equilibrium condition such as that illustrated in Figure 9–2. We may conclude that long-run equilibrium in a monopolistically competitive industry is characterized by zero profits for all firms, just as we saw was true of perfect competition.

However, even though pure profits may be eliminated in monopolistic competition, the efficiency of this industry structure falls somewhat below that of perfect competition. The negative slope of the firm's demand curve causes the point of tangency with the average cost curve to occur to the left of the lowest cost output. Consequently, in long-run equilibrium, the monopolistically competitive firm will produce less output and sell it for a higher price than would a similar firm operating under perfect competition. Only a horizontal line, such as a competitive firm's demand curve, can be tangent to a U-shaped unit cost curve at its minimum value.

One of the main differences between perfect competition and monopolistic competition is that monopolistic competitors usually find it to their advantage to promote their products, while perfect competitors do not. Product promotion allows the monopolistically competitive firm to further differentiate its product in the minds of customers. It matters very little if the differentiation is psychological, accomplished by product promotion, such as advertising, or "real," accomplished by physically altering the product. In either case, the consumer *thinks* the product is different, and so for him it *is* different. Successful product differentiation will simultaneously increase the demand for the product of the monopolistically competitive firm and reduce its price elasticity. To the extent that the firm succeeds in its efforts to differentiate its product through physical changes or promotional activities, it increases its monopoly power. However, any such efforts to differentiate products can only be achieved at a real cost to the producer and to society.

Monopolistically competitive firms attempting to increase their monopoly power by differentiating their products may be successful in doing so at the expense of others. We might suspect, therefore, that a monopolistically competitive industry will be unstable. Moreover, existing firms might be able to restrict the number of firms in the industry by erecting a promotional barrier, putting the output of prospective new firms at a disadvantage compared with established and accepted products. This barrier might appear formidable to a firm considering entering the industry. In other words, the existence of intensive promotional activity in a monopolistically competitive industry might tend to kill off weaker firms and eventually result in the development of "oligopoly," an industry situation characterized by the existence of just a few firms. The automobile industry in the United States was once composed of a great many firms: now there are only four. This suggests that any tendency toward oligopoly is accentuated if there are other economic factors, such as important scale economies, which would give large firms an advantage over smaller ones. The advantage of scale economies is particularly important if a new or existing small firm cannot obtain the necessary capital to build a large-scale plant facility or to engage in national promotion.

OLIGOPOLY

Oligopoly refers to a market structure characterized by interdependence among the firms in the industry. Interdependence exists when the actions of one oligopolist have an effect on one or more of the other firms in the industry. For instance, if firm A lowers its price and thereby draws a noticeable volume of sales away from firm B, then interdependence exists between A and B; or if firm C's advertising campaign results in a noticeable loss of sales by firm D, then firms C and D are interdependent. Where such interdependence exists, each firm, before altering its policies, will assess the effects of its actions on others and then estimate its rivals' most likely response to that change. Returning to our example of firms A and B, A will be less likely to lower its prices if it anticipates that B will match any price decrease.

Because of the similarities between firms in oligopolies and nations at war, or potentially at war, many of the computer models used for war games are based on oligopoly theory. Both situations involve a limited number of rivals engaged in a type of conflict. Often the whole process of interaction can best be simulated using games, and in recent years economists have discovered that the theory of games and game simulation, as an adjunct to decision theory, can help analyze oligopoly behavior. One distinction that is important in a game simulation of firms in competition and countries at war is that firms operate within a more or less effective set of social constraints, so that an oligopolist generally acts on the basis of the *likeliest* response of rivals, without fear of physical destruction if rivals do not react as anticipated. In contrast, countries at war must provide for the possibility that rivals may do the worst they are capable of, because there is some probability, however small, that they will.

Typically, interdependence exists because of the small number of firms in an industry, and strictly, oligopoly means "few firms." The first oligopoly structure to receive widespread attention (in the 1800's) was the case of an industry with two firms, a special case of oligopoly called *duopoly*. With only a few firms in an industry, each firm is likely to have a significant share of the entire market so that if one firm increases its share of the market by reducing its price, one or more rival firms must suffer a reduction in their market share. The rival firms will realize that their market position is affected by the change in policy of the original firm and will not likely remain passive. In general, each firm will continuously observe the behavior of its rivals, because it knows that it is affected not only by its own policies but the policies of others.

Although we typically find interdependence in industries with few firms, fewness is not essential, as an oligopoly might consist of one large, dominant firm and a "trail" or fringe of many smaller firms. Such an industry may be considered an oligopoly because interdependence exists among the firms. However, it may be a one-way interdependence: the policies of the dominant firm can affect the smaller firms, but the reverse may not be true—the actions of any one small firm will not likely affect significantly the larger one. Such a situation is of special interest because, without the large firm, the industry would approximate either perfect competition, if there is no product differentiation, or monopolistic competition, if the products are differentiated. The dominant-firm and duopoly models might be appropriate under certain circumstances, but the typical oligopoly consists of a market structure somewhere between the two extremes, industries with more than two firms, but not many more.

Describing oligopolies and theorizing about their behavior is one of the most interesting aspects of microeconomics, because of both the many oligopolistic industry structures which exist and the variety of ways in which price interdependence is manifested. But oligopoly is, for the same reasons, also the most difficult type of industry structure to theorize about. For one thing, there is no single pattern which describes price interdependence in oligopoly. For example, referring to Figure 9–3, assume that an oligopolistic,

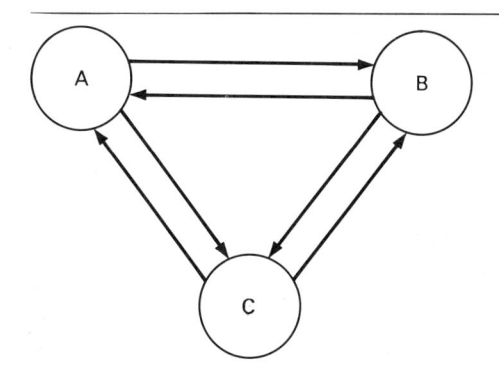

FIGURE 9–3   Lines of Interdependence Among Three Oligopolists

noncollusive industry consists of three firms, A, B, and C, and that we are interested in how firms A, B, and C will react to changes in price initiated by one of the trio. One possible assumption, albeit probably unrealistic, is that firms B and C ignore the price changes of A and of each other, and A ignores B and C. Or B might ignore A's actions but not C's, and A and C might ignore each other's actions but not B's actions. Another possibility is that any one of the firms may respond to any action by any of the other firms. To make it more complicated, A may ignore B and C when they act independently but not when they act together; whereas B may ignore some of C's actions but not other actions initiated by C. Our point is that a large number of possible assumptions could be made about the pattern of interdependence among three firms, and as the number of firms increases, the number of possibilities increases as well, and in greater proportion.

Moreover, simply to know that A will respond to the actions of B is not enough. We must know specifically how A will respond to price changes initiated by B. A might ignore B's price increases but match price decreases by B, or vice versa. The response might be more complicated. For instance, A might lower its price in response to a price increase initiated by B, while if B lowers price, A might reduce its price by two times A's decrease. The *pattern* of response adds a whole new dimension to the problem; once we have determined that firms *will* react to changes in their rivals' policies, we must then determine exactly *how* they will respond.

Given the structure of an oligopoly, and the assumption that each firm is a profit maximizer, we cannot predict what price and output decisions firms will make unless we have complete information about the response behavior of all the oligopolists, that is, how each will react to the price policies of all the others. Since there are many possible patterns of response in a given situation, there are many different models of oligopoly, one for each possible set of assumptions that we could make about oligopoly behavior. Therefore, there exists *no general theory of oligopoly*, only a collection of theories, each applicable to a different situation. For this reason, one economist has remarked that once you turn to oligopoly you leave deductive economics and enter institutional economics.

Since there are a number of different oligopoly models, our task now is to present those which seem most efficient, and in the following sections we will be concerned with three models which appear to many economists to have some predictive efficiency. The first which we will present is called the "Kinked-Demand" model.

The Kinked-Demand Model of Oligopoly—Noncollusive Behavior

In several industries characterized by a competitive, noncollusive brand of oligopoly, changing conditions of demand and costs are often observed to have no effect on output price. The kinked-demand model represents one way of explaining such price stability. And the theory is consistent with the operating criterion of profit maximization assumed to be employed by the firms. The kinked-demand model is based upon a plausible set of assumptions about how oligopolistic rivals might behave in the absence of collusion. In addition to the basic assumption that there is no collusion among firms, we also assume that no firm is an acknowledged price leader in the industry. This model might then be most efficient in predicting behavior in young oligopolistic industries.

The Noncollusive Firm's Concept of Rivals' Response. To illustrate the kinked-demand model, we focus on the decision-making process of one firm in the industry, firm A, as it views its market situation. We assume that a uniform price exists in the industry and that firm A is principally concerned with the effects on its rivals of any price changes A might initiate. In general, A can anticipate one of two possible responses by other firms to a price change: (1) the change might be ignored by others, leaving firm A free to operate independently, or (2) rival firms might react to A's price change, perhaps by following suit.

Following upon the first possible response, if firm A lowers its price and other firms do not respond in any way, the demand for A's output will probably be highly elastic at the original price, because A will not only increase its unit sales by attracting new buyers to the industry with a price decrease but will also lure customers away from its higher-priced rivals. On the other hand, if firm A raises its price and rival firms do not respond, A will rapidly lose business to its rivals.

Considering the second possible response, if A's rivals match price changes initiated by A, then A's demand will be much less elastic at the going price, either for price increases or decreases, because in effect, the entire industry would move up or down the market demand schedule, each firm keeping its market share, as A led the industry in price increases or decreases.

In the absence of any collusion or exchange of information, what assumptions will firm A make regarding the likeliest response by rivals to A's price changes? A plausible assumption is that rivals will ignore price increases but will match price decreases initiated by A, because if they ignored A's price cut, they would lose customers to A; whereas, if they ignored a price increase initiated by A, their market share would increase at A's expense. It is possible that in response to a price cut by A, rivals will cut their price even lower to impress upon the price cutter the evils of boat-rocking. So, in all likelihood, the best firm A can expect with a price reduction is that it will retain its share of the market.

Given the assumption that rivals ignore A's price increases and match price decreases, A's demand schedule will be more elastic for price increases than for price decreases. A's demand curve will, in fact, be kinked at the existing price; hence, the name of the model. The derivation of the kinked-demand curve for firm A is illustrated in Figure 9-4. Price, P_E, is assumed to be the initial

FIGURE 9-4 The Kinked-Demand Model of Oligopoly

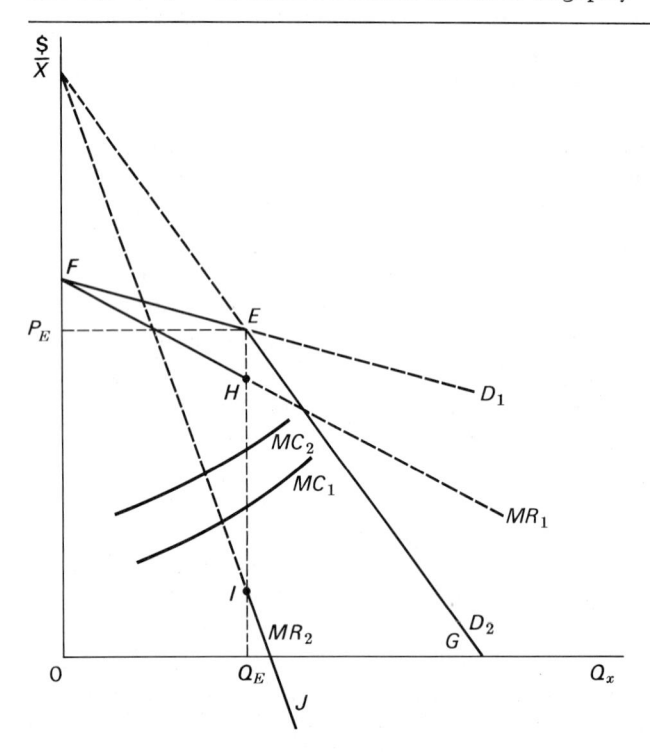

price in the industry and A's market share, Q_E. Curves D_1 and MR_1 are the demand and marginal revenue curves that would be appropriate for A if rival firms did not respond to either price increases or decreases by A; and curves D_2 and MR_2 represent the demand and marginal revenue curves which would face the firm if rival firms matched all price changes initiated by A. Following our basic assumption, segment EF is A's appropriate average revenue curve for prices above E, and segment EG is appropriate for prices below E. A's demand curve is, therefore, kinked at the existing price, P_E, exhibiting much greater elasticity for prices higher than P_E than for prices lower than P_E.

The marginal revenue curve associated with the kinked-demand curve FEG is composed of two segments, FH and IJ. Segment FH is the marginal revenue curve associated with FE and is appropriate for output levels less than Q_E, while segment IJ, the marginal revenue curve associated with EG, is appropriate for output levels above Q_E. A's marginal revenue curve is, then, the two combined segments, FHIJ. The value of marginal revenue is not defined for an output of Q_E and is said to be discontinuous at that output.

Equilibrium Price–Output. If the firm's marginal cost curve cuts across the dashed segment between points H and I, the firm maximizes profits by producing output Q_E at price P_E. For example, if the firm's marginal cost is MC_1, and it is producing an output less than Q_E, MR is above MC_1, so the firm would increase profits by expanding output. Since MR is less than MC_1 for output levels above Q_E, the firm would not produce an output greater than Q_E. If marginal cost intersects marginal revenue along the segment FH, the firm will raise price above the initial price, P_E, and reduce output below Q_E, whereas, it would lower its price and increase output if marginal cost intersected segment IJ above the horizontal axis.

What would happen if A's costs changed or market demand shifted? First, suppose there is a shift in the firm's costs, say, because resource prices change. If the change in cost is moderate, there will be no effect on the firm's price–output decision. To illustrate, marginal cost might shift from MC_1 to MC_2, in Figure 9–4, or vice versa, without affecting the firm's price or output. Of course, the firm's level of profits will be affected. On the other hand, if market demand increases, firm A's demand curve will shift horizontally to the right, but the kink will likely remain at the original price, as illustrated in Figure 9–5. Despite the shift in A's demand from D_1 to D_2, the firm's marginal cost curve will intersect the discontinuous portion of MR_2 between A' and B' if sufficiently elastic. Consequently, the profit-maximizing price is the same as before, though the firm's output would increase from X_1 to X_2. The point is that even if market demand increases, firm A will expect its average revenue curve to be more elastic for price increases than decreases, so it will be reluctant to change price.

FIGURE 9–5 The Effects of Demand Shifts on the Kinked-Demand Model

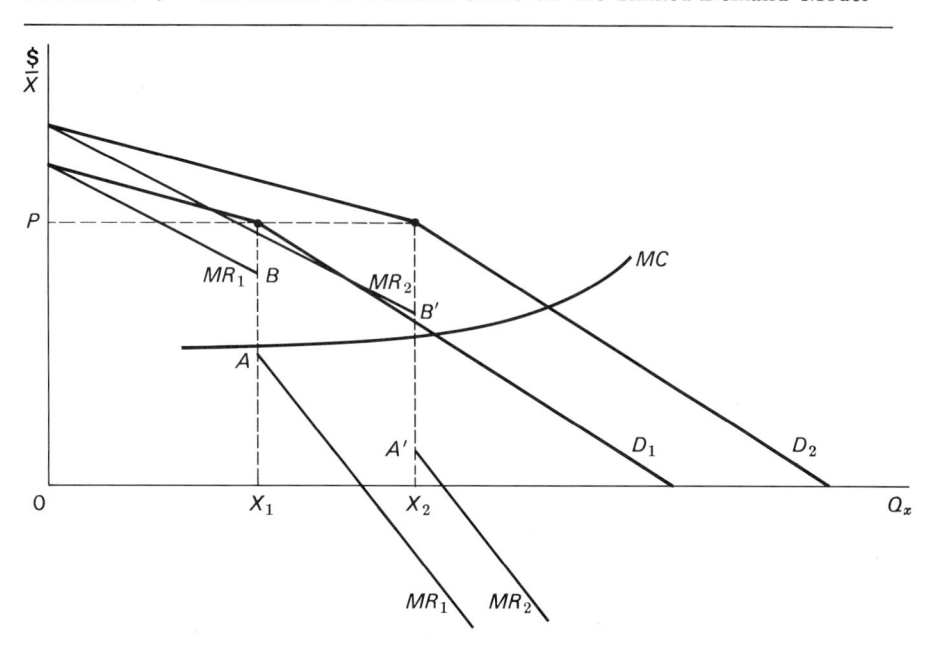

388 A Theory of Producer Behavior

In conclusion, given our assumption that rivals match price decreases but not price increases, a noncollusive oligopoly will be characterized by price–output rigidity in the face of changes in cost, and price rigidity with output flexibility in the face of changes in market demand. For either change, the model reveals considerable price "stickiness."

We should note that the principal weakness of the kinked-demand oligopoly model is that it fails to indicate how the initial price was originally determined. The existing price is simply assumed to be given at the outset.

The Case of Collusion: A Cartel

A cartel is created by a formal agreement among several firms in which each joining firm surrenders control over price and output to the cartel's administrators, who set prices and production quotas so as to realize the greatest possible industry profit. In essence, a cartel operates as a single monopoly firm, dividing the profits of the cartel among its members by a formula previously agreed upon. In return for surrendering its freedom of action, the firm hopes to realize greater profits or, perhaps, increased stability, or both.

The cost curves which are appropriate for the cartel's decision about market price and industry output are derived from those of the member firms. Assume the cartel is composed of four firms, and that MC_1, MC_2, MC_3, and MC_4 in Figure 9–6 are their marginal cost curves. If no scale economies or diseconomies are associated with combining the oligopolists' production activities, the MC function appropriate for the cartel is determined by horizontally summing the individual firm's MC curves. This conclusion follows from the argument that a cartel will allocate production quotas among its members so that the marginal cost of each is equal, for if the MC of any firm is greater than that of any other, the cartel can reduce total costs by reducing the quota of the firm with the higher MC and increasing the quota of the firm or firms with

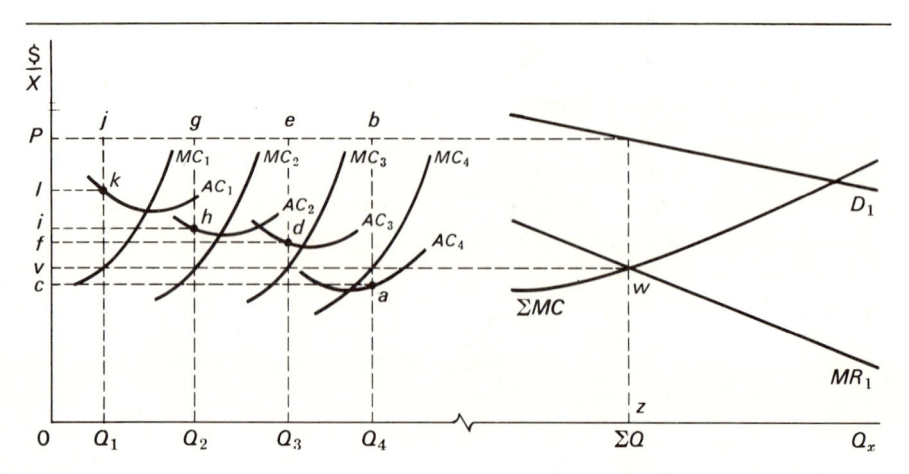

FIGURE 9–6 A Four-Firm Model of a Cartel

lower MC. So the management of the cartel attempting to maximize profits should base its decisions on the aggregate marginal cost curve, ΣMC in Figure 9-6. On the revenue side, the cartel will face the industry demand, D_1, and its related marginal revenue curve, MR_1. Combining the two curves, cartel managers determine the profit-maximizing price and output level by equating ΣMC with MR. Referring to Figure 9-6, ΣQ is the profit-maximizing output and P the associated price.

Production quotas of the several members of the cartel are determined as follows: each firm will produce that output for which its MC equals ZW, the value of ΣMC at the equilibrium output. By drawing a horizontal line back from point W where $MC = MR$, we can determine each firm's quota. Firm 1 will produce Q_1; firm 2, Q_2; firm 3, Q_3; and firm 4, Q_4. Looking at it differently, the profit-maximizing equilibrium quantity, ΣQ, is the sum of Q_1 produced by firm 1, plus Q_2 produced by firm 2, plus Q_3 produced by firm 3, plus Q_4 produced by firm 4.

To determine the total profit of the cartel, we sum the profit contributions of each of the several firms. Firm 4 contributes profits equal to the area of *Pbac*, whereas firm 3's contribution equals area *Pedf*. Firm 2 contributes profits of *Pghi*; and firm 1 contributes profits equal to area *Pjkl*. The sum of those four rectangles represents the total profits of the cartel. Notice that each firm contributes a different amount to the total profits of the cartel. For instance, firm 1 makes a smaller contribution to profits than does firm 4. However, it is likely that the shares of the profits going to the various firms will vary less than their respective contributions to profit. It is probable that the firms will agree before the cartel is formed how profits will be distributed, and each firm's share must be sufficient to insure its continued loyalty.

The difficulties involved in working out a mutually satisfactory arrangement for distributing cartel profits will likely be a stumbling block in the formation of a cartel. There is no theoretical way to predetermine how the cartel's profits will be distributed—even though we can determine theoretically the profit-maximizing output and price for the cartel and its members. The distribution of profits is entirely a matter of bargaining among firms; and disagreements over profit shares arising after formation of the cartel may jeopardize its chances for success.

The distribution of profits is only one of the difficulties facing a cartel. Another problem is that of distributing production quotas among the various firms. Earlier we said that this would be determined by equating the marginal cost of each firm with that value of MR which equals the sum of all marginal costs, ΣMC. Often, however, the market is dispersed and transport cost high, so market allocations are made geographically,[4] with each firm assigned an

---

[4] The international cartels tend to work this way. For example, the aluminum cartels in the past were formed principally to allocate broad market areas among member firms (and also to discourage the entry of new firms).

exclusive territory. Otherwise, if each firm were to sell its output throughout the entire market area, transportation costs would rise due to cross shipping. Under these circumstances, the cartel may be only a weak one in which each firm agrees not to invade the territory of others. Often such agreements are made only to be broken as one or more firms expands its territory. Sharp competition among the firms might then lead to the formation of another such cartel which, again, might have only a brief life.

In general, the biggest difficulty confronting a cartel is that of maintaining effective control over its members. Each firm wants to increase its *share* of the cartel's profits more than it wants to increase the *total* profits of the cartel. A member firm might enjoy a distinct advantage if the cartel holds price up for all the other members, while the given firm chisels by lowering its price. The average revenue curve for the firm would be very elastic for price decreases if all other firms held their prices at the level dictated by the cartel. The incentive for the individual firm to chisel on the cartel is great, and often the opportunity exists to do so without being caught. Probably the most important form of chiseling is *sub rosa* price cutting. Such price cuts may take many forms, such as payment of transport costs, liberal credit terms, or lower prices on other products when bought in conjunction with the given product. Of course, the employment of such tactics jeopardizes the existence of the cartel. In addition to *sub rosa* price cuts, firms may squabble over pooling arrangements or the costs reported to the cartel by member firms. The problems of restricting the entry of new firms may also be insurmountable. For all of the reasons indicated, economists tend to look upon cartels as basically unstable.

On the other hand, there may exist one very cohesive force in any cartel: the power and influence of the small group of managers directing it, coupled with each firm's awareness that without the cartel, the members will likely be worse off. Very often a successful cartel results after a number of unsuccessful attempts, where the dissolutions of the earlier cartels were followed by disruptive periods in the industry. In addition, economists must not overlook the strong control exerted by a group on its members just because the sociological pressures are difficult or impossible to quantify. The group can apply intense pressures on the individual members, such as the threat of a price war against an offending member. Such pressures may be strong enough to withstand any short-run economic pressures for self-enrichment by individual members.

One disadvantage associated with cartels is that they include firms with plant facilities of different scales and efficiencies. Returning to our example illustrated in Figure 9–6, if the cartel had been a monopoly from the start, a plant the size of firm 1 would not have been built, because it is inefficient relative to the size of firm 4. A monopolist would construct one plant large enough to produce the profit-maximizing output at the least unit cost, or several plants of smaller size but equal efficiency. For example, if firm 4's cost curves represented the long-run optimum scale of plant, then the monopolist would have constructed a plant of that size or larger and likely would not have built any plants the size of firms 1, 2, and 3. So we may conclude that several firms with unequal market shares in an oligopoly will not necessarily build the optimum size plant facilities, whereas, a monopolist, who faces the market demand, is likely to do so.

Leadership Oligopolies

One of the limiting cases of oligopoly mentioned in the introduction to this section is that of a dominant firm surrounded by a competitive fringe of smaller firms. The dominant firm may control industry price simply because of its size relative to other firms. Should the dominant firm have the advantages of economies of scale and financial strength, it may enjoy a virtually unquestioned position of leadership. Smaller rivals will avoid provoking the management of the large firm, and the easiest way to put off a confrontation will be to avoid impinging on the large firm's market share. The small firms will likely set their prices at the same level as those of the large firm. However, leadership in an oligopoly is not restricted to those industries where one firm dominates. Even in industries where market power is fairly evenly distributed among a few firms, one firm often assumes a leadership role. This is the case of so-called "administered price." There is no collusion; one firm simply announces its price and all others follow in lock step. The firm which assumes the leadership position might be the oldest or most prestigious or most dynamic.

Simply by tacitly following the industry leader, oligopolists avoid much of the uncertainty and risk which exist under conditions of mutual interdependence. In general, the leader will seek stable conditions in the industry, coupled with satisfactory profits for all firms, and will set prices at a level which other firms will likely find satisfactory. Furthermore, prices will generally be adjusted upward or downward by the leader only when it is clear that other firms will find it advantageous to follow suit. For example, a significant rise in resource prices (say, wages) which affects all firms in the industry will probably cause the leader firm to initiate a price increase. Examples of such behavior may be found in the steel, aluminum, metal can, automobile, and other industries.

The potential benefit to firms in a leadership oligopoly is a stable and dependable price, set high enough so that each firm enjoys economic profits and a stable share of the market. Although any one firm may not realize the greatest possible profits or the largest market share which it might under a different situation, the firm does avoid the risks of intense rivalry with the other firms in the industry. Moreover, the loss of profits a given firm might suffer by following the leader is possibly very small. Firms often feel that less-than-maximum profits or less-than-optimal growth are not too high a price for stability.

Even oligopolies that lack an acknowledged price leader may give results similar to the leadership model, if there is tacit agreement among the firms that higher prices are good for the industry and lower prices bad. Then any firm may raise prices slightly, with the expectation that the rest of the industry will follow its lead. In such cases, the kink in the noncollusive model might disappear. Rival firms would disregard a price increase only when it seemed unreasonably large, but would be quite willing to match reasonable price increases.

Oligopolies and Game Theory

Oligopoly, and its characteristic interdependence, implies that where firms do not actively collude, no firm, even a price leader, can be sure of what its rivals might do in response to any policy change. Therefore, each firm must operate on some expectation of what rivals will do, and management will, in effect, be playing a sort of game with opposing firms. One possible strategy may be to try to avoid any predictable pattern of behavior in order to keep the opposition guessing. In this respect, business can be much like war or football, and it is not surprising that the analysis of decision-making under such conditions has become known as "game theory."

Game theory was introduced in the 1940's with the publication of the *Theory of Games and Economic Behavior* by John von Neumann and Oskar Morgenstern, and a considerable literature has developed on the subject. One basic idea in game theory is that each participant in any given conflict situation should develop each of his possible alternative strategies and determine the expected outcome of each, given his knowledge (or lack of knowledge) of his opponents' capabilities. Game theory analysis will differ depending on how many participants are involved (a two-person game, i.e., a duopoly, is quite different from an n-person game, i.e., classical oligopoly) and on the possible results (a zero-sum game or constant-sum game, in which one participant's winnings must be matched by another's loss, is different from a positive-sum game, in which all may win—or a negative-sum game, in which all may lose). The participants will try to determine a strategy which offers the greatest gains, one which promises the least loss, or perhaps a strategy which offers stability and the promise of continued existence. The various strategies will be ranked and chosen by the participants according to their own preferences (utility functions) and obviously may vary according to the predisposition of the person or group making decisions.

Game theory offers a formal means of determining and ranking the available choices, and is therefore obviously at the heart of oligopoly theory. In fact, we might reverse this sentence and say that oligopoly theory was the start of game theory and that game theory is an extension of oligopoly theory into a generalized theory of decision-making under conflict.

Comparing the Performance of Imperfect and Perfect Competition

We noted in the previous chapter that a profit-maximizing monopolist generally produces less output and sells it at a higher price than would be the case in a perfectly competitive industry. That conclusion can be generalized to include other cases of imperfect competition. Any deviation from perfect competition usually means less industry output and higher market prices than would be the case if the industry were perfectly competitive. For example, given long-run equilibrium in a monopolistically competitive industry, the firms will operate to the left of the low point on their average cost curves. Even though price equals the average cost of production in long-run equilibrium, the monopolistically competitive firm will operate short of the optimum level, so price will be higher and output lower than under perfect competition. It should be pointed out, however, that the difference between perfect competition and monopolistic competition from an efficiency standpoint may be very small if the demand curves facing the individual firms are highly elastic; some economists seem to consider the difference inconsequential.

We noted that all monopolistically competitive industries and many oligopolies sell differentiated products and that product differentiation is achieved at a cost, whether it is accomplished by physically changing the product, by promotion, or by a combination of the two. Therefore, differentiated products cost more than homogeneous products, and we may conclude that one of the inefficiencies of imperfect competition is that costs are higher than they would be under perfect competition by the amount necessary to cover the cost of differentiation. However, we cannot simply conclude that imperfectly competitive industries are inefficient because they may bear a cost which perfectly competitive industries do not incur. That conclusion must be qualified. Product differentiation allows a degree of variety and individuality which homogeneous products would never permit. We must also remember that differentiated products are motivated by private gain and sold in free markets which J. M. Keynes maintains are "the best safeguard of the variety of life, which emerges precisely from this extended field of personal choice, and the loss of which is the greatest of all losses of the homogeneous or totalitarian state."[5] In conclusion, the added costs of product differentiation may be readily apparent, but the benefits might go unnoticed, at least until they are lost.

Like pure monopolists, firms in imperfectly competitive markets may have a more complicated objective function than simply profit maximization. If firms in imperfect markets seek to maximize total sales or production or investment or whatever, perhaps while maintaining a minimum acceptable profit level, the effects on efficiency may be so much the worse. Firms in im-

---

[5] J. M. Keynes, *The General Theory of Employment, Interest and Money* (New York: Harcourt, Brace, 1936), 380.

perfectly competitive markets may become more conservative in their operations. Their attempts to avoid risks and uncertainty may lead them to pursue policies which result in lower output and higher prices than simple profit-maximizing supply and demand analysis would imply. Any such tendency away from profit maximizing might effectively worsen their economic performance. In contrast, firms in other imperfectly competitive situations might sell more output for a lower price, both to discourage new firms from entering the industry and to avoid government charges that they are legally liable for restraining trade as defined in the antitrust laws.

SUMMARY

In this chapter, we have presented theories of the imperfectly competitive industry structures, monopolistic competition and oligopoly. Monopolistic competition exists when a large number of firms produce similar, but differentiated products. A monopolistically competitive firm faces a downward sloping demand curve, like a monopolist, but because of the existence of many close substitutes, it is highly elastic and the firm's market power, small. Monopolistic competition is closer to perfect competition than it is to monopoly for this reason. If there are no barriers to entry, long-run equilibrium in the industry will be characterized by zero profits for firms. The existence of profits attracts new firms and losses cause an exodus, much like the perfectly competitive model. One difference between perfect and monopolistic competition is product differentiation, and the real cost of differentiation of product is manifested in a long-run equilibrium price under monopolistic competition, which is higher than *LRMC* and higher than the minimum average cost of production. These differences are not likely to be great, however, as long as entry into the industry is free and there are no sizable economies of scale. On the other hand, monopolistically competitive firms will be motivated to further differentiate their products through promotion and, if a few are successful, this factor, plus the existence of significant scale economies, may lead to the development of an oligopoly.

Oligopoly exists when there is interdependence in an industry, and interdependence typically arises in those industries with only a few firms. Interdependence means that the action of any one firm in the industry produces a noticeable effect on other firms which is likely to cause them to react. Since there are many possible patterns of response of one firm to another's actions, there are many theories of oligopoly. No one theory will efficiently predict the behavior of all oligopolies. We have presented three oligopoly models which have proven somewhat useful. First is the kinked-demand model, which is based on a plausible set of assumptions about the expected response of one oligopolist to the price changes of another, when there is no collusion. Second is a model of overt collusive behavior among oligopolists, a cartel, which is quite similar to the theory of monopoly. One of the main difficulties of cartels is in maintaining the allegiance of members; failure so often occurs that economists tend to think of cartels as basically unstable. Third is a model describing the behavior of leadership oligopolies, a predominant form in American industry, some of the factors for whose existence we have indicated.

PROBLEMS

1. Answer the following based on the corresponding diagram. AR is the average revenue curve for a monopolistically competitive firm.

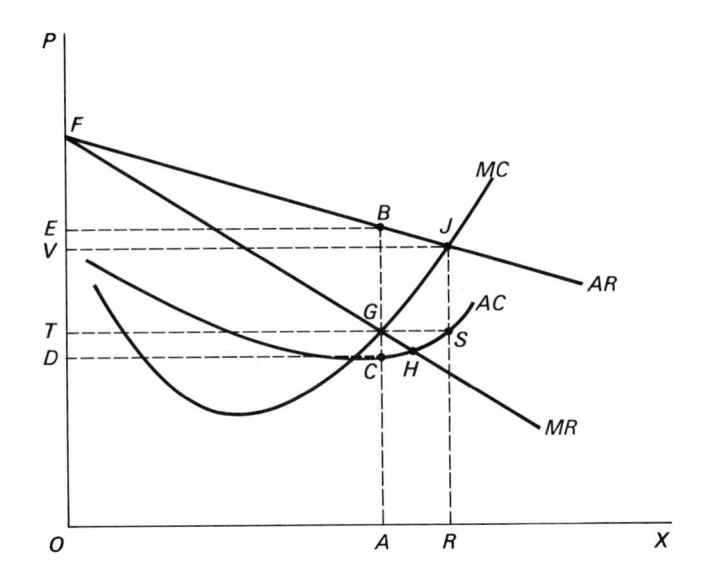

(a) At output OR, MC is (greater than, less than) MR, so the firm would (increase, decrease) output to maximize profits.
(b) The firm would maximize profits by producing output _____ and price _____.
(c) Profit per unit is _____ at the profit-maximizing output.
(d) Maximum profits are equal to area _____.

2. Answer the following based on the accompanying graph.
(a) If an oligopolist faces a demand curve which is more elastic for price increases (line segment AF) than for decreases (line segment FE), then its MR curve for less than OC units is _____ and for more than OC units is _____.

396   A Theory of Producer Behavior

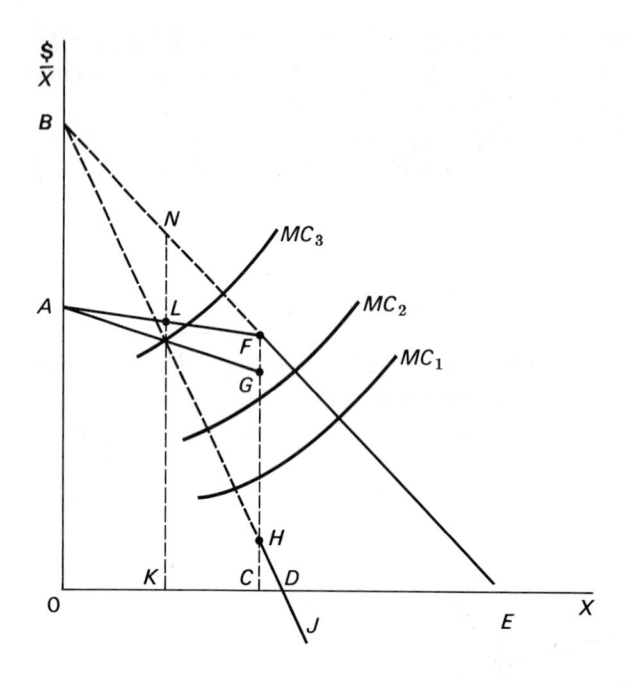

(b) If marginal cost is MC_1, the firm will produce output _____ at price _____.
(c) If marginal cost rises to MC_2, the firm will (increase, decrease, neither increase nor decrease) output and (increase, decrease, neither increase nor decrease) price.
(d) If marginal cost shifts up to MC_3, the firm would charge price _____ and produce output _____.
(e) If all rival firms match the given firm's price changes, whether increases or decreases, and if its marginal cost is MC_3, it would produce output _____ at price _____.

3. Answer the following based on the figure on page 397. Assume an industry with only two firms (a duopoly).
   (a) Suppose market demand is GH and the duopolists agree to share the market equally between them. Then, for any price, the quantity that will be sold by either firm is determined along curve _____.
   (b) The marginal revenue curve for either firm is then _____.
   (c) If the duopolists are identical in size, each with marginal costs along MC_1 and $_2$, then each will want to set price _____ and produce output _____.
   (d) Suppose now that the duopolists merge to form a monopoly. If there are no economies or diseconomies from combining the two firms, marginal cost will be _____.

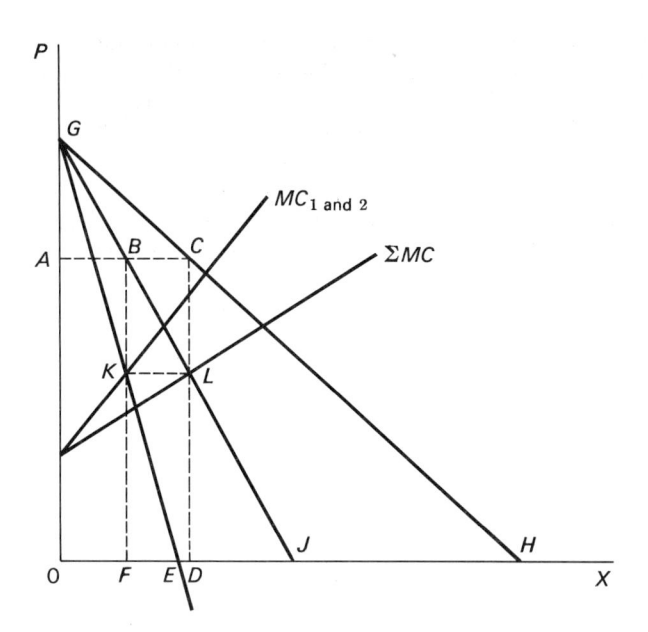

(e) The average revenue curve for the monopolist will be _____, and his marginal revenue curve will be _____.

(f) The monopolist would maximize profits by producing output at price _____.

(g) The difference between industry output under duopoly and monopoly is _____ and the difference in price is _____.

REFERENCES

BAIN, J. S., *Industrial Organization*. New York: John Wiley and Sons, 1959.

BAUMOL, WILLIAM J., "On the Theory of Oligopoly," *Economica*, 25 (August 1958), 187–198.

CHAMBERLIN, EDWARD H., *The Theory of Monopolistic Competition*, 7th ed. Cambridge, Mass.: Harvard University Press, 1956.

COHEN, K. J., and CYERT, R. M., *Theory of the Firm: Resource Allocation in a Market Economy*. Englewood Cliffs, N.J.: Prentice-Hall, Inc., 1965.

DORFMAN, ROBERT, and STEINER, P. O., "Optimal Advertising and Optimal Quality," *American Economic Review*, 44 (1954), 826–836.

PATINKIN, DON, "Multiple-Plant Firms, Cartels, and Imperfect Competition," *Quarterly Journal of Economics*, LXI (February 1945), 173–205.

ROBINSON, JOAN, *The Economics of Imperfect Competition*. London: The Macmillan Co., 1933.

SCHELLING, T. C., "The Strategy of Conflict: Prospectus for a Reorientation of Game Theory," *Journal of Conflict Resolution,* 2 (September 1958), 203–264.

SUPPES, PATRICK, and CARLSMITH, J. MERRILL, "Experimental Analysis of a Duopoly Situation from the Standpoint of Mathematical Learning Theory," *International Economic Review,* 3 (1962), 60–78.

"The Theory of Monopolistic Competition After Thirty Years," *American Economic Review, Papers and Proceedings,* 54, No. 3 (May 1964), 28–57. Papers by Joe S. Bain, Robert L. Bishop, and William J. Baumol; discussants: Jesse W. Markham and Peter O. Steiner.

APPENDIX TO CHAPTER 9

Oligopoly: An Example and a Contrast

E. WARREN SHOWS and ROBERT H. BURTON

There are a number of examples of oligopoly which usually spring immediately to mind, industries such as automobile manufacturing, steel, aluminum, and chemicals. But few would argue that the same degree of oligopoly prevails at the consumer level. When most of us buy a car, we have a choice of many sources: many new car agencies, more used car lots, and still more individuals selling used cars. Similar statements could be made of most other oligopolistic industries; the degree of competition apparently increases as we move from the producer to the consumer. Consequently, many often-cited cases are less than satisfactory as examples of an oligopolistic industry structure. Furthermore, complete price and output data from these industries are not always available, so the industries that are commonly suggested as cases of oligopoly are often poor subjects for study.

One industry does exist which has the characteristics of oligopoly at the consumer level and for which complete data are available. That industry is commercial banking.

It is true that thousands of commercial banks operate in this country, but only a few operate in any market area. More than enough banks exist for the industry to be considered competitive, if the entire country were the market area, but many bank customers do not leave their home town or even their own neighborhood to engage the services of a bank. The cases where customers do look to distant banks for service occur generally because a large customer cannot find a nearby bank with sufficient resources. Consequently, most bank customers operate within a restricted market area served by a limited number of banks. The number of commercial banks is limited because of the restrictions on the entry of new firms. Throughout much of the history of our country, we have, by preventing the free entry of new firms, in effect rejected competition as a means of controlling markets.

Stringent regulations are imposed on banks to insure uniform behavior and standardization of commercial practices. Enforced uniformity of conduct brings about a community of interest which stops short of collusion but which does result in widespread dissemination of information in the banking industry. Market information is further made available throughout the industry by the necessity for cooperation among banks in such matters as clearing-house arrangements, sharing of large loans, and correspondent relationships. If the banks do not collude—and from the evidence most do not—they certainly are well informed and forced into an awareness of interdependence.

If we agree that interdependence exists and that the banking industry is oligopolistic, what results might we expect? How does banking compare with other sectors of the capital and money markets? The market for U.S. Treasury bills (short-term government debt instruments) is a good contrast to the commercial banks' short-term lending, because the Treasury bill market is made up of many buyers and sellers, and with the exception of the Treasury itself and a few other participants, market power is decentralized. All buyers and sellers have access to complete market information. Anyone is free to enter or leave the market. And the product is homogeneous. The conclusion is that the Treasury bill market approximates the competitive model.

Not surprisingly, in light of the theories of perfect competition and oligopoly, we find that the prices of Treasury bills, and thus their yields, change continuously from one trading day to another. In sharp contrast, the bank interest rate is changed so infrequently that when the prime rate does change, it often makes headlines.

Theories cannot be "proved" by such facts. An infinite number of explanations might be consistent with any given set of facts. But we may suggest that facts such as those discussed in this section offer support for theories which lead to the same conclusion. Perfect competition is the most responsive of all market structures; so the daily fluctuations in the price of Treasury bills in response to shifts in supply and demand are to be expected. Noncollusive oligopolies are perhaps among the least responsive industry structures; so whether the banks are considered to be a simple noncollusive oligopoly with a kinked-demand curve or a price leadership oligopoly, the relative sluggishness of the bank rate is what we might anticipate. In the one case, individual banks fear to initiate a change in the interest rate they charge on loans because of the possible response of rivals, and, in the other case, the leaders fear loss of position if too frequent or unjustified rate changes should cause disaffection and revolt among other firms in the industry.

Duopoly, Oligopoly, and Emerging Competition
G. WARREN NUTTER[1]

We have shown that members of cartels have a strong incentive to chisel and that such behavior makes cartels unstable and short-lived. G. Warren Nutter investigates those conditions which make chiseling a rational course of behavior for oligopolists. Moreover, Nutter concludes that if the number of firms in an oligopoly increases, and if each one has an incentive to chisel, the resulting price–output behavior may approach that of competitive equilibrium. In other words, there may be pressures from oligopoly to monopolistic competition, as well as the reverse.

Economic theory has provided few interesting and satisfactory explanations of how competitive pricing could gradually emerge in a market if, beginning with the condition of monopoly, the number of firms were to increase gradually while other relevant factors remained the same. The most familiar and popular explanation is the one provided long ago by Cournot, but most economists are unhappy about the kind of behavior that must be postulated, finding it hardly compatible with good sense on the part of entrepreneurs. The purpose of this paper is to suggest an alternative explanation derived from a line of reasoning first set forth by Edgeworth a number of years ago.[2] The argument is essentially an exercise in logic, showing how a few plausible behavioral assumptions can generate quasi-competitive behavior whenever there is more than one firm in an industry. Naturally, such highly abstract reasoning

From the *Southern Economic Journal*, Vol. XXX, No. 4 (April 1964). Reprinted by permission.

[1] This paper was prepared for the meeting of the Southern Economic Association in November 1962. It was also presented to a seminar at the University of Chicago in the same month. Through continuing discussion over the last two years, my colleagues at Virginia have patiently and generously contributed to the argument as it emerges for better or worse in this paper, and their ideas are interwoven with my own. Professors Ronald Coase, James Ferguson, and Gordon Tullock were particularly helpful in the critical stages of my thinking. Of course, I speak in this paper for myself alone, and nobody else is responsible for my errors.

[2] For a review of Edgeworth's thinking on this subject, see A. J. Nichol, "Edgeworth's Theory of Duopoly Price," *Economic Journal*, XLV (March 1935), 51–66.

can do no more than indicate a possibly fruitful approach to theorizing, and a great deal more would have to be done before a meaningful theory came into being. But it is perhaps useful to start in a vacuum before introducing friction.

I. PRICING WITH IDENTICAL FIRMS AND COMPLETE KNOWLEDGE

Let us imagine an industry with an isolated market demand sufficiently large relative to costs of an individual firm to support a large number of identical firms with independent costs. For simplicity we suppose each firm is limited to only one size and one set of short-run costs. Let the industry operate in a static environment (given wants, resources, and technology) without explicit collusion or combination among firms. We suppose all entrepreneurs and managers to be equally shrewd and quick in their actions, to have complete knowledge of costs and market demand, and to have the single objective of maximizing the net worth of the firm. Consumers are also assumed to have complete knowledge of prices being charged and to be indifferent as to which firm is dealt with, so that each firm has its pro rata share of market demand when a uniform price is charged. To put the analysis in a concrete setting, we may imagine this industry as having a noneconomic barrier (such as a licensing arrangement) that limits the number of firms to those being examined at each stage of the discussion, except in the special case of free entry to be examined separately.

As reference points, it will be useful to define equilibrium prices that would prevail under competitive and monopolistic behavior. The n-firm competitive price is a price such that the market would be cleared if each of n firms in the industry produced the output at which marginal cost equals that price. The n-firm monopoly price is a price such that the market would be cleared if each of n firms in the industry produced the output at which marginal cost equals marginal revenue corresponding to that price, marginal revenue being derived from the firm's pro rata demand. There will be a list of each of these types of equilibrium prices, the level of price descending in each case as the number of firms increases.

A. Pricing with Barred Entry

Imagine the concrete case of duopoly with price established at the two-firm monopoly level, which—for simplicity—is taken to be below the one-firm competitive level. This implies among other things that the marginal cost curve slopes upward over the relevant range of output.[3] (We shall consider the downward-sloping case at a later point.) Now let firm A cut its price ever so

---

[3] The converse is not true. In any case, the relation between the one-firm competitive price and the two-firm monopoly price is not critical to the general argument.

slightly while B does not.[4] A may take his price as fixed no matter how much he sells up to the full amount that will be purchased by the market at that price, and he will therefore expand production until marginal cost equals price. B suffers a loss in the amount he can sell roughly equal to A's expansion. In terms of Figure 1, A's output rises from x_0 to x_1, while B's falls from x_0 to x_2. A's gain from chiseling, expressed as a time rate, is the increase in quasi-rent accompanying the increase in output. In terms of Figure 1, the gain from chiseling, G, may be put as follows:

$$G \simeq p_0(x_1 - x_0) - (x_1 v_1 - x_0 v_0). \tag{1}$$

The gain from chiseling will, of course, persist only as long as B does not cut his price to A's level. If B does so, the gain is replaced by a loss equal to the difference between quasi-rents at the two-firm monopoly price and at the new, slightly lower price. Let us refer to the gain as a temporary gain and the loss as a permanent loss. We may then assert the proposition that, as long as the temporary gain and the discount rate are positive and finite, there is some unilateral cut below a uniform price such that the present value of the temporary gain for the price cutter exceeds the present value of his permanent

FIGURE 1

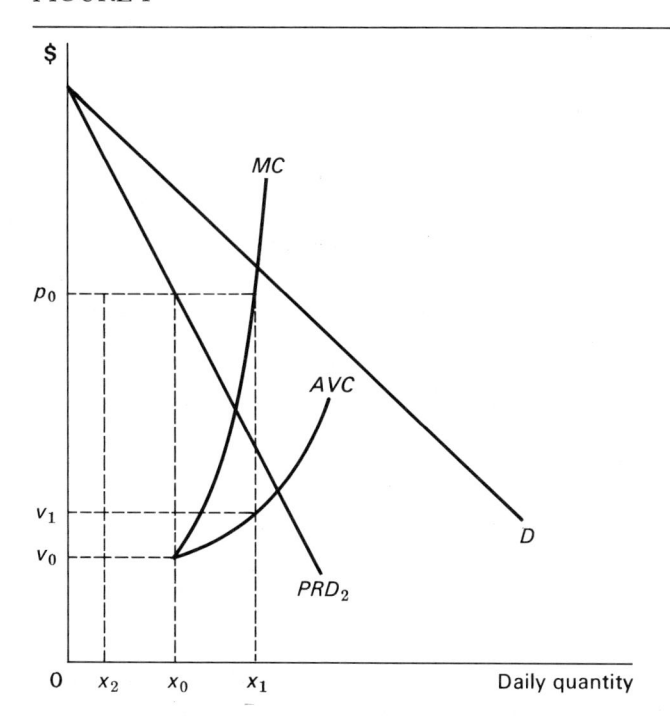

[4] Throughout the argument, A and B (and later C) may be interchanged as desired.

loss. This follows from the fact that the permanent loss can be made as small as desired down to the vanishing point by making the price cut sufficiently small, while a positive and finite temporary gain is not simultaneously made indefinitely small. In fact, under the stipulated conditions the temporary gain is maximized by making the price cut as small as possible.[5]

Before we proceed further, it will be useful to establish the lowest price for which the proposition just stated holds. From Eq. (1) we see that there is a positive and finite gain to A from chiseling as long as, for A,

$$p_0 > \frac{x_1 v_1 - x_0 v_0}{x_1 - x_0}, \qquad (2)$$

where subscripts zero and one identify variables before and after chiseling, respectively. If the interval of output x_0 through x_1 is finite, the right-hand expression represents the finite or arc marginal cost corresponding to that interval. Since the marginal cost curve rises upward over that interval, arc marginal cost must be lower than marginal cost at x_1 and hence lower than p_0. But as p_0 moves downward, the interval x_0 through x_1 becomes increasingly small and arc marginal cost moves increasingly close to p_0 from below. The two become equal at the intersection of the marginal cost curve with the pro rata demand curve—that is, at the two-firm competitive price. As p_0 moves below that level, it becomes less than arc marginal cost. Hence, at the two-firm competitive price the temporary gain from chiseling ceases to be positive and finite. The lower limit to profitable chiseling is fixed at the two-firm competitive level.

Returning to the original line of reasoning, we would suppose that, if it pays for one firm to cut price unilaterally, it should pay for the other as well. Yet if both act this way, neither can be successful more often than the other, and for both the present value of expected gains will be negative. It would seem that, taking the expected net loss into account, both firms should tacitly agree to accept the uniform two-firm monopoly price and to refrain from price cutting. But this will not be the case, for the firms are caught in a strong prisoners' dilemma.[6] If it pays for each to chisel on the assumption that the

---

[5] If the two-firm monopoly price is above the one-firm competitive price, the temporary gain will not be maximized by the minimum cut over that range of prices, but the basic proposition on the relation between the temporary gain and the permanent loss remains valid.

[6] I am indebted to James M. Buchanan for bringing this to my attention. For the dilemma, see R. D. Luce and H. Raiffa, *Games and Decisions* (John H. Wiley, 1957), 95 ff.; and Lester B. Lave, "An Empirical Approach to the Prisoners' Dilemma Game," *Quarterly Journal of Economics*, LXXVI (August 1962), 424–436. Lave offers experimental evidence that college students confronted with a simulated prisoners' dilemma game will in fact tacitly agree to choose the analogue to the monopoly solution. His evidence does not,

other will not, then each will be forced to cut the price by some amount no matter what the other in fact does.

This may be seen by considering the game for alternative courses of action by A and B. We start with both charging the two-firm monopoly price. The situation confronting them may be outlined by the familiar payoff matrix of game theory (see Figure 2). A's relevant possible pricing actions are repre-

FIGURE 2

A \ B	Raise	Retain	Cut	Two-fold cut
Raise	99.9 / 99.9	110.2 / 89.7	110.0 / 89.6	109.8 / 89.5
Retain	89.7 / 110.2	100.0 / 100.0	110.0 / 90.0	109.8 / 89.6
Cut	89.6 / 110.0	90.0 / 110.0	99.9 / 99.9	109.8 / 90.3
Two-fold cut	89.5 / 109.8	89.6 / 109.8	90.3 / 109.8	99.8 / 99.8

sented by the columns, B's by the rows; A's payoff from a combination of actions is listed in the upper right of the appropriate cell, B's in the lower left. The payoff for the status quo is standardized at 100, and the others are set in accord with a rough cardinal scale.

As we view A's possible responses to action by B, we observe that price raising has lower payoffs for every one of B's actions than each of the other three alternatives. In the language of game theory, price raising is dominated

---

however, seem to be directly applicable to the problem here, even if we leave aside the question of qualifications of the participants to play the game. For one thing, in several experiments the participants were notified in advance that play would be limited to a specified number of moves. For another, the courses of action were more restricted and the payoff matrix less refined than in the pricing problem posed here. It is also worth noting that his experiments were limited to pairs of opponents.

Incidentally, contrary to Lave's opening assertion, Adam Smith's invisible hand is a clear case of the prisoners' dilemma in operation: the attempt by each producer to maximize profits defeats the purpose. Lave confuses the gains of consumers, who are benefited bystanders, and the losses of producers, who are the "players."

by other courses of action. Hence we may strike off the "raise" column and row. For the remainder of the matrix, price retaining is dominated by the other two alternatives, and hence we may strike off that column and row as well. Two-fold cutting of price then dominates one-fold cutting, and the former would seem to be the course followed by both A and B. But the matrix could obviously be extended to three-fold cutting, four-fold cutting, and so on; and each would presumably dominate its predecessor. Is there no end to the price-cutting process of the two-firm competitive price?

Let us suppose that an m-fold cut on the part of both A and B would bring price down to the two-firm competitive level, and that the payoff for each firm would be 60 on the scale already established. Under the stipulated condition of rising marginal cost, there is a set of cuts smaller than the m-fold cut that will yield A a higher payoff than 60 even if B undercuts. Moreover, there is one cut within this set that will yield a higher payoff than any other within the set. It is therefore to the advantage of both firms for one of them to set its price at that level and let the other undercut, since the alternative is for price to fall to the two-firm competitive level. That is to say, either of the two firms can unilaterally prevent price from falling to the two-firm competitive level, and it is in that firm's interest to do so even though the other firm will benefit more. The question remains only as to which firm will do its "duty."

The points just made are illuminated more easily through graphic analysis than through the cumbersome payoff matrix, although the latter can equally well be used. We construct a demand curve for A representing the maximum outputs he could sell at indicated prices if at each price B charged an ever so slightly lower price. We shall refer to this as A's residual demand. It is approximated by horizontally subtracting the marginal cost curve from the market demand curve (see Figure 3).[7] Deriving the marginal revenue curve corresponding to residual demand and equating that marginal revenue with marginal cost, we determine the price ($\bar{p}_2$ in Figure 3) at which A earns the highest profit if he allows B to chisel. That profit will in turn be higher than the one each firm could earn if both charged the two-firm competitive price ($\hat{p}_2$ in Figure 3). We shall refer to $\bar{p}_2$ as the conditional optimum price. It will lie below the one-firm competitive and the two-firm monopoly price and above the two-firm competitive price.

The conclusions reached for duopoly extend directly to any number of firms. For expository convenience, we consider the case of three firms—A, B,

---

[7] Residual demand will be recognized to be essentially the same as demand for a price leader in the conventional case. In a somewhat different context, residual demand was introduced into the analysis of duopoly almost three decades ago in a widely overlooked article by Ronald Coase, "The Problem of Duopoly Reconsidered," *Review of Economic Studies*, February 1935. Coase applied the concept to analysis of pricing by firms with different cost conditions, a matter considered in the second part of this paper.

FIGURE 3

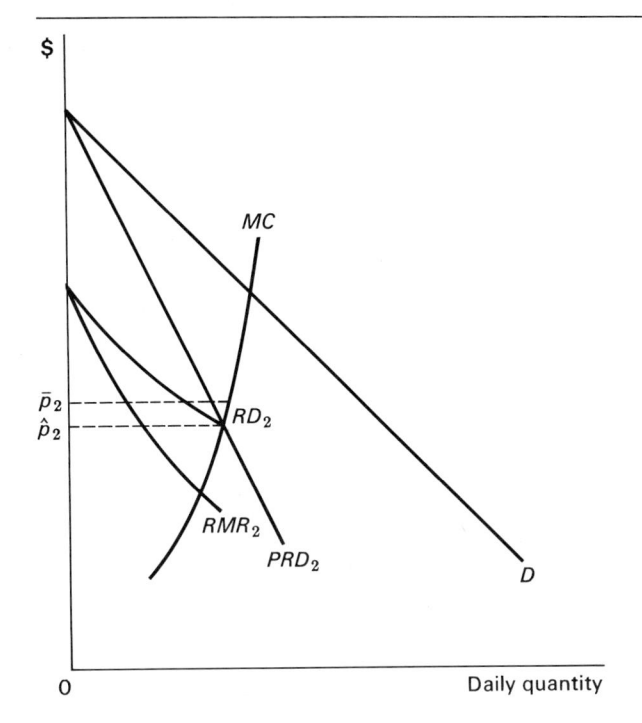

Figure shows axes with $ on vertical and Daily quantity on horizontal. Curves labeled MC, RD₂, RMR₂, PRD₂, D, with $\bar{p}_2$ and $\hat{p}_2$ marked on the vertical axis.

and C—that have established a uniform price at the three-firm monopoly level and below the two-firm competitive level.[8] For each of the relevant possible pricing actions on the part of C, we construct a representative payoff matrix for A and B (see Figure 4). In each matrix, we enter C's payoff (in the center of the cell) only in the case of the optimum pair of actions for A and B given C's action.

We note that, for any price C is expected to set above the three-firm competitive level, A and B are best off to set their uniform price a shade lower. Just as in the case of duopoly, C's profits rise over a range of price cuts and then fall, and there is a conditional optimum price ($\bar{p}_3$ in Figure 5) determined in a similar way. The only difference is that a firm's residual demand is approximated by horizontally subtracting the summed marginal cost curves for the other firms from the market demand curve.

[8] Once again, the relation between the one-firm competitive price and the two-firm monopoly price—or, generally, between the $(n-1)$-firm competitive price and the n-firm monopoly price—is not critical to the analysis, affecting the structure of payoffs in that region of prices but not the outcome of decisions.

FIGURE 4

C raises

A \ B	Raise	Retain	Cut
Raise	99.9 / 99.9	110.2 / 95.0	110.1 / 94.9
Retain	95.0 / 110.2	110.2, 80.0 / 110.2	110.1 / 110.2
Cut	94.9 / 110.1	110.2 / 110.1	110.1 / 110.1

C retains

A \ B	Retain	Cut	Two-fold cut
Retain	100.1 / 100.0	110.1 / 95.1	110.0 / 95.0
Cut	95.1 / 110.1	110.1, 80.2 / 110.1	110.0 / 110.1
Two-fold cut	95.0 / 110.0	110.1 / 110.0	110.0 / 110.0

C cuts

A \ B	Cut	Two-fold cut	Three-fold cut
Cut	99.9 / 99.9	110.0 / 95.0	109.9 / 94.9
Two-fold cut	95.0 / 110.0	110.0, 80.4 / 110.0	109.9 / 110.0
Three-fold cut	94.9 / 109.9	110.0 / 109.9	109.9 / 109.9

C cuts two-fold

A \ B	Two-fold cut	Three-fold cut	Four-fold cut
Two-fold cut	99.8 / 99.8	109.9 / 94.9	109.8 / 94.8
Three-fold cut	94.9 / 109.9	109.9, 80.6 / 109.9	109.8 / 109.9
Four-fold cut	94.8 / 109.8	109.9 / 109.8	109.8 / 109.8

We may then conclude the following. Under the postulated economic conditions (complete knowledge, identical firms, rising marginal costs, and homogeneous product), price will settle in the immediate neighborhood of the conditional optimum price, one firm charging that price and all others another price a shade lower. For the latter firms, marginal cost will equal price; for the former firm, it will not. Given n firms in the industry, the equilibrium price must lie below the n-firm monopoly price and between the $(n-1)$-firm and the n-firm competitive price. With fixed market demand and cost conditions, the latter range normally diminishes as n increases and hence the equilibrium price normally approaches the n-firm competitive level as n increases.[9]

[9] This proposition may be stated too strongly, for there can be exceptions. The argument for the "normal" case runs as follows. Since the marginal cost curve slopes upward and is concave from above, the horizontal shift in the aggregate marginal cost curve brought about by adding a firm will be smaller in absolute size for lower than for higher levels of marginal cost. Hence, as firms are added to the industry one at a time, the vertical distance cut off

FIGURE 5

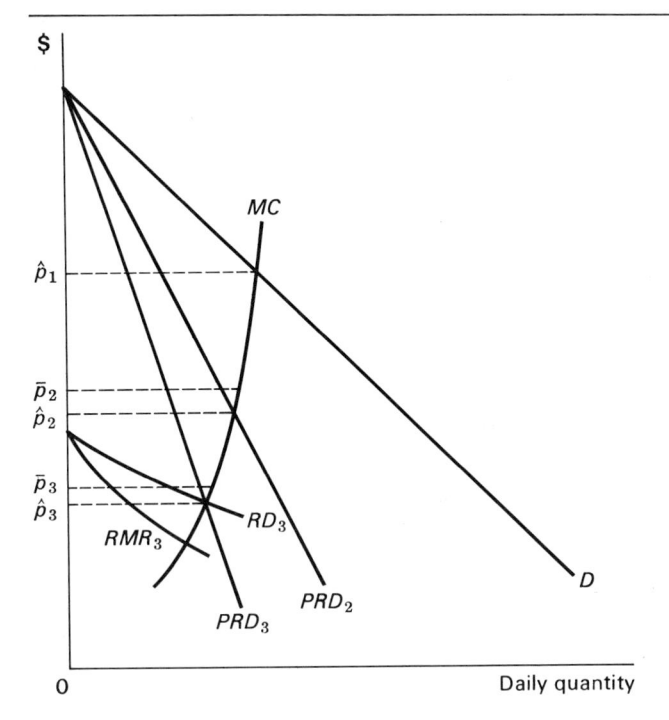

The discussion at the present level of abstraction may be rounded out by considering the case of a downward sloping marginal cost curve over the relevant range of output (see Figure 6). This case may be quickly dismissed because monopoly is the only stable outcome. Suppose that two firms exist in the industry and that the two-firm monopoly price p_0 is being charged by both. That price must be higher than the one-firm competitive price $\hat{p}_1$. If A now chisels, he can sell the entire output x_1 taken by the market, while B can sell nothing. The arc marginal cost for A will be less than marginal cost at x_0 and hence less than p_0. There is a positive and finite gain from chiseling. Let price continue to be cut. The gain from chiseling will continue to be positive and finite as long as marginal costs are declining. Neither firm can keep price from falling to this level, because the firm holding its price fast would simply lose all sales to its undercutting rival. Moreover, neither firm will wish to keep price from falling because each has a positive expected gain from mutual chiseling. But, at the level to which it must fall, price will be lower than average variable cost, and one of the firms will cease producing and leave the industry.

---

by successive intersections of the aggregate marginal cost curve with the market demand curve must become smaller over all segments of a demand curve that are downward sloping and non-convex from above. This will also hold for some convex segments but not for all.

FIGURE 6

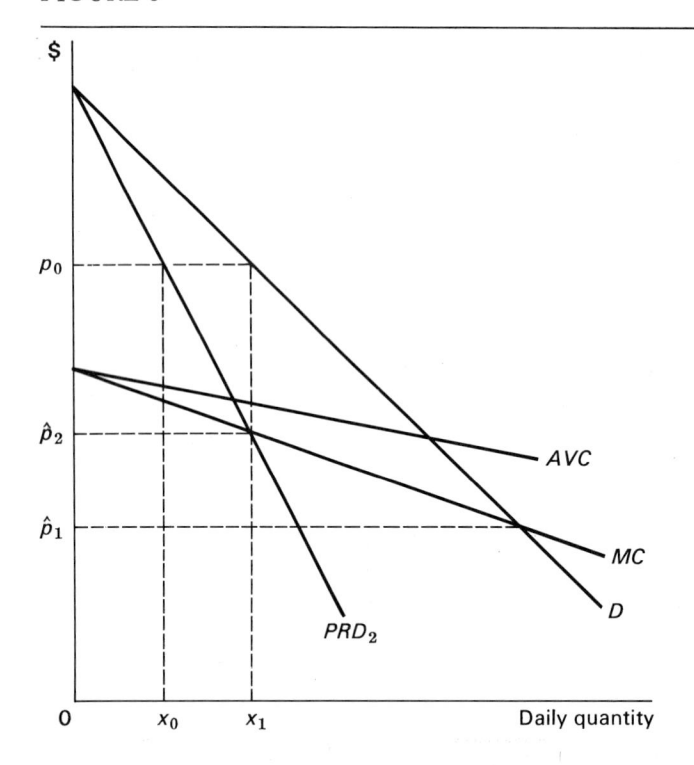

[Figure 6: Graph with vertical axis in $ showing levels p_0, $\hat{p}_2$, $\hat{p}_1$ and horizontal axis "Daily quantity" with points x_0, x_1; curves labeled AVC, MC, D, and PRD$_2$.]

B. Pricing with Free Entry

As long as better than normal profits are being earned, additional firms will presumably be attracted to the industry. But when, for example, minimum average cost is equal to the n-firm competitive price, entry of one more firm will cause every firm to earn less than normal profits even though price settles in the neighborhood of the optimum price under chiseling. In terms of Figure 5, if minimum average cost is equal to $\hat{p}_3$, entry of a fourth firm will push the conditional optimum price below that level. If knowledge is complete, will the additional firm enter the industry?

This depends on the probability that the firm contemplating entry has of surviving and earning greater than normal profits. The larger the number of firms in the industry, the greater the probability that the new entrant can survive. If there are two firms in the industry under the outlined circumstances, the firm contemplating entry has only two chances in three of surviving. If there are a hundred firms, it has 100 chances in 101. Hence entry would be more likely in the latter than in the former case.

But if this is so, firms will continuously be entering and leaving the industry that can support a large number of firms when that industry is in long-run "equilibrium," and nobody is likely to earn better than normal profits over the long run. The firms in the industry would be better off if entry were discouraged by moving price even closer to the n-firm competitive price than it would be at the optimum price under chiseling with n firms. There is therefore this second factor operating in the long run to bring equilibrium price closer and closer to the competitive level as the number of firms that can earn normal profits in the industry becomes larger and larger.

II. PRICING WITH DIFFERENT FIRMS AND INCOMPLETE KNOWLEDGE

In this part, the restrictive conditions applied so far will be relaxed in order to develop a more interesting and general theory. In particular, we shall deal with the cases of different firms, diverse entrepreneurial abilities, and incomplete and unequal knowledge. We continue to assume that there is no explicit collusion, that costs for any one firm are not significantly affected by the number of firms in an industry or by the actions of any given number, and that each type of firm is limited to only one size and one set of short-run costs. The last condition serves merely to simplify analysis; it does not affect basic conclusions. The same applies to the second as far as it refers to effects of the number of firms. The consequences of interdependent costs among a given number of firms are more complex and are not treated here for lack of a theory. Collusion will be considered briefly and separately in part three.

A. Pricing with Different Firms

We start again with duopoly, but let A have lower marginal costs than B over all relevant outputs. This condition makes equilibrium more determinate, for there is no longer likely to be any question as to which firm will set price. Each firm will probably have a different conditional optimum price, and one of these will dominate. Consider the situation as given in Figures 7 and 8. The conditional optimum price is higher for A ($\bar{p}_{a2}$) than for B ($\bar{p}_{b2}$). Which will dominate? The choice is up to the firm with the higher conditional optimum price, in this case A. His alternatives are to set price at his conditional optimum level and let B chisel, or to let B set price at B's conditional optimum level and chisel himself. He will choose the alternative yielding the higher profits. For the situation summarized in the upper left panel of Figure 8, A will let price be set at B's conditional optimum level ($\bar{p}_{b2}$).

The conclusion just reached requires a word of explanation, for it does not follow directly and obviously from the conventional rule for maximizing profits. The demand curve being viewed by A has an upbending kink in it ever so slightly below the point at which B's conditional optimum price $\bar{p}_{b2}$ intersects A's residual demand RD^a_2. That is, A's relevant demand follows the

FIGURE 7

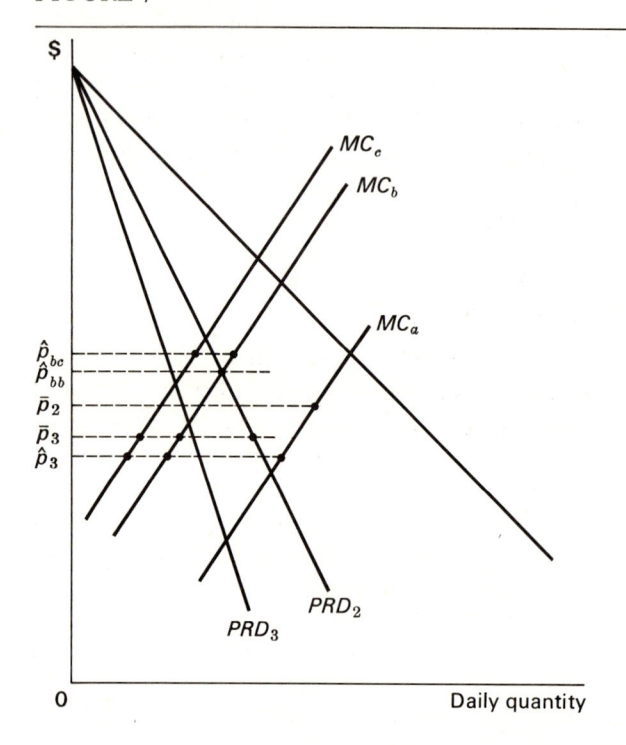

residual demand curve down to the neighborhood of that price and then becomes horizontal. Marginal revenue must be higher to the right of the kink than to the left, and hence marginal cost may equal marginal revenue on both sides of the kink, as it does in the present case. In order to know which equality indicates the output with maximum profits, we need to know the behavior of costs and revenue over the intervening range of output. In the present case, additional revenue exceeds additional costs over that range so that the equality to the right of the kink is the pertinent one. But this will not always be so, depending on the circumstances.

Now let a third firm C with higher costs than B enter the industry. Equilibrium price will be set in the same fashion. Suppose the conditional optimum prices for A, B, and C descend in that order, as they do in Figure 8. A will then either set price or let B do so if that is preferable. Similarly for B with respect to C. If either A or B sets the price, an equilibrium is established. If the task is left to C, an equilibrium is established unless A would be better off setting his own price, in which case he will do so. Hence a definite equilibrium will be established by one of the firms. For the conditions in Figure 8, A is clearly better off to set price and let B and C chisel than to let either B or

FIGURE 8

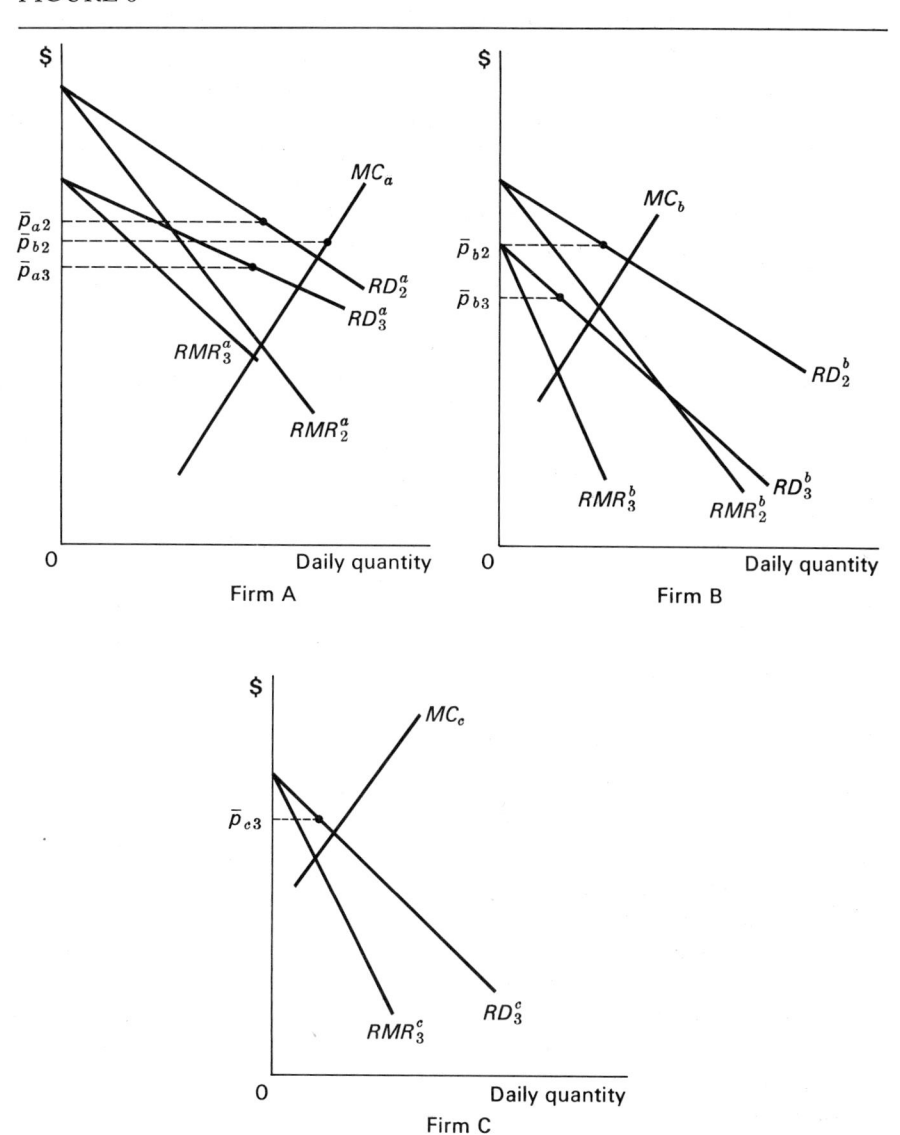

[Figure 8: Three panels showing cost and demand curves for Firm A, Firm B, and Firm C. Firm A panel shows MC_a, RD_2^a, RD_3^a, RMR_2^a, RMR_3^a, with prices $\bar{p}_{a2}$, $\bar{p}_{b2}$, $\bar{p}_{a3}$ marked. Firm B panel shows MC_b, RD_2^b, RD_3^b, RMR_2^b, RMR_3^b, with prices $\bar{p}_{b2}$, $\bar{p}_{b3}$ marked. Firm C panel shows MC_c, RD_3^c, RMR_3^c, with price $\bar{p}_{c3}$ marked.]

C set price and chisel himself.[10] Equilibrium is established at A's conditional optimum price ($\bar{p}_3$ in Figure 7 and $\bar{p}_{a3}$ in Figure 8).

[10] Since the conditional optimum prices for B and C both lie on A's marginal cost curve below A's residual demand curve, there is no problem in determining that they imply lower profits for A than his own conditional optimum price.

In the general case of n firms, equilibrium price will lie between the competitive level applying to all firms but the lowest-cost one and the competitive level applying to all firms. For example, $\bar{p}_3$ lies between $\hat{p}_{bc}$ and $\hat{p}_3$ in Figure 7. As in the case of identical firms, this range will normally diminish, and hence equilibrium price will normally approach the n-firm competitive level as n increases, other relevant things the same.[11] Again, in the long run the price setter may wish to set price even closer to the competitive level—the more so the larger the number of firms the industry will support—in order to deter excessive cyclical entry. No matter how many firms there are, in equilibrium only the price setter will not equate marginal cost with price. Finally, the lowest-cost firm may produce more or less than other firms.

Entrepreneurial talents are also likely to vary among firms, and this will mean that some firms will have higher expected gains than others under mutual chiseling. If one firm has a much shrewder entrepreneur than all others and if its marginal costs are below those for a representative firm, the upper limit to equilibrium price will lie below the competitive level applying to all firms but the lowest-cost one. Consider the case in which the firm with second lowest (or lowest) costs can always succeed in outchiseling every other firm. Then, with n firms in the industry, the equilibrium price can never be above the $(n-1)$-firm competitive level that would exist if all those firms were identical with the one with second lowest costs. An upper limit of this nature would be $\hat{p}_{bb}$ in Figure 7.

B. Pricing with Incomplete Knowledge

Since firms and customers are certain to have incomplete knowledge of relevant economic conditions, the described equilibrium can, at best, be established only over time and through trial and error. This means that those firms with superior knowledge and entrepreneurial ability have added opportunities to exploit gains from chiseling as price wanders toward an equilibrium position. It may well pay other firms always to respond passively and competitively—to accept price set by active chiselers as given—rather than to bear the cost of acquiring knowledge and entrepreneurial talent. Both are expensive, and the potential return from them needs to be high to justify the cost.

With some incomplete knowledge and diversity of firms, every firm in an industry may be expected to try to conceal relevant information under its control: the low-cost and skilled firms will do so in order to enhance exploitation

---

[11] In addition to the qualification given above in 7n, we must suppose that firms increase in such a way that the representative firm does not have increasingly lower marginal costs to a sufficient degree to offset "normal" tendencies. For instance, we may suppose all potential firms to be ranked in accord with the height of their marginal cost curves over the relevant range of output and entry to take place in increasing order of that height, as is the case in our example.

of others; the high-cost and unskilled firms, in order to inhibit exploitation of themselves. When price is above the equilibrium level, each firm will try to inform customers of price cuts without informing its rival firms. And so on. The larger the number of firms in an industry, the more difficult it will be for other firms to know the costs or behavior of any one. Paradoxically, lack of knowledge seems more likely to intensify competitive behavior than to do the opposite.

The same may be true of ignorance on the part of customers. We have argued that, when customer attachment to firms may be taken as a random process, some firm will ultimately halt mutual price cutting by holding its price fast and allowing others to chisel. This is an equilibrium only if the other firms have exhausted all profitable means of expanding production. One such means may be advertising. But if the advertising is successful, it must reduce residual demand for the price setter, causing him almost certainly to reduce his price, which in turn will induce the firms that have advertised to reduce their prices. At some point the gain from advertising will be offset by the loss from price cutting, and a new equilibrium will be established at a lower price. A similar analysis applies to other types of "product differentiation."[12]

III. PRICING WITH COLLUSION

If collusion were costless and fully effective, the optimum procedure would be for the members of an industry to get together and price as if the firms constituted a multi-plant monopoly, the resulting profits being distributed on an earned basis. The trouble is that collusion is never costless and never fully effective in the absence of coercion.

Consider the simple case of duopoly with identical firms and complete knowledge. Then agreement by the two firms to price at the monopoly level would not alter the fundamental prisoners' dilemma facing them unless the agreement were an enforceable contract. This holds true even if one firm were to pay the other to get agreement. In fact, if A knows that B will adhere to the agreement, A is certain that he can gain by chiseling, the more so if he can do it secretly. His best strategy would probably be to cut price and raise it back alternately. Similarly for B. Hence, for the agreement to survive long, it must have teeth: there must be some way to punish the chiseler. When collusive contracts are outlawed, enforceable agreements depend on extra-legal coercion or on some device like the merger or, formerly, the trust.

The larger the number of firms, the shorter the time any unenforced collusive agreement can be expected to be effective. In order for one firm to

[12] For some of my earlier views on this matter, see my "The Plateau Demand Curve and Utility Theory," *Journal of Political Economy*, LXIII (December 1955), 525–528.

adhere, it must be assured that others will also adhere, and this becomes less likely as the number of firms increases. The primary effect of an unenforced agreement may simply be to hasten the chiseling process that would take place in any case, for some firms will act quickly as long as they think there is a likelihood others will not, and in this way a chain reaction is set off.

The costs of making a collusive agreement also increase with the number of firms, because individual firms are in a position to strike a bargain for their participation. For example, the longer a firm delays in joining a cartel, the higher the payment it can demand for doing so. Meanwhile it gains more than whatever the cartel might achieve for its members.[13] Cases may easily be imagined in which it would cost more to organize a cartel (or a merger) than could be gained if it worked optimally once established.

In brief, it is difficult to believe that collusive agreements can long be effective unless they are coercively enforced. They will, of course, exist in the short run, but they will tend to break down for the same basic reason that chiseling will occur without collusion.

IV. CONCLUDING REMARKS

We have argued in this paper that chiseling can be a rational course of action for an oligopolist under certain hypothetical conditions, and that it can lead price to approach the competitive equilibrium as the number of firms increases in an industry. Whether the same conclusions would hold under appropriate modification of conditions remains to be seen, but my own appraisal is that analysis of the chiseling process is the key to development of a truly general theory of price.

---

[13] A related case in point is the so-called "free rider" in a unionized plant.

PART IV. THE THEORY OF DISTRIBUTION

10

THE THEORY OF RESOURCE PRICE

The main thrust of our analysis thus far in this book has been the study of output markets and the supply and demand forces determining output prices and quantities. We have presented the theory of consumer behavior to derive the consumer's demand for goods and services and the theory of the firm to derive the firm's supply of services and commodities for the consumer market. We have not specifically concerned ourselves with the firm's activities in resource markets, except for the discussion in Chapter 4 of the relationship between resource inputs and the firm's cost curves. There we developed the firm's cost curves as representing the lowest achievable cost for each possible level of output. But the firm's decision to produce a given output is inseparable from its decision to purchase the necessary quantities of the factors of production needed to produce this output. The decision to supply a certain quantity of output and the decision to exercise a demand for a certain amount of resources are really two aspects of the same decision. Looking at the supply side of the resource market, a consumer's decision to purchase a given bundle of consumer goods is generally inseparable from his decision to supply a given quantity of resource services (principally labor) with which to earn income to purchase consumer goods.[1]

So, in this chapter, we change our vantage point from the supply and demand for commodities in output markets to the demand for the services of resources by firms, and the supply of these services by consumers or households in the factor market and their subsequent employment in production.[2] Notice that we are drawing a distinction between resource services and the resource itself. The principal resource in our economy is human labor, by

[1] Some consumers, of course, may separate the two in time, saving in one period and dissaving in another, and some consumers may receive transfer payments from government or other persons which are used to buy consumer goods.
[2] We may think of individuals or households as owning all economic resources.

which we mean hours of labor services. In the case of labor, we are interested in the forces determining the price of labor services, rather than the price of a laborer, because buying and selling persons is prohibited by the Thirteenth Amendment to the Constitution. There is virtually no market activity involving human beings as objects for sale.[3] Other resources are different; for example, in Chapter 12, we will be particularly interested not only in the price of the services of the resource, capital, but also in the price of the resource itself. In some cases, the two are inseparable; for example, the services of raw materials used to make products are obtained only by purchasing the resource itself. For convenience, we will often refer to the price of a resource when we are actually concerned with the *services* of the resource. The context of the discussion will indicate whether the service or the resource itself is under investigation; e.g., "the price of labor" will mean "the price of labor services."

The reader will soon discover that our approach to the determination of firms' demand for resources and consumers' supply of these resources is simply another way of looking at profit-maximizing behavior by firms and utility-maximizing behavior by consumers. That is, the firm's decision about the quantity of resources to employ in the production process determines its level of output, and similarly, the consumer's decision to supply certain resources at the market price of these resources determines the consumer's income and his budget constraint. The consumer's decision regarding the size of his budget constraint is governed by his goal of utility maximization, as he trades off leisure for work and income. Of course, the consumer's budget constraint limits the possible combinations of consumer goods which can be purchased. By analyzing the factors governing the supply and demand for resources, we will discover the mechanism whereby resource prices are determined and broaden our understanding of the behavior of consumers and firms. We will begin our analysis of the forces determining the demand for resources by focusing upon price determination, assuming competition in both resource and output markets.

THE SUPPLY AND DEMAND FOR RESOURCES IN COMPETITIVE MARKETS

Competition in Resource Markets

Competition exists in a resource market when there are a large number of buyers and sellers of the resource. All market participants must be so small relative to the market that all are price takers. It is possible, however, for a firm to participate as a small buyer in a perfectly competitive resource market

---

[3] A partial exception to this is found in the practice of making long-term contracts for personal services, e.g., a five-year contract signed by a professional football coach. But even in these cases, the long-term contract is only for the worker's services on his job.

while, at the same time, enjoying a degree of monopoly power in its product market—for example, a cloth merchant who is the sole distributor in a given area. The models which we will develop in the first part of this chapter assume that the resource market and the output market are *both* perfectly competitive. In the second part, we will modify these models to account for those situations in which one of the relevant markets is less than perfectly competitive.

Our purpose in this chapter is to develop the basic analytical apparatus for studying the demand for any resource. Once this is done we will use these tools in the next two chapters to consider the demand for the services of specific resources: labor, land, and capital.

The Derived Demand for Resources

The price of any resource is determined by the market supply and demand for that resource. Therefore, the analysis of resource markets employs the analytical tools of supply–demand analysis, as in the study of commodity markets. Our task then is to determine the principal factors behind resource supply and demand. We begin by showing that the demand for resources is, in effect, derived from the demand for the consumer goods that are produced with these resources.

Consumer goods have two characteristics in common: they all provide utility directly to consumers and all are produced with the use of resources. A commodity may be viewed, therefore, as embodying a bundle of resource services. But how can we define resources so that they are distinguished from consumer goods? Suppose we define a *resource* as anything that does not provide consumers with utility but is useful to produce finished commodities that do. A resource, then, by definition is not consumed directly. Obvious examples of resources are unprocessed tons of pig iron, bales of raw hides, and laborers. All of these resources defy consumption. In other instances, however, usage alone determines whether something is a resource or a product. For example, a car in private use is treated as a commodity, but when used as a taxi, the same car is a resource, which can provide utility to consumers when combined with a dispatcher and a driver. A typewriter used to write personal letters is a commodity, but a typewriter used to write the draft of a book is a resource that does not provide utility directly—the utility is derived from reading the finished product.

If resources do not provide utility because, as such, they are not consumed, why are their services demanded? The answer is that the demand for resources is *derived* from the demand for the commodities that can be produced with them. In one sense, the demand for a consumer good or service is a *joint demand* for a bundle of resource services. If the services of a single resource were consumed, then it might be considered a commodity and not a resource, though it might be considered a resource in other uses. (A man once bought a ton of steel from a mill and put it on his lawn as an ornament. That ton of steel was a commodity, while probably every other ton of steel the mill ever produced was a resource.)

The process of combining inputs to produce outputs we have defined as production, and although consumers engage in some do-it-yourself production, that production which is sold in markets is carried out by firms.[4] The firm is, therefore, the input–output device that combines the services of resources to produce consumer goods. Consequently, the firm must participate in two markets: as a supplier in the market for its output and as a buyer in the market for the resources needed to produce output. We have discussed the theory of the competitive firm's supply in output markets; now we must develop the theory of the competitive firm's demand for resources.

The Competitive Firm's Short-Run Demand for a Single Resource

As a first approximation, a firm's short-run demand for a resource is directly but not exclusively dependent upon the physical productivity of that resource: the greater the productivity of the resource, the greater the demand. Moreover, the physical productivity of a resource is revealed by the short-run production curves associated with it. The total product curve, you will recall, indicates the total output that is derived as a function of the amount of one resource, the variable factor, used along with one or more fixed factors. A hypothetical total product curve, such as that derived in Chapter 4, is shown in panel (a) of Figure 10–1, where output, X, is measured on the vertical axis and units of the variable factor, a, are measured along the horizontal axis. Since our analysis is short run, we assume that all inputs to the production process other than a are held constant. From the TP curve, we derive the average and marginal product curves for resource a, labeled AP_a and MP_a, respectively, in panel (b) of the figure. (For ease of observation, the scale of X measured on the vertical axis is expanded in panel (b).) In short, we have presented in Figure 10–1 the familiar short-run production curves relating to variable input a, assuming all other inputs are fixed. These production curves may be said to describe the productivity of resource a under the short-run conditions assumed, and we will use them to derive the firm's demand for a.

The physical productivity of a resource, however, is only one aspect of its over-all productivity, so far as a firm is concerned. It would be useless for a

---

[4] In some cases, a person is taken to be simultaneously a consumer and a firm. Thus, a homeowner might be considered a businessman who sells the services of his home to himself, and he is so considered by the Department of Commerce in estimating the aggregate level of rental income in the United States economy. However, we are principally interested in production for sale in markets.

FIGURE 10–1 The Firm's Short-Run Product Curves

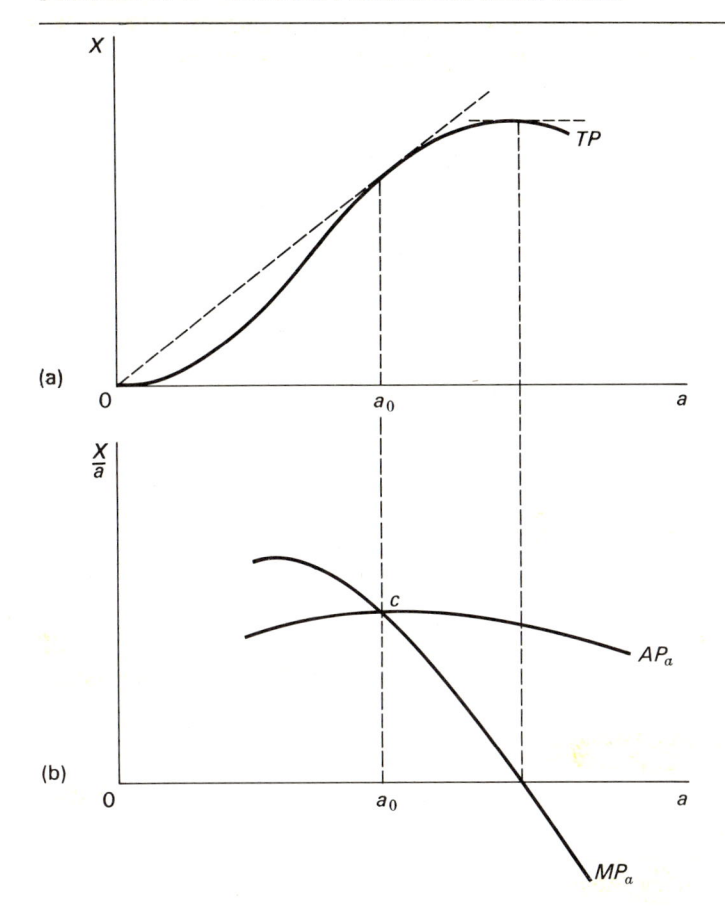

firm to employ a resource that is very efficient at producing a product that cannot be sold for a positive price. The firm demands the variable resource a, because it is used to produce product X, which, when sold, will generate revenue. The firm's demand for resources is analogous to a consumer's demand for commodities: The firm buys resources to obtain revenue, whereas the consumer buys commodities to obtain utility. In other words, completely neglecting costs for a moment, the firm is interested principally in the *revenue productivity* of a resource.

At this point, we introduce a new marginal concept which seeks to measure the revenue productivity of a resource called *marginal revenue product* (MRP). This measure combines the marginal physical productivity of a resource with the revenues obtained from selling output.

> MRP measures the addition to total revenue that occurs when one more unit of the variable factor of production is added to the production process and the resulting increment to output is sold.

The additional revenue which a firm can realize by employing additional units of a variable resource is determined by both (1) the marginal physical product of the resource and (2) the marginal revenue realized from the sale of the finished product. To determine the amount of additional revenue one more unit of a resource will generate, we must multiply the marginal product of the resource by the marginal revenue received from the sale of the finished product. For example, if the fifth unit of resource a employed adds two units of X to total production (marginal product is 2), and if the marginal revenue received from the sale of all X's is $5, then the additional revenue occasioned by the hire of the fifth unit of a is $10.

We can define the additional revenue, or the marginal revenue product, using mathematical symbols, as:

$$MRP_a = MP_a \cdot MR_x,$$

where MRP_a is the marginal revenue product of factor a, MP_a is its marginal product, and MR_x is the marginal revenue derived from the sale of the incremental output. Since we are assuming a competitive output market, the firm's marginal revenue is constant and equal to the market price of X, P_x. Thus, MRP_a for the competitive firm is also determined by the equation:

$$MRP_a = MP_a \cdot P_x.$$

But the multiplication of MP times price is given a special name, the *value marginal product*, VMP. In symbols:

$$VMP_a = MP_a \cdot P_x.$$

MRP_a can be thought of as being equal to the VMP_a, minus the loss in revenue that results when sales of extra or marginal output can be accomplished only by reducing price. The competitive firm need not reduce the price of X to sell additional X's; so MR_x and P_x are always equal, and MRP and VMP are also equal. On the other hand, we will find that MRP and VMP may not be equal in those market structures which are less than perfectly competitive. Furthermore, we will see that the difference between VMP and MRP is one measure of the degree of exploitation of a resource. That is, according to one view, a resource is exploited if it is paid at a rate less than its VMP. Following this reasoning, the marginal unit of a employed should be paid a return no less than the value of its marginal product.

Before considering the question of resource exploitation, however, we must complete our basic competitive model, and to do this we must investigate further the determinants of the marginal revenue productivity of a resource:

MP_a and MR. The marginal product of a, MP_a in Figure 10–1, is dependent upon the number of units of a employed by the firm. Since MR is constant for all output levels under perfect competition, marginal revenue product for a competitive firm is a function of the number of units of a employed. The graph of this functional relationship we call the MRP curve. It can be derived for resource a, using the production curves in Figure 10–1, by multiplying the marginal product of a, MP_a, for each level of a inputs, by marginal revenue. The latter of course equals the market determined price of the product, P_x.

The derivation of MRP_a is illustrated in Figure 10–2, where panel (a) is simply a reproduction of panel (b) of Figure 10–1. If we assume that the firm operates in Stage II only, we restrict the relevant part of MP_a to the negatively sloped portion which falls between the levels of output where $MP_a = AP_a$ and where $MP_a = 0$. It is reasonable to suggest that the firm will normally operate between these two limits, if it produces at all. If the firm employs any units of resource a, it will probably hire at least enough so that the marginal unit is no more productive than the average of all units of a utilized. So, gen-

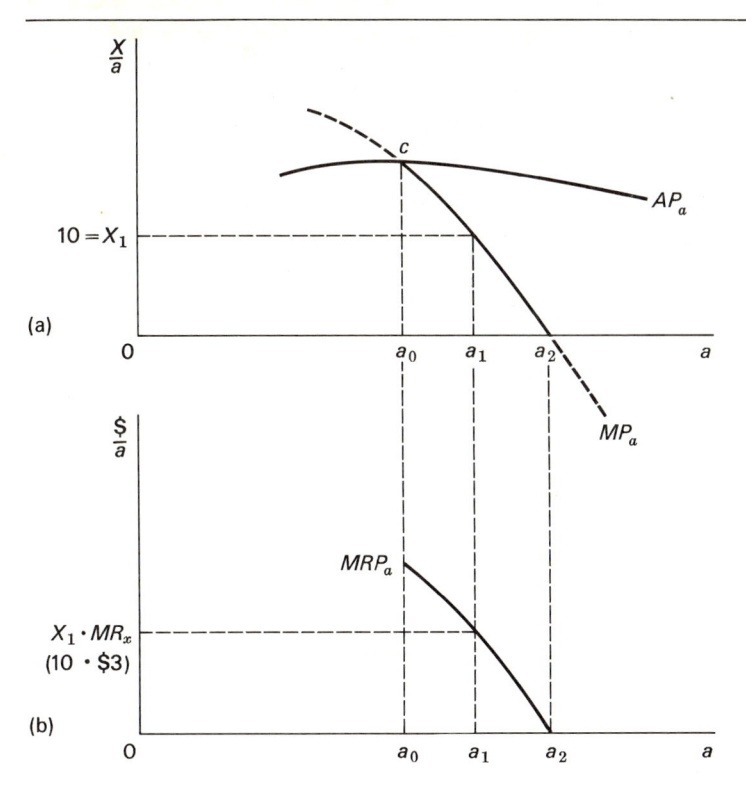

FIGURE 10–2 Deriving Marginal Revenue Product from Marginal Product

erally a_0 in Figure 10–2 represents a lower practical limit to the amount of a that might be employed if any a is used. And it is more reasonable to propose that the firm will stop employing a when the marginal unit employed can no longer increase output at all. In summary, restricting ourselves to Stage II combinations means that only the negatively sloped portion of the curve, below point c, where MP_a is positive, is relevant to the firm. For a_1 units of a, the marginal product is X_1 and, as indicated in the lower panel, MRP is equal to X_1 multiplied by MR_x. MRP_a falls to zero at a_2 units of a since the MP_a is zero at that level of resource hire. Referring again to Figure 10–2, if the marginal product of a is 10 when a_1 units are hired, and marginal revenue is $3, then the marginal revenue product at a_1 is $(10 \cdot \$3)$ or $30. If we continue with these calculations for all values of a between a_0 and a_2, we generate the MRP_a schedule in panel (b).

Marginal Resource Cost and Resource Supply

Since we are assuming competitive conditions in the resource market, the individual firm has, by definition, no control over the prices of the resources that it purchases. Referring to Figure 10–3, the market price of the resource is determined by the market supply and demand schedules in panel (b). (The market schedules will be discussed later in this section.) Equilibrium price is P_{a_1}. Since the single firm can obtain any quantity of a it wishes at this price, the supply of a to the competitive buyer is perfectly elastic at P_{a_1}. Thus, the

FIGURE 10–3 The Resource Supply Curve Facing a Single Firm
(Assuming Competition in the Resource Market)

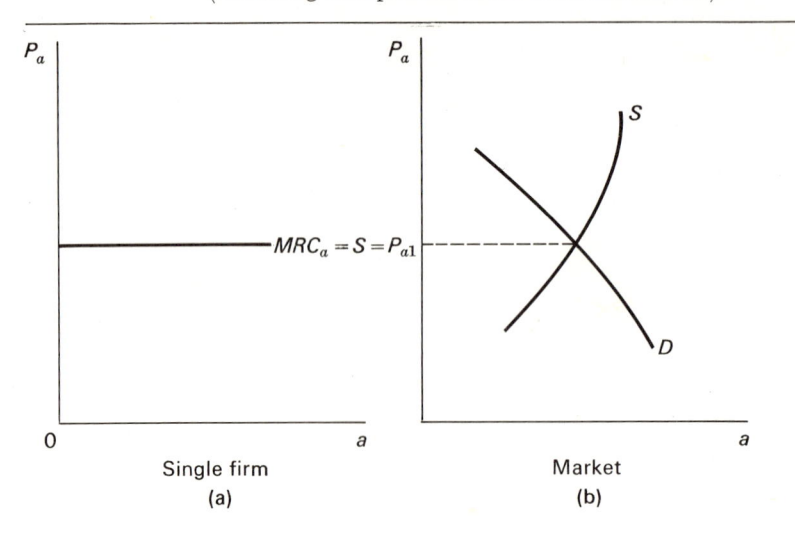

Single firm
(a)

Market
(b)

horizontal line S in panel (a) is the supply curve facing the competitive buyer.

Now we must introduce a second marginal concept, this time relating to resource costs. So far, we have developed a measure which indicates the addition to total revenue that occurs when an additional unit of the variable factor a is hired. Now we develop a new measure which shows the increase in total cost that occurs as the firm purchases an additional unit of a.

> This measure is called marginal resource cost, MRC, and is defined as the change in total cost that occurs as an additional unit of a variable factor is purchased.

In symbols, the marginal resource cost for factor a is:

$$MRC_a = \frac{\Delta TC}{\Delta a},$$

where it is assumed that the quantities of all resources except a are held constant while a is varied.

Assuming perfect competition in the resource market, a firm can always obtain an additional unit of the variable factor at the going market price. Under these conditions, MRC is constant and equal to the market price of the resource. For example, suppose the market price of a is $3 and the firm purchases an additional unit of a. Using the above formula:

$$MRC_a = \frac{\Delta TC}{\Delta a} = \frac{\$3}{1} = \$3.$$

Notice that this calculation would be the same for any marginal purchase of a, whether the firm is employing its first unit or its thousandth. We may conclude that the marginal cost curve for a competitive buyer of a resource is constant, equal to the market price of the factor, and thus coincides with the supply curve to the firm. Curve S in Figure 10–3 is, therefore, additionally labeled MRC_a.

Now we are ready to combine in Figure 10–4 the MRP_a curve and the MRC_a curve to determine the equilibrium quantity of the variable factor a that will be employed by the competitive firm. The reader will recognize that our approach is analogous to the one used to determine the profit-maximizing output, employing MC and MR schedules. For all output levels below a_e, the firm will be motivated to increase its purchases of resource a because the MRP of the factor is in excess of its MRC. To illustrate, at a_0, the MRP of a is in excess of MRC by the amount ab. Therefore, employment of the $(a_0 + 1)$th unit of a will add more to revenue than to cost and will increase the firm's profits. So the profit-maximizing firm would increase its employment of a above the a_0 level. It would not be profitable to increase the number of units of a purchased above a_e units, however, since MRC is above the MRP

FIGURE 10–4 The Profit-Maximizing Quantity of a Employed by the Competitive Firm

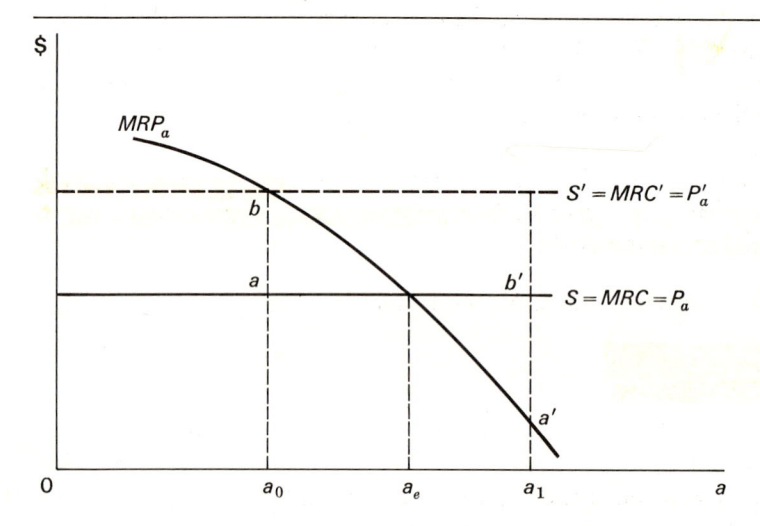

[Figure: Graph with vertical axis $ and horizontal axis a. A downward-sloping MRP_a curve intersects a higher horizontal line $S' = MRC' = P'_a$ at point b (above a_0) and continues through point a, then intersects a lower horizontal line $S = MRC = P_a$ at point b' (above a_e), continuing to point a' above a_1.]

for such levels. Expanding the purchase of units of a beyond a_e to a_1 would entail more extra costs than extra revenues ($a'b'$) and would reduce profits. We may conclude that the profit-maximizing quantity of a is determined at the point of intersection of MRP_a with MRC.[5]

Now let the market price of a rise to P_a' due to a decrease in the market supply of a. Any such change in the price of a resource is, of course, external to the competitive firm. As a price taker, it will simply have to adjust to the price increase, which has the effect of raising the supply curve from S to S'. Notice, though, that there is no reason why this price change should affect the productivity of a or the price of X, so the MRP_a schedule is unaffected by the change. The equilibrium quantity of a that would be hired by the firm will change, however, from a_e to a_0 since MRC' equals MRP_a at a_0. We may note that in both cases, S and S', the quantity of a to purchase at different prices is determined by the point at which S intersects the MRP_a curve. For this reason, we conclude that:

> Given that perfectly competitive conditions exist in the resource market, the MRP_a schedule is the firm's demand curve for resource a, since MRP_a indicates the various quantities of a that can profitably be utilized at different prices.

[5] This is both a necessary and a sufficient condition to establish the profit-maximizing quantity if we assume MRP_a is continuously falling. Otherwise $MRP_a = MRC_a$ is only a necessary condition.

When competition exists in both the resource and output markets, the firm's demand for resource a, d_a, may be stated:

$$d_a = MP_a \cdot P_x.$$

Market Equilibrium in Competitive Resource Markets

If industry X is the only user of resource a, we may obtain a first approximation to the market demand for a by summing all firms' demands. This aggregate demand curve is presented in panel (b) of Figure 10–5 and labeled D_a. We hasten to point out that D_a is only an approximation to market demand, because the summation procedure is incompatible with the *ceteris paribus* assumption that the marginal revenue derived by each firm is constant.[6] In deriving a single firm's MRP schedule, it is permissible to treat MR_x as constant for different levels of firm utilization of a and the associated levels of firm output. However, as we consider alternative levels of *industry* utilization of a, the associated changes in *industry* output will cause market price to change, which will then affect MR for each firm. As we sum a significant number of MRP schedules, industry output changes, market price changes, MR for each firm changes, and the result of all those changes is to shift all firms' MRP schedules. For this reason, D_a in Figure 10–5 is only an approximation of market demand.

FIGURE 10–5 Short-Run Equilibrium in the Market for Resource a and Representative Buyer's Adjustment to Equilibrium Price

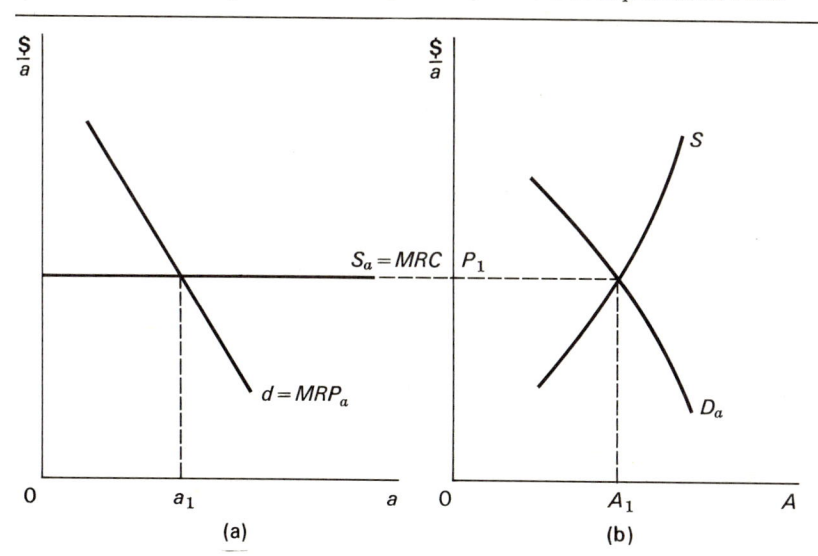

[6] The resulting D_a curve will be accurate only if the *market* demand for the finished product, X, is perfectly elastic.

430 The Theory of Distribution

The approximate market demand schedule, $D_a = \Sigma MRP_a$, intersects the market supply schedule, S, at price P_1. The number of units of a employed in the industry is A_1. Panel (a) of Figure 10–5 shows how the typical firm will adjust to P_1, and the curves should be familiar to the reader at this point. The representative firm equates its MRP_a with S_a and purchases a_1 units. We have assumed the market supply curve to be given. In fact, if resource a is a produced good itself, then S_a is simply the industry supply of a. If a is a resource such as labor, not ordinarily thought of as a produced good, then its supply curve is the aggregate of the supply curves of all laborers. Its derivation we have reserved for Chapter 12, where we discuss in detail the determination of wage rates.

The model presented in Figure 10–5 illustrates the determination of the market price of a, assuming perfect competition and a short-run period in which only the quantity of a can be varied by firms. Now we must expand our analysis to those situations where more than one resource can be varied in quantity. We will explore these situations, still retaining our assumption of perfect competition throughout resource and output markets.

The Demand for More Than One Resource

What is the effect on the formal model just presented of the more realistic assumption that the inputs of several resources may be varied? The effect is fairly predictable. A firm increases its capacity to produce each time it employs more of any resource. Translating this to our product schedules, the firm's total product function for factor a will shift upward whenever it acquires more of complementary resources, b and c. For example, in Figure 10–6, if

FIGURE 10–6   Total Product Curves for Different Quantities of Resources b and c

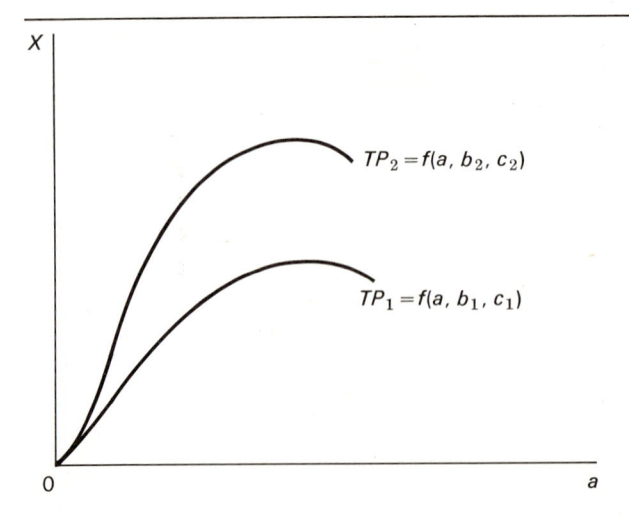

the firm employs fixed amounts b_1 and c_1 of complementary resources b and c, along with various quantities of resource a, then production will vary along TP_1. But if the firm is given sufficient time to increase the amounts of b and c to b_2 and c_2, then it can move along the higher TP_2 curve as it varies its employment of a.

When the firm employs more of resource a, it will choose to increase its employment of complementary resources b and c also, if it is less costly to do so. As successive amounts of b and c are obtained, the TP curve will shift and so, too, will the marginal product curve. Shifts in the marginal product curve will, in turn, cause the MRP curve to shift. Referring to Figure 10–7, let us assume MRP_1 is associated with b_1 and c_1 units of the latter resources. Assume also that the firm is employing the quantity represented by u on MRP_1, and that this represents the profit-maximizing quantity of a, given the corresponding price of a. Now suppose the price of a declines. The lower price will tend to cause more of a to be employed by the firm. If b and c are substitutes for a, more of a will be employed with *less* of b and c. But if resources b and c are complementary, the decline in a's price will not only increase employment of a, but will cause more of b and c to be purchased as well. Suppose b and c are complementary to a so that more of each is purchased as a's price declines. These changes in the employment of a, b, and c will shift the TP curve, the MP schedule, and MRP as well. Suppose the MRP curve shifts to MRP_2, and the quantity of a used to that represented by point v after the firm has optimally adjusted to the decline in a's price. Then points u and v would lie along the firm's demand schedule for a, assuming all resources are variable. We have

FIGURE 10–7   Derivation of Long-Run Demand for Resource a

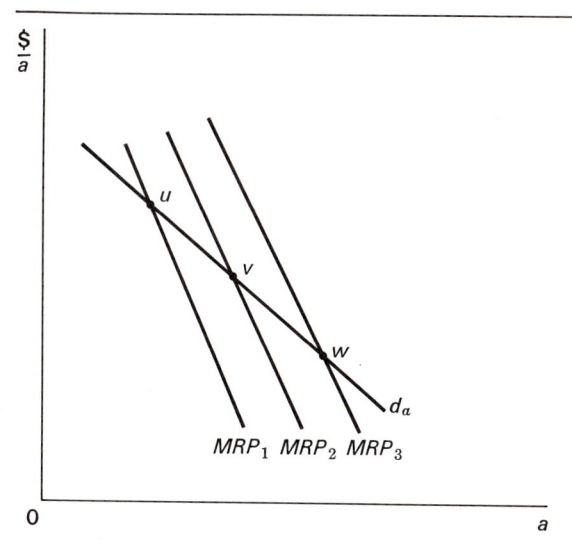

shown still another point, w on MRP_3, which would be appropriate if there occurred still another drop in the price of a. Collecting all such points, we would derive the demand schedule for a, labeled d_a in Figure 10-7.

The result of being able to move onto higher TP curves when several inputs can be varied is that the firm's demand for a is more elastic than when only a can be varied, because the productive process itself is more elastic. That is, the firm will not demand a along one MRP_a function when several resources are variable, because each MRP_a function relates to only one TP curve. A firm's demand schedule for a will pass through as many different MRP_a curves as there are different TP functions.

Given the variability of all resources, the determination of the firm's demand curve for any one resource is more complicated, as the above discussion has suggested. We may think in terms of a number of MRP schedules, one for each resource, but must be prepared to admit that as soon as one resource is varied in amount, the MRP curves for all the others will be shifted, one way or the other. Nevertheless, we can propose a general rule for the profit-maximixing employment of a firm's resources, assuming that all inputs are variable. The rule is an application of the marginal cost–marginal revenue concept and provides that a necessary condition for long-run profit maximization by a firm is the equality of marginal revenue product, MRP, and marginal resource cost, MRC, for each of the resources hired by the firm. Stated in mathematical terms, the general requirement is:

$$\frac{MRP_a}{MRC_a} = \frac{MRP_b}{MRC_b} = \frac{MRP_c}{MRC_c} = \cdots = \frac{MRP_n}{MRC_n} = 1, \qquad (1)$$

where a through n are the resources used by the firm. When the firm equates to one the ratio of marginal benefit to marginal cost for all of the resources used in production, it maximizes profits just as when it equates MR and $LRMC$. In other words, the above equation defines the profit-maximizing combination of inputs, just as $LRMC = MR$ determines the long-run profit-maximizing output. In effect, there are two ways of looking at the same decision process, from the input side or the output side.

Finally, if the firm faces a perfectly competitive resource market, such that the price of each resource remains constant and, therefore, equal to MRC, the formula for profit maximization may be restated:

$$\frac{MRP_a}{P_a} = \frac{MRP_b}{P_b} = \frac{MRP_c}{P_c} = \cdots = \frac{MRP_n}{P_n} = 1, \qquad (2)$$

where P_a, P_b, P_c, ..., through P_n are the respective prices of the resources hired. Note, however, this latter formula applies only if we assume the firm is a price taker in the resource market.

IMPERFECT COMPETITION—RESOURCE AND OUTPUT MARKETS

Imperfect Competition—Output Markets

Now we must discuss resource pricing under less than perfectly competitive conditions, and we will begin by investigating the demand of a monopolistic firm for a single variable resource, a. All other inputs are constant, and we retain our assumption that the resource market is competitive so that the monopoly firm is a price taker in this market. We will see that the only difference between this and the preceding model is found in the determinants of the firm's MRP schedule.

A firm with monopoly power in its output market follows essentially the same decision-making process as the competitive firm in determining its profit-maximizing level of employment of a single variable factor of production. The firm equates the marginal revenue product associated with the resource with its marginal resource cost. Moreover, marginal resource cost will be constant and equal to the market price of the resource, as it was in our previous model, since the monopolist is a price taker in the resource market. The monopolist's MRP curve will be different, however, for it is affected not only by the decline in marginal product as successive a's are employed, but by the decline in price and marginal revenue which results as successive units of the monopolist's output are produced and sold.

If we multiply the marginal product of a by the price of the monopolist's finished product, the resultant is the value of the marginal product of a, VMP_a, but this will not equal the incremental revenue that the sale of the marginal unit of a generates, because the negative slope of the monopolist's product demand curve results in a divergence between its average revenue and marginal revenue. In short, marginal revenue is less than price under monopoly (or imperfect competition), so MRP_a is less than VMP_a. As successive units of a are employed by a monopolist, MRP_a declines for two reasons: (1) the physical productivity of a, MP_a, declines, and (2) the demand for X is negatively sloped so, as the price of X falls, MR_x declines also. By contrast, in perfect competition, firms' average and marginal revenue are equal and constant at all output levels, so MRP_a equals VMP_a and declines only as a result of the decline in MP_a.

We can determine the monopolist's profit-maximizing output level by a model similar to that of a competitive firm. In Figure 10–8, MRP_a is the marginal revenue product curve of a monopolist and $S_a = MRC_a = P_a$ is the resource supply curve. The monopolist will equate MRP_a with MRC_a at output a_1, to maximize profits. If the price of a falls to S'_a, the monopolist would increase its employment to a_2 units as determined by the intersection point of S'_a and MRP_a. We may say, then, that MRP_a is the monopolist's demand for a.

434 The Theory of Distribution

FIGURE 10–8 Monopoly Demand for Resource a (Assuming a Competitive Resource Market)

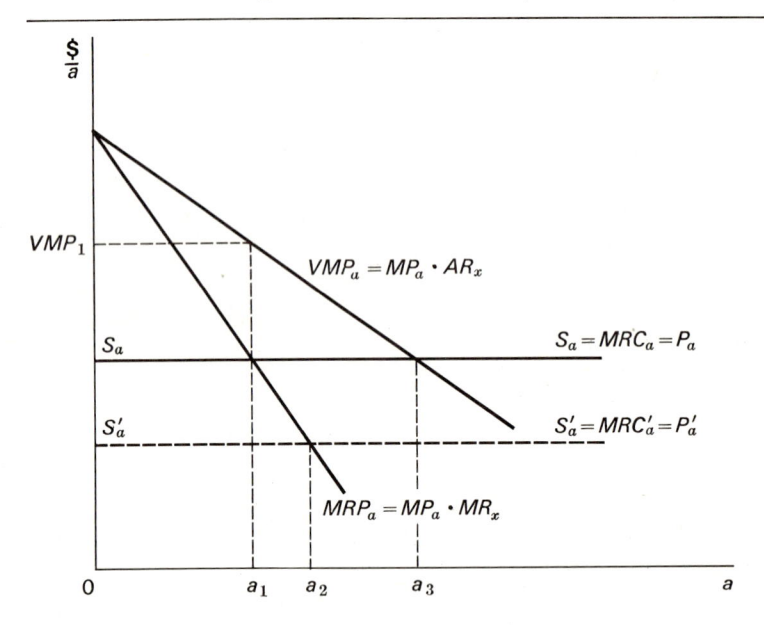

[Figure 10–8: Graph with vertical axis labeled $\frac{\$}{a}$ and horizontal axis labeled a. Shows VMP_1 marked on vertical axis, downward-sloping curves labeled $VMP_a = MP_a \cdot AR_x$ and $MRP_a = MP_a \cdot MR_x$. Horizontal lines $S_a = MRC_a = P_a$ and $S'_a = MRC'_a = P'_a$. Points on horizontal axis: a_1, a_2, a_3.]

The divergence between the value of the marginal product of a and the marginal revenue product of a, for a monopolist, is also shown in Figure 10–8. VMP_a and MRP_a indicate that for any marginal unit of a used by the monopolist, the value of the marginal product of that unit will be greater than its marginal revenue product. At the profit-maximizing level of resource hire of a_1 units, the difference between VMP_a and MRP is equal to $VMP_1 - S_a$. Notice that if competitive conditions prevailed, the VMP_a schedule would also be the firm's MRP_a schedule, and it would hire a_3 units of the variable factor at resource price S_a. Since the monopolist hires only a_1 units, we may think of the difference $a_3 - a_1$ as illustrating the restriction on resource hire that a monopolist interposes because he does not wish to "spoil" his output market.[7] The monopolist's restriction on the hire of the variable factor, a, corresponds with his short-run restriction on the number of units produced and sold in the output market that he monopolizes. In short, output restriction is accomplished by restricting the amount of resources utilized in production.

We can make another analogy. In the short-run monopoly model, the firm equates MC and MR at the profit-maximizing output level. AR exceeds MR

[7] This difference is only illustrative. If the industry in question were made competitive, each competitive firm's $VMP_a = MRP_a$ schedule would be far to the left of VMP_a in Figure 10–8. The VMP_a curve is more accurately a first approximation to the *sum* of the competitive firm's $VMP_a = MRP_a$ schedules and would then be subject to error because of the violation of the *ceteris paribus* assumption.

(equal to MC at the profit-maximizing output) which indicates that consumers' valuation of the last unit of product produced, as measured by the price they will pay, is greater than the extra cost of producing one more unit, as measured by the marginal cost of producing that additional unit. The excess of price over marginal cost under monopoly suggests that monopoly may lead to inefficient resource use. From the resource side, VMP_a will be greater than MRP_a at the profit-maximizing level of resource hire. Consumers value an extra unit of the variable resource, as determined by VMP_a, higher than the monopolist values the contribution of that marginal resource as measured by MRP_a. The monopolist values the marginal contribution of the variable resource less than consumers do, because the monopolist is assumed to be principally concerned with profit maximization and not the utility maximization of his customers.

The basic model which we have just described can be used to analyze the resource demand, not only of the monopolist, but of any firm which realizes a *degree* of monopoly power in its output market, for example, a monopolistically competitive firm. Whenever a firm's average revenue curve declines, marginal revenue will lie below average revenue. As a consequence, the value of the marginal product of the variable factor will be greater than its marginal revenue product. If it is a profit maximizer, the firm will restrict its hire of the variable factor below that level which equates VMP and MRC. We may generally conclude, therefore, that the resource is underutilized by the imperfectly competitive firm.

The Case of Monopsony—A Monopoly Buyer of a Single Resource

In the models we have developed thus far, we have assumed that the resource buyer was a competitor in the resource market, whether a competitor or a monopolist in the product market. That assumption is often a fair generalization, because any resource can be employed to produce several different products. The monopolistic producer of commodity X might then be purchasing resource *a* along with the producers of commodities Y, Z, and any number of others. Now we must investigate those cases where the resource market itself is less than perfectly competitive. The model which we will present in this section is that of monopsony.

A *monopsonist* is simply defined as the sole buyer of a resource (or commodity). Fairly good examples of monopsony are not hard to find. A single textile mill in a small southern town, for example, may dominate the local labor market; or the biggest construction company in a given area may exercise monopsony power when it buys gravel. Where the firm is a monopsonistic buyer of resource *a*, the supply curve which it faces will no longer be perfectly elastic but will be upsloping. That is, the supply curve facing the firm will be the market supply of the resource. Now we must investigate the effects of an upsloping supply curve on the firm's marginal resource cost.

436 The Theory of Distribution

In Figure 10–9, the curve labeled S_a is assumed to be the supply curve for resource a that a hypothetical monopsonist faces in the resource market, indicating that the firm must pay a higher price as it increases its employment of a. In addition, not only must the monopsonist firm pay a higher price for the marginal a it obtains, but the higher price is also applicable to *all* units of a purchased.[8] The extra cost of obtaining that a is therefore higher than its purchase price. Consequently, the marginal resource cost curve for a, MRC_a, no longer coincides with S_a but rises above it, just as any marginal function will lie above the average function, if the latter is rising.

Assuming that MRP_a is the firm's marginal revenue product curve for a, the profit-maximizing monopsony firm will maximize profits by equating MRC and MRP at point e in Figure 10–9. It will employ Q_1 units of a at price P_1. Notice that just as a monopolist sets output price, the monopsonist sets the price of the resource; it is not a price taker in the resource market as the competitive firm is.

At the profit-maximizing quantity of a utilized by the monopsonist, marginal revenue product exceeds the price of a, so VMP_a will exceed the price of a also. Moreover, VMP_a will exceed the price of a whether the monopsonist firm sells its output in a perfectly competitive product market or not, since VMP_a cannot be below MRP_a.[9] Using our previous criterion, the monopsonist would therefore be deemed exploitive. In addition, the inequality of VMP_a

FIGURE 10–9 Equilibrium Price and Quantity under Monopsony

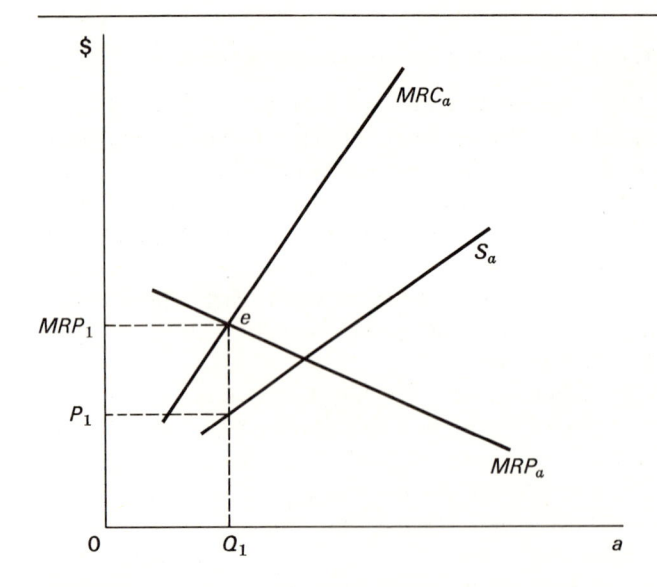

[8] This assumes the monopsonist firm cannot practice price discrimination in the resources it hires.
[9] A possible exception to this is a Gibson good or a Snob good.

and P_a indicates that resource a is underutilized from the standpoint of economic efficiency, since consumers value the marginal product of the next successive a higher than the price of that unit of a.

Finally, we may conclude that the basic monopsony model, or variants of the model, are applicable to any resource market situation in which a buyer faces an upsloping supply curve. If the buyer is not a price taker, MRC exceeds the price of a, which means that at the profit-maximizing level of a obtained, VMP_a exceeds the price of a. The previous conclusions regarding resource exploitation and underutilization of the factor are therefore applicable.

SUMMARY AND CONCLUSION

In this chapter, we have viewed the firm as operating between two markets: as a buyer in the market for resources and as a seller in the product or commodities market. In addition, we have noted that the consumer's decision regarding the purchase of goods and services is inseparable from his decision to supply resources in the resource market. We can diagram the relationship between a firm and its suppliers and consumers as follows:

Resource Suppliers → Resource Market → FIRM → Commodities Market → Consumers

This view of their activities harks back to the real circuit of the circular flow of wealth between firms and consumers.

Our approach to the determination of resource price was to investigate first the forces determining the firm's demand for resources. We found that where competitive conditions existed in the resource market, the firm's demand for a variable factor was identical to the marginal revenue product, MRP, of the factor, where the MRP of resource a equals the addition to total revenue occasioned by the hire of an extra unit of the resource. When knowledge of the MRP of a factor is coupled with that of its marginal resource cost, MRC, the profit-maximizing quantity of a is determined. MRC is defined as the addition to total cost that occurs when a firm purchases one additional unit of a factor. MRC is constant and equal to the price of a if perfect competition exists in the resource market, but is an increasing function if monopsony prevails.

Whether competition exists or not, the firm maximizes profit in the short run by equating the marginal resource cost and marginal revenue product of the variable resource. The point of intersection of MRC and MRP determines the quantity of the variable factor a to purchase to produce the profit-maximizing output. We found also that where all inputs are variable, the firm maximizes profit by equating the MRP of each resource with its respective MRC, which means obtaining that quantity of each resource which makes the ratio

MRP/MRC for that resource equal to 1. Using the tools of marginal resource cost and marginal revenue product, we found that the most efficient allocation of resources occurs when perfectly competitive conditions prevail in both the resource market and in the consumer goods or commodities market. Any degree of monopoly in either the resource or commodity market tends to result in less output and thus less utilization of resources than would occur under competitive conditions. Moreover, the existence of monopolistic or monopsonistic elements tends to result in exploitation of the factor, where exploitation is measured by the difference between the VMP of the factor and its price. As a general conclusion, it may be inferred, therefore, that in the resource market, just as in the product market, competitive conditions provide larger output at a lower price than any degree of monopoly is likely to do. The quantity demanded of a given resource under perfect competition (where the MRP equals the VMP) is greater than the quantity demanded by a firm selling its output in a monopolistic market (where VMP exceeds MRP). So the level of resource use is generally greater under competitive conditions than under monopoly, though there are exceptions.

In the latter part of this chapter we developed the monopsony model, which is applicable when monopoly power is present on the buyer side of the resource market. We found that in the case of monopsony, marginal resource cost rises above the resource supply or the price the resource receives. When the monopsony firm equates marginal resource cost and marginal revenue product to determine the profit-maximizing level of employment, the quantity of the resource used will be less than would be the case under competitive conditions, and the price of the resource will be set less than the VMP of the factor.

In the following two chapters, we employ the models developed in this chapter to investigate the factors influencing the returns to the functional factors of production, land, labor, and capital.

PROBLEMS

1. Why are resources demanded? Can an individual resource be consumed directly?
2. When does VMP measure a firm's demand for a resource?
3. Why is MRP a more general statement of a firm's demand for a resource?
4. If a and b are complementary resources, what will happen to MRP_b if P_a falls and more a is employed?
5. Given the supply curve for resource a (page 439), construct in the lower panel a total resource cost curve ($TRC_a = P_a \cdot a$) and in the upper panel MRC_a.
6. If MRP_a is the monopsonist's marginal revenue product curve, approximately how many units will the firm hire at what price _____?

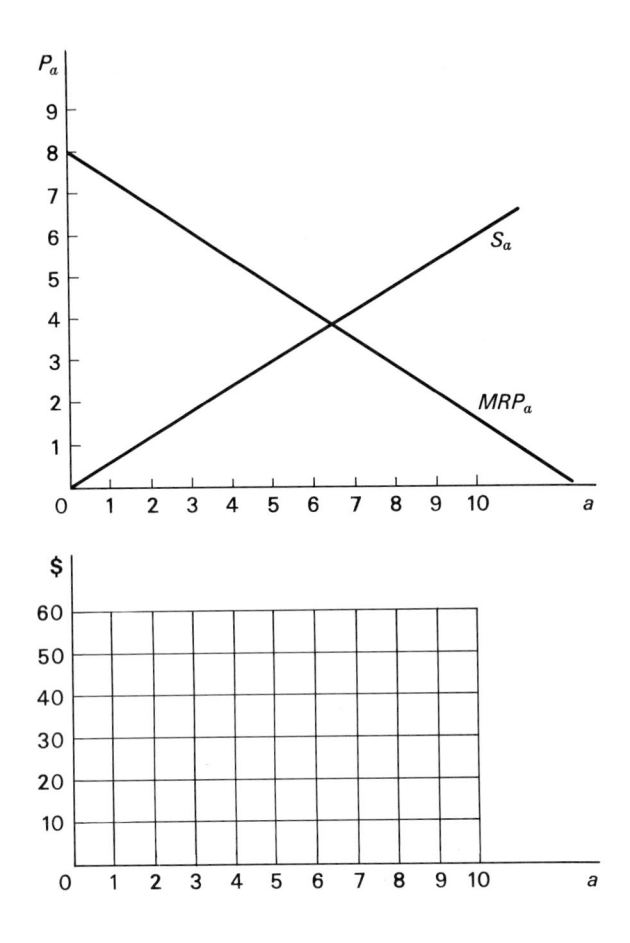

7. If the price of a competitive firm's output is $10 and the marginal product of the first a is 100 units and that of each successive a is 10 units less than the previous a, how many a's will the firm hire if the price of a's is $800?

REFERENCES

BAUMOL, WILLIAM J., *Economic Theory and Operations Analysis*, 2nd ed. Englewood Cliffs, N.J.: Prentice-Hall, Inc., 1965. Chapters 17, 18, and 19.
FRIEDMAN, MILTON, *Price Theory*. Chicago: Aldine Publishing Co., 1962.
FRISCH, RAGNAR, *Theory of Production*. Chicago: Rand-McNally & Co., 1965.
ROBINSON, JOAN, "Euler's Theorem and the Problem of Distribution," *Economic Journal*, September 1934, 398–414.
WEIN, HAROLD H., and V. P. STREEDHARAN, *The Optimal Staging and Phasing of Multi-Product Capacity*. East Lansing: Michigan State University Division of Research, 1968.

APPENDIX TO CHAPTER 10

A Universe of Commodities

KENNETH E. BOULDING

We have at this point in the text covered the major topics in marginal analysis of the firm, including the profit-maximizing conditions in product and resource markets. In the selection below Kenneth Boulding explores the relationship between the economist's marginal tools and the decision-making tools that the businessman uses in an effort to discover why the economist and the businessman do not always communicate effectively. Boulding points out the similarities between the economists' marginal analysis and operations research, a body of mathematical techniques, including linear programming, which has proven so effective in management decision-making.

Can an economist make a contribution worthy of his hire as a member of the staff of a firm? Boulding answers in the affirmative.

> Economists are understood
> To study goods, if not the Good
> Although their goods, we often find
> Are pale obstructions of the mind

I have argued that the skill of the economist lies in the analysis of the behavior of commodities and not the behavior of men. It is not altogether surprising therefore that in spite of the apparently close relationship between their subject matters, the main contributions of the social sciences to the conduct of business have not come from economics but from the more "behavioral sciences" of psychology and sociology. Human relations, industrial relations, public relations, group dynamics, even the psychology of advertising, have all made substantial contributions to the business vocabulary.

The world of the economist and the world of the business man, however, have shown small signs of coming together in spite of the fact that economists

---

From *The Skills of the Economist* by Kenneth E. Boulding. Cleveland: Howard Allen, Inc., Publishers, copyright 1958 by Kenneth E. Boulding. Reprinted by permission.

have spent a great deal of time and effort in developing an elaborate theory of the firm. The vocabulary of the economist seems quite foreign to the man of affairs; all this talk about equating marginal this to marginal that is so much academic gibberish to the great fraternity of "those who have to meet payrolls." Nor on the other hand have the students of management—even the academic students of management—been able to communicate fruitfully with the theoretical economists. The collection of organization charts, platitudes, and maxims which characterize the average textbook on management fills the economist with unrestrained ennui because there is so little relationship to the problems which strike the economist as important.

In part, this unfortunate situation arises because of a difference in point of view. The economist's focus of interest, I must repeat, lies in the world of commodities and not in the world of men. Hence the actual problems of the organization and conduct of business, which are problems in the relations of men rather than in the relations of commodities, do fall more naturally into the realm of the psychologist and the sociologist rather than that of the economist in spite of the traditional association of business with economics.

But I must also regard this persistent inability of economists and business to communicate as unfortunate. On the one hand the economist cannot wholly understand the laws which govern the universe of commodities without knowing something about what governs the universe of men. On the other hand business men do have something to learn from economists, even if it is only from his way of looking at things and at their businesses, which may increase their understanding of what they are doing even if it does not increase their skill. Moreover, recent developments in economics indicate that in the not too distant future economists may have something of great importance to contribute to the theory and practice of the business enterprise as well as other organizations.

Ten years ago I would have said that the marginal analysis, or the theory of maximization, was the only contribution of economics to the theory of the business enterprise. This is no longer true and it is becoming clear that the marginal analysis, as we understood it ten years ago, is a special case of a much more general theory, not only of a more general theory of maximization, as expressed for instance in the theories of linear programming, but also of a more general theory of behavior and organization. Nevertheless, for the purposes of the present argument I propose to neglect much of the work of the past ten years and consider the possible contributions of the marginal analysis as it is conventionally understood.

The marginal analysis is nothing more nor less than the detailed spelling-out of the theory of maximization—that is, the theory that *optimum* position of the variables of any economic organization is that given by the maximum position of that variable which measures desirability or preference. The first basic assumption is that any economic organization is characterized by a set of identifiable variables—prices, quantities, selling costs, and so on—and that these variables are linked in a series of transformation functions which set the *limits* to the possible combinations of the variables. The principal transformation functions are (i) the production function, which reflects the limitations imposed by the nature of the physical world on the amounts of outputs which can be got from specific quantities of inputs, and (ii) the sale and purchase functions which show what quantities of sales of output or of purchase of input are consistent with various prices, selling costs, etc. What these transformation functions do is to delimit the set of *possible* combinations of variables: any set which does not satisfy the limitations laid down by the transformation functions is by definition impossible of attainment. It is not enough, however, to delineate the possible, for even with man a great many combinations are possible, though not all things. Within the range of the possible we need a method of identifying the *optimum* set of variables. To do this we postulate that some quantity, which is a function of all other variables, is a measure of desirability so that any set of variables or position of the organization for which this desirability-measure is higher is *ipso facto* better than a set or position for which the desirability-measure is lower. The bigger the desirability-measure, the better! Then clearly that position of the system (that is, that set of values of all the relevant variables), at which the desirability-measure is a maximum, is the "best."

All this sounds very abstract, but I will illustrate with a very simple case—perhaps the simplest possible case—of an economic organization. Suppose we have a firm which is engaged solely in the business of buying and selling a single commodity—say wheat. We will suppose that the assets of the firm consist of two items only—wheat and money. We will further assume a perfect market for wheat—that is, that the firm can buy or sell as much as it likes at a given market price but that if it raises its price above the market it will not be able to sell and if it lowers its price below the market price it will not be able to buy. Then suppose we plot quantity of wheat on one axis (OW) and quantity of money on the other (OM) as in Figure 1. Then any actual position of the firm can be represented by a point in this field, say T, where KT is the amount of money and HT is the amount of wheat which the firm possesses. The transformation function (or "opportunity line" as it is often called) is the line MTW—the slope of which is equal to the market price of wheat. A movement up this line in the direction of M indicates that the firm is selling wheat and "buying" money: a movement towards W indicates that the firm is buying wheat and "selling" money. The price of wheat is the slope of the line, OM/OW.

We now take the line MW and make it the horizontal axis of Figure 2, the vertical axis now being the desirability or advantage-measure, which I have labeled, following the conventional terminology of economics, "Utility." Utility is a maximum at X and the corresponding position of the firm, L, is

FIGURE 1

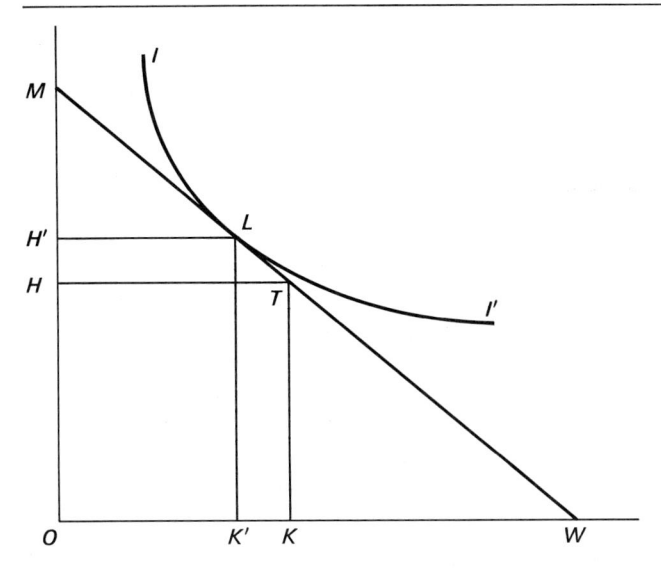

FIGURE 2

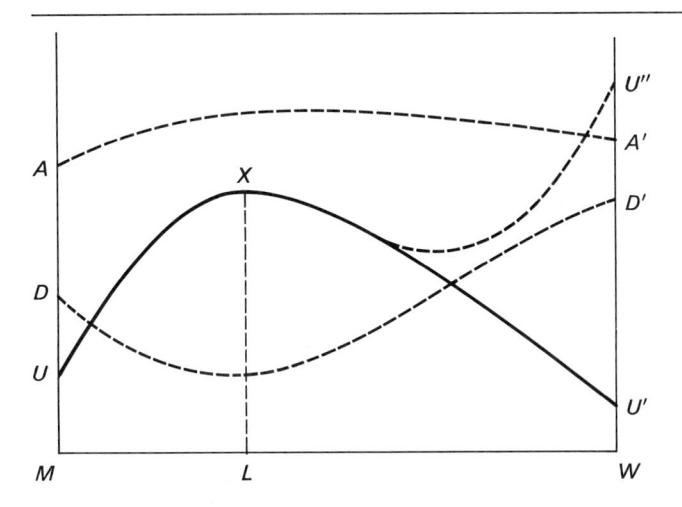

therefore the optimum. Each position in the line MW represents a possible combination of wheat and money but only L is the "best." Measuring ML on Figure 1 equal to ML on Figure 2 we see that the "best" amounts of wheat and money to hold are LH' and LK' respectively. At the maximum point X, and at no other, the *net marginal advantage*—i.e., the slope of the curve UXU' —is zero. We can, if we like, separate the gross advantage from the gross disadvantage—the net advantage being of course the excess of gross advantage over disadvantage. Then we can draw, in Figure 2, gross advantage and disadvantage curves, AA' and DD'. Where the slopes of these curves are the same the net advantage (the vertical distance between them) is the greatest. That is to say, the optimum position is the marginal gross advantage equal to the marginal gross disadvantage.

The reader who is familiar with the marginal analysis will of course recognize the above equality as the general case of all the *marginal conditions*. If gross advantage is measured by revenue and disadvantage by cost, we get the familiar *marginal revenue equals marginal cost* condition for a maximum of net revenue at a point on the output axis, or the equally familiar *marginal revenue product equals marginal cost of input* at a point on the input axis. The final optimum is that combination of variables at which all the various marginal equalities are satisfied simultaneously. We recognize here both the principle of a general equilibrium model and the *method* of partial equilibrium outlined in the first chapter—for the ultimate position of the optimum can be found only by solving all the marginal equations simultaneously, yet it is useful to explore the topography of the model plane by plane.

A number of alternative methods are possible for describing the preference or advantage function. For instance, in Figure 1 we suppose that net advantage is measured in the vertical direction and an advantage-surface is drawn in three dimensions over the plane of the paper. This surface can be represented by a set of contours such as ILI', all points on which represent combinations of equal advantage. These are the familiar indifference curves of Pareto. The optimum point is that at which the opportunity line is *touched* by an indifference curve, for at any point on the opportunity line which is *cut* by an indifference curve it is possible to move to a more advantageous position, represented by a "higher" indifference curve. The point L, however, where the opportunity line is touched by an indifference curve represents the "highest" indifference curve, and therefore the most advantageous position possible while keeping to the opportunity line MW. It may be noted here that the opportunity line is in general a "boundary" rather than a line, in the sense that positions *within* the line are possible by throwing one or the other asset away. Thus, all positions downward and to the left of the opportunity line are possible of attainment; all positions upward and to the right are impossible of attainment.

In general, the transformation functions of all kinds may be thought of as boundaries which cannot be transgressed, rather than as tight ropes to be walked, separating the variable-space into two parts. One part includes all possible sets and another includes all impossible sets. In Figure 1 we can think of the opportunity line as a fence on the "mountain" of the advantage surface. The optimum possible point is the highest point on the fence, which is precisely where the fence touches a contour. There are points, of course, which are still higher up the advantage mountain but since they are on the other side of the fence they are not attainable.

I need not go into all the innumerable ramifications and developments of the essentially simple ideas expressed above. Enough of them will be found even in my own *Economic Analysis* and still more in my *Reconstruction of Economics* to satisfy the most avid thirster after this kind of knowledge. It will suffice here to say that exactly the same principle which I have outlined here can be applied to any and all the variables which are significant in the life of an economic organization, whether costs, inputs, outputs, selling costs, production functions, borrowings, lendings, inventories, capital structures or time structures. In all these cases the principle is the same. First, we postulate some sort of transformation or opportunity function which divides the possible from the impossible. Then we find, within the area of the possible, some technique for describing the most desirable. This may be the selection of one variable of the system, such as profits, as a unique measure of desirability. It may be by setting up a "utility" or advantage function in the form of indifference curves. Even simpler devices may be useful such as the one I have proposed in my *Reconstruction of Economics* expressing preferences in terms of preferred asset ratios. Whatever the application the essential principle is the same.

The main question I raise is why a system of analysis, so self-consistent, so obedient to the great scientific principle of parsimony, so elegant, so persistent in academic teaching, and so admirably adapted to the understanding of students and to regurgitation in examinations, should be so confoundedly useless—useless, that is, to the business man who is supposed to be the prime mover of the whole apparatus. For the business man, alas, either finds the whole rigmarole so unfamiliar that he does not even attempt to master it, or if he does master it (and there are rare business men here and there who have done so) is apt to deny indignantly that he behaves in any such monstrous and outrageously unethical profit-seeking manner as the marginal analysis seems to suggest.

First we examine one or two technical defects in the marginal analysis as usually presented to see if these throw any light on the problem. First we have the problem of the "boundary maximum." Suppose, for instance, in Figure 2, that the net advantage curve, instead of falling continuously from X to U', first fell and then rose to U'' where U'' represents a higher level of advantage than X. Suppose further that the conditions of the problem preclude any position beyond W.[1] Then U'' represents the true position of maximum advantage, not X, though U'' fulfills none of the mathematical conditions for a maximum and none of the marginal equalities or conditions are

[1] We may note in passing that in the example of Figures 1 and 2 the opportunity line may be extended into the fourth quadrant beyond W by borrowing money (in which the individual expands his wheat holdings beyond his net worth by acquiring, as it were, "negative money" in the form of debt). Similarly the line may be meaningfully extended into the second quadrant beyond M by "borrowing wheat" (selling wheat futures) and so increasing the money stock beyond the net worth.

satisfied. The marginal conditions merely represent a maximum "in the small": they may not represent the absolute maximum at all.

A variant of the same problem is presented when there are multiple maxima (dromedaries instead of camels) because the marginal conditions apply equally well at any of the maxima and throw no light on which of the various "humps" is the *maximum maximorum*.

Another variant of the same problem is that presented by discontinuities in the transformation functions. For many reasons these discontinuities can occur in almost all the transformation functions. They can occur in a sales function where a commodity has a number of distinct and non-competing uses at different prices, but where in any particular use below the price at which this use comes into play, the demand is highly inelastic. The sales curve for such a commodity (and the case is not infrequent, especially in raw material industries) will look more like a staircase than a nice smooth demand curve. The resulting discontinuities in the revenue curves are likely to yield advantage-functions with sharp jagged discontinuities, like a saw in profile. The marginal conditions will be formally satisfied even at such jagged peaks but not much in the way of conclusions can be drawn from the analysis except to say that the highest tooth of the saw is the best!

I shall do no more than mention the difficulty that the marginal conditions of the first order apply just as well to minima as to maxima since this is a problem which can be taken care of adequately by the second-order conditions. Indeed, a careful statement of the marginal conditions in a negative sense usually includes implicitly the second-order conditions. Thus, in Figure 2 we might say that the advantage is at a maximum when the marginal advantage, with respect to increase of either commodity, passes from a positive to a negative value with increase in the quantity of the asset.

None of these difficulties in themselves are adequate to explain the deaf ears on which the marginal analysis falls in the business community. There is a deeper problem than any we have mentioned. It is the problem of *what* is maximized—that is, what is the measure of advantage and how is it measured. The answer the economist has usually given to this question, as far as the business enterprise is concerned, is that, considered in its abstract nature as an economic organization, the business should maximize profits. Two problems face us at this point. One is the measure of profit itself. The other is the persistent belief in the business community that a decent, respectable, or even merely cautious and conservative business man would not want to maximize profits even if he knew how to do so.

We will consider first the problem of the *measure* of profits. In the elementary marginal analysis, as it is usually taught in the first course in economics, it is assumed that profits are measured by the *net revenue*. This is the difference between the total revenue, or the value of the product, and the total cost, which consists essentially of the assets (including liquid assets) consumed or destroyed in the production of the product. The maximization of net revenue then gives us the "simple" marginal conditions, such as *marginal revenue equals marginal cost*. The net revenue is only a satisfactory measure of profits as long as we abstract from the time and capital structure of the enterprise. When we try to generalize the marginal analysis to cover the whole time and capital structure of the enterprise, as Friedrich and Vera Lutz have attempted to do, net revenue as a measure of profits must be replaced by some concept of a rate of return on net worth or capitalized value. Two enterprises with the same net revenue of, say, $10,000 a year, would not be regarded as equally profitable if one was capitalized at $100,000 and the other at $200,000. Similarly within a single enterprise the maximum net revenue might appear so "late" in time after the commencement of the enterprise that the rate of return on capital investment would be smaller than if the net revenue were smaller than its maximum but appeared earlier.

Even though it is clear that the net revenue is not an adequate measure of profits over time it is not so clear what should be substituted for it. The Lutzes list four contenders for the throne of the maximand, three of which are serious rivals although their claims are by no means fully resolved even within the fraternity of economists. These are: the rate of return on the total assets of the enterprise; the rate of return on the entrepreneurs' own capital; and the present value of all future net receipts capitalized at market rates of interest.

The idea of a *rate of return* and its relationship to the net worth or the capital value of an enterprise is so fundamental at this level of the theory of the firm that we may well pause for a moment to examine it. Let us consider first the nature of the profit-making process itself. The study of the *process* in this case is probably the best clue to the correct *measure*. Let us return to our simple example of the wheat firm and consider how such a skeleton firm can ever make profits. In order to understand the profits concept it is necessary to develop a concept of a financial balance sheet and a net worth. This can easily be done in the present case if we suppose that a valuation coefficient can be applied to the stock of wheat to reduce it to a dollar value. The dollar value of the wheat and the dollar value of the money would thus be added to form the net worth of the firm. This is shown in Figure 3 in which the axes are the same as in Figure 1. I assume that the value of the amount of wheat $H'L$ is $H'M'$, so that the net worth of the firm at the point L is $OH' + H'M'$, or OM'. The valuation coefficient for wheat is $H'M'/H'L$ dollars per bushel. It will be noticed that I have assumed that the valuation coefficient is different from the market price. This is to emphasize the point that the two concepts are essentially separable, even though closely related.

In Figure 3 the valuation coefficient is greater than the market price (the slope of LM' is greater than the slope of LM). Under these circumstances it is clear that the further the firm moves down towards W, or even beyond if

FIGURE 3

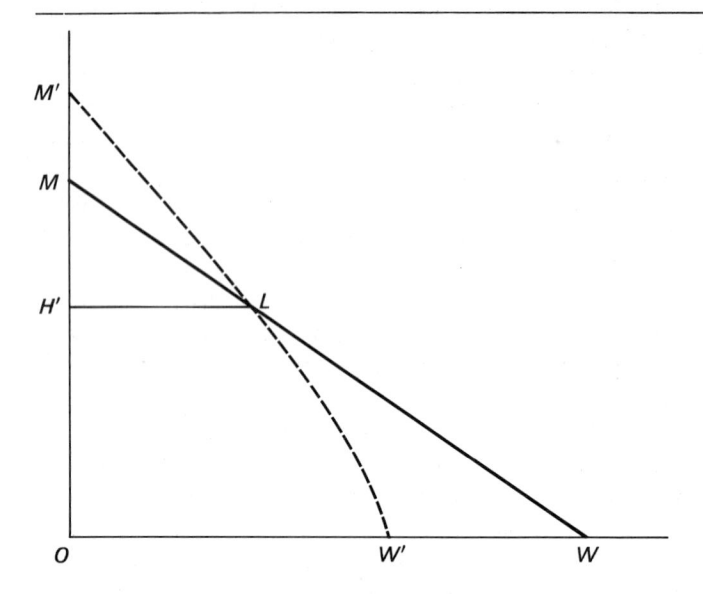

possible, the larger its net worth. If the valuation coefficient had been less than the market price the reverse would have been true—a movement in the direction of M, or beyond, would increase the net worth. If the market price and the valuation coefficient are the same it is clear that no amount of movement along the opportunity line will change the net worth. It is fairly evident that no *maximizing of profit* procedure means anything when applied to a single act of buying and selling. If the valuation coefficient is equal to the market price no profits can be made by buying and selling, because, no matter how much is bought and sold, the net worth remains the same. If the valuation coefficient is not equal to the market price net worth can be increased by moving as far as possible in one direction or the other until either certain boundaries are reached through the inability to borrow money or wheat, or imperfection in the market makes the opportunity curve steeper as the holdings of wheat increase. In this case the maximum net worth is at that position where the valuation coefficient is equal to the (marginal) price of the commodity. Thus, suppose in Figure 3 that after the point L the market became imperfect and the firm could only acquire more wheat by paying higher and higher prices. The opportunity line would curve round as in LW''. If M'L were tangent to this curve LW'' at L, it is evident from the geometry of the figure that OM' is a maximum net worth in the sense that further purchases of wheat beyond H'L would lower the net worth at the given valuation coefficient.

As long as we stick to a single transaction we shall not perceive the essential nature of the profit-making process. Consider then Figure 4, in which the

FIGURE 4

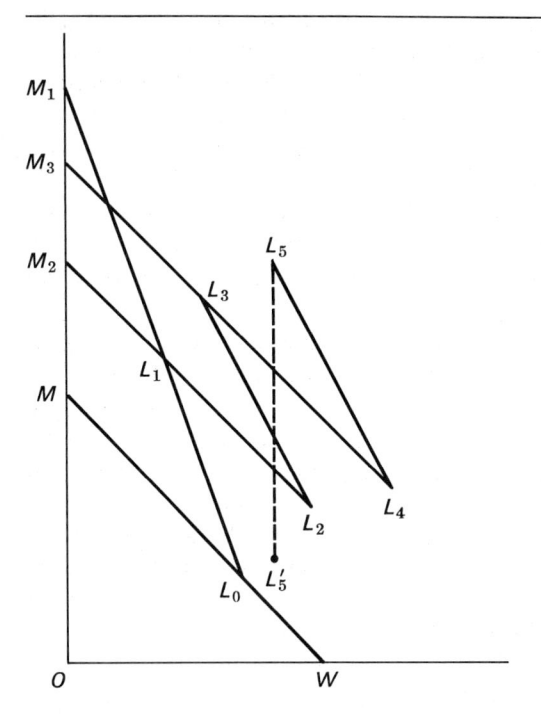

history of the firm is sketched for a few successive operations. We start with the firm at the point L_0, with the price equal to the slope of MW. Now suppose the next day the price rises: the opportunity line steepens to L_0L_1, and the firm sells wheat at this higher price, moving to L_1. The next day the price drops, the opportunity line flattens to L_1L_2, and the firm moves to L_2. So it proceeds to positions L_3, L_4, L_5 and so on. What is happening is that, as a result of successive manipulations of the asset structure, the position of the firm in the asset field is moving further out. L_5, for instance, represents more wheat and more money than the initial position L_0. It would be equally possible for the firm to move from L_5 to L_0, by buying dear and selling cheap—indeed this is frequently done by unsuccessful business men! This is the process of making losses. The profit-making process, then, is a process in which the manipulations of an asset structure through various forms of transformation—production, exchange, consumption, but not distribution[2]—results in an overall increase in the total quantity of assets.

[2] The problem of dividends, distributions out of profits, or of entrepreneurial withdrawals from the accounts of a business should be mentioned briefly here. A "withdrawal" from a business account differs from an asset transformation in that it represents the diminution in one asset (usually money) without any corresponding increase in any other asset. It is a process therefore which differs fundamentally from the processes of asset transformation

Now, however, the inherent difficulty involved in the measure of profits becomes clear. The profit-making process is one in which a complex aggregate of many different kinds of assets is in some way increased. If this increase is to be measured the heterogeneous mass of physical assets must be reduced to a homogeneous financial statement. To do this, however, each item must be multiplied by a valuation coefficient to reduce its "value" to the *numeraire* (dollars). Then the question arises *what* valuation coefficient should be used? The value of the net worth (and hence those changes in the value of net worth which are the measure of profit) depends in large measure on the system of valuation. And the odd fact is that almost any system of valuation will yield some anomalous results.

Consider, for instance, the effects of valuation of inventory at market price. In Figure 4 this would mean that on Day 1 net worth would suddenly rise to OM_1; on Day 2 it would fall to OM_2, even though the move from L_1 and L_2 in response to the lower price is "profitable" in the sense that it lays the groundwork for further advances when the price rises once more. Thus, on this principle, the firm seems to suffer an alteration of profit and loss, profit when price rises, loss when it falls, even though it is precisely these alterations of high and low price which enable the firm to make profits at all! In the short run, at any rate, there is a curious element of inconsistency here even though in the long run the measure may work itself out.

The results of the various methods of inventory accounting (last-in-first-out, first-in-first-out, or constant price variations) can be analyzed by this method. No matter what the method of accounting, there is a certain arbitrariness always implied in the measure of profits because the profit-making process is not a simple linear growth. It is a process whereby the asset structure grows in many dimensions, in some dimensions faster than others and in some dimensions perhaps the quantity of the assets may even be declining. Accounting is the attempt to reduce this multi-dimensional phenomenon to a simple linear scale of dollars. Because the basic phenomenon is multi-dimensional, the attempt to reduce this growth of asset-structures (the essence of the profit-making process) to a simple linear scale, is bound to involve arbitrary assumptions and a certain violation of reality. We run into exactly the same problem in the construction of index numbers, where it is well-known that there is not a single "true" index number of prices or outputs. This is because the reality is multi-dimensional and any attempts to express a multi-dimensional set as

---

by which the diminution in one asset always results in the increase of another. The profit "making" process is that by which the net worth of an organization is increased through successive asset transformations and revaluations. The profit-distribution process is that by which the net worth is decreased through the withdrawal of assets (usually of money). Thus in Figure 4 suppose that at the point L_5 the entrepreneur withdrew a sum of money $L_5 L'_5$ from the business: in the case of a corporation this might represent a cash dividend. The position of the enterprise moves from L_5 to L'_5—from which point the profit-making process may start all over again.

a simple number must involve arbitrary assumptions. It is less well recognized that even the simplest accounting procedures really involve the same problem, perhaps because of the deceptive homogeneity of the dollar-values in financial statements. The arbitrary nature of the procedures involved in either accounting or in the construction of index numbers is no argument against the practice of these procedures. They are necessary because the human mind cannot easily handle many dimensions at the same time. The mind constantly seeks to reduce heterogeneous aggregates to some single homogeneous dimension. Statistical and accounting procedures, while they violate in some degree the nature of the multi-dimensional universe with which they deal, also increase our knowledge of it by a process of rough summarization.

Thus, suppose we were given two long price lists containing a thousand items. We are then asked the difference between the two lists. The mind cannot easily visualize the difference between the two points in a space of a thousand dimensions! If, however, we make a price index and are informed that the index corresponding to the first list is 100 and to the second list is 134, we feel that our knowledge, or at least our perception of an important aspect of the two lists, is increased. This is possible even though the index can only be constructed by making certain arbitrary assumptions about the "weights" of the prices summarized and even though equally plausible assumptions may give us quite widely differing answers.

Similarly, in the case of accounting procedures, if we are faced with two physical balance sheets containing a thousand items—so many tons of this, pounds of that, dollars of debt, and so on—we cannot easily perceive the direct relationship between them. The accountant therefore makes a financial statement, much as the statistician makes an index number, by valuing all the heterogeneous items in terms of a common denominator. If we are then told that one balance sheet represents a net total of $1,000,000 and the other a net total of $1,200,000, again we feel that we know more about them than before. This is in spite of the fact that the two numbers cannot possibly be *substitutes* for the thousand-dimensional complexity of the balance sheets themselves and are necessarily derived from procedures which are arbitrary in the sense that other procedures, giving somewhat different answers, make just about as much sense.

So far we have considered profit merely as an absolute amount and not as a rate of return. A rate of return is a rate of growth and the rate of profit therefore is the rate of growth of net worth. The same difficulties that we encounter in measuring absolute amounts of profit also occur when we are trying to measure a rate of return. On most accounting measures the growth of the net worth through time will be a highly irregular one, alternating rapid leaps in advance with slower movements or even with retreats. If we reckon the rate of growth of net worth simply as a percentage of the net worth at the beginning of each period, the rate of return likewise will exhibit irregular movements which may have nothing to do with the underlying conditions of the enterprise. Between any two points in the history of the enterprise we can calculate an average rate of return—i.e., that rate of growth of the intial value of the net worth which would produce the final value of the net worth, after allowance has been made for withdrawals. We think of the initial value growing at a certain rate, being reduced once in a while by withdrawals, but continuing immediately to grow steadily and finally reaching the level where it actually stands at the end of the period. The actual course of the net worth will be very different from the steady growth course, but the average rate of growth is a summary of its general trend.

The situation is complicated further when there is a debt, for debt also grows at a rate equal to its rate of interest. We have then a kind of race between the assets side and the liabilities side of the balance sheet. The rate of growth of the *net* worth is then dependent on the extent to which the assets can grow faster than the liabilities—that is, on the extent by which the rate of return of the total assets (the "average efficiency of capital") exceeds the rate of interest on the debt. The situation becomes still more complicated when we try to put the problem in marginal terms, comparing marginal efficiencies of capital with marginal rates of interest on increments to assets and to debt respectively.

We can now see some of the difficulties which are inherent in the apparently simple notion of profit maximization. The main difficulty is that the quantity which is supposed to be maximized does not really exist! It would be unkind to call it a figment of the accountant's imagination but it is certainly a product of the accountant's rituals. The difficulty of measurement is seen clearly in Figure 4: the profit-making *process* is the generally outward movement in the field through successive asset-transformations, $L_0 L_1 L_2 L_3$, etc. The measure of profit on the vertical scale $MM_1 M_2 M_3$, etc., depends on the technique of valuations employed. The figure however reveals a yet more fundamental difficulty in the notion of profit maximization. If we knew in advance exactly what the various prices on the various days were going to be, it is evident that the wider the swings (the more wheat is bought on the days of low prices and the more is sold on the days of high prices) the more rapidly on the whole will the firm increase assets—that is, move outward and upward in the field of the diagram.

The maximization of profits, under conditions of certainty in expectations, then becomes a problem in boundary maxima. It is not susceptible to the marginal analysis at all. The rule is simply to move as far as possible in the direction of holding *commodity* when the price is going to rise, and to move as far as possible in the direction of holding *money* when the price is going to fall. If there are perfect capital markets—that is, if it is possible to borrow any amount of money or commodity on terms which do not depend on the amount borrowed—there are no limits at all to the rate of profit. The firm would then borrow an infinite amount of money and hold an infinite amount of commodity whenever the price was going to rise. Likewise it would borrow an infinite amount of commodity and hold an infinite amount of money whenever the price was going to fall, the rate of profit being also infinite! The absurdity of this conclusion points up the fact that one of two things must limit the rate of profit. *Either* there must be some sort of imperfection in markets or in other transformation functions—i.e., the rate of transformation of one asset into another in some sense must "worsen" through price or interest changes as the first asset continued to be transformed into the second. Or there must be uncertainty as to the future, making the possibilities of loss as well as the possibilities of gain greater as assets are transformed one into another. Thus suppose in Figure 4 we proceed upwards from L_0 in the direction of M_1, selling wheat and acquiring money in the expectation of a fall in the price of wheat and a subsequent movement along a path such as L_1L_2. If we are certain that the price of wheat is going to fall then the further we move in the direction of L_0M_1 the better. Suppose, however, that we have an uneasy feeling that there *might* be a rise in the price rather than a fall. Then the further we move along L_0M_1 the more we stand to lose if in fact there is a rise in price, though equally, the more we stand to gain if there is a fall. If now, as we move along the transformation function, the fear of loss rises faster than the hope of gain, at some point the marginal advantage from the hope of gain is just balanced by the marginal disadvantage of the fear of loss. It will not be advantageous to proceed beyond this point because of the uncertainties involved.

We now seem to be back at something much more like the marginal analysis, not maximizing a profit in any accounting sense—this being impossible in the presence of uncertainty—but maximizing utility or advantage in a broad sense.

We run into much the same problem, even under conditions of certainty, if the markets for the various assets are imperfect. It is then not impossible to transform one asset into another in indefinite quantities without loss. Under these circumstances it may well be reasonable to prefer a combination of assets with a lower accounting value to a combination with a higher value. This would be true if the former represents a more desirable *structure* of assets—better proportioned, less open to sudden and unexpected, unfavorable changes, more liquid, etc. The simple profit maximization theory assumes, in effect, that it is only the total value of assets which is significant to the firm, not the form or composition of these assets.

This is to say that the theory of profit maximization is only applicable to the case in which all markets are perfect, where there is no difficulty in transforming any asset into any other, and where the *form* of the asset structure is unimportant. Also, it is applicable only where there is no uncertainty so that we never have to balance lucrativity against security. If, however, under these idyllic circumstances, the maximum profit is to be finite there must be diminishing returns in some sense. In fact, this is precisely the case for which the theory of profit maximization was originally conceived. Economists have not generally realized the damage done to the fundamental principle of profit maximization by the attempt to extend the analysis to imperfect markets and uncertain futures.

If we now reduce the marginal analysis to the maximizing of utility, are we saying anything at all? Utility is such a vague, unmeasurable concept that the reader may be pardoned if he doubts whether the concept is of use for any purpose other than passing examinations. To raise this question, however, is to penetrate the very heart of the marginal analysis. It is to understand not only the strength of the criticisms made against it but also why it persists in spite of these criticisms. Usually the marginal analysis is criticized as an analysis of behavior. However, the marginal analysis, in its generalized form, is *not* an analysis of *behavior* but an analysis of *advantage*. It is not a psychology or an analysis of actual behavior. It is more akin to an *ethic* or an analysis of normative positions. It only becomes an analysis of behavior if we make the further assumption that people always act according to their best advantage. In the case of individuals this assumption is only occasionally true.

People are motivated, even in economic activity, by traditional behavior, by the habit of following well-established rules of thumb, and by response patterns which are derived from sources in the subconscious and have little or nothing to do with the careful weighing of advantage against disadvantage. The passions constantly war with the intellect and even St. Paul complained that, "The good that I would, I do not; but the evil which I would not, that I do." (Rom. 7:19). Nevertheless it is important to have an analysis of advantage even if this is not an analysis of behavior. It is important for two reasons. It is important in itself because it is useful to have some kind of standard by which actual behavior may be judged. If it makes some sense to castigate certain types of behavior as stupid then we must have some notion of the sensible. It then makes sense to clarify the sensible. The analysis of advantage is also important because, in the mass, there must be some tendency for actual behavior to move towards the most advantageous behavior if only because advantageous behavior is likely to have survival value. Those who do not behave in the most advantageous manner do not ultimately survive. If this is the case then the assumption that individuals actually behave to their best advantage is more likely to be true in the aggregate than it is in the individual case. That is to say, aggregative propositions, based on the assumption that individuals maximize advantage, may be quite good descriptions of the behavior of the aggregates. This has been, after all, the economist's primary interest. Even if the original assumption is not a good description of the behavior of any single individual the individual deviations tend to cancel out in the aggregate. This point has been made eloquently by Dr. A. A. Alchian.

We must not, however, be carried away by an enthusiasm for aggregates.

The concept of maximum advantage and the concept of maximum survival value are not the same. They may be equated but they should not be identified. And there is no more necessity in the assumption that behavior drifts toward the position of maximum survival value for organization than there is in the assumption that behavior drifts toward the position of maximum advantage. There are, for instance, *heroic* ethical systems in which advantage is not couched in terms of survival at all (except perhaps in a very long-run sense) and certainly not in terms of individual survival. Individuals who differ as widely as the saint and the soldier may hold ethical systems (as expressed in our terms in advantage or utility functions) which attach high values to sacrifice, to service, and to self-giving, which are certainly not conducive to individual survival. One recalls, for instance, the almost unbelievable story of Canudos and the followers of Antonio the Counselor who, in the otherwise prosaic 1890's, fought off the Brazilian army literally to the last man. Nevertheless, there is at least nothing absurd in the assumption that behavior according to maximum advantage is likely to have survival value and that the firm that succeeds in maximizing its profits (other advantage factors being held constant) is likely to do better than a firm which fails to do so.

From the point of view of behavior theory the great weakness of the marginal analysis, even in its generalized form, is the absence of any information system. It is important to realize, however, that if we cannot *know* where the optimum, or the point of maximum advantage, is located, we obviously cannot move toward it.

Thus the marginal analysis does not describe a true *equilibrium* system. In general the information system of a firm or of any economic organization does not record, except in an extremely vague and broad sense, the divergences between the actual position of the organization and the optimum. As we shall see more clearly in the next chapter some information system of this kind is absolutely essential to any theory of behavior. There can be a marked divergence between the actual position of an organization and its optimum position, measured on any standard, and the organization might be quite unaware of the fact. This is likely to be true in periods of rapid change when the old rules of thumb and traditional modes of behavior (which may have been well adapted to give a position close to the optimum in more stable times) mislead firms into adopting policies very far from the optimum. Thus, when much against their will, the American railroads in the 1930's were forced to reduce their passenger fares, they found to their great surprise that the increase in passenger traffic was so great that their financial returns were improved. Here was a clear case of the inertia of large organizations operating largely by traditional rules which led to a gross failure to reach optimum positions.

It is interesting to observe that there has been an important movement, within the last ten years or less, to improve the information system of organizations in directions which are indicated by the marginal analysis. The movement, which is known as "Operations Research," originated in the armed forces during the second World War but has spread rapidly to the business world. It involves an elaborate set of techniques involving mathematics much more advanced than the simple differential calculus which is used in the marginal analysis. Nevertheless the basic principle of the "optimum"—that is of finding the "best" position of a set of opportunities—lies at the heart of it. It can be applied to the routing of ships, to the hunting of submarines, to finding product mix from an oil refinery, or to inventory control. It is curious that at the very time when some economists were boldly engaged in trying to throw the maximization principle out the front door the engineers were sneaking it in the back door in the form of "linear programming" and Operations Research.

We may once more test the skill of the economist (myself for instance) who is skilled in the techniques of the marginal analysis by supposing that he advises the president of a large corporation. What sort of advice, if any, will his skills enable him to give? In this case the quality of the advice may depend more on an awareness of the concrete reality around him than on his peculiar skill in the marginal analysis. Indeed, if I were the president of a corporation, I would take some care to avoid hiring an economist adviser whose *sole* skill was the marginal analysis! Nevertheless, if the adviser is sensible he knows that a knowledge of the marginal analysis will certainly do him no harm and will give him means for organizing his thoughts; means which are not available to the untrained person.

The marginal analysis will direct his attention towards the *problem* of the optimum even if it gives him no simple rule for finding it. It is useful to be able to "think marginally"—to think in terms of the little bit more and the little bit less, the careful weighing of gains and losses from small changes. The marginal analysis will also direct attention to certain things which are not normally in the information system of a firm such as the nature of the firm's demand and supply curves. At least it may lead to the questioning of the tacit and almost subconscious hypotheses which every business man makes about these subterranean relationships. The marginal analysis will make him suspicious of averages and behavior based on averages—averages being a form of information which is relatively easy to get but which may be highly misleading once obtained.

A familiarity with the marginal analysis may lead to a turn of mind which sees clearly the difference between transformation or opportunity relationships on the one hand and preference functions on the other. Our adviser should always be on the lookout for unexpected relationships among the many variables with which a firm has to deal for the reason that solutions to problems in one place may create three worse problems elsewhere. His should be the warning voice reminding management that the enterprise is a whole and must be looked at as a whole and that the various policies of different departments or different aspects of the enterprise must be coordinated.

Finally, because he has in his head a greatly simplified model of what an enterprise looks like, he may be more sensitive to those changes in environment which make old rules obsolete. These are the changes which force an enterprise, if it is to survive, to make constant adaptations in its products, in its prices, and in its overall policies, to the changing scene around it. Not all these virtues of course can be ascribed solely to a knowledge of the marginal analysis. But skill in the marginal analysis, as a vital instrument rather than as a textbook trick, will contribute to all of them. Perhaps the economist should be hired after all!

11

RENTS AND WAGES

Our objective in this chapter is to employ the analytical tools developed in Chapter 10 to analyze rent, the return to land, and wages, the return to labor. A secondary objective is to present some historical background to the theory of resource pricing as an introduction to the evolution of economic theory. Rent and wages are considered together in this chapter for two reasons: (1) Both draw upon the basic analytical tools of marginal productivity theory, and (2) the classical economists combined their theories of wages, rent, and economic growth into a general theory of resource pricing, so we follow their organization to present the historical development of distribution theory.

THE CLASSICAL AND MODERN THEORIES OF RENT

The Ricardian[1] theory became the generally accepted explanation of rent among classical economists and proved a major step in the development of distribution theory. However, the analytical approach used by Ricardo and his colleagues was not immediately broadened into a general theory of distribution, because of the classical view that the factors of production (land, labor, and capital) were different, and the return to each must therefore be determined differently. Ricardo specifically described the return to land as a special case, concluding that rent was determined by the market price of the finished product, rather than the usual situation in which product price is determined partly by the cost of resources. His widely quoted statement was: "Corn is not high because a rent is paid, but a rent is paid because corn is

---

[1] General reference to "the Ricardian theory of rent" is more a measure of Ricardo's stature than a strict statement of historical fact. Actually, David Ricardo, who published his theory of rent in February 1815, was only one of four economists to develop a rent theory. The others were Malthus, West, and Torrens. The particular model employed in this chapter follows not one of the classical economists but several, including J. H. von Thunen, who based his theory on his own accounts and records of agricultural production, which he maintained from 1810 to the time of his death in 1850.

high; and it has been justly observed that no reduction would take place in the price of corn although landlords should forego the whole of their rent."[2] Understandably Ricardo's followers were discouraged from attempting a general theory of distribution using the analytical approach of rent theory.

What characteristic of land made it unique in the eyes of the classical theorists? First, they saw land as the only resource which was a free gift of nature; it has no replacement cost and no reservation price. Moreover, since it is fixed in amount, its supply is perfectly inelastic; the available quantity cannot be changed regardless of price. Because of this, the classical writers turned their attention to the factors affecting the demand for land, since demand determines equilibrium price if supply is perfectly inelastic.

The classical writers' theory of the supply of land was correct in the sense that the quantity of land resources on this planet is predetermined. Certainly the physical dimensions of the world are fixed, and so is the quantity of coal, iron ore, oil, and all of the other raw materials contained in the ground. Erich Zimmermann quotes a poem from an issue of *John Bull Magazine* in the late 1800's that describes the classical attitude:

> The world is a bundle of hay
> Mankind are the asses that pull.
> Each pulls its own different way
> And the greatest of all is John Bull.[3]

All the world's nonreproducible resources, that "bundle of hay" which is distributed more or less randomly among the different continents of the world, were characterized as "land" by the classical economists.

Today we would say that the quantity of land resources is not fixed as the classical writers thought, but expands with changes in technology. This expansion involves (1) the discovery of new products made from materials formerly not considered resources, such as glass made from silica and (2) the discovery of new or perhaps more productive uses for existing resources, such as man-made fibers from chemical compounds. Judging from recent history, there is no apparent limit to the development of technology as long as human ingenuity is free to work its course; and correspondingly, there is no apparent limit to the possible expansion of the land resource base. However, we must remember that technology in the era of the early classical economists (from the 1700's to the mid-1800's) was closer to that of all the preceding centuries than to the technology of today. It was natural for them to consider technology constant because in their experience it had changed so little. And given a

---

[2] David Ricardo, *The Principles of Political Economy and Taxation* (New York: E. P. Dutton and Co., Inc., 1962).
[3] Erich W. Zimmermann, *World Resources and Industries*, revised ed. (New York: Harper & Row, 1951), 7.

constant level of technology, the assumption of a fixed land resource base and thus a stable, inelastic supply curve for land is understandable.

Since to the classical writers, land had no replacement costs, no return was necessary to insure that it would continue to offer its services to production. Any return accruing to land was a pure surplus. This surplus could arise only if firms' total receipts were in excess of the "legitimate" costs of production. The latter were wages and interest, according to the classical theory, since these payments were necessary for labor and capital to continue offering their services. For example, without sufficient wages to sustain life, workers could not stay on their jobs. No such payment was necessary for land, however, since land is available for use whether it earns a return or not. The following model will show that a key to the understanding of classical rent theory is the classicists' view of rent as a pure surplus or residual.

A Model of Rent Determination

We will present a model of rent determination which draws on the theory of von Thunen.[4] Following von Thunen, we assume an urban market located in the center of a broad plain. Land is used, along with labor and capital, to produce a unique agricultural product, which is sold in the central market place. We assume that technology remains constant and that the product price, wage rate, and interest rate are determined under perfectly competitive conditions. This implies that land is privately owned and land ownership widely distributed. Under the competitive conditions assumed (and which some feel substantially existed in Great Britain at the time the theory of rent was proposed),[5] firms will undertake new production when the price of the finished product just covers all economic costs.

Now suppose the price of the output of land is $1, and the going wage and interest rates result in labor costs of $.30 per unit of output and capital costs of $.30 per unit of output. For simplicity, we will assume that these unit costs, as well as output price, are constant. Constant unit costs imply that firms experience constant scale economies, and a constant output price implies perfectly elastic demand. At first, we may expect that only the land most accessible to the market center will be employed by farmers, because the cost of shipping finished product to market from this land is lowest. As output increases, so that all of this land is being cultivated, it then becomes more valu-

---

[4] Johann Heinrich von Thunen, "Principles for the Determination of the Rent of Land," *Sammlung sozialwissenschaflischer Meister*, Vol. 13 (1910). Cited in J. A. Schumpeter, *History of Economic Analysis* (New York: Oxford University Press, 1954), 466. Schumpeter also gives von Thunen credit for having first discovered the priniciple of marginal productivity. However, his discovery went unnoticed for some time.

[5] Franklin K. Giddings, "The Persistence of Competition," *Political Science Quarterly*, 2 (1887), 62–78.

able than land that is remote. Competition will therefore cause a rent to be paid on the close-in land. In our illustration, we assume there are no transportation costs incurred by farmers cultivating the land immediately surrounding the market, so consequently, total nonland production costs per unit are $.60 ($.30 wages plus $.30 capital). When deducted from the $1 product price, this leaves a *maximum* of $.40 per unit of output, which could be paid as rent in the market area itself. If we define a unit of land as an amount just sufficient to produce one unit of output, when combined with other resources, then firms will not pay more than $.40 rent per unit of land, since a higher rental payment would not leave enough to cover costs. But competition might force firms to pay up to the maximum.

When that land most accessible to the market is fully employed, and there is still a demand for the output of land, then the next most accessible land, that in ring 1 of Figure 11-1, will be put into production. Once it is fully

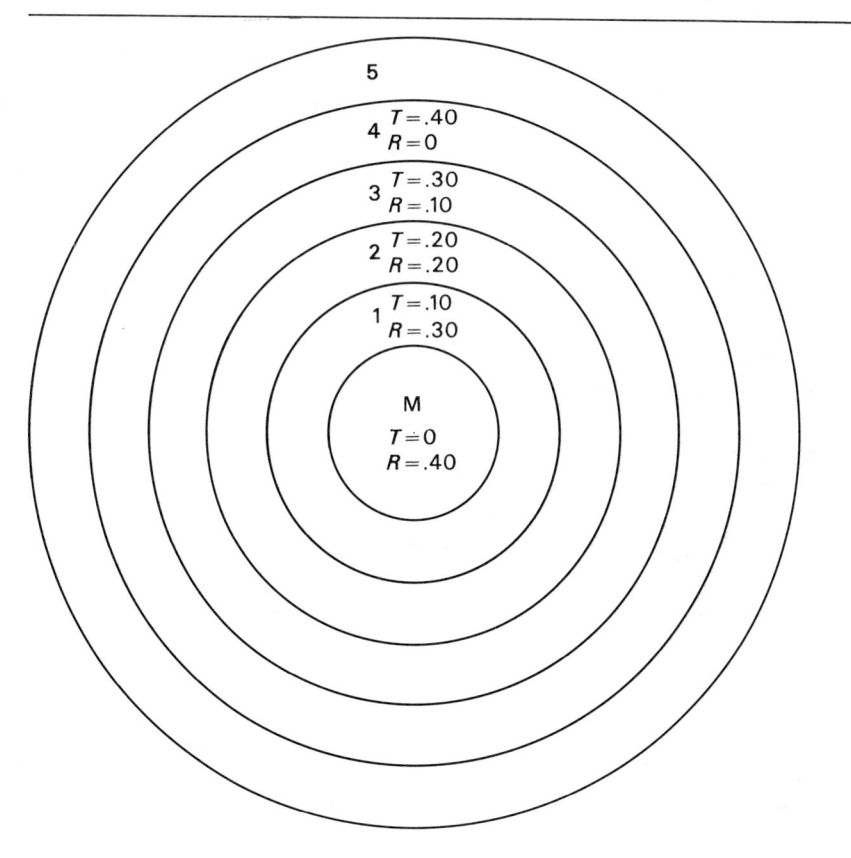

FIGURE 11-1 Graphical Presentation of von Thunen's Theory of Rent

cultivated, the land in ring 1 will now become more valuable than more remote land and will therefore command a rent. But area 1 land is not directly accessible to the market center, and the producer must as a result pay transportation costs to get his output to market. Suppose freight rates increase by $.10 per unit of output each time the distance from the market center increases the width of one ring. Then the rent on a unit of land in area 1 can be bid as high as $.30, but no higher, since $.30 wages, $.30 capital, plus $.10 transportation deducted from $1, leaves a residual of $.30. A farmer will be just as willing to employ land away from the market place, and pay a transportation charge, as to rent land closer in, if the total cost of production in either case (including rent plus transportation cost) is the same. He will, therefore, be indifferent whether he rents land at $.30 per unit in area 1 and pays transportation costs of $.10 per unit, or rents land at $.40 immediately surrounding the market place and pays no transportation costs.

When all the land in area 1 is in use, and competition among potential land users has pushed rent up to $.30 per unit of land, firms will employ land in area 2, assuming product price remains constant at $1.00.[6] Since transport costs are $.20 per unit in area 2, firms will pay a maximum of $.20 rent per unit of land. Rent plus transportation cost in area 2 will then equal that in area 1 ($.30 rent plus $.10 transportation) and in the market area itself ($.40 rent and no transportation charge).

So long as the price of the finished product remains at $1, production will continue to expand in our illustration until it has been pushed out to area 4. Why will expansion halt at this point? Because the total cost per unit in area 4, exclusive of rent, is equal to the price of a unit of output. Since no surplus remains after paying wages, interest, and transportation costs, the rent on the land in area 4 must be zero. It may at first seem unlikely that land in area 4 will be employed if it earns no rent at all, but suppose for the moment that one person owns the entire land area pictured in Figure 11–1. This landowner will, in effect, monopolize the market for X and will be able to capture all of the rents paid on land in the market area and areas 1, 2, and 3. Moreover, he may employ land in area 4, though it earns no rent, since the product price covers all nonland costs of production, including transportation costs, wages, and a normal return on his capital. Even though he will earn no rent on area 4 land, he may increase production out to area 4, if there are no alternative uses for this land, i.e., if the opportunity cost of the land in area 4 is zero.

---

[6] Firms will likely begin to "spill over" into area 2 before area 1 is fully employed and perhaps into 1 and 2 before the area around the market place is fully in use. We will assume, however, that area 2 will begin to be used only when area 1 is fully occupied and that area 3 will be used only when all land closer in has been put to use, and so on.

The model we have developed discloses a pattern of rental payments that ranges from a maximum rent on the land most accessible to the market to a minimum of zero rent on remote land. Now suppose that all available productive land has been exhausted at circle 3 in Figure 11-1 (perhaps because areas 4 and 5 are mountainous or desert land). Then a rent will be earned on land in area 3 to a maximum of $.10 per unit. In that case, rent will be earned even on marginal land. The classicists acknowledged that the unmodified theory applies best to areas where land is plentiful, nonland factors of production relatively scarce, and the same productive techniques applicable to all land. Under these conditions, rent on the marginal land falls to zero. The United States approximated the classical conditions during the colonial period, and we may speculate that, while frontier land earned no rent, the land immediately surrounding the coastal towns and villages did.

In von Thunen's model, a rent differential arose as a result of differences in transportation costs associated with different land. Production on land near the market center means less transportation costs and more rent than production on more remote land. The latter is, of course, associated with higher transport costs but lower rent. We might think of the remote land as being *less productive* (at least less productive of net revenue) at supplying finished product: an agricultural good *delivered to market*. This suggests that the theory of land rent can be applied to land that differs in its physical productivity, e.g., poor land versus rich land, and, indeed, this was the approach Ricardo used to develop his theory of rent. The results are very much like that of von Thunen's model: productive land commands a higher rent than unproductive land. Moreover, if land exists in inexhaustible supply, the last unit employed will be the least productive land, and it can be expected to earn zero rent, analogous to the case of land in ring 4 of Figure 11-1.

A Generalized Theory of Rent and Quasi-Rent

The theory of rent has been generalized since the works of Ricardo and von Thunen, so that it now applies to any resource that is in inelastic supply. Modern rent theory has been most widely used in analyzing short-run factor prices, as we will see. According to the classicists' definition, land consists of all nonreproducible, nonhuman resources available in fixed supply, as distinguished from reproducible, nonhuman resources (capital) and human resources (labor). The principal characteristic of land that set it apart from other resources was that its supply was fixed. But if a very short time period is considered, the supply of almost any resource may be considered fixed, and that resource might then receive a rent.

> *In general, rent may be defined as any payment to a factor of production in excess of its opportunity cost.*

The opportunity cost of any factor of production is zero if a short enough time period is considered; therefore, any factor may, by definition, earn rent. Of course, a time period so short may not be particularly relevant for decision makers. Firms and resource suppliers might have a long time horizon for making decisions. Suppose we consider the short-run possibility that a firm receives revenues in excess of its total production costs, including a normal return on the owner's invested capital. This excess may be considered rent according to the definition. In Chapter 6, we called the excess of receipts over costs short-run economic profits; this profit may now be called "quasi-rent." A positive quasi-rent paid to a factor in short supply encourages its expanded utilization, given enough time, whereas a negative quasi-rent discourages its utilization.

Obvious examples of quasi-rent earned by labor are the salaries of movie stars and the earnings of famous professional athletes. The individuals possessing such skills would probably supply their services as actors or football players for considerably less, if they could be forced to their minimum acceptable wage. Their minimum acceptable wage would likely be about equal to their opportunity cost as determined in an alternative occupation. If these individuals were placed in a situation where they must either accept a lower salary for their special talents or engage in some alternative employment, they would very likely continue to offer their services at the lower salary. The difference between their opportunity cost and the salary they actually receive, is quasi-rent. Other, less obvious examples of quasi-rent may be one explanation for income differences among individuals, as we will describe more fully in the latter part of this chapter.

WAGES

If the theory of rent anticipated marginal productivity theory, the most enthusiastic application of the theory has been to wages. Because of the relative importance of labor among the factors of production, economists have devoted a considerable amount of time and energy to the development of wage theory. On the one hand, wages comprise the largest part of total national income (about two-thirds today) and, on the other, wage earners are numerically the largest group of income recipients. In addition, the human resource has quite naturally attracted considerable attention because of the social, political, and psychological importance of its rate of remuneration.

Marginal Productivity Theory Applied to the Demand for Labor

Marginal productivity theory provides a highly useful framework for understanding the complicated mechanism of wage determination in the real world. The principal shortcoming of the theory is that it applies best to perfectly competitive markets. There is little doubt that in a perfectly competitive world, with highly efficient labor markets, wages would conform closely to the predictions of the theory. However, in the real world are several classes of market imperfections which necessitate modifications in the basic marginal productivity model. To make wage theory more useful, therefore, several modifications will be introduced at certain points in our presentation. Nevertheless, marginal productivity theory isolates the basic forces that determine equilibrium wages and serves as a first approximation to the determination of wages. An additional point: the theory of wages is often presented in real terms, whereas wage negotiations are typically conducted in money terms. But the real wage (money wages deflated by a price index) determines how much real goods and services labor can command. It is important, therefore, to distinguish those situations in which real magnitudes are paramount.

A final introductory point is in order. Wage earners' share of national income, as determined in the market place, may or may not be considered equitable or socially acceptable; this is a question for ethics. Our first efforts are to pursue economics as a positive science, with the initial objective an understanding of how the system, in fact, operates to determine the return to labor. Economic analysis is on firmer ground investigating the market mechanisms that establish wage levels; it is less competent to answer questions of ethics. However, economics is combined with ethical considerations in normative economics, which seeks a socially optimum distribution of income.

The Demand for Labor

The wage rate is a price much like the price of any other resource or commodity and is determined by the market demand for labor and the supply of labor. Our task is to analyze the demand and supply forces in various labor market structures much like the familiar competitive, monopoly, and oligopoly structures in output markets. We will be interested in making comparisons between the equilibrium wage rates expected in the various markets and drawing conclusions regarding economic efficiency. Initially, we assume that all labor is homogeneous, so that employers are indifferent whether they hire one worker or another. Later we will find it convenient to break the total labor supply into a number of separate and noncompeting categories, but now we assume only one class of labor.

Employment and Wages in Competitive Markets. Assume initially that perfect competition prevails among buyers and sellers in both the labor market and in output markets. Under these circumstances, a single firm's short-run demand for labor is the marginal revenue product of labor, (MRP_L), which in turn is equal to the marginal physical product of labor times the marginal revenue derived from selling the finished product. Of course, under

466 The Theory of Distribution

perfectly competitive conditions, marginal revenue equals the market determined price of a unit of output, so the MRP_L schedule for the competitive firm is simply the MP_L schedule multiplied by output price. To illustrate, the marginal product of labor, MP_L, for a hypothetical firm is shown in panel (a) of Figure 11–2, drawn linearly for simplicity. By multiplying the MP_L times the price of the finished product at each and every level of resource use, we derive the MRP_L schedule in panel (b). In symbols, the MRP_L curve is:

$$MRP_L = MP_L \times P_X. \tag{1}$$

MRP_L, shown in panel (b) when $P_X = \$1$, is the competitive firm's demand for labor. We have noted only the downward sloping section of the MP curve

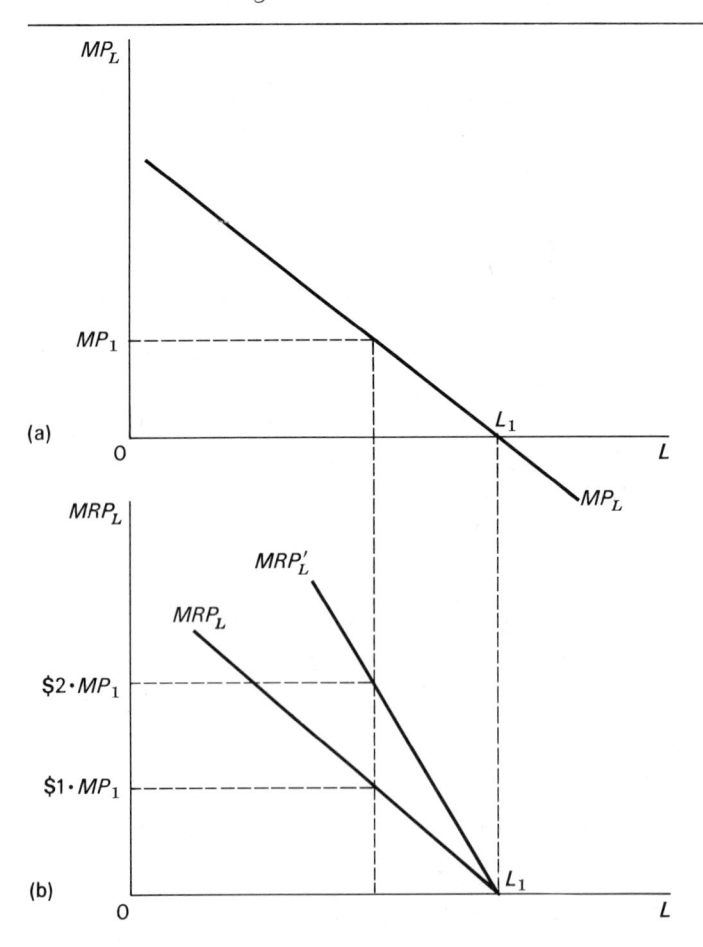

FIGURE 11–2 The Marginal Revenue Product of Labor, Derived from Marginal Product

as relevant.[7] For comparison, MRP_L is the marginal revenue product schedule when P_X equals $2. MRP_L has the same shape as MP_L, because

$$MRP_L = MP_L \times \$1,$$

but MRP_L' is twice as steep, because

$$MRP_L' = MP_L \times \$2.$$

Assuming competition, the firm's demand for labor is directly proportional to both the marginal product of labor and the price of the finished product.

Employment and Wages Under Imperfect Competition in Output Markets. If a firm sells its output in an imperfectly competitive output market, the quantity sold can be expanded only by reducing the selling price. In this case, the average and marginal revenue curves are not equal as they are under competitive conditions. The demand for labor under these circumstances is the marginal product of labor multiplied by the marginal revenue derived from the sale of the finished product, or

$$D_L = MRP_L = MP_L \times MR_X. \tag{2}$$

It is important to distinguish the demand for labor under perfectly competitive output markets from the case of imperfect competition in output markets. In perfect competition, the firm's labor demand is down-sloping because the marginal product of labor diminishes and for this reason only; but in the case of imperfect competition in the product market, the firm's demand for labor is a decreasing function of output, because MP_L falls as additional workers are hired and MR_X falls as the firm increases its unit sales. For the imperfect competition case, the marginal laborer hired produces less than the previous one and his marginal output (as well as all other unit sales) must be sold at a reduced price.

You will notice that Equation (2) above is a general statement for a firm's demand for labor, given competitive conditions in the labor market. It holds whether competition or monopoly prevails in the product market. The firm's demand is:

$$D_L = MRP_L = MP_L \times MR_X. \tag{3}$$

But, since $P_X = MR_X$ under competition, this may be stated as:

$$D_L = MRP_L = MP_L \times P_X. \tag{4}$$

All of this is no more than the application of the models of the previous chapters to labor. To expand our analysis, we must now turn to the other side of the labor market and explore the factors behind labor supply.

---

[7] For a linear MP curve, AP has no peak and Stage I does not exist.

The Supply of Labor

Classical theorists proposed a short-run theory of labor supply based on the theory of marginal utility and the assumption of utility maximization by workers. Workers were assumed to balance the utility of income earned from working with the disutility associated with work. Each worker would offer additional units of employment (hours per day, days per week), so long as the marginal utility derived from spending the earnings from this employment was greater than the disutility associated with the time spent at work. At equilibrium, the worker equates the marginal utility of earnings with the marginal disutility of work.

The marginal utility derived from wages earned is a decreasing function of the amount of earnings, because income is spent on goods and services which are themselves subject to diminishing marginal utility. The marginal utility of the first increments of income earned is likely to be very high, because the first dollars a worker earns will be exchanged for the first few units of consumer goods yielding the greatest utility. Of course, since money can be exchanged for any other good or service, its marginal utility will fall more slowly than the marginal utility of any single consumer good.

The marginal utility or disutility of daily work may be expected to follow a different pattern from that of money earned from working. The first hour or two in the morning probably involves negative utility or disutility. But after the initial discomfort of getting up, going to work, and warming up, workers fortunate enough to have found satisfying jobs may derive positive satisfaction from their work, at least for a time. After that, typically, an individual will begin to tire, and the marginal utility of work will, as a consequence, turn negative again. To illustrate, we have drawn a hypothetical marginal utility schedule which reflects these observations in Figure 11–3. MU_W is first negative, then positive, and finally turns negative again after the worker has put in H_2 hours.

The marginal utility of work will almost certainly decline (and become negative) for nearly all workers at a faster rate than the marginal utility of money earned. For most people, the marginal utility of money, though perhaps a decreasing function of money income, will never turn negative, since it can be used to purchase such a great variety of goods and services. Moreover, since money serves more or less efficiently as a store of value, and there are ordinarily no storage costs (in fact, it grows with interest), it can be held and used for future consumption. MU_E in Figure 11–3 shows the marginal utility which our hypothetical worker derives from spending the wage earned from an additional hour's work. It is computed by multiplying the worker's hourly earnings by his marginal utility of money at various levels of expenditure. For example, when working H_1 hours, the marginal utility which the worker receives from the marginal earnings at that level is MU_1. Since the hourly wage

FIGURE 11-3 The Optimum Quantity of Labor Hours Supplied by a Worker at a Given Wage Rate

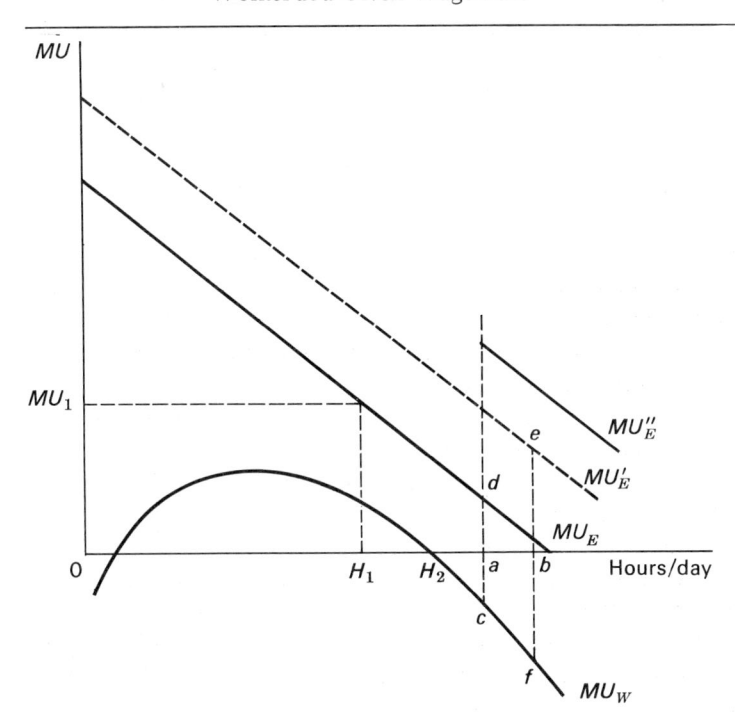

is constant, MU_E declines because of the decline in the individual's marginal utility of money schedule.

In order to determine the equilibrium quantity of hours offered for employment by our subject worker, we must look at both the MU_W and MU_E schedules. We will assume he is free to work as many hours per day as he wishes. Certainly he will find it advantageous to work the first few hours, since the marginal utility of earnings is in excess of the marginal utility of work; indeed, they are both positive for a wide range. However, the marginal utility of earnings, MU_E, just offsets the marginal disutility of work, MU_W, at Oa hours; that is, ca, the marginal disutility associated with Oa hours, just equals ad, the marginal utility of earnings. The worker is just content to work Oa hours per day. He would not work longer, since the marginal disutility of work would be greater than the marginal utility of earnings.

If the firm wants to induce the worker to work longer hours, say Ob hours, it might increase the worker's hourly rate of pay and so increase his MU_E function to the dotted curve, MU_E'. The equality of fb, the marginal disutility of work, would just equal be, the marginal utility of earnings, at Ob hours. As another approach, the firm might offer more pay for the last few hours of work only (e.g., double time for overtime). If overtime is paid for all hours worked beyond Oa, the MU_E schedule for hours above Oa would be MU_E''. (The schedule would be discontinuous at Oa hours.) As an alternative, the firm might try to instill more job pride or improve job conditions, reducing work disutility and increasing the MU_W schedule. Such nonwage programs are somewhat analogous to nonprice product competition and were largely disregarded by classical economists who felt that higher wages were the most effective incentive for enticing more work from individuals.

In conclusion, the quantity of labor offered by each worker may be stated as a function of the wage rate. Generally, a rise in the wage rate increases the marginal utility of earnings, and more hours of work would be forthcoming. Since the quantity of labor supplied increases with the wage rate, the aggregate supply schedule for all workers will generally be a positive function of the wage level. Moreover, a rise in the wage rate might increase the MU_E schedule of some individuals sufficiently that they begin offering their services for the first time; i.e., at a lower wage, they supplied zero hours. Examples might be retired workers and housewives, who will enter the work force only when the wage rate rises above a certain level.

An interesting phenomenon not explicitly incorporated in the model shown in Figure 11–3 is the trade-off each individual makes between work and leisure. Since each hour spent working could be spent at leisure, the disutility schedule for hours spent at work must incorporate the lost leisure time utility. Specifically, MU_W in Figure 11–3 must be net of the utility that would otherwise be enjoyed from leisure but no income. If wages are increased to a very high level and the worker derives utility from leisure time, relative to the utility of additional expenditures, then he may work fewer, not more hours.

The utility pattern which any individual attaches to work is the result of a complex of forces which will differ from person to person. For instance, we usually assume that work involves primarily disutility, but Gordon Hayes has pointed out, no doubt correctly, that many workers—especially businessmen—enjoy their work more than anything else they do. On the other hand, we usually assume that leisure always involves positive utility; but some psychological studies indicate that unstructured time can cause difficulties ranging from emotional disorientation to death.[8] It is no wonder that many employment opportunities are opening up in the "leisure industries." Consequently, it is safe to conclude that the traditional trade-off which economic theory proposes between work and leisure is merely illustrative. Our assumptions that leisure is generally preferred to work at the margin and that workers compare the utility of more income earned to the utility of more leisure are not presumed to apply to everyone: they might apply best to those holding monotonous production-line jobs.

[8] For a survey of such research, see Eric Berne's *Transactional Analysis*.

In any case, an indifference model is a more efficient device in some instances for examining an individual's elasticity of supply of hours of work. To illustrate, we have drawn in Figure 11–4 a family of indifference curves

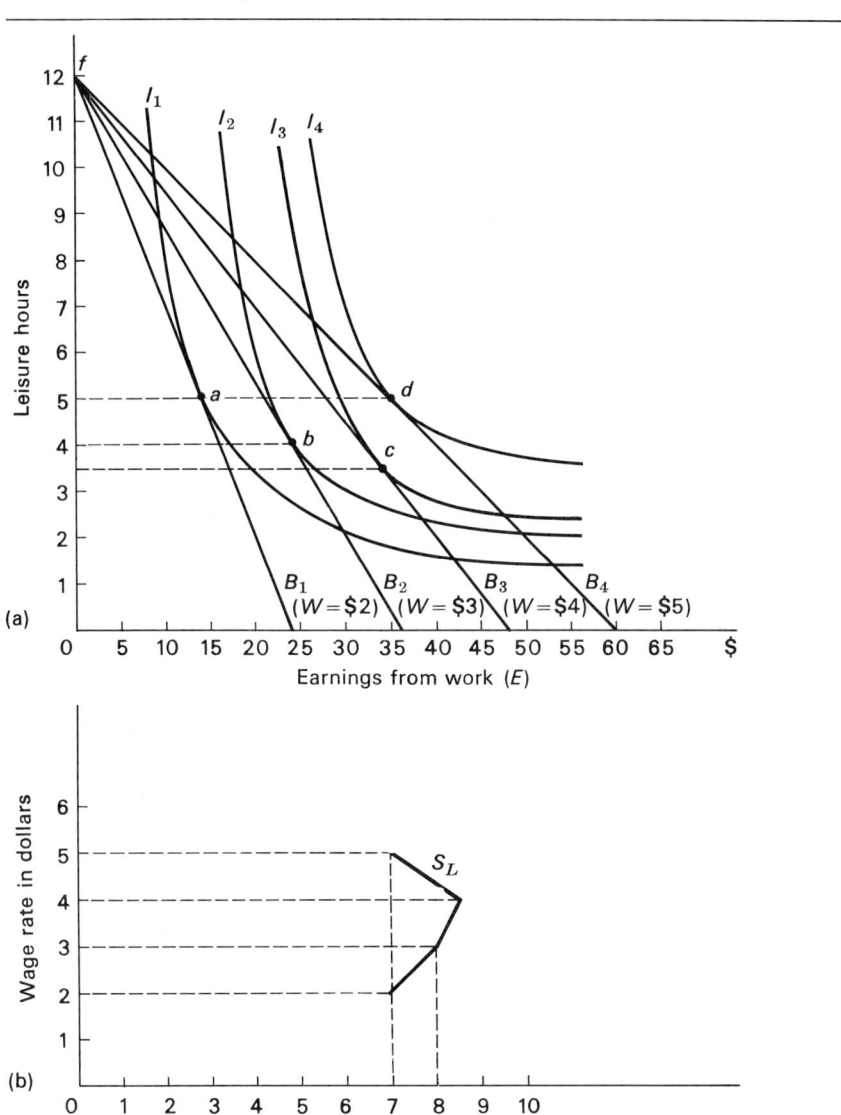

FIGURE 11–4 The Derivation of a Worker's Supply of Labor Using Indifference Curves

which reflect a hypothetical worker's preferences for income from work vis-à-vis leisure time. Each indifference curve shows various combinations of earnings and leisure which result in equal utility and incorporate, therefore, his utilities from consumption and leisure and his disutility from work. These indifference curves "normally" slope downward and to the right, on the assumption that the individual derives positive utility from increased leisure time and income; he will give up income only if compensated by increased leisure and vice versa. The marginal rate of substitution of leisure for work, MRS_{EL}, which equals the absolute value of the slope of an indifference curve at a point, sets the consumer's acceptable rate of exchange. We may expect MRS_{EL} to decline as the ratio of E to L rises, so the indifference curves will be convex to the origin.

The rate at which leisure can, in fact, be exchanged for income is determined by the wage rate. Assume a maximum of 12 hours is available for work and that the wage rate is $2. The constraint line, B_1, shows that the consumer may select either a maximum of 12 hours of leisure or $24 in income or any combination of the two along B_1. B_1 is analogous to a budget line or line of attainable combinations.

The consumer maximizes utility at point a, the point of tangency of B_1 and I_1. He will work 7 hours, receive a $14 daily income, and devote to leisure 5 hours per day of his available 12 hours. If the wage increases to $3 an hour, the line of attainable combinations rotates counterclockwise about point f to B_2, and the new equilibrium combination of leisure and income is found at point b. The new equilibrium combination indicates the worker will work 8 hours and earn $24 per day and devote 4 hours to leisure. If the wage increases again to $4 an hour, the line of attainable combinations rotates further out to B_3, and the new equilibrium occurs at point c, indicating that the individual will work 8½ hours and leave 3½ hours for leisure.

In all of the preceding cases, every time the wage increased, the worker devoted more time to work and less to leisure. However, if the wage is further increased to $5 an hour, the resulting equilibrium at point d indicates that the worker increases his leisure from 3½ to 5 hours and decreases his work time from 8½ to 7 hours. The rise in wage from $4 to $5 increases the "price" of leisure vis-à-vis earnings and decreases the price of earnings vis-à-vis leisure. This will cause the consumer to *substitute* earnings for leisure. However, the rise in wage also produces a positive income effect, and since, for this worker, leisure time is a normal "good," he will tend to "buy" more. In fact, the income effect predominates and the consumer ends up buying more leisure and less earnings. In panel (b), therefore, the supply of labor derived from the various equilibrium points is a normal, positively sloped curve up to a wage of $4 an hour. Then, between $4 and $5, the curve bends backward, indicating that the higher wage results in fewer hours supplied. The worker maximizes his utility by trading off money income for leisure, after money income reaches a high enough level. (American firms with plants abroad have often found that when they raise the rate of pay, natives reduce their work week.)

If we combine all of the individual supply of labor curves, we will derive the aggregate market supply of labor. In general, we will expect the curve to be upsloping for lower wage levels, but possibly backward bending at high levels, because individuals may work less if wages rise to a very high level.

Combining Supply and Demand in the Labor Market

Now we are ready to show how supply and demand combine to determine equilibrium wage and employment levels. This task is accomplished in two steps. First, we analyze the equilibrium conditions for a single firm, given different product and labor market structures. Second, we show how equilibrium is determined in labor markets by the interaction of all buyers and sellers.

Market Equilibrium Under Competitive Conditions in Output Markets. To start with the simplest case, we use the basic competitive model, developed in Chapter 9, to analyze the behavior of a firm which both sells its output in a competitive output market and hires labor in a competitive labor market. Because the single competitive firm is small in relation to the market, its actions (hiring or laying off workers) have no effect on the wage rate, so the supply of labor to it is perfectly elastic at the market-determined wage rate. In Figure 11–5 (panel b), we have shown the market schedules and demand for labor and the equilibrium wage, W_e. The going wage is both the average

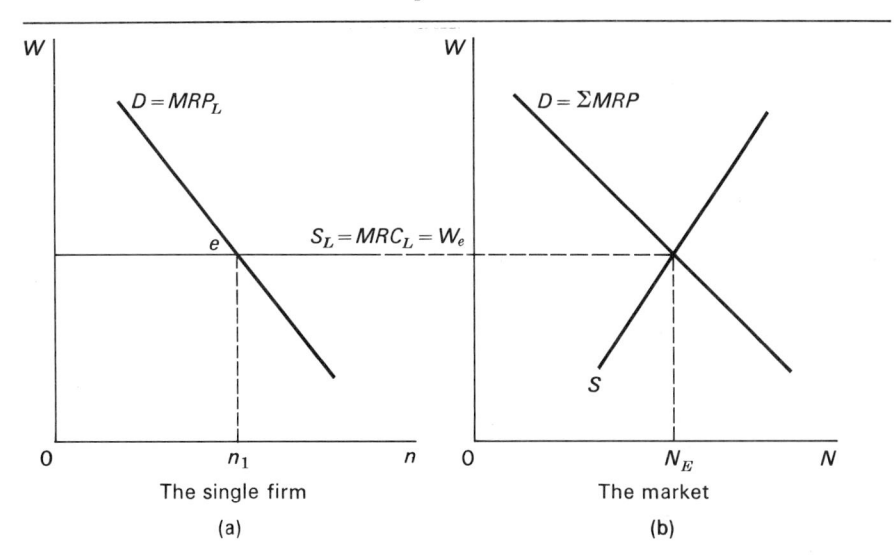

FIGURE 11–5 Wage Determination in a Competitive Labor Market: Firm and Market Equilibrium

cost of labor and the marginal resource cost for labor, as illustrated by curve S_L in panel (a). If the firm is a profit maximizer, it will increase the number of units of workers it hires until point e, where the last worker hired generates an MRP_L just equal to its MRC_L.

Since we assume no market imperfections on the supply side, the market supply of labor is the horizontal summation of the supply curves of all workers. Market demand for labor is also determined by a process of aggregation and, as a first approximation, is the summation of all firm's MRP_L curves. We say it is an approximation, because the assumption of a constant output price, though realistic for the firm, is not realistic for the industry. As the industry increases the quantity of labor it employs and increases unit sales, output price will fall. But as P_X falls, so do the MRP_L schedules of firms in the industry. So a simple algebraic summation of each firm's MRP schedule is inaccurate, because the *ceteris paribus* assumption is violated. However, a horizontal summation of MRP curves is acceptable as a first approximation of the aggregate demand for labor, and in panel (b) of Figure 11-5, we show market equilibrium as the intersection of aggregate supply, S_L, and aggregate demand, $D = \Sigma MRP$. The industry will employ N_E units of labor at a wage of W_e, whereas the representative firm adjusts to the wage rate by hiring n_1 units of labor.

Labor Market Equilibrium, Given Monopoly in Output Markets. A monopolist in the product market, who is a competitive buyer in the labor market, pays the going wage rate just as does the competitive firm and, like the competitive firm, hires up to the point of equality between MRC_L and MRP_L. The only difference is that MRP_L for the monopolist declines both because of a declining marginal product schedule and declining marginal revenue, whereas, for the competitive firm, MRP declines only because MP_L declines. The main difference in the over-all result is that if all firms, or a significant number of firms, in a given labor market are monopolists in the product market, fewer workers will be hired than would be the case if conditions were perfectly competitive in the output market.

Monopoly in the Demand for Labor—Monopsony. An interesting situation occurs when the labor market is monopolized from the employer's side. A possible example would be a large coal-mining firm which is the principal employer in a small town. The monopsonistic employer will face the market supply curve for labor, which means it can obtain additional workers only by paying a higher wage.

An upsloping supply curve means that the marginal resource cost curve for labor will lie above the supply function. To illustrate, S_L in Figure 11-6 is the rising labor supply curve facing a monopsonist, and MRC_L, the marginal resource cost curve. Marginal resource cost is greater than the wage paid to the marginal worker, because additional workers can only be hired by increasing the wage rate, and the new rate is applicable, not only to the marginal

FIGURE 11–6 Wage Determination under Monopsony

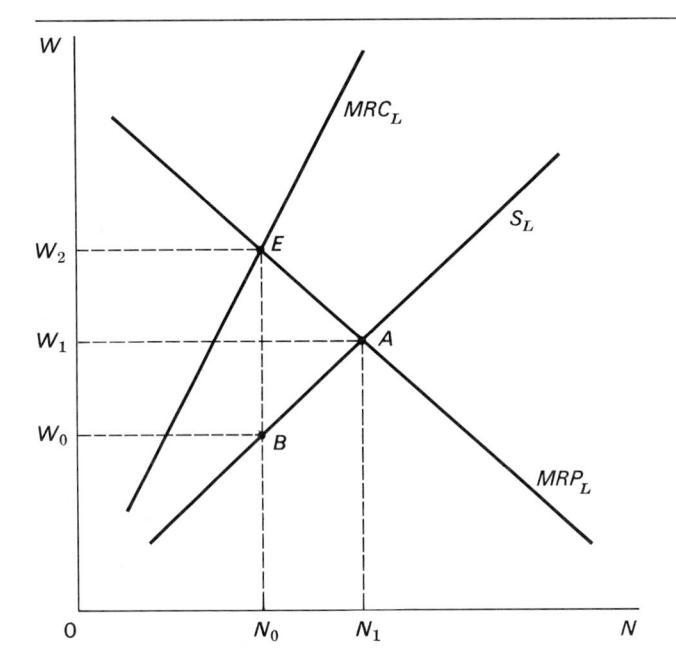

worker, but to all workers. The profit-maximizing wage and quantity will not be determined at the point of intersection of MRP_L and S_L, but at point E, the intersection of MRC_L and the MRP_L. The firm would hire N_0 workers at a wage rate of W_0 and would not find it profitable to hire past the point of equality of MRC_L and MRP_L, since to do so would add more to costs than to revenues.

Bilateral Monopoly. Bilateral monopoly exists in a market when a single buyer, a monopsonist, faces a single seller, a monopolist. Probably the most realistic situation where bilateral monopoly might occur is in a labor market where a single employer hires all of his workers from a single union. In this case the wage rate and the quantity of labor hired cannot be determined deductively. However, we may combine the monopoly model developed in Chapter 8 and the monopsony model developed above to indicate the likely range within which the wage rate and quantity of labor hired will be determined in the bargaining process.

First, let us examine the strategy of the monopsonistic buyer of labor. Referring to Figure 11–7, MRP_L is the marginal revenue product of labor (equal to VMP_L if the monopsonist is a perfectly competitive seller) and S_L is the supply curve of labor. S_L must be interpreted carefully because it shows the quantity of labor which will be forthcoming at different wage rates, assuming workers adjust their quantities of labor supplied to *given* wage rates.

476 The Theory of Distribution

FIGURE 11-7 The Case of Bilateral Monopoly

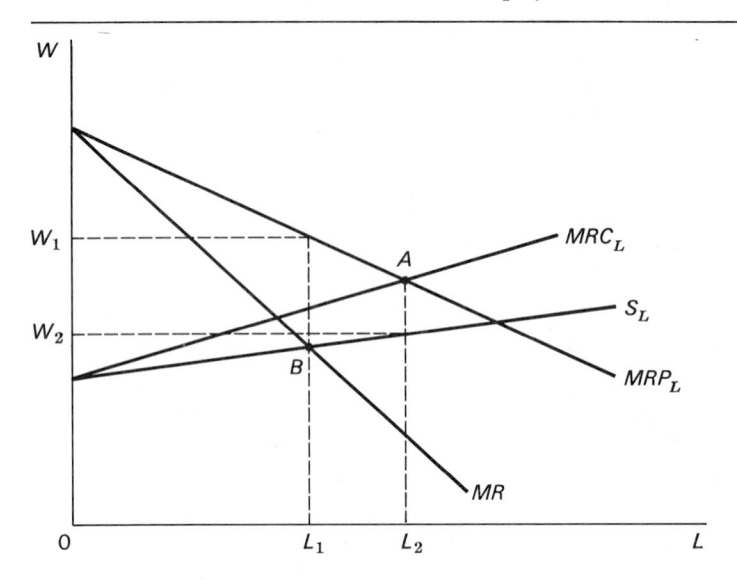

This is the supply curve the monopsonist might anticipate in the absence of a union. Since S_L is upsloping, the monopsonist's marginal resource cost curve, MRC_L, will be above S_L. The monopsonist would then seek to equate MRC_L with MRP_L at point A, setting a wage rate of W_2 and hiring L_2 units of labor. This conclusion follows directly from the monopsony model presented above (see Figure 11-6).

But the monopsonist does not face the labor supply curve S_L; he must deal with the union, so now we must analyze the situation from the point of view of the union. We will assume that the union behaves like a monopolistic seller of labor which considers S_L its marginal cost of "producing" a unit of labor. But what are the union's revenue curves? MRP_L, the marginal revenue product curve of labor, would be the monopsonist's demand for labor if wage rates were determined externally, that is, if the firm were not a monopsonist. So the union might consider MRP_L the demand for labor which it faces, assuming the union sets wage rates. MR, located below MRP_L, is the associated marginal revenue curve. Equating MR and S_L at point B, the union would seek a wage rate of W_1 and offer L_1 laborers for hire.

The union seeks wage rate W_1 and employment L_1, whereas the employer seeks wage rate W_2 and employment L_2. The situation is indeterminate, so there will likely be bargaining between the two and an eventual settlement between the extremes. Notice the dilemma of the union in this particular situation: any settlement above wage rate W_2 will result in fewer workers hired than would occur in the absence of the union. Some workers will gain (higher wages) at the expense of others (no employment). On the other hand, had the supply curve of labor been more inelastic, it is possible that the union could raise the wage rate through bargaining, *plus* increase the quantity of workers hired.

Wage Differentials in the Real World

If labor were perfectly homogeneous and mobile, and if resource markets were free of imperfections and, thus, perfectly efficient, wages would be uniform throughout the economy. But we observe wide differences in the wages received by workers in different occupations, in different geographical areas, and among workers of different races or sexes doing the same job in the same location. Our task now is to examine the causes of those wage differentials.

"Psychic or Implicit Income." Some jobs and certain locations are so pleasant that workers are willing to work for lower money wages, receiving a supplemental, implicit return in the form of congenial work or salubrious climate. An individual might accept a lower wage in Florida than in the Northeast, though the work in the two locations might be identical. As another example of psychic income, college teachers not too many years ago received annual salaries of around $3,000 to $5,000 before education became a growth industry. Most professors accepted wages that were low relative to alternative employments, because the work was satisfying and working conditions congenial. Now that the demand for education has increased the demand for college teachers, their wages have risen and are more in line with the rest of the economy, even though the work is probably not much less pleasant. Such marginal upward adjustments in the wage level for professors were enjoyed by those previously employed professors, who, presumably, began to receive a surplus payment or economic rent.

Labor Mobility. Because of the psychological and monetary costs involved, labor is imperfectly mobile. The pain of leaving familiar tasks and friendly surroundings for another occupation or location is a price many workers are unwilling to bear. In many cases, the individual is inhibited by fear of the unknown. Even an unpleasant situation is at least certain. However, it should be noted that if a significant fraction of all workers are willing to change occupations or move geographically, or both, this might be sufficient at the margin to achieve an efficient equilibrium adjustment in the labor market. Not all workers need be willing to change job or location to correct a wage discrepancy. If only a few are willing to do so, the discrepancy will disappear.

There is a tendency to think of geographical mobility as the main sort of mobility, and it is necessary that workers transfer from labor-surplus to labor-scarce areas if we are to have economic efficiency. However, it is equally important that labor be mobile between different jobs as well as between different locations. And with the increasing urbanization of American society and the growing similarity of American cities, it is probably less difficult to induce workers to move from place to place than from job to job. However, older, less-well-educated workers who have achieved a particular skill over a long period of time may be apprehensive about trying to learn a new job. Farmers are a prime illustration. In contrast, a worker with a broad educational background might feel less reluctant to shift from a glutted occupation into a labor-scarce line of work. On the other hand, the development of retirement programs, stock-sharing arrangements, and seniority rights by modern corporations reduces the interfirm and interindustry mobility of labor.

Noncompeting Groups. In the midnineteenth century, J. S. Mill[9] cited the difficulty most children encounter when they try to do work very different from that of their fathers. He concluded that the population was hardening into distinct groups of workers of different types and that intergroup mobility was very slight. Marshall[10] referred to the "hard-handed" and "soft-handed industries" as an example of a vertical division of labor which is scarcely ever crossed. In our own experience we see particular jobs (and particular types of educations) reserved for certain families, races, sexes, and social classes. Even though there is no economic justification for such artificial impediments to worker mobility, they exist and must be recognized. Public policy designed to foster efficiency should be aimed at removing the artificial restrictions which limit individual access to occupations.

Modifications to Marginal Productivity Wage Determination

The theory of wage determination has gone beyond simple marginal productivity theory to include other factors which also influence the level of wages. Among those other factors we may include management, trade unions, individual workers, and government. On the one hand, managers face certain limits: they must pay wages high enough to attract and retain essential workers, but not so high that wage costs impinge on the profitability of the firm. At what level, between those limits, will wages actually settle? The answer to that question depends first, on the size of the range (under conditions of perfect competition, the range may shrink to zero) and second, on the goals of management. If management is short-run profit-oriented, the wage will be close to the lower limit, but if it is long-run profit-oriented, it may pay a higher wage to attract and keep high quality, more productive workers. Or, if management seeks prestige along with profits, it may pay higher-than-lower-limit wages to help gain the reputation of a "good place to work." The list of qualifications is seemingly endless, because of the wide range of possible

---

[9] John Stuart Mill, *Principles of Political Economy*, Vol. II, revised ed. (New York: The Colonial Press, 1900).
[10] Alfred Marshall, *Principles of Economics*, 8th ed. (London: The Macmillan Co., 1930), 218.

management goals and the existence of many institutions, such as unions and governments, which play a role in wage determination. If the firms in an industry face a powerful union, wage rates may be much higher than marginal productivity theory would predict in the absence of the union. The wages of coal miners are an illustration.

Finally, the government at all levels may become involved in the process of wage determination by setting minimum wages, by offering unemployment benefits, by offering employment counseling, job exchanges, and the like. Even the draft affects the wage levels by removing workers from the labor force.

WAGES AND RENT IN THE LONG RUN IN CLASSICAL THEORY

Finally, we would like to show how classical writers linked their theories of rent and wages with the theory of long-run growth. Suppose the supply of land is small relative to the quantity of labor and the labor supply is growing. Apparently, this was how the classical economists viewed the situation in Great Britain in the early nineteenth century. As the labor supply grows, the ratio of labor to land rises, since the land is worked more and more intensively. The law of diminishing returns indicates that labor's marginal productivity must eventually fall. On the other hand, as the quantity of labor grows and the available land becomes more intensively utilized, rents will rise, until even remote and relatively unproductive land commands a rent.

Thus, the classical writers theorized that as land is worked intensively by an increasing labor supply, rents will increase (due to the growing marginal product of land) at the same time that diminishing returns to labor will cause wages to decrease. As a result, the long-run prospects were rising rents and falling wages. Given the assumption of a fixed supply of land, changes in the supply of labor played a crucial role in the determination of wages and rent. Now to complete the picture we must discuss the classicists' theory of the long-run supply of labor.

The classical theory of labor was first formulated by Rev. T. R. Malthus,[11] a contemporary of Ricardo's. Malthus argued that population growth and the resultant change in the labor supply is a function of the wage rate relative to the subsistence level of wages. If wages fall below the subsistence level, an increase in the death rate and a decrease in the birth rate will reduce the population and, thus, the labor force. A smaller labor supply would increase the marginal product of labor and return wages to the subsistence level or above. Subsistence was thought of as the lower limit to wages in the long run.

Malthus further theorized that due to the passion between the sexes the

[11]Thomas Robert Malthus, *Essay on Population*, 1798 (London: J. M. Dent & Sons, 1914 edition) 69–70.

population and the labor supply would tend to increase whenever wages rose above the subsistence level. There is in other words a persistent tendency for birth rates to rise if workers' incomes rise above the minimum required for human maintenance. But as population increases so does the labor supply, and this decreases the marginal product of labor and forces wages back toward subsistence. Therefore, the long-run tendency is for population to increase or decrease in a manner which keeps the wage rate at or near the subsistence level. No wonder then that Thomas Carlyle called economics "the dismal science." The classical writers linked together their theories of rent and wages to conclude that the economy would move toward a long-run stationary state, with wages hovering around subsistence levels and high rent accruing to scarce land. David Ricardo was consistent in his support of the classical theory's view on rent, despite his own considerable property holdings. Some of his policy prescriptions, had they been adopted, would have deprived him of some of his own wealth.

Interest rates in the stationary state would tend to fall also, because the owners of capital would try to maintain their own incomes by increasing investment. But, as each individual investor increased his capital, the stock of capital would increase relative to land, and as a result, the marginal product of capital would fall, as would the rate of return to capital. In the classical stationary state, interest rates would therefore fall to zero. The individual investor was powerless to improve the situation, because his attempts to maintain his level of income, while rational from an individual standpoint, had the aggregate effect of reducing the rate of interest.

In summary, classical distribution and growth theory predicted a long-run tendency for wages and interest to fall and rent to rise. The landlord was to be the beneficiary of the stationary state, at the expense of labor and capital. The long-run outlook was gloomy to say the least. From our viewpoint two hundred years later, we can pinpoint the principal shortcoming of classical growth theory as its failure to foresee the significance of advancing technology, which tends to raise the marginal product of labor and hence the wage rate, and its underestimate of the possibility that enlightened individuals with rising incomes might limit their family size.

The current concern over our growing world population, and the real possibility of terrestrial overcrowding in many countries makes the classical theory of population, wages, rent, and interest an interesting and worthwhile study. Who can say that the Malthusian nightmare will not occur? Indeed, in some poorer countries today the classical theory is almost directly applicable.[12] And

---

[12] See J. E. Meade, "Mauritius: A Case Study in Malthusian Economics," *The Economic Journal*, LXXI (September 1961), 521–534. Reprinted in abbreviated form in H. Peter Gray and S. Tangri Shanti, *Economic Development and Population Growth, A Conflict?* (Lexington, Mass.: D. C. Heath and Co., 1970).

the Malthusian dilemma could become of more than academic interest for the richer, industrialized nations in the future. There is no guarantee that technological advances will continue to bail us out in the future as effectively as in the past. Moreover, advances in modern technology, already at a highly sophisticated level in the more industrialized countries, often levy a heavy toll in ecological costs.

CONCLUSION

In this chapter, we have considered theories of rent and wages, both drawing upon and contributing to marginal productivity theory. The classical theory of rent anticipated the marginal productivity theory of resource price. The classicists understood that production would be extended to the point where the return on land equaled zero, because the cost of producing the services of land was zero. In current terminology, production would be carried to the point where the marginal revenue product of land equaled its marginal cost of production. However, the classicists failed to generalize their theory of rent into a theory applicable to all resources, since they thought that, because its supply was perfectly inelastic, land was unique among productive resources. Modern rent theory deemphasizes the uniqueness of land and defines rent as any return over opportunity cost, whether to land or any other factor of production.

The theory of wages represents the most direct and complete application of marginal productivity theory to one particular resource. Assuming competition in the resource market, the demand for labor is the MRP of labor, and firms will maximize profits by hiring workers to the point where the revenue brought in by the marginal worker, MRP, just equals its marginal resource cost, MRC, to the firm. Imperfections in the product and labor markets require modifications to the basic model. The first we considered was monopoly in the product market. The firm's MRP curve in this case slopes downward because of declining MP and declining MK. Second, we considered monopsony; an upsloping supply of labor curve means that MRC will lie above supply. The case of bilateral monopoly, one buyer–one seller, turned out to be indeterminate within a range of wages. Finally, we explored the peculiarities of labor markets such as immobility, noncompeting groups, and psychic income derived from certain jobs and locations, which make the actual wage and employment levels less than optimal.

The importance of imperfections in the labor market lies in (1) the reduction in economic efficiency which results from the underproduction of certain commodities and the overproduction of others, that is, the misallocation of resources, and (2) the inequitable distribution of income that is a consequence of both monopsonistic and monopolistic market power and racial, sexual, or class discrimination.

PROBLEMS

1. Why are land and labor demanded?
2. What is the equilibrium level of rent on marginal land, if the quantity of land available exceeds the quantity demanded? Why?
3. If the quantity of land is less than the amount that would be employed if more were available, what determines the level of rent?
4. Why is it unlikely that a firm will stop employing workers as long as MP_L exceeds AP_L?
5. Referring to the graph:
   (a) Plot the demand for labor, D_L, on graph (b), assuming the firm is purely competitive and $P_X = \$1$. Plot D_L if $P_X = \$1.50$.
   (b) How many workers will be employed if the wage is $2 and $P_X = \$1$?

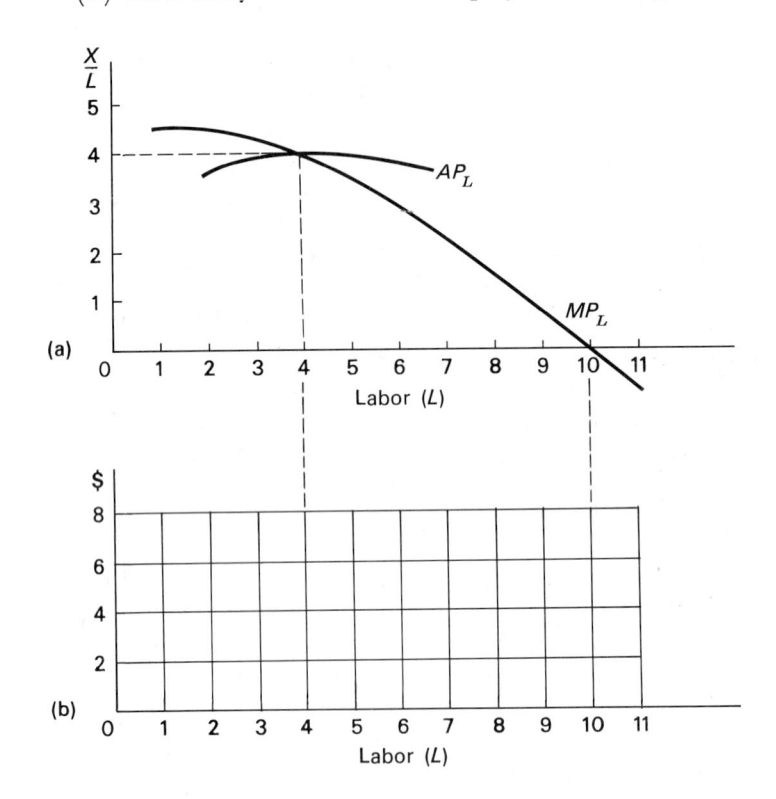

REFERENCES

Bronfenbrenner, M., "Potential Monopsony in Labor Markets," *Industrial Labor Relations Review*, 9 (July 1956), 577–588.

Cartter, Allan, and Marshall, Ray F., *Labor Economics: Wages, Employment, and Trade Unionism*. Homewood, Ill.: Richard D. Irwin, Inc., 1967. 596.

Malthus, T. R., *An Essay on Population*. Everyman Library, No. 692. London: J. M. Dent & Sons, 1914.

Mishan, E. J., "Rent as a Measure of Welfare Change," *American Economic Review*, 49 (June 1959), 386–395.

Rees, A., *The Economics of Trade Unions*. Chicago: University of Chicago Press, 1962.

Ricardo, David, *Principles of Political Economy and Taxation*. New York: E. P. Dutton & Co., Inc., 1941 (originally published 1817). Especially Chapters 1–5.

Robertson, D. H., "Wage Grumbles" in *Readings in the Theory of Income Distribution*. Philadelphia: The Blakiston Co., 1946, 221–36.

Smith, Adam, *The Wealth of Nations*. New York: Modern Library, 1937 (originally published, 1776). Especially Book I, Chapters 1–3, 8, and 10–11.

Stigler, G. J., "The Economics of Minimum Wage Legislation," *American Economic Review* (1946).

Turvey, R., *The Economics of Real Property*. London: George Allen & Unwin, 1957.

APPENDIX TO CHAPTER 11

The Negative Income Tax and the Supply of Work Effort

MICHAEL JAY BOSKIN*

What will be the effects of the negative income tax on the labor supply curves of the poor? The answer to this question would be of great value to policy makers in assessing its merits. Boskin attempts to find the answer with the aid of economic theory and interviews with 103 poor people, largely Negroes, and concludes with a favorable recommendation for the negative tax. We have included a critical comment on Boskin's work by Kesselman so that the student can gain an appreciation for the process of development of economic ideas and the complications that arise when positive and normative considerations are involved in an economic issue.

> I am as poor as Job, my lord, but not so patient.
> —Shakespeare, *Henry IV*

The widespread persistence of poverty in the United States[1] has led many economists both to question the potential adequacy of existing governmental policies (e.g., expansionary monetary and fiscal policy, unemployment insurance, minimum-wage laws, farm-income subsidies, the "War on Poverty," etc.) for ameliorating this problem with a reasonably humane degree of rapidity and to search for other practicable, more effective, measures. One such measure is the negative income tax, or transfer-by-taxation.

The negative income tax is a device designed to use the individual income

From the *National Tax Journal*, Vol. XX, No. 4 (December 1967). Reprinted by permission.

* The author is a graduate student at the University of California, Berkeley. He wishes to thank Professors George Break, Earl Rolph and Gregory Crossman for their valuable advice and assistance.
[1] The Council of Economic Advisers recently counted 35 million poor people in the U.S.; both Michael Harrington and Leon Keyserling have estimated between forty and fifty million.

tax system as a vehicle for closing a portion of the poverty gap, i.e., the differential between the actual income of the poor and poverty-line income.[2] For example, suppose we employ the Johnson Administration's poverty line of $3,000 annual money income for a family of four. If the family has an actual income of just $2,000, the poverty gap is $1,000. The negative income tax would pay the family a direct subsidy equal to the negative tax rate times $1,000;[3] at a 50 per cent marginal rate the family would receive $500.

It is apparent that the tax rate used is the crucial determinant of the proportion of the poverty gap that the negative income tax will close. Why not use a 100 per cent rate and close the entire gap? It seems reasonable to assume that at extremely high rates, the poor might be induced to reduce the supply of work effort they are willing to offer at given wage rates. The view is unfortunately widespread that poor people are poor because they are lazy, that they are inherently freeloaders. Give them a negative income tax allowance, the argument goes, and they will stop working and "live off public funds." A little careful thought leads the ordered mind to question this view of the poor.

The purpose of this paper is to begin to evaluate the hypothesis that the adoption of a negative income tax as an antipoverty measure would lead to a substantial reduction in the amount of work effort supplied by the poor at given wage rates.[4] We will present an intertemporal theoretical analysis of the effects of the negative income tax on the supply of work effort, amending where necessary invalid assumptions of the traditional theory of taxation and work effort; we will conclude that theoretically a negative income tax may either increase or decrease the amount of work effort supplied. We will then present the results of an empirical investigation of the economic behavior of the urban Negro poor; we will conclude that a negative income tax, imposed at a fifty per cent marginal rate, while closing a large portion of the poverty gap, would in all likelihood *not* have a significant effect on the amount of work effort supplied (at least by the urban Negro poor).

I

Theoretical Analysis

For ease in analysis, and for the sake of comparison, we begin by presenting a brief overview of the traditional theory of positive taxes and the supply of work effort.[5] Assume all income is work income and that the worker is free to

---

[2] For a precise operational definition of poverty, see Orshansky, M., "Counting the Poor: Another Look at the Poverty Profile," *Social Security Bulletin*, XXVIII (Jan. 1965), pp. 3–29.

[3] This is only one variant of negative income taxation; for a discussion of others, see "The Negative Income Tax," articles reprinted from *Industrial Relations*, Institute of Industrial Relations, Univ. of California, Berkeley, 1967.

[4] For another attempt and different approach, see Gallaway, L., "Negative Income Taxes and the Elimination of Poverty," *National Tax Journal*, Sept. 1966.

[5] See Musgrave, R., *The Theory of Public Finance*, McGraw-Hill, 1959, Ch. 11.

adjust the number of hours worked.[6] Figure 1 measures income, Y, per unit of time, T, on the vertical axis and leisure, L, per T on the horizontal axis. The amount of work effort, W, equals $T - L$. We assume a set of convexly ordered income-leisure preferences. Before the imposition of a tax, the income-leisure opportunity locus is L_0Y_0; the worker is in equilibrium at C, where he takes L_1 leisure and Y_1 income. If we impose a proportional tax at rate t, the income-leisure opportunity locus swings down to L_0Y_t; the higher t is, the further down the locus swings; the loci associated with a progressive tax and a regressive tax are respectively concave and convex with respect to the origin. The imposition of the tax has an income effect and a substitution effect.[7] On the one hand, the worker will want to increase his work effort to regain some of the income lost as a result of the tax and, on the other, to increase the amount of leisure taken, as a result of the lower cost of leisure, i.e., the lower net wage rate caused by the tax. At rate t, our worker's new equilibrium is at D, where $L_2 > L_1$ and $Y_2 < Y_1$; in general, work effort may increase or decrease depending on the relative strengths of the income and substitution effects.[8]

FIGURE 1

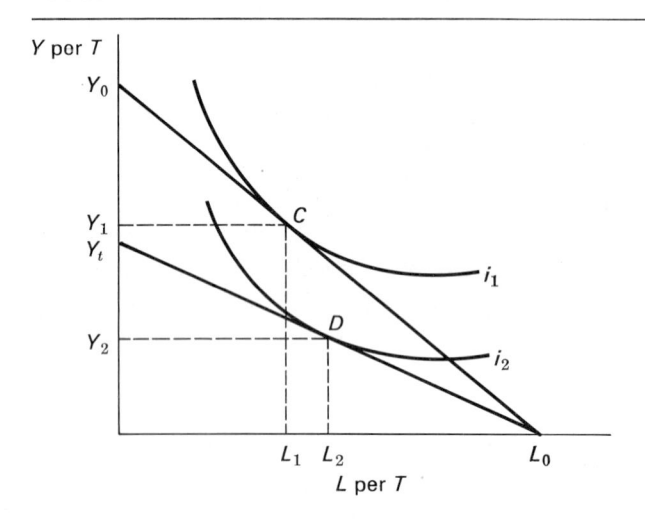

[6] That he often is not in a position to do so is one reason to suspect that a negative income tax will not have a significant work disincentive effect.
[7] The income effect is a function of the average tax rate, whereas the substitution effect is a function of the marginal tax rate.
[8] For empirical evidence on the effects of positive taxes on work effort, see Break, C. F., "Income Taxes and Incentives to Work: An Empirical Study," *American Economic Review*, Sept. 1957, and Morgan, J., Barlow, R. and Brazer, H., *The Economic Behavior of the Affluent*, Brookings, 1967.

The analysis can easily be extended to a negative income tax. Since a negative income tax increases, rather than decreases, the income of the worker, and makes the income foregone by not working less than without the tax, the income and substitution effects *appear* to work in the same direction, i.e., toward inducing more leisure and less work. It seems as if we are in one of those rare but happy situations where the traditional theory can determine *a priori* the direction of change in work effort, where the income and substitution effects lead to predictable results. The traditional theory, however, rests on two rather tenuous assumptions: that the poor are on their supply curve of labor services and that the post-tax *gross* wage rate is the same as the pre-tax rate. For a significant percentage of the poor, these assumptions are not valid.

In Figure 2, the axes again denote income and leisure per T. L_0Y_0 is the pre-negative income tax opportunity locus; X represents the amount of legal exemptions per T; t is the negative tax rate applied to X minus taxable income whenever X exceeds taxable income. The introduction of the negative income tax changes the opportunity locus from L_0Y_0 to $tXPY_0$. It seems reasonable to assume that the practicable *limits* in the alteration of work-leisure equilibrium would be, on the one hand, no reduction at all in work effort, with the negative tax absorbed entirely in added income and, on the other, a reduction in work effort just sufficient to maintain total income (work income plus negative tax) at the pre-tax level, i.e., with the negative tax completely

FIGURE 2

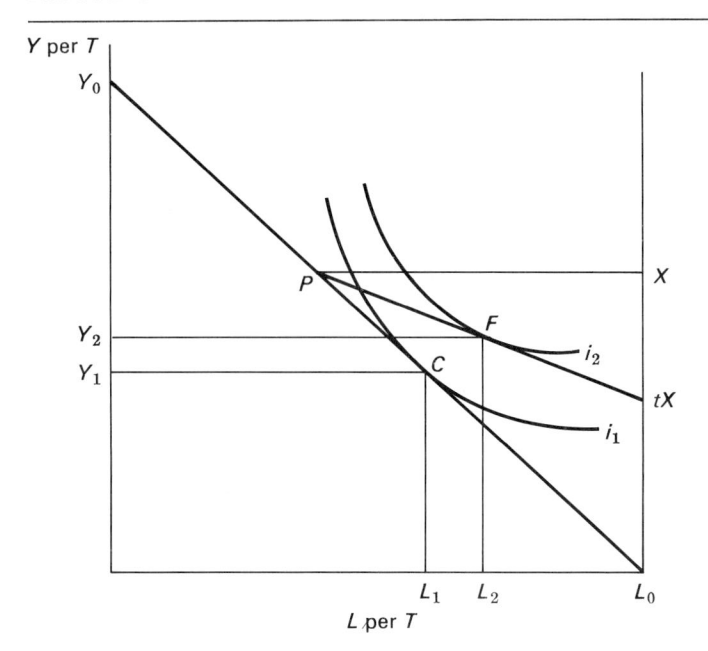

absorbed in added leisure. The general case falls between these limits, part of the tax being absorbed in added income and part in added leisure; this is the case diagrammed in Figure 2.[9] Post-tax equilibrium is at F, where $L_2 > L_1$ and $Y_2 > Y_1$. Again it appears that at best the negative income tax would be absorbed wholly into income, with no work disincentive effects. But the effects of the negative income tax do not end here; the standard theory cannot be applied without taking into account certain effects resulting from the added income which the negative tax puts into the hands of the poor.

There is a high correlation between poor health and poverty and between inadequate training and education and poverty. Two million poor families are headed by a full-time employee—ample evidence of low productivity; one out of every five low-income family heads suffers from some chronic condition limiting his activity; both communicable and non-communicable diseases are far more prevalent among the poor than the national average.[10] We might thus expect a negative income tax to have three effects, each acting on a significant percentage of the poor population, which we name in turn the productivity effect, the restricted activity effect and the investment effect. First, some of the poor will use the added income provided by a negative income tax to improve their health (through better diet, housing and medical care) and education (including vocational training).[11] Better health and/or training will lead to an increase in productivity and therefore to an increase in wage rates. This results not just from the increase in productivity, but also because employers hire those with high rates of absenteeism at lower paying jobs, due to a lack of dependability. As a result of the increased wage rate (which the traditional theory assumes does not occur), the income-leisure opportunity locus swings up from L_0Y_0 to L_0Y_1. Combining the productivity effect with the negative income tax in Figure 3, the opportunity locus is now $tXRY_1$ rather than $tXPY_0$. It is now evident that the productivity effect is part of the more general substitution effect—the higher post-tax gross wage rate makes leisure more costly, perhaps even enough more costly to make the post-tax net wage rate greater than the pre-tax wage rate. If this is the case, the substitution effect induces an increase, not a decrease, in work effort; depending on the underlying preference patterns, *it is quite possible that the new equilibrium will be at an amount of work effort greater than before the negative income tax was imposed*, with $Y_3 > Y_1$ and $L_1 > L_3$. At least we can often expect $Y_3 > Y_2$ and $L_2 > L_3$, i.e., the disincentive effects will probably be less than the traditional analysis might lead us to believe.

---

[9] We should note that a significant percentage of poor workers cannot decrease work at all due to the institutional rigidities surrounding their jobs.
[10] See Pond, M., "Interrelationships of Poverty and Disease," *Public Health Reports*, Nov. 1961, pp. 967–73.
[11] For some scanty evidence on how the poor are likely to spend a negative income tax allowance, see Part II.

FIGURE 3

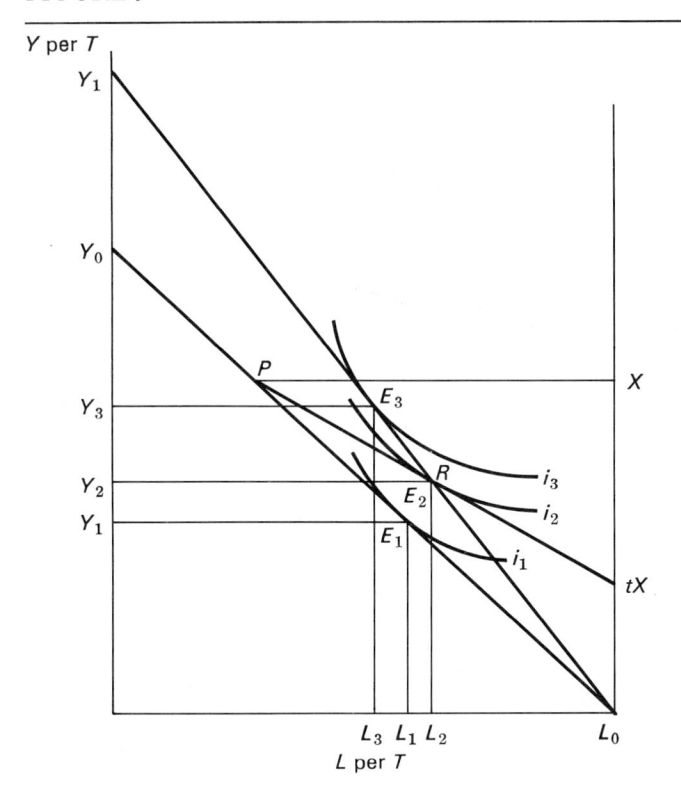

[Figure 3: Graph with Y per T on vertical axis and L per T on horizontal axis, showing points Y_1, Y_0, Y_3, Y_2, Y_1 on vertical axis; points P, E_3, R, E_2, E_1, X, i_3, i_2, i_1, tX in the graph; and L_3, L_1, L_2, L_0 on horizontal axis.]

The second effect is the restricted activity effect. Bergston has shown an inverse relationship between family income and time lost from work due to illness or injury; the National Health Survey of 1957–58 showed a strong inverse relationship between family income and the number of restricted activity dates.[12] Not only are those poor with high rates of absenteeism likely to find lower-paying jobs than they could if they had lower rates of absenteeism, but their physical limitations may place them in a position of disequilibrium at existing wage rates, as diagrammed in Figure 4.

For simplicity, we analyze this effect without a negative income tax in our system. The income leisure opportunity locus is again L_0Y_0. The worker ordinarily would be in equilibrium at G, with Y_1 and L_1. However, his state of health imposes a constraint on the amount of work he can perform per T; this health constraint is represented by the vertical line $L_hL'_h$. By setting an upper limit on the amount of work possible, the worker's state of health imposes a lower limit on the amount of leisure he *must* take. Thus, the income-

[12] See Pond, op. cit.

FIGURE 4

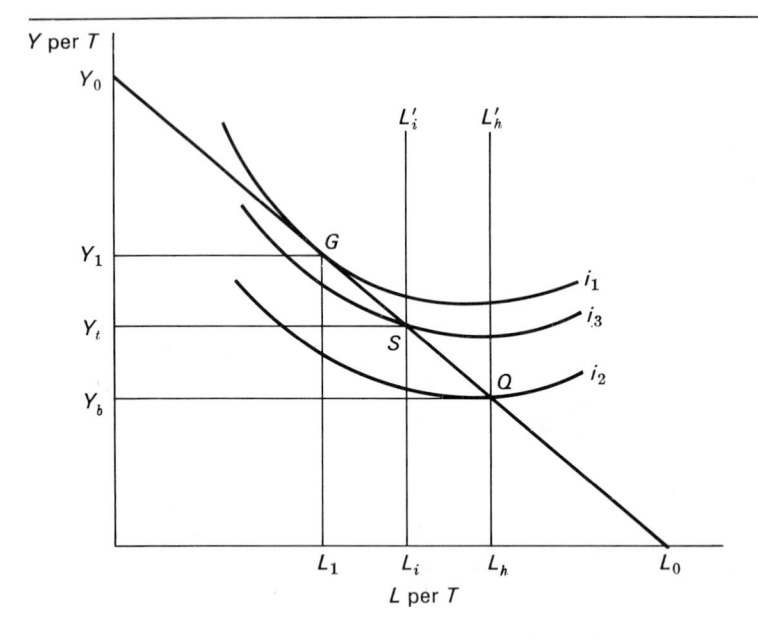

leisure opportunity locus becomes, in effect, L_0Q; unless one of the worker's indifference curves is tangent to L_0Y_0 at, or to the right of, Q, the worker will be forced onto a lower indifference curve, e.g., i_2. He must settle for $L_h > L_1$ and $Y_h < Y_1$ where i_2 meets Q.

Improved health resulting from the better diet, medical care, shelter, etc. procured with the added income provided by the negative income tax can cause $L_hL'_h$ to shift to the left, e.g., to $L_iL'_i$. The further left it shifts, the higher the indifference curve our restricted activity worker can reach (of course i_1 is the upper limit). If the new constraint is $L_iL'_i$, the worker is in equilibrium at S, where $Y_i > Y_h$ and $L_i < L_h$. A similar analysis holds for any obstacle to a worker varying his work effort over the relevant range, e.g., one of the effects of racial discrimination on employment. It should be obvious that the productivity effect and the restricted activity effect may occur simultaneously.

The third, and most important, effect tending to temper the disincentive effects of a negative income tax is the investment effect. Children in low-income families visit physicians less than half as often as other children do; a majority of those between five and fourteen have never been to a dentist. As recipients of the negative income tax allowance spend it on improved diet, medical care and housing for their children as well as themselves, the "investment" will pay off in terms of higher future productivity (and thus wage rates) and lower rates of absenteeism for the children. The theoretical analysis, of course, is analogous to that outlined above for the productivity and restricted activity effects.

We have thus seen three reasons why the distinctive effects of a negative income tax may be significantly tempered, perhaps even entirely overcome or reversed, through time.[13] In the last analysis, however, the disincentive question can only be resolved empirically. We will never be entirely certain of the effects of a negative income tax before we adopt one; uncertainty can become a marvelous excuse for inaction, but the urgency of the problem may compel us to act with less than perfect information. Such may well be the case with the negative income tax, but careful analysis of the economic behavior of the poor can greatly reduce the amount of uncertainty with which we must deal. It is for this reason that in the spring of 1967 the author undertook the investigation of the economic behavior of the urban Negro poor to which we now turn.

II

Empirical Evidence

Why the urban Negro poor? Are they not a very special subgroup of the poor and can we generalize our results to the entire population? It is true that the majority of the poor are white Anglo-Saxon Protestants,[14] but the incidence of poverty among nonwhites relative to whites is increasing rapidly, the number of farm poor is likely to decline sharply when we adopt more precise definitions of poverty which include nonmoney income, the phrase long hot summer has entered our vocabulary—the urban Negro poor do not intend to stay poor forever—violence in the slums of our cities is increasing markedly, and thus the urban Negro poor are the most noticeable poor in the nation, for they are the most vocal. Finally, and most importantly, the urban Negro poor were both interesting and available (they exist in unfortunate abundance in what in Oakland is called the McClymonds district and in Berkeley, the West Oakland Ghetto) to the author.

In several respects the urban Negro poor face a greater economic problem than their white counterparts. Because they live in ghettos, the minority group poor purchase in markets of limited supply to a much greater extent than the general populace; they pay higher rents for equal housing and more for consumer credit; thus, their general purchasing power is less than that of the white poor. Three thousand dollars for the Negro in Oakland, Watts or Harlem may purchase what the white poor can purchase for $2,800 or even

---

[13] The analysis is formalized algebraically in the appendix.
[14] See Orshansky, M., "Who's Who Among the Poor: A Demographic View of Poverty," *Social Security Bulletin*, July 1965.

$2,500.[15] Restricted supply causes another problem; as the negative tax allowance creates an increased demand for certain goods and services, prices may rise, and thus part of the negative income tax allowance may be shared by the poor with *landlords*, credit agencies and local merchants. Another problem is that the economic problems of the nonwhite poor are more intimately interconnected with social and political problems than are those of the white poor.

Extensive interviews were conducted with 103 family heads in the West Oakland Ghetto. Survey research with minority and low-income groups has in general reflected a diversity in the answers obtained depending on whether the interviewer was or was not a member of the same minority or income group. For this reason, the interviews were divided roughly in half between the author and a friend, who is Negro. Several comments concerning the interviews themselves are in order. First, certain definitional problems must be overcome. The word family can mean something quite different in Watts than in Beverly Hills, in Harlem than in Scarsdale. Second, face-to-face communication with the urban Negro poor is not very easy; many have heavy accents; some have difficulty understanding even "grammar school English"; many were nervous or suspicious; sometimes the interviewer had to rephrase or restate a question. This type of interviewing places a tremendous burden on the interviewer; he must be careful both not to bias an answer when he rephrases a question and not to threaten a sometimes tenuous rapport. Third, the concentration span of the urban Negro poor was less than adequate for all but a very brief interview. Usually once or twice during the interview, the interviewee would wander onto another topic; again, the interviewer had to be extremely careful and tolerant in getting the respondent back to the question at hand. Fourth, the author soon found that often the respondent was unable or unwilling to go into great detail in answering a question; fifth, the interviewees became uncomfortable when a relatively lengthy (five or more) series of questions was asked on the same topic, e.g., income. Sixth, the interviewer often had to translate the answers in order to aggregate them in broad categories, e.g., job availability or the type of work. For this reason, the results are the best obtainable from the answers given but certainly are subject to minor errors of omission or over-inclusion. Finally, the interviewer should be prepared for the harsh realities of ghetto life—door-to-door sampling where no doors exist, people wandering through the room where the interviews are taking place, etc.

An area sample was selected as best suiting the needs and purposes of the study. The author had to approach 109 people to obtain 53 interviews, for a 48+ per cent affirmative response rate; his accomplice had to approach 88

---

[15] See Batchelder, A., "Poverty: The Special Case of the Negro," *American Economic Review*, May 1965.

people to obtain 50 interviews, for an affirmative response rate of 61 per cent; the overall response rate was 53 per cent. In addition, there were 51 addresses where no contact was made; how many of these were vacancies and how many repeated "not-at-homes" is not known. How random is the sample? The affirmative response rate was surprisingly high, due primarily, I believe, to the excellent rapport between students at Berkeley and the inhabitants of the ghetto. The interviewers approached the potential interviewees as poor college students (which they are), perhaps eliminating much of the class barrier. When allowed to identify themselves and give their brief sales pitch, the interviewee was usually glad to give a half-hour or so of his time, some (usually the more elderly) were glad to take painfully longer. How safely may we assume that those who refused to be interviewed were not significantly different in their economic behavior than those who consented to the interview? At best, this is difficult to determine; we merely state that we cannot conceive of any differences that could reasonably be expected to lead to differences in economic behavior. How truthful were the responses? Within the limits placed on the knowledge of the interviewee, I believe that the responses were quite truthful. Two checks on the truthfulness of the replies were used. First was the correlation in replies between the two subsamples interviewed by a white and a Negro interviewer respectively. The most noticeable difference was in the response rates. Several other differences involved numbers too small to be statistically significant, and of course there is a small possibility of equal lying to both interviewers. Another check was the use of questions the answer[s] to which were designed to test the reliability of other answers (e.g., asking their marginal tax rate as a check against income); the success of this procedure was partially hampered by a lack of information on the part of the respondents, and the deterioration of rapport between interviewer and interviewee when the former probed too deeply into sensitive areas. Our expertise in the area of survey research does not enable us to claim that our sample is random and our replies perfectly reliable, but we have not been able to uncover any evidence to the contrary. Another question refers to how well people know how they would react in a hypothetical situation, which is crucial to our disincentive estimate. This hypothetical situation (whether they would decrease work effort if given an added income) is certainly one which the poor contemplate, and work is something that is with them all the time. I believe that the poor have a fairly accurate idea as to how they would react to a situation such as the adoption of a negative income tax. With the above in mind, we would like to state that if we would do the study over again, we would opt for a slightly shorter interview (perhaps twenty minutes is optimum) with only the most important questions included; we would also favor re-orienting the wording of the language slightly, more for the ease of the subsequent analysis than for anything else.

Of the 103 interviewees, 101 were Negro; the percentage of non-Negroes in the area was slightly higher, as the Negro refusal rate was lower than the non-Negro refusal rate.

Social and Economic Characteristics

The interviewees were asked the following question:

> Please look at this card. Would you please tell me the letter which comes closest to the amount you earned last year?

Some of the respondents needed help in aggregating their income to a yearly total. Of those who responded, 81 per cent had incomes under $3,000. Of all the questions in the interview, the income questions (which were asked near the end of the interview) were the most hesitatingly received; fourteen per cent refused to answer or hedged so much that the interviewer proceeded to the next question. The results are analyzed in more detail in Table 1. When asked:

> What about the year before?
> The average for the last five years?

several more respondents became edgy or refused to answer. About one in

TABLE 1 Income Distribution of the Sample

Income	Per Cent
Less than $1,500	7%
$1,500– 2,000	12
2,000– 2,500	28
2,500– 3,000	22
3,000– 3,500	9
3,500– 4,000	3
4,000– 5,000	2
More than 5,000	3
Refused	14

every six or seven was subject to enough of an income fluctuation to mention it, and seven claimed to have an income which fluctuated about poverty-line levels. The remaining questions concerning income threatened the rapport of the interview more than was expected and were often skipped. The interviewees were asked:

> In what year were you born?
> Where did you grow up?
> Was that on a farm, in a small town or large city?

> How many different states have you lived in?
> How long have you lived in this locality (the Bay Area)?

Approximately 43 per cent were raised in the southern United States; other important areas included Chicago and New York. The remainder were scattered, with less than 15 per cent native Californians. The incidence of a southern childhood increased with age. About 23 per cent grew up on a farm, 45 per cent in a small town and 23 per cent in a large city; the definition of these terms was left to the respondents. The range as regards number of states lived in was from one to "so many I don't know." The median was between three and four. Sixty-four per cent had lived in the Bay Area for more than ten years. The age distribution is given in rough form in Table 2. Some of the respond-

TABLE 2 Age Distribution

Age	Per Cent
Under 35	17%
36–60	42
Over 60	23
? or refused	18

ents seemed unsure of their age; perhaps the females were just not willing to admit their proper age. Within the poverty group there was a strong relation between income and age; of the seven persons with an income under $1,500, all but one were over sixty, and of the three with an income over $5,000, only one was over sixty. When asked,

> How many grades of school did you finish?

the responses varied predictably. A little less than one-fourth had been through high school; many had quit, some did not remember and some simply refused to answer.

Occupations

The interviewees were asked:

> Are you working now, unemployed, retired or what?

Nine out of ten were members of the work force; 74 per cent were working now, 14 per cent unemployed (a 16 per cent unemployment rate, or four times the national average), the remainder being retired, housewives, students or servicemen. The occupations were almost invariably low-income, unskilled labor, menial and like jobs. A representative list includes laborer, porter, operative, construction worker, dishwasher and parking lot attendant. There were very few managers or foremen. Due to the difficulty some had in defining their jobs and of aggregating the data, the results will not be presented in tabular form.

In order to determine the ease with which the poor could avoid accurate reporting of their income (remember each dollar earned and reported would lose the worker some negative taxes), we asked,

> Do you work for yourself, someone else or what?
> Are you paid in cash or by check?
> Do you receive any non-money payments, such as free room or meals?

The results were conclusive; none of these major avenues of avoidance presents much of a problem at present. Only 5 per cent were self-employed; 12 per cent were paid in cash; 10 per cent received non-money payments. One avenue for increased avoidance would be under-the-table arrangements between employer and employee; on this we were unable to obtain any information.

In order to discover some of the problems the group had in obtaining work, the following questions were asked:

> How long have you been at your current job?
> What did you do before that?
> How did you find out that your current job was available?

The bulk of the respondents had been at their jobs for a relatively brief period (less than three years); 26 per cent had been working at their current job for less than a year. The pattern was unmistakably clear of a group shifting from low-income job to low-income job. Information sources on jobs included, in decreasing frequency of mention, unions, friends, newspapers and public agencies. Many were accustomed to long periods of unemployment; although the answers were spotty and difficult to aggregate, perhaps a rough estimate of the median duration of unemployment would be six to eight weeks.

In order to determine the relative importance of pecuniary incentives in seeking employment, we asked,

> The last time you looked for work, what factors influenced you most in deciding whether or not to accept a particular job?

The overwhelming response was job availability, distantly followed by the type of work, the pay and the location. As accurately as possible, the results are summarized in Table 3.

TABLE 3 Factors Influencing Job Acceptance

Factor	Times Mentioned
Availability	62
Type work	33
Pay	32
Location	17

Work Effort

It was noted above that the view is widespread that the poor are poor because they are lazy. At least in the case of the urban Negro poor, this does not appear to be the case. Demand factors (discrimination, lack of training and education) outweigh supply factors in determining how much the ghetto Negro works. We asked the following questions:

> About how many hours per week do you ordinarily work?
> How many weeks did you work last year?
> Did you take any days off while you were working?
> Do you have any opportunities to earn some additional income by working more at your present job or by taking on another job for a few hours a week?
> Have you ever had two jobs at the same time?
> If more work had been offered to you last year, do you think that you would have taken it on?

The majority work full time *when they work*. Many were unemployed for a substantial part of the year (21 per cent worked 26 weeks or less); the results are summarized in Table 4. Few days off were taken while working, especially

TABLE 4 Weeks Worked

Weeks Worked	Per Cent
0–13	4%
14–26	17
27–39	23
40–52	38
? or refused	18

by those who had been at their jobs less than a year. *Only 15 per cent* said that they had opportunities to work more.[16] Usually they refused such work when it partially conflicted with their main job, when it interfered with their health, or when it was thought to be a potential family problem. About 8 per cent were currently earning money at more than one job, usually having a second part-time job in addition to a fulltime occupation, but in at least one case having two part-time jobs. About 18 per cent had at one time had two jobs at the same time; whether they were both part-time we did not ascertain. One respondent replied, "Man, paint yourself black and try to get just one!" Including the unemployed, 53 per cent claimed that they would have accepted more work had it been offered last year; most wanted to work fulltime all the time; another 24 per cent were undecided if they would have accepted additional employment. Less than one respondent in four said that they would

---

[16] The author overlooked the possibility of asking if they could work less if they desired.

not have accepted additional employment had it been offered, and this group was composed, partially, of the higher-income and higher-weeks worked members of the sample. The evidence indicates that a substantial percentage of the urban Negro poor are not on their demand for employment schedules at given wage rates.

Retirement Decisions

To determine if a negative income tax might cause some poor to retire earlier than planned, we asked,

> Have you had any opportunities for paid employment since you retired?
> Looking towards the future, do you plan to keep on working as long as your health permits, or retire at a certain age, or haven't you thought about it much? (Asked only of those who appeared to be over 45.)

The retired (who numbered only six) to a man did not have any opportunities for paid employment since they had ceased working. As for the retirement plans of the relatively elderly working poor, most thought that they would work as long as their health permitted, or had not given the matter much thought; very few thought that they would retire at a certain age. When asked if they were covered by social security, most did not know!

Tax Disincentives

We have thus far presented numerous qualitative information relating to potential tax disincentives among the poor; institutional rigidities surrounding their jobs, lack of employment opportunities outside their regular jobs, and a strong commitment to maintain or improve pre-tax levels of consumption and saving all point to minimal disincentive effects. To more directly determine the extent of the potential work disincentive, a series of direct and indirect questions was asked to determine the extent of indebtedness among the poor, how satisfied they are with their present stock of consumer durables and savings, what they would be likely to do with an added income, and whether they thought they might decrease their work effort if given an added income. Among the questions asked were:

> Do you own a television or a car?
> Did you pay cash or make payments?
> Suppose a friend or relative left you a gift or inheritance of $500, what would you most likely do with it?
> Suppose you received an additional $500 per year, what would you most likely do with this added income?
> Do you think you might work less because of this added income?

If a friend or neighbor came to you for advice and asked you what you thought would be a safe savings cushion to have set aside for emergencies, what would you tell him?

What about your own savings goal, are you satisfied with the amount you have saved?

About 29 per cent of the interviewees owned a television and 24 per cent owned a car. Of those who would say, two-thirds purchased the car on payments; making payments will commit the worker to a continued stream of income, and would temper the disincentive tendencies of the negative tax. As for the most likely thing to do with $500, anything and everything was mentioned. Only 14 per cent mentioned the possibility of saving all or part of the gift; the most frequently mentioned items fell into two broad categories: consumer durables such as radios, televisions, hi-fis, and occasionally even cars, on the one hand, and non-durables such as food, clothing, medicine, etc., on the other. Also frequently mentioned was the payment of debt (19 per cent); for those in debt, we can again expect minimal disincentive effects. As expected, answers to the safe savings cushion covered a remarkable range, from $100 or $200 to the ambiguous "as much as you can." The data was difficult to meaningfully aggregate; perhaps $400 to $500 was the median. The majority were not satisfied with the amount they had saved, but judging from the low response to the $500 questions, were not prepared to sacrifice consumer goods in favor of saving. On the $500 per year question, three persons brought up the possibility of working less (although none had on the $500 gift question). This forms what I call the strong disincentive group. When directly asked if they thought that they *might* work less, only four more responded in the affirmative, forming the middle disincentive group; 66 per cent flatly declared that they would not; 18 per cent were undecided. To make sure that we included all those who might be subject to a disincentive, the undecided group was winnowed on the basis of their answers to other questions, and the weak disincentive group of three more persons was added. The results are summarized in Table 5. It should be noted that the results are a practicable upper limit; first, we have *not* winnowed the strong and middle groups (for example, to include those above poverty incomes) and second, the question was carefully worded to obtain a yes response from those who thought only

TABLE 5 Disincentive Group—Hypothetical

Type Disincentive	Per Cent
Strong (3/87)	3+%
Middle (4/87)	5
Weak (3/87)	3+
Strong + Middle (7/87)	8
Strong + Middle + Weak (10/87)	12

that they *might* be subject to a work disincentive, not just from those who thought that they *would* be subject to one. One problem remains; how do we know that more people would not have answered in the affirmative had we used the sum of, say, $1,000 per year, instead of $500? We believe that when contemplating an improved economic condition, the poor do not usually think in fixed amounts, but rather in terms of "a lot more dough" or "a bundle." For this reason, they may not distinguish as sharply between $500 and $1,000 as more wealthy people might. Second, we had to employ a single figure. Median income among the poor is approximately $1,900. A negative income tax at a 50 per cent rate would give the median poor person $550; $500 was selected because of the rounded nature of the figure. We thus have a rough measure of a practicable upper limit to the percentage of the poor subject to a work disincentive (at least with a marginal rate of 50 per cent) based on their own evaluation of how they would react in a hypothetical situation. We know that about 12 per cent of our sample might be subject to a work disincentive; what we really want to know is the amount by which total work effort will decrease. We will again adopt the technique of figuring a practicable upper limit. We reasoned above that the practicable upper limit to the decrease in work effort for an individual would be a decrease just sufficient to equate pre-tax and post-tax income. A worker behaving in this manner will have a decrease in work effort function that is a function of the tax rate t and his pre-tax income. Depending on the tax rate, up to a certain limit the worker can decrease his work effort by 100 per cent; with a 50 per cent tax and a $3,000 poverty line, any worker earning $1,500 or less can stop work entirely and receive the same, or more, income. Above $1,500 (or in general, tX), the possible decrease declines rapidly, reaching two-thirds at $1,800, one-half at $2,000, and one-fourth at $2,400. Remember these are unlikely practicable upper limits. Assuming an average decrease in work effort of two-thirds, which we believe overstates the decrease by well over 100 per cent, we present the results in their most highly reformed manner in Table 6. Again, the estimates are arrived at by taking the upper limit of those who believe that they *might* be subject to a disincentive and assuming that every single one of them reduces his work by the maximum practicable amount. Even with these upper limits, our estimate of the decrease in work effort is only 8 per cent!

TABLE 6   Total Decrease in Work Effort

Type Disincentive	Per Cent	At	Decrease
I. Strong	3	2/3	2%
II. Middle	5	2/3	3.3
III. Weak	3	2/3	2
IV. Strong + Middle	8	2/3	5.3
V. Strong + Middle + Weak	12	2/3	8

Several comments are in order. First, recall the problems of randomness, reliability and generalizability. The study was primarily conducted on weekends, and we probably missed some domestic workers; we also have not been able to accurately determine what the effects on second earners in a family might be (about three-fourths of those interviewed had a husband or wife who had worked during the last five years). However, we do not believe either of these considerations would significantly alter the results. We have much qualitative evidence to support the order of magnitude of our quantitative estimate. The poor are not satisfied with their levels of consumption or saving, many are in debt, some have institutional rigidities surrounding their job, few have opportunities to obtain additional work and perhaps most importantly their wives do not want them at home. At least a dozen times during interviews with wives, they claimed that they did not want their husband to receive welfare, that it was socially degrading to have the neighbors see him around the house during the day, and that they only wanted him to work fulltime all the time. As far as generalizing from the urban Negro poor to the poor as a whole, we will merely state that their common suffering probably overwhelms any significant differences. Even if the poor as a whole were subject to a fifty per cent greater work disincentive (and there is just as much reason to believe that they will be subject to the same or less of one) than the urban Negro poor, we would still estimate only 12 per cent as a dubious upper limit; if the average reduction factor is one-third rather than two-thirds, the estimate drops to 6 per cent; in either case, it is hardly translatable into quitting work and living off the public.

III

Our conclusion, like the lives of the poor, shall be comparatively brief. First, let us establish what amount of resources a 50 per cent negative income tax might transfer to the poor. Assume a $750 per person per year exemption for poor persons; total exemptions for the poor (based on 35 million people) total $26.2 billion. Other income amounts to $16.4 billion, composed of $12.4 billion in earned income and Lampman's estimate of $4 billion of OASDHI benefits going to the poor alone.[17] The poverty gap totals $9.8 billion. With no disincentive effects a negative income tax at a 50 per cent rate would transfer $4.9 billion to the poor. Assuming that an 8 per cent reduction in work effort is reflected in an 8 per cent reduction in earned income, earned income drops from $12.4 billion to $11.4 billion, and the poverty gap increases to $10.8 billion. The 50 per cent negative income tax thus transfers $5.4 billion to the poor, or one-half billion dollars more than it would if there were no disincentive effects.

[17] Based on 1963 data.

Second, the extent of the work disincentive depends on how the tax is implemented; will it replace or supplement existing welfare programs? How will it be integrated into our present system of income maintenance if it only supplements existing programs? To the extent that existing programs are eliminated, the relevant magnitude is the differential between the work disincentives of a negative income tax and those of the displaced programs. A negative income tax might cause problems both in relocating redundant labor now in the "distressed industries" and in frictional unemployment. The tax would ease the financial pressure to relocate and/or find a job, acting not unlike severance pay. Better job information and additional financial incentives for those who will relocate would do much to alleviate these undesirable side effects of the tax. Finally, the composition of any disincentive may be as important as its magnitude. The taxpayer and politician would find it more palatable if the disincentive fell mostly on the old and sick rather than on the young and healthy.

In conclusion, we state only that the negative income tax is an attractive device for closing the poverty gap substantially and quickly, and that, although additional research is needed among other poor groups, it appears feasible from the disincentive standpoint. Perhaps more important, when the poor were asked,

> Would you rather see the government provide free services such as housing, education, etc., or spend the same amount of money by giving it directly to poor people to spend as they wish?

the respondents voted two-to-one in favor of the negative income tax.

APPENDIX

We have traced through the productivity, restricted activity and investment effects geometrically; let us briefly formalize them algebraically. Assume that the worker's satisfaction depends on income and leisure. His utility function is

$$U = f(L, Y), \qquad (1)$$

where L denotes leisure and Y income. Both L and Y are desirable. We assume that U is continuous and has continuous first and second order partial derivatives. In constructing (1), we assumed that the worker derives utility from the commodities he purchases, and that he buys them in fixed proportions at constant prices. The rate of substitution of income for leisure is

$$-\frac{dY}{dL} = \frac{g_1}{g_2}, \qquad (2)$$

where g_1 is the partial derivative of U with respect to L and g_2 is the partial derivative of U with respect to Y. The amount of work done is W, so $L = T - W$, where again T is time available in the period. The budget constraint is $Y = rW$, where r is the prevailing wage rate. Substituting the values of L and Y into (1),

$$U = f(T - W, rW). \qquad (3)$$

Maximizing utility, we set the derivative of (3) with respect to W equal to zero:

$$\frac{dU}{dW} = -g_1 + g_2 r = 0 \qquad (4)$$

and therefore

$$-\frac{dY}{dL} = \frac{g_1}{g_2} = r. \qquad (5)$$

The second-order condition for a maximum is fulfilled when

$$\frac{d^2 U}{dW^2} = g_{11} - 2g_{12}r + g_{22}r < 0. \qquad (6)$$

We impose a negative income tax levied at rate t against the difference between unused exemptions, X, and taxable income, whenever X exceeds taxable income, on our system. Income now equals $rW_1 + t(X - rW_1)$, where W_1 refers to after-tax equilibrium, and so

$$U = f[T - W_1, rW_1 + t(X - rW_1)] \qquad (7)$$

and

$$\frac{dU}{dW} = -g_1 + g_2(r - rt) = 0 \qquad (8)$$

and

$$-\frac{dY}{dL} = \frac{g_1}{g_2} = r(1 - t) \qquad (9)$$

with the appropriate second-order constraints. We now introduce the productivity effect; with the after-productivity effect wage rate $r_2 > r$ and equilibrium work effort W_2, Equation (7) becomes

$$U = f[T - W_2, r_2 W_2 + t(X - r_2 W_2)] \qquad (10)$$

and

$$\frac{dU}{dW} = -g_1 + g_2(r_2 - tr_2) = 0 \qquad (11)$$

and

$$-\frac{dY}{dL} = \frac{g_1}{g_2} = r_2(1 - t). \qquad (12)$$

Equations five, nine and twelve are relations in terms of W and r based on the worker's optimizing behavior; each is therefore an offer curve of work and states what W he will work at any wage rate. Since the offer of work is equivalent to the demand for income, these equations provide demand curves for income. We can readily assume a utility function where equations four, eight and eleven yield a W that is a function of r. Depending on the nature of the preference patterns and the amount of increase from r to r_2 caused by the productivity effect, we can obtain a $W_2 > W$, i.e., a post-tax work effort exceeding pre-tax work effort.

The restricted activity effect works by easing the constraint on the amount of work the worker can do. Ill health causes the worker to maximize his utility subject to the constraint that $L \geqslant L_h$. As health improves the constraint becomes $L \geqslant L_i < L_h$. If health improves enough, he may maximize without constraint.

Again, the analysis of the investment effect is analogous to that of the other two effects, as outlined above.

The Negative Income Tax and the Supply of Work Effort: Comment

JONATHAN KESSELMAN*

In an article on the negative income tax in this *Journal,* Michael Jay Boskin asserted that "uncertainty can become a marvelous excuse for inaction, but the urgency of the problem may compel us to act with less than perfect information."[1] Many would share these feelings about the urgency of providing some form of income maintenance for the impoverished. But, in his eagerness to make a compelling case for the negative income tax, Boskin has only made our knowledge of the incentives problem more imperfect. Insofar as there are alternative approaches to income maintenance, it seems imperative that we learn their true relative incentive effects. Boskin's study does not advance this needed endeavor and may be seriously misleading if taken at face value. His opening section of theoretical analysis seems to be defective at several points. The survey technique of the study, and particularly the key questions asked interviewees, are subject to strong criticism.

Boskin hypothesizes the existence of three dynamic incentive effects which might overcome the static disincentives under a negative income tax (*NIT*). Any dynamic improvement in the quality or quantity of work which the poor would be able to supply is undoubtedly an important aspect of a *NIT*. However, by failing to mention any other form of income maintenance, Boskin has left us with the vague implication that these dynamic effects are peculiar to the *NIT*. Yet, one might make an equally tenable case for similar dynamic effects arising under a program of family allowances or wage supplements.[2] Furthermore, improved diet, health care, housing, education, and job training might be more effectively secured for the poor by improved programs for

From the *National Tax Journal,* Vol. XXII, No. 3 (September 1969). Reprinted by permission.

* The author is a graduate student in economics at the Massachusetts Institute of Technology.
[1] "The Negative Income Tax and the Supply of Work Effort," *National Tax Journal,* Vol. XX, No. 4 (December, 1967).
[2] Jonathan Kesselman, "Labor-Supply Effects of Income, Income-Work, and Wage Subsidies," *The Journal of Human Resources,* Vol. IV, No. 3 (Summer, 1969).

505

these explicit purposes than by giving the poor an equivalent sum of extra income. We have no reason to believe that poor people's marginal propensity to spend on human-capital items is unity, and we do have reasons to question the market's ability to provide these services to the poor. Whether income maintenance is to be preferred to the provision of public services will hinge more upon judgments about the value of consumer choice to beneficiaries and the accompanying welfare effects.

To what extent would the *NIT* induce the dynamic effects which Boskin hypothesizes? His justification for positing substantial favorable effects rests on an observed "high correlation between poor health and poverty and between inadequate training and education and poverty" and "an inverse relationship between family income and time lost from work due to illness or injury." Boskin does not attempt to evaluate the direction of causation in these relationships, but his hypotheses require that poverty have a significant causal influence on the observed effects. Yet, if poverty is not a major factor in the poor health and low skills of the impoverished, then removing poverty will not improve these deficiencies of the poor. Even if lack of income is a major determinant, and if the poor were to spend a major part of *NIT* benefits on investment in themselves—the expenditures might still be too small to reverse the deficiencies. This is not to take a substantive position on these matters, except to suggest that it is incumbent upon an objective economist who makes hypothetical assertions to specify the opposing possibilities as well.

In two separate footnotes, Boskin states that the poor worker often cannot adjust his hours of work downward, due to institutional rigidities. He argues that this provides "reason to suspect that a negative income tax will not have a significant work disincentive effect." As Peter Diamond has observed, however, the absence of continuous adjustability by the individual in his hours of work will not prevent the aggregate labor supply from diminishing.[3] That is to say, those workers who are more sensitive to changes in the net wage rate will leave the market entirely if they are subjected to additional disincentives. Their welfare is diminished by the rigidity on hours, since they are forced to over-respond to the disincentive. Also, those who decide to continue working full-time suffer a fall in welfare from the rigidity, insofar as they would have liked to reduce their hours of work somewhat.

In his "restricted activity effect," Boskin contends that poor health may place an individual "in a position of disequilibrium at existing wage rates." By this it is meant that the individual is at a point where his income-leisure opportunity locus *intersects* his highest attainable indifference curve. This seems to be stretching the conventional income-leisure utility analysis in an unwarranted and unnecessary fashion. It is more reasonable to consider that, even

---

[3] Peter A. Diamond, "Negative Taxes and the Poverty Problem—A Review Article," *National Tax Journal*, Vol. XXI, No. 3 (September, 1968).

though the individual is in poor health, he is in static equilibrium so that he maximizes his welfare, given his preferences. His preferences are, to be sure, molded by objective constraints on his existence, including poor health, as they are subjectively perceived. Even a very ill person *could* work more than some stipulated "maximum"; but he *chooses* not to, on account of his preference to conserve his health. There is no reason to treat one person's poor health differently from another's alienation or sloth as influences on their respective income-leisure preferences. Although we may reject Boskin's original exposition of the "restricted activity effect," the effect still remains. Instead of the individual's leisure constraint shifting with improved health, it is his preferences which change.

Boskin's theoretical analysis has a tenuous relation to his empirical evidence. The sole item which appears to connect the two is the response by interviewees as to how they would dispose of an additional $500 per year. It is recorded that "the most frequently mentioned items fell into two broad categories: consumer durables ... and non-durables such as food, clothing, medicine, etc." We are given no hint as to what proportion of the $500 would be spent on food and medicine, nor is there any mention of expenditures on education or job training. Yet, this would seem to be a crucial question, if the dynamic effects which are the substance of Boskin's theoretical treatment are to work effectively. Aside from this one point of contact, the empirical evidence becomes a series of ad hoc observations about how the life patterns and economic environment of the poor militate against much reduction in their work effort.

Now, there remains one conceivable justification for the choice of a survey technique to plumb the dynamic side of the incentives problem. This would be the possibility that, in responding to the "$500 question," the poor were making careful estimates of how their increased human-capital expenditures out of income subsidies would affect their ability to work. The assumption of such foresight seems too far-fetched to be credible, and indeed Boskin does not indicate in his questions or responses that this kind of calculation was intended or occurring. It thus appears that the study has not measured the likely dynamic effects of a *NIT* either directly or indirectly. The remainder of the present comment will treat Boskin's empirical evidence as it relates to the static incentive effects of a *NIT*.

Boskin's reasons for feeling that a survey approach might provide a tolerable measure of the likely incentive effects of a real *NIT* are not persuasive. He says, "This hypothetical situation (whether they would decrease work effort if given an added income) is certainly one which the poor contemplate, and work is something that is with them all the time. I believe that the poor have a fairly accurate idea as to how they would react to a situation such as the adoption of a negative income tax." He provides no further support for this belief. Little evidence which bears directly on the evidence is available, but analogous examples may not be totally irrelevant. Classroom experiments with students playing the roles of warring duopolists have evoked much different behavior when the stakes were tangible rewards rather than hypothetical victories.

Boskin says he believes "that when contemplating an improved economic condition, the poor do not usually think in fixed amounts, but rather in terms of 'a lot more dough' or 'a bundle.' For this reason," he adduces, "they may not distinguish as sharply between $500 and $1000 as more wealthy people might." It seems equally plausible to conjecture that people's contemplations of economic well-being often take the form of fantasy, which may tell us little about their behavior when they are confronted with real changes. We might also suspect that most poor people would distinguish *more* sharply between $500 and $1000 than wealthier people would. This should be revealed by their relative intensities of preference in situations which make them sacrifice other "goods" in which they are (more or less) equally endowed, such as leisure, freedom, or life.

NIT payments would be a considerable fraction of current income for many recipients, and it is simply not established that people can accurately predict their work response to such changed conditions. If the average income of the interviewees was in fact $1900—which Boskin seems merely to assume—then the proposed negative-tax payment would be about $500 (rounded from $550). This is a 26 percent rise in income and will lie outside the range of experience for many of those interviewed. Moreover, while he thinks he is talking about a *NIT* with $3000 break-even income and 50 percent tax rate, Boskin confronted all of his interviewees with the same $500 prospect. For poor people with earned income less than $1900, however, the negative-tax payment would be larger—and presumably work disincentives would be greater, too. The interviewees had preference patterns of people with more income than $1900 and of people with less. What, then, is the justification for assuming that the greater disincentives for families earning less than $1900 will be just offset by lesser disincentives for those with incomes greater than $1900? Such an asymmetry would add to the unreliability of the study's aggregate estimates of work disincentives.

In particular, Boskin's conclusions about the effects of the *NIT* on retirements from the workforce must be rejected. His survey offered payments of $500, instead of the actual $1500 which a beneficiary family could collect upon withdrawing from work. Presumably, the *NIT* payments would be geared to family size in addition to earnings, so that the $1500 payment would be granted to a non-working family with four members. For an elderly family, usually smaller than four people, the retirement payment would thus be less than $1500 but still substantially more than $500. Individuals aged over 60 constituted 23 percent of Boskin's sample, and to this we might add part of the 18 percent who did not know their age or refused to tell. Since only six percent of those interviewed were already retired, the potential for elderly retirements may be substantially larger than the proposition of $500 would indicate.

Boskin's survey formulation of the NIT obliterates the important distinction between income and substitution effects of the program.[4] *The interviewees are posed with the prospect not of a NIT, but rather of a $500 lump-sum subsidy with no substitution effects.* This leads to an under-estimate of the extent of deterioration in work incentives, and perhaps a very serious one. Figure 1 shows the initial equilibrium of a worker earning $1900 with no subsidy. A $500 lump-sum subsidy raises the individual's leisure-income opportunity locus from AB to CD. The worker seeks his new equilibrium by increasing his consumption of leisure from L_0 to L', which is a reduction in work hours. The budget locus offered by a true NIT is depicted by EFB, which shows the $3000 break-even level and 50 percent tax rate which Boskin believes he is using. Substitution and income effects of the NIT together induce the beneficiary to reduce his work effort to L''. The true measure of work disincentive under a NIT will be $L'' - L_0$, which in general will exceed $L' - L_0$ that Boskin has estimated. The substitution effect of the NIT unambiguously raises work disincentives beyond those of the income effect common to the NIT and the lump-sum subsidy.

FIGURE 1

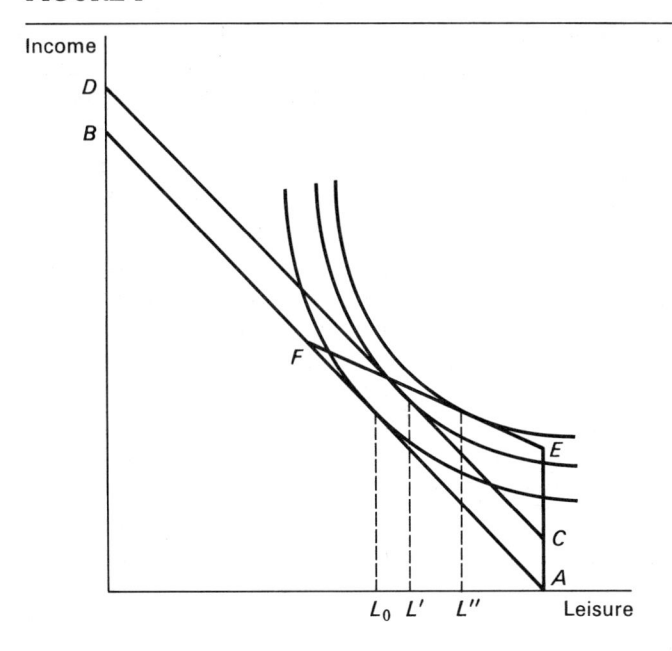

[4] Christopher Green, "Negative Taxes and Monetary Incentives to Work: The Static Theory," *The Journal of Human Resources*, Vol. III, No. 3 (Summer, 1968).

Ironically, Boskin is aware of the undesirable substitution effects which may occur at high tax rates. He writes, "Why not use a 100 percent rate and close the entire gap? It seems reasonable to assume that at extremely high rates, the poor might be induced to reduce the supply of work effort . . ." Yet, no aspect whatever of a tax rate on earnings appears in the "NIT" which is posed to the interviewees. Nonetheless, Boskin seems to believe that he has accounted for this effect: "We thus have a rough measure of a practicable upper limit to the percentage of the poor subject to a work disincentive (at least with a marginal rate of 50 percent) based on their own evaluations of how they would react in a hypothetical situation." What is his justification for claiming that he has employed a 50 percent tax rate? It is true that $500 is about 50 percent of the difference between $1900 and $3000. But $500 is also 100 percent of the difference between $1900 and $2400, or any percentage of the difference between $1900 and another figure. In the survey, the interviewee was told nothing about a $3000 break-even level or a 50 percent tax rate.

It is unfortunate that Boskin devoted more care to the administration and interpretation of his survey than to its proper formulation. He says, "the question was carefully worded to obtain a yes response from those who thought only that they *might* be subject to a work disincentive, not just from those who thought that they *would* be subject to one." The survey would have been more meaningful if it had posed to each interviewee the true alternatives under a NIT—even if the question would have been much clumsier to handle. For then, the poor person would have known that the NIT does not involve solely a lump-sum cash payment. He would have seen that the NIT also cuts in half the net-wage returns to working, because the "lump" payment varies with his income.

As a last line of defense for his contention of minimal disincentives under a NIT, Boskin has the qualitative evidence from his survey. This is probably the most useful part of the entire study, if it is dissociated from any conclusions about work incentives. Yet, Boskin argues in an objectionable fashion: "We have much qualitative evidence to support the order of magnitude of our quantitative estimate." There is no reason to dispute his finding that "the poor are not satisfied with their levels of consumption or saving, many are in debt," and so forth. (And we might well reach similar conclusions in surveying families with median income of $15,000.) Can these influences act as an independent constraint on the willingness of the poor to work less? Or are the poor not still subject to work disincentives if the marginal return to working declines? We might hope that the influence of life patterns and real-world rigidities would be reflected in the responses to a properly constructed NIT survey or to an experimental NIT program. But it is a hazardous undertaking to argue directly from the qualitative evidence to the magnitude of change in work incentives under a NIT.

This critique of Boskin's article should not be taken as an outright rejection of all that his work represents. Numerous problems in economics will only be cracked when applied economists become more willing to soil their hands, as Boskin has, by undertaking difficult and time-consuming surveys to obtain information. And some of the most important questions of economic-social policy, including income maintenance, require careful qualitative studies of habits, institutions, and environments for their intelligent handling. This aspect of Boskin's article stands intact as a useful study bearing on the *NIT*. The gathering and interpretation of surveys and qualitative evidence are probably more susceptible to the injection of value-views than the traditional tools of economic analysis which eschew non-quantifiable information and relationships. In fact, it may be inevitable that the survey-qualitative approach will be molded by the preconceptions of the practitioner.

Even recognizing the room for subjective elements in a study of this nature, though, this comment cannot help concluding that Boskin has gone beyond the unavoidable degree of judgment and viewpoint. He has stumbled into an error of methodology which can be recognized on purely technical grounds; yet, its origins seem to lie in a prejudgment of the incentive effects of a *NIT*. The reasoning would seem to be that, *since the beneficiary can be expected not to reduce his work effort with a NIT*, his earnings would not drop from $1900, so that $500 would be the correct figure to offer him—in a survey intended to determine whether he would in fact reduce his work effort. Some of us may hope that economists become more impelled by their social concern to choose to treat neglected problems of genuine social import. Let us also hope that such studies be conducted so as to spare readers the uncertain and tiresome task of having to disentangle substance and author's viewpoint.

12

INTEREST AND PROFITS

Interest and profits are considered together in this chapter mainly because of historical precedent. Some classical economists lumped interest and profits together and considered both a return to the owners and managers of businesses. Since interest and profits return to the same factor of production, capital, some classical economists felt that no distinction need be made between the two. Modern economics attempts to distinguish between the two types of factor returns, and it is the purpose of this chapter to explain that difference.

INTEREST

Much like wages paid to labor and rent paid for the use of land, interest is payment for the use of capital. Capital is defined as any reproducible, nonhuman resource used in the production of output. Though humans, and even more, human skills, may reasonably be considered capital, since they are capable of producing output, they are excluded by this definition. We do this for pedagogical reasons only. In fact the distinction is dropped in the selected reading for this chapter. Concentrating on nonhuman capital is a simplification which allows us to ignore the problems associated with imputed costs and returns that arise when analyzing human capital.

The interest rate is different from other factor returns, for it is not the purchase price of capital assets, but rather a kind of rent which must be paid for the use of funds necessary to acquire capital. Furthermore, interest is unique, because it is stated not as a sum of money but as a pure number. Rather than denominated in dollars per hour, or dollars per acre, the rate of return on capital is expressed as a percent, the ratio of the number of dollars earned to the number of dollars of capital employed. An interest rate of 5 percent means the use of $100 will require a $5 annual rental.

For the most part, capital is demanded because, without it, production would be less efficient. Imagine a production process which produces a consumer good directly, using labor and the necessary raw materials, but without capital. Now consider a second production process for the same product, using capital in addition to the same amounts of labor and raw materials. Obviously, the second process using capital will not be employed unless the resulting output is greater than that of the first process. In fact, a measure of the return to capital is the difference between (1) total output over the life of the capital asset using the second process, over and above the cost of replacing the capital, and (2) total output produced by the same resources without capital. For almost all goods and services produced, roundabout production techniques (capital-using techniques) are more efficient than direct production. It is virtually always more efficient to use resources to produce tools, and then the tools, along with labor and raw materials, to produce output, because tools increase the efficiency of other resources. There is an opportunity cost associated with acquiring capital, however, measured by the amount of consumption goods given up because productive resources are used to make tools rather than consumable output. Decision makers within an economy must balance this cost of acquiring capital with the returns to capital. The rate of growth of the stock of capital and the interest rate which achieves this balance result from the interaction of forces of supply and demand. In the following paragraphs, we will focus upon the principal determinants of the supply and demand for new capital and the characteristics of the capital market.

We begin by studying the effects of changes in the interest rate on the consumption behavior of consumers. The principal assumption underlying the models we will develop is that consumers seek to maximize utility over their entire life cycle. Consumers' decisions about consumption levels largely determine the volume of saving in an economy, the principal source of supply of funds for forming new capital. In the United States, usually about 93 percent of aggregate consumer income is spent on consumption, leaving 7 percent of income unspent and therefore, by definition, saved.

The Time Dimension and Consumer Saving

In Chapter 3, we analyzed consumer behavior on the assumption that consumers' incomes and budgets were identical. The consumer had only to decide, for an upcoming period, how to spend that period's income, without a thought given to his consumption in subsequent periods. We concentrated on the consumer's allocation of expenditures among the many consumer products and services that he might buy. But if we introduce the possibility of borrowing and lending, then the consumer's budget for any one decision period may be more or less than his income in that period. He may borrow future income and augment his present budget or save now so that his future budget will be greater than future income. Once borrowing and lending are introduced, *time* enters explicitly into the utility-maximizing decision process of consumers.[1] So, too, does the interest rate, for it sets the terms on which consumers can exchange present for future income and future for present income. To see how the interest rate affects consumer's consumption decisions, we will develop a two-period model of consumer behavior.

A Two-Period Model

To keep our model simple let us make the following assumptions: (1) The time horizon for consumers is two periods long. Consumers make their consumption decisions at the beginning of the first period for both periods and, once made, the decisions are unalterable. (2) Any amount budgeted for expenditure in a given period is spent in its entirety in the given period. (3) Consumers' incomes are uniform from period one to period two, and are known in advance. (4) Consumers are free to borrow and lend at the prevailing interest rate; however, any amount borrowed in period one must be repaid in period two.

A Zero Interest Rate. To begin, suppose the interest rate is identically zero for lending and borrowing, admittedly an unrealistic case but useful as an introduction, and suppose a consumer's *income* is Y_1^P, equal to Y_1^F, in periods one and two. If the consumer neither borrows nor lends, his *budget* will be Y_1^P for the first upcoming period and Y_1^F for the second. This combination of first period–second period budgets is represented by point a on line B in Figure 12–1. But this is not the only combination of first- and second-period budgets possible. By borrowing all of his second-period income, the consumer's first-period budget can be doubled from Y_1^P to Y_2^P. This would reduce the second period's budget to zero, since all of the latter period's income would be needed to repay the loan, at zero interest. The combination of Y_2^P and zero is represented by point T, the vertical intercept of line B. Now suppose the consumer budgets and spends nothing in period one. Then period one's income can be loaned (or hoarded) at zero interest, so that the second period's budget will be doubled to Y_2^F. The second-period budget would equal the income in the second period and the savings from the previous period, with zero interest earned. The combination of zero budget in period one and Y_2^F budgeted for period two is plotted as point V, the horizontal intercept of B. Finally, all the combinations of period one–period two budgets open to the consumer lie along the constraint line B. The slope of B is determined by the rate at which present income can be exchanged for future income. With a zero interest rate, the slope is -1: one dollar of period two's income can be exchanged for a dollar now, or a dollar given up now will result in one extra dollar in period two.

---

[1] The theories presented here derive largely from Irving Fisher, *The Theory of Interest*. Reprints of Economic Classics. (New York: Augustus M. Kelley, 1961), especially Chapters 4 and 5.

FIGURE 12-1   A Two-Period Consumer Model (Assuming Zero Interest and a Neutral Time Preference)

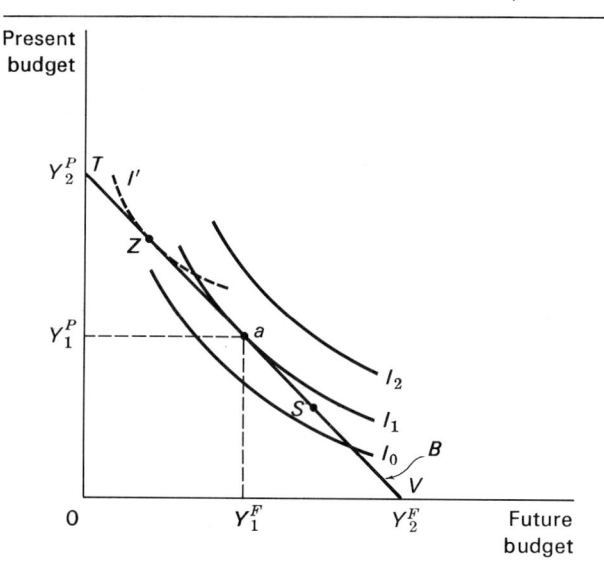

Curves I_0 through I_2 are the consumer's indifference curves for present and future budgets. Since, by assumption, any amount budgeted in a period is spent in its entirety in that period, we may think of these curves as reflecting the consumer's preferences for future versus present consumption. The curves will generally be downward sloping, since a consumer will willingly give up present consumption only when compensated by increased future consumption. The slope of one of these indifference curves at a point is the consumer's *marginal rate of substitution of present for future consumption*, MRS_{PF}, at that point. Following the arguments advanced in Chapter 3, we may expect that the MRS_{PF} will decline as the ratio of future to present consumption rises, so the indifference curves will be convex to the origin.

To maximize utility, the consumer will choose that combination of present and future consumption for which the constraint line is tangent to an indifference curve. This occurs in Figure 12-1 at point a, where I_1 is tangent to B. The consumer maximizes utility by budgeting and spending all of the first period's income in period one and the second period's income in period two. The consumer, in this case of a zero interest rate, would neither save nor borrow: he has a *neutral* time preference for consumption. On the other hand, it is quite possible that a consumer with a *positive* time preference would achieve an optimal combination at point z, the point of tangency of B with the dashed indifference curve I'. This latter consumer would budget and spend in the first period an amount greater than his income, through borrowing, because *ceteris paribus*, he prefers present to future consumption. Of course, he must be prepared to budget and spend less in the second time period because he must repay his loan. As still another possibility, a third consumer faced with the same constraint line, B, might maximize his utility by choosing the combination at point S. This consumer exhibits a *negative* time preference, for he would rather save in period one, so that consumption in period two can be increased.

Which pattern of behavior can we expect? There can be no general answer to this question, for some people will have a positive and some a negative time preference, and we cannot predict, a priori, which will apply in a given circumstance. We might expect, however, that those consumers in the early phases of their life cycle will have a positive time preference for consumption, while during the years just prior to retirement one is likely to have a negative time preference, as funds must be accumulated to finance retirement. Finally, during retirement, an individual will likely have a positive or neutral time preference. In other words, a consumer's time preference for consumption will vary over his life cycle. In addition, a consumer's level of income will influence his pattern of preference for present versus future consumption, and we might expect that those with low incomes will have a positive time preference. On the other hand, an individual with a positive time preference at a low level of income may have a neutral or negative time preference at a higher income level. Expectations about the level of future income will play an important role in shaping present consumption. If an individual's income is expected to rise, he will possibly exhibit a positive time preference for present consumption and a negative time preference if future income is expected to fall. Thus consumers' incomes and their expectations about future income levels are important in shaping present expenditure plans.

A Positive Interest Rate. Now let us assume a more realistic situation: that the interest rate is not zero but some positive amount. A consumer can now expect to pay interest on funds borrowed and earn interest on funds saved and loaned. As an arithmetic illustration, suppose a consumer's income is $1,000 in each of periods one and two and that he wishes to borrow all of period two's income to spend in period one. He will have available in the first period $1,000, his income earned in that period, plus $1,000, the amount borrowed, *less* an amount set aside to pay interest. (Or perhaps the loan will be discounted, the interest subtracted, at the time the loan is made.) On the other hand, if he saves all of period one's income, he will have available in period two, $1,000, his income in that period, plus $1,000, the amount saved, *plus* the interest earned on his savings. All of the combinations of first- and second-period budgets possible with a positive interest rate lie along constraint line B_2 in Figure 12–2. For comparison, we have also presented constraint line B_1 appropriate for a zero interest rate. The difference between the vertical intercepts of B_1 and B_2, $Y_2^P - Y_3^P$, is the interest charged if all period two's

FIGURE 12-2 The Effects of an Increase in Interest on Saving: Neutral Time Preference

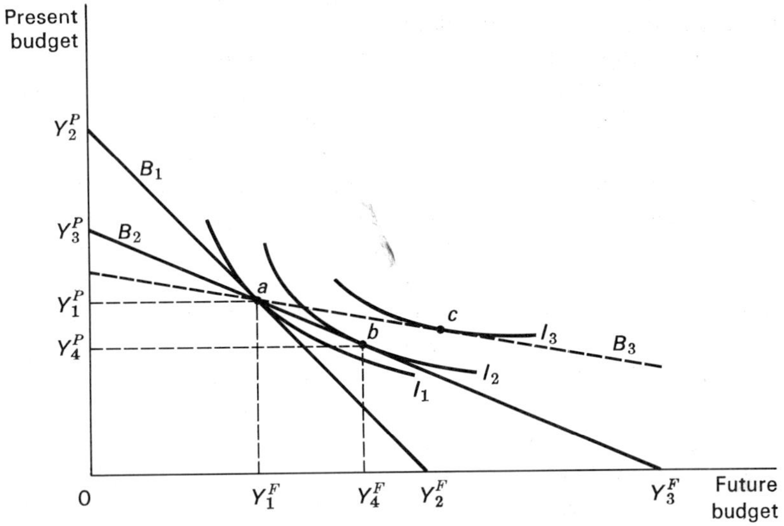

income is borrowed, and the difference between the horizontal intercepts of B_2 and B_1, $Y_3^Y - Y_2^F$, is the interest that would be earned on all of period one's income.[2] B_2 intersects B_1 at its midpoint, point a, since the consumer can always choose neither to borrow nor lend, in which case he will have Y_1^P available to budget in period one (that period's income) and a like amount, Y_1^F, to budget in period two.

We have shown in Figure 12-2 the indifference curves of a consumer with a neutral time preference for consumption; at a zero rate, I_1 is tangent to B_1 at point a and saving and borrowing are zero. But at a positive rate, the same consumer would choose the consumption combination at point b, the tangency point of B_2 and I_2. The consumer would save in period one, Y_1^P minus Y_4^P. The rise in interest rate from zero to a positive amount increases this consumer's saving in period one. However, if the interest rate rises again, we cannot be certain that he will increase his saving. For instance, if the constraint line rotates to the dashed line, B_3, due to a further increase in interest rate, the consumer would maximize utility with combination c. Consumption in period one will rise from what it was at point b, and saving will fall. The rise in interest rate, which is a fall in the price of future vis-à-vis present consump-

[2] The vertical intercept of B_2 is equal to $Y_1 - [Y_2/(1+r)]$, where Y_1 is the present year's income, Y_2 is next year's income, and r is the interest rate. The horizontal intercept is $Y_1(1+r) + Y_2$.

tion, has caused the consumer to *substitute* future for present consumption, but the income effect has caused him to increase present consumption. Obviously, the income effect of the rate change is greater than the substitution effect for this consumer and this particular rate change.

But what would happen if the interest rate rose from zero to a positive amount for an individual with a positive time preference? The case is illustrated in Figure 12–3. B_1 is the constraint line, assuming a zero rate of interest, and B_2 applies for a positive interest rate. Initially, the consumer maximizes utility with the first period–second period budget combination at point b. Since the amount budgeted for period one is Y_4^P, which is greater than income, Y_1^P, saving in period one is negative. The rise in interest rate rotates the constraint line to B_2, and the consumer's optimum combination changes from that at point b to that at c. At the new combination, first-period consumption has fallen to Y_5^P, and saving has risen from a negative amount, $Y_1^P - Y_4^P$ to a positive amount $Y_1^P - Y_5^P$. The interest rate increase has raised the individual's saving in period one. The change from point b to c has left the consumer's utility unchanged in our illustration since both points lie along I_1. It is possible, however, that the consumer might gain or lose utility as a result of the rate change. Moreover, any further rises in the interest rate may increase or decrease the individual's rate of saving depending on the strengths of income and substitution effects.

Our two models of consumer behavior have indicated that the rate of in-

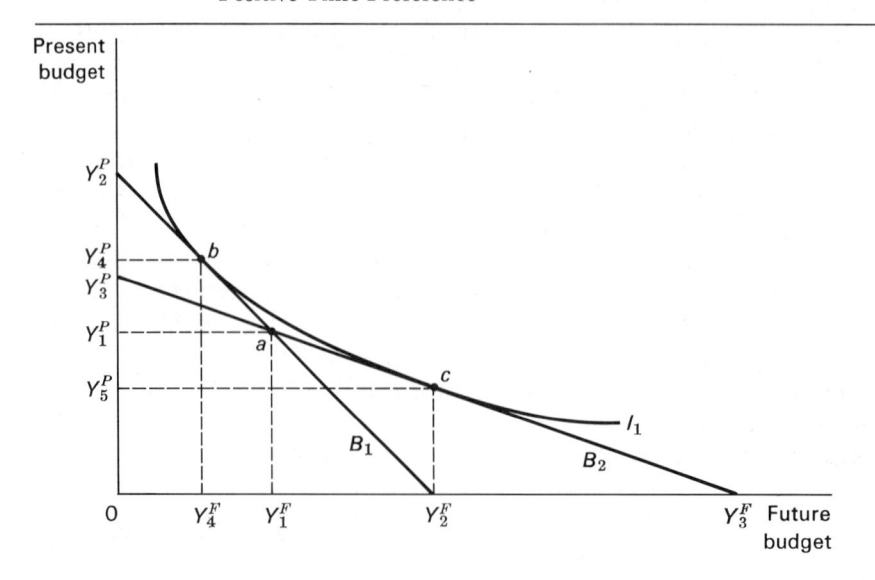

FIGURE 12–3 The Effects of an Increase in Interest on Saving: Positive Time Preference

terest is one of the determinants of consumer expenditures. In general, consumers with a positive or neutral time preference for consumption will exhibit an inverse relationship between consumption and the rate of interest and a direct relationship of interest to saving. It is left as an exercise at the end of the chapter for the student to show that an individual with a negative time preference for consumption may increase or decrease his consumption with a rise in interest from zero to a positive amount. In any case, our two-period models indicate that we must now expand our conception of consumer behavior to recognize that consumers seek to maximize utility *over time*. The interest rate is an important price in consumers' decision-making, because it determines how the consumer's lifetime earnings may be distributed over time. For each consumer, we may imagine a schedule showing the level of saving which will be forthcoming in any given period at different interest rates. And we may construct a schedule for an economy to show the volume of saving that would arise in the whole economic system at different rates, by summing the schedules of individual consumers.

The conclusion that the aggregate supply of savings is a simple summation of individual savings ought to be modified. People acquire with their savings titles to future consumption which eventually generate utility. In other words, savings, as well as the financial assets which people buy with their savings, eventually give savers utility. It may be easier to picture a consumer deciding at the margin whether to "spend" his last $18.75 on a pair of slacks or on a government savings bond. If he chooses the latter, it is because the discounted utility anticipated from spending the saving, plus interest, is greater than the present utility of the slacks. But the utility that any individual gets from saving may be affected by aggregation. The effects are similar to the aggregation effects mentioned earlier in our discussion of the aggregate market demand for commodities. Some individuals will be influenced by the bandwagon effect. Those people may try to increase their saving if they feel "everyone is saving" or decrease their saving to "keep up with the Joneses." Other individuals are influenced by the Veblen effect. If they have any way of letting the world know the size of their savings, and if savings are a superior good, those individuals will save more than they would otherwise. Still other people are subject to a snob effect. That group might try to buck what they see as a popular trend. If they feel that the popular attitude is to provide for the future by saving, the group subject to the snob effect might dissave, since saving would appear gauche to them precisely because it was the popular attitude. The point is that savings decisions of consumers are interdependent, so that aggregation could affect the saving curves of the individuals being aggregated.[3]

Although there may be considerable interdependence among savers, we

---

[3] See James S. Duesenberry, *Income, Saving and the Theory of Consumer Behavior* (New York: Oxford University Press, 1967).

may expect that most individuals' savings patterns will be governed by the objective of utility maximization over time and, since the interest rate is the principal economic variable that relates the present with the future, it will be an important force affecting peoples' savings decisions. In Figure 12–4, we have drawn the aggregate supply of savings as a positive function of the rate of interest for interest rates less than r_1. The curve is drawn inverse for higher rates, however, to indicate that supply of savings may be backbending, like a labor supply curve.

FIGURE 12–4 Aggregate Supply of Saving

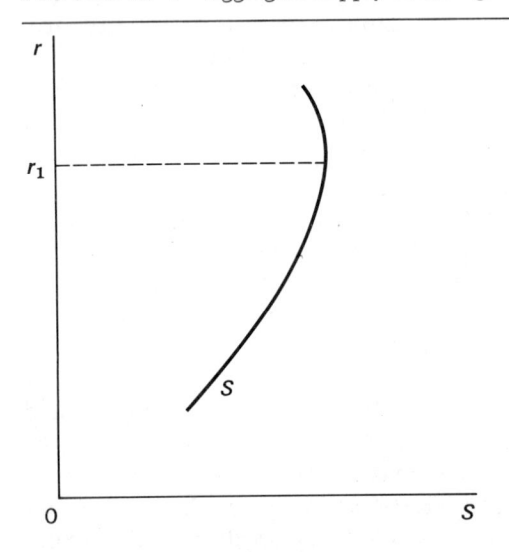

The Time Dimension and Firms' Investment

We have looked at the effects of changes in interest rates and changes in other factors on consumers' decisions to save. But what becomes of income that is not consumed? Suppose aggregate income is $1,000 and consumption $900, leaving $100 in saving. What form does the $100 saving take? It must be that some produced goods are "carried over" to be used in a subsequent period (not consumer services, since these cannot be stored). Such goods are called investment goods, and they add to the stock of capital in an economy, by increasing either the quantity of machines, equipment, buildings, or businesses' inventories. By not consuming all of an economy's income, consumers "release" resources for use in producing capital goods. Now we must investigate the demand side of the capital market to see what factors influence decisions to invest. We concentrate on the firm's decision-making process, assuming firms account for all investment in the economy, though a major proportion of investment in the United States is accounted for by consumers (that is, consumers' new home purchases).

The Demand for Investment

The Motive to Invest: Our task in this section is to isolate the principal factors influencing a firm's demand for new capital. Generally, firms demand capital because capital earns a return over its life that is greater than its original purchase price. Suppose a piece of capital, which never wears out, costs $1,000 and produces $100 of net income per year. Should the firm buy a machine which recovers its purchase price in 10 years, yet continues to produce? To simplify the problem, suppose the firm has no funds of its own but must borrow from others to get the $1,000 to buy the machine and that the interest rate is 20 percent. Then, if the firm borrows the $1,000, it must pay $200 in interest the first year and each year thereafter, if the principal is not reduced. But the machine only brings in $100 per year; so, obviously, its purchase will not be profitable. Notice that this conclusion is unchanged, even if the firm has its own funds. It would be more profitable to loan the funds to others at a 20 percent rate than invest in the machine.

Apparently, the firm's decision to purchase the machine or not turns on two factors: (1) the productivity of the machine and (2) the rate of interest. What is needed is a measure of the productivity of the machine that can be compared directly with the interest rate. One measure often used is variously called the *marginal efficiency of investment* or the *marginal productivity of investment*. For our perpetual machine, it is easy to compute for:

$$MEI = \frac{R}{P}, \tag{1}$$

where MEI is the marginal efficiency of investment, R, the perpetual annual return attributed to the machine (in excess of operating costs), and P, its purchase price. For our numerical illustration, $MEI = \$100/\$1,000 = .10$ or 10 percent. Now we can directly compare the rate of return on the machine with the interest rate. The firm would not borrow funds at a cost of 20 percent to purchase a machine which has an MEI of only 10 percent. On the other hand, if the rate of interest, i, drops to 5 percent, the firm would increase profits by borrowing $1,000 and purchasing the machine, since $MEI > i$.

In reality, the expected life of any capital investment is finite, and the annual expected returns of the investment over its life are likely to differ. In this case, the marginal efficiency of investment is defined by the formula:

$$P = \frac{R_1}{(1+MEI)} + \frac{R_2}{(1+MEI)^2} + \frac{R_3}{(1+MEI)^3} + \cdots + \frac{R_n}{(1+MEI)^n}, \tag{2}$$

where R_j is the expected annual receipts in year j, less expected operating costs, but including depreciation; n is the number of years the capital is expected to produce; P is the purchase price of the asset; and MEI is its rate of return or the marginal efficiency of investment. If the annual R's are equal and continue indefinitely, the formula reduces to $P = R/MEI$, the one used for the perpetual machine. But since the R's may differ and eventually become zero as capital wears out, the formula is more complicated. MEI is the rate of discount that equates the expected annual returns over the life of a capital asset to its purchase price. In other words, the MEI is the rate of return over operating cost that an investor anticipates earning on an investment over its expected life. The MEI concept, developed by Irving Fisher and J. M. Keynes, has proved a useful analytical device for measuring the anticipated return on invested capital.

Ranking Investment Projects. Typically, a firm may have under consideration a number of investment opportunities, each yielding a different MEI. Perhaps it has several proposed projects that are very promising, and thus have high expected MEI's, and additional projects in mind with lower anticipated returns. In general, however, diminishing returns will accompany an increase in investment in an activity. For instance, as investment is increased in a given industry, the price of investment goods is apt to rise, and a glance at the formulas above indicates that this lowers the MEI. Furthermore, the increased output associated with expansion will lower output prices, and this reduces MEI. There simply is not an unlimited number of high-yielding investment opportunities available to a firm.

The firm will likely consider some scheme for ranking its proposed investment projects, and there are three generally recognized techniques for accomplishing this—payback, present value, and MEI.

1. Under the payback method, the firm determines the number of years required to recover the original cost of an investment. For the perpetual machine this will be ten years. The shorter the payback period, the higher the rank given a project. The payback method suffers from two main weaknesses: (1) it disregards income that may be earned after the payback period, and (2) it fails to discount future earnings; that is, it fails to recognize that a dollar received today is more valuable than a dollar to be received next year.

2. The present value approach may be used when management knows the interest rate it must pay for investment funds. The present value of a project is determined by the formula:

$$A = \frac{R_1}{(1+i)} + \frac{R_2}{(1+i)^2} + \frac{R_3}{(1+i)^3} + \cdots + \frac{R_N}{(1+i)^N}, \quad (3)$$

where A is the present value of the asset, R_j is the return over operating cost expected to be earned in year j, and i is the interest rate which the firm must pay for borrowed funds. The subscripts 1, 2, 3, . . . N represent the years in which the investment project yields a return. Notice that this formula, like that for MEI, specifically recognizes that capital assets wear out eventually. Notice also that the increasing size of the denominator in each more remote year reduces the present value of that expected return. A dollar expected many years hence is not worth so much now. The firm may rank its investment opportunities in descending order according to their present value.

3. The final approach, and the one that we will employ, simply ranks investment projects according to their respective MEI's as determined by formula (2). Applying the formula to each potential investment project allows management to determine its rate of return, and once the rate of return is determined for each project, all can be ranked in descending order. The resulting ranking should match the ranking derived from the present value approach, if the same assumptions hold in both cases. Of course, in either case, the MEI's computed represent only an approximation based upon management's *expectations* about the returns to capital. The future dollar returns attributed to a piece of capital can never be known with certainty; they can only be estimated.

Using the third approach, a firm generates a collection of investment levels and MEI's, which can then be plotted in a graph like that of Figure 12–5. Curve MEI is the firm's investment schedule. If I_1 dollars are invested, the MEI will be r_1; if I_2 dollars are invested, the MEI will fall to r_2. Notice that the MEI curve shows the return on the *marginal* dollar invested. The average return on an investment of, say, I_2 dollars will be higher, since the MEI is higher for all dollars invested below I_2. Now we can determine the level of investment that will be undertaken by the firm at different interest rates. To begin, supose the market rate of interest, i_2, is equal to r_2 and that the capital market is perfectly competitive, so that the supply of funds is perfectly elastic

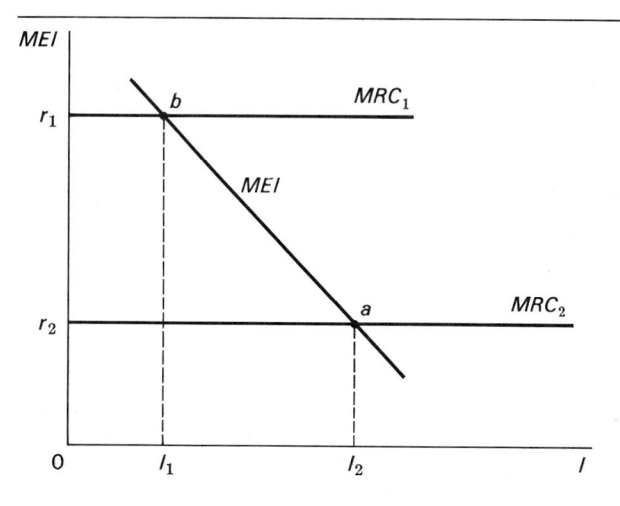

FIGURE 12–5 The Profit-Maximizing Level of Investment of the Firm Using Marginal Efficiency of Investment and Marginal Resource Cost Schedules

to the firm. Then the horizontal line, MRC_2, is the firm's marginal resource cost curve expressed as a percentage. The firm will find it profitable to expand its investment so long as $MEI > r_2$. All investment projects out to I_2 dollars will be undertaken, but no more, since beyond I_2 the MEI's would be less than the marginal cost of loanable funds. If the interest rate rises to r_1, the firm's marginal resource cost curve will shift up to MRC_1, and the firm will contract its investment to I_1. In effect, MEI is the firm's investment demand curve.

Aggregate Investment Demand. By summing the MEI curves of all firms, we may derive an aggregate investment demand schedule. Of course, we must allow for the possibility that the summation process will not be consistent with the *ceteris paribus* assumption made in the derivation of the separate MEI curves, as we have noted before, and for the possibility that some firms are not perfectly competitive. But if these qualifications are accepted, we can conceive of an MEI schedule for the economy as a whole, which shows the levels of aggregate investment that will be undertaken at different interest rates. It will generally be a downward sloping curve, reflecting the inverse relation between investment levels and interest.

Savings and Investment

In Figure 12–6, we have combined the aggregate supply of savings and demand for investment schedules. At interest rate $r_1 = i_1$ and savings level $S_1 = I_1$, the savings intentions of savers are in equality with the investment plans of firms. Excess supply and demand are zero, thus the interest rate is an

FIGURE 12–6 Saving-Investment Equilibrium

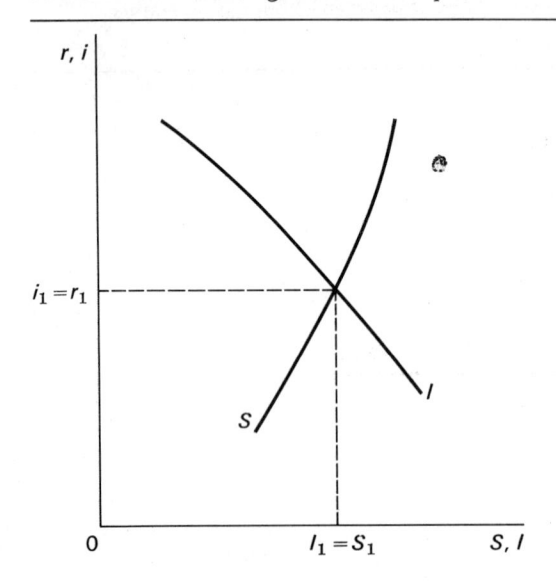

equilibrium one. It is tempting to leave the theory of the interest rate at this point, since we have a complete model of interest rate determination. This "completeness" is only apparent, however. The model which we have presented, called the *classical theory of interest*, is only a first approximation to a general interest theory. In many cases, it is not efficient as a predictive tool, because it does not include a number of other variables that also influence the rate of interest. Our task now is to indicate the nature of the refinements needed to make the theory a more useful predictive device.

We ordinarily think of interest as payment on *loans*, not rented real capital. The interest rate, then, may be defined as the rate of return on loans made in the financial capital market, and a complete theory of interest must relate savings–investment equilibrium to capital market equilibrium. There cannot be a savings–investment interest rate greater than the capital market rate if there is to be a "general" equilibrium. There must be one rate, which makes the excess supply and demand for savings and investment zero and the excess supply and demand for loanable funds zero as well. The *loanable funds* theory of interest attempts an extension and refinement of simple classical interest theory by focusing upon the aggregate supply and demand schedules for loanable funds. Saving is the major source of supply and investment the major source of demand; but the loanable funds theory makes no particular distinction as to whether loans are made to finance investment, consumption, or anything else. The loanable funds theory is a theory of the rate of interest in financial markets. One advantage of loanable funds theory is that it incorporates the role of the banking system as a source of new funds for lending.

If we view the interest rate as the marginal return on assets, whether real or financial, then the interest rate on all such assets must in equilibrium be equal. For if capital markets are competitive, competition will cause the marginal efficiencies of all assets to be equal. One asset cannot earn a higher return than another, for increased demand for the first and decreased demand for the second will raise the price of the first and lower its yield and lower price on the second and raise its yield until the rates are equal. For a general equilibrium, the interest rate on real assets must equal the interest rate on financial assets. Of course, interest rate differences will always arise due to different risks of assets. But general equilibrium requires that the interest rate (adjusted for risk) be an equilibrium one in every market for which there is a two-way influence.

It is one thing to state the requisites for an equilibrium interest rate, but quite another to describe the adjustment mechanisms which come into play when there is disequilibrium. When we discussed the equilibrating mechanism in commodity or resource markets, we were reasonably justified in assuming that the adjustments that take place in other sectors would not unduly upset our conclusions. In other words, the *ceteris paribus* assumption seemed a valid simplification in most of the models we discussed. But we cannot be so confident with the *ceteris paribus* assumption when we investigate the forces determining the interest rate. To illustrate, suppose there is an excess demand for investment goods over saving at the prevailing interest rate. This will tend to raise the interest rate and decrease the quantity of investment. But the decrease in investment may lower aggregate income, which will in turn have an effect on people's saving rates. This will shift the aggregate savings supply schedule. In other words, the saving supply and investment demand schedules are interdependent. This greatly complicates the problem of finding an equilibrium interest rate with the partial equilibrium tools of supply and demand.

And interdependence is just the beginning of the complications. Another arises due to the effects of the *flow* of investment on the *stock* of capital. At the prevailing interest rate, saving and investment rates may be in balance. But if investment adds progressively to the stock of capital, raising the ratio of capital to other resources, the rate of return on capital must "eventually" fall, an application of the law of diminishing returns propounded by Karl Marx. Some economists distinguish, therefore, between short-term equilibrium of the flow of saving and investment and long-term equilibrium of an economy's stock of capital.

We have indicated the main forces which affect consumers' decisions to save and firms' decisions to invest, and some of the complications that arise in a general theory of interest. It is beyond the scope of this text to explore the subject further. In fact, the reader will find that the theory of interest is one of the bridges between microeconomics and macroeconomics. Macroeconomics builds upon micro principles of interest rate determination to show how the interest rate affects the over-all level of resource use in an economy.

PROFITS

We have saved until last our consideration of profits, largely because there is no general theory of profits acceptable to all economists. In fact, marked differences exist in the way economists have approached the theory of profits, reflected in their definitions of profits and the economic functions ascribed to profits. As a consequence, several different theories of profit prevail. However, these are not altogether conflicting, and each theory makes a contribution to our understanding of the role of profits in the economy.

Economic Profits in Competition

As you will recall from our discussion of competitive markets in Chapter 7, economic profits may be realized by firms in the short run, if the selling price of output, though equal to the marginal cost of production, is above each firm's average cost. Although profits may exist in short-run competitive equilibrium, payment to all productive factors is, nevertheless, equal to the marginal product of each factor. Furthermore, short-run competitive profits perform a useful function. For, given time, they induce firms to enter a competitive industry, increasing supply and decreasing price. Eventually, after a sufficient number of firms have entered the industry, firms' profits will be erased. Economic profits in competition, therefore, perform two functions: (1) an incentive function—they induce firms to enter an industry and (2) an allocative function—the short-run appearance of profits causes resources to flow into those industries experiencing increased demand and out of those industries for which demand is relatively less. Therefore, in competitive industries, profits are a transitory phenomenon and disappear in the long run.

Profits as a Symptom of Market Imperfections

Another view is that profits arise because of market imperfections. In this view, profits are not a flow to a factor of production for services rendered and, consequently, perform no incentive function, as do wages and interest. Nor do profits perform an allocative function if they persist through time, as the following discussion will show.

How can a firm receive a money payment in excess of the opportunity cost of the resources it employs? We discovered in Chapters 8 and 9 that the answer lies in the nature of the market in which the firm operates. Profits cannot occur in an industry for any appreciable time if perfectly competitive conditions exist; however, profits can occur, even in long-run equilibrium, if firms are able to exploit monopoly power. Such profits are restricted, therefore, principally to monopolies and oligopolies, and represent a "reward" for restricting output. Monopoly profits are inefficient for two reasons: (1) They result in an inefficient distribution of income, because the monopolistic firm receives a return over and above all economic costs of production, providing the firm's owners with a claim on the current output of the economy in excess of their contribution to that output. The firm's owners gain, therefore, at the expense of others in the economy. (2) The existence of economic profits means consumers favor an increase in the output of the monopolized industry, just as in the short-run competitive case. However, the essence of monopoly is exclusion of other firms from the industry. Though the existence of economic profits may attract new resources into the industry, resources are precluded from entry because of one or more of the barriers to entry discussed in Chapter 8. Thus, monopoly profits are a sign of misallocation of the economy's resources.

Other Theories of Profits

Still other views of profits might be taken. For example, profits that cannot be ascribed to any visible factor of production have been ascribed by some economists, most notably the eminent Harvard economist Joseph Schumpeter to effective enterprise or to successful innovation.

According to this third theory, profits are beneficial. They reward those individuals who are not only imaginative and forward-looking, but also willing to bear the risks of developing new products and production methods. Profits are, therefore, the motive force behind successful economic change, since firms are innovative in the hope of gaining profits. Thus, profits might be viewed as a return to entrepreneurs, and entrepreneurship becomes a fourth factor of production. There is some negative evidence favoring this concept of profits as a return to invisible but, nevertheless, productive factors. The evidence is provided by studies of the determinants of economic growth. For when the contributions to growth of the various identifiable factors of production are summed, they fall short of actual growth in the economy. That is, a portion of economic growth remains unaccounted for.

Some economists theorize that profits might play a positive role in an economy, even if they are generated by monopoly elements, because profits allow a firm to engage in research and development activities that lead to the discovery of new products and more efficient ways of producing existing products. Only firms realizing a positive surplus over all costs will have funds available for research and development. Moreover, according to these theorists, only monopolists or oligopolists have the incentive to engage in research and development activities. Competitive firms will not only lack funds for research, but will also lack the incentive for R and D expenditures, because any new discoveries regarding either new production methods or new products would, under competitive conditions, become available to all firms in the industry. Thus, a single competitive firm would not be willing to bear the costs of R and D, if any benefits generated thereby become available to all. Following this view, firms that are profitable are the main sources of new products and improvements in productive technique.

Since there is a lack of consensus regarding the nature and role of profits in the economy, it is entirely possible that each separate theory is at least partly true. They are not necessarily mutually exclusive. All three types of profits could exist simultaneously in an economy, and probably do. The different types of profits should, however, be identified for purposes of establishing public policies designed to improve economic efficiency and social welfare.

PROBLEMS

1. Refer to the figure and answer the following:
    (a) If the vertical intercept OA equals the horizontal intercept OB of constraint line AB, the interest rate must be _____.
    (b) The interest rate associated with constraint line CD is (greater than, less than) that of AB.
    (c) If AB is the constraint line, then consumer saving is _____.
    (d) If CD is the constraint line, then consumer saving is _____.
    (e) A rise in interest rate has caused an (increase, decrease) in saving from _____ to _____.

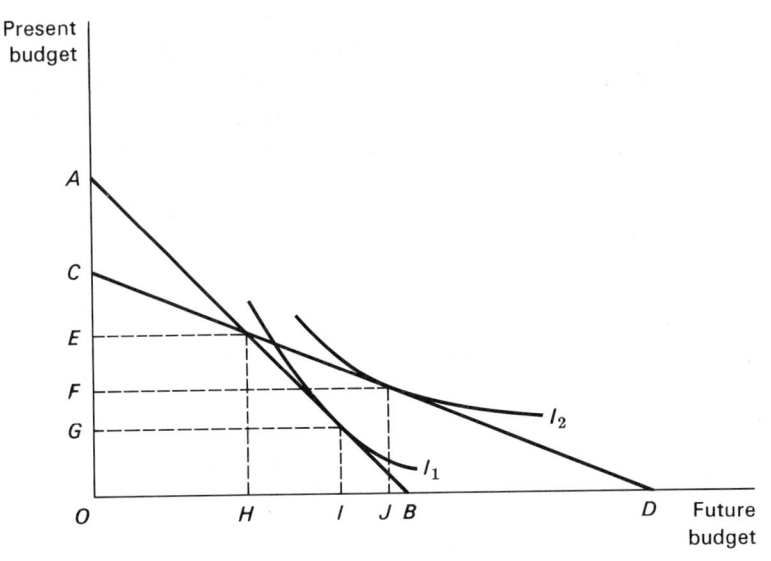

2. Answer the following based on the corresponding diagram.
   (a) If AB is a zero interest constraint line, the consumer must have a (positive, negative, neutral) time preference for consumption.
   (b) Constraint line CD must be for a (positive, zero, negative) interest rate.
   (c) This consumer (increases, decreases, neither increases nor decreases) his saving with a rise in interest above zero.

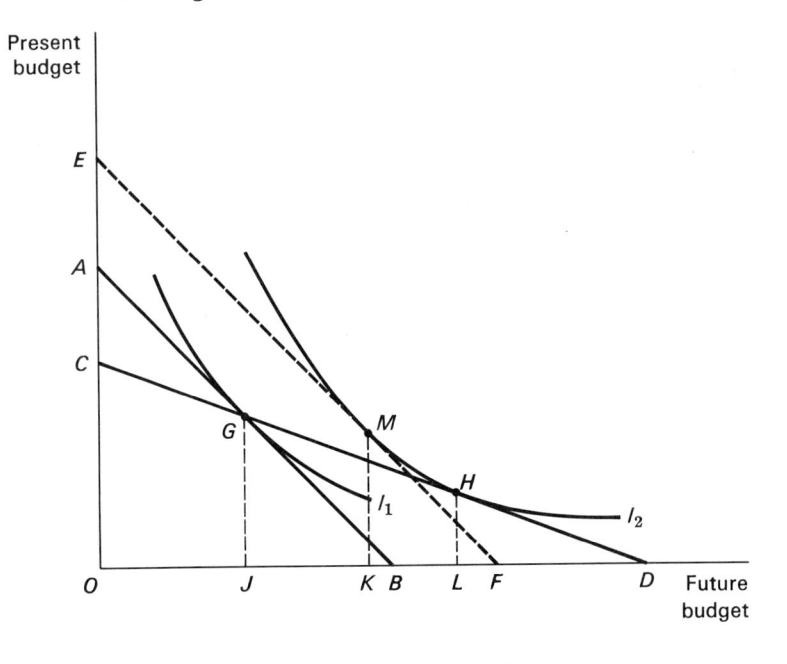

(d) If the consumer is at equilibrium at point H and interest falls to zero, his new combination of present and future budgets will be at point _____ representing (less, more, the same) utility as before.
(e) We remove the income effects of the rate change in d (above) by shifting constraint line AB out to the dotted EF. The consumer would then choose the combination at point _____.
(f) The substitution effect of the rate change is represented by the shift from point _____ to point _____.
(g) The income effect of the rate change is represented by the shift from point _____ to point _____.
3. Suppose a firm is expecting to receive from one of its investment projects $11,000 in one year. How much is this worth to the firm now, if the interest rate is 5 percent?
4. A consol is a bond which pays an annual sum in perpetuity. Suppose a consol pays $1,500 annually and costs $20,000. What is its yield? If the interest rate changes to 30 percent, what will this consol sell for?

REFERENCES

Fisher, I., *The Theory of Interest*. New York: The Macmillan Co., 1930.

Friedman, M., *Price Theory*. Chicago: Aldine, 1962.

Hicks, John R., *Value and Capital*, 2nd ed. Oxford, England: The Clarendon Press, 1946. Chapters 1–2.

Hirshleifer, J., "On the Theory of Optimal Investment Decision," *Journal of Political Economy*, August 1958.

Knight, Frank H., *Risk, Uncertainty, and Profit*. Boston: Houghton Mifflin Company, 1921, 94–104.

Modigliani, F., and Miller, M. H., "The Cost of Capital Corporation Finance and the Theory of Investment," *American Economic Review*, June 1958.

Solomon, Ezra, "Measuring a Company's Cost of Capital," *Journal of Business*, October 1955.

Solow, Robert M., "The Production Function and the Theory of Capital," *Review of Economic Studies*, 23 (1955–1956), 101–108.

APPENDIX TO CHAPTER 12

The Optimum Lifetime Distribution of Consumption Expenditures

LESTER C. THUROW*

Using the Bureau of Labor Statistics' *Survey of Consumer Expenditures and Income in 1960–61*, Thurow develops an estimate of the pattern of distribution of lifetime income desired by families, and compares this to the actual time distribution of income. He finds that people would prefer to have their highest income in the years 20 to 35 rather than between 40 and 55, but are prohibited from distributing their income optimally through time because of institutional rigidities in the capital market; for instance, lenders are reluctant to lend because of the high risks of expected future earnings. He suggests that public policy be directed toward removing the institutional rigidities in order to increase social welfare.

The actual lifetime distribution of consumption expenditures may have little relation to the optimum lifetime distribution. Individuals can easily redistribute consumption into the future by saving, but they cannot easily borrow for present consumption. The high risks associated with expected earnings make borrowing difficult. Without slavery there is no effective way to mortgage expected future earnings. Consequently the current flow of income rather than the total lifetime flow of income may dominate current consumption expenditures. The individual is unable to optimize his distribution of consumption expenditures.

The importance of the institutional constraints upon lifetime redistribution depends upon how much individuals wish to redistribute consumption expenditures away from their actual income stream. For the average person con-

From the *American Economic Review*, Vol. 59, No. 1 (June 1969). Reprinted by permission.

* The author is an associate professor of economics and management at the Massachusetts Institute of Technology. The ideas for this paper were developed while working on a project at the NBER. The author would like to thank the anonymous referee for his excellent comments. The remaining errors are those of the author.

sumption and expenditures move closely together (see Figure 1), but this may not be by choice.[1] Since there is no a priori method to determine the optimum distribution of consumption, this paper develops an empirical technique for estimating the optimum lifetime distribution of consumption expenditures.

FIGURE 1   Average Money Income After Taxes and Expenditures for Current Consumption

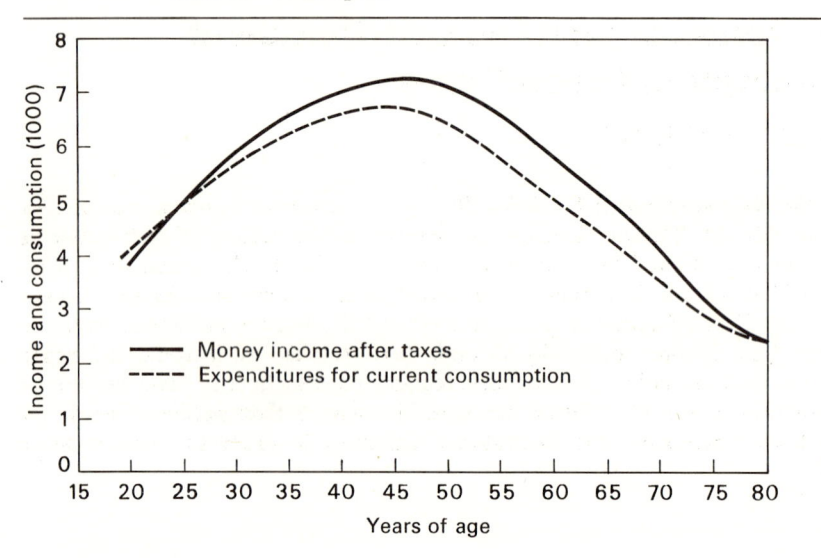

I. THE THEORY

Given an expected lifetime budget constraint, an individual maximizing utility will arrange his lifetime consumption pattern in accordance with the well-known Fisherian conditions (see Equation 1).[2]

$$\frac{MU_c^i}{MU_c^j} = (1 + r_1 - r_2)^{j-i}, \tag{1}$$

where:

MU_c^i = marginal utility of consumption in year i
MU_c^j = marginal utility of consumption in year j
r_1 = market rate of interest between years i and j
r_2 = individual rate of time preference between years i and j

[1] All data in this paper come from the U.S. Department of Labor, Bureau of Labor Statistics, *Survey of Consumer Expenditures, 1960–61. Consumer Expenditures and Income Cross-Classification of Family Characteristics, Urban United States,* Supp. 2—Part A to BLS Report, July 1964.
[2] Fisherian conditions assume that the individual is neutral with respect to risk and that he can estimate his expected lifetime income.

The ratios of the marginal utilities of consumption in any two years must be equal to the individual's personal discount differential, $(1 + r_1 - r_2)^{j-i}$.[3] The personal discount differential is composed of two elements, the market rate of interest (r_1) and the individual's subjective rate of time preference (r_2). If the personal discount differential is one $(r_1 - r_2 = 0)$, the utility maximizer will arrange his consumption pattern to make the marginal utility of consumption equal in each year. Such procedures maximize expected lifetime utility, but they do not necessarily lead to equal consumption in all periods.

An individual may have a varying positive or negative rate of time preference. If he prefers to consume goods and services while young, his rate of time preference is positive. Enjoyment may also fluctuate over a lifetime rather than being a smooth function of time, but the higher the rate of time preference and the lower the market rate of interest between any two years, the more consumption will occur in the earlier year.

Consumption will also be higher in those years where the marginal utility of consumption expenditures is higher. Needs differ over the course of a lifetime.[4] Consumption of medical services rises at particular times of life; expenditures on children occur while an individual is raising his family. Education expenditures may be high when young and again when children are being educated. Other expenditures are lumpy. Durable goods purchases are large when setting up a household. If these goods are to be enjoyed, they must be purchased in a limited period of time.

If individuals save only for future consumption,[5] positive savings indicate that the individual wishes to transfer some of his income from present consumption to future consumption. Negative savings indicate that the individual wishes to transfer consumption from the future to the present. If a person is neither dissaving or saving, he has reached his desired consumption level given his personal discount differential and his consumption preferences.

As mentioned there are institutional constraints on dissaving. They are not absolute, however. Dissaving is severely limited but not prevented.[6] Consequently empirical observations on dissaving cannot indicate how much the individual would like to dissave, but they do indicate that the individual is not at his desired consumption level. He wishes to consume more than his current income allows. Individuals will continue to dissave as their income rises until current income equals desired current consumption. Thus if it were

---

[3] In the standard expression of the Fisherian conditions, the subjective rate of time preference affects the marginal utility of income schedules rather than appearing explicitly. Consequently the marginal utility of income schedule for any year depends on the year from which it is being viewed. This is not the case under the formulation in Equation (1). The marginal utility of income schedule in any year is invariant to the year from which it is being viewed. The influence of time preference appears explicitly.
[4] A rising probability of death may reduce the utility of consumption while elderly, if the individual is a risk averter.
[5] In this paper, future consumption is assumed to be the only motive for saving.
[6] In every age group there are substantial amounts of dissaving at low income levels.

possible to estimate the income at which an individual becomes a zero saver for each year of his life, it would be possible to determine his optimum lifetime distribution of consumption.

Individuals undoubtedly differ, but consumer expenditure and income surveys make it possible to determine the income at which the average person in a particular age group neither saves nor dissaves. Using these surveys it is possible to determine the average desired lifetime distribution of consumption expenditures. The technique, however, has several limitations or problems.

1. Using cross section data, the actual average lifetime income does not equal the lifetime income calculated by summing the income levels at which savings are zero. If the lifetime distribution of income is independent of the absolute level of lifetime income, the problem can be solved by scaling consumption expenditures at each age up or down by a constant fraction so that they sum to the actual average lifetime income. With this assumption the marginal utility of consumption may still depend upon total consumption, but the ratios of consumption at different points in a lifetime are assumed to be independent of lifetime income. The proportion of total consumption spent in any one year is assumed to remain constant as total consumption varies. This may be untrue. A higher lifetime income, for example, may lead to a more than proportionate increase in education expenditures (and total expenditures) while young. For lack of a better assumption, a constant scaling fraction is used in the following empirical analysis. Some empirical evidence for this assumption is presented in footnote 14.

2. Using cross section data assumes that individuals in older age brackets are similar in all relevant aspects with those in younger age brackets. This is obviously not true. The average older individual has a lower lifetime income than the average young person. Ignoring this factor biases the results toward too much consumption in the early years of an individual's lifetime since it is assumed that the young will consume the same amounts when elderly as the current elderly. In all probability they will consume more since they have a higher lifetime income. There may be other systematic differences which affect consumption patterns. Education may differ, time preferences may differ, etc. These factors bias the results, but the direction of the bias cannot be determined theoretically.

3. If total dissaving as well as the annual increments to dissaving are limited, savings may occur to repay previous debts even though the individual would like to continue dissaving. Thus a position of zero savings would not indicate a position of equilibrium. This would bias the results towards too little consumption while young. Empirically this possibility does not seem to be an acute problem. Individuals are increasing assets rather than reducing liabilities at the point where they become zero savers.

4. Individuals within the same age group are not homogeneous. Different individuals may have very different patterns of income. Laborers reach an in-

come plateau much earlier than professional workers. Thus it may be possible to have an income class composed of laborers with balanced budgets while higher income classes are dissaving because they are composed of professional workers. This would bias the results toward too little consumption while young. Empirically there are no age groups with double points of equilibrium or where savings decline as income increases, but there may be some biases in this direction.

5. The income class with zero saving in aggregate may be composed of individuals who are either large savers or dissavers. They simply cancel each other. The dissaving of professional workers with higher lifetime incomes and more slowly rising incomes could exactly balance the saving of laborers with lower lifetime incomes and faster rising incomes. In this case the average optimum lifetime distribution of consumption might not look like the optimum distribution of consumption for any actual person. It is simply a weighted average of two distinct curves where the weights depend not only on the numbers of individuals but their relative incomes. If laboring income is higher relative to professional income while young, the results will be biased toward too little consumption while young and too much consumption while elderly.[7]

6. The procedure assumes that the lifetime utility function has annual utility levels as its sole arguments. In addition the annual utilities are assumed to be independent and additive. Consumption in year one is assumed not to affect the utility of consumption in year two. If there are complementarities between consumption at different points in time, it is impossible to compare individuals at different points of time unless they have the same history of previous and future consumption.

7. Since goods need not be totally consumed in the year in which they are purchased, the procedure estimates the optimum distribution of consumption expenditures and not the optimum distribution of consumption.

8. Given optimum consumption expenditures in any two years, it is not possible to separate the effects of the personal discount differential and differences in the marginal utilities of income. There are many combinations of marginal utilities and personal discount differentials that are compatible with the estimated equilibrium.

II. THE DATA

The Bureau of Labor Statistics' *Survey of Consumer Expenditures and Income in 1960–61* provides the data base. Since there are errors in the BLS survey any systematic over- or under-reporting for different age groups of either income or consumption expenditures will bias the results.

---

[7] An alternative, if the sample were larger, is to find the central tendency of all those families with balanced budgets.

536   The Theory of Distribution

Two definitions of zero savings are used.[8] In the first, savings are zero when expenditures for current consumption equal money income after taxes. In the second, savings are zero when expenditures for current consumption plus gifts and contributions plus personal insurance payments equal money income after taxes.

The second definition was used for two reasons. (1) Positive consumption benefits are derived from being able to provide gifts and contributions to family members, friends, and charities. Benefits may also vary over the lifetime of an individual. Consequently gifts might be considered consumption expenditures. (2) No allowance has yet been made for risk and uncertainty. If risk and uncertainty differ systematically by age, the marginal utilities of income might not be equal at the point where consumption equals income. At different ages the individual must be making provisions for different amounts of risk. Risk may lead to a need for liquid assets and the consequent depression of consumption expenditures. There is no a priori method to determine when risk is highest. Risks may be higher when old since the probability of death and sickness is higher, but they might equally well be higher when young since fewer assets have been accumulated and there are more dependents who would suffer for a longer period of time.

To the extent that insurance premiums are not savings but are payments for pure insurance designed to eliminate the effects of risk and uncertainty, insurance premiums are consumption expenditures to reduce risk and uncertainty. If the insurance market is in equilibrium, including insurance premiums in consumption expenditures should correct for differences in risk at different ages.[9]

III. THE RESULTS

Using the first definition of zero saving, a desired distribution of consumption emerges which is quite different from the actual distribution of income (see optimum distribution #1, Figure 2).[10] If the family head lives from age 19 to 80, the average family has a lifetime income of $342,246 in 1960–61. The average family prefers to redistribute $30,242 into the years between 19

---

[8] Linear interpolation was used to find the precise point of equilibrium and free hand interpolation was used to interpolate optimum consumption curves between the midpoints of income classes.

[9] If the proportions of observed insurance premiums that are pure insurance and the proportion that are savings vary over a lifetime, this will bias the results toward too much consumption in years with a greater than average amount of insurance savings.

[10] Since potential dissavings is small and all income is not actually consumed the optimum distributions of consumption will be compared with the actual distribution of income. The distribution of income is a good estimate of potential consumption possibilities.

FIGURE 2 Actual and Optimal Distributions of Income for Urban Families

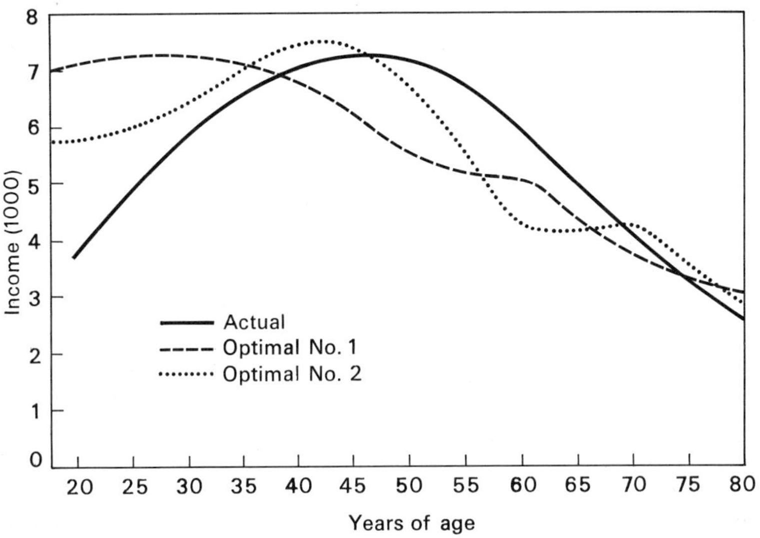

——— Actual
---- Optimal No. 1
········ Optimal No. 2

Income (1000)
Years of age

and 35 and $1560 into the years between 75 and 80 by borrowing from the years between 35 and 75.[11] Instead of having its highest income years between 40 and 55 years of age, the average family prefers to have its highest income years between 20 and 35 years of age. Possible reasons are not hard to find. During the 20 to 35 age period, the family is faced with problems of raising a family and building up its stock of consumers durables. Enjoyment of consumption goods may also be highest in these years.

The second definition of zero savings provides a slightly different optimum consumption curve (see optimum distribution #2). The average family prefers to redistribute $18,134 into the years between 19 and 46, and $3484 into the years between 69 and 80. The total amount of redistribution falls from $31,802 under the first set of assumptions to $21,618 under the second. Less is desired in the early years; more is desired in the later years. Allowing for risks, uncertainty, and gifts leads to relatively less need for income between 19 and 35 and relatively more need between 35 and 46 and between 69 and 75.[12]

[11] In terms of time preference, there is a positive rate of time preference between the ages 19–35 and the ages 35–75, and a negative rate of time preference between the ages 35–75 and the ages 75–80. These rates of time preference, however, are not based on a zero rate of interest. They reflect the rates of interest actually existing in the economy in 1960–61.
[12] Since there is a substantial amount of insurance savings and since the proportion probably rises with age, these results are probably much closer together than the numbers would indicate.

IV. THE CONCLUSIONS

Both sets of assumptions yield the same basic conclusions. Families desire a substantial amount of lifetime income redistribution over and above that done in 1960–61 and this redistribution is heavily weighted toward the younger years of a family's life.[13,14] The actual lifetime pattern of income is a severe constraint on the desired lifetime distribution of consumption expenditures. Based on the results of this analysis, lifetime welfare levels might be substantially increased if the constraints on lifetime income redistribution could be lifted. Consequently social planners should investigate methods of eliminating the institutional constraints.

Perhaps proposals like the educational opportunity bank ought to be expanded to permit loans for current consumption expenditures other than education. Consumption loans could be secured through incurring a liability to pay a higher income tax rate until repayment is made. Only a governmental institution such as the educational opportunity bank can provide a method of securing expected future earnings as collateral and be large enough to eliminate the risks associated with the large variance in the income distribution of any particular group. As a second best solution, the Social Security system might be expanded to include children's allowances. Children's allowances are ineffective instruments to eliminate poverty, but they do redistribute income into the age brackets that want it. Alternatively, tax rates might be made to vary with age.

---

[13] This conclusion might be modified if there were systematic differences in inherited wealth by age group. Greater wealth would lead to higher consumption. Although wealth is a possible source of bias, it should not be important. The survey contains no information on wealth, but it was supposedly drawn to avoid such problems.

[14] The two definitions of zero saving make it possible to provide some information to substantiate the assumption that the ratios of consumption expenditures are independent of total lifetime consumption. With the first definition of consumption, a lifetime income of $254,946 is necessary to insure that money income after taxes equals expenditures for current consumption at each point in time. With the second definition of consumption an income of $423,621 is necessary. Since the actual average lifetime income in the survey was $342,246, annual consumption expenditures are scaled up under the first definition and down under the second. Since both definitions indicate that families desire substantial amounts of lifetime income redistribution and that this redistribution is heavily weighted toward the younger years, these qualitative results are invariant with respect to whether the results are scaled up or down. Thus the central conclusions only depend on the assumption that the distribution of consumption changes monotonically between income levels of $254,946 and $423,621. Within this constraint ratios may vary without altering the qualitative conclusions.

Student Finance in Higher Education
STEPHEN MERRETT[1]

In the text, we defined capital as nonhuman in character, but only as a pedagogical convenience. In fact, since humans generate income streams just as machines do, we might generalize our concept to consider the rate of return on human capital. Stephen Merrett does just this in his effort to devise an efficient scheme of finance in higher education. Educational expenditures are essentially investments in human capital and should optimally be carried to the point where the rate of return on education matches the interest rate. Difficulties arise because students do not usually have perfect access to the capital market and, thus, public financial aids are typically set up as supplements. The student will find particularly interesting Merrett's proposed meritocratic system of financing higher education.

The object of this paper is to arrive at a set of principles for governments to adopt in directing the money flows reciprocating the cost and benefit streams of higher education. The results of adopting these principles would be to make present systems both more efficient and more equitable. The methodology I shall employ is unusual: it is a form of comparative statics in which the initial difference between two economies, or a single economy in two time periods, is not an economic phenomenon such as a difference in tastes or a change in the rate of growth of population, but rather it is a dissimilarity in their political structures. The manufacture of human capital is examined in two idealised polities, which for want of better words are called capitalist and socialist.

First, the process of education is described in a highly stylised fashion. A number of factors of production, including land, buildings, teaching staff and of particular importance the "primary labour unit," the student, are integrated over a certain gestation period to produce a bundle of physical and intellectual skills to be known as the "machine." Once construction is completed, the

From *The Economic Journal* of the Royal Economic Society, Vol. LXVII, No. 306 (June 1967). Reprinted by permission.

[1] The first draft of this paper was written during 1965, when the author was a Research Fellow of the Institute of International Education at the Centro de Investigaciónes Económicas of the Instituto Torcuato di Tella in Buenos Aires. I am grateful to Oscar Braun, Robert Ferber, Michael Kaser and Fred Stephenson for their comments on that draft. All value judgments and any errors of analysis are entirely the responsibility of the author.

"machine" is indissolubly associated in a spatio-temporal sense with the "primary labour unit," and is rented out to the economy for the rest of its working life.

In the capitalistic society all capital, whether human or physical, is privately owned, and "machines" are owned only by their respective "primary labour units." Higher education is a commodity and, like all other commodities, is freely bought and sold. The young student draws his funds from the following sources: familial financial support; familial real income support, such as free food and lodgings; self-finance from part-time work and vacation earnings; finally, loans from the banking system. Additionally, he will in his entrepreneurial role engage in the exploitation of labour through personal asceticism. In this way he can maintain himself and purchase the services of other co-operating factors, and with good luck and judgment eventually emerge with a recognised qualification. He then hires the "machine" out to business, using the income he receives to indulge his fancies, pay back outstanding loans and perhaps reimburse his family.

In the socialist society all capital, whether human or physical, is owned by the State. The output of the education sector will be geared to the estimated future needs of skills in different industries and occupations. The State pays the costs of education, including the rent of land, the construction expenses of buildings, the salaries of teachers and the wages of the "primary labour unit." The "machine" is later rented out to the publicly owned companies, which pay for its use directly to the State Bank.

The financial framework in these two idealised polities is not matched very closely by what takes place in actual socialist and capitalist countries. This is not to be expected, since education finance is not determined alone by the logical relations between ideological conceptions and capital formation. Nevertheless, it will be interesting to examine briefly what parallels with the U.S.S.R. and the United States do exist.

In the Soviet Union education has been recognised as a form of investment since the 1917 Revolution. In fact, it was the Soviet economist Strumilin who first attempted to calculate a rate of return to education. DeWitt[2] informs us that:

> . . . there are no private educational establishments, no private sources of support, no endowments, no revenue-creating investment funds, no charitable foundation or individual contributions, no long-term bond financing, no local or regional tax-supported funds. Most of the funds for education in the Soviet Union originate from a single national budget. . . .

About 35% of current expenditures on higher education take the form of stipends to individual students; in 1927 they were awarded to 42% of all

---

[2] Nicolas Dewitt, "Soviet and American Higher Education: Magnitude, Resources, and Costs," *Economic Aspects of Higher Education* (Paris: O.E.C.D., 1964), 134.

full-time students, and after reaching a peak in the mid-'thirties declined again to over 79% in 1956. They are regarded by the Soviet authorities as wage payments. On average they are lower than the wages paid to workers in industry of the same age as students. This wage system can be looked upon as the necessary concomitant of the formation of the physical and mental skills required to make possible the enormous expansion in industrial output which began in 1928/29. If the State was to transform the economy into an industrialised society it was clear that both physical and human capital had to be created on an enormous scale, which involved state control of the education sector and wages for the "primary" labour force.

On the production side the match between model and reality seems to be good; this is not true when the "machine" comes to be rented out. The State Committee on Labour and Wages with the assistance of the All-Union Central Council of Trade Unions divides all jobs into grades. The lowest grade is allocated a certain wage-rate. For higher grades the basic rate is multiplied by defined coefficients. Each industry publishes a "tariff-qualification manual" setting out the qualifications for each grade. Since the more highly educated workers are more likely to be capable of holding a higher-grade job, then it follows that workers receive the income paid to the "machine" they possess, and therefore income owed to the State. Intangible capitalism still flourishes in the U.S.S.R.

In the United States the structure of university finance is much less monolithic than it is in the Soviet Union, just as the model suggests. However, education cannot be realistically regarded as freely bought and sold in the open market. It is clear that students do not pay the full cost of their education: tuition fees just about offset capital costs, so that all current expenditures in institutions of higher learning can be regarded as subsidies. College students' expenses consist primarily of tuition fees, maintenance and travelling costs. In 1959 they were derived from the following sources: 40% from family income, 20% from long-term family savings, 25% from part-time and summer earnings of students themselves and the remaining 15% from scholarships, veteran benefits and loans. Personal asceticism certainly characterises a large number of students and their families.

The high rate of subsidy, including scholarships, and the rather negligible use of loans matches poorly with the capitalist model. However, there is a strong trend of opinion amongst American writers on education towards formalising the resemblance between education expenditures and investment in physical assets by increasing tuition fees to a more realistic level and setting up large-scale loan programmes. Some of these writers have also proposed an increase in the number of scholarships and subsidised loan interest rates, often on the ground of the presumed external economies of education. Vickrey has set out the details of a loan system, with repayment made as a share of that part of post-graduation income deemed the income of the "machine." The maximum size of the annual loan would equal tuition fees plus the student's estimated earnings forgone per year. Goode has suggested that higher tuition charges and long-term credit facilities should be complemented in the following way. One should have the opportunity of writing off educational expenditures, through current deductions or amortisation allowances, against taxable income attributable to that education, as is done for the purchase of capital assets in the business sector.

On the selling side, the match with the model is precise: after graduation all "machine" income is credited to the owner, he who was so recently the "primary labour unit." In the United States many attempts have been made to measure the private rate of return on such capital.

In choosing an efficient and equitable system of student finance, it can be shown that both polities have such deep-running faults that neither system can be accepted. The difficulties of the socialist system arise on the selling side—that aspect of the model with no parallel in the Soviet Union. First, state ownership of human capital implies that the skills a person acquires at university, although possessed by him, are the legal property of the Government. Many people would find this morally offensive. Second, every individual's income would have to be divided into two shares: one going to the unadulterated labour power of the "machine" possessor, the former "primary labour unit," the other share going to the "machine" as payment strictly for the university-acquired skills. But such a separation, defining the net returns to education, is an extraordinarily complex business. Income is a function of age, experience, education, occupation, intelligence, psycho-motor skills, effort, sex, class and race. (In our socialist society the last three categories would be irrelevant.) The return to education cannot be extracted from such a complex relation, since the independent variables are non-additive, inter-correlated, non-parametric and open to large measurement errors. Finally, if the worker were to receive an income equivalent only to the value of his unadulterated labour power there is no reason why he should seek to use his acquired skills to the full, unless doing so were a reward in itself. "Machines" would work below full capacity—the most common problem of any egalitarian income-distribution pattern.

The difficulties of the capitalist system arise on the production side—that aspect of the model which corresponded less well with practice in the United States. In this case financial resources derive from loans to students, familial contributions, part-time and vacation earnings and personal asceticism. Loans to make possible the construction of human capital will not be raised easily, partly because financiers have no experience in providing resources for study at university, and partly because investment in education is not embodied in a saleable asset which may be offered as security. Nevertheless, this problem may be overcome fairly easily in a mixed economy by setting up a state finance company specifically with this kind of investment in mind. If it were felt that there exist significant external economies or diseconomies to education, then the loan rate of interest could be correspondingly lowered or raised.

Much more fundamental objections can be lodged against a loan system. First, those people with the intellectual and psychological talents necessary to carry through successfully the *production* process at university will have a very wide range of personal characteristics. But it is unlikely that the capitalist instinct, that is the willingness to undergo present sacrifice and enter into long-term financial commitments in order to realise a long-run gain, would exist in more than a small percentage of them, particularly since the majority are very young, usually between 18 and 24. Certainly working-class children have little or no experience of financial manoeuvres, even in those countries with a socially extensive hire-purchase network. They especially would be unwilling to saddle themselves with future debts, to indenture themselves. The resulting bias on entry into higher education to the sons and daughters of the wealthy, who can also risk a failure in their entrepreneurial judgment with greater equanimity, would lead to a form of social ossification with obvious moral and technical disadvantages. Second, the penalties will be great for those people who after graduation either enter professions which, although of great importance to the community, do not receive such recognition in terms of salary payments, or enter professions in which the risk of low incomes is very significant, such as the writing of poetry. Both groups will have to face fixed repayment obligations, possibly very severe as a percentage of their money incomes.

If loans as a method of finance are unsatisfactory, even more so is family support. Parental contributions are clearly a function of the socio-economic status of the family head. The great majority of the world's adult population can be classed as peasants or low-income proletariat. Therefore the great majority of the world's children have negative, zero or barely positive family support. (Parental support is negative when the child is expected to bring money into the home, an extremely common phenomenon amongst poor people.) Assuming that intelligence in children is independent of their social class, then if university finance rests largely or entirely on money and real income donated by the family the great majority of those intellectually qualified will be excluded. The finance system and selection for entry into higher education are intimately related.

In the great majority of countries outside the Socialist world students' part-time and vacation earnings form an important, often vital, part of their income. This means that the length of degree courses is extended. For instance, a study of the Faculty of Engineering of the University of Buenos Aires has shown that 60% of the student body have an income-earning occupation. Amongst these students there is a statistically significant negative correlation between hours of work and hours of study per annum. Furthermore, it is shown that academic performance varies directly with hours of study, and *independently of the association between hours of study and hours of work*, a negative correlation exists between hours of work and academic performance.

Is it economically efficient to have a financing system based largely on part-time earnings, which leads to the extension of degree courses and a high rate of drop-out? To answer this question one would have to compare the excess of the present value over the present cost of these mutually exclusive investment projects. The investment costs of a student doing part-time study and part-time work and graduating in, say, 7·5 years are spread over a longer time period, and his opportunity costs are probably lower than a full-time student graduating in say 5 years. However, the benefit stream of the latter commences 2·5 years earlier. Second, one would have to compare the excess of the present values of a full training and an uncompleted degree over their respective present costs.

Intuitively I suspect very strongly that the longer gestation period is less efficient, since it involves a highly qualified worker, in intellectual terms, undertaking an unskilled occupation. In the United States and the United Kingdom, for instance, the student clips grass or sweeps hospital floors during the long vacations when he could be employed full-time in a profession for which he is uniquely qualified: creating a valuable bundle of skills. Here, however, I have ignored a potentially most valuable non-monetary social benefit: the likelihood that manual labour on the part of the future economic *élite* will leave them with lasting impressions and a vivid sympathy with those who spend their lives shovelling coal or cutting sugar-cane. The Cuban Universities send their students into industry and agriculture for six to seven weeks each year, not only for the value of their labour but also to strengthen the social cohesion of the nation. The People's Republic of China has the same policy.

I wish to put forward an alternative set of arrangements for financing higher education: it takes account of these fairly damning criticisms of socialist and capitalist mechanisms by combining the purchasing system of the former with the selling system of the latter plus an "equity condition." The necessary and sufficient condition for entry into university is that the performance of the "primary labour unit" in tests of "need achievement" and intellectual and psycho-motor abilities show that the probability of his passing the degree course is very high. The actual minimum level of probability acceptable should ensure that the number of accepted students multiplied by the average probability of success equals the number of degrees required, by specialisation, in the light of the country's anticipated occupational requirements at the degree-holder level.

One could use a multiple regression equation using past entrants to the university system as observations, and adopting as the dependent variable the dummy variable success or failure in the degree course. This will give an estimate of the probability of a student's success for given scores in pre-university aptitude and motivation tests. Johnston has described this procedure in some detail, illustrating how it can be adapted for dealing with interaction effects, and Feldstein has proposed the model for the very similar problem of minimising perinatal mortality rates.

During the gestation period the student will be regarded as working in a State-owned industry, constructing not a machine but a "machine"; a bundle of skills. He will work all the year, reaping the presently neglected benefits of specialisation and the division of labour; there is no reason why his holidays should exceed those of a lathe-maker or steel-ladler.[3] Annual wages will equal those of the age-cohort outside the university who work full-time. In the short-run education will be completely free, for no fees whatsoever will be charged. Incomes of teachers and auxiliary staff, current materials and capital costs will be covered from government funds.

Graduates receive on average much higher incomes than the non-graduate population, and this is clearly in part a return on their additional education. Glick and Miller have shown that annual income for American men in the 45–54 age range rises with every additional year of primary, secondary and university education; the marginal increment jumps when any given level of instruction is terminated. University graduates will not be required to pass over to the Government their "machine" income. However, since they benefit in money terms from such public expenditures, an "equity condition" will be set up. "Machine" owners will be required to pay in taxes a percentage of their gross annual income for some fixed period after graduating.[4]

If it were felt that the first years of work outside the university were particularly trying financially because of marriage and setting up a home, then a moratorium of, say, five years could be allowed. The percentage charge on income would be adjusted so that the discounted value of all receipts from all students in the country were in aggregate sufficient to pay off the full costs of their education, including the wages paid to the "primary labour unit." It might be objected that the graduate should not be expected to pay back his

---

[3] If psychologists were to show that a 2,000-hour study year induced "staleness," inefficiency in the student's performance, this would demonstrate that the economic cost of attempts by a country such as Cuba to engender mutual respect and understanding amongst different occupational groups has a very low, possibly negative, cost.

[4] In any economy with a proportional or progressive income-tax system, part of the income deriving from university education will automatically be credited to the State in taxes without the need for a tax on graduates, which is what is being advocated here. However, the repayment of education costs has a quite different rationale to that of the redistribution of income introduced by income taxation, and there is no reason why the existence of one should preclude the existence of the other. The graduate tax would be on gross income, and the income tax on income net of the graduate tax. For given income-tax rates the total debt of the graduate would clearly be greater under the two-stage tax, since the total tax liability on net income would be the same in both cases, whereas the tax liability on gross minus net income in the two-stage case is by definition 100%, and therefore inevitably greater than the income-tax liability on this slice under a single income tax.

own wages; but in a long-run equilibrium situation the income of the average graduate should be sufficient to cover the full cost of "machine" construction, and wages to the "primary labour unit" will make up about half of this.

As Blaug has pointed out, it is a widely held belief that the indirect benefits of education are very large. In this case the student should not be expected to pay back the full cost of his education, since society also benefits from "machine" production. In order to make some adjustment for these external economies the rate of interest at which the cost repayment stream is discounted should be reduced below the market rate to a level lying between, say, 0 and 5%, depending on estimates of the importance of such economies. Eckstein has estimated that with payments at a 4% rate of interest up to the age of 67 the average graduate would be paying 2% of his income for tuition costs of $1,000 per annum for four years.

In the short-run the student has no financial problems to overcome, and he can devote himself in tranquillity to his studies. Nor need there be any anxiety about repayment in the long-run: since the tithe is a percentage of gross income, the risk associated with a low income after graduation is pooled amongst the entire graduate body. Society provides an efficient and easy channel to attaining the highest qualifications and merely asks those who benefit to cover the costs. Income is provided when it is needed, and repayment made when it can be afforded.

One of the criteria by which any education system is judged is the success it has in encouraging social mobility. It will be important for economists and sociologists to examine the effects of these proposals for student finance in higher education on the occupation and education mix of graduates from the entire educational system by their social class. In a society where social mobility is complete the occupational and educational mix for its members would be invariant with the social class of their parents. I believe that these proposals would encourage social mobility for two reasons:

1. 100% State finance during one's university career eliminates the budget constraint on undertaking these studies, and this constraint has obviously been lower for children of working-class parents.
2. Where their high time discount rate was discouraging them from entering university, working-class children will now find that outlays during their study years are zero, whilst the costs of education (which admittedly to the average student will be higher) are spread over their entire working life.

Of course, it is widely recognised that there is a correlation between performance in aptitude tests and social class, which will introduce a bias into the acceptance of children for enrolment in university courses, quite apart from the fact that there will be a social class bias in those children desiring university places. The existence of a comprehensive school system and the abolition of all private education may do a great deal to correct differential performance in aptitude tests by controlling the school environment. If the desire to enter higher education is to be invariant with social class, then the State will inevitably have to devise publicity campaigns, hold public meetings and set up parent advice centres with the specific objective of influencing the taste structure of working-class parents. Clearly the proposed financial system is not a sufficient—although I believe it is a necessary—condition for achieving complete social mobility.

I now wish to anticipate three possible criticisms of this essay. First, that mine is an egregiously meritocratic approach; second, that to insist on payment for education is a reactionary measure; third, that education is not "machine" construction.

The continuing meritocratic trend of this paper is founded *on strictly technological grounds*. First accept education as a "machine"-producing process. In its production the "machine" requires a number of only partially substitutable factors: teachers, land, classrooms, laboratory equipment, books, writing materials and "primary man-power"—the students. Teaching costs of production will be defined as total costs less earnings forgone of the "primary labour unit." In producing any given "machine" the qualities of the student, his ability and desire to learn, are vitally important. Therefore the teaching costs of production vary inversely with these qualities, and probably not in a linear fashion, for the marginal rate of substitution of the "primary" factor for teaching factors will almost certainly increase. This implies that if students are less able or willing there must be a correspondingly greater expansion of the other factors to compensate. Similarly, as the complexity of the "machine" increases, that is to say as we move higher up the education scale in terms of the present value of the "machine," the marginal returns to increases in the volume of teaching factors with the quality of the student population held constant are likely to be diminishing. Therefore in selecting the "primary" man-power, the students, from an economic point of view one wishes to choose intelligent, physically skilled, highly motivated individuals. Meritocracy makes good economic sense (see Appendix).

There seems to have been a trend general in many countries during this century of increasing subsidisation of education, particularly at the primary and secondary levels. Vaizey, for instance, has documented this carefully for the United Kingdom. To that extent my proposal to charge the student body in aggregate the full costs of higher education is quite definitely reactionary. Nevertheless, it is important to understand *why* repayment was requested. First, human capital was assumed to be a meaningful concept: the point of education was taken to be the production of "machines," "bundles of skills," qualified man-power. From this an economic conclusion was drawn: meritocratic selection procedures. Alongside the two was placed an implicit moral premise: no one in the society receives an economic good free unless on the basis of their need. Making the further assumption that more intelligent people do not *need* further education (in the sense that hungry people need free food, flood-stricken people need free homes), it follows that education should be paid for. I suggest that the premises and therefore the conclusion are not "reactionary" in the loaded sense of the word, although they certainly run against the trend of the times.

The third possible criticism mentioned was that it is incorrect and positively misleading to regard education as "machine" construction. The refashioned concept of human capital used here seems such a powerful and useful tool that it would be obscurantism of the worst kind to reject it outright. But it does make good sense to refuse to apply it wholesale to every educational level, every speciality of interest and every community. Let us dispense with the human capital model: education, we say, cannot possibly be looked upon as a "machine"-forming process. The rationale of payment for education disappears. But much more interesting is that the rationale established in this paper for a meritocratic selection procedure, technological efficiency, also disappears.

In that case how can higher education be distributed freely to a selected proportion of the university-age population? The number of possible schemes are as infinite as the ideas of men. One of these is very common amongst education policy makers and writers on education: free or subsidised higher education should be available only to the intelligent. The case often rests on a very simple fallacy of equivocation involving the systematic terminological abuse of the phrase "higher education." Here the word higher can have one of two meanings which although distinct are frequently co-extensive:

1. *Tertiary*, or post-secondary education, higher in the sense that 3 is higher than 2.
2. *Advanced*, in the sense that the level of ability required to deal with the subject matter is higher than that required for the subject matter with which one compares the advanced stream.

One frequently comes across a thesis such as: "all those and only those able to benefit from higher education should be so educated, without social or economic hindrance." From this is drawn a fallacious argument: since only clever children can benefit from higher (advanced) education, only clever children should receive higher (tertiary) education. Summarising this section: if education is not an economic good we urgently need to know why we are trying to fill our universities with clever people. An egalitarian would say: free tertiary education should be available only to those who need it most, the unintelligent, to compensate them for natural disadvantages.

The objective of this paper was to arrive at an efficient and equitable system for financing higher education, with particular emphasis on the problems of students. The methodology adopted was to impose the refashioned concept of human capital on two idealised polities: socialism and capitalism. The similarities and differences between the socialist economy and that of the U.S.S.R. were pointed out, as were those between the capitalist economy and the United States. The disadvantages in terms of efficiency and equity of the socialist selling method and the capitalist production method were discussed. A meritocratic solution was proposed, having the State pay for all university costs including market-rate wages to the students. An equity condition was imposed, involving repayment by the student body of their education costs. Three possible criticisms were anticipated: that one should not adopt meritocratic selection procedures; that students should not be required to pay for their education; that university education is not "machine" producing. The replies were intimately inter-related—the most interesting conclusion was that meritocratism makes good economic sense. If education is *not* an economic good we need to know why we are allowing only the most intelligent to enter the later stages of education, especially tertiary education.

In general, I believe that the lower the *per capita* income of a country, the greater is the utility of income, and therefore the greater the need to establish economically efficient education systems. Low-income countries should organise tertiary advanced education in the meritocratic fashion described above. Similarly, high-income countries should introduce a tax on graduates where their selection procedures are meritocratic, although in the case of these countries they are more easily able to afford education systems or sub-systems where the objective of investment in human capital does not predominate.

APPENDIX

Figure 1 represents the production map of two "machines." The isoquants can be regarded as having either an ordinal or a cardinal relation. In the former case the two products are defined in terms of educational attainments qualifying the student for two sets of occupations, one set requiring a higher degree of skill than the other. In the latter case the isoquant represents the present value of the discounted receipts on the investment in a particular piece of human capital.

Teaching units are measured on the vertical axis: they are an aggregate of teaching time, capital and material costs over the gestation period. On the horizontal axis labour power units are the inputs of time, effort and the intellectual talents of a single "primary labour unit." A fixed number of hours of study over the gestation period is assumed for all students, so that the value of the labour power units is determined by effort and ability alone.

The shape of (1) and (2) indicate, of course, the substitutability between the student's qualities and the aggregate of all other inputs. Curve (1) drops down almost vertically until above H_1 it starts a gentle curve, after which for

FIGURE 1

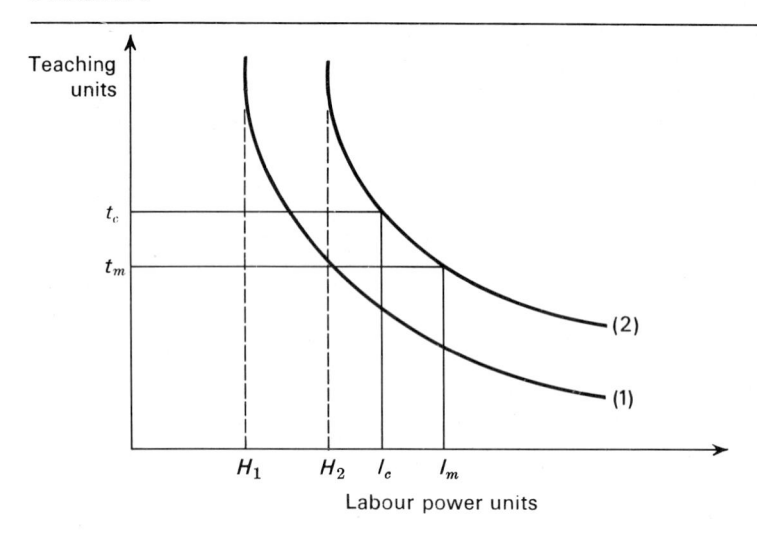

[Figure 1: Graph with "Teaching units" on vertical axis showing t_c and t_m levels, and "Labour power units" on horizontal axis showing H_1, H_2, l_c, l_m. Two downward-sloping convex curves labelled (1) and (2), with (2) to the right of (1).]

most of its course it is only negligibly convex to the origin. This indicates in this case that a learning threshold exists, H_1, defined by the intelligence and drive of the pupil, which is a necessary condition for the successful completion of this level of education with a given teaching technology. However, once this threshold is passed the marginal rate of substitution between the two factors is almost constant, except when teaching factors—in particular *teachers*—fall to a very low level, when non-substitutability again reasserts itself.

Curve (2) does not have quite the same shape. There exists a learning threshold, H_2, where $H_2 > H_1$. Once this is passed the two factors are substitutable, but the marginal rate of substitution is constantly changing, perhaps because at advanced levels of education increases in student ability cannot make up so easily for the reduction of lecture time, specialised text-books and laboratory equipment. I do not claim this as an immutable law; I merely wish to illustrate the educational-psychological implications of curves with different shapes and positions.

Suppose there exist two methods of selecting the students to enter sector (2): one is meritocratic, the other capitalist. It is clear from our criticisms of the capitalist financing methods that the average meritocratic student is more highly qualified than the average capitalist student, or in the figure $l_m > l_c$. The difference in teaching costs involved in educating n students in each society to level (2) will equal $n(t_c - t_m)$, the job being done more cheaply in the meritocracy.

But for the difference in total costs to equal $n(t_c - t_m)$ one must assume that the social opportunity cost of the average student in either society is the same, which implies that the additional labour-power units in the "primary labour unit" of the meritocracy have an opportunity cost equal to zero. This is most unlikely to be true: the earnings of hard-working, clever people will, *ceteris paribus*, exceed those of less-hard-working and less-able people. Conceivably the extra teaching costs required by the average capitalist student may be more than offset by his lower income forgone; in this case meritocratic selection procedures are economically *inefficient*.

Although the possibility does exist, it seems unlikely to occur. In order to establish the technological efficiency of the meritocracy it is not necessary to assume that income forgone is independent of student qualities, but merely that the rate of increase in the student's wage-rate is more than compensated by the rate of decrease in teaching costs. This is illustrated in Figure 2. Here l_t indicates the quality of the average student chosen by any selection procedure, i: it is always the case that $l_i < l_m$, since the whole object of the meritocracy is to maximize the quality of the average student. Let us drop the previous assumption of constant incomes amongst "primary labour units" and now assume that labour power units have constant opportunity cost, so that the ratio of the opportunity costs of any two students is equal to the ratio of their respective holdings of labour power units. The line b_1–b_2 is an equal cost curve expressing the ratio of the prices of the two factors.

FIGURE 2

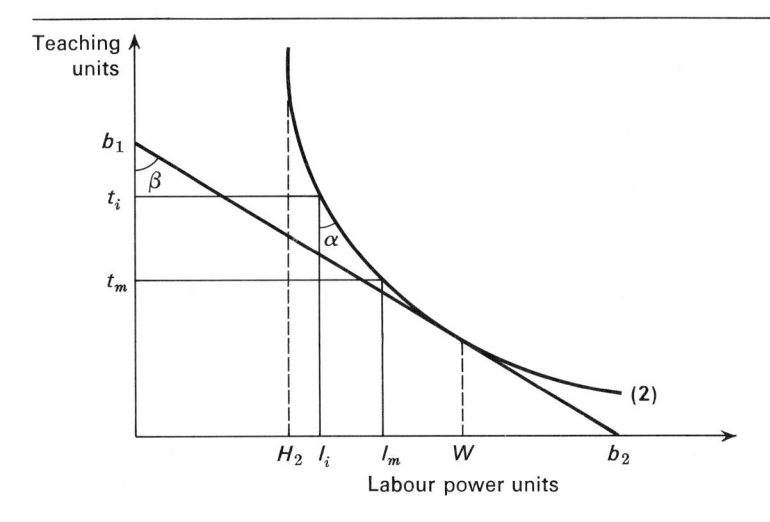

For a meritocratic system always to be the most efficient it must be true for any part of the curve that:

$$\frac{(t_i - t_m) \cdot \text{Price of a teaching unit}}{(l_m - l_i) \cdot \text{Price of a labour power unit}} > 1.$$

This is close to the familiar micro-economic rule for minimising the cost of production of any given level of output. The marginal rate of substitution of labour units for teaching units must always be less than the inverse ratio of their prices:

$$\frac{(l_m - l_i)}{(t_i - t_m)} < \frac{\text{Price of teaching unit}}{\text{Price of labour power unit}}.$$

Since

$$\tan \beta = \frac{\text{Price of 1 teaching unit}}{\text{Price of 1 labour power unit}},$$

and $\tan \alpha$ = Marginal rate of substitution of labour power units for teaching units, the condition reduces to $\tan \alpha < \tan \beta$.

This is clearly the case in Figure 2.

This condition will hold as l_i approaches H_2, since $\tan \alpha$ tends to zero. However, as soon as $l_m > W$ the condition will not hold, for as l_m increases $\tan \alpha$ tends to infinity. But as long as $l_m < W$, meritocratic procedures will always optimise the solution.

If it is likely that a meritocratic system will produce an average student so brilliant that his earnings forgone as a student more than outweigh the reduction in teaching costs involved in producing his given skills, the following method of minimising total costs can be adopted. Let there be three education levels, producing 3 products: 1, 2 and 3. Let there be required the following output of these products respectively: n_1, n_2 and n_3, where all n_3 students are educated to level 2 and all n_2 students to level 1. (That is to say a necessary condition of university education is a secondary education, and a necessary condition of a secondary education is a primary education.) Let there be n members of the student age-cohort, where $n > n_1 > n_2 > n_3$.

On the x-axis of these graphs the n individual students are placed in order of their quality so that as x approaches zero the intellectual, psycho-motor skills and desire to learn of the student decrease. On the y-axis plot for each student the total costs, i.e., teaching costs and earnings forgone, of educating each student at that level. Establish the parameters of the three cost functions. Minimise the following sum: [(Area under curve 1 for any student range n_1) + (Area under curve 2 for any student range n_2) + (Area under curve 3 for any student range n_3)], with the following constraint: all the members of n_3 are members of n_2, and all the members of n_2 are members of n_1. The diagram [Figure 3] presents a non-meritocratic solution. It is amusing to note that with education as an economic good, one *might* do best to keep some of the very best potential students out of university, especially where the relation between "machine" income and the independent variables labour power units and teaching units is additive.

FIGURE 3

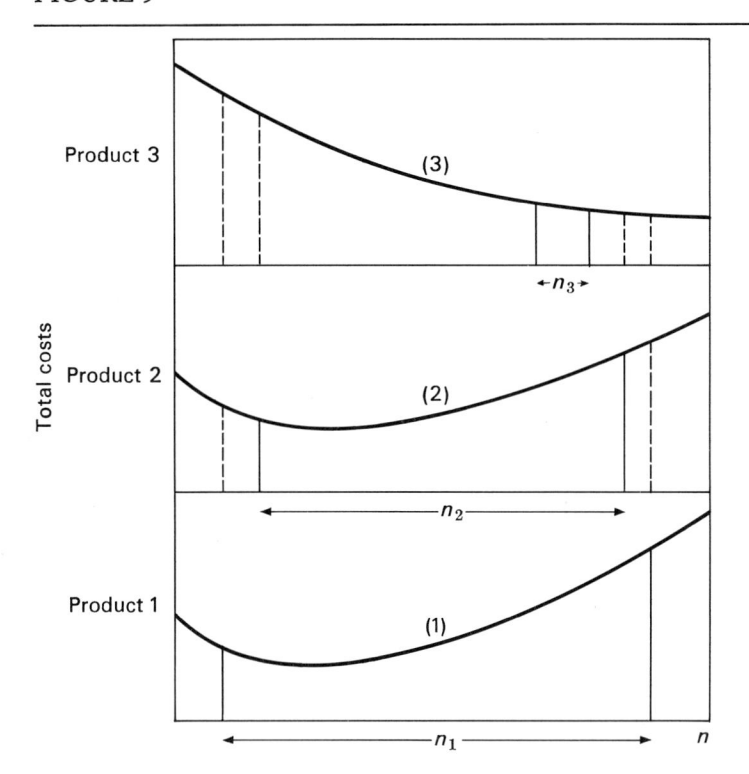

PART V. GENERAL EQUILIBRIUM

13

GENERAL EQUILIBRIUM AND SOCIAL WELFARE THEORY

Throughout this book we have employed the static partial equilibrium approach developed by Alfred Marshall. Each product market and each resource market has been studied in isolation—for the most part, treating each market as though it were independent of the others and, in effect, assuming that if each market could reach equilibrium, then the over-all economic system composed of many markets would reach a general equilibrium. But if there is one essential lesson to be learned from our study of microeconomics, it is that everything depends on everything else; that is, the parts of a market economy are mutually interdependent. The study of this mutual interdependence of the parts of the economy is general equilibrium analysis.

As an introduction to the problems involved in general equilibrium analysis, let us assume that a market economy starts in equilibrium, with supply and demand equal for all commodities and all resources, and let us then disturb this equilibrium to see what happens. Assume that the economy reacts to any disturbances which occur by smoothly and quickly restoring equilibrium in all product and resource markets. Now suppose that the demand for one commodity, X, increases and the demands for Y and Z decrease, simultaneously. The increase in demand for X raises the price of X. Suppliers will respond to X's higher price by increasing quantities supplied. This will follow an increase in the demand for resources used to produce X, which will cause their prices to rise. The rise in resource prices will affect the costs of producers of other products, their supply curves, and ultimately the prices of these goods. Looking at the markets for goods Y and Z, the decrease in demand reduces the demand for resources used to produce the two goods, at the same time that the demand for resources needed to produce X is increasing. (Of course, it is probable that some of these resources are used to produce X's, Y's, and Z's, in which case there would simply occur a transfer of resources from one activity

557

to another, with little change in their prices.) In effect, the increase in the demand for X and the decrease in demand for Y and Z cause a whole chain of reactions, which spread to both factor markets and consumer goods markets. Presumably, these reactions will steadily diminish in amplitude as we consider markets more remote, and we might expect that eventually a new pattern of equilibrium prices will be established.

Leon Walras, who published his version of general equilibrium analysis in two parts in 1874 and 1877, pictured the over-all effect of a change in any market as similar to the effects of a rock dropped in a pond of water.[1] A pebble will cause small ripples to spread; a stone will cause large waves. But there will always be some effect, large or small, in nearly all parts of the pond, as a result of the initial disturbance. General equilibrium analysis is concerned with the over-all effects of a given change in the economy (all the ripples) and must, therefore, be concerned with the way the parts of a market system relate to each other. As an introduction: general equilibrium analysis pictures the economy as a system of interdependent markets for goods and services and resources, rather than as a system of separate and distinct parts to be analyzed in isolation.

Partial equilibrium analysis is not rendered useless by these observations about the interrelatedness of an economy, however. Rather, the partial equilibrium approach should be viewed as a *first approximation* to a general theory of markets. In many situations, partial equilibrium analysis gives a very good approximation to market behavior, because the sector under investigation is indeed quite isolated from most other sectors. For example, it is difficult to conceive of any close links either in product or resource markets between the market for hairpins and the market for ice cream cones. These markets are so separated that the *ceteris paribus* assumption, which holds constant the latter while investigating the former, is seemingly perfectly valid. For any market under investigation, the links with some product markets are closer than for others. Considering for example the market for ice cream cones, the relationship to the market for bottled milk will be closer than for hairpins. The complete market demand function for ice cream cones must include the prices of all other consumer goods in the economy, however remote the substitute or complementary relationships. But the cross elasticities of demand for cones and most other goods like hairpins will approach zero. Thus, very little in accuracy is gained by including them in the model, for partial equilibrium analysis would yield satisfactory predictions of market behavior. One of our collateral objectives in studying general equilibrium theory is to know when economic analysis is "too partial"; that is, when important factors have been excluded by the *ceteris paribus* assumption which should not have been.

---

[1] Leon Walras, *Elements of Pure Economics*, trans. W. Jaffe. (Homewood, Ill.: Richard D. Irwin, Inc., 1954).

Our basic objective, however, is to gain some understanding of how a market economy functions to answer the basic economic questions of production and distribution, and that understanding requires a knowledge of how all the different sectors of an economy are related to each other. The underlying theme of this book has been how most efficiently to allocate the scarce resources of an economy among all the various competing alternative uses for these resources, to obtain the maximum possible satisfaction for the members of society. This means we must study resource and product markets as an integrated system and analyze the way the system functions to economize on the economy's scarce resources. However, even though our discussion of general equilibrium theory is necessary to an understanding of microeconomics, at best, our presentation can only be an introduction to the subject. A complete treatment of general equilibrium theory is beyond the scope of this book.

We will begin by describing a very simple general model of an economy, followed by a discussion of the properties of the model.

GENERAL EQUILIBRIUM ANALYSIS: A TWO-COMMODITY–TWO-RESOURCE MODEL

Let us suppose, for simplicity, that a hypothetical economy is composed of only two industries which separately produce consumer goods, X and Y, and that each employs two resources, A and B, to produce the two products. The resources are wholly owned by consumers, who supply these resources to firms and demand finished output. The consumer goods are produced and supplied by firms in the two industries and are the source of demand for the two resources. In this economy there are, then, four equilibrium prices and four quantities to be determined. Probably the best, if not the only way, to describe a general equilibrium model is with simple algebraic equations; this is certainly true if the model includes many different outputs and many inputs. For this reason, we will use the algebraic approach to describe our highly simplified model.

The Demand Functions for X and Y

The market demand functions for the two goods X and Y might initially be written:

$$D_x = f(P_x, P_y), \tag{1}$$
$$D_y = f(P_y, P_x), \tag{2}$$

to reflect the interrelatedness of the market demand for X with Y's price and vice versa. But a consumer's demand for X or Y will depend not only on the prices of X and Y, but on the consumer's income which, in turn, will depend on the prices of A and B and the quantities of A and B supplied by the consumer. Presumably, one of the resources the consumer will supply is his own labor services, and the quantity of labor supplied will be a function of the individual's preferences for income in relation to his aversion to work and his preferences for leisure time. An individual consumer's income will be determined by the equation:

$$Y = a \cdot P_a + b \cdot P_b, \tag{3}$$

where a and b are the quantities of the two resources that the consumer supplies, and P_a and P_b are their respective prices. Our principal behavioral assumption is that consumers seek to maximize the utility they derive from consuming X's and Y's, subject to the constraints of limited resource supplies and output price constraints, as well as to the disutilities associated with work. An individual consumer's demand functions for X and Y should then look like this:

$$d_x = f(P_x, P_y, P_a, P_b), \tag{4}$$
$$d_y = f(P_y, P_x, P_a, P_b), \tag{5}$$

where d_x is the quantity demanded of X and d_y is the quantity demanded of Y. Now when we aggregate the demands of all individuals we get the market demand functions:

$$D_x = f(P_x, P_y, P_a, P_b), \tag{6}$$
$$D_y = f(P_y, P_x, P_a, P_b). \tag{7}$$

In general, the quantity of X demanded in the market will be directly related to the prices of A and B and inversely related to the price of X (see footnote on page 561). The cross elasticity between D_x and P_y will depend upon the strength of the substitute or complementary relationship between X and Y.

The Supply Functions for X and Y

Viewing the firm as an input–output device with profit maximization as its principal objective, we may describe its supply functions for products X and Y as:

$$s_x = f(P_x, P_y, P_a, P_b), \tag{8}$$
$$s_y = f(P_y, P_x, P_a, P_b), \tag{9}$$

where the quantity supplied by the firm of X or Y is a function principally of output prices and input prices. For example, the quantity supplied of X will vary directly as the price of X and inversely as the prices of A and B. The quantity supplied of X may also vary directly as the price of Y if the firm produces and supplies both products. When aggregated for all firms we get:

$$S_x = f(P_x, P_y, P_a, P_b), \tag{10}$$
$$S_y = f(P_y, P_x, P_a, P_b). \tag{11}$$

Now we have the supply and demand functions for output. We must now turn to the supply and demand functions for inputs, for we cannot determine equilibrium output prices without determining equilibrium input prices, since the latter appear as arguments in the supply and demand functions for X and Y.

The Demand and Supply of Resources

Again viewing the firm as an input–output device, we can write its demands for resources a and b as:

$$d_a = f(P_a, P_b, P_x, P_y), \tag{12}$$

and

$$d_b = f(P_b, P_a, P_x, P_y), \tag{13}$$

where the quantity demanded of resource a (resource b) will vary inversely with the price of a (resource b) and directly with output prices and directly or inversely with the price of b (resource a). Of course, if the firm produces only one product, say X, the coefficient of the price variable, P_y, will be zero. Aggregating, we get the following market demand functions for resources:

$$D_a = f(P_a, P_b, P_x, P_y), \tag{14}$$
$$D_b = f(P_b, P_a, P_x, P_y). \tag{15}$$

Now we turn to a determination of the market supply functions for resources. Assuming a given pattern of preferences for goods X and Y and a given preference for leisure time versus time spent at work, the individual's supply functions for resources may be expected to vary directly as the prices of a and b and inversely as the prices of consumer goods.[2] The supply functions for the individual may be written:

$$s_a = f(P_a, P_b, P_x, P_y), \tag{16}$$
$$s_b = f(P_b, P_a, P_x, P_y), \tag{17}$$

where the coefficient of P_b in Equation (16) may be zero in some cases and that of P_a in (17), likewise; e.g., there may be no reason for a consumer to increase or decrease the quantity supplied of A if the price of B rises. Aggregating we get:

$$S_a = f(P_a, P_b, P_x, P_y), \tag{18}$$
$$S_b = f(P_b, P_a, P_x, P_y). \tag{19}$$

This completes the determination of market supply and demand functions for both resources and both consumer goods.

---

[2] The quantity supplied of one of the resources may not vary in all cases directly as resource prices or inversely with output prices; e.g., there may be a backward bending segment of a consumer's supply schedule for labor.

The Complete Model

Now we may put all of the aggregate supply and demand functions in one general equilibrium model of the economy. Since, for simplicity, we have assumed that there are two goods and two resources and supply and demand equations for each, we obtain the following 8 equations:

$$D_x = f(P_x, P_y, P_a, P_b), \tag{6}$$
$$D_y = f(P_y, P_x, P_a, P_b), \tag{7}$$
$$S_x = f(P_x, P_y, P_a, P_b), \tag{10}$$
$$S_y = f(P_y, P_x, P_a, P_b), \tag{11}$$
$$D_a = f(P_a, P_b, P_x, P_y), \tag{14}$$
$$D_b = f(P_b, P_a, P_x, P_y), \tag{15}$$
$$S_a = f(P_a, P_b, P_x, P_y), \tag{18}$$
$$S_b = f(P_b, P_a, P_x, P_y). \tag{19}$$

Notice that there are 8 equations and also 8 unknowns, including the 4 equilibrium prices and quantities. A basic principle of algebra tells us that, in general, to derive a unique solution to a set of equations, there must be as many independent equations in the set as there are unknowns. Our model apparently fulfills this requirement, since there are 8 unknowns and 8 equations, and this fact suggests a unique equilibrium solution to all of the unknowns in the model: a set of prices and quantities that would make all excess supplies and demands equal to zero.

However, despite appearances, the equations in the system are not independent; there are only seven independent equations and eight unknowns, which implies that there is no unique solution set. That one of the equations in our model is not independent can be easily demonstrated. To begin, we note that one of the characteristics of the model is that consumers' total expenditures for X and Y must equal the total receipts of all suppliers which, in turn, equals the total cost of production. There is no profit, as such, and no saving. In other words: $P_a \cdot A + P_b \cdot B = P_x \cdot X + P_y \cdot Y$. Once the prices and quantities of inputs A and B are determined, so also is aggregate income. Moreover, once aggregate income is given and the total expenditure on one good, say X, is given, the expenditure on the other good, Y, is predetermined. The demand function for Y, then, is not independent of the other functions taken together. This means there are only 7 independent equations and 8 unknowns, and this precludes a unique solution to the system, unless we can reduce the number of unknowns to 7.

We can reduce the number of unknowns in the system by predetermining the value of one of them, specifically by setting the price of one of the goods (or one of the inputs) to 1. The commodity selected is called a *numéraire*, and this commodity serves as the unit of account, i.e., as money. The creation of a *numéraire* means we have 7 equations and 7 unknowns and suggests the possibility of a unique, equilibrium solution to the model. Of course, this suggests only the possibility; it says nothing about the mechanism for establishing equilibrium or even if an equilibrium can be expected. The setting of a *numéraire* is acceptable, since what we are principally interested in determining in an economy is *relative* prices, e.g., the price of one good relative to others. The *numéraire* implies that the prices of all goods will be stated in terms of some one other commodity. For our simplified two-commodity–two-input model, the determination of all prices in terms of one commodity is not particularly advantageous (we might just as well dispense with the *numéraire* and work with a limited number of price ratios, as would be the case in a barter economy); but it becomes more advantageous, indeed essential, when the model is expanded to include many produced goods and many resources.

What do the solution values of the model imply? First, the solution values of price are equilibrium values in the sense that excess supplies and excess demands in all markets are zero at these prices. We infer from the lack of any excess supply or demand in any market that inputs are being efficiently rationed among the various producers, and that, simultaneously, outputs are being efficiently rationed among all the consumers via the market mechanism. (More on this later.) In addition, equilibrium means that all prices have gravitated to levels that will, in the absence of changes in supply or demand in any market, be maintained through time. The solution values are, in other words, stable. In conclusion, it appears that despite the interrelatedness of all the separate resource and commodity markets, there may exist a set of prices and quantities which bring all the parts into harmony, i.e., into a general equilibrium.

An Expanded Model

The general equilibrium model can be expanded to include many outputs and resources. Such a model can be handled conceptually only with mathematics, and there can be no pretense of fitting such a model empirically to the real economy. There are entirely too many products produced and too many different resources in the real world and, thus, too many markets and too many interrelationships, even for large-scale data processing facilities, to allow us to develop a comprehensive general equilibrium model and fit it to an economy. The main benefits to be derived from general equilibrium models are the theoretical conclusions that may be generated from the conceptual manipulation of the models and the questions which these models stimulate about the structure and stability of an economy. The principal conclusion that we may state from our brief survey is that a market economy is an exceedingly complex entity, with exquisite interrelationships and links between various product and resource markets. The principal questions raised are: Is a unique equilibrium solution to be expected? If so, what are its properties, particularly regarding stability? Finally, are the solution values optimal from the standpoint of economic efficiency? We will explore the first of these questions below, that is, the arguments *pro* and *con* for the possibility of a general equilibrium and, in the latter portion of the chapter, we will investigate whether such solution values imply economic efficiency.

THE EXISTENCE OF A UNIQUE GENERAL EQUILIBRIUM

Our simile likened the effects of a disturbance in a general equilibrium system to dropping a rock in a pond, where the ripples created by the rock spread to every part of the pond. But the analogy is imperfect. In the pond, each subsequent ripple must be smaller than the preceding one, so that the ripples most remote from the impact point will be smallest. Moreover, the surface of the pond will always become smooth again, eventually, though at a higher level, whether the original disturbance was as small as a pebble dropped from the shore or as great as a boulder dropped from an airplane. However, we have no advance assurance that an initial disturbance in the economy will always be followed by a condition of stability. We cannot be confident beforehand that general equilibrium, once disturbed, will always be restored.[3] It is possible that the reaction to the disequilibrium may be as strong or stronger than the initial disturbance, which may then cause the system to fluctuate violently or even collapse. In short, the economic ripples may not necessarily always become smaller over time.

We can propose four different possibilities:

1. An initial disturbance might result in fluctuations which continually increase in amplitude and move the economy continually further from equilibrium.
2. An initial disturbance could lead to continuous fluctuations of the economy around equilibrium.
3. The economy, like the pond, could react to the initial disturbance by producing fluctuations which diminish in amplitude until equilibrium is restored.
4. Finally, a disturbance to an equilibrium condition might be followed by a steady adjustment to new equilibrium values of prices and quantities, with no tendency for fluctuations to occur.

Under what conditions will each of these results occur, and how stable is the equilibrium of a general model if once attained? We will illustrate these cases using partial equilibrium models on the presumption that if we demonstrate continuous disequilibrium in one or more markets of a general equilibrium model, this is tantamount to saying that the system is unstable. We will begin by analyzing the first three of the possibilities listed above.

[3] The basic stability of the United States economy over a long period of time, however, lends some confidence to the belief that the system is inherently stable.

Instability Due to Shapes of Supply and Demand Curves

Suppose that one or more of the supply functions for commodities in an economy are negatively sloped, like that shown in Figure 13–1. An initial equilibrium condition is assumed to exist with demand D and supply S; the equilibrium price is P_1 and quantity Q_1. Suppose there is then a reduction in demand for X, a shift in demand from D to D'. If price would rise to P_2, equilibrium would be restored. But with the shift in demand, AB represents an excess supply at price P_1, which would tend to lower price. The disturbance sets up forces that tend to make price move in the wrong direction. In this model, any initial movement away from equilibrium will induce continual disequilibrium. In addition, the continuous changes in price and quantity in the market for X (and all other similarly unstable markets) will, in their turn, cause continual changes in the related resource markets, which will cause further instability. In other words, the system responds inappropriately to change. Even if the system were to be in equilibrium at a point in time, it would be an "unstable equilibrium," because a shift in demand would cause price and quantity in one or more markets to behave erratically.

FIGURE 13–1 Supply–Demand: Price Instability

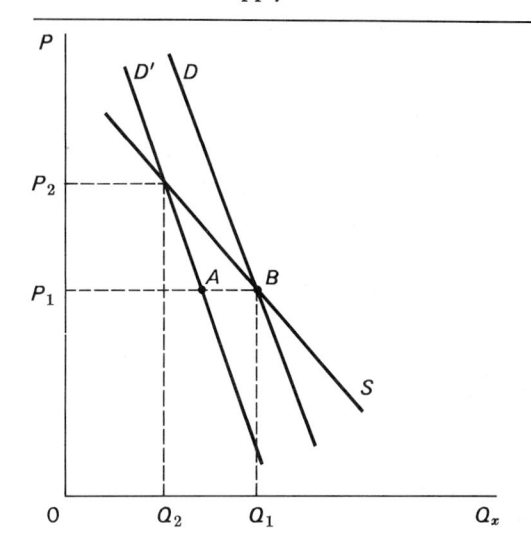

The Cobweb Theorem: Instability Due to Time Lags

Another situation in which general equilibrium is theoretically unobtainable is demonstrated by the cobweb model, aptly named for the visual appearance of the graphical demonstration of the model. (See Figure 13–8.) Suppose we have a competitive market for a product that is in every way identical to the competitive models we have discussed before, except for one

566   General Equilibrium

FIGURE 13–2   The Cobweb Model—Constant Cycles

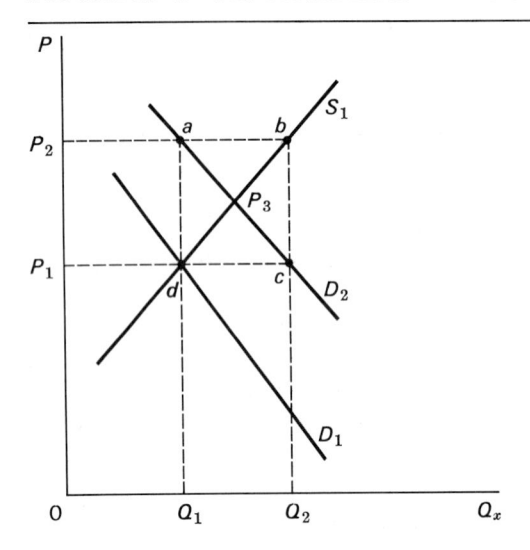

feature: There is a lag in production such that suppliers supply a given quantity of product in period $t+1$ based upon production decisions made in period t. Moreover, we assume production decisions are made in period t based upon prices existing in period t, and that once production plans are made, based on current prices, they are irreversible and will not be complete until the following period. Figure 13–2 demonstrates the model, where D_1 is the initial demand for X, and S_1 the supply, resulting in equilibrium price P_1 and quantity Q_1. D_1 is to be interpreted as usual, but S_1 is different, for it shows the quantity of output supplied by firms in the *subsequent* period, given *this* period's price.

Now suppose equilibrium price P_1 and quantity Q_1 are disturbed by a shift in demand from D_1 to D_2. This will raise price from P_1 to P_2 (point a on D_2) in the immediate period, since the quantity supplied cannot be increased above Q_1, except after a period of elapsed time. According to our assumption about supply, price P_2 will cause a quantity of Q_2 to be supplied in the next period, which will fetch a price of P_1, as determined by point c on D_2. Price P_1 will, in turn, cause the quantity supplied in the next period to be Q_1. The new quantity is consistent with a price of P_2 in that period (point a on D_2). But this is where we began. Evidently, if there are no other changes, price will fluctuate between P_1 and P_2 and quantity, between Q_1 and Q_2, indefinitely. This illustrates the second possibility listed above. The specific requirement for continuous oscillation of price and quantity is that the absolute value of the slope of S_1 equal that of D_2. Otherwise, price will either explode, if D_2 is steeper, or gradually approach the equilibrium price P_3 if S_1 is steeper. The latter would illustrate the third possibility that we listed.

To summarize, it is possible that under certain circumstances a general equilibrium in a market economy will be unattainable. We saw that this is true if the supply curves in output markets exhibit a certain shape in relation to demand, and that it may also be true if lagged relations exist in producers' responses to output prices.

The Arguments for a General Equilibrium Solution

So far we have pointed out those situations in which a stable pattern of prices in an economy is unattainable. What about the fourth of our possibilities? If a number of simplifying assumptions are made concerning a general equilibrium model, then an equilibrium solution to the models is theoretically attainable. This has been proved by L. Walras and A. Wald[4] and also by K. J. Arrow and G. Debreu.[5] The Arrow–Debreu general equilibrium model employs only one set of markets for resources and commodities. This makes the model more convenient for handling the theoretical problems associated with intermediate goods and output which may be employed either as a commodity or a resource. In addition, the model assumes a finite number of firms with nonincreasing returns to scale, thus ruling out downward sloping long-run supply curves. Also, it assumes consumers have defined consumption preferences and cannot be satiated with attainable levels of output. The general equilibrium model of Arrow–Debreu leads to the conclusion that the attainable states of the economy are bounded by the *production set* on one side and the *consumption set* on the other.

One argument which supports the inherent stability of a market economy is the *theory of approximations* or *tâtonnements* as advanced by Walras. Walras suggests that suppliers and demanders would "discover" equilibrium through a process of successive approximations. That is, through a process of "groping," the buyers and sellers will try out different prices and quantities until an effort to find equilibrium is successful. Walras' theory of *tâtonnements* is essentially a theory of the dynamics of a market system, of how an equilibrium condition, once disturbed, will return to equilibrium. It is based upon trial and error. If a given price–quantity is in error (not an equilibrium price and quantity), the actions of suppliers and demanders will cause a new price–quantity combination to be tried, and the process will continue until an equilibrium price and quantity are achieved. The successive price–quantity combinations tested are presumably determined in a systematic manner in which the existence of excess supply or demand is given only a partial role. An objection to this theory, first raised by Edgeworth, is that not enough detail is furnished about the path of the system as it seeks to establish an equilibrium.

[4] Leon Walras and A. Wald, "On Some Systems of Equations of Mathematical Models." *Econometrica*, 19 (1951), 368–403.
[5] K. J. Arrow and G. Debreu, "Existence of an Equilibrium for a Competitive Economy," *Econometrica*, 22 (1954), 265–290.

GENERAL EQUILIBRIUM AND ECONOMIC EFFICIENCY

Suppose we can be reasonably confident that, in a perfectly competitive market economy, a general equilibrium will result, either because the elasticities of supply and demand are such that all markets will return to equilibrium after a disturbance or because the system, through a process of *tâtonnement*, adjusts to changes in a manner that avoids unnecessary disruption. What can we say about the likelihood that the resulting general equilibrium will be an economically efficient or optimal one? Before we proceed any further, we should set out our basic criteria for optimality. This criteria was first developed by Vilfredo Pareto, an Italian economist who lived from 1848 to 1923. Pareto's criterion is not that the pattern of prices and quantities in the system be ethically correct or socially acceptable. Rather, the criterion is described as follows:

> *A Pareto optimum exists if no person can improve his utility without reducing someone else's utility. By the same token, a given state of an economy is not Pareto optimal if the utility of at least one person can be improved without lowering that of another.*

In the following sections of this chapter, we will attempt to prove that a perfectly competitive economy will be Pareto optimal. To accomplish this objective, we will set out the criteria for Pareto optimality in three separate parts. The first concerns the criteria for efficiency in the use of resources. The second concerns the criteria for efficiency in the distribution of a given output among consumers, and the third concerns the production of an optimal mix of consumer goods. Only when an economic system is efficient on all three counts can it be said to be Pareto optimal. We will then show that the three basic criteria are satisfied under conditions of perfect competition. We will have to qualify our conclusion at a later point, but, for the time being, we will ignore the qualifications.

Efficiency in the Use of Resources

We begin by retaining our simplified model, in which there are two goods produced, X and Y, using two resources, A and B. Though there may be many firms producing X's and many firms producing Y's, for the present, think of one firm producing X's using A's and B's and another producing Y's using the same two inputs.[6] In Figure 13–3, we have presented in what is called an Edgeworth Box diagram, the isoquants for the firm making X's and the isoquants for the firm making Y's. The isoquants for good X are read in the conventional way, with the number of units of resource B read along the vertical $O^X B$ axis and A's read along the horizontal $O^X A$ axis. I_3^X represents an

---

[6] In fact, it is probable that some firms will produce both X's and Y's.

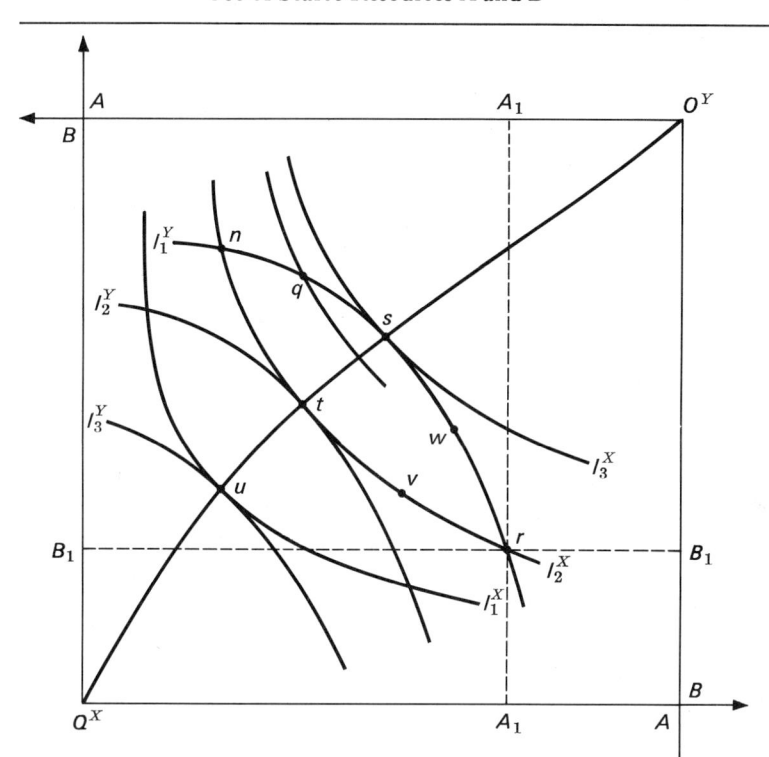

FIGURE 13-3 An Edgeworth Box Used to Demonstrate Efficiency in the Use of Scarce Resources A and B

output of X's greater than I_2^X, which is greater than I_1^X. We have drawn only three representative isoquants from the family of isoquants for X. On the other hand, the isoquants for Y's, I_1^Y, I_2^Y, and I_3^Y, can be read in the conventional way, only by inverting the page, since the origin for these isoquants is O^Y, in the northeast corner of the graph. I_3^Y, which represents a greater output of Y's than I_2^Y or I_1^Y, is furthest from the O^Y origin, as to be expected, but closer to the O^X origin. To read larger quantities of A used to make Y's, we read *right to left* along $O^Y A$, and more B's used to make Y's is read *down* the $O^Y B$ axis. Again I_1^Y, I_2^Y, and I_3^Y represent only three of the family of isoquants for Y.

The sides of the box, $O^X B$ ($O^Y B$) and $O^X A$ ($O^Y A$), measure the total amount of resources, B and A respectively, which are available to the two firms.

Now suppose the division of the resources between the two firms is represented by point r. Notice that once a single point is designated, the distribution of A's and B's between the two firms is determined. Firm 1 is employing

$O^X A_1$ units of A and $O^X B_1$ units of B to produce an output of X's represented by I_2^X. Simultaneously, firm 2 is employing $O^Y A_1$ units of A and $O^Y B_1$ units of B to make an output of Y's represented by the isoquant I_1^Y. Suppose the allocation of A's and B's were changed, giving more B's to the firm making X's and more A's to the firm making Y's, a movement on the graph from point r to w to s. The production of Y's would be unaffected, since this is a movement along the isoquant I_1^Y. But the production of X's would rise if the allocation is changed to point s; specifically the output of X's would increase from that associated with I_2^X to I_3^X. Clearly, this would be a desired reallocation of A's and B's from the standpoint of over-all productive efficiency in the system, since the output of X rises with no reduction in the output of Y. In other words, the resource allocation at point r is not Pareto optimal, since, by switching to s, we can increase one output, X (and thus someone's utility), without lowering the output of Y.

Once the allocation represented by point s is achieved, there can be no further gains in the output of X (or Y) from the reallocation of inputs A and B, except at the expense of reductions in the output of Y (or X). For instance, if we continued to reallocate A's and B's until we got to point q, we would not have affected the production of Y's (we are still on I_1^Y), but we would have fallen to an isoquant for X's representing a lower output than I_3^X. Point s is unique because isoquant I_1^Y is tangent to isoquant I_3^X.

Our analysis could have proceeded just as well with a reallocation of inputs along I_2^X from point r to v, then to t. In this case, the output of X's would remain unchanged, while the output of Y's would increase. But the basic conclusion is still the same: productive efficiency is improved by a reallocation from point r to point t. In fact, any reallocation of A's and B's away from points like r, w, v, or n is desirable, since at least one of the outputs can be increased without reducing the output of the other. Points u, t, and s are unique because they are points of tangency between the isoquants for X and those for Y. All the combinations of A and B along $O^X uts O^Y$ have the property that any reallocation of inputs to points off the line will either (1) lower output of X while keeping output of Y the same, (2) lower output of Y while keeping X the same, or (3) lower output of both X and Y. On the other hand, a change from one point on line $O^X uts O^Y$ to another point still on the line $O^X uts O^Y$ will necessarily increase the output of one good while decreasing the output of the other. We may summarize by saying *all* allocations of A's and B's along $O^X uts O^Y$ are Pareto optimal and all allocations off the line are Pareto inferior.

The points along $O^X uts O^Y$ are the points of tangency of isoquants for good X with those for Y. If the isoquants for X and Y are tangent for the efficient allocations, then their slopes must be equal. But the slope of an isoquant for X equals the marginal rate of substitution of A for B in the production of X and the slope of an isoquant for Y equals the marginal rate of substitution of

A for B in the production of Y. Using superscripts to distinguish the two rates of substitution, we get:

$$MRS_{AB}{}^X = MRS_{AB}{}^Y \qquad (20)$$

as the basic Pareto requirement for production efficiency.

From Chapter 6, we know that a firm which minimizes the cost of production will equate the MRS_{AB} with the ratio of the prices of the inputs A and B. That is, the cost-minimizing combination of A and B for any given output is determined by the tangency of the firm's isoquant with its isocost curve, and at that tangency point, $MRS_{AB} = P_A/P_B$. But if we assume that all users of resources A and B pay the same price, then all firms' isocost curves have the same slope. Any one firm, say the firm making X's, will equate:

$$MRS_{AB}{}^X = \frac{P_A}{P_B},$$

and the firm making Y's will equate:

$$MRS_{AB}{}^Y = \frac{P_A}{P_B},$$

and since the ratio, P_A/P_B, is the same for all firms by assumption, then:

$$MRS_{AB}{}^Y = MRS_{AB}{}^X.$$

We may conclude that this condition holds, and the situation is Pareto optimal, if all users of the resources pay the same prices for them. Of course, one of the characteristics of perfect competition in resource markets is that all buyers are price takers, since each is small relative to the market. This means the Pareto optimal condition for the efficient use of resources is satisfied in competitive resource markets.

Efficiency in Distribution

Many economists believe that there exist no valid means of directly determining society's well-being as measured by the total utility people derive from consumption. So even though the maximization of social utility might be an ideal goal, it is generally unachievable since social utility is not measurable, because either (1) the techniques for measurement do not yet exist, or (2) they cannot exist. The measurement of total social utility probably falls into the second category. There is simply no way of determining whether A gets greater utility than B from spending a dollar's income. Even if we could enter everyone's head to determine objectively how much utility each person derives from consumption (and, of course, we cannot at present, although the possibility cannot be completely ruled out), the criterion of social utility maximization would seemingly require that the person with the largest capacity for enjoyment from consumption receive the largest share of output. There is no reason to be confident that distribution on this basis would be socially acceptable or equitable. Equity as regards economic policy almost defies definition. For this reason, economists have tended to focus on distribution efficiency rather than equity. In other words, since it is well-nigh impossible to determine when social utility is being maximized, and since it is equally difficult or impossible to reach a satisfactory consensus regarding what is an equitable distribution of income, we tend to concentrate on distribution efficiency as our primary concern.

As the discussion above implies, to develop the criteria for a Pareto optimal allocation of consumer goods and services, we must use ordinal rather than cardinal utility. We will find that a Pareto optimum exists when no one person can increase his utility (move to a higher indifference curve) without reducing someone else's utility (by shifting him onto a lower indifference curve). Our model for presenting the conditions for distribution efficiency looks much like the Edgeworth Box model used earlier. We begin by assuming two consumers and two commodities, X and Y, and we further assume that the total amount of consumer goods X and Y available to both consumers is fixed. The model is presented in Figure 13–4. The indifference curves for consumer number one are presented in the usual way, with increased consumption of X represented by a left-to-right movement along O^1X and increased Y consumption by an upward movement along O^1Y. Indifference curve I_3^1 represents more utility for the first consumer than I_1^1 or I_2^1. (The superscript indicates the curves are for the first individual.) Increased consumption of X by the second consumer is represented by a right-to-left movement along the O^2X axis, and increased consumption of Y by a downward movement along O^2Y. As conventionally viewed, the indifference curves for the second individual appear concave, but with respect to the YO^2X plane, they would be convex, as expected. I_3^2 represents greater utility to the second consumer than I_2^2, which represents more utility than I_1^2. In general, a northeast movement in the diagram means more X and Y consumed by the first individual and less X and Y consumed by the second individual, and thus more utility enjoyed by the first and less by the second.

The lengths of the respective sides of the rectangular box equal the total available X and Y for the two consumers. That is, O^1X (equal to O^2X) is the maximum amount of X available for both consumers, and O^1Y (equal to O^2Y) is the maximum amount of Y.

Now we begin by supposing that the distribution of X and Y between the two consumers is represented by point r in Figure 13–4. Consumer one has O^1X_1 units of X and O^1Y_1 units of Y, whereas consumer two has O^2X_1 units of X and O^2Y_1 units of Y. Consumer one enjoys a utility level represented by his indifference curve I_2^1, whereas individual two would be on I_1^2. Suppose that the first consumer exchanged X's for Y's with consumer two as shown by a movement from point r to point w and then to point s in the diagram. Con-

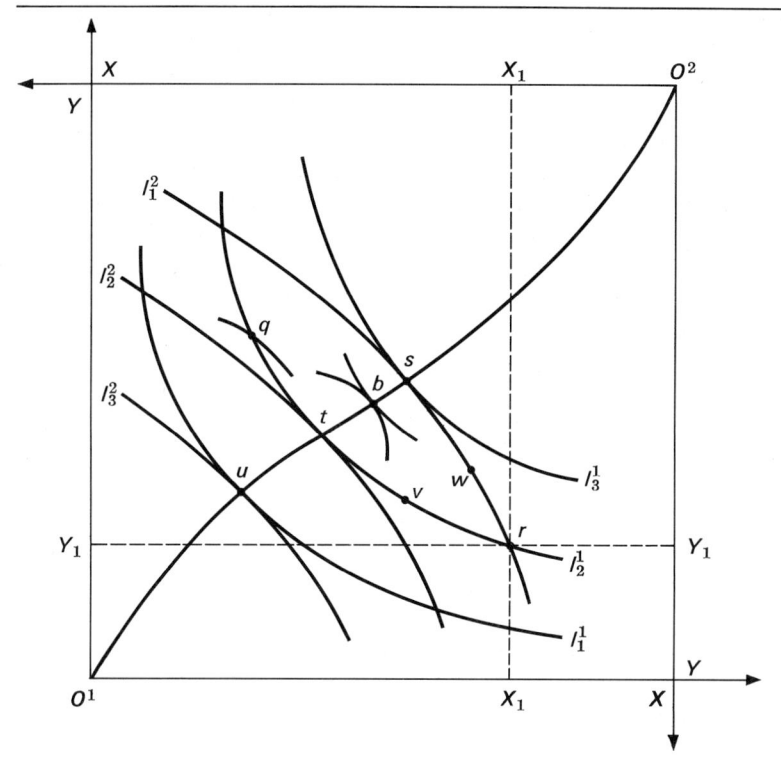

FIGURE 13-4 An Edgeworth Box Used to Demonstrate Efficiency in the Allocation of Products X and Y Among Two Consumers

sumer two's utility level would not be affected by this pattern of exchange, because all three points lie along his indifference curve I_1^2, but consumer one would gain utility because these points lie on indifference curves further from origin, O^1. At point s, consumer one would be on indifference curve I_3^1, representing greater utility than I_2^1, while consumer two is still on I_1^2. As another possible pattern of exchange, consumer two might swap Y's for X's with consumer one, as represented by moving from point r to points v and t. In this case, consumer two would gain utility, moving from curve I_1^2 to I_2^2, whereas consumer one's utility would be unaffected, since he would stay on his indifference curve I_2^1.

Once at point t, the point of tangency of consumer one's I_2^1 curve with two's I_2^2 curve, it is not possible to increase the utility of one individual except by reducing the utility of the other. For instance, a change in the distribution away from point t to that represented by point q would leave consumer one unaffected (he is still on I_2^1) but would lower two's utility level since point q lies on an indifference curve lower than that of I_2^2. This same conclusion would apply for any redistribution away from all other points of tangency between consumer one's indifference curves and consumer two's curves. Collecting all these points of tangency we get O^1utbsO^2, called a *contract curve*.

The two patterns of exchange described above (movement from point r to either s or t) would either (1) increase consumer one's utility and leave consumer two unaffected or (2) increase consumer two's utility and leave consumer one unaffected. If the two individuals are free to exchange with each other on terms mutually agreeable, and if we begin with a distribution at r, it is unlikely that either of these two patterns will emerge, since in either case one person would gain nothing. More likely a bargain will be struck which will benefit both, such as a movement from point r to point b on the line O^1utbsO^2. In any case, once the distribution of the two consumer goods is represented by any point on the contract curve, there is no possibility for improving one consumer's utility without reducing the other's, and thus no basis for any further exchange between the two consumers.

We may summarize by saying that any distribution of goods X and Y along line O^1utbsO^2, the contract curve, has the characteristic that if this distribution is changed in any way, either by a move to a point off the line or to another point on the line, the level of utility of one or both of the consumers will be lowered. Moreover, for any distribution of the two goods not on this line, an exchange (freely entered into by both parties) that results in a new distribution of the goods on the line O^1utbsO^2 will either (1) raise the utility of one consumer and not affect the other or (2) raise the utility of both. From the standpoint of distributive efficiency, then, a combination of consumer goods off of line O^1utbsO^2 can be improved upon by a redistribution of consumer goods back on the contract curve. We may conclude that all distributions along the contract curve are Pareto optimal and all those not on the curve are Pareto inferior.

The efficient distributions of X and Y along the contract curve are determined by the tangency points of consumer one's indifference curves with consumer two's curves. At these tangency points, the slopes of the indifference curves are equal. But the slope of consumer one's indifference curves equals the marginal rate of substitution of Y for X for consumer one, and the slope of consumer two's indifference curves (as viewed from the YO^2X plane) equals the marginal rate of substitution of Y for X for consumer two. We may indicate, therefore, the requirement for Pareto optimality, using symbols as:

$$MRS_{YX}{}^1 = MRS_{YX}{}^2,$$

where the superscripts 1 and 2 indicate consumers one and two, respectively.

From Chapter 3, you will recall that a consumer maximizes utility by choosing that combination of consumer goods for which his indifference curve is tangent to his budget line. The slope of the budget line is equal to the ratio P_X/P_Y (neglecting signs), which is fixed to the consumer if he is a price taker. If all consumers of goods X and Y are price takers, and there is one price for all, then all will face budget lines of identical slope. Any given consumer, say consumer one, will equate:

$$MRS_{YX}{}^1 = P_X/P_Y.$$

But consumer two (or any other consumer) will also equate:

$$MRS_{YX}{}^2 = P_X/P_Y,$$

and since the ratio P_X/P_Y is the same for both consumers, we can write:

$$MRS_{YX}{}^1 = MRS_{YX}{}^2.$$

Moreover, we can generalize this result for any two consumers of X and Y as long as all face given prices for the two goods. To summarize, we may say that a distribution of consumer goods is Pareto optimal if all consumers face the same prices for these goods. The latter condition is, of course, satisfied in perfectly competitive consumer goods markets.

The Pareto Optimal Production Mix

The Pareto optimality criteria which we have discussed thus far have concerned efficiency in the use of resources and efficiency in the distribution of a given output of X and Y. We have not yet established, however, the criteria for a Pareto optimal output mix. Suppose we retain our assumption that there are only two commodities, X and Y, and two inputs in our system. What, then, is the Pareto optimal combination of the two goods to produce? We will attack this problem by introducing (1) a production possibilities curve for the economy and (2) the notion of a community indifference curve.

First, what are the possible combinations of X and Y that can be produced, given the fixity of resources in the economy? Referring to Figure 13–3, the efficient combinations of resources A and B are those along the curve $O^X uts O^Y$. If all resources are used to make X's, output will be that associated with the X isoquant which passes through origin O^Y, whereas if only Y's are made, the maximum possible output would be that associated with the isoquant for Y's through origin O^X. Suppose X_M is the maximum X's possible and Y_M is the maximum Y's possible. Another possibility is to distribute the resources between X and Y production as represented by point t in Figure 13–3. This would give an X output associated with $X_2{}^X$ and a Y output associated with $I_2{}^Y$. If we continue and collect all the possible X–Y combinations along $O^X uts O^Y$, we generate the curve labeled PC_E in Figure 13–5, called the economy's production possibility curve or *transformation curve*. This name derives from the fact that the economy can transform resources into either X's or Y's and that Y's, then, can be transformed (by not producing Y's) into X's or vice versa. The transformation curve is identical in concept to the production possibilities curve presented in introductory economics courses in which, typically, guns are measured on one axis and butter on the other.

FIGURE 13–5 The Production Possibilities Curve and Community Indifferences Curves

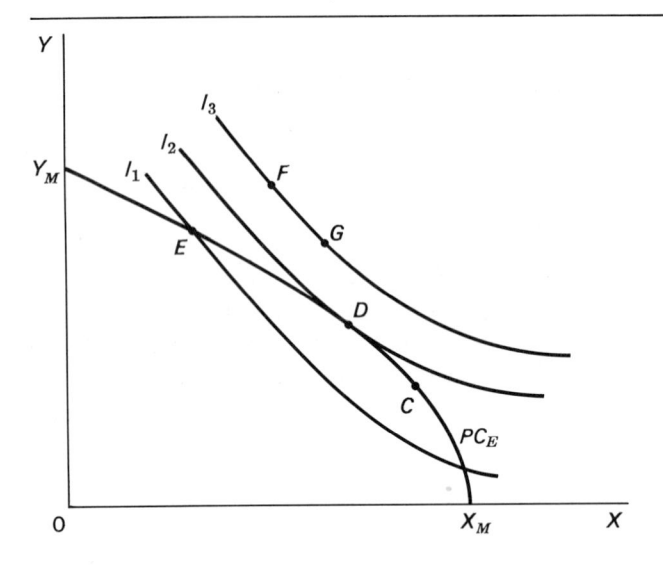

The slope of the PC_E curve at any point, say point E, measures the marginal rate of transformation of one good for the other. In symbols:

$$MRT_{YX}{}^C = \frac{\Delta Y}{\Delta X}.$$

$MRT_{YX}{}^C$ measures the rate for the whole community at which one good can be "transformed" in production for the other. It also measures the real opportunity cost of producing one product as the reduction in the production of the other which is necessary to produce the first.

The curves labeled I_1, I_2, and I_3 in Figure 13–5 are called community indifference curves. We may note that they are derived from the indifference curves of consumers in the economy. Their derivation, however, is beyond the scope of this book.[7] We may, nevertheless, describe their basic characteristics. First, note that these curves are drawn up on the assumption of a *given income distribution* among consumers that is efficiently distributed in the sense that Pareto optimality criteria are satisfied. Given the distribution of income, different combinations of goods X and Y along one of the community indifference curves results in equal utility for consumers in the economy; for example, a move from point F to G along I_3 would leave each consumer's level of utility unaffected. If a community indifference curve is drawn for two consumers, neither may be dislodged from his own indifference curve as we move from

[7] See E. J. Mishan, "A Survey of Welfare Economics, 1939–1959," *Economic Journal* (1959).

point to point along the community indifference curve. The combination at G on I_3 in Figure 13-5 represents more X and less Y than point F. Some consumers must be giving up Y's (some more than others) in a move from F to G, but to keep each consumer's utility constant, these consumers are compensated by giving them more X's. Like the indifference curves we have already worked with, there is a family of community indifference curves, those further from the origin representing more utility than those closer. That is, I_3 in Figure 13-5 represents greater social utility than I_2 or I_3.

We may define the marginal rate of substitution of good Y for X along a community indifference curve as:

$$MRS_{YX}{}^C = \frac{\Delta Y}{\Delta X},$$

which is thus defined much like the MRS_{YX} for any consumer. The superscript designates the MRS for a community indifference curve. The difference between the MRS for a consumer and the MRS for the community is that, for the latter, the changes in Y and X are such that all consumers' utilities remain unchanged; e.g., ΔX and ΔY are changes along a community indifference curve.

Now we are ready to combine community indifference curves with the production possibilities curve for the community. Referring again to Figure 13-5, we can say that the production of the commodity bundle at point E is not Pareto optimal since, by switching to the bundle at point D, we can improve community welfare; i.e., point E is on I_1 whereas D is on I_2. With the limitations on available resources, output combinations along I_3 are not possible. The combination at D is optimal, since it is on the highest community indifference curve attainable. Combination D is Pareto optimal, since it is not possible to increase anyone's utility without reducing someone else's. The Pareto optimum at point D is determined by the tangency of PC_E with I_2. This means the slopes of the two curves are equal, which, in turn, means the marginal rate of substitution of Y for X along the community indifference curve equals the marginal rate of transformation along the production possibilities curve. In symbols:

$$MRS_{YX}{}^C = MRT_{YX}{}^C.$$

In words, for a production mix to be Pareto optimal, the marginal rate of transformation of Y for X must equal the marginal rate of substitution of the two goods. If the two rates are not equal, it will be possible to raise community utility by switching to a new commodity bundle at which the rates coincide.

The optimality criterion established above is satisfied in a two-commodity economy with many consumers and many firms if the marginal rate of trans-

FIGURE 13-6 The Profit-Maximizing Output of a Firm

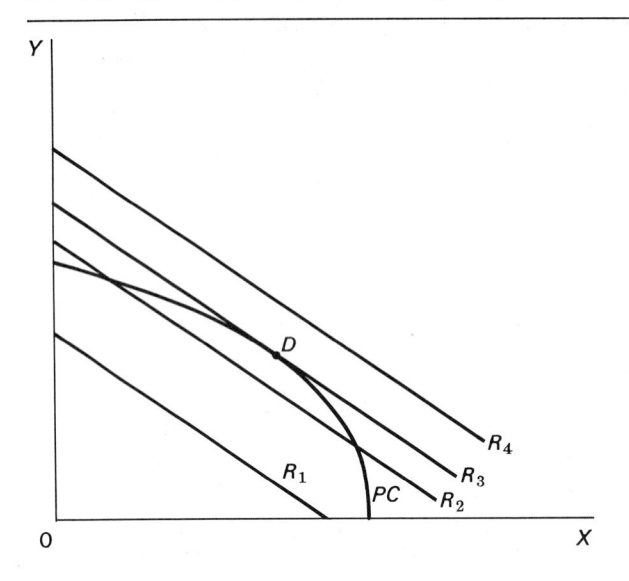

formation for any producer is equal to the marginal rate of substitution for any consumer.[8] That is, the equality:

$$MRS_{YX}{}^V = MRT_{YX}{}^V$$

must be satisfied, where the superscript indicates any consumer and any firm. We will now show that this last equality will indeed be satisfied in a perfectly competitive economy.

First, recall that a consumer maximizes utility by purchasing that quantity of X and Y for which his indifference curve is tangent with his budget line. At that point of tangency, the consumer's MRS_{YX} equals the ratio of the prices of the two goods. That is, for any consumer:

$$MRS_{YX} = \frac{P_X}{P_Y}.$$

Now we must turn our attention to the firm to show that to maximize its profits it will equate its MRT_{YX} with the ratio of the prices of X and Y. We assume at this point that the firm produces both X's and Y's and seeks to produce the most profitable combination of the two. A profit-maximizing two-product model is demonstrated in Figure 13-6. PC is the production pos-

[8] For an advanced discussion of those criteria, see Francis M. Bator, "The Simple Analytics of Welfare Maximization," *American Economic Review*, Vol. XLVII (March 1957), 22–59.

sibilities curve for the firm drawn on the basis of a given quantity of resources available to it. The lines R_1 through R_4 are called *isorevenue lines*. These latter curves show the combinations of X and Y that result in a given revenue for the firm. Isorevenue curves to the north and east represent greater total revenue than those to the south and west. Assuming constant output prices, the slopes of all isorevenue curves are identical and equal to P_X/P_Y (neglecting signs). This model, though nonlinear, is analogous to a linear programming problem: The solution is found at point D, since the revenue associated with R_3 is the largest attainable with the firm's given quantity of resources. At point D, the firm's MRT_{YX} equals the slope of R_3, so:

$$MRT_{YX} = \frac{P_X}{P_Y}.$$

Now we have determined that any one consumer equates $MRS_{YX} = P_X/P_Y$ to maximize utility, and any one firm equates $MRT_{YX} = P_X/P_Y$ to maximize profit. If we assume perfect competition throughout, the prices of X and Y are given to all firms and all consumers. This means both firms and consumers are price takers and that the ratio P_X/P_Y is the same for all. The budget line of any consumer has the same slope as the isorevenue curve of any firm. We may therefore equate:

$$MRT_{YX} = MRS_{YX}$$

for all firms and consumers in the economy, which is, therefore, consistent with the equality of:

$$MRT_{YX}{}^C = MRS_{YX}{}^C,$$

the rates of substitution for the community. This discussion may, therefore, conclude that the existence of perfect competition is consistent with production of a "mix" of consumer goods that is Pareto optimal.

Pulling the various parts together, we can summarize by saying that a perfectly competitive economy implies Pareto optimality regarding (1) resource use, (2) distribution of output, and (3) the production mix. Under these conditions, it is not possible to increase the welfare of any one person in the economy without reducing the welfare of someone else.

It is important to point out that Pareto optimality associated with perfect competition does not necessarily imply an equitable or socially acceptable income distribution. In fact, Pareto optimality is consistent with different income distributions. An income distribution that is highly unequal can, nevertheless, be Pareto optimal. Referring again to Figure 13–4, a point on the contract curve close to the origin O^2, which means greater real income for consumer one than for consumer two is, nevertheless, consistent with Pareto optimality, as is a possible distribution close to O^1. Many might consider inequality in the distributions of income as inequitable. Pareto optimality criteria can contribute little to the determination of criteria for an equitable distribution. Pareto criteria are useful largely as a test for economic efficiency.

Externalities—A Qualification

We must make one major qualification to the general conclusion that we have developed. That qualification is that for Pareto optimality to exist in a competitive economy, there must be no externalities (costs or benefits) in the economy. Recall from Chapter 4 our definition of external costs as those costs which arise because of the actions of one individual (or firm) which are borne by one or more other persons. Examples are the smoke emitted by a firm or sewage by a municipality, which results in costs borne by the public. There may also arise certain benefits, due to one person's actions, which are enjoyed by another, and these are called external benefits. An example often given of the latter is that of a beekeeper whose bees may, in the course of gathering honey, pollinate the trees of an orchard keeper. The beekeeper cannot easily collect from the orchard keeper for the services of his bees, any more than the public can easily charge for the costs imposed by the firm for emitting noxious smoke.

Suppose a perfectly competitive economy has achieved a general equilibrium and that in this economy there exist certain external benefits and/or costs associated with the economic behavior of people. As a microillustration, suppose individual A's activities generate external costs, borne largely by individual B, and that B's actions result in considerable external benefits, enjoyed largely by A. The situation is very probably Pareto inferior, since a reduction in A's activity and an increase in B's activity would very likely improve the utility of both. Of course, if A and B are close enough together, they will likely effect an exchange: B will agree to reduce his activity somewhat, thereby lowering the costs imposed upon A, in exchange for an expansion in A's activity that benefits B. But, in many situations involving externalities, the exchange mechanism will not function at all or, at least, not efficiently in this respect. For example, it may be that an external benefit associated with an activity is widely distributed among many individuals. Singly, these individuals have no effective way to register their demands for these benefits. Neither is there a market mechanism for individuals to collect for external costs imposed upon them by others. Externalities involve extramarket phenomena; e.g., no markets exist for quiet neighborhoods or clean rivers.

Individuals in a competitive economy make their decisions on the basis of the private costs and benefits which attend their actions. Any external effects of their activities, they will possibly ignore or, at any rate, these external effects will not influence the decision in the desired direction, as they would if the decision maker paid *all* costs and received *all* benefits. As a result, we can generalize as follows:

> *Activities resulting in considerable external costs will be carried to excessive levels, whereas activities tending to produce considerable external benefits will not be carried far enough.*

Our conclusion that a perfectly competitive economy is Pareto optimal assumes the absence of externalities. Now we must conclude that where externalities exist, general equilibrium in a competitive economy may not be Pareto optimal.

WELFARE ECONOMICS

Since before Adam Smith, economics has been concerned not only with the positive aspects of the discipline, but also with the normative. Of course, it is positive economics that has laid claim to being the scientific branch of economics, for the theories of positive economics seek only to systematize observable economic behavior by developing principles or generalizations about economic events. Empirical testing, in the tradition of the physical sciences, leads to refinements in positive economic theories, making them more efficient predictive devices. But economics has never taken, for long, a neutral stand on normative questions. Underlying all economic analysis is the objective of improving things. Spending resources to acquire knowledge about economic systems makes little sense, unless we somehow put this knowledge to work. But what is the role of positive economics? Positive economics should provide a basis for distinguishing between "good" states of the economic system, where social welfare is high, and "bad" states of the system, where it is low, so we can opt for the former through economic policy. Unfortunately, economic theory will not always give us a firm "ruling" on whether one state is better than another, as we shall see.

The Pareto optimality criteria, which we have discussed throughout most of this chapter, provide one basis for distinguishing good and bad states of an economy. Few would argue against the conclusion that social welfare had increased if an economic change increased A's utility without decreasing B's or anybody else's, or if it raised A's and B's utility without reducing anyone else's in the economy. Since perfectly competitive conditions throughout an economy give assurance that Pareto's criteria will be met, many economists prescribe competition in preference to monopoly. But, typically, it is not possible to make a selection on an "all or nothing" basis. More likely, policy decisions will concern smaller adjustments in particular sectors of the system.

But can we be assured of improving things if we make a system "more" competitive? *The Theory of Second Best* answers this question in the negative.[9] In general, if an economic system is Pareto inferior, we can make it Pareto optimal by transforming it so as to satisfy all of the Pareto criteria for optimality. But if only a partial fulfillment of the criteria is possible, we cannot be *assured* of a gain in social welfare, according to the theory of the second best. In fact, we might make things worse. But such "piecemeal" policy adjustments are typical, for example, United States anti-trust policy. There can be little hope for a "once and for all" readjustment in an economic system to perfect competition or any other system guaranteeing Pareto optimality. Indeed, most economic systems cannot efficiently be made perfectly competitive throughout for reasons of scale economies.

In any case, Pareto criteria provide weak guidelines for economic policy. First of all, they are consistent with a highly unequal income distribution, and for this reason tend to favor the existing state of a system, whether bad or good on equity grounds. Secondly, from a practical policy standpoint, it is well-nigh impossible to tamper with the state of an economy without improving the welfare of some people and worsening that of others. Most policy changes do both, for instance, adjustments in the tax structure, expenditures for public goods, and the like. But such changes are a violation of Pareto criteria. If the change is initiated anyway, who is to say that the gains outweigh the losses? When two people or two groups of people are affected by a policy change, one made better off and the other worse, there can be no assurance of a net gain for society. Positive economics does not provide us with a measuring stick for making *interpersonal comparisons* of utility. If the rich are taxed to pay the poor, is social welfare increased? There can be no definitive answer to this question, since we cannot measure the rich man's loss or the poor man's gain. The policy maker may strongly feel that there is a net gain, but there are no scientific grounds for this belief. Policies may be formulated on the basis of judgment alone.

[9] See R. G. Lipsey and R. K. Lancaster, "The General Theory of Second Best," *Review of Economic Studies*, 24, No. 63 (December 1956).

PROBLEMS

1. Answer the following based on the corresponding graph. O^1 is the origin for the first consumer and O^2, the second. The initial distribution of X and Y is at point B.

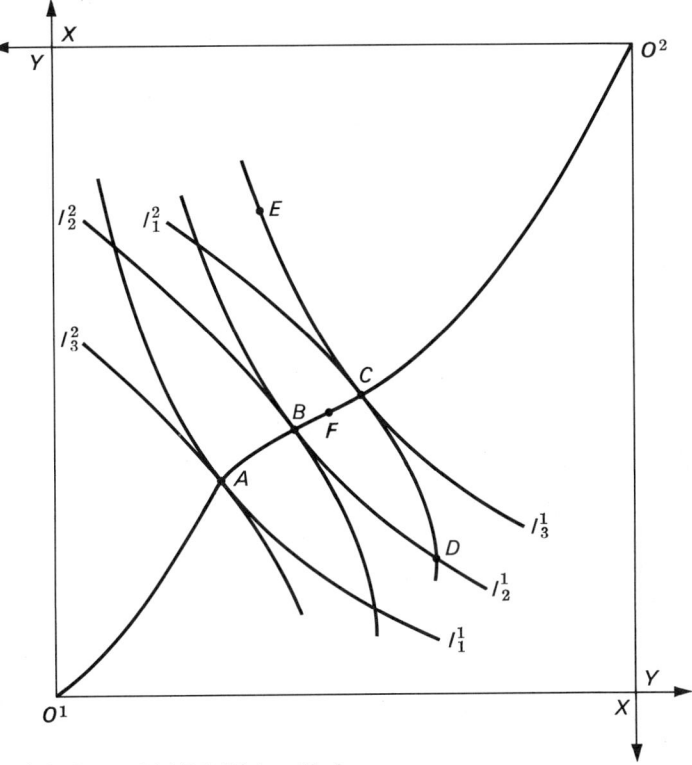

(a) Line O^1ABCO^2 is called a _____.
(b) A move from point B to point D would (increase, decrease, neither increase nor decrease) one's utility and (increase, decrease, neither increase nor decrease) two's utility.
(c) Point E is Pareto (inferior, superior, neutral).
(d) A move from B to C (lowers, raises) one's utility and (lowers, raises) two's utility.
(e) Given an initial distribution at point D, one and two are likely to enter into trade, after which the distribution is apt to be at (A, B, F, C).

2. Answer the following based on the accompanying figure. Assume a cobweb model, in which S_x shows the lagged supply.
(a) If the quantity supplied is initially OA, then price will initially be _____.

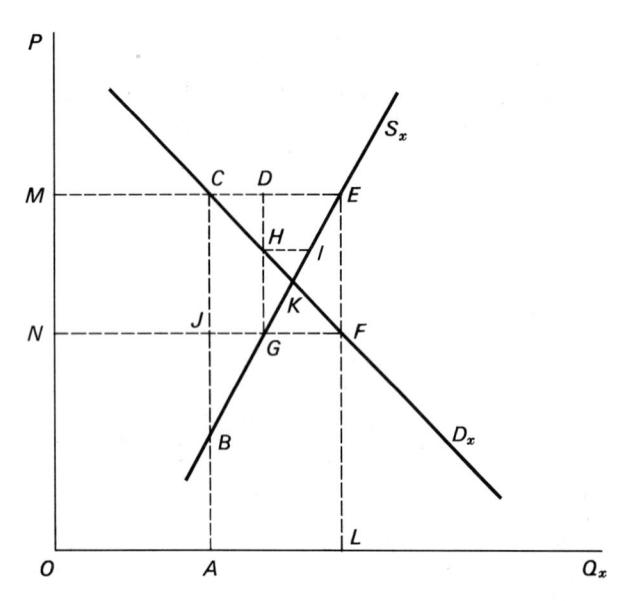

(b) This will cause _____ to be supplied in the subsequent period.
(c) This quantity supplied, in turn, will fetch a price of _____.
(d) And cause the quantity supplied in the following period to be _____.
(e) In this model, price will (explode, implode) and (never, eventually) reach price K because the absolute value of the slope of S_x is (greater than, less than, equal to) the slope of D_x.

3. If four goods exist in a barter economy, how many output price ratios will exist?
4. If an economy contains many industries characterized by large external diseconomies, perfect competition (is, is not) likely to assure Pareto optimality.
5. If one industrial activity is associated with large external diseconomies and another industry produces equal external benefits, it (is, is not) probable that there will be a balancing-out so that no public policy is needed.

REFERENCES

ARROW, KENNETH J., and DEBREU, GERARD, "Existence of an Equilibrium for a Competitive Economy," *Econometrica*, 22 (July 1954), 265–290.
BAUMOL, W. J., "External Economics and Second-Order Conditions," *American Economic Review*, 54 (1964), 358–372.
DAVIES, OTTO A., and WHINSTON, ANDREW, "Externalities, Welfare, and the Theory of Games," *Journal of Political Economy*, 70 (1962), 241–262.

Kaldor, Nicholas, "Welfare Propositions in Economics and Interpersonal Comparisons of Utility," *Economic Journal*, 49 (September 1939), 549–552.
Lange, O., "The Foundations of Welfare Economics," *Econometrica*, 1942.
Lipsey, R. G., and Lancaster, R. K., "The General Theory of Second Best," *Review of Economic Studies*, 24, No. 63 (December 1956).
Little, I. M. D., *A Critique of Welfare Economics*, 2nd ed. Oxford: Oxford University Press, 1957.
Pigou, A. C., *The Economics of Welfare*, 4th ed. London: Macmillan & Co., Ltd., 1932.
Samuelson, Paul A., "Social Indifference Curves," *Quarterly Journal of Economics*, 70 (1956), 1–22.
Scitovsky, Tibor, "The State of Welfare Economics," *American Economic Review*, 41 (June 1951), 303.

APPENDIX TO CHAPTER 13

Production, Consumption, and Externalities

ROBERT U. AYRES and ALLEN V. KNEESE*

We have indicated that perfect competition will not insure Pareto optimal conditions in an economy if there are significant externalities involved in the actions of people and firms. Before the explosion of interest in atmospheric, water, and other forms of pollution, economists tended to consider the problems of externalities as exceptions to be dealt with on a piecemeal basis. Here, Robert Ayres and Allen Kneese seek to integrate external effects into a general equilibrium framework. Rather than treating externalities as exceptions, they consider them natural adjuncts to production and the environment's ability to absorb them as a valuable natural resource. One conclusion is that policy based on a partial equilibrium approach to problems of externalities may be inefficient.

Students unfamiliar with simple matrix algebra may omit Section II without an undue loss of continuity.

> For all that, welfare economics can no more reach conclusions applicable to the real world without some knowledge of the real world than can positive economics. [E. J. Mishan, "Reflections on Recent Developments in the concept of External Effects," Canadian Jour. Econ. Pol. Sci., Feb. 1965, 31, 1–34.]

Despite tremendous public and governmental concern with problems such as environmental pollution, there has been a tendency in the economics literature to view externalities as exceptional cases. They may distort the allocation

From the *American Economic Review*, Vol. 59, No. 1 (June 1969). Reprinted by permission.

* The authors are respectively visiting scholar and director, Quality of the Environment Program, Resources for the Future, Inc. We are indebted to our colleagues Blair Bower, Orris Herfindahl, Charles Howe, John Krutilla, and Robert Steinberg for comments on an earlier draft. We have also benefited from comments by James Buchanan, Paul Davidson, Robert Dorfman, Otto Eckstein, Myrick Freeman, Mason Gaffney, Lester Lave, Herbert Mohring, and Gordon Tullock.

of resources but can be dealt with adequately through simple *ad hoc* arrangements. To quote Pigou:

> When it was urged above, that in certain industries a wrong amount of resources is being invested because the value of the marginal social net product there differs from the value of the marginal private net product, it was tacitly assumed that in the main body of industries these two values are equal. [A. C. Pigou, *Economics of Welfare*. London 1952.][1]

And Scitovsky, after having described his cases two and four which deal with technological externalities affecting consumers and producers respectively, says:

> The second case seems exceptional, because most instances of it can be and usually are eliminated by zoning ordinances and industrial regulations concerned with public health and safety. The fourth case seems unimportant, simply because examples of it seem to be few and exceptional. [T. Scitovsky, "Two Concepts of External Economies," *Jour. Pol. Econ.*, Apr. 1954, 62, 143–51.]

We believe that at least one class of externalities—those associated with the disposal of residuals resulting from the consumption and production process—must be viewed quite differently.[2] They are a normal, indeed, inevitable part of these processes. Their economic significance tends to increase as economic development proceeds, and the ability of the ambient environment to receive and assimilate them is an important natural resource of increasing value.[3] We will argue below that the common failure to recognize these facts

---

[1] Even Baumol who saw externalities as a rather pervasive feature of the economy tends to discuss external diseconomies like "smoke nuisance" entirely in terms of particular examples.

[2] We by no means wish to imply that this is the only important class of externalities associated with production and consumption. Also, we do not wish to imply that there has been a lack of theoretical attention to the externalities problem. In fact, the past few years have seen the publication of several excellent articles which have gone far toward systematizing definitions and illuminating certain policy issues. . . . However, all these contributions deal with externality as a comparatively minor aberration from Pareto optimality in competitive markets and focus upon externalities between two parties. Mishan, after a careful review of the literature, has commented on this as follows: "The form in which external effects have been presented in the literature is that of partial equilibrium analysis; a situation in which a single industry produces an equilibrium output, usually under conditions of perfect competition, some form of intervention being required in order to induce the industry to produce an "ideal" or "optimal" output. If the point is not made explicitly, it is tacitly understood that unless the rest of the economy remains organized in conformity with optimum conditions one runs smack into Second Best problems."

[3] That external diseconomies are integrally related to economic development and increasing congestion has been noted in passing in the literature. Mishan has commented: "The attention given to external effects in the recent literature is, I think, fully justified by the

may result from viewing the production and consumption processes in a manner that is somewhat at variance with the fundamental law of conservation of mass.

Modern welfare economics concludes that if (1) preference orderings of consumers and production functions of producers are independent and their shapes appropriately constrained, (2) consumers maximize utility subject to given income and price parameters, and (3) producers maximize profits subject to the price parameters; a set of prices exists such that no individual can be made better off without making some other individual worse off. For a given distribution of income this is an efficient state. Given certain further assumptions concerning the structure of markets, this "Pareto optimum" can be achieved via a pricing mechanism and voluntary decentralized exchange.

If waste assimilative capacity of the environment is scarce, the decentralized voluntary exchange process cannot be free of uncompensated technological external diseconomies unless (1) all inputs are fully converted into outputs, with no unwanted material residuals along the way,[4] and all final outputs are utterly destroyed in the process of consumption, or (2) property rights are so arranged that all relevant environmental attributes are in private ownership and these rights are exchanged in competitive markets. Neither of these conditions can be expected to hold in an actual economy and they do not.

Nature does not permit the destruction of matter except by annihilation with anti-matter, and the means of disposal of unwanted residuals which maximizes the internal return of decentralized decision units is by discharge to the environment, principally, watercourses and the atmosphere. Water and air are traditionally examples of free goods in economics. But in reality, in developed economies they are common property resources of great and increasing value presenting society with important and difficult allocation problems which exchange in private markets cannot resolve. These problems loom larger as increased population and industrial production put more pressure on the environment's ability to dilute and chemically degrade waste products. Only the crudest estimates of present external costs associated with residuals discharge exist but it would not be surprising if these costs were in the tens of billions of dollars annually.[5] Moreover, as we shall emphasize again, tech-

---

unfortunate, albeit inescapable, fact that as societies grow in material wealth, the incidence of these effects grows rapidly . . .," and Buchanan and Tullock have stated that as economic development proceeds, "congestion" tends to replace "co-operation" as the underlying motive force behind collective action, i.e., controlling external diseconomies tends to become more important than cooperation to realize external economies.

[4] Or any residuals which occur must be stored on the producer's premises.

[5] It is interesting to compare this with estimates of the cost of another well-known misallocation of resources that has occupied a central place in economic theory and research. In 1954, Harberger published an estimate of the welfare cost of monopoly which indi-

nological means for processing or purifying one or another type of waste discharge do not destroy the residuals but only alter their form. Thus, given the level, patterns, and technology of production and consumption, recycle of materials into productive uses or discharge into an alternative medium are the only general options for protecting a particular environmental medium such as water. Residual problems must be seen in a broad regional or economy-wide context rather than as separate and isolated problems of disposal of gas, liquid, and solid wastes.

Frank Knight perhaps provides a key to why these elementary facts have played so small a role in economic theorizing and empirical research.

> The next heading to be mentioned ties up with the question of dimensions from another angle, and relates to the second main error mentioned earlier as connected with taking food and eating as the type of economic activity. The basic economic magnitude (value or utility) is service, not good. It is inherently a stream or flow in time. . . .[6] [*Risk, Uncertainty and Profit*. Boston and New York, 1921.]

Almost all of standard economic theory is in reality concerned with services. Material objects are merely the vehicles which carry some of these services, and they are exchanged because of consumer preferences for the services associated with their use or because they can help to add value in the manufacturing process. Yet we persist in referring to the "final consumption" of goods as though material objects such as fuels, materials, and finished goods somehow disappeared into the void—a practice which was comparatively harmless so long as air and water were almost literally free goods.[7] Of course, residuals from both the production and consumption processes remain and they usually render disservices (like killing fish, increasing the difficulty of water treatment, reducing public health, soiling and deteriorating buildings, etc.) rather than services. Control efforts are aimed at eliminating or reducing those disservices which flow to consumers and producers whether they want them or

---

cated that it amounted to about .07 percent of GNP. In a later study, Schwartzman calculated the allocative cost at only .01 percent of GNP. Leibenstein generalized studies such as these to the statement that ". . . in a great many instances the amount to be gained by increasing allocative efficiency is trivial. . . ." But Leibenstein did not consider the allocative costs associated with environmental pollution.

[6] The point was also clearly made by Fisher [I. Fisher, *Nature of Capital and Income*. New York, 1906]: "The only true method, in our view, is to regard uniformly as income the *service* of a dwelling to its owner (shelter or money rental), the *service* of a piano (music), and the *service* of food (nourishment) . . ." (emphasis in original).

[7] We are tempted to suggest that the word consumption be dropped entirely from the economist's vocabulary as being basically deceptive. It is difficult to think of a suitable substitute, however. At least, the word consumption should not be used in connection with goods, but only with regard to services or flows of "utility."

not and which, except in unusual cases, they cannot control by engaging in individual exchanges.[8]

I. THE FLOW OF MATERIALS

To elaborate on these points, we find it useful initially to view environmental pollution and its control as a materials balance problem for the entire economy.[9] The inputs to the system are fuels, foods, and raw materials which are partly converted into final goods and partly become waste residuals. Except for increases in inventory, final goods also ultimately enter the waste stream. Thus goods which are "consumed" really only render certain services. Their material substance remains in existence and must either be reused or discharged to the ambient environment.

In an economy which is closed (no imports or exports) and where there is no net accumulation of stocks (plant, equipment, inventories, consumer durables, or residential buildings), the amount of residuals inserted into the natural environment must be approximately equal to the weight of basic fuels, food, and raw materials entering the processing and production system, plus oxygen taken from the atmosphere.[10] This result, while obvious upon reflection, leads to the, at first rather surprising, corollary that residuals disposal involves a greater tonnage of materials than basic materials processing, although many of the residuals, being gaseous, require no physical "handling."

Figure 1 shows a materials flow of the type we have in mind in greater detail and relates it to a broad classification of economic sectors for convenience in our later discussion, and for general consistency with the Standard Industrial Classification. In an open (regional or national) economy, it would be necessary to add flows representing imports and exports. In an economy undergoing stock or capital accumulation, the production of residuals in any given year would be less by that amount than the basic inputs. In the entire U.S. economy, accumulation accounts for about 10–15 percent of basic annual

---

[8] There is a substantial literature dealing with the question of under what conditions individual exchanges can optimally control technological external diseconomies. A discussion of this literature, as it relates to waterborne residuals, is found in Kneese and Bower [A. V. Kneese and B. T. Bower, *Managing Water Quality: Economics, Technology, Institutions*. Baltimore, 1968].

[9] As far as we know, the idea of applying materials balance concepts to waste disposal problems was first expressed by Smith. We also benefitted from an unpublished paper by Joseph Headley in which a pollution "matrix" is suggested. We have also found references by Boulding to a "spaceship economy" suggestive. One of the authors has previously used a similar approach in ecological studies of nutrient interchange among plants and animals.

[10] To simplify our language, we will not repeat this essential qualification at each opportunity, but assume it applies throughout the following discussion. In addition, we must include residuals such as NO and NO_2 arising from reactions between components of the air itself but occurring as combustion by-products.

FIGURE 1 Materials Flow

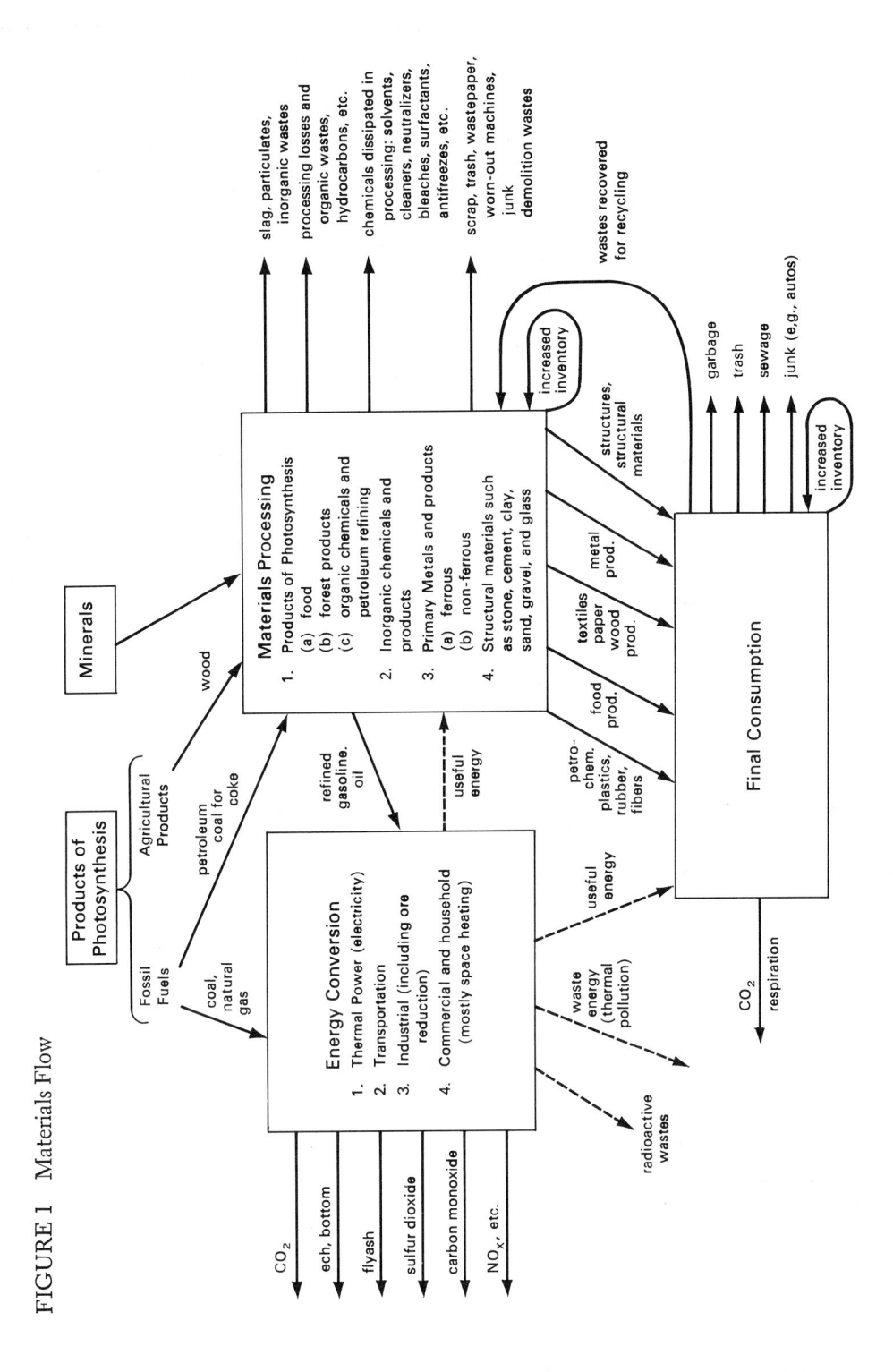

inputs, mostly in the form of construction materials, and there is some net importation of raw and partially processed materials amounting to 4 or 5 percent of domestic production. Table 1 shows estimates of the weight of raw materials produced in the United States in several recent years, plus net imports of raw and partially processed materials.

Of the active inputs,[11] perhaps three-quarters of the overall weight is eventually discharged to the atmosphere as carbon (combined with atmospheric oxygen in the form of CO or CO_2) and hydrogen (combined with atmospheric oxygen as H_2O) under current conditions. This results from combustion of fossil fuels and from animal respiration. Discharge of carbon dioxide can be considered harmless in the short run. There are large "sinks" (in the

TABLE 1 Weight of Basic Materials Production in the United States Plus Net Imports, 1963 (10^5 tons)

	1963	1964	1965
Agricultural (incl. fishery and wildlife and forest) products			
Food { Crops (excl. livestock feed)	125	128	130
{ Livestock	100	103	102
Other products	5	6	6
Fishery	3	3	3
Forestry products (85 per cent dry wt. basis)			
Sawlogs	53	55	56
Pulpwood	107	116	120
Other	41	41	42
Total	434	452	459
Mineral fuels	1,337	1,399	1,448
Other Minerals			
Iron ore	204	237	245
Other metal ores	161	171	191
Other nonmetals	125	133	149
Total	490	541	585
Grand total[a]	2,261	2,392	2,492

[a] Excluding construction materials, stone, sand, gravel, and other minerals used for structural purposes, ballast, fillers, insulation, etc. Gangue and mine tailings are also excluded from this total. These materials account for enormous tonnages but undergo essentially no chemical change. Hence, their use is more or less tantamount to physically moving them from one location to another. If this were to be included, there is no logical reason to exclude material shifted in highway cut and fill operations, harbor dredging, land-fill, plowing, and even silt moved by rivers. Since a line must be drawn somewhere, we chose to draw it as indicated above.
Source: R. U. Ayres and A. V. Kneese.

[11] See footnote to Table 1.

form of vegetation and large water bodies, mainly the oceans) which reabsorb this gas, although there is evidence of net accumulation of CO_2 in the atmosphere. Some experts believe that the latter is likely to show a large relative increase, as much as 50 percent by the end of the century, possibly giving rise to significant—and probably, on balance, adverse—weather changes.[12] Thus continued combustion of fossil fuels at a high rate could produce externalities affecting the entire world. The effects associated with most residuals will normally be more confined, however, usually limited to regional air and water sheds.

The remaining residuals are either gases (like carbon monoxide, nitrogen dioxide, and sulfur dioxide—all potentially harmful even in the short run), dry solids (like rubbish and scrap), or wet solids (like garbage, sewage, and industrial wastes suspended or dissolved in water). In a sense, the dry solids are an irreducible, limiting form of waste. By the application of appropriate equipment and energy, most undesirable substances can, in principle, be removed from water and air streams[13]—but what is left must be disposed of in solid form, transformed, or reused. Looking at the matter in this way clearly reveals a primary interdependence between the various waste streams which casts into doubt the traditional classification of air, water, and land pollution as individual categories for purposes of planning and control policy.

Residuals do not necessarily have to be discharged to the environment. In many instances, it is possible to recycle them back into the productive system. The materials balance view underlines the fact that the throughput of new materials necessary to maintain a given level of production and consumption decreases as the technical efficiency of energy conversion and materials utilization increases. Similarly, other things being equal, the longer that cars, buildings, machinery, and other durables remain in service, the fewer new materials are required to compensate for loss, wear, and obsolescence—although the use of old or worn machinery (e.g., automobiles) tends to increase other residuals problems. Technically efficient combustion of (desulfurized) fossil fuels would leave only water, ash, and carbon dioxide as residuals, while nuclear energy conversion need leave only negligible quantities of material residuals (although thermal pollution and radiation hazards cannot be dismissed by any means).

Given the population, industrial production, and transport service in an economy (a regional rather than a national economy would normally be the relevant unit), it is possible to visualize combinations of social policy which could lead to quite different relative burdens placed on the various residuals-receiving environmental media; or, given the possibilities for recycle and less residual-generating production processes, the overall burden to be placed

---

[12] There is strong evidence that discharge of residuals has already affected the climate of individual cities.
[13] Except CO_2 which may be harmful in the long run, as noted.

upon the environment as a whole. To take one extreme, a region which went in heavily for electric space heating and wet scrubbing of stack gases (from steam plants and industries), which ground up its garbage and delivered it to the sewers and then discharged the raw sewage to watercourses, would protect its air resources to an exceptional degree. But this would come at the sacrifice of placing a heavy residuals load upon water resources. On the other hand, a region which treated municipal and industrial waste water streams to a high level and relied heavily on the incineration of sludges and solid wastes would protect its water and land resources at the expense of discharging waste residuals predominantly to the air. Finally, a region which practiced high level recovery and recycle of waste materials and fostered low residual production processes to a far reaching extent in each of the economic sectors might discharge very little residual waste to any of the environmental media.

Further complexities are added by the fact that sometimes it is possible to modify an environmental medium through investment in control facilities so as to improve its assimilative capacity. The clearest, but far from only, example is with respect to watercourses where reservoir storage can be used to augment low river flows that ordinarily are associated with critical pollution (high external cost situations).[14] Thus internalization of external costs associated with particular discharges, by means of taxes or other restrictions, even if done perfectly, cannot guarantee Pareto optimality. Investments involving public good aspects must enter into an optimal solution.

To recapitulate our main points briefly: (1) Technological external diseconomies are not freakish anomalies in the processes of production and consumption but an inherent and normal part of them. (2) These external diseconomies are quantitatively negligible in a low-population or economically undeveloped setting, but they become progressively (nonlinearly) more important as the population rises and the level of output increases (i.e., as the natural reservoirs of dilution and assimilative capacity become exhausted).[15] (3) They cannot be properly dealt with by considering environmental media such as air and water in isolation. (4) Isolated and *ad hoc* taxes and other restrictions are not sufficient for their optimum control, although they are essential elements in a more systematic and coherent program of environmental quality management. (5) Public investment programs, particularly including transportation systems, sewage disposal, and river flow regulation, are intimately related to the amounts and effects of residuals and must be planned in light of them.

[14] Careful empirical work has shown that this technique can fit efficiently into water quality management systems.
[15] Externalities associated with residuals discharge may appear only at certain threshold values which are relevant only at some stage of economic development and industrial and population concentrations. This may account for their general treatment as "exceptional" cases in the economics literature. These threshold values truly were exceptional cases for less developed economies.

It is important to develop not only improved measures of the external costs resulting from differing concentrations and duration of residuals in the environment but more systematic methods for forecasting emissions of external-cost-producing residuals, technical and economic trade-offs between them, and the effects of recycle on environmental quality.

In the hope of contributing to this effort and of revealing more clearly the types of information which would be needed to implement such a program, we set forth a more formal model of the materials balance approach in the following sections and relate it to some conventional economic models of production and consumption. The main objective is to make some progress toward defining a system in which flows of services and materials are simultaneously accounted for and related to welfare.

II. BASIC MODEL

The take off point for our discussion is the Walras-Cassel general equilibrium model, extended to include intermediate consumption, which involves the following quantities:

$$\overbrace{r_1, \ldots \ldots \ldots \ldots, r_M}^{\text{resources and services}}$$

$$\overbrace{X_1, \ldots \ldots \ldots \ldots, X_N}^{\text{products or commodities}}$$

$$\overbrace{v_1, \ldots \ldots \ldots \ldots, v_M}^{\text{resource prices}}$$

$$\overbrace{p_1, \ldots \ldots \ldots \ldots, p_N}^{\text{product or commodity prices}}$$

$$\overbrace{Y_1, \ldots \ldots \ldots \ldots, Y_N}^{\text{final demands}}$$

The M basic resources are allocated among the N sectors as follows:

$$r_1 = a_{11}X_1 + a_{12}X_2 + \cdots + a_{1N}X_N,$$
$$r_2 = a_{21}X_1 + a_{22}X_2 + \cdots + a_{2N}X_N,$$
$$\vdots$$
$$r_M = a_{M1}X_1 + a_{M2}X_2 + \cdots + a_{MN}X_N,$$

or

$$r_j = \sum_{k=1}^{N} a_{jk}X_k, \ j = 1, \ldots, M. \tag{1a}$$

In (1a) we have implicitly assumed that there is no possibility of factor or process substitution and no joint production. These conditions will be discussed later. In matrix notation we can write:

$$[r_{j1}]_{M,1} = [a_{jk}]_{M,N} \cdot [X_{k1}]_{N,1}, \tag{1b}$$

where $[a]$ is an $M \times N$ matrix.

A similar set of equations describes the relations between commodity production and final demand:

$$X_k - \sum_{l=1}^{N} A_{kl} Y_l, \quad k = 1, \ldots, N, \tag{2a}$$

$$[X_{k1}]_{N,1} = [A_{kl}]_{N,N} \cdot [Y_l]_{N,1}, \tag{2b}$$

and the matrix $[A]$ is given by

$$[A] = [I - C]^{-1}, \tag{3}$$

where $[I]$ is the unit diagonal matrix and the elements C_{ij} of the matrix $[C]$ are essentially the well-known Leontief input coefficients. In principle these are functions of the existing technology and, therefore, are fixed for any given situation.

By combining (1) and (2), we obtain a set of equations relating resource inputs directly to final demand, viz.,

$$\begin{aligned} r_j &= \sum_{k=1}^{N} a_{jk} \sum_{l=1}^{N} A_{kl} Y_l = \sum_{k,l=1}^{N} a_{jk} A_{kl} Y_l \\ &= \sum_{l=1}^{N} b_{jl} Y_l, \quad j = 1, \ldots, M, \end{aligned} \tag{4a}$$

or, of course, in matrix notation (4b):

$$\begin{aligned} [r_{j1}]_{M,1} &= [a_{jk}]_{M,N} \cdot [A_{kl}]_{N,N} \cdot [Y_{l1}]_{N,1} \\ &= [b_{jl}]_{M,N} \cdot [Y_{l1}]_{N,1}. \end{aligned} \tag{4b}$$

We can also impute the prices of N intermediate goods and commodities to the prices of the M basic resources, as follows:

$$p_k = \sum_{j=1}^{M} v_j b_{jk}, \quad k = 1, \ldots, N \tag{5a}$$

$$[p_{1k}]_{1,N} = [v_{1j}]_{1,M} \cdot [b_{jk}]_{M,N}. \tag{5b}$$

To complete the system, it may be supposed that demand and supply relationships are given, a priori, by Pareto-type preference functions:

$$\text{Demand:} \quad Y_k = F_k(p_1, \ldots, p_N), \quad k = 1, \ldots, N \tag{6}$$
$$\text{Supply:} \quad r_k = G_k(v_1, \ldots, v_M), \quad k = 1, \ldots, M, \tag{7}$$

where, of course, the p_j are functions of the v_j as in (5b).

In order to interpret the X's as physical production, it is necessary for the sake of consistency to arrange that outputs and inputs always balance, which implies that the C_{ij} must comprise *all* materials exchanges including residuals. To complete the system so that there is no net gain or loss of physical substances, it is also convenient to introduce two additional sectors, viz., an "environmental" sector whose (physical) output is X_0 and a "final consumption" sector whose output is denoted X_f. The system is then easily balanced by explicitly including flows both to and from these sectors.

To implement this further modification of the Walras-Cassel model, it is convenient to subdivide and relabel the resource category into tangible raw materials $\{r^m\}$ and services $\{r^s\}$:

$$\begin{bmatrix} r_1 \\ r_2 \\ \vdots \\ r_L \end{bmatrix} \quad \text{becomes} \quad \begin{bmatrix} r_1^m \\ r_2^m \\ \vdots \\ r_L^m \end{bmatrix} \right\} \text{raw materials (units)},$$

$$\begin{bmatrix} r_{L+1} \\ \vdots \\ r_M \end{bmatrix} \quad \text{becomes} \quad \begin{bmatrix} r_1^s \\ \vdots \\ r_p^s \end{bmatrix} \right\} \text{service (units)},$$

where, of course,

$$L + P = M. \tag{8}$$

It is understood that services, while not counted in tons, can be measured in meaningful units, such as man-days, with well-defined prices. Thus, we similarly relabel the price variables as follows:

$$\begin{bmatrix} V_1 \\ \vdots \\ V_L \end{bmatrix} \quad \text{becomes} \quad \begin{bmatrix} V_1^m \\ \vdots \\ V_L^m \end{bmatrix} \right\} \text{raw material (prices)},$$

$$\begin{bmatrix} V_{L+1} \\ \vdots \\ V_M \end{bmatrix} \quad \text{becomes} \quad \begin{bmatrix} V_1^s \\ \vdots \\ V_p^s \end{bmatrix} \right\} \text{labor and service (prices)}.$$

The coefficients $\{a_{ij}\}$, $\{b_{ij}\}$ are similarly partitioned into two groups, e.g.,

$$\begin{matrix} b_{1j} \\ \vdots \\ b_{Lj} \end{matrix} \quad \text{becomes} \quad \begin{matrix} b_{1j}^m \\ \vdots \\ b_{Lj}^m \end{matrix}$$

$$\begin{matrix} b_{L+1,j} \\ \vdots \\ b_{Mj} \end{matrix} \quad \begin{matrix} b_{1j}^s \\ \vdots \\ b_{pj}^s \end{matrix}$$

598 General Equilibrium

These notational changes have no effect whatever on the substance of the model, although the equations become somewhat more cumbersome. The partitioned matrix notation simplifies the restatement of the basic equations. Thus (1b) becomes (9), while (5b) becomes (10).

$$M\left\{\begin{bmatrix}\vdots\\r\\\vdots\end{bmatrix}\right\} \equiv \begin{bmatrix}\cdots & r^m & \cdots\\ \cdots & \cdots & \cdots\\ \cdots & r^s & \cdots\end{bmatrix}\begin{matrix}\}L\\ \\ \}P\end{matrix} = M\left\{\begin{bmatrix}\}L & b^m\\ \cdots & \cdots\\ \}P & b^s\end{bmatrix}\begin{bmatrix}\\Y\\ \end{bmatrix}\right\}N, \qquad (9)$$

$$[p_1, \ldots, p_N] = [v^m \vdots v^s]\begin{bmatrix}b^m\\ \cdots\\ b^s\end{bmatrix}\begin{matrix}\\ \end{matrix}M$$
$$\underbrace{}_{M}\quad \underbrace{}_{N}$$

$$= [\ldots v^m \ldots]\begin{bmatrix}\cdot & b^m & \cdot\\ & \vdots & \\ \cdot & \cdots & \cdot\end{bmatrix} \qquad (10)$$

$$+ [\ldots v^s \ldots]\begin{bmatrix}\cdot & b^s & \cdot\\ & \vdots & \\ \cdot & \cdots & \cdot\end{bmatrix}$$

The equivalent of (5a) is:

$$p_k = \underbrace{\sum_{j=1}^{L} b_{jk}{}^m v_j{}^m}_{\substack{\text{prices imputed}\\\text{to cost of raw}\\\text{materials}}} + \underbrace{\sum_{j=1}^{P} b_{jk}{}^s v_j{}^s}_{\substack{\text{prices imputed}\\\text{to cost of}\\\text{services}}} \qquad (11)$$

where $k = 1, \ldots, N$.

We wish to focus attention explicitly on the flow of materials through the economy. By definition of the Leontief input coefficients (now related to materials flow), we have:

$C_{kj}X_j$ (physical) quantity transferred from k to j
$C_{jk}X_k$ quantity transferred from j to k.

Hence, material flows *from* the environment to all other sectors are given by:

$$\sum_{k=1}^{N} C_{0k}X_k = \sum_{j=1}^{L} r_j{}^m = \sum_{j=1}^{L}\sum_{k=1}^{N} a_{jk}{}^m X_k$$
$$= \sum_{j=1}^{L}\sum_{k=1}^{N} b_{jk}{}^m Y_k, \qquad (12)$$

using Equation (1), as modified.[16] Obviously, comparing the first and third terms,

$$\underbrace{C_{0k}}_{\substack{\text{total material}\\\text{flow }(0\text{ to }k)}} = \underbrace{\sum_{j=1}^{L} a_{jk}{}^m}_{\substack{\text{all raw materials}\\(0\text{ to }k).}} \qquad (13)$$

Flows into and out of the environmental sector must be in balance:

$$\underbrace{\sum_{k=1}^{N} C_{0k}X_k}_{\substack{\text{sum of all raw}\\\text{material flows}}} = \underbrace{\sum_{k=1}^{N} C_{k0}X_0 + C_{f0}X_0}_{\substack{\text{sum of all return}\\\text{(waste) flows.}}} \qquad (14)$$

Material flows to and from the final sector must also balance:

$$\underbrace{\sum_{k=1}^{N} C_{kf}X_j}_{\substack{\text{sum of all}\\\text{final goods}}} = \underbrace{\sum_{k=1}^{N} C_{fk}X_k}_{\substack{\text{sum of all}\\\text{materials}\\\text{recycled}}} + \underbrace{C_{f0}X_0}_{\substack{\text{waste residuals}\\\text{(plus accumulation}^{17}).}} \qquad (15)$$

Of course, by definition, X_j is the sum of the final demands:

$$X_j = \sum_{j=1}^{N} Y_j. \qquad (16)$$

Substituting (16) into the left side of (15) and (2a) into the right side of (15), we obtain an expression for the waste flow in terms of final demands:

$$C_{j0}X_0 = \sum_{j=1}^{N}\sum_{k=1}^{N} (C_{jf} - C_{fj}A_{jk})Y_k. \qquad (17)$$

The treatment could be simplified slightly if we assumed that there is no recycling per se. Thus, in the context of the model, we could suppose that all residuals return to the environmental sector,[18] where some of them (e.g., waste paper) become "raw materials." They would then be indistinguishable

---

[16] Ignoring, for convenience, any materials flow from the environment *directly* to the final consumption sector.

[17] For convenience, we can treat accumulation in the final sector as a return flow to the environment. In truth, structures actually *become* part of our environment, although certain disposal costs may be deferred.

[18] In calculating actual quantities, we would (by convention) ignore the weight of oxygen taken free from the atmosphere in combustion and returned as CO^2. However, such inputs will be treated explicitly later.

from new raw materials, however, and price differentials between the two would be washed out. In principle, this is an important distinction to retain.

III. INCLUSION OF EXTERNALITIES

The physical flow of materials between various intermediate (production) sectors and the final (consumption) sector tends to be accompanied by, and correlated with, a (reverse) flow of dollars.[19] However, the physical flow of materials from and back to the environment is only partly reflected by actual dollar flows, namely, land rents and payments for raw materials. There are three classes of physical exchange for which there exist no counterpart economic transactions. These are: (1) private use for production inputs of "common property" resources, notably air, streams, lakes, and the ocean; (2) private use of the assimilative capacity of the environment to "dispose of" or dilute wastes and residuals; (3) inadvertent or unwanted material inputs to productive processes—diluents and pollutants.

All these goods (or "bads") are physically transferred at zero price, not because they are not scarce relative to demand—they often are in developed economies—or because they confer no service or disservice on the user—since they demonstrably do so—but because there exist no social institutions that permit the resources in question to be "owned," and exchanged in the market.

The allocation of resources corresponding to a Pareto optimum cannot be attained without subjecting the above-mentioned nonmarket and involuntary exchanges to the moderation of a market or a surrogate thereof. In principle, the influence of a market might be simulated, to a first approximation, by introducing a set of shadow (or virtual) prices.[20] These may well be zero, where supply truly exceeds demand, or negative (i.e., costs) in some instances; they will be positive in others. The exchanges are, of course, real.

The Walras-Cassel model can be generalized to handle these effects in the following way:

1. One can introduce a set of R common-property resources or services of raw materials $\{r_1^{cp}, \ldots, r_R^{cp}\}$ as a subset of the set $\{r_j\}$; these will have corresponding virtual prices $\{v_j^{cp}\}$, which would constitute an "income" from the environment. Such resources include the atmosphere; streams, lakes, and oceans; landscape; wildlife and biological diversity; and the indispensable assimilative capacity of the environment (its ability to accept and neutralize or recycle residuals).[21]

---

[19] To be precise, the dollar flow governs and is governed by a combined flow of materials and services (value added).

[20] A similar concept exists in mechanics where the forces producing "reaction" (to balance action and reaction) are commonly described as "virtual forces."

[21] Economists have previously suggested generalization of the Walras-Cassel model to take account of public goods. One of the earliest appears to be Schlesinger. We are indebted to Otto Eckstein for calling our attention to this key reference.

2. One can introduce a set of S environmental *disservices* imposed on consumers of material resources, by forcing them to accept unwanted inputs $\{r_1^u, \ldots, r_s^u\}$ (pollutants, contaminants, etc.); these disservices would have negative value, giving rise to *negative* virtual prices $\{u_j\}$.[22]

The matrix coefficients $\{a_{ij}\}$ and $\{b_{ij}\}$ can be further partitioned to take account of this additional refinement, and equations analogous to (9), (10), and (11) can be generalized in the obvious way. Equation (6) carries over unchanged, but (7) must be appropriately generalized to take account of the altered situation. Actually, (7) breaks up into several groups of equations:

$$r_k^m = G_k^m(p_1, \ldots, p_N), \quad k = 1, \ldots, L, \tag{18}$$
$$r_k^s = G_k^s(p_1, \ldots, p_N), \quad k = 1, \ldots, P. \tag{19}$$

However, as we have noted at the outset, the supplies of common-property resources and environmental services or disservices are *not* regulated directly by market prices of other goods and services. In the case of common-property resources, the supplies are simply constants fixed by nature or otherwise determined by accident or noneconomic factors.

The total value of these services performed by the environment cannot be calculated but it is suggestive to consider the situation if the natural reservoir of air, water, minerals, etc., were very much smaller, as if the earth were a submarine or "spaceship" (i.e., a vehicle with no assimilative and/or regenerative capacity). In such a case, all material resources would have to be recycled,[23] and the cost of all goods would necessarily reflect the cost of reprocessing residuals and wastes for reuse. In this case, incidentally, the ambient level of unrecovered wastes continuously circulating through the resource inventory of the system (i.e., the spaceship) would in general be nonzero because of the difficulty of 100 percent efficient waste-removal of air and water. However, although the quantity of waste products in constant circulation may fluctuate within limits, it cannot be allowed to increase monotonically with time, which means that as much material must be recycled, on the average, as is discarded. The value of common resources plus the assimilation service performed by the environment, then, is only indirectly a function of the ambient level of untreated residuals per se, or the disutility caused thereby, which

---

[22] The notion of introducing the possibility of negative prices in general equilibrium theory has apparently been discussed before, although we are not aware of any systematic development of the idea in the published literature. In this connection, it is worth pointing out the underlying similarity of negative prices and effluent taxes—which have been, and still are being considered as an attractive alternative to subsidies and federal standard-setting as a means of controlling air and water pollution. Such taxes would, of course, be an explicit attempt to rectify an imbalance caused by a market failure.

[23] Any consistent deviation from this 100 per cent rule implies an accumulation of waste products, on the average, which, by definition, is inconsistent with maintaining an equilibrium.

depend on the cost efficiency of the available treatment technology. Be this as it may, of course, the bill of goods produced in a spaceship economy would certainly be radically different from that we are familiar with. For this reason, no standard economic comparison between the two situations is meaningful. The measure of worth we are seeking is actually the difference between the total welfare "produced" by a spaceship economy, where 100 percent of all residuals are promptly recycled, vis-à-vis the existing welfare output on earth, where resource inventories are substantial and complete recycling need not be contemplated for a very long time to come.

This welfare difference might well be very large, although we possess no methodological tools for quantifying it. In any case, the resource inventory and assimilative capacity of the environment probably contribute very considerably to our standard of living.

If these environmental contributions were paid for, the overall effect on prices would presumably be to push them generally upward. However, the major *differential* effect of undervaluing the environmental contribution is that goods produced by high residual-producing processes, such as papermaking, are substantially underpriced vis-à-vis goods which involve more economical uses of basic resources. This is, however, not socially disadvantageous per se: that is, it causes no misallocation of resources unless, or until, the large resource inventory and/or the assimilative capacity of the environment are used up. When this happens, however, as it now has in most highly industrialized regions, either a market must be allowed to operate or some other form of decision rule must be introduced to permit a rational choice to be made, e.g., between curtailing or controlling the production of residuals or tolerating the effects (disservice) thereof.

It appears that the natural inventory of most common resources used as inputs (e.g., air as an input to combustion and respiratory processes) is still ample,[24] but the assimilative capacity of the environment has already been exceeded in many areas, with important external costs resulting. This suggests a compromise treatment. If an appropriate price could be charged to the producers of the residuals and used to compensate the inadvertent recipients—with the price determined by appropriate Pareto preference criteria—there would be no particular analytic purpose in keeping books on the exchange of the other environmental benefits mentioned, although they are quantitatively massive. We will, therefore, in the remainder of the discussion omit the common-property variables $\{r_j^{cp}\}$ and the corresponding virtual-price variables

---

[24] Water is an exception in arid regions; in humid regions, however, water "shortages" are misnomers: they are really consequences of excessive use of water-courses as cheap means of waste disposal. But some ecologists have claimed that oxygen depletion may be a very serious long-run problem.

$\{v_j^{cp}\}$ defined previously, retaining only the terms $\{r_j^u\}$ and $\{u_{jk}\}$. The variable $\{r_j^u\}$ represents a physical quantity of the jth unwanted input. There are S such terms, by assumption, whose magnitudes are proportional to the levels of consumption of basic raw materials, subject to the existing technology. However, residuals production is not immutable: it can be increased or decreased by investment, changes in materials processing technology, raw material substitutions, and so forth.

At first glance it might seem entirely reasonable to assert that the *supplies* of unwanted residuals received will be functions of the (negative) prices (i.e., compensation) paid for them, in analogy with (7). Unfortunately, this assertion immediately introduces a theoretical difficulty, since the assumption of unique coefficients $\{a_{ij}\}$ and $\{C_{ij}\}$[25] is not consistent with the possibility of factor or process substitution or joint-production, as stated earlier. To permit such substitutions, one would have to envision a very large collection of alternative sets of coefficients: one complete set of a's and C's for each specific combination of factors and processes. Maximization of any objective function (such as GNP) would involve solving the entire system of equations as many times as there are combinations of factors and processes, and picking out that set of solutions which yields the largest value. Alternatively, if the a's and C's are assumed to be continuously variable functions (of each other), the objective function could also, presumably, be parameterized. However, as long as the a's and C's are uniquely given, the supply of the kth unwanted residual is only marginally under the control of the producer, since it will be produced in strict relationship to the composition of the bill of final goods $\{Y_j\}$.

Hence, for the present model it is only correct to assume

$$r_k^u = G_k^u (Y_1, \ldots, Y_N). \tag{20}$$

This limitation does not affect the existence of an equilibrium solution for the system of equations; it merely means that the shadow prices $\{u_{jk}\}$ which would emerge from such a solution for given coefficients $\{a_{ij}\}$, $\{b_{ij}\}$, and $\{C_{ij}\}$ might be considerably higher than the real economic optimum, since the latter could only be achieved by introducing factor and process changes.

Of course, the physical inputs are also related to the physical outputs of goods, as in (21).

$$[r] = \begin{bmatrix} r^m \\ r^s \\ r^u \end{bmatrix} = M \underbrace{\left\{ \begin{bmatrix} a^m \\ \vdots \\ a^s \\ \vdots \\ a^u \end{bmatrix} X \right\}}_{N} N = \begin{bmatrix} b^m \\ \vdots \\ b^s \\ \vdots \\ b^u \end{bmatrix} Y . \tag{21}$$

---
[25] Or $\{b_{ij}\}$ and $\{Ai_j\}$.

Written out in full detail (21) is equivalent to:

raw materials
$$r_k^m = \sum_{j=1}^{N} a_{kj}^m X_j = \sum_{j=1}^{N} b_{kj}^m Y_j, \quad k = 1, \ldots, L, \quad (22)$$

labor and technical services
$$r_k^s = \sum_{j=1}^{N} a_{kj}^s X_j = \sum_{j=1}^{N} b_{kj}^s Y_j, \quad k = 1, \ldots, P, \quad (23)$$

unwanted inputs
$$r_k^u = \sum_{j=1}^{N} a_{kj}^u X_j = \sum_{j=1}^{N} b_{kj}^u Y_j, \quad k = 1, \ldots, S, \quad (24)$$

where, of course,

$$L + P + S = M. \qquad (25)$$

The corresponding matrix equation for the prices of goods, in terms of production costs, is

$$[p_1, \ldots, p_N] = [v^m \vdots v^s \vdots u] \begin{bmatrix} b^m \\ \cdots \\ b^s \\ \cdots \\ b^u \end{bmatrix}. \qquad (26)$$

Written out in the standard form, we obtain

$$p_k = \underbrace{\sum_{j=1}^{L} b_{jk}^m v_j^m}_{\text{cost of raw materials}} + \underbrace{\sum_{j=1}^{P} b_{jk}^s v_j^s}_{\text{cost of labor and technical services}}$$

$$+ \underbrace{\sum_{j=1}^{S} b_{jk}^u v_j^u}_{\substack{\text{cost (compensa-}\\ \text{tion) for pro-}\\ \text{viding environ-}\\ \text{mental disser-}\\ \text{vices,}}} \quad k = 1, \ldots, N. \qquad (27)$$

Evidently, the coefficients b_{jk}^u are empirically determined by the structure of the regional economy and its geography. It is assumed that a single overall (negative) price for each residual has meaning, even though each productive sector—and even each consumer—has his own individual utility function. Much the same assumption is conventionally made, and accepted, in the case of positive real prices.

All of the additional variables now fit into the general framework of the original Walras-Cassel analysis. Indeed, we have $2N + 2M - 1$ variables (r_i, Y_i, p_i, v_i) (allowing an arbitrary normalization factor for the price level) and $2N + 2M - 1$ independent equations.[26] If solutions exist for the Walras-Cassel system of equations, the arguments presumably continue to hold true for the generalized model. In any case, a discussion of such mathematical questions would carry us too far from our main theme.

IV. CONCLUDING COMMENTS

The limited economics literature currently available which is devoted to environmental pollution problems has generally taken a partial equilibrium view of the matter, as well as treated the pollution of particular environmental media, such as air and water, as separate problems. This no doubt reflects the propensity of the theoretical literature to view externalities as exceptional and minor. Clearly, the partial equilibrium approach in particular is very convenient theoretically and empirically for it permits external damage and control cost functions to be defined for each particular case without reference to broader interrelationships and adjustments in the economy.

We have argued in this paper that the production of residuals is an inherent and general part of the production and consumption process and, moreover, that there are important trade-offs between the gaseous, liquid, or solid forms that these residuals may take. Further, we have argued that under conditions of intensive economic and population development the environmental media which can receive and assimilate residual wastes are not free goods but natural resources of great value with respect to which voluntary exchange cannot operate because of their common property characteristics. We have also noted, in passing, that the assimilative capacity of environmental media can sometimes be altered and that therefore the problem of achieving Pareto optimality reaches beyond devising appropriate shadow prices and involves the planning and execution of investments with public goods aspects.

We have exhibited a formal mathematical framework for tracing residuals flows in the economy and related it to the general equilibrium model of resources allocation, altered to accommodate recycle and containing unpriced sectors to represent the environment. This formulation, in contrast to the usual partial equilibrium treatments, implies knowledge of all preference and production functions including relations between residuals discharge and external cost and all possible factor and process substitutions. While we feel that it represents reality with greater fidelity than the usual view, it also implies a central planning problem of impossible difficulty, both from the standpoint of data collection and computation.

[26] There is one redundant equation in the system, which expresses the identity between gross product and gross income for the system as a whole (sometimes called "Walras law").

What, if any, help can the general interdependency approach we have outlined offer in dealing with pollution problems effectively and reasonably efficiently? A minimal contribution is its warning that partial equilibrium approaches, while more tractable, may lead to serious errors. Second, in projecting waste residuals for an economy—a regional economy would usually be the most relevant for planning and control—the inter-industry materials flow model can provide a much more conceptually satisfying and accurate tool for projecting future residuals production than the normal aggregative extrapolations.[27] The latter not only treat gaseous, liquid, and solid wastes separately, but do not take account of input-output relations and the fact that the materials account for the region must balance.

We think that in the next few years it will be possible to make improved regional projections of residuals along the lines sketched above. Undoubtedly, there will also be further progress in empirically estimating external costs associated with residuals discharge and in estimating control costs via various alternative measures. On the basis of this kind of information, a control policy can be devised. However, this approach will still be partial. Interrelations between the regional and national economy must be treated simplistically and to be manageable, the analysis must confine itself to a specific projected bill of goods.

The basic practical question which remains to be answered is whether an iterated series of partial equilibrium treatments—e.g., focusing on one industry or region at a time, *ceteris paribus*—would converge toward the general equilibrium solution, or not. We know of no theoretical test of convergence which would be applicable in this case but, in the absence of such a criterion, would be willing to admit the possible relevance of an empirical sensitivity test more or less along the following lines: take a major residuals-producing industry (such as electric power) and parametrize its cost structure in terms of emission control levels, allowing all technically feasible permutations of factor (fuel) inputs and processes. It would be a straightforward, but complicated, operations research problem to determine the minimum cost solution as a function of the assumed (negative) price of the residuals produced. If possible industry patterns—factor and process combinations—exist which would per-

[27] Some efforts to implement these concepts are already underway. Walter Isard and his associates have prepared an input–output table for Philadelphia which includes coefficients representing waterborne wastes (unpublished). The recent study of waste management in the New York Metropolitan region by the Regional Plan Association took a relatively broad view of the waste residuals problem. Relevant data on several industries are being gathered. Richard Frankel's not yet published study of thermal power in which the range of technical options for controlling residuals, and their costs, is being explored is notable in this regard. His and other salient studies are described in Ayres and Kneese [R. U. Ayres and A. V. Kneese, "Environmental Pollution," in U.S. Congress, Joint Economic Committee, *Federal Programs for the Development of Human Resources*, Vol. 2, Washington, 1968.]

mit a high level of emission control at only a small increase in power production cost, then it might be possible to conclude that for a significant range of (negative) residuals prices the effect on power prices—and therefore on the rest of the economy—would not be great. Such a conclusion would support the convergence hypothesis. If, on the other hand, electric power prices are very sensitive to residuals prices, then one would at least have to undertake a deeper study of consumer preference functions to try to determine what residuals prices would actually be if a market mechanism existed. If people prove to have a strong antipathy to soot and sulfur dioxide, for instance, resulting in a high (negative) price for these unwanted inputs, then one would be forced to suspect that the partial equilibrium approach is probably not convergent to the general equilibrium solution and that much more elaborate forms of analysis will be required.

ANSWERS TO PROBLEMS

Chapter 2 (p. 37)

1. (a) OB
   (b) supply, DE
   (c) suppliers, down
   (d) demand, GH
   (e) purchasers, up
   (f) have no effect
   (g) shortages
2. (a) $3
   (b) $3
   (c) $3
   (d) $3.50
   (e) $2.50

Chapter 3 (p. 88)

1. (a) 4X's, 7 Y's
   (b) 9X's, 6Y's
   (c) 4X's at $4, 9X's at $2
2. (a) budget lines or lines of attainable combinations
   (b) lower, X
   (c) decreases, Giffen
   (d) decrease, more, normal
3. (a) 5X's, 2Y's
   (b) $.8
   (c) X, increased
   (d) 3X's and 1Y
   (e) $1.6 to $4.0, 5X's to 3X's
   (g) is not
4. (a) FEDC, 3750 utils
   (b) AFCB, 4250 utils
   (c) No, the loss in utils is greater than the gain.
   (d) yes

Chapter 4 (p. 139)

1. drop of approximately 245,000 units

2. (a) 3
   (b) 1
   (c) $3
   (d) 2
3. inelastic
4. (b) ⅗ or .6
   (c) .2
5. X = 25
7. increase

Chapter 5 (p. 190)

3. at ½X, AFC = $20, at ¼X, AFC = $40. AFC is hyperbolic.
4. AFC curve would be unaffected up to the short-run output capacity.

Chapter 6 (p. 239)

1. (a) constant
   (b) optimum expansion path
   (c) $P_a = \$80$, $P_b = \$60$, $TC_{200} = \$480$
2. Resources are perfect substitutes and may be used in any combination to produce a given output.
3. (a) 5, 4
   (b) 2
   (c) 6.5/5
   (d) 1
   (e) 35/25, 3/2
4. (d) LRAC = $4

Chapter 7 (p. 303)

1. (a) X_4, profits, $cbbaP_4$.
   (b) zero, losses, fixed cost
   (c) loss, greater than
   (d) zero, X_3
   (e) MC, e

608

2. Short-run fixed factors have increased less in proportion to variable.
3. (a) contraction
   (b) stability
   (c) expansion

Chapter 8 (p. 349)

1. (a) OC, X_2
   (b) hf
   (c) $X_2 h$
   (d) loss, gf
   (e) loss, $cgfd$
   (f) cge
2. (a) X_3, OC
   (b) $X_3, smgc$
   (c) X_4, zero
   (d) X_5, zero
3. (a) decrease, 1, increase, 2
   (b) $6, $6
   (c) 50, 20, 30
   (d) 100, 40, 60
4. produce some small, fractional output

Chapter 9 (p. 395)

1. (a) greater than, decrease
   (b) $OA, AB = OE$
   (c) CB
   (d) $DCBE$
2. (a) AG, HJ
   (b) OC, CF
   (c) neither increase nor decrease, neither increase nor decrease
   (d) KL, OK
   (e) OK, KN
3. (a) GJ
   (b) GKE
   (c) OA, OF
   (d) MC
   (e) GH, GJ
   (f) OA
   (g) zero, zero

Chapter 10 (p. 438)

6. 4.25, $2.6
7. 31 units

Chapter 11 (p. 482)

5. (b) 7 workers

Chapter 12 (p. 528)

1. (a) zero
   (b) greater than
   (c) GE
   (d) FE
   (e) decrease, GE to FE
2. (a) neutral
   (b) positive
   (c) increases
   (d) G, less
   (e) M
   (f) H to M
   (g) H to G
3. $10,476
4. 7.5%, $5,000

Chapter 13 (p. 583)

1. (a) contract curve
   (b) neither increase nor decrease, decrease
   (c) inferior
   (d) raises, lowers
   (e) F
2. (a) AC
   (b) ME
   (c) LF
   (d) NG
   (e) implode, eventually, greater than
3. 12
4. is not
5. is not

INDEX

Adaptable and indivisible capital, 227
Aggregate investment demand, 524
Allen, R. G. D., 68
Aluminum industry, 279
Arc elasticity, defined, 121
Arrow, K. J., 567, 567n.
Average cost
   long-run, defined, 179
   short-run, defined, 173
Average product, 164
Average total cost, short-run, 174
Average variable cost, short-run, 174

Baumol, William J., 343, 343n.
Berne, Eric, 470n.
Bilateral monopoly, 28, 475
Budget line, 68, 76
   intercept of, 79
   slope of, 78
Budgetary constraint, 60

Capital
   adaptable but indivisible, 227
   defined, 512
   nonhuman, 512
   rate of return on capital, 512–26
Cardinal measuring systems, 66
Carlyle, Thomas, 480
Cartel, 388–90
Ceteris paribus, defined, 8
Chamberlin, Edward, 377, 377n.
Classical rent and wage theory, 279–81
Cobweb theorem, 565–66
Community indifference curves, 576–77
Comparative statics
   contrast with dynamics, 10
   defined, 10
Competition
   characteristics of, 279–82
   competitive equilibrium with free entry and exit, 293

firm's demand curve for a variable resource, 428
firm's short-run demand for a single resource, 422
long-run equilibrium, characteristics, 294
long-run firm equilibrium, 291
long-run supply
   constant cost industry, 295–97
   decreasing cost industry, 298–99
   increasing cost industry, 297–98
perfect competition *vs.* pure competition, 281
profit-maximizing output, short-run, 284
rationale for competitive model, 278
short-run firm equilibrium, 284
short-run firm supply, 288–90
short-run industry supply, 290–91
short-run revenue curves, 282–84
Competitive resource markets, 420–33
  defined, 420
  market equilibrium, 429
Complementarity and indifference curves, 74
Complementary goods, 131–34
Constant cost competitive industry, 295
  derivation of long-run supply, 296
Constant returns to scale, 179–80, 226
Consumer surplus, 64–66
Consumers, 49–87
  a two-commodity model of behavior, 59
  consumer's life cycle, 516
  objectives of, 51
Contract curve, 574
Cross elasticity of demand, 132–34

Debreu, G., 567, 567*n.*
Decreasing cost industry, 299
  relation to external economies, 300
Decreasing returns to scale
  defined, 183–85
  relation to long-run average cost, 225–26
Demand
  consumer surplus, 64–66
  demand curve, for individual, 63, 78
  demand function, individual, 63
  derivation of market demand, 116
  derived demand, 421
  determinants of demand, 30

   for investment, 521
   for more than one resource, 430
   for output of monopolist, 324
   for output of monopolistic competitor, 378–82
   for output of oligopolist, 384–85
   for single variable resource, 422–26
   law of downward sloping, 86
   market demand, 30, 116–138
   market demand function *vs.* demand curve, 128–30
   measurement of market demand, 118–28
Diamond-water paradox, 58
Duesenberry, James S., 519*n.*
DuPont antitrust case, 321
Dynamics, 10

Economic policy
   role of, 10
   and welfare economics, 581
Economics, defined, 3
Economies and diseconomies of scale, 186
Economy, defined, 7
Edgeworth, F. V., 68*n.*
Edgeworth Box
   efficiency in distribution, 571–72
   efficiency in use of scarce resources, 569
Elasticity
   arc elasticity, 120–22
   concept of, 119
   cross elasticity, 132–33
   defined, 120
   determinants of, 134
   income elasticity, 130
   of expectations, 136
   of supply of hours of work, 471
   point elasticity, 122–26
Empirical studies, of cost functions, 187
Engel, Ernest, 82
Engel curve
   defined, 82
   derivation of, for consumer, 80
Engel's Law, 82
Equilibrium
   concept of, 9
   of supply and demand, 31–32

Equilibrium combination
  consumer goods, 77
    equilibrium of the firm, 284–86
    excess demand, 32
    excess supply, 32
Expansion paths, 221
External economies, decreasing cost industry, 300
Externalities, costs and benefits, 580–81

Feasible region (linear programming), 223
Firm, defined, 160
Fisher, Irving, 514, 514n.
Fisherian two-period model, 514
Fixed costs, defined, 173

Game theory and oligopolies, 392
General equilibrium, 557–80
  contrast with partial equilibrium, 7–8, 557–59
  and efficiency, 568–80
  existence of a unique general equilibrium, 564
  general equilibrium model, expanded, 563
  a two-commodity–two resource model, 559–63
General inflation, 138
Geographic market area, 115–16
Giddings, Franklin K., 460n.
Giffen, 86
Giffen's paradox, 86
Gossen, Herman Heinrich, 50n.
Gray, H. Peter, 480n.

Hayes, Gordon, 470
Hicks, J. R., 68, 84, 137n.
Hicksian technique, substitution and income effects, 84
Homogeneous product, competition, 280
Human needs and wants, 3–4

Imperfect competition, 433
Implicit income, 477
Increasing returns to scale, 182–83
  defined, 182
  illustrated, 185, 223, 226
Indifference curves, 68–87
  characteristics of, 71
  definition of, 69
  family of, 74
  slope of, 70

used to derive demand, 78–80
used to derive Engel curve, 80–82
used in Fisherian two-period model, 514–20
Indivisibility of resources, 187–88
Industry, defined, 114–16
Inferior good, 82, 131
Initial basic feasible solution (linear programming), 246
Input coefficients, fixed versus variable, 218
Instability
due to shapes of supply and demand curves, 565
due to time lags, 565
Interdependence
among individual demand curves, 117
among oligopolists, 383
Interest
classical theory of, 525
and consumer saving, 514, 520
defined, 512
and the demand for investment, 521
in the stationary state, 480
Interpersonal comparisons of utility, 582
Isocost curves, 218–29
defined, 218
as a restraint, 229
slope of, 219
Isoproduct curve, 213
Isoprofit line, 233
Isoquants, 212–29
characteristics of, 215
defined, 213
family of, 217
and least-cost combination of resources, 220
linear isoquants, derivation, 235
short-run production adjustments, 227
Isorevenue lines, 579

Jevons, W. S., 50n.

Keynes, J. M., 377, 393
Knight, Frank, 343, 343n.

Labor, 464–81
demand for, 464–67
equilibrium supply and demand, 473–75
mobility, 477

monopoly in output markets, 474
supply of, 468–73
Lancaster, R. K., 582n.
Law of diminishing returns, defined, 166–67
Law of downward sloping demand, 86
Leadership oligopolies, 391
Least-cost combination of resources, 220
Leibenstein, Harvey, 118n.
Limited resources and the fundamental economic problem, 5–6
Line of attainable combinations, 76
Linear isoquants, derivation, 235
Linear programming, 229–38
   algebraic approach to linear programming, 242
   constraints, 230
   feasible solution to a linear programming problem, 233
   graphical solution of a linear programming problem, 232
   minimization of cost, example, 237
   simplex solution to a linear programming problem, 242–48
   statement of linear programming problem, 231
   theorem of, 234
Lipsey, R. G., 582n.
Loanable funds theory of interest, 525
Long-run competitive equilibrium, 291
Long-run competitive supply
   constant cost industry, 295
   decreasing cost industry, 298
   increasing cost industry, 297
Long-run costs, 179–89, 223–27
Long-run defined, 162, 179
Long-run equilibrium
   the competitive firm, 294
   competitive industry, 300–302
Long-run monopolistic competition, 380–82
Long-run monopoly behavior, 328
Long-run supply
   competitive constant cost industry, 295
   competitive decreasing cost industry, 298
   competitive increasing cost industry, 297

Malthus, Thomas, 458n., 479, 479n.
Marginal cost
   defined for long-run, 181
   defined for short-run, 176
   relationship between marginal product and marginal cost, 177

Marginal disutility of work, 468
Marginal efficiency of investment, 521
Marginal physical product, 177
Marginal productivity of investment, 521
Marginal productivity theory of labor, 464–68
Marginal rate
  of substitution
    of consumer goods, 69
    of leisure for work, 472
    of present for future consumption, 515
    in production, 214
  of transformation, 576
Marginal resource cost, 427
Marginal revenue, 284
Marginal revenue product, 423–24
  of labor, 466
Marginal utility, 52–54
  defined, 53
  diminishing marginal utility, 54–56
Marginal utility theorists, 50
  goals of, 67
Marginal utility theory, 50–68
  criticisms of, 66
Market, defined, 28–30, 114–15
Market demand
  defined, 28
  derivation of, 116
Market demand curve, 128–38
Market demand function, 28, 128–38
Market supply, defined, 30–31
Markets, classification of, 27
Marshall, Alfred, 8, 478, 478n., 557
Marx, Karl, 526
Mathematical relationships, 56–57
Mathematics, use in microeconomics, 11
Meade, J. E., 480n.
Menger, Karl, 50n.
Methodology, in economics, 6–12, 557–58
Mill, J. S., 478, 478n.
Minimization problem, linear programming, 234
Mishan, E. J., 576n.
Modified elasticity coefficient, 126
Monopolistic competition, 378–82
  defined, 378

   long-run equilibrium, 380
   short-run equilibrium, 378
   short-run profit maximization, 379
Monopoly, 320–46
   cost curves, 325
   defined, 28, 320
   in the demand for labor, 474
   demand for variable resource, 433
   long-run behavior, 328–30
   maximization of sales and profits, 340
   natural monopolies, 330
   price ceiling, effects on, 332
   and price discrimination, 334–39
   public utilities, 331
   revenue curves, 322–24
   short-run loss minimization, 328
   value of the marginal product, 434
Monopsony
   behavior, 435–38
   defined, 28, 435
   in labor market, 474–75
Morgenstern, Oskar, 67, 67*n.*, 392

Natural monopolies, 330
Negative time preference, 516
Neutral time preference, 515
Noncompeting groups in the labor market, 478
Nonprofit-maximizing behavior of firms, 339–47
   effects of risk and uncertainty, 343–46
   sales maximization, 340–43
Nonsatiety assumption, 72
Normal good
   and market demand, 131
   defined for consumer, 82
Normative economics, 10–11, 581
Numeraire, 562–63

Objective function (linear programming), 229
Objectives of consumers, 51
Objectives of firms, 340–46
Ohlin, Bertil, 377
Oligopoly, 382–94
   cartel, 388
   defined, 28
   interdependence, 383

kinked-demand model, 384–85
leadership oligopolies, 391
noncollusive behavior, 384–88
Opportunity cost, defined, 187–88
Optimum combination
  of consumer goods, 77
  of resources, 220
  of risk and return, 345
Ordinal measuring system, 66–68

Pareto, Vilfredo, 68*n.*, 568
Pareto inferior, 570
Pareto optimality, 568–80
  defined, 568
  and distribution, 572–74
  and production mix, 575–79
Partial equilibrium analysis, 8, 558
Partial equilibrium and *ceteris paribus*, 114
Payback method of ranking investment projects, 522
Perfect competition. *See* Competition.
Perfect competition *vs.* imperfect competition, 393
Point elasticity, 122–28
  defined, 122
  for curvilinear demand curve, 125
  and total expenditures, 126
Positive economics, 10–11, 581–82
Positive time preference, 515
Present value approach, of ranking investment projects, 522
Price, functions of, 33–36
Price ceiling effects on monopoly behavior, 332
Price change, effects of income and substitution, 82
Price discrimination, 334–39
  first-degree price discrimination, 335
  second-degree price discrimination, 337
  third-degree price discrimination, 338
Price elasticity. *See* Elasticity.
Price expectations, 138
Price takers, defined, 280–82
Production, 159–173, 212–218
  and isoquants, 212–13
  and law of diminishing returns, 166
  production function, 161
  short-run production function, 162
  stages of production, 168

Profit maximization
    necessary and sufficient conditions for, 284–87
    and other objectives of the firm, 340–46
Profit-maximizing level of investment of the firm, 523
Profits, 526–28
    in competition, 284, 291, 526
    in monopolistic competition, 379
    in monopoly, 325–30
    in oligopoly, 384–88
    as a symptom of market imperfections, 527
    other theories of, 527
Public utilities, 331
Pure competition *vs.* perfect competition, 281

Quasi-rent, 463–64

Rent, 458–64
    classical theories of, 458
    defined, 463
    generalized theory of rent and quasi-rent, 463
    von Thunen's model of rent, 460–63
Resource pricing, 419–38
    competitive supply and demand for resources, 420–26
    demand for more than one resource, 430
    imperfect resource markets, 433–37
    market equilibrium in competitive resource markets, 429
Resource transformation function, 161
Resources, 419–38
    complementary resources, 430
    defined, 421
    efficient allocation of, 5
    and their exploitation, 424
    supply, 426, 468–73
Ricardo, David, 6, 7, 458*n*., 459*n*., 463, 479, 480
Risk, 343–44
Robinson, Joan, 377, 377*n*.

Saving-investment equilibrium, 524
Schumpeter, Joseph, 460*n*., 527
Shanti, S. Tangri, 480*n*.
Short-run competitive firm supply, 288
Short-run competitive industry supply, 290
Short-run cost curves, monopolist, 325
Short-run costs, 171–79
Short-run defined, 162

Short-run equilibrium, in the market for a variable resource, 429
Short-run product curves, 165–66, 227–28
Short-run production function
   with capital divisible and unadaptable, 169–70
   with capital indivisible and adaptable, 162–68
   defined, 162
Short-run profit-maximizing output of a monopolist, 326–28
Short-run profits of a competitive firm, 282–88
Short-run revenue curves, competition, 282
Short-run unit costs, 173–79
   average cost, 173
   average total cost, 174
   average variable cost, 174
Simplex Method, 244
Sirkin, Gerald, 138n.
Slack variables, 244
Slutsky, Eugen, 85
Slutsky technique, 85
Small industry assumption, 291
Smith, Adam, 6
Snob goods, 78
Statics and dynamics, 9–10
Substitute goods, 74, 131–34
Superior goods, 82
Supply
   of labor, 468–73
   long-run competitive
      constant cost industry, 295–97
      decreasing cost industry, 298–99
      increasing cost industry, 297–98
   market, 30–31
   of monopolist, 320–46
   of monopolistic competitor
      long-run, 380
      short-run, 378
   of oligopolist, 383–85
   short-run firm supply, 288–90
Supply and demand
   excess demand, 32
   excess supply, 32
   interaction, 27–37

Tax, on cigarettes, 36
Theory, role in economics, 6–7

Theory of approximations or *tâtonnements*, 567
Theory of second best, 582
Time dimension
  consumer saving, 513
  and firm's investment, 520
Torrens, Robert, 458n.
Total cost, 172
  fixed, 173
  variable, 171
Total expenditures, 126
Total profits, 282
Total utility, 53–55
  maximization of, 61
Transformation curve, 575

Uncertainty, 343–44
Utilities, public, 331
Utility, defined, 51
Utils, 52

Value marginal product, 424
Veblen effect, 519
Veblen goods, 78
Viner, Jacob, 3
von Neumann, J., 67, 67n., 392
von Thunen, J. H., 458n., 460, 460n., 463n.

Wage determination
  in a competitive labor market, 473
  in competitive markets, 465
  under imperfect competition, 467
Wage differentials in the real world, 477
Wages, 464
Wald, A., 567, 567n.
Walras, Leon, 50n., 558, 567, 567n.
West, Sir Edward, 458n.

Zimmermann, Erich, 459, 459n.